THE
PREROGATIVE
OF THE HARLOT

Press Barons & Power

HUGH CUDLIPP

THE BODLEY HEAD
LONDON SYDNEY
TORONTO

British Library Cataloguing
in Publication Data
Cudlipp, Hugh, *Baron Cudlipp*
The prerogative of the harlot.
1. Newspapers—Great Britain—Ownership
2. Newspapers—United States—Ownership
I. Title
301.5'5   PN5124.09

ISBN 0-370-30238-9
© Hugh Cudlipp 1980
Printed in Great Britain for
The Bodley Head Ltd
9 Bow Street London WC2E 7AL
by Redwood Burn Ltd, Trowbridge & Esher
Photoset in Plantin
by Woolaston Parker Ltd, Leicester
First published 1980

CONTENTS

ACKNOWLEDGEMENTS

The sources I have consulted and quoted are acknowledged, with gratitude, throughout this book.

In a number of instances the courtesy of the traditional footnote is insufficient. I wish to place on record my special indebtedness to the following:

W. A. Swanberg, the American biographer and historian, and his publishers Charles Scribner's Sons, New York. Mr Swanberg's *Citizen Hearst* and *Luce and his Empire* are indispensable in any critical analysis of publishing power in the United States.

Sir Denis Hamilton, for permission to reprint material from *The Times* and *The History of The Times*, and for the availability of the archives of *The Times*.

Hedley Donovan, to whom Henry Robinson Luce finally yielded the Editorship-in-Chief of *Time*, *Life* and *Fortune*, for permission to use essential material from Robert T. Elson's two volumes *Time Inc., The Intimate History of a Publishing Enterprise, 1923-41*, and its successor *The World of Time Inc., 1941-1960*, both copyright Time Inc., 1968, 1973.

A. J. P. Taylor, FBA, and Hamish Hamilton, the publishers of his massive biography, *Beaverbrook*.

Sir Geoffrey Harmsworth and Reginald Pound, the authors, and the publishers Cassell of London, of the official biography, *Northcliffe*.

T. S. (Tom) Matthews, for permission to quote his perceptive and entertaining assessments of Henry Robinson Luce in his autobiography, *Name and Address*, Anthony Blond, London.

The author of *My Life* by Sir Oswald Mosley for passages which detail his political association with Viscount Rothermere; the Beaverbrook Library for quotations from David Lloyd George's *War Memoirs*, and *The Truth About the Peace Treaties*; finally Hodder and Stoughton, publishers of *Richard Burdon Haldane, An Autobiography*.

My thanks, too, to Sydney Jacobson for commenting upon the manuscript.

The copyright-holders of the pictures are: William Randolph Hearst, Camera Press. Viscount Northcliffe, a portrait study by Bassano, Camera Press; Northcliffe with Wickham Steed, Radio Times Hulton Picture Library. The first Viscount Rothermere, from Sir Geoffrey Harmsworth's family archives. Henry Robinson Luce, with Clare Boothe Luce, Camera Press; Henry Luce, Burt Glinn, Camera Press. Lord Beaverbrook, Baron, Camera Press.

H.C.

'The newspapers attacking me are not newspapers in the ordinary sense, but engines of propaganda for the constantly changing policies, desires, personal wishes, personal likes and dislikes of two men. What the proprietorship of these papers is aiming at is power, and power without responsibility – the prerogative of the harlot throughout the ages.'

Stanley Baldwin, Prime Minister, rebuking Lord Beaverbrook and Lord Rothermere

INTRODUCTION

An all-embracing study of each of the five newspaper and news-magazine creators and proprietors here caught under the microscope would overflow five volumes. The object of this book is to trace the origin of their power, analyse their personalities and motives, and investigate their policies and political machinations where any national or international significance was apparent. The right and duty of the Press to investigate and expose in the public interest is not argued here. The emphasis is on the misuses and abuses of that privilege by individuals who were often less concerned with the public interest than their own.

Lord Northcliffe's insistence until it was too late that the generals were right in the First World War, his destruction of Lord Haldane, his feud with David Lloyd George, rate here more attention than his promotion of the *Daily Mail* hat when he was going mad in 1921. ('It is about time men had a new hat. Offer £100 for a new design.') Henry Luce's grand delusion over China and his lobbying for Chiang Kai-shek at the White House are examined more diligently than his domestic bias in *Time* and *Life* against the Democrats. Lord Rothermere's enthusiasm for continuing the Ideal Home Exhibition does not matter by the side of his support for the creed of Mussolini and Hitler and his attempt to foist Sir Oswald Mosley's British Union of Fascists on his compatriots. Lord Beaverbrook's propaganda for isolation and appeasement when collective security was the only answer, and the anaesthetising effect of his campaign 'There will be no war', are treated as of more importance than his quarrel with the Co-operative Wholesale Society and other raillery.

They were all multi-millionaires in pounds sterling or us dollars, and for the most part—notably the Harmsworths—seclusive and sensitive about their own affairs. The common factor between them is the intention and the means to exercise power or influence or both. That was why Beaverbrook went into the newspaper business; the others succumbed to the temptation once they were in the business and successful. Three of them contrived to establish that there should exist outside elected parliaments an omnipotence higher than within. What is particularly observed is the pursuit of the personal vendetta, usually but not always against politicians, under the guise of high-minded national interest. Deception of the reader, and news-manipulation on matters of importance reaching war and peace, are recurrent themes. What they aim at, said the British Prime Minister Stanley Baldwin of Beaverbrook and the first Rothermere, 'is power, and power without responsibility—the prerogative of the harlot throughout the ages.' Other statesmen in most countries have made unflattering remarks about their adversaries in the Press without the aid of Rudyard Kipling, Baldwin's cousin, in polishing the indictment.

Inescapably, in the post-mortems on Hearst, Northcliffe and Rothermere, megalomania emerges as the vocational disease: Luce, on the best evidence available, was satisfied with autocracy and occasionally a tyrannical attitude to his editors. Beaverbrook remained William Maxwell Aitken, the Canadian buccaneer, and that was sufficient to inspire an extraordinary heap of abuse and suspicion.

Hugh Cudlipp 1980

I

WILLIAM RANDOLPH HEARST

'Please remain. You furnish the pictures and I'll furnish the war.'

'The force of the newspaper is the greatest force in civilisation ... The newspapers control the nation because they REPRESENT THE PEOPLE.'

William Randolph Hearst: 'Truth to him was a moving target.'

Some years before William Randolph Hearst was a household name in America, and a decade before he was known throughout the white world, he had a curious encounter with Ambrose Gwinett Bierce, a man still recorded in literary lore as 'a difficult genius who never attained full stature'. Bierce was a journalist, poet and writer of short stories, a friend of Mark Twain, Bret Harte and Joaquin Miller, a torch in a literary coterie in San Francisco at a time when culture didn't figure in the city's social priorities.

When they first met Hearst was twenty-four, the new proprietor of the 'Frisco *Examiner*. The mordant Ambrose Bierce was forty-five, a writer of wit and invective so offensive that he packed a pistol for his own protection. He was a pioneer in the United States of the same brand of instant lethal journalism later practised in Britain by William Connor ('Cassandra') and by Malcolm Muggeridge and Bernard Levin, those rarefied blooms who often to their own surprise can be transplanted into the vulgar soil of the popular press from the highbrow weeklies, their natural habitat.

Hearst had sailed from San Francisco across the bay to Oakland with the audacious notion of signing up Mr Bierce as his columnist. The author of *The Devil's Dictionary* described the meeting:

> 'I heard a gentle tapping at my apartment door. I opened, and I found a young man, the youngest young man, it seems to me, that I had ever confronted. His appearance, his attitude, his entire personality suggested extreme diffidence. I did not ask him to come in, install him in my better chair (I had two) and inquire how we could serve each other. If my memory is not at fault, I merely said, "Well?" and waited results. "I am from the San Francisco *Examiner*," he exclaimed in a voice like the fragrance of violets made audible, and backed away a little. "Oh," I said, "you come from Mr Hearst." Then that unearthly child lifted his blue eyes and cooed, "I am Mr Hearst."'[1]

Hearst's credentials as a rich playboy were notorious among his

[1] *The Life of Ambrose Bierce* by Walter Neale, W. Neale, New York, 1929.

acquaintances. Everyone in 'Frisco who could read knew that his sudden appearance as a newspaper owner and editor at that tender age, dangling his cheque book before thirsty writers and hungry artists, was not due to any genius of his own so far unveiled. Fortunes were his toys, but the gaudy *Examiner*—to the surprise of those who had heard or viewed him—was already threatening to become the first success in a rampaging career of power and irresponsibility in publishing.

William Randolph Hearst was dictating the policies of his newspapers until his death at eighty-eight in 1951. He was in a wheelchair in his final home in Beverly Hills when he held his last editorial conference two weeks before a nurse checked that his pulse had stopped. His mistress, the actress Marion Cecilia Davies, was asleep in a room nearby when the end came, exhausted by the vigil. She began her professional career in the chorus line of *Chu Chin Chow* in New York and was now the châtelaine of his ostentatious estate, castle and art treasury at San Simeon in California.

The last conference was with Warden Woolard, editor of a local newspaper.

'Mr Woolard,' he said, 'who owns the Los Angeles *Examiner*?'

'Well, you do, Mr Hearst.'

'Well, if I own it, and I want something in it, why can't I have it?'

The item Mr Hearst required, a minor story about a local playhouse, had in fact appeared in the previous day's issue.

'Mr Woolard,' he said, 'please forgive me. I'm an old man, and I'm sick. I don't notice things as well as I used to. Please drop in when you can. I want to keep in touch.'[1]

Hearst had been accustomed to wanting something all his life, and having it.

The severing of the umbilical cord a few minutes after he emerged at Stevenson House in San Francisco was a surgical formality, but his mother suffered torment in labour and the psychological bond with her only child was never severed. Their relationship was obsessionally cosy during his babyhood. It endured over the years in a tiny ill-assorted family where his father was usually away prospecting for a fortune in gold or silver, living with buccaneers and cut-throats and their camp followers, and surviving. There was a whiff of the Oedipus complex in the early rapport between mother and son, the shadow if not the substance; *Oedipus Rex* without the murder and the incest. His childhood was abnormal.

[1]*Citizen Hearst* by W. A. Swanberg, Charles Scribner's Sons, New York, 1961.

On 'Willie's' insistence he and his mother slept together in her bed until he was nearly four. 'He was very much put out when his Papa came home because he could not sleep with me. I told him when his Papa went away again he could sleep with me. He said, well, he wished he would go.' His gurgling, prattling and antics, monitored in minutia, were a source of pride and wonderment to her in letters to Papa, relatives and friends. Willie seemed to understand everything. He was very sweet, very good, very wise, so cunning, a great comfort, a little calf.

The maternal influence caused or stimulated the defects in his character. He was petulant, selfish, arrogant and occasionally callous, and in later life his associates and victims were to suffer from his tantrums. He was also the beneficiary of American momism in a material form. His parents, father George cautiously and mother Phoebe lavishly, gave him millions of dollars to play with in his early manhood.

George Hearst was a tobacco-chewing semi-literate, six feet tall and craggily handsome with a shaggy, unkempt beard, a roughneck nobody would have wagered a dollar on daring to woo the daughter of Missouri aristocrats. He was a self-taught geologist, rated by his cronies as the best assessor of a mine in the business. What the vivacious, cultivated Phoebe Elizabeth Apperson had to offer as a bride was plain to see. She was comely, brimful of prim ideals, conventional, a schoolteacher acquiring an understanding of the arts and foreign languages. They married when George was forty-one and she nineteen, and among the society of Franklin County the gossip about his hidden wealth compensated for the incongruity of the match. Nobody, except perhaps Phoebe, thought she would become one of America's significant women, California's uncrowned queen and the great lady of New York, hostessing Royalty, giving ten million dollars to noble causes, financing the lioness's share of 'Sweet Willie's' early newspaper escapades, and still leaving a legacy of five million.

William Randolph Hearst first passed through the Golden Gate of San Francisco as a foetus. George took his bride to the city in style from Missouri via Panama, and Willie was born in 1863. Phoebe had to establish herself in a raw sin-city of boom and panic with more brothels than schools or churches, more gun-toting crooks and freebooters than Bible punchers. Business deals were clinched over the toss of a coin or the click of a safety catch as often as in a lawyer's chamber. Since the Gold Rush of 1849 the city had been ruled by gangs and demagogues, with vigilantes from among the slightly less tainted citizens striving to establish some caricature of law and order to protect their families. Rogues and adventurers from all over the world had come to California to seek their fortunes and slit the throat of any other rogue staking a rival claim or muscling in on a dame or a racket. The better restaurants provided food on the ground floor and vice upstairs.

> The miners came in forty-nine,
> The whores in fifty-one;
> And when they got together
> They produced the native son.

In 'Frisco, even in the Sixties, a woman needed a man to protect her. George's absences were frequent, usually on horseback filling his saddlebags with sample minerals, but the family's progress to grander houses shielded them from the lewdness and perils of the roaring city. Phoebe's maternal affection, overwhelming in its intensity, would have satiated a large brood; all was lavished on her one and only child. The blue-eyed boy could do no harm. He was denied nothing that female attention could furnish or George's silver buy. 'His being with me so constantly has made him perfectly devoted to me. He never wants anybody else to do anything for him, and I think I love him better than ever before.' A child reared on self-indulgence could only become an all-demanding adult, narcissistic, assured the world was his oyster and its inhabitants his servants to yield to his whims.

George was engrossed in mining and real estate, roaming Nevada and Utah in search of more silver. Phoebe was tutoring herself in the arts in preparation for her supervision of Willie's education, teaching him many of his lessons herself. She mingled with the more refined—well, less vulgar—of the wives of other adventurers. The ladies were more concerned with the muscle of their husband's money than its source: some of them, bejewelled and tastefully gowned, were gangsters' molls or politicians' dolls with their names, albeit temporarily, on a marriage certificate and an eighteen-carat gold ring on their finger. The risk that their men might disappear without trace, abruptly, was a domestic hazard to be taken in a lady's stride. They were sisters under the skin, members of the adaptable sex that will supply, without notice, the wife for a Pope if the Vatican changes its rules.

Phoebe was addicted to culture, studying reproductions of the European masters in the local art gallery, but there were two factors at this time that disturbed the domestic scene. The munificent mother learned she was now infertile. She also learned to her distaste that George had secretly, but not secretly enough, bedded down with another woman more to his earthy liking, a liaison that was not swiftly broken. It was a blow to Phoebe's pride and perfectionism, though George was still the benefactor who could enable her to see the originals of the masters in Europe instead of the copies in San Francisco. The alternative, a return to the philistines of Missouri, resolved the family crisis and encouraged her to forgive, or at least strive to forget. In her sadness her love for Willie, already at full tide, overflowed.

The Grand European Tour was a torture imposed upon well-to-do middle-aged Americans by their wives before the days of package tours and Freddie Laker: the status symbol. Few who survived the business rat race without thrombosis were granted immunity. They visited in comparative opulence the lands from which they or their forebears had been driven by pogrom, poverty or avarice. Willie's first European tour was bestowed upon him at the age of ten. The journey was officially George's idea, doubtless planted in his mind during pillow-talk; his preoccupation with the Ontario mine in Utah was one reason for the prolonged parting, his generosity another. His marital guilt prompted the lavishness of the cavalcade.

The mastermind of the globetrot was Mrs Hearst. She hired a classics graduate from Harvard named Mr Barry as mentor to her son for the eighteen-month cultural orgy, and planned 'to study all the time and improve all we can'. There were ten days of ice-cream-and-jelly parties for Willie and his friends and a firework farewell.

No ancient city from Edinburgh to Florence was by-passed, no cathedral, museum or art gallery unvisited. The raids were preceded by a teach-in with the Harvard mentor, followed by a talk-in with Phoebe, and the journey fashioned the boy's future. Mother and son were upset by the poverty they saw in Dublin, and Phoebe reported to her husband back in California that 'the poorer classes are so *terribly* poor. Willie wanted to give away all his money and his clothes, too.' She was unaware, ironically, that George's fortunes at this time were also at a low ebb, nudging bankruptcy.

Willie was not allowed to dwell too long on the misfortunes of others. He was impressed by Windsor Castle and told Mama he would like to live there. In Hanover he wanted to buy the royal horses. In Paris he wanted her to buy the Louvre. In Rome the Pope placed his hand on Willie's head and blessed him. And there was 'study all the time'; daily German lessons in Dresden, French in Geneva, and drawing lessons at his own request twice a week. Phoebe chronicled home that he was picture-crazy, but added that she wouldn't wish him to be an artist unless he were a great one.

Willie was not an average boy. There was more to him than his mother's pride. Others have been born with a silver spoon in their mouths and accomplished nothing. Willie was already exhibiting the curiosity and perception of the born reporter and editor, precocious in his interest in antiques and architecture. When most little boys are collecting conkers and playing marbles he was harvesting stamps and coins and clocks in Switzerland. He also hoarded colourful picture books for children, called *Bilder Bücher*, later to become the inspiration for the American comic strip, the Katzenjammer Kids.[1]

To Phoebe education, studying all the time and improving all we can, was everything in life: to Willie it was something. There was another side to his character, a glimpse of the future 'Mr Hearst'. He was aggressive and rebellious, a practical joker with a yearning for fireworks: father called him Buster Billy. His pranks damaged their apartments during the tour, occasionally with experimental fires, all fondly forgiven by Phoebe who paid the bill.

Mr Hearst the sensationalist and showman was as apparent in embryo as Mr Hearst the collector of *objets d'art*. The shy connoisseur, in knickerbockers, a white frilled blouse and velvet jacket, was fashioned by Phoebe. He was also the sprig of the gritty, wayward George and a native son of 'Frisco.

Mother and son returned from the tour to the only period of financial stringency they experienced. The change in George's circumstances was abrupt and he could not conceal it from them or the neighbours. Phoebe now knew why her hint from Florence, 'We are always busy. I like it and wish we could remain another year,' brought no response. The residence and the carriage were sold, servants dismissed and Phoebe and Willie lived as boarders in the modest house of a friend while George set off again for the mines. This was not at all to Phoebe's liking, but the humiliation lasted only a year and she never recalled it. George struck lucky again in silver in Utah and was suddenly rich indeed.

The geological genius discovered that what he had bought with his partners as a potential silver mine in Montana also tapped the world's richest vein of copper. Phoebe could now graduate from her social position as an exponent of the arts to collector, patron and philanthropist. The blue-stocking from the country school in Franklin County had arrived, enthroned, underwritten by the lucre George later dug out of the ground in Mexico, Chile and Peru.

At seventeen Willie was launched on his second European tour, displaying a serious interest in newspapers, critically comparing

---

[1]*William Randolph Hearst, a New Appraisal* by John K. Winkler, Hastings House, New York, 1955.

London's with their continental counterparts and learning more about everything. He was essentially the product of mother's own 'intensive care' teaching unit. Between world tours and other distractions he had some sort of formal education at private and grammar schools, but these spasmodic periods were further interrupted by his ceaseless rebellion against discipline. The records of his formal education were destroyed in the San Francisco earthquake and fire of 1906, not, so far as is known, started by Hearst himself.

The second tour ended for Willie with a crucifying year at St Paul's, an exclusive Episcopal private establishment in New Hampshire. Even Phoebe had now come to realise that discipline might be necessary; in Willie's own words it was thought desirable to untie him from his mother's apron strings.

'For God's sake please ask me to New York,' he cabled a relative, and to his mother he said the only comfort was that the time was getting shorter every day until she would be there to release him. The time was shorter than intended: he was expelled. The only distinction he achieved at St Paul's was to subscribe to the London *Times* and present it to the study room. His next education appointment was with private tutors back in 'Frisco.

Hearst's world in babyhood, boyhood and teen years might have produced tendencies to homosexuality. There was no need for concern on that score. On a visit to the Southern Pacific at eighteen he had been captivated by a charming brunette named Sybil Sanderson, daughter of a State Supreme Court judge. Their headstrong engagement was ended when Sybil was sent packing to Paris to continue her studies in singing. Not long after his rapture cooled, Willie was writing to his mother:

> 'On the train I saw the prettiest girl . . . Every love including Sybil sank into the dimness of obscurity when the fair unknown beamed upon me.'

A decision by George Hearst at that time resolved the future of his son. George was already contributing to Democratic Party funds, and the idea of becoming 'Senator Hearst' appealed to him. The San Francisco *Examiner*, Democratic but broke, was the Party banner-waver in the city, and in 1880 he changed his role from creditor to proprietor to promote the cause of George, the unlikely politician.

'Willie' became 'Will' Hearst at nineteen when he began his three riotous years at Harvard, and his appearance at that time is portrayed by W. A. Swanberg:

'A tall, slender, gangling, pink-and-white young man with big feet and hands and a voice of such girlish timbre that it seemed that there must be a ventriloquist in the offing . . . Strangers were startled by his eyes, blue-grey in colour but with the irises swimming in whites so large as to give him a startling effect—an impression accentuated by his habit of looking directly, with the most unwavering concentration, at anyone speaking to him. Despite his shyness, he ran to showy plaids and screaming neckties.'

With a modicum of application, never forthcoming, and the use of his first-class mind, never over-extended, he could have seized all the honours Harvard had to offer. Buffoonery, usually at a childish and tasteless level, was more to his liking. With two enduring exceptions, boyhood friends Eugene Lent and Jack Follanshee, who at that time had dollars of their own to squander, he bought his friendships with George Hearst's largesse, liberally dispensed by Phoebe and replenished whenever he asked for more or she figured he might need it. He was the only undergraduate with an elastic allowance, but the story that his father occasionally sent him solid gold nuggets was a college joke. He was polite by nature, restrained, yet paradoxically only happy and uninhibited in the limelight he organised around himself.

The evidence of the princeling's arrogance and rejection of convention cannot be dignified as a rebellion against authority. He did not like Harvard, then at a golden period of academic quality, and the university establishment couldn't tolerate him; he was 'awfully tired of this place' within a few weeks, incensed by discipline of any kind. One of his diversions was pelting the actors at the Boston Howard Atheneum with custard pies. 'Of what use is a biography?' he wrote to Gene Lent, 'which does not record our rides back to Cambridge from Boston on the top of a hack, and our friendly but forceful distribution of oranges to policemen on route, and the dire consequences? "Them was the good old days."'

The good old days and nights when the tall, handsome Jack Follanshee was obliged to leave Harvard because of the financial collapse of his benefactor, his uncle, and Jack was concerned about the future of his mistress, Miss Tessie Powers. It was tenderly guaranteed by Will Hearst, an act of loyalty that appalled the academics who were paid to educate him.

The Harvard period is significant because it marked the birth of Will Hearst the journalist and of Mr Hearst the shrewd management man. From Jack Follanshee he acquired the hard-up mistress, from Eugene Lent the liability of an insolvent magazine, the college communicator known as *Lampoon*, a satirical weekly. Lent's parents were wealthy but also wise, and he could no longer shoulder the losses. Will could have solved the problem by opening his wallet or writing to Phoebe, but for the first occasion in his life he set to work, launching a circulation push, harrying former Harvard men for donations and annual orders, squeezing advertisements from merchants in Boston who one way or another had grown fat on the trade from the campus. This was the first sighting of a Will Hearst with zest, a sense of purpose and a sound business instinct. He reported his success to his mother with a prophetic footnote: 'Show this to Papa, and tell him just to wait until Gene [Lent] and I get hold of the old *Examiner* and run her in the same way.'

The boy who knew how to get what he wanted had already as a young man decided what he would do with his life. He received his father's *Examiner* regularly and studied it. He was a frequent visitor to the *Globe* in Boston, near Harvard, pestering the staff in every department with questions. He was fascinated by Joseph Pulitzer's boisterous trans-formation of the New York *World*. It was all part of what he called his 'journalistic investigations', not strictly part of the Harvard curriculum. It was his first foray into politics—not squalid politics, he said, but exalted politics—that curdled his relationship with the university's President Eliot.

Will Hearst called it a flag-raising for Grover Cleveland, then running for the White House, a very loud and conspicuous occasion with speeches, punch, a Boston brass band, a banner stretched across the street, fireworks and 'Democratic gamecocks' in all the windows of Mrs Buckman's boarding house. The gamecocks crowed at dawn and roused the Harvard assembly, including President Eliot. Hearst was rusticated. Yet the last straw was not politics. He was expelled a year later, after a brief return, for organising the delivery of chamber pots, known locally as thunder mugs, to all his instructors with their names elaborately inscribed at the target point.

Curiously, Hearst worked energetically during his rustication from college. He spent the time at Washington once more under the surveillance of the indulgent Phoebe. His political experience so far was tenuous. When Will was thirteen he had been patted on the head in New York by the great reformer, Samuel J. Tilden, and instructed to be a good Democrat, like his father. At twenty-one in Harvard Will had cast his first vote for the Presidential Democratic candidate. Now in Washington, jauntily enjoying his academic penance, he studied politics, attended sessions in Congress, swotted up American history, met some politicians, and became engaged to Eleanor Calhoun, an actress. The romance was the second in his life to be severed when the talented young lady was spirited away to Europe to continue her Shakespearean studies, a trip Phoebe was suspected of financing. Like Sybil, Eleanor later became a star.[1]

In Washington he also wrote to his father. He denounced the *Examiner* as 'our miserable little sheet' and proclaimed his conviction that he could run a newspaper successfully. 'Now,' he wrote, 'if you should make over to me the *Examiner*—with enough money to carry out my schemes—I'll tell you what I would do!' The transformation of the paper's presentation he outlined was sound and progressive. He thought the illustrations then appearing nauseated rather than stimulated the imagination. He wanted to imitate only some such leading journal as the New York *World*

'. . . which is undoubtedly the best paper of that class to which the *Examiner* belongs—that class which appeals to the people and which depends for its success upon enterprise, energy and a certain startling originality and not upon the wisdom of its political opinions or the lofty style of its editorials.'[2]

He expressed his longing for the *Examiner*:

'I have begun to have a strange fondness for our little paper—a tenderness like unto that which a mother feels for a puny or deformed offspring, and I should hate to see it die now after it had battled so long and so nobly for existence; in fact, to tell the truth, I am possessed of the weakness which at some time or other pervades most men; I am convinced that I could run a newspaper successfully.'

This communication is preserved in the anthology *The World's Great Letters*.

Phoebe had hoped Will's senior year at Harvard would lead to a sedate career as a diplomat; expelled, he spent that year as a reporter on the New York *World*, studying Joseph Pulitzer's methods but never catching a glimpse of the eccentric genius himself. Hearst mingled with newspapermen day and night, and worked under Ballard Smith, a lively operator he later tried to lure to 'Frisco as his editor.

[1]Hearst was stage-struck. As a boy he wanted to be an actor; at Harvard he appeared in a university show as a black comic; vaudeville was his relaxation as an editor. The two girls he became engaged to were actresses in embryo. Millicent Willson, the wife who bore him five sons, was a New York dancer. His mistress Marion Davies was a chorus girl he turned into a mediocre Hollywood star with the aid of ecstatic reviews in his newspapers.

[2]*William Randolph Hearst, A Portrait in His Own Words* edited by Edmond D. Coblentz, Simon and Schuster, New York, 1952.

George's response was initially adamant. He was also on record as saying: 'There's only one thing that's sure about my boy Bill. I've been watching him and notice that when he wants cake, he wants cake, and he wants it now. And I notice that after a while he gets the cake.' He took Will to see the million-acre cattle ranch Babicora he had bought for a song in Mexico through his dubious acquaintance with President Porfirio Díaz; the ranch needed developing. Or would Will prefer some of the mines? Will merely wanted that damned newspaper.

Senator-elect Hearst became a full-time Senator in January 1887, and among his mail was another letter from his son. 'I want to see you about the paper,' he wrote. 'We must be alarmingly enterprising, and we must be startlingly original. We must be honest and fearless.' The crucial meeting took place in San Francisco. George was pleased that Will was not content merely to be a rich man's son, that he wanted to do something on his own. He caved in, explosively: 'Great God! Haven't I spent money enough on that paper already! I took it for a bad debt and it's a sure loser.' He had been saving the *Examiner* to unload on some enemy, but—'If you are still set, Will, and want it, go ahead. Only I want you to promise that you will go into it seriously and earnestly.' He didn't know that Will had arrived from New York with bound volumes of Pulitzer's *World*.

On 4 March 1887 George Hearst occupied his Senate seat in Washington for his first six-year term, received by the Press with contempt as an illiterate, a man whose sole claim to preferment was his wealth. He was no more or less altruistic than the other Senators who had bought or fought their passage into America's most influential lobby to crown their careers or nurse their vested interests. The same day an announcement appeared in the *Examiner*:

'The *Examiner* with this issue has become the exclusive property of William Randolph Hearst, the son of the former proprietor. It will be conducted in the future on the same lines and policies which characterised its career under the control of Senator Hearst.'

That prim declaration was strictly for George's consumption. In the raw and rough city where nothing was sacred, especially religion, George Hearst's Buster Bill raised a horse-laugh. The custard-pie clown despatched in disgrace from Harvard after his episode with the thunder mugs, with Jack Follanshee's waitress-mistress still occasionally tucked under his arm in California and the Senator's bank within easy reach, had assumed the mantle of newspaper proprietorship and editorship. The *Examiner*, holding the attention of only thirty thousand citizens, was now his toy. Its demise, overdue, seemed a certainty in the hands of the playboy with the multi-coloured cravats, the high-pitched voice and the higher-pitched giggle.

William Randolph Hearst was twenty-four. No valid assessment of him could be struck without a glimpse into his sumptuous youth; his bizarre excesses must also be judged in the context of the times and country in which he operated. He promoted an international war for self-gratification and self-interest. He propelled Franklin Delano Roosevelt into the Presidency and might have become President himself. He exercised more influence on affairs for good or ill through his loud-mouthed newspapers than any other publisher in American history. America at the turn of the century would have taken a different course if George Hearst's attempt to deflect his son's ambition with the offer of the Babicora cattle ranch had succeeded. And none of it would have happened if Phoebe Apperson, the schoolmarm in Franklin County, Missouri, had told the maverick George, twice her age, to be on his way.

It was the decade of unbridled big business, a capitalist bonanza in which the buccaneers were licensed to make a killing without government restraint. The rich mineral deposits generated multi-millionaires by the handful. Commerce, piratically conducted, offered similar awards for the desk-bound entrepreneurs. Monopoly was the major political issue. Public opinion was aware and angry, but the businessmen's Party, the Republicans, initially averted their eyes or were too busy helping themselves. The first of their Presidents in that period was William McKinley, and they were the masters of national government for fourteen years until they lost their majority in the House of Representatives.

The standard bearer for the monopolists was John D. Rockefeller, who pioneered the Trusts with Standard Oil, harnessing the competitive companies in refining and distribution, eliminating rivalry, promising jucier dividends for the stockholders and hammering the consumer with no harassment from the courts because no law was being defied. The ploy was simple, though unctuously presented as a new concept of corporate organisation. Competing companies deposited a controlling slice of their stock with trustees in consideration of stock from the Trust: the trustees were John D. and his puppets. Half a dozen signatures on a document at the tail-end of a convivial club dinner transformed free enterprise into an exercise in public extortion. What was good for the oil business was good for whisky, sugar, lead, even salt, with monopolies or near-monopolies holding the reins of supply, price and quality. When 'Trust' became a dirty word they were declared illegal in a number of States and the demand for national action accelerated: the monopolists responded by changing the rules of the monopoly game and the next move was mergers. The American Sugar Refining Company achieved control of ninety per cent of sugar refining, virtually stifling competition. The American Tobacco Company had similar unsavoury objectives, and central government could no longer ignore the public unrest.

In a country, an age, and an economy which favoured the survival of the fittest, Will Hearst opted for the cause of the underdog. There were more of them. Underdogs buy more newspapers than top dogs. Most of his biographers have striven, in an attempt to balance the rapacious and domineering overtones of his personality, to ascribe to him a compassionate concern for the underprivileged. He was emotional, and his sympathy for causes that could not benefit him one jot was easily roused. He relished the role of the rich spokesman of the poor people, the crusader, dedicating himself and his newspapers to public service. He fought for reform in cities riddled with corruption and run by political bosses who held power by seeking and taking backhanders and doling out patronage and franchise in return. Was he merely a gangster with a printing press, noisily threatening the establishment? He may have sided with the masses for personal gain and aggrandizement; he was certainly regarded by his own class as an enemy, a capitalist who hated capitalists. The men and women who served him for ample rewards in financial terms were reluctant to talk about him, even after his death; the more freely they spoke the more they wished to preserve anonymity. They remembered his private kindnesses to his staff, especially those who were sick or in trouble. The Hearst publishing empire still exists, now conducted with a regard for the truth and an acceptance of current ethical standards that would be scorned by its founder as degeneracy and cowardice.

The formula Hearst adopted was Joseph Pulitzer's, the man who had resurrected the New York *World* from a falling sale of fifteen thousand to an expanding quarter of a million in three years. Pulitzer's target was the victims of the monopolists and the bait a raucous mixture of sensationalism and sincerity, stunts and crusades, with a piercing appeal to the basic instincts and passions. Scandal and crime were the sugar on the pill, but commercial brigandry was courageously exposed and the paper fought against injustices. To discerning readers the *World* was impulsive and vulgar, but it became the Bible of those whose interests it espoused.

Hearst calculated that the congregation in America was large enough to need and support two Messiahs. The shy man who liked fireworks, practical jokes and brass bands blossomed into a front-page braggart without inhibition, but he was an extrovert only in cold metal and headlines: his *alter ego* did not die.

The readers of San Francisco's *Examiner* were promised the earth in fun and games, and Hearst kept his word. It was now described under the masthead as 'Monarch of the Dailies. W. R. Hearst, Editor and Proprietor.' The clients were informed that because the *Examiner* had THE MOST ELABORATE LOCAL NEWS, THE FRESHEST SOCIAL NEWS, THE LATEST AND MOST ORIGINAL SENSATIONS it was indisputably THE LARGEST, BRIGHTEST AND BEST NEWSPAPER ON THE PACIFIC COAST. He gave the public what it wanted, unadorned, and it did not take him long to fathom what they wanted in bawdy, bustling 'Frisco. The *Examiner* modestly described itself as A GREAT PAPER.

He had told his father 'We must be alarmingly enterprising and startlingly original.' When the fabulous Del Monte Hotel blazed to the ground at Monterey, two hundred miles down the coast, Hearst hired a Southern Pacific train and rushed at two in the morning to the scene with a team of writers and sketch artists to produce a special fourteen-page issue. The first two-column headline appeared, and what a headline, written by W.R.H. himself:

HUNGRY, FRANTIC FLAMES
'LEAPING HIGHER, HIGHER, HIGHER,
WITH DESPERATE DESIRE'
RUNNING MADLY RIOTOUS THROUGH CORNICE,
ARCHWAY AND FACADE
RUSHING IN UPON THE TREMBLING
GUESTS WITH SAVAGE FURY . . .

There were illustrations three columns wide.

When five fishermen were marooned on a rock in a gale outside the Golden Gate, abandoned by the government life-saving services, Hearst hired an ocean-going tug and led a team of volunteers to rescue them. A strong swimmer plunged into the sea and succeeded in reaching the rock with a line. The fishermen were laughing their heads off on the front page of the *Examiner* while the other papers were still describing their plight. The services of the same strong swimmer[1] were enlisted to expose the

[1] The hero of these exploits was an Englishman, Henry R. Haxton, who later became a Member of Parliament.

inadequacy of the life-saving apparatus and drills on the Southern Pacific ferries. He jumped overboard while reporters monitored the time it took to rescue him and fish him back on board. Both adventures led to public concern and swift reforms.

Other examples of the alarmingly enterprising were an interview with train bandits on the run, and the discovery of the route across the Canadian border where thousands of Chinese, plus opium, were illegally entering the United States.

Hearst took time off to traverse San Francisco harbour in a balloon and describe the wonders of the city to his readers. The trade unionists, flexing their muscles, were wooed with a column called 'The Workingman'. The blood and guts department was macabre, specialising in gory piffle.

Human appeal was dispensed in large doses. A girl reporter obliged Hearst by 'fainting' in the main street to expose the conditions of the City Receiving Hospital, and the hearts of the readers were regularly massaged by appeals for good causes, the *Examiner* generously dipping its hand into its own pocket, and more frequently into Senator George Hearst's. When there wasn't any news Will would create it: when he couldn't create it his staff, on occasion, would fake it. 'The Last of the McGintys', a tear-jerker about a newsboy's valiant efforts to rear his orphaned brother and sisters, had only one flaw: there were no McGintys. Allen Kelly, who crossed the States from New York to become the paper's city editor, asked to be moved to a job as an individual writer because he could no longer connive at Hearst's slanting of news and 'unwarranted insinuations'.

Above all, the *Examiner* became a crusader. It defeated a new city charter handing too much power to the ruling clique. It harried the water and electricity utility companies. It exposed criminals sheltered by the city's underground network. There was a commendable sense of purpose behind the circus appeal. The paper campaigned for the construction of the Panama Canal and exposed the danger spots in the Pacific naval defences. In a campaign that lasted years and was conducted with courage Hearst challenged the baleful influence of Collis Potter Huntington, one of America's most powerful men and California's *most* powerful. Huntington bossed the Southern Pacific railroad, whose subsidiary, the Central Pacific, held a stranglehold on California and on the rail link with the East. Governors were not elected—or, if they were, did not long survive—without Huntington's approval. He rigged political appointments in a city where corruption was the way of life. His grip on the State's principal newspapers was operated by subsidies and by his influence over the big advertisers. Bribery and intimidation were his mode of business. The supplies he controlled with his railroad monopoly could make or break and the service to the public was regulated by avarice. Nobody, except Hearst, fought Big Collis Huntington, but Hearst considered journalism as an 'enchanted playground in which giants and dragons were to be slain simply for the fun of the thing'. Minor mishaps on the monopoly railroad were portrayed as major tragedies; even if all escaped unbruised they were interviewed as survivors.

Hearst expanded his editorial staff, recruiting talent from the *Lampoon* team of Harvard days. Eugene Lent, who later became a prominent attorney in the city, covered society gossip and financial news. Famous writers and artists were hired, including Ambrose Bierce.

The formula worked and the *Examiner* succeeded. Within two years it was selling sixty thousand a day, still gathering one thousand new readers a week and showing a substantial profit. Senator George Hearst had lost a fortune on the *Examiner* before Will had taken over, and had been relieved of another three-quarters of a million dollars since that day. But before he died in Washington in 1891 he knew that feckless Will had gone into it seriously and earnestly. A slice of the forty million dollars he bequeathed Phoebe enabled his son to pursue his hobby even more seriously.

Hearst, Jr, remained a true Californian. He was born and bred and died there. But California was too small for him, too remote from the centres of federal influence and power politics; besides, Phoebe had handed over $7,500,000 acquired by the sale of some of the family mining interests. He bought the *Journal* in New York City in 1895, eight years after 'W. R. Hearst, Editor and Proprietor' first appeared on the front page of the *Examiner*. The *Journal* was a paper with a lurid and chequered history, floundering with a sale of 77,000 copies. The deal cost him a paltry $180,000, yet within a year he was able to announce an increase in circulation to 430,000 for the daily edition, with the *World* only 200,000 ahead of him, and an increase from 54,000 to 400,000 for the Sunday version.

Again he applied the Pulitzer formula, with the brasher Hearstian embellishments concocted in San Francisco; he called it the New Journalism. At this stage he also perfected the *modus operandi* with his editorial staff to apply throughout his life and theirs. Fellow performers in his circus they might be, walking the same tightrope without a safety-net, performing feats of journalistic bareback riding, entering unarmed the dens of the forest-bred lions of monopoly and Tammany Hall, dedicated to the same codes of honour and dishonour, spitting in the same sawdust; there the *bonhomie* ended. During the excitement or panic of the moment the fun and exhilaration were mutual, but he was the circus master, withdrawn in his demeanour at a second's notice, to be treated with courtesy. When the lights went out in the big tent and the dung was swept from the ring for the second house, he was aloof, a loner.

He kept his distance with the same fastidious caution exercised over the years by the newspaper owners in London's Fleet Street, notably the Harmsworths. The ritual and mystique of proprietorship preclude intimacy with journalists on the pay roll; metaphorically, they are expected to use the tradesmen's entrance. Familiarity might breed contempt, over-familiarity might erode authority, the weapons of instant dismissal or reward might be blunted. Personal shyness, which he never overcame, was a factor in Hearst's autocracy, but an assumption of superiority born of power and wealth played its part. He had the first and last word and was the court of appeal against his own judgements. Will, alias Buster Bill and Willie, became 'Mr Hearst' in and out of the office. He also liked to be called 'The Chief', like Northcliffe.

The Spanish–American War of 1898 was Spain's last international conflict and America's first with a nation outside its own continent. The issue was the agony of Cuba. It was, and should have remained, the final confrontation between a European power in eclipse and its misgoverned colony. The Press in New York City was responsible for escalating a situation that could have been resolved by American diplomacy and pressure into a war, brief almost to the point of absurdity but with historic consequences in the twentieth century.

Columbus discovered the largest island in the Caribbean, and it was milked by the Spanish for five centuries. The classic cruelties and blunders of colonial history were committed by Spain in Cuba with scarcely a traceable omission. The events that starred Hearst in the protracted tragedy were the climax to a century of exploitation, discontent and turmoil. Madrid's resources of insensibility and obscurantism were inexhaustible, and the fact that the Spanish premiership at this time was a prize in a game of musical chairs between the dictatorial Antonio Cánovas and the liberal Práxedes Mateo Sagasta, alternating in power, added inconsistency to insanity. The United States made its own contribution to the gathering crisis in 1894 by restoring punitive duties on imported sugar, imposing a depression on Cuba which exacerbated the situation.

At the moment that called for magnanimity Cánovas chose the arid policy of no concessions without submission, and worse still despatched

General Valeriano Weyler to Cuba as his instrument. In a colony now in open revolt he obeyed his orders with military precision to a degree that was explosively foolish and inhuman. He herded the non-combatants into reconcentration areas under conditions of squalor that caused disease and starvation for women and children in their tens of thousands; no treatment more certain of arousing American sympathy could have been devised. The rest of the population were arbitrarily classed as the enemy and isolated by every contrivance of primitive infantry defence such as barbed wire and blockhouses.

The conflict was now petrified. For twenty-five years Spain had failed to maintain law and order under a regime that was harsh and mean; she was unable to achieve a military victory over the Cuban rebels, unwilling to yield the concessions that would defuse the dispute. The insurgents had no chance of success and independence without direct foreign aid. In the United States there was a rift between jingoism and calm counsel, popular emotion over the plight of the Cubans and vested interest.

Until Mr Hearst breezed into New York as a newspaper proprietor, backed by Senator George's legacy, hungry for circulation, a crusader in search of a cause, the American attitude to Cuba was manipulated by big business leaning on the administration and officials in Washington. Banking and industrial tycoons had just emerged breathlessly from a depression and were in no mood to contemplate war. US investments in Cuba topped fifty million dollars and annual trade with the island nudged one hundred million. They sought the panacea of The City in all countries—stability and security; the investors wanted no truck with direct or indirect aid to insurgents to generate more destruction. American-Spanish tension undermined stock prices on Wall Street, appeasement spurred a rally: it was as simple as that. The suffering of the Cubans aroused the compassion of the average American citizen but was of no concern to businessmen on the make.

Grover Cleveland, Democrat President, steadfast for peace, offered mediation to establish a compromise settlement with the insurgents, leaving Spanish sovereignty unperturbed. The offer was scorned by Mr Hearst's newspaper as a conspiracy with the Spanish government whereby the United States became its efficient ally! The truth was, of course, that Cleveland would have been gratified if Cuba were submerged or towed a thousand leagues away provided American investment remained inviolable.

His successor's attitude was certain the moment he hung up his topper in the White House on 4 March 1897, one year before the war. The nomination and election to the Republican Presidency of William

McKinley, and the financing and fiddling thereof, were engineered by Mark Hanna, the personification of the political power of industrialism in the United States. Hanna's opposition to war with Spain was legendary. McKinley ('the advance agent of prosperity') was committed to the official Republican policy announced before the election, that the US should 'actively use its influence' to restore peace in Cuba with independence for the Cubans. He was perturbed about the Cuban insurrection as soon as he took office, but firmly against armed intervention in a partisan role.

Yet the war happened because of popular clamour fomented by the popular newspapers of New York City. The campaign was conducted in a shrill key with scant regard for truth and less for justice. William Randolph Hearst was the arch-villain of the plot to ennoble the rebels, denigrate the Spanish, and embroil America. He relished the accolade of 'the journalist who liberated a country' and basked in the gratitude of the Cubans; his methods reduce the trickery of the propagandists on both sides in World Wars One and Two to energetic amateurism. The solitary decency which emerges was his sympathy for the suffering. The trouble was that a circulation marathon was raging in New York City between the *Journal* of the audacious Mr Hearst and the *World* of the cunning Joseph Pulitzer. Nothing, including human misery, was sacred.

Newspapers mounted a campaign of support for the Cubans and vilification of the Spanish government, its colonial administrators and military forces. Both sides were guilty of barbarity, but the rebels were presented as righteous freedom-fighters and their masters as tyrants. The Spanish–American collision course engineered by Hearst and Pulitzer was the first and last newspaper circulation contest in history to be fought with navies and armies, shells and bullets. When Hearst's sole weapon was the San Francisco *Examiner*, three thousand miles away from the scene of operations, he had advocated American intervention. Now his domain extended to New York, the olive-skinned Cuban activists operating on American territory were encouraged to wander through the doors of his newspaper headquarters whispering the password *Cuba Libre*, assured of a prompt hearing. They were mentally well-equipped to create or connive at gruesome tales of child murder, mother rape, or eye-gouging, and they had perfected their own propaganda machine.

Their 'Doctor Goebbels' was Señor Tomás Estrada Palma, an able, imaginative schoolteacher who headed the Cuban junta in New York and doled out bulletins to the reporters every evening in the Broadway offices of Horatio S. Rubens, US lawyer. He specialised in tales of Cuban advances, Spanish retreats, and bloodcurdling atrocities. He saw to it that in his communiqués Havana was frequently captured by the rebels; in fact it was never entered or even threatened. Because of Mr Rubens's generosity in feeding the Press from a box of peanuts, Estrada Palma's HQ was known as the Peanut Club. Never again in the history of manufactured news were so many lies swallowed for so humble a bribe as a peanut, but the reporters knew any story that was pro-Cuban or anti-Spanish would be welcomed by Mr Hearst and Mr Pulitzer.

Hearst's readers were already conditioned by the stimulus of a horrific diet. They were informed that Spanish troops had resumed the inhuman practice of beating Cuban prisoners to death, that it was the daily practice of the Spanish gaolers to take several prisoners from the forts and prisons and shoot them, that unarmed peasants, women and children, were beaten mercilessly. Twenty-five Catholic priests, they were told, had been roasted alive. 'FEEDING PRISONERS TO SHARKS' was one of the headlines. Even when events that could be substantiated occurred they were presented with maximum bias. Weyler's troops successfully ambushed a rebel force led by General Maceo; the general was killed in battle, but the readers of the *Journal* were told the Spanish had entrapped Maceo and murdered him. The newspaper boasted that 'The New Journalism prints what is new and prints it first'. In practice it printed what was false and printed it first.

Mr Hearst reacted vociferously when two of his reporters were temporarily detained by the Spanish bureaucrats. It was regarded as an unpardonable affront, this minor formality, and the *Journal* protested:

'No surer road is open for popularity of the new President than the abandonment of the cold-blooded indifference to Cuba to which Cleveland committed our government.'

As soon as its correspondents were expelled they were replaced. Nor did Mr Hearst hesitate to raise the circulation war to the level of simulated statesmanship. He invited the governors of every State to express their views on America giving material aid to promote a Cuban war of independence, and on the probable supply of volunteers from each State in the event of an American war with a foreign power.

Mr Hearst arranged for one of his new reporters, Ralph D. Paine, a Harvard man, to join a small ship sailing from Florida to land arms and combatants. He bought a sword in Fifth Avenue to be presented to 'the greatest living soldier'. It was inscribed 'To Maximo Gomez, Commander-in-Chief of the Army of the Cuban Republic'. The hilt was gold-plated, embellished with diamonds, and the sword was mounted in a mahogany case.

Paine recorded the story and the dialogue with Hearst:

Paine: Very handsome. Old Gomez will be tickled to death, when he gets it.

Hearst: That is the idea, *when he gets it*. I have been trying to find somebody foolish enough to carry this elegant sword to Gomez. I am perfectly frank with you. These inscriptions [the sword also bore the legend *'Vive Cuba Libre'*] would be devilish hard to explain to the Spanish army, if you happened to be caught, wouldn't they?

Paine: And do you want me to present this eighteen-carat sword to Gomez, with your compliments?

Hearst: If you don't mind . . . Of course if you are nabbed at sea, you can probably chuck it overboard in time . . .

Paine: And if I get surrounded on land, perhaps I can swallow it, Mr Hearst. Never mind that. I am the damn fool you have been looking for . . .[1]

Joseph Pulitzer had his share of the luck. He was able to express his outrage in the *World* at the arrest of his ace correspondent, Sylvester Scovel. Mr Hearst did not support Pulitzer in his Free Scovel campaign; instead, he increased his own team in Cuba with the elegant author Richard Harding Davis and the illustrator Frederick Remington. They joined the other journalists at the Hotel Inglaterra in Havana, though Davis was stated to be with the insurgents. Remington forthwith specialised in the portrayal of iniquities (Spanish) and heroism (Cuban). In an early example of his work the caption was signed by the artist though probably written by Davis:

'The acts of the terrible savages, or irregular troops called guerrillas, employed by the Spaniards, pass all understanding by civilised man. The American Indian was never guilty of the monstrous crimes that they commit. Their treatment of women is unspeakable, and as for the men captured by them alive, the blood curdles in my veins as I think of the atrocity, the cruelty practised on these helpless victims. My picture illustrates one case where the guerrillas saw fit to bring their captives into the lines, trussed up at the elbows, after their fashion.'

Remington was enjoying his fee of $3,000, but was soon running out of atrocities that curdled the blood in his veins. From Cuba he cabled The Chief:

[1]*Roads of Adventure* by Ralph D. Paine, Houghton Mifflin, Boston and New York, 1922.

W. R. Hearst, New York *Journal*, NY.
Everything is quiet. There is no trouble here.
There will be no war. I wish to return. Remington.

Mr Hearst replied:

Remington, Havana.
Please remain. You furnish the pictures and
I'll furnish the war. W. R. Hearst.

Popular causes thrive on personalities, good or bad, and the Cuban situation needed General Valeriano Weyler. De Lome, the Spanish Minister in Washington, endeavoured to cool the temperature by stating some obvious facts. He explained, reasonably, that the single aim of Estrada Palma's propaganda in New York was to antagonise the United States towards Spain. He said that the rebels hoped to create bad blood and ultimately war between Spain and the United States, with the idea of having their fighting done by American troops. Among those who disbelieved him was Mr Hearst's New York *Journal*. On 23 February 1896 it published a special Sunday feature portraying General Weyler as 'the prince of all the cruel generals this century has seen':

'Spain has at last produced her trump card and sent on the field of battle her most ferocious and bloody soldier . . . the fiendish despot whose hand Cuba well knows . . . A panic has spread over Cuba . . . Hundreds of Cuban women, maids and matrons, shudder . . . it is not only Weyler the soldier but Weyler the brute, the devastator of haciendas, the destroyer of families, and the outrager of women . . . Pitiless, cold, an exterminator of men . . . There is nothing to prevent his carnal, animal brain from running riot with itself in inventing tortures and infamies of bloody debauchery.'[1]

The *Journal* called him Butcher Weyler.

In February 1897 Mr Hearst published a five-column headline: 'DOES OUR FLAG PROTECT WOMEN?' The story, from Richard Harding Davis, related the experience of three Cuban girls who boarded an American vessel bound for New York. The *Olivette* was flying, no less, the Stars and Stripes. As published, Davis related that the three girls were pretty; further, that before the ship sailed they were

[1] *The Cuban Crisis (1895–1898)* by Joseph E. Wisan, Columbia University Press, New York, 1934.

stripped to their skins by Spanish policemen suspecting them of carrying despatches from the rebels. No documents were found. Frederick Remington portrayed the scene, and in his illustration one of the girls was starkers, ogled by prurient officials rummaging among her underclothes. On 17 February Pulitzer's *World* interviewed the three Cubans when they arrived in New York. They were shown Davis's story. No, they said, they had not been undressed by men; the officers had waited outside while they were searched by matrons. The headline was: 'THE UNCLOTHED WOMEN SEARCHED BY MEN WAS AN INVENTION OF A NEW YORK NEWSPAPER'.

In *Facts and Fakes about Cuba* George Bronson Rea wrote that Davis sent an explanatory letter:

'I never wrote that she was searched by men . . . Mr Frederick Remington, who was not present, and who drew an imaginary picture of the scene, is responsible for the idea that the search was conducted by men. Had I seen the picture before it appeared, I should never have allowed it to accompany my article . . .'

The despatch from Davis had been doctored in the *Journal* office to authenticate the Remington illustration.

The case of Ricardo Ruiz was another welcome stimulus to war hysteria. He was a Cuban revolutionary who had fled to America with his skin intact during earlier troubles. He became a graduate of a dental college in Philadelphia, was naturalised as an American in 1880, returning to Cuba to practice. The tedium of dentistry was relieved by his hobby as an insurrectionist. As the *late* Dr Richard Ruiz in 1897 he was the next sensation in the series.

The arrest of Ricardo on a charge of train robbery would have passed unnoticed. The arrest of Richard, American citizen, and his subsequent fate were a different matter. He was placed in solitary confinement in a prison a few miles from Havana and two weeks later was found dead in his cell. Even in less excitable times, and without a newspaper circulation war in New York, the official statement of the gaolers that Ruiz had committed suicide by bashing his head against the wall would have aroused suspicion. Murder, with no evidence, was assumed.

Under the headline 'THE UNITED STATES MAY FIGHT SPAIN YET', the *World* on 21 February 1897 reported that the US Consul-General in Havana, Fitzhugh Lee, had been refused permission to exhume the body. 'The murder of Dr Ruiz, an inoffensive American citizen in a Cuban gaol, sharply illustrates the peril in which Sylvester Scovel [its detained reporter] is placed.' Hearst evidently considered this tepid and colourless, and the next day's *Journal* alloted its front page and many inside pages to the case. The principal headline was 'SHERMAN FOR WAR WITH SPAIN FOR MURDERING AMERICANS'. It reported what purported to be an authorised interview with Senator John Sherman of Ohio, a key figure in Washington, already nominated by the incoming President McKinley as his Secretary of State. The Senator cautiously said that his only information came from the *Journal*, but added less cautiously: 'If the facts are true, as reported, and American citizens are being murdered in Cuba in cold blood, the only way to put an end to the atrocities is to declare war on Spain.' The New York *Evening Post* the same day reported Sherman's denial of the interview: 'It is a lie from beginning to end. I am surprised that the *Journal* should make such a statement.' The *World* enthusiastically published the same rebuttal.

The issue of the *Journal* also carried a report from its Havana correspondent, George Eugene Bryson. Contrary to what was said in the previous day's *World*, Consul-General Lee had obtained permission for an autopsy and it showed that Ruiz's death had been caused by head injuries. A few days later Bryson had news of the dentist's last message he claimed was found scratched on a chair in the cell: 'I shall be killed.'

Hearst was badgering William McKinley before he took office and persistently when he was President to escalate America's 'influence' in Cuba from diplomacy to high explosives. He accused him of listening with eager ear to the threats of the Big Business interests. When McKinley attempted to sober the situation with a smattering of statesmanship in his inaugural address—'We want no wars of conquest. We must avoid the temptation of territorial aggression'—Hearst trounced the speech as vague and sapless. He had already cabled dollars to Mrs Ruiz to enable her to cross to the States with her children with an offer to join the newspaper's staff. 'My Life in Cuba' by Mrs Ruiz duly appeared, with the Spanish prison system as its theme. She was sent to Washington (with children), and McKinley and Sherman were cajoled into receiving her. Sherman ordered an investigation into her husband's death.

All newspapers in New York reported that Spain herself had undertaken to investigate the suicide/murder of Dr Ruiz; only the high-minded *Evening Post* published the fact that the Spanish War Minister had promised to punish the guilty ones if it were established that the man had been ill-treated in prison. But Richard, formerly Ricardo, was ushered into the wings as the stage was cleared for the next sensational act—Señorita Evangelina Cosio y Cisneros.

In August, five months after the President's inaugural speech, Mr Hearst saw a cable from his man in Havana, George Bryson:

'Evangelina Cisneros, pretty girl of seventeen years related to President of Provisional Cuban Republic, is to be imprisoned for twenty years on African coast for having taken part in uprising of Cuban political prisoners on Isle of Pines.'

'Sam,' said Mr Hearst to the news editor, Sam Chamberlain, 'we've got Spain. Look at this! Get every detail of this case from Havana. Let's draw up a petition to the Queen Mother of Spain for this child's pardon. Enlist the women of America . . . Have distinguished women sign first . . . Notify our Minister in Madrid . . . This girl must be saved if we have to take her out of prison by force or send a steamer to meet the vessel carrying her to Africa—but that would be piracy, wouldn't it?'[1]

Pages were devoted to the cause of Miss Cisneros day after day, and the *Journal* announced: 'THE WHOLE COUNTRY RISING TO THE RESCUE'.

In June 1895 her father, an insurgent, had been arrested and sent to prison in Cienfuegos on the south coast of Cuba. The girl's plea for mercy through an intermediary resulted in the reduction of his death penalty to life imprisonment. A second appeal by the girl directly to General Weyler brought about a further amelioration in her father's plight: he was moved to the penal settlement on the Isle of Pines and the girl and her sister were allowed to accompany him and live in 'moderately pleasant circumstances', a tolerable existence until the arrival of Colonel Berriz as the new military commander. Evangelina's story, later published without corroboration but accepted in every detail by the *Journal*, related that Berriz had attempted a brutal sexual assault upon her; other Cuban exiles had rushed to her aid, physically assaulting the Colonel who in turn was rescued by his own Spanish soldiers.

Evangelina was charged with sedition and removed to the Recojidas gaol in Havana. Her sister, also arrested, was freed after three weeks. Not a word appeared in any newspaper about the experience of Miss Cisneros or her father until Mr Hearst's George Bryson visited her six months after her imprisonment. The *Journal* scoop became an international *cause célèbre*, and the prose, the tactics and the highjinks were vintage Hearstian throughout.

On 18 August the *Journal* said:

'This tenderly nurtured girl was imprisoned at eighteen among the

[1]James Creelman in an article on Hearst, *Pearson's Magazine*, September 1906.

most depraved negresses of Havana, and now she is to be sent in mockery to spend twenty years in a servitude that will kill her in a year.'

On 19 August:

'The unspeakable fate to which Weyler has doomed an innocent girl whose only crime is that she defended her honour against a beast in uniform has sent a shudder of horror through the American people.'

On 22 August:

'Miss Cisneros is, according to all who have seen her, the most beautiful girl in the island of Cuba . . . She was reared in seclusion and, almost a child in years, is as ignorant of the world as a cloistered nun.'

On 24 August:

'This girl, delicate, refined, sensitive, unused to hardship, absolutely ignorant of vice, unconscious of the existence of such beings as the crowd in the cells of the Casa de Recojidas, is seized, thrust into the prison maintained for the vilest class of abandoned women of Havana, compelled to scrub floors and to sleep on bare boards with outcast negresses, and shattered in health until she is threatened with an early death.'

On 26 August Colonel Berriz was described as a lecherous and foiled scoundrel. The Americans devoured the romantic tale, spread throughout the nation by the Associated Press news agency, without asking questions.

Distinguished women in the United States including the mother of President McKinley and others close to authority were persuaded to petition the Pope and the Queen-Regent Maria Christina of Spain. The names of the women who signed were inscribed in the *Journal*'s Roll of Honour; two hundred thousand signatures were harvested in England by Lady Rothschild. Governors, ex-Governors and Senators acclaimed the *Journal*'s solicitude for Evangelina, and Hearst personally cabled to General Weyler, whom the *Journal* had denounced as the prince of all cruel generals, imploring mercy. There is no other example of a bogus story arousing such pity and anger on an international scale. The meticulous organising and timing of spontaneous public indignation was one of the publisher's specialities.

On 21 August the *World*, united in the cause of the rebels but anxious for its cut in the circulation harvest, published a telegram from General

Weyler. He denied that the case against Evangelina had been resolved; sentence had not been passed. He gave a different version of the episode involving the Colonel: Miss Cisneros had 'deceitfully lured to her house the military commander of the Isle of Pines, had men posted secretly who tied him and attempted to assassinate him'. Same opera, new libretto; for Scarpia read Calvaradossi. The *World* said: 'The Spanish in Cuba have sins enough to answer for, but nothing is gained for the Cuban cause by invention and exaggerations that are past belief.' The next day the *Journal* promised that the women of America would save her yet, in spite of Weyler and the *World*.

The Spanish Minister in Washington, Dupuy de Lome, wrote to the petitioners deploring the conduct of newspapers 'desiring to increase their circulation by their usual slanderous methods'. He reiterated Weyler's version of events and declared that 'The Queen-Regent is favourably disposed to your plea.' He said that because the girl had not been sentenced no interference could take place until the trial had been completed; instructions, however, had been communicated to the Governor-General 'to bring a speedy trial and to grant Miss Cisneros all possible consideration'. The Queen-Regent received an appeal from His Holiness Leo XIII, but her order to Weyler to move the girl to a convent until her trial was over was ignored.

The furore continued with stories of Spanish spies active along the American eastern seaboard, investigating forts and naval defences. Nothing was left to the imagination; nothing that could be imagined was left out.

When Fitzhugh Lee, the US Consul-General, arrived in New York on 8 September, he said:

'I wish to correct a false and stupid impression which has been created by some newspapers. I refer to the Señorita Cisneros. This young woman has two clean rooms in the Casa de Recojidas, and is well clothed and fed. It is all tommyrot about her scrubbing floors and being subjected to cruelties and indignities. She would have been pardoned long ago if it had not been for the hubbub created by American newspapers.

'I do not believe the Spanish government ever for one moment intended to send her to the penal colony in Africa or elsewhere. I believe her name is now upon the roll for pardon.

'That she was implicated in the insurrection on the Isle of Pines, there can be no question. She herself, in a note to me, acknowledged that fact, and stated she was betrayed by an accomplice named Arias.'

39

The *World* the next day reported Lee's statement fully; the *Journal* omitted his comments about tommyrot.

On 7 October Evangelina escaped from prison and the next day the New York newspapers reported the event. On 9 October some newspapers, including the *Journal*, disclosed that she had been assisted by aid from outside the prison. On 10 October the *Sunday Journal* revealed the astonishing news that it had rescued the girl single-handed.

Mr Hearst had selected Karl Decker, his star correspondent in Washington, as the man for the mission. Accustomed to intrigue and political skulduggery, he had the additional qualifications of being a tough, cool Virginian who had earlier served in Cuba and knew the scene. The Chief told him he was determined to rescue Miss Cisneros at any hazard and Decker accepted an assignment that could have landed him in the same prison for an uncomfortable period. He reckoned on an ample reward should he succeed.

Other reporters in Cuba studied the prison and laid plans for Decker's arrival in late September to replace George Bryson, expelled by Weyler for his earlier part in the Evangelina affair. The gamble was to effect the rescue with the co-operation of the prisoner herself, and unaccountably Decker was allowed to visit her.

He had two allies. He rented a house next door to the prison, strangely vacant, and a secret room where the prize when kidnapped could be hidden and disguised. His props were a ladder, a hacksaw, a .44-calibre revolver, a forged visa, an outfit of male clothing and a carriage parked nearby. He used the ladder to cross from the house to the roof of the gaol and the saw to sever the bars of the cell, identified by a fluttering white handkerchief.

Karl Decker's account of the escape was as colourful as a rainbow, exhausting every cliché, embellishment and titillation known to romantic fiction. He knew his Hearst. As soon as he got to work with the saw (no five-second chore, with three bars still to go) 'She gave one glad little cry and clasped our hands through the bars, calling upon us to liberate her at once' (an imperious command for one so delicate and refined). What about the other prisoners, the most depraved negresses of Havana, with whom the *Journal* told the world she was banished? They couldn't sound the alarm, even if they were so inclined, because they were sleeping heavily under the effect of drugged bonbons Evangelina had generously given to them. Decker had slipped her the candies during his official visit. The Spanish guards had in fact been bribed, and some at least of his mushy fiction may be attributed to his desire to divert official attention from their treachery.

Decker did liberate the captive. He described how he dressed her in a sailor's uniform, stuck a Havana cigar in her mouth, walked her to the wharf and put her aboard the steamer *Seneca* bound for New York. A coded message reached the excited Hearst as Decker boarded another ship, the *Panama*. In the compositors' room at the *Journal* the dust was blown off the biggest blackest type to unveil the scoop on pages one, two and three of the Sunday issue:

EVANGELINA CISNEROS
RESCUED BY THE JOURNAL
An American Newspaper Accomplished at a Single Stroke
What the Best Efforts of Diplomacy Failed
Utterly to Bring About in Many Months

More headlines followed: 'Taken from Her Loathsome Havana Prison by a Courageous Correspondent; Now on Her Way to New York Under the Shelter of the Stars and Stripes'.

And then, when the most beautiful girl in Cuba arrived in New York on 13 October:

EVANGELINA CISNEROS REACHES
THE LAND OF LIBERTY

The contrast between Hearst's public image and his private demeanour, in print the lusty demagogue and histrionic sensationalist, in conversation the bashful, softly-spoken, courteous introvert, was again apparent during the reception he staged for Miss Cisneros in the grand ballroom of the Delmonico restaurant. It was followed by a monster open-air jamboree with 100,000 New Yorkers yelling their heads off or shedding a tear in Madison Square—searchlights, fireworks, brass bands, all Willie's favourite toys. The gay scene was dominated by shimmering electric lights announcing 'THE JOURNAL'S WEL- COME TO EVANGELINA CISNEROS'. Mr Hearst nervously popped in to the Delmonico for a handshake with the heroine he had created and hastened back to his waiting carriage, vanishing into the night, alone.

In Washington the *Journal*'s men stage-managed the presentation of the girl to William McKinley. It was seemly that the President who had shaken the hand of the widow of Dr Ruiz, the 'murdered' dentist, should also receive the Cuban Joan of Arc who had not been condemned to the stake or sentenced to twenty years' servitude in Africa.

Miss Cisneros, thus anointed, toured the principal cities to propagate her cause while, coincidentally, the *Sunday Journal* published for three months its version of her life. Then she was dropped into Mr Hearst's garbage bin with all the other page-one sensations, busted generals, diplomats, politicians, criminals, ersatz heroines and Queens for a Day.

It was time for political musical chairs again in Madrid. An uprising in the Philippines, and the continued failure to pacify Cuba, led to the fall of the right-wing Cánovas government[1] and brought Sagasta back for his second term as premier in the autumn of 1897. His anxiety was to appease the Americans and subdue rather than suppress the Cuban rebels. The mild General Blanco replaced Butcher Weyler as Military Governor. The Cubans were promised self-government. The policy was forbearance, to avoid American armed intervention at all costs. America was offered a treaty granting all the advantages enjoyed by Spain in trading in the West Indies. Spain's consuls now resembled Don Quixote more than Hernando Cortés. But—the final folly—the autonomy offered to the Cubans was circumscribed: self-government under the surveillance of General Blanco with the last word still in Madrid. The plan was initially welcomed by President McKinley, but with reservation. War he wished to avoid, strenuously, but he would settle for nothing short of the Republican Party policy—total independence for the Cubans.

The *Maine* carried twenty-four guns and a crew of three hundred and fifty officers and men. On 15 December 1897 the battleship arrived at Key West, the largest of the islands in the reef that stretches westwards from the tip of Florida, provocatively opposite Cuba. The newspapers were aware of the mission in store for her. Should it become necessary to protect American people and property in Cuba she was to sail immediately for Havana on receipt of a coded signal from Consul-General Lee, 'Two Dollars', repeated. Five weeks later, in spite of Lee's advice that the visit should be delayed, Washington ordered the *Maine* to sail to Havana on a 'friendly naval visit' and instructed the Consul-General to arrange for an interchange of social calls with the authorities. Blanco told Lee that the visit would obstruct autonomy, produce excitement, and most probably a demonstration; the Spanish suspected an ulterior motive but made no official protest. The *Maine* anchored in Havana harbour on 25 January 1898, and the *Journal*'s headline did nothing to reassure the Spanish: 'OUR FLAG IN HAVANA AT LAST'. The Peanut Club were joyful.

[1]The assassination of Cánovas on 8 August was a further impediment to his continuation in office.

There was one advocate of persistent sanity in the New York Press, and he will be heard occasionally in this narrative. Edwin Lawrence Godkin was acknowledged as America's finest editorial writer, and his mouthpiece was the *Evening Post*. 'What,' he asked, 'has moved the President to take this step? There is much guessing, but the strong possibility is that he was told that he had to do something to appease the Republicans in Congress. If the Spanish are excitable, what is our Press, our legislators, our Congress? A warship is a curious kind of oil on troubled waters, though the Administration would have us believe the *Maine* to be about the most unctuously peaceful ship that ever sailed.' The *Evening Post* sold only twenty-five thousand copies a day.

At 9.40 on the balmy, tropical night of 15 February the *Maine* blew up.

Two hundred and sixty men were killed in the explosion, more than two-thirds of her crew. The battleship lights were gouged in the same momentous second of time in which the ancient harbour defences of Morro Castle and La Punta fortress, erected to shield Havana from the French and English prowlers of the sixteenth century, were illuminated with the old and new cities in a gruesome *son et lumière*. The moans of men torn apart could not be heard by the rescuers until the tattoo from the small-arms ammunition store, ignited by fire, petered out. The wounded and dying unable to jump into the sea were not located until the smoke and stench cleared away and the horror of it all was grasped as the hull of the *Maine* slowly settled in the mud.

America was shocked and the dwindling advocates of a peaceful solution were dismayed. There was a sick discord between the reactions of the serving men of both nationalities on the spot and of the warmongers in New York City, far away from the reality, confusion and remorse.

Captain Charles Sigsbee, who commanded the *Maine*, was a professional to his fingertips. When the catastrophe occurred he was in his cabin writing a letter to his wife. He sent an instant cable from another vessel, *City of Washington*, to the Secretary of the Navy in Washington urging that public opinion be suspended until further report. He added, to encourage calm: 'Many Spanish officers including representatives of General Blanco now with me to express sympathy.' He later wrote that Blanco, head of the autonomous government, wept when he heard the news and sent his officers not only to convey his regret but to organise assistance. Consul-General Lee also acted promptly with a similar injunction for patience. 'Hope our people will repress excitement and calmly await decision.' The Spanish cruiser *Alfonso XII* despatched boats to save the survivors who had leapt overboard, and serving men of both nationalities worked together in rescue parties.

A moment's reflection could lead only to the conclusion that on any reckoning, unless it were the work of unofficial Spanish maniacs, the Spanish authorities were the last to be suspected. Their attitude throughout the Cuban revolt was to avoid American armed intervention; sabotage of the *Maine*, with the ghastly death toll, was the maddest provocation that could be conceived. The Spanish Empire was now a clutch of ill-assorted remnants. Spain itself was tottering to her grave as a world power. For centuries the wealthiest nation in the world, she was now facing bankruptcy and the disintegration of her society at home. A war with the United States, more powerful and with short lines of communication, could not offer a hope in heaven or hell of victory, deadlock, or an honourable peace. Spain could not muster sufficient resources to rout the native Cubans in her own colony and base of operations; she was now sustained merely by pride and tradition. Premier Sagasta besought the courts and governments of Europe to mediate: they were polite but busy, not over-anxious to intercede in Washington. The US Minister in Madrid informed his government that Spain was willing to accede to all American demands granted time to do so with traditional Iberian dignity.

Those with everything to gain, the Cuban rebels, would be highest on the suspect list of any impartial investigator, but they were not implicated then or thereafter. The probability of accident was in fact overwhelming, and the assumption and public proclamation by Hearst of official Spanish guilt was evil. He was more responsible than any other person, or government, or agency for channelling the shock of the nation into war hysteria.

President McKinley and Navy Secretary Long, in an exercise of unusual statesmanship, expressed the view that an explosion in the *Maine*'s magazine had caused the disaster. Hearst's attitude was best described in his own words in an article he published in his own newspapers in July 1940:[1]

'Your columnist had worked late . . . made up a satisfactory front page, and had gone home.

'On arrival he had found George Thompson, conscientious major-domo, at the door.

'Said George: "There's a telephone from the office. They say it's important news."

The office was called up.

[1] *William Randolph Hearst, a Portrait in his own Words*, edited by Edmond O. Coblentz.

'"Hello, what is the important news?"

'"The battleship *Maine* has been blown up in Havana Harbour."

'"Good Heavens, what have you done with the story?"

'"We have put it on the front page, of course."

'"Have you put anything else on the front page?"

'"Only the other big news."

'"There is not any other big news. Please spread the story all over the page. This means war."'

Mr Hearst did not hesitate to exploit the *Maine* tragedy with stunts for the good and glory of the *Journal*. His contempt for the truth is recorded in his newspaper's headlines, day after day.

16 February: 'CRUISER MAINE BLOWN UP IN HAVANA HARBOUR.' *True.*

17 February: 'THE WARSHIP MAINE WAS SPLIT IN TWO BY AN ENEMY'S SECRET INFERNAL MACHINE.' *Nobody knew the cause of the explosion nor whether an enemy was involved.*

Another headline: 'Captain Sigsbee Practically Declares that His Ship was Blown Up by a Mine or Torpedo.' *Fiction.*

Another headline: 'Strong Evidence of Crime.' *There was no evidence.*

The newspaper correctly reported that the government had set up an investigation and added: 'The *Journal* has independently undertaken another.' Between them, it said, the truth would be known. In one of his favourite roles as Santa Claus, Hearst announced a reward of $50,000 for information furnished to the *Journal* exclusively 'which shall lead to the detention and conviction of the person, persons or government criminally responsible for the loss of the lives of American sailors'. The offer was conceived, written and signed by W. R. Hearst. Few could have thought the government he had in mind was Iceland's.

18 February: 'THE WHOLE COUNTRY THRILLS WITH WAR FEVER.'

The paper reported there were many among the Spanish officers and privates who hated Americans to the point of frenzy. An artist's illustration, seven columns wide, showed the *Maine* anchored over sunken mines connected by wiring to a fort on the shore. *The illustration was fictional.*

The caption said:

'The Spaniards, it is believed, arranged to have the *Maine* anchored over one of the harbour mines . . . If this can be proven, the brutal nature of the Spaniards will be shown in that they waited to spring the mine until after all men had retired for the night. The Maltese Cross shows where the mine may have been fired.'

It is believed . . . if this can be proven . . . may have been.

There were messages, gathered by reporters and printed in this issue, announcing the readiness and anxiety of American militia for service.

19 February: a no-news day, but that did not silence Hearst. A fund was launched to set up a monument in memory of the dead men, and glittering personalities were willing to lend their names to the enterprise; except one, ex-President Grover Cleveland, who declined to allow his sorrow for those who died to be perverted to an advertising scheme for the New York *Journal*.

20 February: 'HOW THE MAINE ACTUALLY LOOKS AS IT LIES WRECKED BY SPANISH TREACHERY, IN HAVANA BAY.'

There was still no evidence of treachery, Spanish or otherwise. A headline promised proof of a submarine mine. *The news item referred to omitted the heralded proof.*

This was the day on which the official Court of Inquiry, announced in Washington on 17 February by Secretary Long, left to begin its investigation in Havana. In the same issue the newspaper regaled its readers with a new game for four persons with cards called 'Game of War with Spain'.

21 February: 'HAVANA POPULACE INSULTS THE MEMORY OF THE MAINE VICTIMS.'

The evidence was that Spanish officers had been heard to boast that any other American ship visiting Havana would follow the *Maine*. Three days before this invention the naval, military, church and civil leaders in Havana, both Spanish and Cuban, had organised and attended a State funeral of impressive solemnity for the American dead. The plots where they lay were dedicated in perpetuity to the United States.

23 February: 'THE MAINE WAS DESTROYED BY TREACHERY.'

The Court of Inquiry had not yet heard a witness.

That Hearst succeeded in his objective is established by the circulation figures of the morning *Journal*.

The week of 9 January, an average of 416,885.
On 17 February, two days after the *Maine* blew up, 1,025,624.
On 18 February, 1,036,140.
For the week beginning 27 February, an average of 632,217.

The *Evening Journal* reached 519,032, announced as a record. The *Sunday Journal* increased its sale by 200,000 in six weeks.

The *World* was not prepared to allow Mr Hearst to monopolise the war; patriotism was profitable, and Pulitzer was also hungry for circulation. He lampooned Hearst's war news as 'written by fools for fools', and then surpassed Hearst in foolery. The *World* warned on 16 February of the damage possible from the Spanish cruiser *Vizcaya*, that day visiting New York on its reciprocal goodwill cruise. It said that while lying off the Battery, 'her shells will (sic) explode on the Harlem River and in the suburbs of Brooklyn'.

There was still no war; hence the resolve of Hearst to sustain the pressure while the nation awaited the official report on the *Maine*. Two weeks before it was completed the *Journal* falsely anticipated its findings. 'The Court of Inquiry finds that Spanish government officials blew up the *Maine*.' The warship 'was purposely moved where a Spanish mine exploded by Spanish officers would destroy it'. On 27 March, the day before the Court's findings were made public, the *Journal* predicted that the report would call for immediate war. It staked its reputation as a war prophet on this assertion: 'There will be a war with Spain as certain as the sun shines unless Spain abases herself in the dust and voluntarily consents to the freedom of Cuba.'

Mr Hearst at his own expense sent three Senators and two Representatives to the colony as his special commissioners. They duly reported on the circumstances the people were enduring. Senator Gallinger, one of the party, told the Senate that the cruel Spanish policy had resulted in the death of six hundred thousand Cubans. The demise of Mrs Thurston, wife of another Senator and a member of the party, was attributed by the *Journal* to the horrors she had witnessed. The lady succumbed to a heart attack aboard Hearst's yacht, but not until she had penned this homily for his women readers:

'Oh! Mothers of the Northland, who tenderly clasp your little ones to your loving hearts! Think of the black despair that filled each [Cuban] mother's heart as she felt her life-blood ebb away, and knew

47

that she had left her little ones to perish from the pain of starvation and disease.'

Edwin Lawrence Godkin put this aspect of the Hearst Cuban Circus into perspective in an attack on 'the yellow journals':

'When one of [them] offers a yacht voyage with free wine, rum and cigars and a good bed, under the guise of philanthropy, or gets up a committee for Holy purposes, and promises to puff it, it can get almost anyone it pleases to go on the yacht voyage and serve on the committee—senators, lawyers, divines, scholars, poets, presidents and what not . . . Every one who knows anything about 'yellow journals' knows that everything they do and say is intended to promote sales . . . No one—absolutely no one—supposes a yellow journal cares five cents about the Cubans, the *Maine* victims, or any one else. A yellow journal office is probably the nearest approach to hell in atmosphere existing in any Christian state. A better place in which to prepare a young man for eternal damnation than a yellow-journal office does not exist.'[1]

The Court of Inquiry into the *Maine* was an exclusively American exercise conducted by officers of the US North Atlantic Squadron. Predictably, the request of the Spanish government to participate was rejected. Its plea that American newspaper correspondents would not be drafted to the tribunal *was* granted. The investigation in Havana took twenty-three days and the secrecy sustained was unique in official affairs. There were no press interviews with the divers sent down day after day to examine the hull.

The man on the diplomatic tightrope while Washington and Spain anxiously awaited the findings was Stewart Woodford, US Minister in Madrid. On 19 March he telegraphed McKinley urging delay in action on the report to allow more time for negotiation. The reply next day was unequivocal. The report must go to Congress soon; feeling in the US was very acute; the loss of the *Maine* might be settled peacefully if full reparation were made, but conditions in Cuba demanded immediate action by the US unless Spain restored an honourable peace that would stop starvation of people and give them the opportunity to take care of

---

[1] N.Y. *Evening Post*, 17 March 1898.

The origin of the contemptuous phrase 'yellow journalism' was a strip cartoon character, The Yellow Kid, so called because of his colouring from head to foot. He appeared for a time in both the *World* and the *Journal* comic supplements. The taunt came to be used generally for the type of journalism in which Hearst and Pulitzer at that time indulged. The Yellow Kid himself was a lovable scamp.

themselves. The *Journal* dismissed the peace efforts of Minister Woodford as twaddle.

The report was in President McKinley's hands on 22 March. On 26 March Woodford received a summary. On 27 March he was telegraphed from Washington to attempt to obtain an armistice in Cuba between the Spanish and the Cubans until 1 October, and if possible acceptance of the President of the United States as final arbitrator if terms of peace were not satisfactorily settled by 1 October. A third request was for the immediate revocation of the reconcentration order. These cables, not disclosed until later in *United States Foreign Relations Reports*, establish the anxiety of McKinley to avoid war with Spain even at the eleventh hour: they also explain his delaying tactics over the *Maine* report.

The note to Madrid was garbled by the *Journal* as: 'OUR POSITIVE ULTIMATUM SENT TO SPAIN—"HOSTILITIES MUST CEASE AT ONCE".' It forecast, with no evidence, an intervention message by the President the following week. A move unknown to the Press was Washington's suggestion to Spain a week earlier that the *Maine* loss might be peacefully settled if full reparation were made, with the important rider that general conditions in Cuba could no longer be endured and would 'demand immediate action on our part unless Spain restores honourable peace which will stop starvation of people . . .'[1] Minister Woodford's frank discussion with the Spanish government on the possibility of an American purchase of Cuba[2] was also a well-preserved secret. The headline 'US BUYS CUBA', a one-day wonder, would not have appealed to W. R. Hearst.

On 28 March the President submitted the Inquiry's findings to Congress. The destruction of the vessel was unanimously attributed to the explosion of a submarine mine which caused a partial explosion of two or more of the forward magazines. The Court was unable to pin responsibility upon any person. Many questions were left unanswered. The mining of a home-based harbour was manifestly hazardous in wartime and lunatic in peacetime. Was the submarine mine laid in the harbour or did it drift in from the Gulf of Mexico? An explosive device with sufficient destructive power to blow a battleship asunder was too heavy and too bulky a toy to be rolled along the sandy bottom by a trio of unofficial Spanish loyalists or fanatical Cuban rebels.

The findings neither convicted nor wholly exonerated the Spanish government. Congress received the report in a 'deeply anxious silence'. In

[1] and [2] *United States Foreign Relations Reports.*

his message the President asked for deliberate consideration, debate was postponed, and the matter was referred to the Committee on Foreign Affairs. Congress received the message with 'great disappointment and dissatisfaction'.[1]

The circulation war excluded the popular press from the considerations of patience and restraint that Congress was prepared to exercise for a day or two. Two cartoons in the *Journal* of 30 March ridiculed the Administration's delay. One showed Uncle Sam, his hands manacled with rope, defenceless against missiles labelled '*Maine* Disaster' and 'Ruiz', hurled at him by Spain. The other depicted Mark Hanna with a shrivelled President McKinley tucked in his rump pocket, depositing the White Feather of Dishonour into Uncle Sam's hat. The readers were urged to plague their Congressmen with letters of protest. On 2 April it published the lie that 'the suppressed testimony shows Spain is guilty of blowing up the *Maine*' and said that the truth was being hidden from the public.

Hearst and his editor Arthur Brisbane (salary, plus commission on circulation) were goading the President into war with a cynical contempt for truth, justice or any semblance of decency. An illustration showed Spanish soldiers bayoneting Cubans. The caption said: 'The wires bring news of the butchery of two hundred more *reconcentrados*. Two hundred murders more or less is of little importance in Spain's record, and McKinley can hardly be expected to get excited about this.' Hearst and Brisbane instructed their reporters to interview, nearly two months after the tragedy, the mothers of sailors who were killed. 'How would President McKinley have felt, I wonder, if he had a son on the *Maine* murdered as was my little boy? Would he then forget the crime and let it go unpunished while the body of his child was lying as food for the sharks in the Spanish harbour of Havana?'

The *World* castigated the Inquiry's report as an inadequate and chilling document and the President's message as lacking a touch of natural sympathy or a word of honest indignation. Pulitzer decided the time had come to stop the deliberating and proceed to action... 'If Spain will not punish her miscreants, we must punish Spain.' The *Sun*, *Times* and the *Herald*, and the *Mail* and *Express* were united in demanding freedom for Cuba and were ready for war if necessary to gain that objective. Three newspapers only still pressed for peace—the *Evening Post*, *Journal of Commerce* and *Tribune*. Godkin's *Post* urged the 'hotheads' in Congress to consider the unfavourable financial condition

[1] The Washington correspondent of the *Herald*. He added that the war spirit was rapidly rising and that party lines were being laid aside.

of the nation, and disregard warmongering letters from individual constituents. It strove to counteract the 'pure hysteria which goes by the name of patriotism'. For Mr Hearst individually Godkin reserved a unique Oscar of opprobrium:

> 'A blackguard boy with several millions of dollars at his disposal has more influence on the use a great nation may make of its credit, of its army and navy, of its name and traditions, than all the statesmen and philosophers and professors in the country. If this does not supply food for reflection about the future of the nation to thoughtful men, it must be because the practice of reflection has ceased.'

There were indeed hotheads in Congress. The ominous silence for the *Maine* report and the President's message on 28 March was the lull before the gale. Within twenty-four hours, roused by public opinion (roused by the Press), the nation's representatives in the House and Senate were offering resolutions that if passed would have meant war.

In Spain the olive branch was being waved with equal fervour. Premier Sagasta was progressively yielding to American demands and the diplomacy of us Minister Woodford in Madrid was on the brink of success. On 30 March General Blanco abolished the concentration areas in Cuba. On 31 March the Spanish government was prepared to submit the *Maine* dispute to arbitration, would grant a truce if the rebels asked for one, and proposed that the terms for permanent peace in Cuba be negotiated by the ('autonomous') government of the island, it being understood that the powers reserved by the constitution of the central government (Madrid) were not lessened and diminished. There was no offer of an immediate end to hostilities. In Woodford's view a declaration of armistice would have provoked a revolution in Spain. The concessions were rejected by the New York Press with varying degrees of contempt or dissatisfaction and summarily dismissed by the *Journal* as an insulting evasion.

Spain made another move for peace when the Pope proposed mediation. On 5 April McKinley was informed by Woodford that the Queen-Regent was willing to proclaim immediate cessation of hostilities in the island of Cuba, to become effective as soon as accepted by the insurgents. There was no assurance, even by secret diplomacy, of total independence for Cuba, nor did Washington or Woodford insist. He informed McKinley:

> 'They cannot go further in open concessions to us without being overthrown by their own people here in Spain. They want peace if they

can keep peace and save the dynasty. They prefer the chances of war, with the certain loss of Cuba, to the overthrow of the dynasty.'

The Press as a whole, ignorant at this stage of the Spanish concessions, paid small attention to the Vatican's offer of mediation; the *Journal*, to whom no concession was acceptable, predicted that armed soldiers were soon to take the place of talking diplomats. The pages of all the newspapers were filled with war news, real or imaginary, and bellicose pronouncements by public men ranging from Congressmen to college presidents.

On 9 April Woodford cabled that General Blanco had been authorised to proclaim an armistice unconditionally, the final concession Woodford believed would preserve peace. 'I hope,' he cabled, 'that nothing will now be done to humiliate Spain as I am satisfied that the present government is going, and is loyally ready to go, as fast and as far as it can. With your power of action sufficiently free, you will win the fight on your own lines.' On 11 April the insurgents in Cuba issued a proclamation refusing point-blank to suspend hostilities.

The same day McKinley made a decision, or decisively reached an indecision, which triggered the course of events.

The man on the cross lived in the White House. William McKinley was twenty-fifth in the line of Presidents, the first of those against whom Hearst flexed his muscles and tested the power of his newspapers. In the Civil War he had been courageous in battle; as an attorney in Ohio he earned the permanent affection of labour by volunteering, in spite of hostile public opinion, to defend thirty-three rioting miners and achieving the acquittal of thirty-two. His election and re-election as Governor of Ohio led to his nomination with Mark Hanna's blessing as Republican President. McKinley's humble origins, the seventh of nine children of the small-time operator of a few pig-iron furnaces, appealed to the imagination of the American people. Stern, righteous and forbidding in his official photographs, he was a father figure whose sincerity was accepted by the majority with the votes.

As a lawyer in his fifty-fifth year he was accustomed to sifting evidence and assessing the difference between stupidity and criminal intent. As a politician he was not deaf to the siren call of public popularity. As a President he was aware of the difference between leading a reluctant nation into a necessary war and a jingo nation into an unnecessary war. The choice was between lonely statesmanship and vote-assured acclaim. Hanna was pressing for a peaceful solution and Woodford in Madrid could achieve peace with honour. There was still one card to play—a guarantee from Spain of Cuban independence even if at that stage, for internal reasons in Spain, the pledge must remain secret. With the threat of immediate war as the alternative, Woodford might well have achieved that goal.

Could the President defy the Press, now baying for war? The *Journal* dismissed Spain's offer of armistice as a ruse to gain time. On 11 April the *Herald* reported that Congress looked unfavourably on the offer and was likely to pay no attention to it. On 11 April the *World* said: 'Our national duty is plain. The President might make light of a hideous insult to our flag, a hideous crime against the people of the United States, but the Senate and the House of Representatives refuse to go down with him to everlasting execration.' It was the morning of the Presidential decision and the Press were derisively rejecting the armistice offer.

Could he lead or dominate Congress? The *Herald* reported the day after his message intended for 6 April had been postponed: 'The House was in an uproar yesterday. Men of both parties were suspicious of the President, distrustful of his policy ... In the Senate there was amazement.' The President had his own daily reports on the mood of the Senators and Representatives.

He surrendered to the warmongers. His political sidestep on 11 April signified the victory of William Randolph Hearst. In a message bereft of leadership, relegating the new Spanish offer to his closing words, William McKinley abandoned the historic decision to Congress. His statesmanship was exposed as spineless by the vote in the upper house, the Senate: the resolution for war was passed on 19 April by the narrow majority of four. The reality of the President's fear of unpopularity if he continued to press for a peaceful solution, demonstrably within his grasp, was indeed proved by the emotive decision in the House of Representatives, a majority of 294 for war with only six voting against. A Republican President genuflected to a rabble-rousing Democrat newspaper.

The *Evening Journal* of 20 April 1898, several days before the formal declaration of war by both sides, proclaimed in type four inches deep:

NOW AVENGE THE MAINE!

Mr Hearst's gift for acquisition exhibited a new dimension. He was already the owner of the San Francisco *Examiner* and the New York *Journal*. He now became the owner of the Spanish-American War, and his ecstasy reached its climax. On two successive days in May he used the front page of his newspaper to ask his readers:

HOW DO YOU LIKE THE JOURNAL'S WAR?

He later described it as a war of adventure, a knight-errant war, a war in the ancient manner, a war of the old school. He hired the yachts *Buccaneer* and *Anita*, with a tug and steamers for good measure; his private fleet sped to Havana to accommodate his battery of special correspondents.

Madison Square and Fifth Avenue were bedecked with flags. The jobbers in Wall Street stiffened their shoulders and sported patriotic rosettes in their lapels. The seedy entertainers in the clipjoints of Broadway prowled around the second-hand music shops for traditional jingoistic songs and ditties. The restaurants were plugging Victory cocktails and ice-cream moulded into battleships. Special editions of the papers, 'Extra! Extra!', were littering the streets like confetti and Mr Hearst and Mr Pulitzer were selling their million copies a day. The aloof *Atlantic Monthly* startled its readers by slapping the Stars and Stripes on its cover. A Chamber of Commerce in Ohio voted unanimously to boycott the Spanish onion.

The Spanish-American War was a brief encounter, pathetically one-sided. It began in the last week of April and ended in August, in time for the summer holidays. It was an international mugging, principally conducted on the high seas; luckily for the United States, because its army at that time was noted more for its prowess on the baseball field than the battlefield and its State Department was in poor shape. The four new battleships of the US North Atlantic Squadron were replete with fuel and ammunition, ready for action. The Spanish Navy could do little more than exercise the freedom of ordering their last breakfast; they scarcely had time to write their farewell letters home.

Commodore George Dewey, commanding the Asiatic force, led his ships into Manila Bay in the Philippines before daylight on 1 May and spent the morning in sporting fashion sinking that part of the Spanish fleet by superior gunfire. (US casualties: seven men slightly wounded.)

The Spanish Admiral Cervera, who favoured a more spirited final manoeuvre, dashed from the Cape Verde Islands with his four cruisers and three destroyers and tucked them into Santiago Harbour on the south of Cuba, which the US Atlantic Squadron promptly blockaded. When Cervera's ships were ordered out of the bay on 3 July by some unthinking landlubbers in command in Havana, the hope was that they would escape to the west. They all finished up stranded on the beaches, sinking or afire, out-gunned. It was like harpooning dolphins. (US casualties: no report.)

The US Army, ill-prepared, was not geared to armed combat with foreigners and the account it gave of itself in the field was erratic. Tropical disease and climatic exposure notched more victims than the enemy's infantry, but the expeditionary forces achieved their objectives. They occupied Santiago in Cuba in the third week of July and Manila in the second week of August. A third force grabbed Puerto Rico, a sitting duck.

On 18 July before the US Army had completed its missions, the Spanish government asked France to bring about a cessation of hostilities. The war ended on 12 August. Spanish rule ceased on 1 January 1899, and Cuba became an independent republic after three years of US military rule and magnaminity.

The war Hearst promised Remington to furnish lasted 115 days, with minimal US casualties. Its consequences were historically portentous. The United States established its status and confidence as a world imperialist power strategically dominating new spheres of influence. The pledge of independence for Cuba was honoured, but Puerto Rico, the Philippines, and Guam in the Marianas were possessed. The annexation of Hawaii, a peaceful negotiation, was a by-product. The Caribbean Sea became an American pond and the Pacific, with no objection from Britain or Japan, a private ocean. Access to new foreign markets was assured, the American interests in China protected, and the US achieved a leading role in Far Eastern affairs. Within six years a fifty-mile canal was cut and opened through the isthmus of Panama, linking the Pacific and the Atlantic for ocean-going ships, and the US leapt from sixth place to second in the league of world war fleets. The US Army was reformed and reorganised. In the brutal computation of warfare, the cost in white human life had been negligible. 'In God We Trust': the American eagle spread its wings.

Nor was the three-month war disastrous in the long term for Spain. It retired ignominiously from its jumble sale of imperialist remnants in the western hemisphere, jettisoned the scrap value of its sunken fleets and embarked upon two decades of industrial and cultural renaissance. Wisely, in World Wars One and Two, it basked in neutrality.

William McKinley was renominated in 1900 for a second term with no opposition. He trounced the Democrats and was able to say with some smugness and conviction: 'I can no longer be called the President of a party; I am President of the whole people.'

Tomás Estrada Palma, the schoolteacher head of the Peanut Club, who used Hearst and was used by Hearst, became the first President of the new Cuban republic. He cabled the publisher: 'I do not believe we could have secured our independence without the aid you rendered.' In 1949, two years before his death, Hearst was honoured by the Grand Cross of the Order of Carlos Manuel de Cespedes, Cuba's highest decoration.

Evangelina Cosio y Cisneros became Señora Carlos Carbonel; the bridegroom was a member of Karl Decker's rescue party. Decker himself was under The Chief's orders to liberate Captain Dreyfus from the French in Devil's Island, studying the map and costing an expedition that never sailed.

General Gomez met up with his Fifth Avenue sword but not until the war was over. He did not want it. He berated the imbeciles in New York who had wasted two thousand dollars that would have bought 'shoes for my barefooted men, shirts for their naked backs, cartridges for their useless rifles'.

For William Randolph Hearst the war was the orgasmic experience of his sixty-year reign as a newspaper potentate, nostalgically savoured in his old age. He appeared at the front as his own war correspondent, demanding a receipt from a US warship for twenty-nine shipwrecked Spanish sailors they didn't want to hear about. He ordered James Creelman to buy a big British steamer and make preparations to sink it in the Suez Canal to obstruct naval reinforcements sailing from Spain. When it was all over bar the boasting he reached an armistice of his own with Joseph Pulitzer; henceforth no internecine strife, each granting the other immunity from personal attack. Hearst was still the incurable adolescent, yet his name was now known throughout the world. Triumphant and content, he set off on another of his European pleasure tours, buying up paintings, statuettes, porcelain, minatures, ancient German armour, a gilded Egyptian mummy case and Cardinal Richelieu's bed, an array of art treasures for display in later years in his palace San Simeon, or storage in vaults where they were never to be seen again; he delayed his visit to Spain in search of loot until a later trip, but then made up for lost time by dismantling a Spanish castle in numbered stones to send home by ship. He took his leave for the journey with this hymn of praise in the *Journal* of 25 September:

'The force of the newspaper is the greatest force in civilisation.

'Under republican government, newspapers form and express public opinion.

'They suggest and control legislation.

'They declare wars. They make and unmake statesmen.

'They punish criminals, especially the powerful. They reward with approving publicity the good deeds of citizens everywhere.

'The newspapers control the nation because they REPRESENT THE PEOPLE.'

The Spanish-American War set the seal on his creed as a newspaper operator. Truth to him was a moving target; he never aimed for the bull and rarely pierced the outer ring. The playboy expelled from Harvard for pisspot raillery at twenty-one graduated in megalomania in New York City at thirty-five. Hearst's 'New Journalism' had established itself as a war veteran while still in its infancy, and within a year, when William McKinley's second term of office was ended abruptly by a bullet, his successor Theodore Roosevelt was publicly indicting Hearst's newspapers for complicity in the tragedy.

Senator Hearst's son was nursing political ambitions of his own, certain that the Democratic Party, given the right policies and the right leadership, could oust the Republicans. William Jennings Bryan, about to be nominated by the Democrats for the Presidency, had no difficulty in persuading him to launch a new paper in Chicago. It was a newspaper cemetery with half a dozen ailing journals and only two (Republican) that were successful. 'All right,' said Hearst, 'if the leaders will recognise that I am doing it for the Party's sake, not for the money.' In that hazardous exercise the circulation war was fought by gangs of thugs hired by the rival proprietors; the journalistic ethics of the time are reflected in the play and film *The Front Page*. The Chicago *American* materialised in thirty days, the product of Hearst's energy and talent at organisation, on the eve of Bryan's nomination. A Hearst newspaper was inevitable at some time in Chicago but doing it for the Party's sake was rewarded by Hearst's appointment as president of the National Association of Democratic Clubs, a power-base more significant than Bryan or the Democratic hierachy realised when placed in the hands of a thruster who now owned newspapers in three major cities and was soon to launch the Boston *American*. Hearst's personal control over the clubs' activities and loyalties was guaranteed by his own man as secretary, Maximilian Ihmsen. He was a long-standing stalwart of Hearst's Washington bureau, destined to become The Chief's own campaign manager, and eventually, political pallbearer.

With the result of the election a certainty, Hearst saved his ammunition until the battle was over. The *Evening Journal* conceded Bryan's inevitable defeat on the day the votes were cast and before they were counted, acknowledging McKinley's 'irreproachable character' and declaring that the United States would be safe whichever side won. The campaign against McKinley materialised soon after his victory. He grappled with the big business Trusts with the low-key enthusiasm that might be expected from a Republican President created by big business, and was therefore a legitimate target for the Democratic Press. The campaign started with a recurring headline on the editorial page, 'DESTRUCTION OF THE CRIMINAL TRUSTS', backed by cartoons depicting the Trusts as an evil gorilla and McKinley as their tool in office. The onslaught then became wildly irresponsible.

There was already one skeleton in Hearst's cupboard; one that was to rattle for many a year. On 4 February 1900, shortly after Governor-elect William Goebel was shot dead in an election fracas in Kentucky, the *Journal* had published this quatrain by Ambrose Bierce:

> 'The bullet that pierced Goebel's breast
> Can not be found in all the West;
> Good reason: it is speeding here
> To stretch McKinley on his bier.'

Now Arthur Brisbane was writing that McKinley was 'the most hated creature on the American continent', and on 10 April 1901 the first edition of the *Evening Journal* published the following words in an editorial generally attributed to Brisbane: 'If bad institutions and bad men can be got rid of only by killing, then the killing must be done.'

On 5 September President McKinley visited Buffalo in New York State to speak at a trade and cultural fair, the Pan-American Exposition, an event to be followed the next day by a public reception in the Temple of Music. The occasion was planned as the climax to a policy speech-making tour in the Western States, and there was a cogent reason why precautions of an extraordinary nature were taken for his safety. The previous year King Humbert of Italy had been assassinated by G. Bresci, a man of Italian descent whose original hometown was traced to Paterson in New Jersey, where he had worked as a silk weaver. It was an inner secret among the security services of the principal countries that anarchists in Europe were conspiring to obliterate one by one the rulers of the world. They had drawn up their death list: Austria first, then Italy, Russia, Britain, America. The discovery by the US Intelligence Bureau of a cell of anarchists at Paterson was the cause of alarm, and there was fear of an assassin's bullet during the election. Mark Hanna thought McKinley might not survive his second term.

On 6 September in the Temple of Music the President was shaking hands at the reception with admirers, enjoying his popularity, closely cosseted by his guards, but not closely enough. The hand of Leon Czolgosz, a twenty-eight-year-old psychopathic anarchist, was wrapped in a scarf that concealed a revolver. He shot the President twice at close range.

Hearst was in Chicago nursing his new newspaper when he heard the news. 'Things are going to be very bad,' he said to his Chicago publisher. They were. In spite of Hearst's frantic efforts to do all the right things, he knew what the repercussions might be. An editorial oozing remorse appeared in all his newspapers:

'The hopes and thoughts of every American mind are fixed upon the President battling courageously, patiently, for life. Earnestly he longs to live:

'First, and above all, that he may not leave his much loved wife alone behind him.

'Second, that he may devote his days and his strength to the programme of national duty and national prosperity which his latest speech outlined.'

Homer Davenport, the principal cartoonist, had depicted McKinley that week as a dancing Negro in a Big Trust Minstrel Show with Mark Hanna in the lead part, conducting. A new contribution by the same artist showed a disconsolate Uncle Sam standing respectfully at the President's bedside, holding his hand.

The President rallied, but then died from his wounds nine days after the shooting. Hearst himself now became the most hated man in America; the muckraker was raked. Other newspapers exhumed the 'killing must be done' editorial published five months before McKinley's assassination and Ambrose Bierce's sombre quatrain written nineteen months before.

The first blow was struck by the Grand Army of the Republic; every member excluded from his household the New York *Journal*, a 'teacher of anarchism and a vile sheet', unfit for perusal by any respecter of morality and good government. Other organisations, church groups, clubs, and libraries announced a boycott. In a number of towns Hearst was hanged or burned in effigy and his life was threatened; like Ambrose Bierce, he now considered it prudent to carry a revolver and took care his mail was screened for bombs.

Was Hearst culpable? To what extent? One newspaper alleged that when the Polish-American gunman Leon Czolgosz was seized, a *Journal* was found in his pocket, a copy containing an editorial attack on McKinley. If he had read that copy he might well have read the 'killing must be done' editorial in another issue, or Bierce's four foreboding lines. There was *no* newspaper in Czolgosz's pocket. The assassin was offered $10,000 that might be useful to his family for a confession that his inspiration for the deed came from a paper published by Hearst. No, he hadn't read a Hearst newspaper; what had inspired him was a talk by Emma Goldman, the notorious American anarchist. The grilling by the police, the trial, even his approaching execution did not change his story.

Ambrose Bierce's quatrain was perhaps ambiguous. His own explanation of those four prophetic lines was that Goebel's assassination might be a perilous precedent if unpunished. Bierce's name was not mentioned at the trial. 'As to Mr Hearst,' he wrote, 'I dare say he first saw the lines when all this hullabaloo directed his attention to them . . . Hearst's newspapers had always been so unjust that no injustice could be done to them, and had been incredibly rancorous toward McKinley, but no doubt it was my luckless prophecy that cost him tens of thousands of dollars and a growing political prestige.'

The important point was that the proprietor was away in Europe when the quatrain was published. He never mentioned the matter to the poet: 'I fancy there must be a human side to a man like that,' said Bierce.[1] Hearst did not complain to Brisbane when he described McKinley as the most hated creature on the American continent. Nor did he dismiss him on the spot when he wrote, or caused to be written and certainly published, the inflammatory words: '*If bad institutions and bad men can be got rid of only by killing, then the killing must be done.*' Hearst did personally tone down the outrageous gospel in the succeeding editions.

The new President, Theodore Roosevelt, referred to the national tragedy in his first message to Congress, portraying his predecessor's assassin as a . . .

'. . . professed anarchist, inflamed by the teachings of professed anarchists, and probably also by the reckless utterances of those who, on the stump and in the public press, appeal to the dark and evil spirits of malice and greed, envy and sullen hatred. The wind is sowed by the men who preach such doctrines, and they cannot escape their share of responsibility for the whirlwind that is reaped.'

William Randolph Hearst had his say in the *Journal*:

'From coast to coast this newspaper has been attacked and is being attacked with savage ferocity by the incompetent, the failures of journalism, by the kept organs of plutocracy heading the mob.

'The Hearst newspapers are American papers for Americans. They are conservative papers, for the truest conservatism is that radicalism which would uproot revolution-breeding abuses . . . All the enemies of the people, all who reap where others have sown, all the rascals and their organs, and many fools caught by the malignant uproar, are yelling at the *Journal*. LET THEM YELL.

[1] *The Life of Ambrose Bierce* by Walter Neale.

'Note the thrift of the parasitic press . . . It would draw profit from the terrible deed of the wretch who shot down the President.'

Hearst was not away in Europe when that humbug was printed; he wrote it. Nobody was sacked. There was no public contrition for what had appeared in his newspapers. The one and only gesture he made was to change the name of the New York *Journal* to the New York *American*, no doubt hoping that the less savoury episodes in its past would be interred with the remains of William McKinley.

In 1902 Hearst began to covet the White House, regardless of the vocational hazard, the assassination of three Presidents within thirty-six years. The Democrats sought his financial help and were hungry for the support of his newspapers. They cared little for his own pretensions as a vote-getter and resented the contempt in which he held professional politicians at all levels. His newspaper colleagues were also discouraging. They considered the White House an absurd goal for one so tongue-tied and gauche on the platform; the Gettysburg Address itself would raise a laugh intoned by a physical giant with a soprano voice, an irrepressible giggle and stage-fright. There was doubt whether the sensationalist who had projected himself as a front-page reformer and warmonger would be accepted as a serious statesman.

Yet his hopes were not forlorn. He had the flair to spot and exploit in America's interest as well as his own the big national or international situation. Early in 1901, photographing on a holiday cruise up the Nile, he saw a paragraph in a well-thumbed English newspaper that excited his interest and action. Hearst knew that the United States and Great Britain had been negotiating over the construction of a canal linking the Pacific and Atlantic oceans, but the English newspaper disclosed that:

'The treaty has been signed and ratified by the British Cabinet. All that remains is ratification by the American Senate. The United States and Great Britain agree the proposed canal *shall not be fortified*.'

Hearst didn't agree. His editor in New York received a cable of instruction: 'Better no canal than an unfortified canal. Marshal every resource at your command. Fight ratification of the Treaty.' Theodore Roosevelt, then Governor of New York, knew Hearst was right. The controversy was not resolved when McKinley was assassinated, but was resolved when Roosevelt succeeded him as President. 'I despise Hearst,' he said to Secretary of State Hay, who had negotiated the treaty, 'but dammit, this time Hearst is right. We must have a fortified canal.' On such judgements as that, scrawled on the back of an envelope, conveyed to a cable office seventy miles away by a Nubian courier, there was no intrinsic reason why a newspaper proprietor whose parish was the world should be less effective at the White House than any of the cavalcade of lawyers and soldiers who preceded Theodore Roosevelt or the lawyers and soldiers and peanut farmer who succeeded him.

One setback to Hearst was his moral 'complicity', believed and deplored by many, in the McKinley tragedy: the instability of his character was another. The Daughters of the American Revolution would not have been impressed had a rival newspaper located and publicised Miss Tessie Powers to whom, loyally and graciously, he was sending monthly cheques when she was seventy and in need. Even if she had been in direct lineal descent of a soldier of the period she would have been blackballed on one rigid rule, 'personal acceptability to the society'. There was no escape clause for newspaper proprietors' mistresses.

On domestic American problems the people's champion initiated or blessed the causes that appealed to the people. Each move, backed by his newspapers, was organised with his usual flamboyance. Under his leadership the National Association achieved a strength of 12,000 Democratic Clubs with 3,000,000 members, and 'President W. R. Hearst' was prominent on every battle order or information sheet they received. There was a noticeable transformation in his appearance on political occasions; he shed his flowing bow ties and gaudy suitings. Money had bought everything he had wanted so far: why not the White House?

From 1903 to 1907 Hearst endured two terms in the United States House of Representatives, responsible for more editorials than speeches. In 1905 he nearly, but didn't, become mayor of New York. The next year the White House seemed a trifle nearer when the Democrats nominated him for Governor of New York State. He was defeated, and defeated again more decisively on his second attempt for the mayoralty in 1909. He remained in the political ring until 1922, often proposed but never nominated, and then a row in 1932 shattered his allegiance to the Democrats. The public had Mr Hearst's word for it that the force of the newspaper was the greatest force in civilisation, with the formation of public opinion and the making and unmaking of statesmen among its run-of-the-mill miracles. A deal with Tammany got him into Congress, but the greatest force in civilisation failed to upgrade him to mayor, Governor or President. The mis-use of his Press power in his abortive political career was not unique in the twentieth century though unsurpassed in sordid wheeler-dealing.

As the richest and most courageous newspaper operator in the United States he exposed time and again the municipal corruption of Tammany Hall, headquarters of the executive committee of the Democratic Party in New York County; as a statesman-in-waiting he was ready to connive with the Tammany bosses when he figured it suited him. He once attended a Tammany fund-raising jamboree graced by the presence of a politician once accused of murder, a Sing Sing expatriate found guilty of murder, a fire commissioner who had murdered a political opponent, and a notoriously fraudulent divorce lawyer.

Hearst entered into an alliance with the new Tammany boss Charles Murphy, a New York East Sider, a former shipyard worker, street-car conductor and saloon keeper, who—to be fair to 'Silent Charlie'—was more honest than his immediate predecessor but by no means immune to temptation once he was in the saddle. Their initial deal was of some simplicity: the Hearst newspapers would support Murphy's nomination of Bird S. Coler for Governor, then cosmetised as 'New York's Honest Comptroller', and Hearst in return would be nominated for a safe Democratic seat in the House of Representatives for the district where he lived.

On the night of the election of the new Congressman his editors faced a startling problem in the assessment of news values. It was an election he couldn't lose, but he wanted all the voters to know who was winning. He had booked Madison Square Park for another firework display and unfortunately nearly a hundred of the public, there to cheer the fun, were killed or injured when a mortar exploded: the device was supposed to ignite the fireworks not massacre the sightseers.

Hearst celebrated his victory and also his marriage to Millicent Willson, twenty years his junior, with a holiday in Europe. He attended Congress only nine times during the first six-month session, but when he was in Washington the man with his eye on the 1904 Presidency did not waste his time. The Bills he introduced had a familiar ring about them and his programme for reform was well publicised in his newspapers: shorter hours for men engaged on government work, better roads, bigger salaries for Supreme Court judges. He harassed the sugar Trust, sought to curb the Standard Oil monopoly, and pressed for the Federal ownership of the cable and telegraph services. Many of the measures he presented in his cavalier, Robin Hood fashion with no success were later passed by Congress when sponsored by more painstaking advocates who mastered the parliamentary techniques. Organising Christmas relief funds was more to his liking than the routine work on Capitol Hill.

One of the principal functions of his newspapers during this political period was shamelessly promoting The Chief. The name 'W. R. Hearst' was displayed under the titles; contents that justified any prominence bore the warning 'Copyright, W. R. Hearst'. He was the pioneer of subliminal advertising, repeating his name a score of times in every issue and blazoning it in the headlines when he appealed for funds during national disasters. His newspapers glorified his charitable donations and quoted all who praised him. In a single issue of his New York *American* his name appeared in headlines three times on the same page, and the diminutive *W. R. Hearst* soon burgeoned into William Randolph Hearst. Who had ever heard of G. Washington or A. Lincoln?

The more the public, especially his constituents, were excited by his stunts the less impressed was Congress. He made enemies where he needed friends by ignoring the Democratic Party line, offending the skilled stalwarts, and above all by his audacity in trying to gallop to the White House before he had learned how to walk humbly in the House of Representatives. He had not waited until his first appearance as a Congressman in Washington before he initiated the William Randolph Hearst Clubs in every State, using the Democratic Club membership as a mailing list.

James Creelman, a former Hearst man who served in Cuba with his boss but was now no longer on the payroll, wrote thus of Congressman Hearst: 'So intense is the distrust of his Congressional colleagues that it is doubtful whether he could secure an endorsement of the Ten Commandments in the House.' In 1904 the New York *Evening Post*, still keeping its enemy in range, was also assessing Hearst in disparaging terms:

> 'It is not a question of politics, but of character. An agitator we can endure; an honest radical we can respect; a fanatic we can tolerate; but a low voluptuary trying to sting his jaded senses to a fresh thrill by turning from private to public corruption is a new horror in American politics. To set the seal of contempt upon it must be the impulse of all honest men.'

Hearst could not expect, other than by a fluke, to be nominated by the Democrats to stand against Theodore Roosevelt in the 1904 Presidential election but—honest or otherwise—the disparagers were somewhat alarmed at his initial successes as his bandwagon rolled from State to State drumming up radical delegates to support him at the convention in St Louis where the final choice would be made. He had scores of agents and there were rumours of money changing hands. He launched the Boston *American* at a propitious moment, but more than two hundred newspapers outside his control in the United States favoured his candidacy. The loner, with no party machine behind him except his own, carried the Democratic conventions in fourteen States.

The serious Democrats were more perturbed than the Republicans at the possibility of Hearst's nomination. Senator Carmack of Tennessee, who favoured the chief judge of the New York Court of Appeals, Judge Alton Brooks Parker, said, 'The nomination of Hearst would compass the ruin of the Party. It would be a disgrace, and if Hearst is nominated we may as well pen a despatch and send it back from the field of battle: "All is lost, including our honour."' Undeterred, the frock-coated Hearst continued his electioneering tour in a private railway coach while his newspapers dutifully boosted his public triumphs and personal virtues. He was formally nominated by California at the national convention and the New York *American* was loyal to The Chief as long as it could pretend he had any chance of victory:

HEARST IS CHEERED FOR 38 MINUTES
CONVENTION IN WILD TUMULT OF APPLAUSE
CHEERS FOR HEARST CAME FROM THE
HEART, SAY DELEGATES

In spite of the fireworks and bands, the massive photographs of Hearst and the tonnage of posters and pamphlets, the conventional and conservative Judge Parker won the nomination and the dejected Hearst was in the train for New York before the convention ended.

William Jennings Bryan had nominated a third candidate who didn't have a chance. He and the Tammany boss Charles Murphy would always kow-tow to gain the support of Hearst's newspapers, but running the man himself for President was a different matter. There was in any case no doubt, whoever the Democrats nominated against him, that Roosevelt would be staying at the White House.

That was not the end of the story for a campaigner as resourceful and impatient as Hearst. He decided to prepare his position for the Presidential election of 1908 by methods more subtle than the frontal attack. He accepted from Tammany a second term as Congressman while laying plans to grab from Tammany one of its rich plums, the mayoralty of New York City, directly opposing the Tammany incumbent and nominee for 1905, George B. McClellan. His base was the Municipal Ownership League and his objective was simply to slay the racketeering bosses who ran the city hand-in-glove, though Democrats, with the

Republican Wall Street and industrial wizards who wangled the contracts that mattered.

Any idea that his papers in their news pages should present both sides was alien to the people's champion and the great reformer. The duties of his staffs during his candidatures extended far beyond boosting The Chief in his newspapers as America's saviour, the white hope of New York and eventually of the White House. Maximilian Ihmsen master-minded his campaigns, Arthur Brisbane spoke for him; the office legal advisers, hired as experts on libel and company law, drafted his Bills for presentation before Congress. His secretaries ran his electioneering headquarters. His reporters sought out causes he could espouse and political scandals he could expose. They also investigated the activities and backgrounds of his opponents. During a prolonged anthracite strike that deprived the poor of heating in their homes Hearst brought the stuff to New York City in barges and dragooned his reporters into selling it from carts at next to nothing a bucketful.

The stunts should certainly not detract from the justice of his campaigns. He wanted municipal ownership instead of public utility companies. He exposed insurance scandals. On several occasions he took his battles against the exploitation of the public to the courts. The rich boss was serving up some aspects of socialism, piping hot, in his newspapers.

Hearst was unanimously nominated for mayor by the Municipal Ownership League on 4 October 1905, modestly declined, and then accepted five days later as a public duty because the situation in the city was 'very grave'. The hustings lasted twenty days and culminated in a Madison Square Garden rally the Sunday before polling day where he made his final speech with more platform panache than he had ever shown before: 'I greet you tonight not as Democrats or Republicans but as friends . . .' Long after the Garden was crammed to capacity 100,000 people were still trying to get in to join the 40,000 already there; they had to be content with hearing the mighty orchestra and joining in the frantic cheers, but they had already heard his promises of better wages and lower taxes, better schools, better transportation.

The vote was close and a recount gave McClellan a lead of only 3,472 over Hearst. 'Boss' Murphy, who had begun the election with the confident prediction that 'the Californian will be licked hands down', soon changed his tune, set up his election headquarters in the Fifth Avenue Delmonico restaurant and personally directed the Tammany Hall machine; he marshalled the spellbinders and ran Mayor McClellan off his feet, making ten times as many speeches as he had planned.

Murphy's lieutenants organised the thugs for voting day, invalidating ballot forms that opted for Hearst, herding phoney voters, and hurling ballot boxes into the river. The election was fraudulent and held to be so by an official investigation. Some wag said that even cats and dogs voted in New York in that memorable fight for the mayoralty.

Immediately after the election the *Evening Journal* cartoonist Tad Dorgan had Murphy as a convict in striped prison garb with cropped hair: 'LOOK OUT MURPHY! IT'S A SHORT LOCKSTEP FROM DELMONICO'S TO SING SING.' The editorial accompanying the cartoon said:

'Every honest voter in New York wants to see you in this costume. You have committed crimes against the people that will send you for many years to State prison, if the crimes can be proved against you . . . an awakening is ahead of you. *You know that you are guilty. The people know it . . .*'

The official investigation into the election frauds hadn't even begun, and when it was completed the half-handful of miscreants who went to Sing Sing did not include 'Boss' Murphy. Some reforms in voting procedures, enforcing personal signatures, were introduced by law. But Murphy, who had described Hearst as 'a debauchee of a peculiarly depraved type', was offended.

The *New York Times* said: 'The election of Mr Hearst to be Mayor of New York would have sent a shiver of apprehension over the entire Union.' Its deep sigh of relief echoed the thoughts of those in the city who detested Hearst personally and deplored the brutality of his newspapers, especially the conservatives and the élite who felt that his radicalism was unnervingly akin to European socialism. How would he behave in office?

An inkling of Hearst's next move in the power game surfaced when his newspapers were ordered during his absence on holiday in New Mexico to remind the public frequently and vehemently that the Democrats and the Republicans were equally corrupt and therefore incapable of cleansing State government. The same year, 1906, he stood for Governor of New York State, first nominated by the Independence League, formerly the Municipal Ownership League, and later officially by the Democrats at a State Convention at Buffalo after a feat of political skulduggery that inspired the chairman of the Membership Committee, Senator O'Grady, to remark: 'Boys, I have done the dirtiest day's work of my life.'

We are concerned with the use Hearst made of his newspapers rather than the use the politicians made of him. As soon as District Attorney Jerome indicated a personal interest in the governorship the Hearst newspapers wanted to know why he hadn't taken a band of transport racketeers to court. He was denigrated as 'The Brass-buttoned Bellhop of the Trusts' and photographed asleep at his desk with his feet up and mouth open; an *Evening Journal* cameraman had happened to be passing by the office door at that embarrassing moment. Concurrently, Hearst was loftily reminding his editors that the problems that faced the State must be solved 'not by partisanship but by patriotism'.

There was a sharp change in the attitude of the Hearst press to Mr Charles Evans Hughes. The unemotional, aesthetic advocate had been much praised for his skill in nailing the insurance frauds, honoured as the enemy of the grafters. As soon as he was nominated by the Republicans to fight Hearst for the governorship, the bearded Hughes was lampooned by the *Journal*'s cartoonists as the 'animated featherduster' for the big corporations, an outrageous caricature of the truth. Backed by Tammany Hall, Hearst did not hesitate to attack its bosses and the official Democratic and Republican parties:

> 'I decline to fuse with Tammany Hall . . . the old parties are infested with the vermin of bossism, corruption, and rascals in office who mouth empty words about civic righteousness while the dollars of their corporate masters are jingling in their pockets.'

The anti-Hearst Press—that is, the newspapers not owned by Hearst—did not on this occasion miss the opportunity of the gubernatorial election to revive the malodorous incidents from his past. 'These articles,' he wrote to his mother, who was upset, 'are outrageous, but don't read them. Any kind of success arouses envy and hatred. The best punishment is to succeed more. I shall try to do that. After a while when people understand what my papers are trying to accomplish everything will be all right . . .'[1] Phoebe soothed, and thus reassured, her son cast aside his Christian forbearance and forgiveness and dashed off to an election meeting in Brooklyn to denounce Mr Pulitzer of the *World* as a coward, a traitor and a sycophant, and Mr Laffan of the *Sun* as the mortgaged menial of J. P. Morgan. His audience was informed, correctly,

[1] *William Randolph Hearst, American* by Mrs Fremont Older, published by Appleton-Century-Crofts, Inc., 1936. Mrs Older was the wife of a San Francisco editor and an intimate friend of the Hearsts. Her biography is semi-official and often gushing, but her possession of five trunkfuls of letters by and between Hearst and his mother Phoebe established her as the fountain of domestic Hearstiana, variously interpreted by different authors.

that James Gordon Bennett of the New York *Herald* had lately been indicted for printing obscene and indecent advertising and that Mr Villard of the *Evening Post* had been sued by his own sister who was alleging that he tried to rob her of her share in her father's estate. The legend that dog doesn't eat dog in the newspaper business must have been inaugurated some decades later.

The Republicans had even more reason than the Democrats to resent the publisher's incursion into professional politics, and not the least concerned was Theodore Roosevelt with the next Presidential election only two years ahead. Hearst's racket-busting operations were also being conducted by his newspapers in San Francisco, Chicago, Boston and Los Angeles, his newest and most profitable publishing base. He was conducting with startling success a nation-wide campaign against the influences and millionaires who provided the life-blood (money) of the Republican Party at federal, state, and municipal level. It was not surprising that Roosevelt took seriously the growing possibility of Hearst's election as a Governor; the Hughes-Hearst combat was more than a local difficulty. Roosevelt despatched a trio of his Cabinet from Washington to give the kiss of life to Charles Evans Hughes's tepid but worthy appeal to the public, with the flinty Secretary of State Elihu Root as the star performer.

When the International Guild of Political Blockbusters, Character Assassins and Hatchetmen is formally inaugurated, Elihu has prodigious claims to be anointed their patron saint. His opening remarks were sober and philosophical, enumerating the salient points of Hearst's 'qualities' as a demagogue, a capitalist masquerading as the friend of labour, and as a newspaper tycoon 'specialising in the incitement of hatred'. As a Congressman, said Elihu Root, he had been absent at 160 of 185 rollcalls. As a politician he was a corruptionist 'covered all over with the mark of Tammany'. He dealt with Hearst's morals in a perfunctory manner:

> 'Of his private life I shall not speak further than to say that from no community in this State does there come concerning him that testimony of lifelong neighbours and acquaintances as to his private virtues, the excellence of his morals, and the correctness of his conduct which we should like to have concerning the man who is to be made the Governor of our State . . .'

In this final speech for Hughes, Elihu Root rattled the skeletons in Hearst's cupboard and recalled the words of President Theodore Roosevelt about the assassination of McKinley by a professed anarchist inflamed 'probably also by the reckless utterances of those who, on the stump and in the public press, appeal to the dark and evil spirits of malice and greed, envy and sullen hatred'. The Secretary of State said:

> 'I say, by the President's authority, that in penning these words, with the horror of President McKinley's murder fresh before him, he had Mr Hearst specifically in his mind. And I say, by his authority, that what he thought of Mr Hearst then he thinks of Mr Hearst now.'

It was a devastating attack on the eve of the election, but it did not devastate Hearst. The White House, confident of the power of the knock-out blow, had issued Mr Root's speech in advance to the Press, including the New York *Evening Journal*. When Mr Root and Mr Hughes were conveyed together from the railway station to the meeting hall they were handed copies of the newspaper. On the front page was a huge cartoon entitled: 'ROOT THE RAT', with the Secretary of State as the rodent gobbling up the people's rights. There were as many jeers as cheers at the meeting when Root gnawed at the people's champion.

Hearst spent half a million dollars on the campaign against his rival's $619, and he lost by 60,000 votes. His parting words as he set off on a trip to Mexico with Millicent and their first son were: 'I congratulate the bosses on their foresight in defeating me, for my first act as Governor would have been to lift the dishonest officials by the hair of their unworthy heads.'

Hearst never bade farewell to politics, yet the next two encounters marked the end of his career as an election candidate or active campaigning sponsor. The worst that can be said of him at this time is that he used unscrupulous methods for scrupulous ends: the best that can be said of him is that he was one of the few powerful men in public life then in America who dared expose commercial shadiness without the fear of exposure himself. The cynical view that it is harder to bribe a multi-millionaire is not the explanation.

He cannot be faulted on his radicalism. There was a wild and revolutionary, even anarchical, dimension in his character that alarmed the free-enterprise society of the United States. A cartoon by Robert Carter in the New York *American* on Labour Day, 1906, the year Hearst was commending himself as State Governor, seemed to be a further justification of Theodore Roosevelt's castigation of 'the reckless utterances of those who appeal to the dark and evil spirits of malice and greed, envy and sullen hatred'. In the cartoon Labour was represented by a handsome, worthy man in harness, driven by a fat capitalist wielding a whip. The caption said: 'The Harness is Not Very Strong. The Big Man is Getting a Little Tired of the Small Man's Horseplay. The Workmen are to have THEIR Say.'

Every issue of every Hearst newspaper was still designed to shock the reader, but he did make one genuflection towards respectability during his candidatures: his editors were instructed to refrain from using the words *rape, abortion* and *seduction* in the headlines. There was evidence, new and surprising, of a puritanical streak in the editorial policy. His newspapers described in some detail the iniquities and salacities that offended their Instant Morality, but Broadway's licentious plays were frowned upon, the suppression of magazines containing nudes even for art's sake was applauded, and even gambling was tut-tutted. Hearst's artists were now ordered to paint track-suits and gym-slips on nubile female athletes. The brief encounter with puritanism was regarded with as much levity by his staff as by his rivals.

The editors knew that getting The Chief into the White House was a priority in their selection of news and expression of views, and they were relieved when he no longer saw himself as a contender in the 1908 Presidential stakes. The role he selected was more to their liking, backing Thomas L. Hisgen as the Independent League nominee against William Howard Taft, Theodore Roosevelt's successful Republican choice, and the Democrat's shopworn Bryan, thrice loser. For three years Hearst had had a time-bomb ticking away in a safe in New York that he had wrongfully concealed but was now ready to allow to explode.

Standard Oil had been systematically bribing and influencing the legislators of both parties to operate in its favour. Hearst had the evidence to prove it, and the evidence to prove that the Republicans had begged electioneering funds from Standard Oil. He claimed that the letters in his possession had been 'given to me by a gentleman who has intimate association with this giant of corruption, but whose name I may not divulge lest he be subjected to the persecution of this monopoly'. The letters had in fact been filched from the private files of John D. Archbold, executive vice-president of the company and a deacon of the Methodist Church, by two lowly employees who removed them at night, photographed them, returned them at dawn, and sold the copies to the New York *American*. Hearst disclosed them to the American voters during the 1908 Presidential election and at intervals during a period of four years after. 'He entertained and astonished the country, paralysed the politicians, and tantalised his foemen,' wrote John Winkler. 'Plain as was his purpose, his manoeuvres were feline in their ferocity; and without consideration for conventional ethical standards.' The defenders of investigative journalism in the 1970s would not fault Hearst's reply to his critics:

'If I discover any more letters which tend to show that the people's representatives are in the pay of the privileged interests, and are traitorously betraying the people to these privileged interests, I will certainly inform the people of these dangerous and disgraceful conditions.

'There has been a good deal of hypocritical cant, chiefly from those whose rascality has been exposed, about the impropriety of publicly reading private letters. I do not consider that letters written to public men on matters affecting the public interests and threatening the public welfare are private letters. I do not consider that the offer of a bribe by a privileged corporation to a public servant to betray a public trust is a private transaction.'

There was nervousness even in the White House at what might be revealed from Standard Oil's files. Hearst's revelations *proved* that what many suspected was true, and the result was legal reform at state and national level concerning corrupt practices and the disclosure of campaign revenue. He established the unfitness of the principal parties for office and power but, predictably, failed to enhance the White House prospects of the Independence League's Tom Hisgen.

Hearst's own last-minute appearance in the 1909 mayoralty election was merely a protest, without any chance of victory, against a judge who stood as an anti-Tammany independent Democrat until 'Silent Charlie' talked him into accepting Tammany recognition and the support of the party regime.

Apart from the problems caused by Hearst spending as much as his newspapers produced in profit, his publishing empire was flourishing with an extension into magazines. He founded *Motor*, copying the idea from England, and then bought *Cosmopolitan, Good Housekeeping*, a future goldmine, and two London publications, *Harper's Bazaar* and *Nash's Magazine*. His growing family now shared with his art treasures the three top floors of the Clarendon, a sumptuous apartment house, and Mr Hearst was always happy in his role as the best-known American, though not the most respected or best liked. The new nest and treasure trove was christened with a fancy dress ball at which Millicent presented herself as a demure milkmaid and 'W. R.' made his entry as Napoleon, with cocked hat.

His antipathy to Woodrow Wilson began as soon as the first Democratic President for sixteen years took office in 1913. Wilson's political economy was denounced not only as 'British' but as *passé-*

British. He was cartooned as a dippy 'Professor Wilson' twisting American history to American children. He was accused of Anglophilia on the fragile grounds that he chose to address Congress in person (like the sovereign in Britain at the opening of Parliament) instead of 'sending a message', and that he admitted an admiration for the foreign reports in the London *Weekly Times*. Hearst's new campaign of denigration brought this rebuke from the New York *World*:

'Day after day Mr Hearst, in word and caricature, is picturing the President of the United States as a traitor to the United States . . . Mr Hearst apparently has learned nothing from the assassination of William McKinley . . . Indeed, his attacks upon President Wilson are even more malicious, mendacious and incendiary than were his attacks upon President McKinley.'

Hearst fiercely opposed any American interest in the First World War, adopting a curiously xenophobic attitude for an educated man so widely travelled. There was nothing ambiguous in the message thumped out in his newspapers' editorials. The war was merely a struggle for the European domination of the world markets with Britain and Japan more dangerous to American neutrality than Germany. American men, munitions and money must be kept out of the conflict. No Entangling Alliances. America First. He encouraged independence and revolutionary movements in Ireland and elsewhere in the British Empire. He told the Canadians and Australians they were stupid to fight in a cause that was none of their concern. Hearst, accused of being pro-German because he was overtly anti-British, protested that he was merely pro-American, an innocent stance not borne out by the evidence: two men he personally employed at that time, one as a writer of editorials and the other as his correspondent in Germany, had every qualification except impartiality. The confrontation between the Hearst newspapers and the Allies erupted in the autumn of 1916 after his publication of a series of news and picture scoops that flagrantly broke the British censorship. The British Government denied the use of cables and mails to Hearst unless he guaranteed that news of the war would be published as censored. Having been invited by the American publisher to go to hell, the British fulfilled their threat, so did France, and Canada vetoed the entry of all Hearst publications. He didn't give in; he was entitled as a member to the news service of Associated Press and contented himself with that. Nor did he capitulate in his attitude to the war when his top executives threatened, but only threatened, to resign *en masse*. 'Sorry,' he said, 'I hate to lose good men.'

The Hearst campaign unquestionably delayed the entry of the United States into the war. From 2 April 1917, when the new world was embroiled in the old world's conflict, the passionate pacifist Woodrow Wilson fought like a lion for victory. Hearst still said: 'Let us keep our men, money and supplies on this side of the water.' The hero who liberated Cuba appeared to have a higher regard for the Kaiser Wilhelm's divisions than he ever displayed for the wretched colonial troops of General Weyler. Less than four months after America's declaration of war Hearst's newspapers were calling for immediate peace rather than sending 'a million of our splendid young Americans every year to a war which may last seven to ten years to be offered up in a bloody sacrifice'. He did not succeed in any considerable measure in whipping up hatred for the British and French and sympathy for the Germans; instead, public opinion turned against Hearst himself, especially when by the start of winter a number of us divisions had safely landed in France. A mass meeting at Carnegie Hall denounced him as a traitor and a national menace, and his newspapers were publicly burned in several cities.

The end of the war, when Hearst was fifty-six, produced the first two major setbacks he experienced in his life of bluster, glitter and power. The first was a blow to his prestige as the paramount newspaper tycoon: the *Daily News* was launched in 1919 as an illustrated tabloid in direct rivalry to Hearst's *American* and by 1922 achieved a sale of 600,000, equalling the total sale of Hearst's morning and evening newspapers. The second setback was a blow to his political pride: in 1922 Al (Alfred Emanuel) Smith, a truckman's son who became a fish-market checker and subsequently served four times as Governor of New York, felled Hearst as an ogre to fear and buried him politically.

Al Smith was a son of Tammany, groomed and educated by the bosses in their image; a gentle, wily 'natural' with star quality as a platform performer. There was a massive lovability about the man that survived prominence in office. The cause of the battle was a characteristic attack by the *American* on Governor Smith when the milk barons upped the cost to the public. Hearst demanded action and the Governor replied he had no jurisdiction over commodity prices. Whereupon he was assailed by the Hearst newspapers as a tool of the bosses and pilloried in cartoons with the milk barons winking at him, saying 'You know me, Al.' Other cartoons portrayed emaciated kids begging milk from the callous Governor. 'This was too much for Smith. He saw red,' writes John K. Winkler:

'He tramped aboard a train for New York and told Murphy and the other Tammany chieftains: "I am going to say what I think of Hearst openly and publicly." The Governor issued a challenge to Hearst to meet him in joint debate in Carnegie Hall. His only stipulation was that Hearst might ask him any questions concerning his public or private life if the same privilege was accorded the Governor in respect to Hearst.'[1]

When Hearst declined, Al Smith continued with his meeting, denouncing his traducer as an enemy of the people and demanding the setting up of a committee 'to protect public servants and citizens generally from Hearst's irresponsible methods of misrepresentation and slander'. The homely phraseology of his indictment proved to be more damaging than the rhetoric of Arthur Brisbane and the wicked wit of the *American*'s cartoonist.

'In the last analysis there is nothing very remarkable about the assault upon me,' said Al Smith. 'Follow back the history of this man's newspapers since he came to this part of the country and you will have to read out of his newspapers this remarkable fact: that in this great democracy, in this land of the free and in this home of the brave, there has never been a man elected to office yet that has not been tainted in some way ... If the Hearst newspapers were the textbooks for the children of our schools, they would have to spell out of its every line that no man can be trusted in this country after he is put in public office; that no man thinks enough about it; no man has enough regard for his country; no man has enough of real Christian charity to do the right thing; no man that ever held great public office had enough of respect and regard for his mother and his wife and his children and his friends to be right in office. About that, there can be no question, because no public man in this state from Grover Cleveland right down to today, has ever escaped this fellow. We all know that. The children on the street know it.'

The speech was widely reported and acclaimed throughout the United States. Al Smith's blunt refusal, rejecting every pressure, to run for Governor in 1922 on the same Tammany ticket as Hearst for Senator, ended Hearst's political career.

In 1927 at the age of sixty-four Hearst was again in the headlines with his publication of the notorious Mexican Documents which he alleged

[1] *William Randolph Hearst, a New Appraisal* by John K. Winkler.

proved that the governments of Mexico and Japan conspired against American security and that the Mexican treasury had earmarked $1,215,000 for the bribery of four US Senators and other prominent American personalities. The documents were forgeries, established as such by a senatorial investigation and by Hearst's own handwriting experts *after* publication. They were 'apparently quite authentic', said Hearst. There was, in fact, no evidence that any American had accepted or been offered Mexican bribes. Charles Lindbergh's world fame as an aviation hero had to be harnessed by the Administration to restore a relationship with the countries maligned by Hearst's newspapers and thus avoid war.

His private attitude to the political extremists of right or left was rational, best expressed in a letter he wrote from Germany in September 1934 after an interview with Hitler:

'I only hope that he and the Germans may have sense enough to keep out of another war. Fascism seems to be spreading over here. We have got to keep crazy *isms* out of our country. If we can keep out Communism we can keep out Fascism. Fascism here and elsewhere has sprung up to prevent the control of countries by Communism. Both are despotisms and deprive people of the liberties which democracy assures.'

He recognised Hitler's qualities—his energy, enthusiasm, dramatic oratory and organising ability: he also recognised that those qualities could be misdirected. Hitler did the wooing, worried that he was 'so misrepresented, so misunderstood' in America, and Hearst did not see him until his Jewish friend Louis B. Mayer had approved. Hearst frankly told the Führer that the American people were antagonistic to his regime because of its treatment of the Jews. He was hoping to achieve some amelioration in the harsh Nazi attitude, but he paid dearly for that contact with Hitler. When he published articles by the Nazi leaders including Goering, the Jewish population of the United States rose against him, boycotting his newspapers and applying advertising sanctions. He was denounced as pro-Fascist and anti-Semite.

The trouble over what he regarded as his greatest crusade, anti-Communism, was not the righteousness or otherwise of his cause but the lack of principle with which he pursued his principles. He returned from Europe convinced that Russian Communism, because of its declared intention to inflame world-wide revolution, was a greater danger than Italian Fascism or German Nazism. He launched his crusade in a coast-to-coast radio speech in January 1935, warning against the underground activities of the Communist International: 'Does anybody,' he asked, 'want the bloody despotism of Communism in our free America except a few incurable malcontents, a few sapheaded college boys and a few unbalanced college professors, who teach the young and inexperienced that the robbery and rapine of Communism is ideology?'

The policy was summarised by a cartoon showing a sinister-looking pedagogue labelled 'Red Teacher' instructing a class of innocent young boys in an American school. On the blackboard these words were blazoned:

READIN

RITIN

RITHMETIC

and

REVOLUTION

There were certainly Communists among the educators, but Hearst's campaign developed into a witch-hunt that terrorised the campuses and tarnished the names of intellectuals who in any other country at that time would have been regarded merely as progressives or orthodox liberals. Confidential talks with professors were contrived by reporters posing as prospective students and published as authentic interviews.

There is no example more bizarre of the contradictions that added up to William Randolph Hearst than his record with Franklin Delano Roosevelt. He made Roosevelt President in 1932 by persuading his own candidate to withdraw at a dramatic moment at the Democratic national convention so that F. D. R. could achieve the requisite two-thirds majority for nomination; the President remained forever grateful. However, Hearst consistently opposed Roosevelt's New Deal and National Recovery Act and attacked most of his ministerial appointments. In 1936 he backed the Republicans against F. D. R., boosting as contender an inconspicuous Governor he hadn't even heard of a few months before the vote and who carried only two States in the election. In 1940, still opposing the Roosevelt policies and fanatically against American intervention in the war, Hearst wrote of the President: 'The United States has never had in the Presidential chair an abler, keener, more resourceful or more relentlessly ambitious politician than Mr Roosevelt.' Yet in the election that year he supported the Republican Wendell Willkie.

The aerial bombardment of Pearl Harbor brought not only the President and the United States into the war but Hearst as well, solidly committing himself and his newspapers to total war against Japan and Germany. When Roosevelt died in April 1945, deprived of the political fruits of victory, Hearst was grief-stricken, for there was a bond between them, privately acknowledged but unspoken. Hearst, a few weeks off eighty-two, wrote of F. D. R.:

'The work and name of Franklin Delano Roosevelt will live on in all the annals of recorded time . . . He loved his country above all else and laboured in its service with utter disregard of his own well-being, of his own comforts and convenience, of life itself.'

During the closing decades of his long life Hearst conducted the affairs of his newspaper and magazine empire from San Simeon, the estate in central California he called his little hideaway. San Simeon began as George Hearst's forty-thousand-acre cattle ranch and became his son's kingdom within a nation, expanding to 420 square miles, much larger than half of Buckinghamshire. It was guarded by triple gates and sentries. Hearst and Miss Marion Davies, his mistress for thirty-four years, occupied the castle known as La Casa Grande, an edifice with carilloned towers, floodlit at night and fringed by guest houses with Spanish names that catered in ostentatious luxury for a hundred guests at a time. There were farms, a movie theatre, America's biggest private zoo, and swimming pools with telephones installed at the edge. La Casa Grande, where the people's friend sojourned in feudal splendour and dictated orders to his editors ('The Chief says' or 'The Chief suggests'), was his personal Fort Knox where collections of the world's treasures were exhibited above ground or stored, forgotten, in vaults below.

It is arguable whether the Spanish-American War was the starkest manifestation of his predilection for evil; connoisseurs still differ over whether he was a better character assassin than warmonger. The old man talked about that war of his in an interview on his seventy-fifth birthday with the sardonic Damon Runyon, one of his writers. 'Ah, well,' said Mr Hearst, 'we were young. It was adventure.'

He died in 1951 in his eighty-ninth year. His last campaign, in 1950, was in pugnacious support of General Douglas MacArthur's wild plan to escalate the Korean War and carry the fight into Red China.

II

NORTHCLIFFE

Alfred Charles William Harmsworth

'God made people read so that I could fill their brains with facts, facts, facts—and later tell them whom to love, whom to hate, and what to think.'

'Heaven forbid that I should ever be in Downing Street. I believe the independent newspaper to be one of the future forms of government.'

'What you have to do is perpetually to insinuate into the public mind suspicion and hatred of Lord Haldane, so that the moment there is a question of his reappearance in public life, public opinion may automatically howl him down.'

The young Alfred Harmsworth with an early copy of the *Daily Mail*.

Wickham Steed, Editor of *The Times*, with his chief in America
a year before Viscount Northcliffe died insane.

The achievements and iniquities of Alfred Charles William Harmsworth, Viscount Northcliffe, were orchestrated on a grandiose scale, *fortissimo*. He exulted in the title of Napoleon of Fleet Street, trying on the Emperor's hat during a visit to Fontainebleau and finding it too small. As the result of his influence, and the desire of politicians to placate him, he and his brothers harvested more titles than any family living then or since. The baubles became so prolific that even the family had to laugh. When brother Harold arranged that sister Geraldine's husband should be knighted she wrote to brother Leicester: 'In view of the paper shortage, I think the family ought to issue printed forms like Field Service postcards, viz: "Many congratulations on your being made Archbishop of Canterbury/Pope/Duke/Viscount/Knight, etc."' At one time there were five Lady Harmsworths, causing confusion in the account departments of Harrods, and Fortnum and Mason. Alfred was the one and only Lord Northcliffe because all his children were illegitimate, a fact not recorded in his official biography.

As a young man he had no assets apart from good looks, creative energy and his wits. He was the eldest of a family of fourteen children, three dying in infancy. His father was a personable, gregarious barrister, a mediocrity in his profession who died young because he met too many cronies over too many bottles in too many clubs. One of Harmsworth Senior's fantasies was that the family were descended from kings. Fortunately, Alfred's mother was a dauntless woman, to whom (like Hearst) he was obsessionally attached throughout his life, addressing her as 'Sweet Mother', or 'Most sweet and Precious', and signing his letters 'Your devoted firstborn' when he was more than fifty. She did not gush so freely. '*Alfred*,' she cabled him in New York, '*I cannot make up my mind which of your two principal papers is the more vulgar this morning.*'

Mary ('Molly') Milner, the woman he married in 1888, was the most comely and cultivated of the Harmsworth brothers' brides. She was more refined than her husband, a petite beauty, a hostess of acknowledged charm and personality and also a fearless character, among the first of her sex to ride in motorcars and fly in aeroplanes. Alfred never neglected his 'little lion-heart' or deprived her of mansions or money. The slightest discourtesy towards her by others would provoke his rage, but the marriage was childless and her influence on his life after their first twelve years together was peripheral.

His publishing achievements establish Northcliffe as a major creative force of the early twentieth century. He launched scores of magazines when he was acquiring his journalistic craft, notably *Answers*, on borrowed capital, which specialised in titbit knowledge, e.g. that three Members of Parliament had glass eyes and one a cork leg. 'I was five years old when the Education Act was passed,' said Northcliffe, 'fifteen when education for children was made compulsory, and twenty-two when I first cashed in with *Answers to Correspondents*. God made people read so that I could fill their brains with facts, facts, facts—and later tell them whom to love, whom to hate, and what to think.' He invented the popular national daily newspaper, was the saviour of the London *Evening News*, the founder of the *Daily Mail*—the first daily newspaper to reach a million sale—and the *Daily Mirror*, and was the Chief Proprietor of *The Times* for fourteen years from 1908 until his death. Despite the fear and chagrin of its editorial staff, whom he bullied and insulted, he rescued and rebuilt The Thunderer. Before his journalistic revolution only one person in six read a daily paper regularly; today only one person in six does not. He enriched drab lives. He fashioned one of the crutches of British democracy, an independent Press with its own financial resources from advertisements—not an unmixed blessing, as he was also early to foresee: 'It is not pleasant to think that . . . newspapers are now for the first time in their history entirely subordinate to advertisers. I see no way out of this impasse, other than by maintaining a great daily net sale and thus keeping the whip hand of the advertiser.'

Until Northcliffe, daily newspapers catered for the minority with the leisure, education and vested interest to wade through columns of Parliamentary reports and meandering editorials. He brought *news* into newspapers. He was swift to publicise the potentialities of motoring and flight, seeking out Orville Wright, the first man to fly, and Santos Dumont, the first man to fly over Paris. He perceived what was not seen by many others, including the peril to Great Britain of the German militarism which led to the First World War. During that war he defied the censorship which concealed 'bad news', headed the British Mission to the United States, and in 1918 directed British propaganda in enemy countries. The Germans, notably the fallen Emperor and General Ludendorff, preferred to attribute their collapse to his ingenious and demoralising activities than to their defeat by force of arms.

Harold Harmsworth, who became the first Lord Rothermere, was the financial brain of the newspaper enterprise until their ways parted. Together they transformed the losses of the *Evening News* into a profit with Alfred's innovations. He changed the type overnight, threw out the tedious politics, printed three short editorials instead of one long dissertation, and introduced a woman's column. It was the rehearsal for Northcliffe's *Daily Mail*, where again he made the contents briefer and simpler than his rivals. He knew his readers shared his tastes. They wanted to know about new modes of travel, inventions, new ways of living. They needed a topical daily encyclopedia. So Northcliffe broadened the concept of the newspaper, creating feature journalism— chatty, informative, provocative. The *Daily Mail* was not, as Lord Salisbury gibed, a paper written by office boys for office boys: it was written for men like Northcliffe himself, men of push and go, the enterprising lower middle class of both sexes. The ingredients were crime, love, health, money, diet. Every day there had to be a new surprise, something to make people talk. He insisted his reporters asked Who? Why? How? Where? and got the answers right—well, sometimes right. He raised the status of his craft. He was often tyrannical with his staffs but he improved the pay of journalists, enhanced their expertise, and would not stand for their obstruction by secretive bureaucrats.

The last years of Northcliffe's life and his end were uncompromisingly grim, but there were manifestations of the darker side of his character long before he was signing his encyclicals with the preposterous pseudonym 'Lord Vigour and Venom'. His signet ring bore the emblem of dagger and mailed arm. He expected his underlings to stand respectfully when 'The Chief' entered their room. He humiliated his senior staff before their subordinates. Telephone wires in the office were tapped by his spies. He used his newspapers as instruments of political power and political blackmail. His hobby of character assassination injured a variety of people for a variety of reasons.

He did not look with favour on the principal character in James Bernard Fagan's play *The World*, a newspaper tycoon who resembled himself. When Mr Fagan was involved in a divorce case there were instructions from The Chief on how the case should be reported and presented in the *Daily Mail*. 'Fagan put me on the "boards",' he told a secretary, 'I'm going to put him on the bills!'—newspaper placards boosting the contents.

Marshall Hall, a barrister reaching for fame as a King's Counsel, endured obloquy and tumbling fees for several years because he incurred Alfred Harmsworth's displeasure in a libel claim against the *Mail*. When he won a case his name was omitted or he was referred to as 'Mr Hall', or

'Mr M. Hall'; when he lost he was identified as 'Mr Marshall Hall'. The headline on a minor swindling case was 'A BIT OF A MUG—MR MARSHALL HALL'S CLIENT LOSES HIS CASE.' The headline on a divorce hearing was 'MR MARSHALL HALL AGAIN.' The vendetta, which reduced the future Sir Edward Marshall Hall to penury, continued until he sent a letter of grovelling apology to the publisher. The offence, which he had forgotten until reminded by the *Mail*'s editor, was that when he appeared in court for an attractive actress in the libel case against the *Daily Mail*, he said, in a rhetorical flourish, 'My client may have to work hard for a living, but her reputation is entitled to the same consideration as that of any lady in the land, including Mrs Alfred Harmsworth.'

Northcliffe was also responsible for driving a Lord Chancellor from public life by insinuating base and unpatriotic motives to an honourable man.

Viscount (Richard Burdon) Haldane was a Scottish lawyer, philosopher and politician, Secretary of State for War from 1905 to 1912 and subsequently Lord Chancellor in the years when the Liberal Party ruled Britain with its greatest majority. He earned his place in history by welcoming the ministry which Campbell-Bannerman, the Prime Minister, told him nobody would touch with a barge pole. 'He was by common agreement the best War Minister since Cardwell,' wrote David Lloyd George later; 'the subtlety, efficiency and celerity with which the British Expeditionary Force was transported to the Belgian frontier without the knowledge of the German Staff was almost entirely due to the genius of Lord Haldane.' Haldane founded the Territorial Army as a reserve to the Regular Army, founded the Officers' Training Corps and created the Imperial General Staff, the Army's 'think tank'. The BEF helped to save Paris, and without Haldane's reforms Britain would have collapsed early in the First World War. In 1914, then Lord Chancellor for two years, he was the obvious man to return to the War Office when war with Germany was imminent—no one was more qualified to expand the fighting machine he had marshalled. Haldane also had another qualification unrivalled in the Cabinet or the Foreign Office. He understood the German mind and had a unique knowledge of the mentality of the Emperor and his principal ministers. He was familiar with the organisation of the German Army, more so than any professional British soldier. Yet he was driven from office, humiliated, thrown on the political scrapheap. His affinity with the nobler aspects of German culture was misrepresented by malevolent men to arouse the suspicion that he was an enemy of the people.

Haldane was born in Edinburgh into a Scottish family noted for its intellect. He moved from Edinburgh Academy to the universities of Edinburgh and Göttingen in Saxony and became absorbed by a set of ideals, one of them based on 'the moulding influence on education of the German literature of the beginning of the nineteenth century'. Goethe's creed fascinated him, and as a Liberal Member of Parliament he spent the Easter recesses in Germany with a kindred spirit pursuing his studies. These sojourns continued when he became War Minister, then travelling incognito. 'Probably they thought later that we came to look at their defences!' he wrote in his autobiography.

He made no secret of his efforts to influence the antipathy of the British people towards their Continental neighbours. He deplored the ignorance, even in the Foreign Office, of German history, language and literature, but in his official capacity he behaved with circumspection, reporting to his colleagues in detail. Some of his predecessors at the War Ministry had been invited to Germany by the Emperor to witness the annual army manoeuvres, but Haldane did not accept in 1906 until he was assured the Foreign Office raised no objection. On his journey to Berlin he spent three days with King Edward at the Hotel Weimar in Marienbad, later at his request sending him a diary of all he saw and heard. Some 'uneasiness' expressed in the French Press about the wisdom of the visit caused the Foreign Office in London, in the absence of the Foreign Secretary Sir Edward Grey, to ask him to call it off at the last moment. The King and the Prime Minister, Campbell-Bannerman, also sipping the medicinal springs in the Bohemian spa, said 'Carry on'. Nor were objections raised by the French Ambassador in Berlin.

During this visit, the first of two official journeys to Berlin, Haldane accompanied the German Emperor to the parade on the Tempelhofer Feld, and during the review Wilhelm II galloped up to his carriage. 'A splendid machine I have in this Army, Mr Haldane, now isn't it so? And what should I do without it, situated as I am between the Russians and the French? But the French are your allies, so I beg pardon.'

The object of Haldane's visit was to study organisation at the German War Office. He had discussions with von Moltke, Chief of the German Staff, and lunched with the Emperor when he told him that 'Things he [the Emperor] had said had caused uneasiness in England, and that this, and not any desire of forming a tripartite alliance of France, Russia and England against him was the reason of the feeling there had been.'

An incident at Windsor Castle in 1909 during a visit of the Emperor and members of his Cabinet affords an example of Haldane's ability to understand the mentality of the nation Britain was soon to engage in war.

He was appointed the go-between in negotiations between Britain and Germany about the Baghdad Railway.

'The [German] Ministers were divided, and the argument grew so hot that I interrupted it and said to the Emperor that it was not right that a foreigner, who was outside his Cabinet, should remain present. But the Emperor had a keen sense of humour, and besides he wanted my support. "Be a member of my Cabinet for tonight and I will appoint you." . . . I remained.'[1]

Haldane acted in these talks with the full assent of Grey and the Foreign Office. In 1911—the year of the Agadir incident—he sought and obtained permission to spend sufficient money to perfect Britain's mobilisation arrangements and to make ready the Expeditionary Force. In 1912, following overtures conducted by two powerful private citizens of Germany and Britain, the Emperor sent a message to London expressing his concern at the tension between the two countries and suggesting an improvement might arise from a direct and personal exchange of views. Haldane did not seek to go to Germany; the British Cabinet decided that his mastery of the language and his relationship with some of the principal statesmen there made him the obvious choice. 'You must go,' said the Foreign Secretary. Haldane's plan that Grey should go, accompanied by him, was rejected by Grey, by the Prime Minister, Herbert Henry Asquith, and by the Cabinet. His instructions were to discuss freely and to indicate the mind of the government, not to conclude an agreement or go further than to bring back information for final decisions in London. On his return Haldane reported to the Cabinet. He conducted himself as a lawyer with a brief.

On Friday, 8 February he told the German Chancellor Bethmann-Hollweg that he had come to Berlin officially with the approval of the King and Cabinet to talk over the ground and not to commit either himself or his government to any propositions. He spoke in accordance with his own conversation with Grey before leaving London. He was not questioning Germany's policy but reviewing the events that had caused drift between Germany and Great Britain. He stated unequivocally Britain's position in relation to France. He said that Britain could accept no formula of neutrality which could tie Britain's hands if Germany threatened to attack France. He rejected the formula of unconditional neutrality of both nations whatever war might arise.

There was a discussion on the relative naval strengths of the two

---

[1]*Richard Burdon Haldane, An Autobiography,* Hodder and Stoughton, London, 1929.

86

countries and on the feasibility of an unrestricted neutrality agreement which would be consistent with their treaty and moral obligations. What was the point, Haldane asked, of entering into a solemn agreement for concord and against attack if Germany at the same moment was going to increase her battle fleet as a precaution against Britain and Britain had consequently to increase her battle fleet as a precaution against Germany? 'We should certainly have to proceed at once to lay down two keels to each one of the new German additions.' Haldane repeated his statement in the presence of the Emperor and Admiral Tirpitz the next day.

The 1912 mission to Berlin was the last international duty he performed as War Minister. His version of what occurred was confirmed after the war by Bethmann-Hollweg and Tirpitz and by the published German Foreign Office documents. No historian has ever doubted the authenticity of Haldane's account of those meetings and deliberations.

There was at this time one particular speech on his theme of 'internationalism' for which he paid dearly. In 1913 as Lord Chancellor he was invited to address the Bar Association of the United States at a meeting in Montreal with the Bar Association of Canada. The Prime Minister and the King agreed he should accept. His philosophical speech, of high-minded idealism, advocated the international acceptance of ethical standards which as a code of personal behaviour were expressed by the German word *sittlichkeit*, implying custom and a habit of mind and action. He quoted Fichte's definition of *sittlichkeit*, and Rudolph von Jhering's. He also quoted Grotius and Immanuel Kant. The speech, entitled 'The Higher Nationality', was acclaimed by intellectuals throughout the world, but not by the Little Englanders who included Northcliffe. Haldane's respect for the German philosophers encouraged a friend to say of him, but in no unkindly fashion, 'Germany is his spiritual home,' a remark later attributed to Haldane himself as saying 'Germany is my spiritual home.'

The first Parliamentary attack on Haldane was in March 1914 during an acrimonious debate on the Irish Home Rule Bill. There were questions about his visit to Berlin in 1912 carrying the implication that he had gone there on his own initiative without Cabinet authority, proposing a deal against the interests of Britain. It was the green light for the anonymous letter-writers whose abuse grew to ugly proportions over the next two years.

A sample of what was in store occurred after Haldane foolishly 'corrected' or 'got rid of the ambiguity of' a Hansard proof of a speech of his on Irish affairs; he altered the official report instead of clarifying his position openly on the floor of the House. A page-one cartoon in the *Daily Express* portrayed him in his Lord Chancellor's robes saying, 'Now, Gentlemen, remember, whenever you make an awkward speech you can always alter it in the Hansard reports afterwards. "What I have said I have said" is merely a silly formula.' Displayed behind him was a map of Europe labelled 'Greater Germany' and the motto *'Gott segne Deutschland'*. His platform consisted of portentous books labelled 'Schopenhauer', 'Nietzsche' and 'Kant Cant'. In other cartoons in the same newspaper during his crucifixion he usually appeared as a pot-bellied academic in cap and gown.

The record of injustice and persecution which follows is rendered even more chilling because Haldane's plight was unrelieved by a single act of imaginative compassion by his two close friends and colleagues, the Prime Minister and Foreign Secretary, though Grey frequently lodged under his roof in London and was staying with him when war was declared. They mourned with him in private and consoled him, but never cleared his name in public. One speech by either of them stating the facts would have ended his agony: it was never delivered.

What was immediately at stake was the first major appointment on the side of the Allies in the First World War. Who should become the British Secretary of State for War? The post was temporarily overseen by the Prime Minister. In Downing Street, Westminster and Fleet Street there was indecision and intrigue, and the course of events over a very few days has the fascination of a political whodunit. The option was between an able, proven minister who knew German weaknesses as well as strengths, and a brave, unsmiling, inflexible, celebrated warrior who had served his country overseas for forty years but knew naught of Cabinet work and regarded civilian ministers with contempt. Haldane or Kitchener, the hero of Omdurman, Khartoum and Fashoda? Northcliffe's intention, and the ruthlessness with which he pursued it, is on record in *The History of The Times* and in the files of his newspapers. Asquith's denial in his memoirs that he had been affected in the appointment of Kitchener by either Press or personal influences is unconvincing.

The Balkan crisis sparked by the assassination of the Hapsburg archduke escalated into a war alert throughout Europe when Austria–Hungary declared hostilities against Serbia. The Russians and the Germans mobilised but no frontiers were violated. On 3 August 1914 Belgium rejected the ultimatum demanding the free movement of German troops through her territory, and King Albert appealed to King George. That morning Colonel C à C Repington, military correspondent of *The Times*, suggested in that newspaper that Kitchener would make the best War Minister. It was an impulsive idea, put to the editor Geoffrey Dawson, who agreed. Repington said in his book *The First World War* that Kitchener sent an intermediary to him 'to find out what political game was behind my suggestion. I told him that I knew of none, and that I had made the suggestion in the public interest without any prompting from anybody.' Haldane, though Lord Chancellor, was already engaged in work at the War Office organising mobilisation; Asquith agreed with his friend the previous evening that as Prime Minister during the crisis he would have no time himself for War Office affairs, then under his wing.

There is no doubt that Haldane's initial view was that he was the man for the job and Kitchener was not. He realised the public would be comforted by the Field-Marshal's appointment but doubted whether the soldiers would: 'They know what they want and like working with me.' He sent a message to Sir Ian Hamilton saying he had taken the War Office expressly to keep Kitchener out. There is also no doubt that the High Command of the Army were already welcoming Haldane's reappearance at the War Office. Field-Marshal Lord Nicolson, the first Chief of the Imperial General Staff, wrote: 'I need hardly tell you what a delight it would be to serve under you again.' Douglas Haig hoped Haldane would return to the War Office for as long as war lasted and preparations were necessary. Yet late that night Haldane wrote to Asquith a letter which suggests he was already aware his detractors were active. He was able to report that everything was going without fuss or flurry and that the proclamation announcing mobilisation would go out the following day. He urged the Prime Minister to hand over the War Office at once, expressing his willingness, if Asquith wished, to stay on in his old office. He also expressed the opinion that Kitchener should be made War Minister: 'He commands a degree of public confidence which no one else would bring to the post.'

On 4 August, the day Britain declared war on Germany, Kitchener was *en route* from London to return to his military command in Cairo, but at Dover received a message about the situation of the railways in France which caused an immediate about-turn. Haldane was still busy at work at the War Office. That morning, so Lord Milner told Lady Edward Cecil, whom he subsequently married, Asquith appointed Haldane to the War Office. All that Kitchener received that day from Asquith, according to Lady Edward Cecil, was a note suggesting he should stay and help in England. The same lady said that at a meeting with Kitchener at Belgrave Square, Milner advised him not to answer so indefinite a proposal and persuaded him to go at once and see Asquith and force him to change his mind. Milner was a man of influence, governor of the Cape during the South African War and later a member of Lloyd George's wartime Cabinet. Kitchener was recorded in *The Times* the next day as among the callers at 10 Downing Street between 7 p.m. and 8 p.m. on 4 August.

The History of The Times comments that the story of Kitchener's appointment to the War Office is 'not perfectly clear' and that neither Haldane's *Autobiography* nor Sir Frederick Maurice's two volumes on Haldane throw much fresh light. Yet there is no inconsistency. If Asquith did appoint Haldane on 4 August he changed his mind on 5 August. The note Kitchener received from the Prime Minister on the evening of 4 August suggesting he should stay and help in England would hardly have been couched in such vague terms by a man who had already resolved that Kitchener should be appointed to the vital post.

The History of The Times records that concurrently 'Northcliffe, ever sensitive to the possibility of German influence, ordered a sharp attack on Haldane to be coupled with support for Kitchener's candidature.'

On 5 August *The Times* began its demolition with an editorial written by Lovat Fraser under an ominous headline, 'Lord Haldane or Lord Kitchener?' Suspense was removed in the first sentence:

> 'While there is yet time, we desire to enter an emphatic protest against the proposal that the Government should appoint the Lord Chancellor as Secretary of State for War. We are convinced that our protest will be instantly echoed throughout the length and breadth of the land. At this supreme crisis in the Empire's history we cannot afford to deal tenderly with the susceptibilities of any individual, however eminent. Any mistake made now may perhaps never be corrected. The eve of battle is the time for plain words. We object to the selection of Lord Haldane for the War Office because, in our belief, and in the belief of the enormous majority of his countrymen, he is not the best man available for the post. The best man is unquestionably Lord Kitchener . . .'

Kitchener's experience of organising warfare, said *The Times*, was unequalled. His lack of Parliamentary experience 'may be instantly swept aside'. The objection that he had no Cabinet experience was 'readily answered' with a mention of his membership for seven years on the Viceroy of India's executive council. The unsuitability of Haldane for the post was stated more explicitly:

> 'There are other objections to the appointment of Lord Haldane which we must state with absolute frankness, though with due

qualification. We do not doubt that England has a faithful patriot in the Lord Chancellor, and that if, like all of us, he contemplates the advent of this mighty conflict with sorrow and reluctance, he nevertheless faces it with calm readiness and resolute determination. But there are manifest difficulties about his translation to the War Office, the chief of which is that such a step might be seriously misconceived by France. Lord Haldane has been long and honourably known for his warm predilections for Germany. He was partially educated in that country, he has frequently spent his leisure there, his mind is coloured by his unremitting study of German literature and philosophy, he cherishes many close German friendships. Those tendencies are natural and innocuous enough, but there are other and more important factors which, in our view, render him ineligible. He has been constantly strenuous in his efforts to promote Anglo–German friendship, and in pursuing this course he has unwittingly contributed to cloud British perception of the arrogant dominating aims of German national ambition. He has repeatedly been on confidential missions to Berlin, and we now see how fruitless and illusory these missions were . . . To France Lord Haldane has seemed the friend of Germany, and she would regard his appointment to the War Office with dismay. It would be an entirely unnecessary dismay; but when we go forth to war, shoulder to shoulder with our neighbours, these things must be taken into account. Not because England would have the slightest doubt, but because misapprehensions might arise in France, we hold that Lord Haldane should remain upon the Woolsack . . . [Lord Kitchener's] appearance at the War Office would fill the nation with a confidence which Lord Haldane could never hope to inspire . . .'

The *Daily Mail*, lacking Mr Lovat Fraser's suave hypocrisy, expressed the same thoughts, and the *Daily Express* was indignant at 'the return of Lord Haldane to the War Office. This is no time for elderly doctrinaire lawyers with German sympathies to play at soldiers.'

That afternoon a council of ministers and generals was held at No. 10 Downing Street, attended by Haldane and Kitchener, and Asquith stated in his *Memories and Reflections* that he took the decision that day to appoint Kitchener as 'the emergency man'. Sir George Arthur, Kitchener's official biographer and a close friend, had no doubt that 'The Prime Minister's mind was largely made up for him by the persistence of Lord Northcliffe and the insistence of the public.' How the public was able to make up its mind on that occasion so decisively and quickly, and how it was able to express its mind, remains as on similar occasions unexplained. The public was brainwashed by the Press. There could not have been any public 'insistence' prior to the decision.

There are skeletons in every newspaper's cupboard and it is a healthy exercise to rattle them. *The History of The Times*, dealing in 1952 with what happened in the Northcliffe era, makes no attempt to defend that editorial:

> 'No one in the office felt strongly enough in Haldane's favour to resist the order, though the editor [Dawson] regarded it with distaste. The Haldane incident was not one of which *The Times* felt proud. The editor was able to make some indirect amends for it in a leading article of 30 October, in which he stigmatised a similar agitation against Prince Louis as "part of it honest if ill-timed, part of it monstrously unjust".'

The amends were certainly indirect. There was no similarity between the monstrous injustices to Prince Louis Alexander of Battenberg and Richard Burdon Haldane. Prince Louis, who became a British admiral and was British First Sea Lord in 1914, was the grandson of a Grand Duke of Hesse; he was obliged to resign because of anti-German feeling. Haldane, the Lord Chancellor, was born in the castle at Gleneagles where his family had been seated for seven hundred years. The guilty tears of *The Times* brought no solace to either. Its remorse over Haldane was transient in Northcliffe's time, but after his death troubled the newspaper's conscience. In 1926, reviewing the pre-war documents of the German Foreign Office, it acknowledged that it had wrongly interpreted Haldane's mission in 1912. In his Haldane Memorial Lecture in 1976 the present chairman and editor-in-chief of the newspaper, Sir Denis Hamilton, described the editorial which stitched Haldane to the Woolsack as a classic example of assassination by leader-writer. There is the trick, he said, of establishing a notion in the reader's mind by plucking it out of the blue to deny it; the technique of supporting an unprovable charge by proving something else; the device of sheltering one's own prejudices behind someone else's. Hamilton deplored the use of all these practices in the editorial of 5 August 1914, published four years before he was born.

A number of references to the anti-Haldane crusade echo the opinion at the time of another Hamilton, Sir Ian, who commanded the forces at Gallipoli the following year. He believed 'this reptile Harmsworth' was the instigator and orchestrator. Northcliffe's role, judged in perspective, was even more reprehensible. Among its unsavoury aspects was his exploitation of the anti-German hysteria prevalent as soon as the war began. He wasn't responsible for all of it and Haldane wasn't the only sufferer. Sir Ernest Cassel, a German-born London financier who was a friend of Edward VII and Haldane and well known to the German Emperor, was suspected of treason. The scoundrel Horatio Bottomley attacked in *John Bull* officers with German names who held commissions in the British Army. He published a weekly up-to-the-minute guide to prominent but usually patriotic people who were anglicising their names. Sunlight Soap was advertised as 'typically British' and Bovril was 'British to the Backbone'. German chauffeurs and governesses and maids were dismissed. Ford Madox Hueffer, English novelist, editor and critic, ironically the author of *The Good Soldier* and *No Enemy*, became Ford Madox Ford. George V publicly abandoned all his German titles, the house of Saxe-Coburg-Gotha became the house of Windsor, and the Battenbergs the Mountbattens. Haldane, insensitive to public opinion, still called his dog 'Kaiser'.

Northcliffe was the most effective but neither the first nor the most virulent or persistent of Haldane's persecutors; that stigma was earned by Leo Maxse, editor of the *National Review*, eccentrically biased and a life-long enemy of Germany. Within a year of welcoming Haldane as War Minister in 1905 as a bulwark against pacifism he denounced him as a member of the 'Potsdam Party' in the Liberal Cabinet, a Germanophile minister, and didn't again change his mind. *Blackwood's Magazine*, a strange literary bedfellow for *John Bull*, was also a zealous anti-Haldane agitator. In addition to Northcliffe's newspapers, the *Daily Express* and *Morning Post* were in the arena. In March 1909, when his column appeared in the Manchester *Daily Dispatch*, Arnold White exalted Haldane as a War Minister whose achievement 'stamps him as one of the masterminds of our era'. During the war, when that achievement was being put to the test, the piper was playing a different tune, paid by the *Daily Express*. Early in 1915 he wrote to Leo Maxse: 'If we do not destroy Haldane there is no reason why the Radical boches should not go on for thirty years.' In public, in his Monday morning column in the *Express*, White reiterated until some or all of his readers believed him that Haldane had reduced the British Army by 40,000 men, cut down the field artillery and extinguished the Militia. 'The Militia must have had something that answered to our national military needs,' he wrote, 'it lasted a thousand years.' His attacks in the *Daily Express* mounted in malevolence and mendacity.[1]

---

[1] Lord Beaverbrook played no part in this. As Sir Max Aitken, MP, he acquired a substantial financial interest in the newspaper in 1913—in Beaverbrook's own words 'a considerable

Northcliffe's unique shame was that he deployed *The Times* to bestow credence and respectability upon the slanderers, and the *Daily Mail* to disseminate the slanders to the widest public; his popular newspaper outstripped its rivals in circulation. He also conducted a vendetta against Haldane behind the scenes, determined not only to keep him out of the War Office but to drive him from the Woolsack and prevent his return to any Cabinet office.

The campaign, conducted by allegation in Parliament, innuendo in the Press, and malicious gossip in and around Westminster and Fleet Street, did not subside when Kitchener was appointed to the War Office. The realities of the first year of war on the Western Front could not be totally camouflaged by jingoistic songs, flag-waving, patriotic orations and the censorship of bad news. There were no victories to cheer. Had some evil influence in a high place delayed or sabotaged Britain's preparations, and was that evil influence still at large?

The *Daily Mail* was ordered by Northcliffe to keep the Lord Chancellor on the rack. A selection of items published in former years was put out in book form to salute 'the paper that foretold the war' and insult the critics who had condemned in the past its 'jingo-journalism'. The title was *Scare Mongerings from the Daily Mail, 1886–1914*, compiled by a writer with the foreboding name of Twells Brex. Haldane's vote, among that of other Liberals, to reduce naval expenditure four years before the war was exhumed from the files. Mr Brex also discovered that on some formal occasion as Secretary of State for War, over-stretching the insincerities of diplomacy, he had toasted the Kaiser as one 'who has given his country that splendid fleet that we who know about fleets admire': Twells Brex did not recall, because he did not know, that Haldane had warned the Emperor in 1912 that Britain would lay down two keels to each of the German additions.

The *Daily Express* was also active. On one day 2,600 letters of protest against Haldane's supposed disloyalty to the nation arrived at the House of Lords; he recorded disdainfully that they were sent over to his house in

---

connection of an indefinite character' (*Politicans and the Press*). He did not own the controlling shares until the war was nearing its end and did not commence his vigorous control of the *Daily Express* editorially until he ceased to be Minister of Information when the Armistice was signed. The paper was conducted during the war by Ralph D. Blumenfeld as editor. In the Haldane collection at the National Library of Scotland there is a letter from Beaverbrook to Haldane written on 26 May 1915 which establishes his attitude: 'But for your preparations the victorious advance of Germany would today have submerged Calais, Boulogne and Dunkirk and the existence of England as a power independent of Germany would have been menaced by mortal peril.'

sacks, the opening and disposal of the contents being entrusted to his kitchenmaid. The letters were written in response to an appeal in the *Express*.

On 17 October 1914 *The Times* reproduced a letter written by a Munich academic, Professor Quidde, to a professional friend in Italy; he had never met Haldane, but praised him for remaining within the British Cabinet as a pro-German influence. The letter was published without comment but was grasped by the *National Review* as a succulent titbit for a thunderous new attack.

In the autumn of 1914 Lord Haldane told the Prime Minister that it would probably be better that he should not remain in office. He knew that a formidable section of the public had turned against him and felt this was no good for the Government.

> 'He [Asquith] laughed at the idea of this, but I took a more serious view of it . . . As time went on, and the storm raised against me increased, I saw that the Prime Minister was not likely to be able to form a Coalition Ministry if I remained as Lord Chancellor, and I wrote to him saying so.'[1]

That winter there were catcalls as he took his seat in a London theatre. When he chaired an intellectual discussion on international relations at the Sociological Society a woman shouted, 'Shame on you, Haldane! What do you know about international law or politics? You are a pro-German.' Another lady at the same meeting called him a traitor. Some society hostesses asked their guests in advance whether they objected to meeting Lord Haldane, others spread rumours about the Lord Chancellor's scientist brother experimenting with bombs to blow up the kingdom, and about Haldane holding the Foreign Secretary under a hypnotic influence. He was threatened with assault in the street and was in some danger of being shot at. Scotland Yard detailed an officer to guard his house. He was called a spy.

The storm increased at the turn of the year with such fury that Northcliffe's assistance was not required. The *National Review* criticised him for having been so 'demonstrably and hopelessly astray on every single point on which he professed to be an authority'. The *Daily Express* castigated 'the man who knew Germany best' for doing 'the least to protect Britain'. The same newspaper published a series of four articles by Arnold White entitled 'The Case Against Haldane'; he had 'deceived the public about the Army, about Germany, and about spies'. Between

[1] *Richard Burdon Haldane, An Autobiography*.

the appearance of the first and second of these diatribes Haldane gave a choice example of his inability as a lawyer to defend himself or present his own case in a favourable light. On New Year's Day, standing in for his younger brother, a physiologist, at a modest benefit concert in Scotland for Belgian refugees, he preened himself with the reflection that 'Few people had known Germany as he had known her', excusing her present activities by saying that 'lately she has gone mad'. In an attempt to be homespun and human, of which he was notoriously incapable, he told the simple folk of Auchterarder of a favourite dog of his which suddenly vanished and worried nine sheep. 'That was a sudden outbreak in an otherwise blameless career. And what was true of him is true of Germany.' It was a gift to his pursuers: was it 'Kaiser'? asked *John Bull*.

His only wartime speech which did him any good was delivered in the Lords on 8 January 1915, bulging with caution and casuistry, but none the less positive—even stirring—on the vital question of conscription, which was unwelcome to the Liberals. He saw no reason to anticipate the breakdown of voluntary service, but he wanted it to be understood that in the event of a great national emergency he would consider it the government's *duty* to resort to compulsion. He noted a great reaction in the newspapers in his favour, perhaps even a turning of the tide. But his joy and relief were shortlived. It was the eye of the storm. The exhausted pirates were resting.

What he sought, and Northcliffe and his editor Geoffrey Dawson would not grant, was vindication by *The Times*. Letters from his friends presenting him in a true light were not printed, and even books which spoke of him with respect were ignored; no space appeared to be available for the Case for Haldane. When he gave patriotic interviews to foreign journalists in the hope that they would be reprinted in British newspapers, only the Liberal Press, hardly audible, obliged. The astute Leo Maxse observed that the Lord Chancellor 'divulges information to neutrals that he apparently lacks the courage to share with his countrymen'. Haldane's efforts at rehabilitation were clumsy and naïve; newspapers don't publish second-hand whitewash, as Northcliffe could have told him, and Northcliffe now had another idea in mind, his best or worst.

On 23 April 1915, when the wartime Liberal Government was tottering, *The Times* published a disclosure concerning Lord Haldane calculated to stimulate the maximum mischief. At first glance the item concerned only *The Times* and Herr Albert Ballin, but the appearance of Ballin's name in the headlines could not have been welcomed by the Lord

Chancellor. Ballin was the leading German ship owner, chairman of the Hamburg-Amerika Line, a formidable personality of commercial genius whose Jewish extraction was overlooked by the Kaiser and his principal ministers because of his power, wealth and connections. He had contacts in America and Britain, and access to decision-makers in or near foreign governments. He was one of the two influential men, the other being Sir Ernest Cassel, who instigated the Anglo-German talks of 1912.

In June 1914, at the Kiel regatta, Ballin entertained John Walter IV, whose family had controlled *The Times* for more than a century. Exploiting that friendship he telegraphed Walter on 2 August 1914 expressing astonishment at the idea that the German Emperor contemplated an aggressive war, saying that Russia alone was forcing the war upon Europe, and that Russia alone must carry the full weight of responsibility. The communication, delivered via Ballin's own London office, was in the form of a letter or article he hoped would appear in the newspaper; it was read out at the Sunday editorial conference, presided over by Northcliffe and attended by Walter, but not published because of the editor's view that it would hamper the Foreign Secretary in his negotiations. It was published, some days later, with the sender's and recipient's names suppressed. That was not the end of the incident of the Ballin Telegram, however.

Herr Ballin had rejected the offer of a ministerial post in Germany because he believed he was of greatest use to his Emperor operating alone. The offices of the Hamburg-Amerika Line were, for instance, the headquarters of German propaganda in the United States and Ballin's views on the war were sought by the American Press. Eight months after he had told John Walter that Russia alone had forced the war on Europe the New York *World* published an interview with him in Berlin in which he cast the whole blame of the war upon England and in particular upon Grey: 'We all feel,' he said, 'that the war has been brought about by England. We honestly believe that Sir Edward Grey could have stopped it.' His case now was that the British Foreign Office had failed to make clear its commitments to European states. On 15 April 1915 *The Times* reported the interview and reprinted Ballin's telegram to Walter blaming the Russians, this time revealing the authorship and exposing his contradictory views in an editorial. On 23 April *The Times* published in facsimile Ballin's telegram of 2 August 1914 to his London office containing instructions about his message for Walter. It had been handed to the newspaper that week by a former employee of the Hamburg-Amerika Line. It also contained a reference to a letter Ballin said that he had addressed to Lord Haldane.

The Chancellor's three-month respite ended savagely with *The Times* disclosure and a *Daily Express* headline the next day asking: 'What Did Herr Ballin Write to Lord Haldane?' Maxse expressed no surprise in the *National Review* that Haldane had engaged in last-minute correspondence with the enemy and suspected that incriminating evidence was being concealed; why should not the full text of the letter be published? He hoped some peer would put a question in the Upper House.

'Of course,' said Lord Hylton in the Lords on 5 May, 'I have not the remotest idea whether that letter ever reached the noble and learned Viscount on the Woolsack or whether it is of a public or a private character. It may be of a public character, in which case it is possible that the noble and learned Viscount may think proper, if he is able, to confirm the point that I have endeavoured to make—namely, that from the original telegram of 2 August it was at that time the policy of the German Emperor, through his official and unofficial agents, that Russia, and Russia alone, was responsible for the war. But quite apart from that I shall be well content to show up the methods of Herr Ballin in particular and of German diplomacy in general.'

Lord Hylton's probing was silky, but lethal. Haldane *had* received the letter from Herr Ballin on the eve of war and their contact had been more intimate than a one-sided correspondence. Ballin had interrupted his holiday in July 1914 to go to Hamburg and set off immediately for London to negotiate, so the *Vossische Zeitung* said, with English shipping companies about the supply of oil for ships; in fact to pour an oil slick on troubled waters. He sent the telegram to John Walter on his return, but what happened in the interim was more significant. On 25 July in London he dined at Haldane's house in Queen Anne's Gate with Grey and Lord Morley, Lord President of the Council until he resigned when Britain declared war. Two evenings later Ballin was the guest of Winston Churchill. Haldane and Grey both told Ballin that the maintenance of good relations between Germany and Britain was dependent upon Germany not attacking France; in such a situation, they said, Germany 'could not reckon on our neutrality'. On 1 August Herr Ballin addressed a letter of thanks to Haldane, reiterating the conversation and expressing the hope that it would be possible for England to preserve a friendly neutrality in return for 'certain guarantees', and that it would still be possible to find a peaceful way out of the terrible chaos. The letter was delivered within a matter of hours before Britain declared war on Germany on 4 August. His mission had obviously been conducted with the knowledge of, or with the connivance of, or on the orders of, the German Emperor.

Grey and Lord Crewe, leader of the Upper House, had seen the letter and concurred that there was no reason why it should be made public. Haldane rose from the Woolsack on 5 May to deal with Lord Hylton's concern about 'the Ballin business' which, he later told Edmund Gosse, 'went off peacefully this afternoon. I dealt with it myself.' This was his first and last opportunity to clear his name. Yes, he said, the curious incident which *The Times* had brought to light unquestionably had been able to demonstrate complete inconsistency between two views expressed by Herr Ballin.

'All one can say is that Herr Ballin has been very unfortunate.
'He is a man of distinction in his own country and I find it difficult to bring myself to believe that there has not been some lapse of memory, some treachery of recollection in his handling of this matter, because the proximity of the two documents and the divergence of view is a divergence of view which cannot be otherwise explained without making a great reflection on his sincerity. I myself have had the pleasure of knowing Herr Ballin in the past—not well—I have met him two or three times, and I have always thought him a man of the most interesting personality and of great eminence in his own country.'

After that citation to the distinction, sincerity, pleasurable sociability, personality and eminence of an enemy who could be briefly and accurately described as a two-faced liar and opportunist, Haldane continued to demonstrate that as his own advocate he was a disaster. What about the reference in the Ballin telegram to the letter sent to himself?

'Well, in July, before the Serbian Manifesto, and when the political sky stretching between Germany and this country was clear and unbroken, Herr Ballin was in London and dined at my house. I did not know him well, but he called on me, and I asked him to meet certain people. The letter to which he referred was written after his return to Germany—some time subsequently—referring to the peaceful character of the occasion, and referring to the peaceful disposition of the German nation. There was nothing which remotely resembled the accusation against Russia ... It was a private note. I have a great objection to publishing private correspondence. I think it wrong in principle, and I think, even in the case of an alien enemy, there are some considerations to be extended to the moral right of those who wrote letters at a time when they were not alien enemies, and the letter was written at a time of peace . . . It was a brief private communication written to me after he had dined with me in London.

'I have told your Lordships all there is bearing on the matter for the purpose of making it clear that no State document, nothing of importance, is in my possession which could be disclosed and that would interest the public . . . The letter I received I did not think it necessary to answer. Indeed, I have had no correspondence at any time in my life with him or with any other distinguished personage in Germany on public affairs. I think it right to make that statement, because there have been suggestions, I notice from the papers, that I might be in possession of correspondence with high personages in Germany. I have never in my life had any such correspondence. On three or four occasions, which are known to the public, and when I have been acting officially as a Minister, I have had intercourse with high personages connected with the German Government. All these are cases in which the communications were with the cognisance of my colleagues and in which the circumstances were known to the public. I have known Germany well, and have been a keen student of her literature during most of my life, and I have often been there, but my friends there are men of letters whose occupations are not political. The noble lord will appreciate why I have risen to make this statement. I wish no misapprehension to be in his mind with reference to the communication to which he has referred.'

Northcliffe had put Haldane on the spot, and Haldane in his reply to Lord Hylton could not have been more helpful to his critics had Leo Maxse himself written the speech. Haldane published the contents of the letter after Ballin's death and years after the war had ended. The brief private communication after he had dined was a 496-word document in which the excellence of the wine and quality of the food at Haldane's table were not even mentioned. 'The atmosphere which then surrounded us,' wrote Ballin, 'was so pure and beneficial that it was not even disturbed by the serious political conversation that we carried on after dinner.' There *was* a serious political conversation and Herr Ballin set it down with reasonable accuracy. The two embarrassing phrases—(1) 'You know our Emperor personally and are aware that he has made it the task of his life to preserve peace for Germany' and (2) 'I know the high esteem and friendship you feel for our Reichskanzler Herr von Bethmann-Hollweg'—were within his competence as a lawyer to defuse with sardonic asides. The importance of the letter was that Ballin repeated what he had been told by Haldane and Grey that Britain would martially intervene if Germany were to hazard France: it was a complete rebuttal of his current allegation that Grey and the British Foreign Office had failed to make clear its commitments to European States. Haldane had also made Britain's commitment to France emphatically clear during his 1912 mission to Berlin. Why didn't he read out the letter there and then and expose Northcliffe's plot?

In his autobiography, published fifteen years after the event, he disclosed the only valid reason. He said he regarded Ballin's letter as harmless and a little foolish. He did not want Grey, the fellow-guest at the dinner, to be dragged into the attack on himself. He felt, retrospectively, that apart from that consideration the 'least evil would have been to have disregarded Ballin's legal right and published the letter'. His observance of such a courtesy in wartime, and the concurrence of Grey and Crewe, were naïve in the circumstances: or was Grey, in a lapse of his usual scruples, protecting himself? Instant publication would have removed suspicion; instead, the Lord Chancellor became the target for further calumny.

No one other than Haldane thought the Ballin business went off peacefully that afternoon, including Northcliffe. *The Times* could not believe that the Lord Chancellor had found nothing stronger to say than that Herr Ballin had been very unfortunate. The *Mail* considered his statement damning enough merely to publish it in full, returning to the scene a week later with an article by Lovat Fraser: 'No man not endowed with the skin of a rhinoceros,' he wrote, 'would in his place have clung to office for a single day after the purpose of Germany was revealed.' The *Express* repeated its headline, 'What DID Herr Ballin write to Lord Haldane?', and offered £100 to any reader who could relate what Bal had said to Hal from Haldane's 'spiritual home'.

Two major events, the first an unexpected disaster at sea and the second an expected political crisis at Westminster, removed Herr Ballin's name from the headlines. Plying from New York to England on its lawful business the British Atlantic liner *Lusitania* was torpedoed by a German submarine operating off the coast of Ireland on 7 May, sinking it within twenty minutes, drowning 1,198 passengers including 124 Americans. An eruption of Hun-hatred, in some places uncontrollable except by force, occurred throughout Britain. German-owned shops were looted and wrecked in London and the Army was called in to quell the rioting in Southend and Liverpool. The same month Asquith's Liberal Government expired and the Tories joining the Coalition administration that followed, still headed by Asquith, refused to serve if Haldane were a member. He was dropped. It was his head they wanted, not his seal of office; his successor as Lord Chancellor was another Liberal, the complacent Lord Buckmaster, a dwarf by comparison in the legal profession. Asquith was too upset, or too ashamed, to tell his friend personally that he had betrayed him without a fight.

As a lawyer Haldane was aware that a personal denial of all the charges against him would merely lend credence; the refutation had to come from elsewhere. In his autobiography he considered that his speeches on the theme of greater understanding between the two nations had been more appreciated in Germany than by his own countrymen, and conceded that some of them were possibly indiscreet. He recalled the attacks upon him affecting public opinion. His motives and the nature of his negotiations in Berlin in 1912 were 'grossly misrepresented' and 'every kind of ridiculous legend about me was circulated'.[1]

The bachelor was said to have a German wife.[2] The son of a pious Scottish family was alleged to be the illegitimate brother of the Kaiser. He had corresponded secretly with the German government and concealed from his Cabinet colleagues his knowledge that the Germans intended war. He had delayed the mobilisation and despatch to the Continent of the British Expeditionary Force; in fact, he had urged speedy mobilisation and went to the War Office to set it in motion. He was accused of not wanting to send the BEF in full strength when he had been insisting, unsuccessfully, on just that. He had intrigued with Ballin and other German friends without informing the Foreign Office. He had diminished the Regular Army, especially the artillery; in fact he had greatly increased the artillery of the Expeditionary Force. The most serious charge, recurrently made but false, was that in 1912 he had gone to Berlin on his own initiative. The minister whose loyalty to his own country was questioned because of his knowledge of German culture was too gentlemanly to mention that two of the sisters of Northcliffe's Irish mother had married Germans and were living in Germany during the war

---

[1] *Richard Burdon Haldane, An Autobiography.*

[2] Haldane was as unlucky in love as in politics. In March 1900 he announced his engagement to Miss Valentine Munro Ferguson, a novelist and sister of a political friend, eventually Lord Novar. Five weeks later he received a note from the lady saying all was over. Her conduct, he told his mother in a fragment of their voluminous correspondence, indicated some sudden breakdown of feeling due simply to some 'physical cause' and also to a 'mental aberration'. The evidence suggests that Miss Ferguson was a lesbian, romantically involved with another woman. She died, unmarried, seven years later. Haldane told an aunt he never judged her nor blamed her. He told Lord Rosebery that his old love remained and would not end in her grave, but in his. Every spring throughout his life he recalled in family letters his brief engagement to Valentine.

as widows. Through the good offices of an American journalist Northcliffe sent money during the war to Aunt Frau Borntraeger and Aunt Frau Sels, the £125 to be handed cautiously to Frau Sels because her German husband had been a naturalised Englishman. It was illegal to send money to Germans, and Northcliffe's newspapers were loud in their condemnation of British sentimentalists whose consciences were troubled by stories of starving German women and children. R. D. Blumenfeld, chairman and editor of the *Daily Express* when it was accusing Haldane of Germanophilia, was a British naturalised American-born subject of German descent. The newspaper assured its readers that 'He is not and never has been a German.'

Why did Asquith and Grey not come to Haldane's rescue? They were close friends as well as colleagues. A few days after war was declared Asquith visited him at Queen Anne's Gate. 'If the country is prepared for this war,' he said, 'it is to you more than to any other person that it owes it.' Had he repeated in public what he had said in private, or half of it, the outcry against his minister would have been stillborn and the slanderers silenced. Grey's trust in Haldane was so established that on two occasions in 1914 he asked him to take over the Foreign Office on his behalf so that he could rest in Northumberland. It is true that when the Conservative leaders believed a scurrilous story that during his second 'stand in' at the Foreign Office Haldane had released a ship loaded with copper which Grey had seized at Gibraltar, and the ship had subsequently reached Germany, Grey exposed the lie. It is also true that when the fallen Chancellor made his farewell speech to his supporters at the National Liberal Club, Asquith wrote 'an admirable letter which was read out on the occasion. He did more, for without my knowledge he and the King arranged that I should have the Order of Merit. I had not thought of such a thing, and I was a little doubtful about accepting it.' But neither Asquith nor Grey spoke out in public to clear Haldane's name. The Prime Minister was contemptuous of Press criticisms, and he and Grey did not consider the attacks important enough for official denials. The Foreign Office were not in favour of publishing the records on their files of what precisely occurred during Haldane's official mission to Berlin in 1912, and Asquith and Grey concurred with the Foreign Office veto. They were prepared to seal their lips and see Haldane driven from public life, unshielded.

On 5 July 1915, no longer in office, Haldane spoke in public in defence of a general he considered wrongly criticised over the shell shortage. 'I have not come,' he told his audience, 'to talk on personal matters'; he appealed to the nation for self-restraint and pleaded that the public 'should not be led astray by this craving for scapegoats'. *The Times* editorial of 8 July was written by Geoffrey Dawson, the editor:

> 'Lord Haldane's speech of Monday evening—the speech which has apparently been hailed by his friends as the prelude to his return to office—seems likely to produce some very different consequences . . .
>
> 'We have not commented before either on Lord Haldane's retirement or on his singularly unwise *apologia*. We would gladly leave them to speak for themselves if he would not insist on provoking public controversy. But this at least must be said, since he seems utterly unable to understand it for himself. The strong pressure of public opinion which drove him from office was based at bottom neither upon his administration of the War Office nor upon his work as Lord Chancellor. Much can be said, and has been said, for both. It was based, first and foremost, upon the fact that he stands to the British public as the supreme instance of a man who professed to know Germany and the Germans through and through, who went on secret diplomatic missions to Germany, and who, though he now claims to have been aware of the reality and the imminence of the German peril, not only failed to give his country a word of warning in *public*, but opposed and denounced the efforts of Lord Roberts and others to awaken it in time to a sense of its danger and its duty. For such a man, in the public view—and it is a sound view—there was no place in a Cabinet which was called upon to meet the German peril when it came.'

The *Daily Mail* the same day published an item proposing an Anti-Haldane League dedicated to preventing him forcing his way back into the Cabinet.

The solitary official gesture towards the salvage of his reputation was the publication by the Foreign Office on 26 August 1915 of a summary of the documents so barren that to clear up the further misunderstandings it created another memorandum was issued on 6 September. Haldane's peers as well as the Press still pursued their quarry remorselessly. In the Lords, which traditionally deplores questions phrased offensively and even 'asperity of speech', the members were roused when the seventh Duke of Buccleuch intervened at the outset of a debate on education on 12 July 1916. Haldane, no longer Lord Chancellor, occupied a place on the front Opposition bench from which he rose to move a motion dealing with the educational training of the nation and the need for reform. He got no further than his opening two words, 'My Lords,' when the Duke intervened: 'Before the noble Lord directs your Lordships' attention to foreign policy I suggest he should explain his past conduct in misleading Great Britain upon the German danger, and in misleading Germany upon British policy.'

Haldane replied: 'We are not here to discuss foreign policy and I have only to say in answer to the question of the noble Duke that nobody more than myself desires that the whole facts should be brought out as to what was done before the war and the preparations that were made. There has been an extraordinary stream of misrepresentation, untruths, inaccuracies, and the sooner these things are brought to the test the better. Nobody desires the moment to come for the most complete judgement of the nation on the full facts more than I do. That is all that I have to say to the noble Duke.'

On 21 July, nine days after the unusual scene in the Lords, it seemed that an end to his agony was in sight. Grey visited him, indignant and sympathetic, talking of initiating a debate in his defence. Haldane told his sister that he spoke 'pretty plainly' to Grey about the delay of the Foreign Office in releasing at least a summary of the events which culminated in his visit to Berlin in 1912, making it clear that the full facts were not withheld in his interest. Grey was still adamant in refusing to publish the documents but had no objection to the facts being stated *unofficially*. It was agreed by Asquith that Haldane's 1912 memorandum could be seen and used in his defence by 'discreet friends', and there were friends available. Harold Begbie wrote a book to put the record straight, or as straight as it could be put while the war was still on. The *Manchester Guardian* published a series of articles judiciously based on the Haldane 1912 memorandum. Winston Churchill and Edmund Gosse came to his aid with articles in his defence, and Lord French enthusiastically spoke in the Lords of his great military reforms as Secretary of State for War before war broke out.

None of this was to the liking of Northcliffe, who was now prepared to project his campaign beyond his own newspapers. In October 1916 he called a number of prominent journalists to a private luncheon at the Aldwych Club. Edmund Gosse, who was informed of what occurred by a friend important in the journalistic world, wrote to Haldane:

'I have some information to give you which is very unpleasant. The hounds of Hell are again being laid on to your track . . . [Northcliffe] made a speech entirely directed against you. After the bitterest diatribes he adjured all those newspaper men to see to it that you never regained political power in this country. He told them there was a campaign afoot to reinstate you, but that they must combine by all means known to them to defeat it. He assured them that you were the greatest enemy to the English state ... "What you have to do," he went on, "is perpetually to insinuate into the public mind suspicion and hatred of Lord Haldane, so that the moment there is a question of his reappearance in public life, public opinion may automatically howl him down."

'I think you should make this odious conspiracy known amongst your friends.'[1]

Lloyd George's verdict on the fate of Haldane, 'driven in disgrace into the wilderness', was uncompromising:

'His abandonment by men who were his devoted friends—at least by men to whom he was devoted—at the instigation of the fussy and noisy patriots that always danced around the flag as if they owned it, was one of the meanest betrayals in British history. Haldane was a brave and unselfish man. He never whined or complained about his treatment. All the same it shook him. I rarely saw him after he left office. But I have the memory of seeing a man bent and bowed, walking slowly from his house in Queen Anne's Gate towards the Privy Council, where he sat as a judge.'[2]

Haldane's family motto was 'Suffer'. The brave and unselfish man wrote that he was never depressed by even the most violent abuse, but this was autobiographical bravura; his sister Elizabeth admitted to Gosse that he 'really felt these attacks more than he should'. He endured because he believed that if the Army came home victorious it would return with witnesses in his defence whose testimony would be irresistible. The Foreign Office's refusal to publish the documents was, he thought, 'unwise', and it was 'unfortunate' that it was not made known to the public at the time. 'I had gone to Germany too often, and had read her literature too much, not to give ground to narrow-minded people who say that Germany was my "spiritual home".'

The irony was that the man regarded as suspect by the Press and by the Tories and ostracised as a traitor by the deluded public, was still held in esteem by the Army. French immediately pressed him to visit the British Forces under his command in France. On a second visit he carried out a mission for Kitchener. In December 1916 King George consulted him privately on constitutional aspects when Asquith's final government was overthrown. Lloyd George as Prime Minister consulted him over major

[1]*Haldane* Vol II by Major-General Sir Frederick Maurice, Faber & Faber, London. 1939.
[2]*War Memoirs of David Lloyd George*, Vol II, Ivor Nicholson and Watson, London, 1933.

Army affairs and dined with him at Queen Anne's Gate. In April 1917 he told Haldane: 'You must come in. All the difficulties must be put aside for the nation needs your brains.'[1] On no occasion did he invite him to join his government; Haldane the philosopher was still political dynamite, still stalked by Northcliffe.

When the war was over there was a tumultuous parade in London with the King and the Commander-in-Chief, Field-Marshal Douglas Haig, riding side by side at the head of the victorious British troops. Haldane was alone in his study that evening. His only visitor, unexpected, was Haig, who called to leave a book in which he said he had written something. It was a volume of Haig's despatches, with this inscription: 'To Viscount Haldane of Cloan—the greatest Secretary of State for War England has ever had.' Six more years passed before he again attained high office, again as Lord Chancellor and then as Leader of the House of Lords, this time in the first Labour Government of 1924.

Another vendetta conducted earlier by Northcliffe appeared to spring from a nobler motive, a crusade to protect the public from commercial exploitation. The readers of the *Daily Mail*, the *Daily Mirror* and the London *Evening News* were given every reason to believe that the great publisher was unable to sleep at night because of his anxiety over the retail price they were being charged for a bar of household soap. So far as Northcliffe was concerned in this exercise, cleanliness was not next to godliness. There were even overtones of blackmail. The hunger of the *Daily Mail* for 'causes' was only part of the story, the most salubrious part.

The victim was Mr William Lever, Member of Parliament, later Lord Leverhulme, wealthy soap manufacturer, producer of Lux, Vim and Sunlight. Newspaper combines were one thing, soap trusts another. With the power of advertising, of which Northcliffe's newspapers received their share, Lever had introduced pure soap into the hands of the masses, boosting one brand after another. He was doing as well out of soap suds as Northcliffe was doing out of popular papers until the margarine manufacturers also needed the oil, Lever's raw material; in addition there was competition from rival soap operators for the same oil. Lever secretly set up a soap combine to eradicate frontal rivalry, reducing expenditure on overheads and advertising.

Daily Mail reporters ferreted out shopkeepers ready to complain at the dangers the soap combine held for them, and angry employees who were

[1] The Haldane Papers.

sacked or likely to be sacked when the industry was rationalised. The broadside which landed the newspaper in trouble was the accusation that Lever's Port Sunlight factory was using inferior fish-oils and short-weighting the public: 'Prices have been artfully raised to the public,' said the *Mail*, 'not always in a straightforward manner, but by the subtler process of diminishing the quantity in the packets and packages, and giving the ignorant customer fifteen ounces, or even less, to the pound . . . If ever hunger and poverty followed upon the ruthless operation of a great "combine", it waits upon the Soap Trust. It goes straight at the throat of people living on the verge of starvation.'

The venom, predictably an ingredient of a Northcliffe campaign, escalated over the months. W. K. Haselden drew a series of cartoons in the *Daily Mirror* portraying 'Mr Soap Trust' picking pockets and giving short weight, and 'Signor Soapo Trusti, the celebrated conjuror from Port Moonshine', removing two ounces from a sixteen-ounce bar of soap by sleight of hand. 'You didn't see me do it !! !' shouted the signor to the audience, who hollered back, 'We did see you do it,' 'Robber' and 'Humbug', as his stage stooge murmurs 'I told him it wouldn't wash.' One of the contributions to the campaign in the *Evening News* was in the form of a reader's letter, monstrously libellous:

> 'I'm a tradesman in a small way, and I'm thinking of trying a short-weight Lever dodge, just to make ends meet. There's my yard measure; well, I've cut six inches off that. Then my scales; I've stuck a chunk of putty below the end I weigh the soap in; no, I made a mistake, not soap, cheese I mean. Then I'm getting a false bottom put in my gallon measure. And the painter is coming in the morning to add to my sign above the door, "Yard measure, scales and gallon according to Lever." I'm not greedy for money, but I must make ends meet. (signed) A Would-be MP, West Kensington.'

When Lever MP challenged the authenticity of the letter the paper replied that it had been received without name and address, protesting that *they* hadn't written it. The *Daily Mail* wrote to Lever giving the 'sincere assurance' from Northcliffe that the 'strictest impartiality' would be maintained, but his three popular newspapers pursued their crusade in the public interest with zest. The headlines indicate the tone: 'Cruel Blow to the Poor,' 'Squeezing the Public,' 'How Fifteen Ounces Make a Pound.' Northcliffe wrote a good deal of the material himself. Lever Brothers' sales and shares slumped sixty per cent. The soap combine was dismantled. The sixteen-ounce bar was restored to the shelves of the retail shops. The *Daily Mail* was able to announce on its front page that public opinion had smashed the soap trust and W. K. Haselden's valedictory cartoon in the *Mirror* depicted the British lion roaring triumphantly over the prostrate figure of Signor Soapo Trusti.

Paul Ferris[1] summarises the morals of the campaign:

'There was certainly a case for investigating Lever and the soapmen. The manufacturers were reorganising the industry. Bars of soap had got smaller without most people realising, whatever Lever said about small print on the retailers' cartons. Newspapers rightly suspected that the soapmen, whatever they were up to, were acting in their own interests. But only large-scale villainy would have justified Northcliffe's attack. No evidence of this was forthcoming.'

The Times, which did not enjoy the benefit of Northcliffe's proprietorship and guidance at that time, pointed out that a classic trust with evil intentions would hardly begin by raising prices and so alarming the public. And there was one conspicuously odious aspect of the campaign. Lever received a message through an advertising agency at the height of the crusade that if Lever Brothers considered it prudent to resume their advertising in the Harmsworth newspapers there would be an end to the attacks. It was a verbal message. As on future occasions when Northcliffe was invoking the law of the jungle, there was nothing in writing.

The lawyers and the accountants now took over from the word-spinners and cartoonists. William Lever's solicitors consulted Lord Birkenhead, then F. E. Smith, who dealt with the case with customary aplomb. After a day's hunting in Leicestershire he sat up all night studying the documents, fortified by champagne and oysters, and pronouncing by breakfast time that there was no answer to an action for libel and that the damages must be enormous. The Napoleon of Fleet Street retreated to France for many months to escape from the process servers acting not only for Lever Brothers but for other soap manufacturers. Officially the word was spread that his prolonged absence was due to medical, not legal advice.

Edward Carson appeared in court for Lever and Rufus Isaacs for the *Daily Mail*, with the opening hearing at Liverpool Assizes. The bravado of the Northcliffe crusade was lacking in the Northcliffe defence. Lever's answer to the offer of a public apology before the case began was No, and Rufus Isaacs's opening ploy for the defence that a threepenny bar of Sunlight Soap was supposed to weigh a pound failed to get off the

---

[1]*The House of Northcliffe* by Paul Ferris, Weidenfeld & Nicolson, London, 1971.

ground. Lever persisted in the witness box that because of evaporation the bar was sold as threepennyworth of soap, not sixteen ounces; if anyone had thought anything else that was not Lever's intention. When the case for the defence was disintegrating on the third morning Isaacs was offering to settle outside the court for £10,000, swiftly raising the price to £50,000, an offer Lever felt he couldn't refuse. Damages awarded against other Northcliffe newspapers, or claimed and paid to other soap manufacturers, brought the bill to be settled by the champion of the poor to a sum in excess of £200,000, by 1980 values £4,200,000.

In British journalism no single figure exercised more power, or more ruthlessly, than Northcliffe. Newspapers at that time were the sole source of public information. The monopoly of broadcasting was not granted by the government to the British Broadcasting Company until the year of his death.

His principal adversary was David Lloyd George, the most astute politician of the time, at the summit of his own authority as wartime Prime Minister from 1916 and in the post-war years when the peace terms were imposed upon Germany. Few would now contest the necessity of Lloyd George's 'interference' with the conduct of the war by the generals, or question his reluctance to exact from the Germans a forfeit they could not pay, thus sowing the seeds of the Second World War. Northcliffe, on both issues, was myopic. He was also at the peak of his influence when in Churchill's words 'The sun of newspaper power began to glow with unprecedented heat.' In the arena where Parliament and Press meet as rival forces no conflict was more savage than between these formidable gladiators. Politically, the confrontation was between a reactionary and a radical; psychologically, it was a battle of wills. The publisher threatened but could not savage the politician. There were also periods of uneasy reconciliation, finally shattered when the dignity of the Prime Minister's office was assaulted.

They were flexing their muscles before the war when Lloyd George was Chancellor of the Exchequer. He was more concerned in his 1909 Budget with social reform than with Northcliffe's demands for a bigger navy, and their first meeting took place a few months after Northcliffe had informed the hierachy of *The Times* editorial staff that 'The emptiness of Lloyd George's head is becoming painfully apparent to the country.' The Chancellor heard that Alfred had wandered into the peers' gallery in the Commons before joining his brother Cecil for tea. He invited them to his private room, flattering his guest for an hour, extolling the virtues of his Budget, dismissing with a wave of the hand all who put their heads around the door to interrupt. The Harmsworths were now rich. They had erased all memories of their humbler origin as if by a snobbish conspiracy. Northcliffe was therefore impervious to the charm and eloquence of the Welshman and his passion for social reform, but much impressed by a calculated act of political irresponsibility staged during the conversation by the Chancellor for his benefit. He produced his draft speech on the Development of Roads Bill he was to present in the Commons next day, urged Northcliffe to take the document away with him and gave him *carte blanche* to publish his proposals the next morning. Cecil Harmsworth, a Liberal MP, recorded that his brother 'delighted in Ll.G.'s splendid imprudence'. It was an astonishing genuflection to Press power and an affront to his Parliamentary colleagues.

The first public clash between the two occurred when Lloyd George introduced his first National Insurance Bill in 1911, the keystone of the future Welfare State. The upper-class response was predictable, deliciously lampooned in a cartoon of a duchess declaring: 'What! Me lick stamps?' Northcliffe was no less reactionary. The solicitude he lavished upon the poor, the hungry and the unemployed when they were deprived of an ounce of their threepenny bar of soap (and he was deprived of his advertising) was not repeated when the first meaningful attempt was made by Parliament to alleviate their insecurity. The insurance, financed by a State grant (2d. per worker covered) and a compulsory weekly levy on employers (3d.) and employees (4d.), covered all earning less than three pounds a week. 'Ninepence for Fourpence' was Lloyd George's slogan. Instead of backing this modest beginning, Northcliffe used his popular newspapers to mislead and frighten his readers. The *Daily Mail* smoothly sided with the better-off, middle-class housewives who were bothered about stamping their servants' cards. They were scared by stories of the menace of government inspectors knocking on their doors to check that the cards were regularly stamped. Nor did the *Mail* neglect the servants themselves, who acquired a coffee-stained copy of the newspaper when madam discarded it later in the day: they were warned they might be sacked when they qualified for sickness benefit.

The Times, then in its third year of Northcliffe ownership, was allotted an even more dubious role when the Bill was passed. It advised its readers not to observe the new Act, assuring them that the fine would be only a shilling. The newspaper was guilty of a grave contempt of Parliamentary democracy, but Lloyd George belittled the affair by using it as fodder for his oratorical gifts. Were there now to be *two* classes of citizens in the land—*one* class which could obey the laws if they liked; the *other*, which must obey whether they liked it or not? Some people seemed to think that the Law was an institution devised for the protection of their property, their lives, their privileges and their sport—it was purely a weapon to keep the working classes in order. This Law was to be reinforced. But a Law to insure people against poverty and misery and the breaking up of homes through sickness or unemployment was to be optional. Was the Law for the preservation of game to be optional? Was the payment of rent to be optional?

An outbreak of foot-and-mouth disease gave him the opportunity to press his point more mockingly:

> 'Defiance of the law is like the cattle plague. It is very difficult to isolate it and confine it to the farm where it has broken out. Although this has developed first of all among the Harmsworth herd, it has travelled to the office of *The Times*. Why? Because they belong to the same cattle farm. *The Times* is just a tuppenny ha'penny edition of the *Daily Mail*.'

In 1912 Northcliffe, setting off on a golfing holiday, instructed Thomas Marlowe, editor of the *Daily Mail*, to 'Keep Lloyd George off the contents bill during my absence.' Yet the following year he displayed extraordinary magnanimity towards his adversary during what became known as the Marconi Scandal.

The facts emerged tortuously in a libel action and during an investigation by a Select Committee in Parliament. They were capable of the blackest interpretation. The British Government, at the urging of the Committee of Imperial Defence, decided to develop Empire links with a world-wide chain of radio stations, a technical undertaking demanding the skill and resources of one of the few major companies in wireless telegraphy. Mr Herbert Samuel, the Postmaster-General, accepted the tender of the English Marconi Company, the managing director of which was Mr Godfrey Isaacs, brother of Sir Rufus Isaacs, now the Attorney-General. There were rumours that members of the government had speculated in Marconi shares, and a political hurricane which roared for a year broke out when *Eye Witness*, a scurrilous anti-Semitic weekly, alleged that Samuel was about to hand over large sums of public money to the English Marconi Company for the private enrichment of the Isaacs brothers, and of Herbert Samuel himself. The 'three Jews' were indicted by *Eye Witness*, but no mention was made of Lloyd George except by slanderers in the City—'These sinister rumours,' said Lloyd George, 'that have been passed from one foul lip to another behind the backs of the House.'

Sir Rufus rose in the Commons, declaring categorically that he had never taken part in the Marconi negotiations and had never had one single transaction in the shares of the company concerned; that, he said, went equally for the Postmaster-General and the Chancellor of the Exchequer. What he did not disclose to the Commons was that he, Lloyd George, and Alexander Murray, the Government Chief Whip, but not Herbert Samuel, had acquired shares in the Marconi Wireless Telegraphy Company *of America*. It could have been claimed, and was vehemently claimed, that the American Marconi Company was not in a position to benefit from the British government's hefty contract with their parent company English Marconi. That was the sole defence for an act of reckless indiscretion by senior Ministers of the Crown which excited the suspicion of corruption. What was incredible was that Rufus Isaacs and Lloyd George, both lawyers of more than average perception, resolved at the outset to tell the truth, but not the whole truth and nothing but the truth; certainly, in modern parlance, the mercenary details of their personal transactions would earn the stricture of the 'ugly face of Liberalism'. Equally incredible was the insensitivity of Prime Minister Herbert Asquith, another lawyer, to the explosive nature of the dealings, and the connivance of Northcliffe in presenting the affair in the most innocent light in his newspapers.

The English Marconi Company, which landed the contract by tender, held more than half the shares in its subsidiary, the American company. They were selling the same patents and were financially interlocked to the degree that Godfrey Isaacs and two other English directors graced the board of the American company. Concurrently, the American end of the business was undergoing a financial reconstruction involving the issue of new shares. The English Marconi Company guaranteed to market nearly 100,000 of the shares and Godfrey Isaacs obliged by undertaking personally to place fifty thousand more. A third Isaacs brother, Harry, in the fruit-broking business, acquired fifty-six thousand of the English company's slice. Assured that American Marconi had no financial interest in the English company, which was true though the converse was not true, Rufus accepted Harry's offer of ten thousand shares and favoured his friends Lloyd George and Alexander Murray with a thousand of those shares apiece. The price and the gain were soaring before the flotation to the public in the States. On the purest of appraisals the deals illustrated the value of being born with the right relatives or acquiring friends in the know. The eminent politicians who were making a fast buck did not seemingly grasp the enormity of the danger involved. Nor did the Prime Minister; when Lloyd George,

Rufus Isaacs and Murray confided in him that they had bought Marconi American shares, and that the American company had no financial interest in the English company, that was the end of the matter so far as he was concerned. The first the House of Commons and the British public knew of the deal was a libel action against *Le Matin* by Rufus Isaacs and Herbert Samuel. Samuel, the Postmaster-General, had never bought, sold, or had an interest of any kind in *any* Marconi company; Sir Edward Carson, counsel for the Attorney-General, disclosed the facts about Sir Rufus, Lloyd George and Murray.

Northcliffe received a letter from his brother Harold, the first Lord Rothermere, saying that he knew Alfred had always thought it 'judicious and prudent' to help Rufus Isaacs if the occasion arose, and that in *his interests* (Northcliffe's) he should help him now; Harold bluntly pointed out that Isaacs was destined for high judicial office, and all that was wanted was a soft pedal in *The Times* and *Daily Mail*. Not for the first or last time the public interest was subjugated to the Harmsworth interest. The readers would be told what was good for them, or good for the Harmsworths.

The other interceder was Winston Churchill, telephoning Northcliffe early in the morning and arriving in his bedroom, giving his word that there was 'nothing behind it all'.

Northcliffe held the power to suppress or submerge as well as to expose. He gave a pledge to handle the Marconi affair in a friendly way and thereby placed two men in high office in his debt. Isaacs, the future Lord Chief Justice, Special Ambassador to Washington, Viceroy of India and Marquess of Reading, wrote to express in fulsome terms his gratitude for the 'generous treatment'. Lloyd George, who was to become Minister for Munitions, then Secretary of State for War, succeeding Asquith in 1916 as wartime Prime Minister, wrote to Northcliffe on 21 March 1913:

'I feel I must write to thank you for the chivalrous manner in which you have treated the Attorney-General and myself over the Marconi case. Had we done anything of which men of honour ought to feel ashamed we could not have approached you on the subject. But although the transaction was in itself a straightforward one, we were only too conscious that it was capable of exciting unpleasant comment.'

Northcliffe replied:

'I am neither a rabid party man nor an anti-Semite. I was particularly glad to do so, inasmuch as I feel that you will now know that I am not personally hostile to you, as was twice suggested last year by mutual friends.'[1]

Defending himself in the House, Lloyd George said: 'If you will, I acted thoughtlessly, I acted carelessly, I acted mistakenly, but I acted innocently, I acted openly and I acted honestly.' He later claimed that all the charges were exploded, though 'the deadly after-damp remained'. The anxiety of this personal crisis turned his mane white and his reputation for integrity was permanently fractured.

Northcliffe's first campaign in the First World War was against the censorship rigidly imposed by the Government and the Service chiefs; he called it 'a foolish conspiracy' of which the newspapers were made to be part to hide 'bad news'. A significant contribution was his exposure of the shell shortage in 1915. The information came to his newspapers in letters and also directly to him from officers and men at home from France as casualties or on leave. On a visit to the British HQ in France he heard of the problem directly from Sir John French. The massive bombardment at Neuve Chapelle at dawn on 10 March, designed to prepare the way for an infantry attack which briefly pierced the German line, petered out after two hours and had to be limited to four rounds a day. The result was needless slaughter. The cost of one square mile of enemy-occupied territory was nearly thirteen thousand dead.

Lloyd George was threatening to resign unless decisive action was taken over munitions. Northcliffe's attempt to disclose the truth was systematically blocked out of the proofs of *The Times* and the *Daily Mail* by the censors, but he stressed to the leader writer of *The Times* that the paper had a tremendous duty and responsibility to avoid any white-washing of the Cabinet. The Cabinet certainly lost no time in whitewashing themselves.

In a public speech in Newcastle on 20 April 1913 the Prime Minister denied a statement he had seen that the operations, not only of our army but of our Allies, were being crippled or at any rate hampered by a failure to provide the necessary ammunition: 'There is not a word of truth in that statement,' he said. Yet, after all the demands to the War Office from Sir John French at the front, when the Battle of Festubert began on 9 May less than eight per cent of the shells supplied were high explosive, restricting the artillery preparation for the attack to forty minutes.

[1]The correspondence is published in *Northcliffe* by Reginald Pound and Geoffrey Harmsworth, Cassell, London, 1959.

On 14 May 1915 *The Times* appeared with the headlines:

NEED FOR SHELLS
BRITISH ATTACKS CHECKED
LIMITED SUPPLY THE CAUSE

Colonel Repington, the military correspondent, reported in a heavily censored despatch: 'The attacks were well placed and valiantly conducted. The infantry did splendidly but the conditions were too hard. The want of an unlimited supply of high explosive was a fatal bar to success.'

The *Mail* began a series of critical editorials which culminated in a piece written by Northcliffe himself for the issue of 21 May. His staff warned him of the possible consequences, including imprisonment, but that day the *Mail* on his orders carried one startling contents placard for all editions: 'KITCHENER'S TRAGIC BLUNDER'. When he took the proof of the editorial into Thomas Marlowe's room, the editor said, 'You realise, I suppose, that you are smashing the people's idol?' Northcliffe replied, 'I don't care. Isn't it all true? I don't care twopence for the consequences. That man is losing the war.' The same day he declared that he didn't care if the circulation of the *Mail* went down to two and of *The Times* to one. Nor did he care that the man upon whose name he focused his attack was the Minister whose appointment *The Times* at his instigation had urged, instead of Haldane, at the opening of hostilities. Kitchener's inadequacy, autocracy, secretiveness and obduracy as Secretary of State for War were now common knowledge in Westminster and Whitehall and among the high command in France. It was his job to see that the fighting men had the right weapons to fight with; an illustrious leader himself on the field of battle he failed them as Minister.

The Government was shaken by the personal attack and the public shocked. The service clubs in London banned the two newspapers from their premises. Copies were burned on the London Stock Exchange and destroyed at exchanges in the provinces. The sale of the *Mail* fell by nearly a quarter of a million before the campaign subsided, and the office at Carmelite House was guarded by police. In *Punch* there was a classic example of the brand of unctuous, blimpish cartoon in which that magazine excelled until Malcolm Muggeridge shattered its smugness in 1953. It depicted John Bull trampling upon the *Daily Mail* with contempt, patting Kitchener's shoulder, and saying, 'If you need assurance, sir, you may like to know that you have the loyal support of all decent people.' Winston Churchill in *The World Crisis* saw Northcliffe as 'a swaying force, uncertain, capricious, essentially personal, potent alike for good or evil'. He was an ardent patriot with an intense desire to win the war, but 'He wielded power without official responsibility, enjoyed secret knowledge without the general view, and disturbed the fortunes of national leaders without being willing to bear their burdens.' In his revelation of the shell scandal Northcliffe had been potent for good, but Churchill, then still at the Admiralty quarrelling with Admiral Fisher, urged the Prime Minister to close down *The Times* as an independent newspaper and re-launch it as a government organ. His rule for an obstreperous Press in both world wars was 'square or squash'.

The collapse of Asquith's Liberal Government was attributed by the *Mail* to 'The failure of Sir John French's appeals to the War Office for a larger proportion of high explosive shells and to the resignation of Lord Fisher on account of disagreements with Mr Churchill.' The Fisher resignation was the more significant factor, but Northcliffe's exposure hastened its demise. Unfortunately, the new Coalition Government also had no resemblance to a war-winning team. Asquith remained Prime Minister and Lloyd George was moved from the Exchequer to be Minister for Munitions, a task calling for his energy and leadership. Kitchener continued at the War Office, with a large slice of his realm moved to the new Chief of the Imperial General Staff, Sir William Robertson. Churchill, bearing the brunt of the Dardanelles disaster, costly in men and material, was dropped from the Admiralty and Haldane vanished from the Lord Chancellorship. Bonar Law and other leading Unionists joined the Cabinet. At the end of the year Haig replaced French as commander-in-chief of the Western Front. Conscription, for which Northcliffe had pressed, was at last introduced.

Northcliffe's official biographers describe his relationship with Lloyd George as one of friendliness but not of friendship, but the 'friendliness' was frequently severed by hostility. He was ever ready to draw his sword for the generals against the politicians, urging Lloyd George to visit the British armies in France to admire their organisation. What in fact was at issue was Lloyd George's mounting scepticism of the war of attrition which culminated the following year in Passchendaele. He favoured diversions to harry the enemy on other fronts, for instance at Salonika.

Nobody knows what transpired at a secret meeting at Lord Milner's house in London on 6 October 1916 between Lloyd George, then War Minister, Northcliffe, and an unnamed third person. That month Northcliffe was conniving with Sir William Robertson against civilian questioning of the wisdom of the brasshats, and on 16 October he suddenly presented himself in the room of Lloyd George's personal secretary, J. T. Davies, at the War Office in an irate and blustering mood. Davies rose politely from his desk and moved towards the Secretary of State's inner room. 'I don't want to see him—you can tell him from me that I hear he has been interfering with strategy and that if it goes on I will break him.' Lloyd George's own reference to the scene was given in a personal sketch of the publisher in *The Truth About the Peace Treaties*:

> 'When I subsequently disagreed with the senseless and sanguinary offensives in France and urged a reconsideration of the strategy of the war, he came to the War Office and told my Private Secretary that unless I ceased harassing Sir William Robertson and Haig he would expose me in his papers. I took no notice of his warning and he withheld his support from me for several months.'

Northcliffe frustrated the elected politicians in their duty to exercise any sort of civilian control over generals whose raw material was the lives of civilians. But he assumed the right because he owned newspapers to interfere with politicians and strive to liquidate those who did not conform to his prejudices, whims and vanities; first Haldane, then Lloyd George as War Minister, and later Asquith as Prime Minister.

December 1916 was the crucial month in the political career of David Lloyd George. It began with a reconciliation with Northcliffe though he was still telling his friend George Riddell of the *News of the World* that 'An alliance with Northcliffe is something like going for a walk with a grasshopper.'

An indictment of Asquith's Coalition was published by the *Daily Mail*, based on promptings from Northcliffe himself:

> 'Greatest characteristic of this government is indecision. More than one hundred committees making up its mind for it. Idle septua-genarians like Mr Balfour and Lord Lansdowne and semi-invalids, such as Lord Grey of Fallodon. Government by twenty-three men who can never make up their minds a danger to the Empire.'

The criticism was justified and overdue.

Just before midnight on 3 December, Asquith announced from No. 10 the belated reconstruction of his government. 'Who killed cock robin?' Northcliffe asked his brother, and Cecil dutifully replied, 'You did.'[1] But Northcliffe was not responsible for the fall of Asquith's Coalition Government at the end of that month.

[1] *Northcliffe* by Reginald Pound and Geoffrey Harmsworth.

The Cabinet was weary as well as wearisome. It had lost Parliament's confidence, the nation's, and its own. The qualities which had made Asquith for nearly nine years one of the notable peacetime leaders of his country—his scholarship, serenity, his legal clarity of mind—were small in a situation which called for desperate and instant measures. He could not force the pace. He was aloof at all times from the Press, incapable of harnessing its power and oblivious to its criticism, however valid. He lacked imagination and could not fire the imagination of others, or inspire public response. He was a man of law, not war, a man for all seasons except winter. Orator he was, and a skilful departmental administrator, the amiable chairman of a political contrivance, a cabal of dinosaurs, most of them in office to preserve an irrelevant political party balance. It was a Cabinet of lawyers in search of a brief, seven of them monopolising the highest offices. There was something in Leo Maxse's gibe that if a German army corps landed in Britain Lord Haldane would apply to the Court of Chancery for an injunction to restrain the invader.

Neville Chamberlain was not in Asquith's league, but the inertia which ousted the umbrella man from No. 10 in 1940 and brought forth Churchill beset Asquith's Coalition in 1916 and brought forth Lloyd George. Distrusted as he was, he possessed the qualities of a war leader, charisma, energy, evangelical eloquence, and the capacity to cajole the doubters into subservience. On an earlier occasion when Lloyd George had first pressed for an inner War Cabinet he was accused of trafficking with the Press, a pardonable suspicion. Asquith recalled in his memoirs that Ll.G. swore with tears in his eyes that sooner than take part in such disloyalty to his leader 'he would prefer (i) to break stones, (ii) dig potatoes, (iii) be hung and quartered. And I am sure that he was quite sincere.'[1] On this occasion, in the last month of the first wartime Coalition, Asquith's cronies suspected that the widespread Press demand for a new direction in the conduct of the war had been orchestrated. It was led by the Northcliffe newspapers and Northcliffe had been seen in Lloyd George's company. The campaign stimulated the demand for a change already simmering among the leading politicians of both parties and fanned the feeling in the country that the listless Government was dominated by events. *The Times* credited itself for having nudged the change. Northcliffe did not personally claim to have brought Lloyd George to power, nor did he dispel the notion, but Lloyd George disavowed any connivance in one sentence in his memoirs: 'When I became Prime Minister without his help he made up the quarrel . . . he

[1]*Memories and Reflections*, by the Earl of Oxford and Asquith, Vol II, Cassell, London, 1928

was always an unreliable helper.' Lloyd George did discuss with Northcliffe the allocation of some ministerial appointments, certainly the question of who should be President of the Board of Trade, but he took care in public speech and private conversation to affect an indifference to Northcliffe whenever opportunity arose. During his spirited appeal to a deputation of Labour MPs and the Labour Party Executive to participate in his government he was questioned about the apparent fear of prosecuting the powerful national newspapers while harassing the less important. He replied that he would treat Lord Northcliffe in the same way as he would treat a labourer. He was unconcerned, at any rate at that moment, that the remark would be reported to the labourer; that may have been his intention.

He became Premier on the evening of 7 December after a great deal of political intrigue in which Beaverbrook, then Max Aitken, played the leading role in bringing Bonar Law to the starting post. Lloyd George was virtually dictator for the remainder of the war, initiating, improvising, contriving. He revolutionised its conduct with a Cabinet of five members as his instrument. He listened as well as talked; he knew the art of hearing all sorts of advice, accepting that which suited his purpose; a long spoon to sup with the Devil was in his briefcase, and the Devil was wise enough to use the same cutlery.

The one man impervious to the dictatorship was the chief proprietor of *The Times* and *Daily Mail*. Lloyd George nonchalantly conceded to a delegation of Conservative ex-Ministers he was wooing to join his coalition that he had no intention of removing Field-Marshal Sir Douglas Haig from the post of C-in-C in France, and no intention of inviting either Mr Churchill or Lord Northcliffe to join his government, but at the end of his first day in No. 10 Downing Street, 8 December, he asked in a personal phone call to see Northcliffe. The reply was that Northcliffe saw no advantage in any interview between him and the Prime Minister at this juncture: on this and other occasions, he was indicating that he did not seek a government office that could compromise the freedom of his newspapers. The one way to muzzle him, or achieve some measure of his allegiance for a limited period, was to involve him in government, but Northcliffe was as aware of this snare as the man who set the trap. The new Prime Minister also knew that Northcliffe had great ability and drive. 'It is the wisdom of successful government,' he wrote, in a prime example of the gobbledegook of ministerial memoirs, 'that it should harness the powerful but unruly natural elements to some beneficient staff.' Less pompously, he also admitted, 'I never believed in costly frontal attack either in war or politics if there were some way round.' He was as devious as his adversary was ruthless.

In April 1917, when the United States declared war on Germany, he asked Northcliffe to accept the appointment of Ambassador and Minister Plenipotentiary to the US, with no success. The next month he pressed him to go there as head of the British War Mission to maintain liaison with the American government and to co-ordinate the activities of independent British buying agencies who were muddling through, often in rivalry. Northcliffe knew that as a controversial figure he was not the man for the task; he felt it was a post for a businessman like his brother Harold, and suggested Rothermere's appointment in his place. He was also certain that no one could emerge with credit. Reluctantly, he undertook the mission, and during the period of his absence the readers of *The Times* and the *Daily Mail* were forbidden to read a single word criticising anything American; Northcliffe's orders, and another example of news manipulation.

There are few passages in the history of mass warfare more chilling than Lloyd George's verdict on the battles of Verdun, the Somme and Passchendaele, responsible for the slaughter or mutilation of between two and three million brave men of three nations:

> 'In each case it was obvious early in the struggle to every one who watched its course—except to those who were responsible for the strategic plan that wrought the grisly tragedy—that the goal would not be reached . . . It is the story of the million who would rather die than own themselves cowards—even to themselves—and also of the two or three individuals who would rather the million perish than that they as leaders should own—even to themselves—that they were blunderers.'[1]

The battle of Passchendaele, a British exercise, was launched to clear the Flanders coast and its German submarine bases. It took a year to prepare, during which time Lloyd George was either War Minister or Prime Minister, and it achieved only one-sixth of its objective with nearly 400,000 British casualties, of whom 17,000 were officers. The Cabinet had agreed to the plan with heavy doubt. Lloyd George wrote bitterly of Passchendaele:

> 'It is said that I ought to have taken the risks, and stopped the carnage. Let me confess that there were, and still are, moments when I am of the same opinion. But let those who are inclined to condemn me

[1] *War Memoirs of David Lloyd George*, Vol II.

and the War Cabinet for not taking the hazard, weigh carefully the conditions at the time.'

One of his considerations was the Press:

'GHQ could not capture Passchendaele ridge, but it was determined to storm Fleet Street, and here strategy and tactics were superb. The Press Correspondents were completely enveloped and important publicists and newspaper proprietors were overwhelmed. Lord Northcliffe had, ever since 1916, been the mere kettledrum of Sir Douglas Haig, and the mouth organ of Sir William Robertson. *The Times* reports were therefore ecstatic.'

Throughout the Passchendaele holocaust during the second half of 1917, Northcliffe was operating in and from the United States, but his absence meant no amelioration of his policy, 'No interference with the generals.' Why should the strategy and tactics of the generals be more superb in Fleet Street than those of a wily statesman with the status of wartime Prime Minister? Why was a Field-Marshal in France able to overwhelm newspaper proprietors at a time when the leader of His Majesty's Government theoretically had the power to dismiss or kick upstairs the Field-Marshal and imprison the principal newspaper proprietor, or shut down his newspapers and leave him at large to rail in the House of Lords to a dwindling audience? If Northcliffe was Haig's kettledrum and Robertson's mouth organ, Lloyd George was Northcliffe's reluctant accompanist.

There were considerations other than the blind submission of the Press to the military, and of one newspaper proprietor in particular, which prevented the Prime Minister from ordering the breaking off of the battle. The Flanders campaign had been long planned and he had already expressed his misgivings. He had no expert military counsel to weigh against the confidence of the British officers in supreme command. He was unaware at the time that the French generals and even some British generals considered the attack a mistake. He was a layman, and 'in matters of military strategy did not possess the knowledge and training that would justify me in overriding soldiers of such standing and experience'. The dismissal of Haig, which would have provoked the resignation of the CIGS, Robertson, would not have commanded Cabinet support and would have shocked the hierarchy of the Army and outraged the Palace. He had given an undertaking to the Tory delegation while forming his government that he had no intention of removing Haig. Protected by King George, who had promoted Haig a Field-Marshal the moment the new Premier took over, and by 'King Alfred' and the more gullible of the Tories in the Government, the generals had nothing to fear from the amateur strategist. Whatever else he achieved, including victory, Lloyd George failed to prevent what he described as 'the most gigantic, tenacious, grim, futile and bloody fights ever waged in the history of war'.

What Northcliffe could and would say in his newspapers for the worst of reasons, his subservience to the generals, was an abiding concern to the Prime Minister. He not only admitted the anxiety as one of the factors which prevented him from halting the carnage on the Western Front. Northcliffe's protection of the British generals also delayed the creation of the Allied Joint Council with permanent staffs to produce a united war strategy for submission and approval to the Allied governments. It meant 'interference'. Northcliffe did not comprehend. The advocacy of his newspapers was misdirected. Therefore his readers did not know.

The Cabinet was misled by Haig's radiant optimism from the battlefield, by the loyalty of his GHQ subordinates, and by his superior at home, Robertson, in camouflaging the enormity of the error. Minor advances at disproportionate cost were magnified into victories. Deepening despair was attributed to the Germans. British casualties were minimised and the enemy's multiplied, claimed as enormous. The shells and the rain churned the earth into muck, making any real progress so uncertain that the Germans diverted divisions for more useful and menacing employment elsewhere. Yet the daily message from GHQ in France through the CIGS to the Ministers was that the enemy were visibly cracking, that Haig must be supported at all costs. When Lloyd George visited General Headquarters he found 'an atmosphere of unmistakable exaltation'. The horror was not known until later.

The public were deceived by the newspapers, notably Northcliffe's. The man who had boasted that he cared naught for censorship did not even whisper in *The Times* until the carnage of 1916 and 1917 was over that the hour had come to reappraise the strategy. His newspapers were the tool of the generals in the great cover-up. They were the willing propagandists in anaesthetising the parents and families of the men who were being uselessly slaughtered in hundreds of thousands, publicising the mythical victories claimed by GHQ. No newspaper was more idolatrous of the generals who conceived and commanded those disasters than *The Times*, accepted by its readers as sober and reliable; no newspaper was more assiduous in disguising failure or deadlock. The orchestra Northcliffe still conducted from his official government mission in America knew the music he wanted the public to hear. The generals knew best. No meddling by the politicians, especially by Lloyd George.

In September 1917 *The Times* published the headline 'GERMAN DEFENCE IS BROKEN' over a report from its special correspondent. His despatch claimed that 'in the battle we have broken the elaborate scheme of defence which was the last blossom and ultimate triumph of German strategists. This is, from the strategic point of view, the most signal triumph of this attack. It is not merely that it is ground of the first importance that we have taken, or the number of German regiments we have shattered, *but we have broken, and broken at a single blow*, in the course of some three or four hours, the German system of defence.'

The truth was that after a fierce battle the enemy had been forced back a thousand yards on a narrow front with heavy British casualties and around three thousand German prisoners taken. The Passchendaele ridge, the objective, remained in enemy hands. A second battle conquered another kilometre of mud and picked up three thousand wounded Germans. A third battle in the same sector early in October seized another few hundred yards. There was no tactical and certainly no strategic gain, but this last sanguinary struggle was announced by *The Times* as 'the most important British victory of the year. In short, the particular task which Sir Douglas Haig set his armies has been very nearly accomplished.' The truth was that ten weeks of fighting with heavy losses had not gained for Haig one-sixth of his first objective, the Passchendaele ridge.

An example of the euphoria with which *The Times* was deceiving the public, not only in its 'news' reporting but in editorials, occurred during the so-called Broodseinde victory. Two leading articles were devoted to the occasion, congratulating the British public that they were now in sight of Bruges (in fact, still fifteen miles away) and eulogising Haig for recovering what was lost in the first battle of Ypres 'with a tenacity and a calm, unhurried persistence which compel the admiration of the world . . . With each successive stride the arrangements grow more exact, the results more certain, the losses lighter.'

Writing of those battles which achieved so little at such horrendous cost, Lloyd George said: 'It is one of the bitter ironies of war that I, who have been ruthlessly assailed in books, in the Press and in speeches for "interfering with the soldiers" should carry with me as my most painful regret the memory that on this issue I did *not* justify that charge.' There is no record of Northcliffe's remorse or regret for his part in the deception of the British public at that time, or of any acknowledgement of his portion of guilt for the squandering of lives. The Harmsworths did, however, suffer grievously as a family during the war. Harold Rothermere lost two sons. Cecil King, the son of Northcliffe's sister Geraldine, lost two of his brothers. The eldest son of another brother, Leicester, was severely wounded.

Northcliffe's unquestioning acceptance of the war of attrition was alarming in an innovator of his imagination. The story of the First World War could have been different, the war itself shorter and the casualties lower, if he had sided with Lloyd George in the probing of an orthodox strategy which no professional soldier would now attempt to endorse or defend. Brute belligerence, patently misdirected, was a facet of his own nature. It was not until December 1917, when the facts about the Passchendaele failure and the lies that had poured from GHQ could no longer be concealed, that *The Times* at last spoke out—too late— demanding a prompt, searching and complete inquiry. 'We can no longer rest satisfied with the fatuous estimates, e.g., of German losses in men and morale, which have inspired too many of the published messages from France.'

Northcliffe also sought to bend the minds of his readers to a total rejection of any outcome of the war short of the unconditional surrender, humiliation and the protracted subjection of the enemy. It was seemly at this juncture of a war which was grinding to a standstill that sensitive minds might contemplate without dishonour a negotiated peace. The German system of defence had been broken at a single blow only in the news columns of *The Times*. Lloyd George regularly reaffirmed in public his own undying defiance and militance, but even he was telling C. P. Scott of the *Manchester Guardian* that there was 'a good deal of feeling in the War Cabinet towards peace'. 'King Alfred', who would have none of it, decided the public should never hear of such heresy. He ordered *The Times* to keep the word 'pacifist' out of the newspaper. Pacifism? The word also occurred too often in the *Daily Mail*: 'Let it be dropped.' He did not acknowledge the difference between a man who would not fight for any cause and a patriot who would fight with his life for victory and, failing in his objective or rating the cost too high, strive for an honourable compromise. Sir Norman Angell, unaware at the time of Northcliffe's personal instructions, was right in his assertion that Northcliffe had decided that the British people—or as many of them as his papers reached—should not be allowed to know that responsible people were making such a suggestion.

The Communicator Extraordinary was never hesitant to communicate about himself in his public activities. The nation, certainly that section that read any newspaper, was aware that Northcliffe was again in circulation in Britain in November 1917. He had endured the exile in America from his newspapers for barely six months. He made his mark there as a publicist, explaining Britain's role in the war and the needs of the Allies, countering the efforts of the Germans to promote tension and dissension. The Prime Minister was happy to pay tribute to his 'invaluable work', awarding him with a viscountcy. The price was immaterial. Nobody was more cynical about honours and awards than Ll.G.; in the post-war years he sold them over the counter to swell party funds. What he did not calculate was that for reasons of instant expediency he was massaging the ego of the Harmsworths and founding a dynasty that would exercise Press power for three-quarters of the century.

Lloyd George had already broken his pledge to the Tories by bringing Churchill back into office as Minister of Munitions; now he planned to break another pledge and bring Northcliffe into the government as head of the new independent Air Ministry; it was a conceivable role for a man who more than any other in Britain had prophesied and propagated the efficacy of aircraft and its war potential. The notion was discussed privately between the two men at lunch in Downing Street, and though Lloyd George had the impression that Northcliffe would accept, the publisher asked for time to think it over. What followed was a breach of confidence, a flagrant insult to the Prime Minister, and an exhibition of petulance and arrogance uninhibited even by Northcliffian standards. Protocol was for lesser men and common decency for common people.

That evening Beaverbrook phoned Lloyd George to inform him that the Press Association had announced on the tapes that Northcliffe had rejected the offer. Next morning the Prime Minister read in the newspapers the full text of a letter addressed to himself as 'Dear Prime Minister' but not yet received at No. 10 Downing Street. It stated that Northcliffe had given anxious consideration to 'your repeated invitation', and that the reasons impelling him to decline the great honour and responsibility were in no way concerned with the new Air Ministry, now rightly to be set up. There followed a proclamation, virtually a far-ranging indictment of Lloyd George's Government though not of Lloyd George. The spirit of the men and women of Britain was still as eager and splendid as ever and we had the finest army in the world led by one of the greatest generals. But Northcliffe felt that in present circumstances he could do better work if he maintained his independence and was not gagged by a loyalty he did not feel towards the whole of the Prime Minister's administration. He said that he had none but the most friendly feelings towards Lloyd George. There was no suggestion in his letter that he would have regarded the Prime Ministership itself as beneath his dignity or vanity or an abasement of his own talents.

The rebuff, publicly delivered, was not the last encounter between the Harmsworths and Lloyd George. When Northcliffe refused, the Prime Minister appointed Lord Rothermere as the first Secretary of State for Air. Was this an act of lofty impartiality, a resolve to get the best man available for the job, or a further genuflection to the most powerful man in the land? Colonel House, a friend and confidant of President Woodrow Wilson and then head of the American Mission in London, was told by Northcliffe at the end of that year that he paid no attention to the censorship; he considered it stupid and useless and said that the British government dared not interfere with him. House recorded in his diary: 'He certainly is an unruly member . . . He handles himself just as if he were Dictator of England, and, in a way, he is, for the Government are afraid of him.' That night House dined with the Prime Minister and Lord Reading (the former Sir Rufus Isaacs) and added in his diary: 'We talked of Northcliffe. He [Lloyd George] is evidently afraid of him and, unfortunately, Northcliffe knows it.'

David was still resilient or incautious enough to enter the lion's den again, with no guarantee of divine deliverance. His tormentor's next and final government appointment, from February 1918 until the end of the war, was Director of Propaganda in Enemy Countries. It did not banish him to enemy countries or separate him from his newspapers, the crucible of his power. He maintained his independence, untrammelled by a loyalty he did not feel towards the whole of the Prime Minister's administration. Some at least of his spleen was reserved for the enemy in his new role, and the War Cabinet benefited from his ingenuity. First with balloons and then with planes he bombarded German civilians with news of Allied power and success, and their front-line troops with certificates guaranteeing safe conduct and good treatment for those who surrendered.

The appointment concurrently of Beaverbrook, who had acquired control of the *Daily Express*, as Minister of Information and Chancellor of the Duchy of Lancaster was more than some of the politicians could bear. Maybe the politicians were running the country, but were the publishers running the politicians? Lloyd George was closer to the Press barons than any Prime Minister in the first half of the century, including Churchill. There were others, besides the Harmsworths. George Riddell (later Lord Riddell) of the *News of the World* was his Press adviser, go-between and golf-course crony. Dalziel of *Reynolds News* (later Lord

Dalziel) was also in his intimate circle. Those who were not harnessed were placated. A *Daily News* editorial warned that the newspaper proprietor was advancing from the sway of opinion to the throne of actual power: 'We are in some danger of having a newspaper Administration in this country.' Bonar Law told Lloyd George there would be trouble. The Unionist War Committee passed a resolution against newspaper proprietors holding government office. In a speech in the Commons Austen Chamberlain said the Prime Minister should sever the connection with newspaper proprietors. He mentioned recent attacks in the *Daily Mail* on naval and military leaders and recalled the 'insolent and offensive patronage of the Prime Minister by Northcliffe over the affair of the Air Ministry'. Why should people guilty of such practices be found indispensable to the Government shortly afterwards? He said it must also be invidious for a Minister of Information to receive the most confidential information in his Ministry and forget all about it when he returned to his newspaper office. Chamberlain's attack was grounded by a spirited defence by the new Minister of Information, and Chamberlain did not hesitate soon to join the Government in which Beaverbrook and Rothermere held office.

Rothermere, overwhelmed by personal grief and in conflict with his chief of staff, Trenchard, resigned as Secretary of State for Air after less than six months. Both Northcliffe and Beaverbrook wanted to resign, Northcliffe with the customary threat, saying that he wished to escape from any connection with the 'alleged War Cabinet' so that he could publish what he thought about it, Beaverbrook because the Foreign Office blocked his plans and opposed his methods. Lloyd George managed to hold them by the coat-tails, but only just, until the Armistice in November 1918. As soon as victory was achieved his attitude to Northcliffe abruptly changed, but there began in August a series of demands which can only be explained by the megalomania which clouded the last years of the publisher's life.

The evidence for the first demand came from Beaverbrook. Northcliffe sought to be Lord President of the Council in a Lloyd George–Northcliffe administration, using Beaverbrook and Lord Reading as his intermediaries with the Prime Minister. The most unstatesmanlike and apolitical of men wanted to be a statesman, a member of the War Cabinet, no less, without troubling to be a politician first. The notion was ill received at Downing Street.

A month before the Armistice Northcliffe wrote to Riddell saying he would be glad to help Lloyd George in the forthcoming general election; the threat on this occasion was that he did not propose to use his newspapers and personal influence to support a new government unless he knew definitely and in writing, and could conscientiously approve the Cabinet list. It was a novel and audacious stipulation. The answer, through Riddell, was that Lloyd George 'would not dream of such a thing'.

Northcliffe's refusal to support a return to power of the 'Old Gang' was reasonable enough. His ultimatum to vet or veto a Cabinet was the product of an unbalanced mind, but it did not seem that way to the other prominent Harmsworth, Harold Rothermere. 'Of course,' he wrote to his brother, 'Lloyd George may be elated at the outlook and have a fit of independence.'

Lloyd George recalled that he 'fell in and out' with Northcliffe several times both before and during the war. The most savage and bizarre of the 'fallings out' was now to occur. The ceasefire between the Allies and Germany in exhausted Europe was the signal for the outbreak of war between Northcliffe and Lloyd George over the general election in Britain and the peace terms in Europe.

Northcliffe's official biographers, his nephew Geoffrey Harmsworth and Reginald Pound, do not go out of their way to mention the morally unconventional aspects of his character. There was no space in their mammoth work for the youthful lapse when the young Alfred was turned out of the family home for getting the family servant in the family way; 'the child, a boy, was an undistinguished member of the Amalgamated Press staff . . . an embarrassment shipped to Australia, where he eventually died of drink in an asylum some time between the wars.' Nor, in the many pages devoted to their subject's creativity, genius and patriotism, is there the opportunity to mention Kyrle Bellew, 'whose show or shows he boomed in the *Mail*'; or 'his principal amorous interest in a Mrs W - - [Mrs Kathleen Wrohan, his Irish mistress], by whom he had three children'. Northcliffe was as adept at concealing his private life as most other communicators. One must turn for such indiscretions to *Strictly Personal*, a book by another nephew, Cecil Harmsworth King, published in 1969. But Geoffrey Harmsworth and Pound do not drape all the warts; they 'tell all' about his brutality in dealing with his minions, including successive editors of *The Times*. They also give this example of his behaviour at No. 10 Downing Street during the post-war election:

'Lloyd George had never intimidated him but he had intimidated Lloyd George and was capable for that reason of treating him with personal disrespect. During the general election preparations that December, for instance, he had taken Alexander M. Thompson, the *Daily Mail* writer on Labour, to see the Prime Minister at Downing Street . . . Lloyd George, who had not met Thompson before, clapped him genially on the back and began to talk of Russia. Northcliffe intervened almost at once. "I didn't bring Thompson here to talk about Russia !" Thompson said that Northcliffe's voice was "like the crack of a whip".'

There is conflict of opinion over his next demand and a denial by Northcliffe in a private letter. There was no doubt in Lloyd George's mind, however, that the publisher had 'conceived the idea that he must be one of the official delegates of the Empire at the Peace Conference'. In *The Truth About the Peace Treaties* the Prime Minister wrote:

'I had to refuse Northcliffe's request. I knew what this refusal meant as far as his powerful support at the coming election went, and afterwards in my conduct of the Peace negotiations. He was visibly astonished and upset by my declining to accede to his request. He sent an emissary who was a mutual friend to ask me to reconsider my decision. This peacemaker left no doubt what consequences would ensue if I persisted. I must expect the implacable hostility of the Northcliffe newspapers at the impending electoral contest and afterwards. But I resolved not to give in. Had I done so I should have been his man in possession at Downing Street, and he would want to make it clear to his readers that I was his nominee. That position was incompatible with the independence and dignity of the high office I held. I elected to break with him.'

There was one more personal confrontation. Northcliffe called on the Prime Minister to outline another plan, to organise the whole of British official propaganda during the Peace Conference from the Hotel Majestic in Paris. 'I thought the suggestion dangerous in the extreme,' wrote Lloyd George. 'Indirectly it would have given him great power in the direction and control of our policy. So once more I rejected his offer. He became angry and threatening. I curtly told him to go to Hades. And as poor Bonar Law said afterwards: "He came straight to me at the Treasury" . . . and that was the last either he [Law] or I ever saw of Northcliffe.' One historian has raised a doubt as to whether the publisher was told to go to Hades because of his bid to be official propagandist in Paris or of a repeated demand to know the composition of the future

Government; no one has doubted that he was assigned to Hades, merely why.

It was the last they saw, but not heard of Northcliffe. His feud with the Premier proceeded remorselessly until Northcliffe's death three years later. The vendetta of the most powerful journalist of the time against the greatest Briton of the time led him to forsake any semblance of impartiality in dealing in his newspapers with the issues at stake in the election and at the Peace Conference. In his vendettas the first casualty was truth. Lloyd George might have been afraid of him in 1917, as Colonel House claimed, but this was the end of 1918.

That final meeting was on 3 November. The following day, a week before the Armistice, Northcliffe published his own peace terms in a 3,500-word article in *The Times* and the *Daily Mail*, called 'From War to Peace'. He circulated it at his own expense to the world's leading newspapers, including Germany's. The declaration had obviously been prepared in advance with the aid of experts on his staff in Printing House Square and Crewe House, the propaganda HQ. It had been waiting in a drawer of his desk for sudden release at the moment of maximum mischief. 'Whatever Northcliffe intended,' says *The Times* historian, 'the publication could not fail to appear to the Prime Minister and others as a piece of blatant egotism and as an attempt to force his hand and dominate the British Peace Delegation from outside.'

The election was announced in the Commons by Bonar Law on 14 November 1918, three days after the Armistice, polling day to be in one month's time. Northcliffe's newspapers supported the anti-Government candidates, though most of them tended to be Labour. He appealed to the men in uniform to vote against the Government, flooding the silent battlefields with hundreds of thousands of free copies of the *Daily Mail*. Lloyd George faced the electorate at the outset with the declaration that 'Germany shall pay to the limit of her capacity', which the *Mail* rudely pointed out meant anything or nothing. Northcliffe was demanding a public trial for the Kaiser and 'fullest indemnities', and he called it peace with justice. The magnanimity of Alexander the Great in victory was not for Alfred the Great. He was suspicious of Liberal sentimentality, and publicly pressured Lloyd George into a pledge he did not want to make, that 'Those who started the war must pay to the uttermost farthing.' The Prime Minister jettisoned his qualifying phrase 'to the limit of her capacity' for the jingoistic cry of searching the pockets of Germany for the whole cost of the war. Northcliffe's message was the noisy advocacy of vindictive and punitive measures, revenge against Germany and malice against Lloyd George. He had no intellectual grasp of the problems of peace. He did not know that without the Germans Europe could not be rebuilt. His last attempt to dictate to Lloyd George during the election brought the reply: 'Don't always be making mischief.'

When the man who won the war also won the election, Northcliffe established himself and a team in Paris with the objective of spreading propaganda against him and therefore against the British government. The anxious deliberations at Versailles merely stimulated his potency for evil. Throughout the peace talks he was nagging that Lloyd George was 'going soft' on war indemnities. He conducted propaganda behind the scenes and instructed the *Daily Mail* to publish regularly in April, May and June of 1919 the slogan: 'THEY WILL CHEAT YOU YET, THOSE JUNKERS!' In one of his own magazines he flayed Lloyd George for not possessing 'that high moral courage which enables a man to stand alone. The most perilous defect in his character is that he is not sure of himself.' He instructed Rothermere, who was due to see the Prime Minister, to tell him that the uncertainty as to who was to pay for the war was exasperating people. Early in April, when the Big Four of the Allies went into secret session, *The Times* and the *Daily Mail* daily published what they claimed to be the inside story of what was going on, slating Lloyd George for letting down the British to the advantage of the Germans. Some of the titbits, which wholly misled the public, were supplied by the proprietor himself.

There were hazards enough for the quarrelling statesmen at their private conclave in the Rue Nitôt. Now came another irritation in the form of a telegram to the Prime Minister in Paris signed by the 370 Tory Coalition Members of Parliament complaining that the greatest anxiety existed throughout Britain at the persistent reports from Paris. Lloyd George concocted with Bonar Law a reassuring reply, and then returned to London to face his Parliamentary critics and deal with Northcliffe in the same speech.

The organiser of the back-bench revolt was Kennedy Jones, a brilliant editor and newspaper executive who had earlier made a fortune out of his association with Alfred Harmsworth and was now an MP. The anxiety had been caused or reinforced by a telegram to Jones from Paris. The French Sûreté had in fact shown Lloyd George the message before it was transmitted; and it was signed 'Northcliffe'.

Lloyd George pictured vividly in the Commons the magnitude and gravity of the Peace Conference settling the fate of five continents. 'You are not going to solve these problems by telegram.' He questioned whether any body of men with a difficult task had worked under greater difficulties, with stones clattering on the roof and crashing through the windows, and sometimes wild men screaming through the keyholes. He had come back to say a few words, and he meant to say them. He asked for calm deliberation for the rest of the journey. 'I beg, at any rate, that the men who are doing their best should be left in peace to do it, or that other men should be sent there.' It was a far-ranging script dealing with the future of the small states ('Yes, it was the quarrel of small states which made the war'), of the ancient empires of Russia, Austria and Turkey. With Churchill, the man who wanted to strangle Communism in its cradle, sitting at his side he dealt with the perils of military intervention in Russia, then in the throes of the Bolshevik experiment; 'a country very easy to invade, but very difficult to conquer . . . very easy to get into, but very hard to get out of'. He shared the horror of all Bolshevik teachings, but would rather leave Russia Bolshevik until she saw her way out of it than see Britain bankrupt. We had had quite enough bloodshed. 'We want a stern peace, because the occasion demands it. The crime demands it. But its severity must be designed not to gratify Vengeance but to vindicate Justice.'

He demolished the irresponsibility of the Northcliffe policies, without mentioning his name. Then he demolished Northcliffe. He did not object to the telegram from the 370 members, but did object to the information on which it was based. He was told that the telegram was based on information from a 'reliable source'. He knew the 'reliable source' and would tell the House something about it.

'There were some peace terms published in November as a model for us to proceed upon . . . we must have everything—the cost of the War, damage to all sorts of property—hanging everybody all round, especially members of the Government! In December there were hundreds of thousands of newspapers circulated freely, at somebody's expense, among the soldiers in France, asking them to return candidates. If those candidates had been returned, the two peace delegates in Paris now would certainly not have been the Foreign Secretary [Mr Balfour] and myself, but perhaps Mr Ramsay Macdonald and Mr Philip Snowden. Who issued that appeal? The "reliable source".

'Then the war is won without him. There must be something wrong. Of course it must be the Government! Then, at any rate, he is the only man to make peace . . . so he publishes the Peace Terms, and he waits for the "call". (*Loud laughter.*) It does not come. He retreats to sunny climes, waiting, but not a sound reaches that far-distant shore to call him back to his great task of saving the world. What can you expect?

He comes back, and he says, "Well, I cannot see the disaster, but I am sure it is there! (*Laughter*). It is bound to come." Under these conditions I am prepared to make allowances; but let me say this, that when that kind of diseased vanity'—Lloyd George hesitated at this point and tapped his head—'is carried to the point of sowing dissension between great Allies, whose unity is essential to the peace and happiness of the world . . . then I say that not even that kind of disease is a justification for so black a crime against humanity.' (*Loud cheers.*)

Cecil Harmsworth offered to resign his post with the Government, but Northcliffe affected to laugh the matter off. He said the incident had simply brought him a great deal of amusement and public congratulation and had substantially increased the sale of his newspapers. Lloyd George was angry because 'we' had found out what was going on in Paris. He added, on a meaner level: 'The attack was a little ungrateful in view of the abject letter of thanks the PM wrote to me for my assistance during the Marconi case.'

The pursuit of his quarry became an obsession with 'King Alfred' until his death in 1922, the year in which Lloyd George lost power for ever. In his newspapers' reports of the various international conferences which followed the peace there was malevolent criticism of the Government policies. His journalists were forbidden to attend Press conferences called by Lloyd George. The source of the Northcliffe news service was French, understandably biased against the British. In January 1921, in one of his increasingly tedious and acrimonious messages to *The Times*, Northcliffe observed: 'Our sometimes tactless pinpricking of the Prime Minister in leading articles has created the impression—especially in clubs—that we have a personal vendetta against him.' The impression possibly lingered on because *The Times*, in another pinprick in July, described the Prime Minister as 'probably the most distrusted statesman in Europe'.

Lloyd George was not alone in welcoming Northcliffe's much-heralded world tour, which began the same month. He had become as odious to his associates as to the politicians, except to the most ingratiating in each sphere. Stripped of his power he would have been a candidate for mirth or pity, but the power remained. At an editorial conference on the eve of his departure he demanded of a *Daily Mail* sub-editor what was the best story in that day's newspaper. There was an ominous silence when the brave man replied, 'Viscount Northcliffe is leaving tomorrow on a world tour and will be away for several months.'

But The Chief, still unpredictable, was able to his own satisfaction to transmute this insult into a prayer for a fleeting delivery from his superman genius and drive. In an aside he said to a minion, 'See that man gets a bonus.'

The tour lasted seven months, regarded by the traveller as an opportunity for the world to see Northcliffe as much as for him to see the world. He was a sick man, mentally and physically, motivated by fantasies and furies. On his orders he was photographed on board the *Aquitania* arm-in-arm with the unhappy editor of *The Times*, Wickham Steed, hijacked at the last moment to accompany him to New York. The Chief also ordered that the picture must be published the next day in the *Daily Mail* and *The Times*, 'not less than 4½ inches square'. Among his baggage was a medicine chest stuffed with sufficient drugs, potions and palliatives, ointments and bandages, to treat the whole of the passengers and crew for any conceivable malady. Strange despatches were cabled to Carmelite House, including the complete menus of the *Aquitania* for all classes of travel with the instruction, obeyed, that the *Mail* should print them. In New York he announced he was willing to answer any questions from anybody, including passers-by, who might wish to call at his hotel. The newspapers riotously reported his views on chewing-gum, free love and women's stockings. The once-great man was treated by the Press with ribaldry, exploited as a Silly Season buffoon. Lord Curzon, British Foreign Secretary, warned the White House that the visit was unofficial. Northcliffe cabled King George V, 'I am turning Roman Catholic,' and received a reply: 'I cannot help it.' From China he ordered *The Times* to press for an end to the Anglo-Japanese Treaty, and it did so. In Bangkok, where he was the guest of the king, he flung his secretary Harold Snoad down the palace steps because he couldn't find a newspaper; the king's guards picked up little Snoad and dusted his suit. In India, Northcliffe wrote a circular letter wondering why Britain wanted the place. He thought all Oriental servants were spies. He sailed past Napoleon's Elba, which was covered in snow. The journey ended in February 1922 with a few days of rest on the French Riviera. Back in London, the daily bombardment of messages, complaints and imperious orders began again. His abusiveness caused revolt and threats of resignation. There were rumours among his executives and journalists about his health, the more courageous among them saying he was mad.

There was time for a final clash with David Lloyd George over the international economic conference of thirty-four nations held at Genoa in April. On the agenda was recognition of Bolshevik Russia ('shaking hands with murder', Northcliffe called it) and the rehabilitation of Europe.

Lloyd George requested the journalists assembled in Genoa to ask the British public not to believe any statements about the conference made in *The Times* or the *Daily Mail*, promising to deal with them personally in Parliament. A few days later he reinforced the message in a more spectacular manner when Wickham Steed, forced by Northcliffe to report the conference though he was still editing the newspaper, reported that the Prime Minister had informed M. Barthou that the *entente* between Britain and France would be at an end if France insisted on continuing its intransigent attitude over Russia's debts. The headlines were:

WRECKING THE ENTENTE
PREMIER'S THREAT TO FRANCE
STORMY INTERVIEW

Steed always maintained that the story was substantially true, but Lloyd George told the pressmen at Genoa that the statements made in *The Times* were 'just ravings of a person who is insane with the desire to wreck the Conference'. Austen Chamberlain delivered in the Commons a severe blow to the traditional reputation of *The Times* for accuracy: 'I have seen the report published in *The Times* this morning, a summary of which appears to have reached the Prime Minister . . . He has asked me to say that the account is a deliberate and malicious invention, and to contradict it at once. The Lord Chancellor, who is also mentioned in *The Times* report, has already repudiated it.' *The Times* historian, while claiming that Steed's despatch was nearer the truth than Lloyd George wished to admit, summed up the discomfiture of the newspaper of record: 'The combination of denials by the Prime Minister, Chamberlain and Barthou placed Printing House Square in a situation that was as uncomfortable as it was unfamiliar.'

As early as 1915 Dawson had referred in his diary to Northcliffe's 'lunatic rages'. In April 1922 Wickham Steed was 'struck by the incoherence of his talk and the sensitivity of his nerves. The slightest noise startled him as though it had been a pistol shot.' The same month Northcliffe objected to the 'coarse, abominable and offensive' advertisements in the *Daily Mail* and appointed one of the commissionaires at Carmelite House as censor.

The twilight of Alfred Harmsworth was a brief and grotesque interlude, with darkness following swiftly. In June he told the station master at Boulogne there had been an attempt to assassinate him. He bullied the railway officials and insulted the conductor on the train to

Paris. Steed entered Northcliffe's suite on the fifth floor of the Plaza-Athénée the next day on the evening of Sunday, 11 June.

> 'He found him in bed, scantily dressed, obviously excited . . . His lower lip bore a dark scar as if he had been burned. Seizing Steed's hand he said how keenly he had felt the separation from him, and rehearsed in a gabbling voice the circumstances of his poisoning by the Germans, and the attempted assassination by his Secretary at Boulogne.'[1]

During Steed's absence from the apartment Northcliffe perceived the shadow of his dressing-gown hanging on the door and mistook it for an intruder. Steed returned to find him waving a Colt pistol at the shadow with his right hand. Seven chambers were loaded and his finger was constantly on the trigger. In his left hand he clutched a book of piety entitled *Daily Light on the Daily Path*. Except when under sedation he talked incessantly, or shouted or groaned, until 10.12 a.m. on the morning of 14 August 1922, the hour of his death in a guarded hut on the roof of the next-door neighbour in Carlton Gardens at the age of fifty-seven.

The controversy over the cause of death was still the subject of medical correspondence in *The Times* in 1971, and of continuing strife among the second generation of newspaper Harmsworths, his nephews. Sir Geoffrey Harmsworth attributed Northcliffe's delirious mental state in the last months solely to bacterial (or ulcerative) endocarditis—an inflammation of the inner lining of the heart—as diagnosed by his last physician Lord Horder. Stanley Morison, *The Times* historian, gave the diagnosis and added the nose-tapping qualification 'according to the doctors': the phrase was deleted by Printing House Square because of the angry objection of Esmond, the second Viscount Rothermere. Morison believed in the widely-held suspicion that Northcliffe died of general paralysis of the insane, the only cause of which is syphilis. Cecil Harmsworth King, a third nephew, always asserted in private and public that GPI was the cause; among its manifestations are derangement of the mind and delusions of grandeur. Endocarditis and tertiary syphilis may be present in the same body.

Morison's statement that Northcliffe was certified insane was not deleted but was challenged by representatives of the family and denied by Geoffrey Harmsworth, who produced an emphatic and written refutation by Horder. Whether he was formally certified is academic. From 18 June to 14 August 1922 he was under constant vigilance and

---

[1] *The History of The Times.*

protection, with three attendants near his bedside and the telephone line severed. He was talking gibberish.

'Northcliffe aspired to power instead of influence, and as a result forfeited both.' A. J. P. Taylor's epitaph is true of the final years, but Northcliffe exercised both until he ceased to be reasonable and eventually lost his reason. Milner wrote to Carson: 'I believe myself that he is only a scarecrow, but still the fact remains that most public men are in terror of him.' Lloyd George wrote of Northcliffe: 'Most politicians bowed their heads . . . When he supported me I always expected to hear the arrow that flies in the noon-day sun hiss past my ear from behind, an arrow always dipped in poison.' Lloyd George also bowed his head until their final parting and there were times when his attitude to Press power was craven. Yet Northcliffe never exercised either influence or power on the scale he sought or imagined.

The brilliance of his earlier years must certainly not be overshadowed by the Learean ravings of the final act. His creation of the popular newspaper ranks with television in advancing the access of the masses to knowledge about the world they live in. He breathed life, energy and enterprise into the moribund Press of his time. He introduced modern technologies and produced better newspapers, more quickly and cheaply, than existed before. He championed creditable causes as well as conducting discreditable vendettas. He was immune to the flattery of political leaders and despised party dogma. He did not fear public opinion, or anything or anybody. He was the only man in the world of journalism who justified the accolade of genius.

Power and wealth corrupted him. He revolutionised the technique of journalism but desecrated its standards by using his newspapers for personal ends and purveying processed information. On almost every issue which excited his personal interest his readers were bamboozled by exaggeration, suppression or by selected news. Public enlightenment was not the first of his priorities. The pursuit of political power, unguided by political prescience, was the dominant motive. Too impatient to persuade, he discarded the spur for the bludgeon. He saved *The Times* financially but polluted it editorially. His influence on the voters in the post-war election and on the government they chose, indeed his influence on the post-war world, was nil. The popular press in Britain never recovered from the suspicion, distaste and obloquy engendered by the worst of Alfred's policies and the imbecilities of the first Lord Rothermere who acquired the *Daily Mail*.

'Heaven forbid,' Northcliffe wrote to a correspondent in 1917, 'that I should ever be in Downing Street. I believe the independent newspaper to be one of the future forms of government.' So did Hearst. But Northcliffe failed in his hilarious design to establish newspapers as the final arbiter of human destiny; he merely demonstrated that the fiat of the Press lord was circumscribed, that he could not marshal events or adjust the course of history.

Towards the end of 1918 he was talking in private about the feasibility or desirability of setting up a military dictatorship after the war, and it may be assumed there was no doubt in his mind who would be dictating to the generals. Was it a preliminary step in this direction when, three days after the Armistice, he instructed *The Times* to publish the name of Field-Marshal Sir Douglas Haig in the newspaper as frequently as they had formerly published Kitchener's?

The Harmsworth descendants who through family pride or personal loyalty sought to establish that Northcliffe was sane to the end did no service at all to his memory. Insanity, in the clouded years, was his alibi.

III

ROTHERMERE THE FIRST

Harold Sidney Harmsworth

'Does Britain need a Mussolini?'

1926

'I urge all British young men and women to study closely the progress of this Nazi regime in Germany. They must not be misled by the misrepresentation of its opponents.'

1933

'Hurrah for the [British] Blackshirts!'

1934

'There is nothing more I can do to help my country now.'
(Rothermere's dying
words in Bermuda in 1940
when Sir Oswald Mosley was
interned and the Luftwaffe
was blitzing London.)

The first Viscount Rothermere, 'growling among the ermine'.

The hilarious tale of how Harold Sidney Harmsworth, the first Viscount Rothermere, might have become the King of Hungary may be disposed of painlessly because on that occasion the only mind being bent was his own. The episode has some clinical interest, however, as a case history in this study of the uses and abuses of Press power.

Why should an archetypal tycoon whose principal interest in life was to be the richest man in Britain, embroil himself in the tribulations of a Central European peasant state encircled by Czechoslovakia, Russia, Romania, Austria and Yugoslavia? Why should the Treaty of Trianon of 1919, which dealt sternly with Germany's ally Hungary, re-aligning her borders and re-classifying millions of her inhabitants, later arouse such ire in the mind of a man rarely moved by the under-privileged or dispossessed, especially foreigners? Princess Hohenlohe-Waldenburg alone knew the answer. A chance social meeting with the lady led Rothermere to make a clown of himself and also of his newspaper, the *Daily Mail*, which he acquired from his brother Northcliffe's executors.

The year after the General Strike in Britain Rothermere was more concerned about the rehabilitation of Hungary than of South Wales or the north-east of England. At Whitsun in 1927 he and his entourage were touring Vienna, Budapest and Venice in a convoy of Rolls-Royces, and we are invited to take the romantic view that the briefest of dallyings in the capital of Hungary, astride the Danube, set him aflame with the sufferings of the people of the Great Plain. On 21 June the Viscount requisitioned the leader page of the *Daily Mail* to awaken his English readers to the cause of 'Hungary's Place in the Sun'. He signed the proclamation: who wrote the article, which displayed a knowledge of mid-European affairs beyond its faded aristocracy, is irrelevant, but nobody was fooled by the fact that Rothermere had founded and endowed the King Edward VII Chair of English Literature at Cambridge. His readers had his word for it that the post-war frontiers, which scythed off choice portions of Hungary to its neighbours, some of them states newly created by the peacemakers, must be revised forthwith. The British, socially embittered after the first confrontation between unions and government, were ordered to concern themselves with the mugging of Hungary. There was also a hint from the illustrious tourist that international finance, via Wall Street, might consider the cancellation of the pawn tickets they held from the countries who, with the blessing of Versailles, were doing Hungary down.

For months that year the readers of his newspapers, less those who deserted in droves to the *Daily Express*, were nourished on a diet of Hungarian goulash. Only the Hungarians were delighted, not merely with his decision to allot them a place in the sun but with the gifts he showered upon them. Some of the story was narrated in *My Campaign for Hungary* by Lord Rothermere. Everything imaginable, except a gentleman's convenience, was named after him in Budapest. The single act of common sense he displayed in this Ruritanian farce was his reluctant refusal to accede to the request of a group of Hungarian monarchists that he should accept the Crown of Saint Stephen. He despatched his son Esmond to accept on his behalf the endowment of a university honorary doctorate. The last of the Hapsburgs was not succeeded in Hungary by Harold, the third-born of the Harmsworths.

Writing of *Myself and the King Question*, Rothermere said: 'I have never discovered how or when the proposal that this high honour should be offered to myself first took place ... I was assured that, in the prevailing enthusiastic mood of the Hungarian people, a plebiscite in my favour would be practically unanimous.' He accepted many gifts which were 'pathetic evidence of the place I had attained unsought in the imagination of the mass of the people'.

Princess Hohenlohe-Waldenburg's spell lost its potency, though another role in her admirer's European fantasies was still in store for her.

Harold was educated at the Philological School in Marylebone Road, London, later a grammar school. 'Particularly good at arithmetic,' said one of his early reports. He began his Civil Service career as a boy clerk at twelve shillings a week in a fusty Board of Trade office in Tower Hill, where an imprudent rat once ran up his trouser leg. He rated twenty-five shillings a week at twenty-one. Then he moved, with misgivings but on his mother's orders, to the bizarre publishing world of *Comic Cuts* and *Forget-me-Not* when his elder brother Alfred was launching on borrowed money his first successful satellite, *Answers to Correspondents*. Harold, worrying himself into a state of depression because of a warning from a superior civil servant that he was parting from a pension, became company secretary of Answers Company, Ltd, crossing his fingers. Mother was right, because Harold's 'particular goodness' at arithmetic made him a natural complement to her creative, unpredictable Alfred.

In later years after Northcliffe's death Rothermere told Lady King, his sister Geraldine, the second truculent baby in the Harmsworth family, that Alfred owed everything to him and that without his management Northcliffe would never have been heard of. In a less expansive mood in 1937 he told Bernard Falk, one of his editors who visited him in old age: 'In the great business we built up Alfred was No 1 and I No 2—*the runner up*. He was the creative genius. I looked after the business end and saw that his wonderful ideas were properly marketed.' Harold pruned the roses Alfred grew. Without Northcliffe, Harold would never have been heard of, not at any rate in the publishing world. He would have plodded on in the Board of Trade, breast-stroking forward through a million cups of civil-service tea, immune from the risk of final decision, secure behind the shield of anonymity, until he earned his gong and pension.

He was shy when young, developing in later life a suspicion of his fellow men and an unsavoury attitude to women. Alfred described Harold as particularly obstinate and determined, and he had none of his elder brother's charm; his sense of humour was sardonic. The blue-eyed blonde he married was pretty and frivolous, but sharp-witted and no fool. Chattering as a child, she had told her sister of a secret prayer that she would marry a rich man and have three sons. Lilian Share married a rich man, but realised that Harold fell short of her idea of romance at their first honeymoon breakfast when he summoned his secretary to deal with urgent business. She had three sons, found the going hard, shut up shop, and meandered for the rest of her life around the French Riviera in luxury and in more congenial and artistic company, all expenses paid. They went their separate promiscuous ways.

Cecil King, the only rebel in the second generation of the Fleet Street Harmsworths, was no flatterer, but nothing known about his Uncle Harold before or after death would seem to require an application of cosmetics to King's portrait. Rothermere's decision that his own documents and letters should be destroyed does not suggest they contained much that would present him in a more laudatory light to posterity. Even the customary tribute to his generosity and patriotism is omitted in King's stark unveiling.

In the eyes of his nephew, Rothermere was a forceful, able man, disgusted by the ineffectiveness of governments between the wars. He was an ugly man with a powerful bulldog look about him in later life. His Wall Street gambling was 'presumably' financed by the sale of some of the family shares in the publishing business. He was an incredibly inept politician, and King could not believe he would have made a good Minister because he was 'inarticulate and no administrator'. He was a very unhappy man after the death of his two elder sons in the First World War, fighting off despair, with really nothing to live for, taking refuge in drink. King recalled among Rothermere's many mistresses a secretary who used to clatter away at her typewriter wearing a ring containing a diamond the size of a pigeon's egg. 'Evidently she became a nuisance, and Geoffrey Harmsworth told me Rothermere offered him ten thousand pounds a year to marry her.' Most of his affairs were one-night stands with girls who were astonished to receive mink coats or diamond brooches for their services. He once told King that old mistresses were much more expensive than old masters, 'and he had plenty of experience of both'. Rothermere's morale depended apparently on his immense success in making money. 'He was not a man of integrity.'[1]

'Ugly' is a lazy description of Rothermere, especially in maturity. There was no trace of asymmetry, or of the sort of physical blemish which arouses sympathy. His face at once conveyed the considerable judgement that everyone and everything had a price he could afford to pay. The first impression of arrogance and obduracy was confirmed on closer examination. The crudeness of his features advertised a capacity for the ruthless and brutish. The calculating eyes were disconcerting. The plump sensual lips turned down at the corners, pointing to a bull neck as wide as his skull. It is all to be seen, growling among the ermine, in his photograph as the First Viscount Rothermere, fatuously topped by a circlet of nine visible pearls with the cap of estate tucked inside.

There was certainly evidence for what Cecil King called his lack of integrity. He used his newspapers to beguile the readers into buying shares in the *Daily Mirror* to boost them to a phoney price at which he could (and did) sell out. City speculators studied the financial columns of Rothermere's publications not to know what happened the previous day but what was likely to happen tomorrow. When Northcliffe was traducing in the *Daily Mail* the alleged perfidy of Lever Brothers, a gigantic libel, Harold was buying the soap shares at their slumped value in anticipation of the verdict going against his brother, and making a killing. He purchased the private favours of actresses for favourable reviews of their public performances. He was patriotic in the sense that an England that cosseted the few, including himself, must be conserved at all costs: if there were always an England there would always be a Rothermere.

[1] *Strictly Personal, Some Memoirs of Cecil H. King*, Weidenfeld & Nicolson, London, 1969.

His rise to power may be briefly sketched without injustice. He was commercially stingy, absorbed as a young man with the cost of glue, paper clips and string, but generous later on with his own money. Rolls-Royces came as Christmas presents for his sisters-in-law. Fivers for beggars. Tenners, handfuls of them, for the appeal box in a cathedral where he was delayed by a shower. The fortunes the family made out of the business materialised because of Harold's skills, but without Alfred's buoyancy and originality there would have been no business, no cheese to pare. Harold was quick to write to Alfred when a trade paper said that *Answers* was semi-bankrupt until Harold was hi-jacked from the Civil Service to control the commercial side; 'silly', he said. But the complaint frequently on Alfred's lips was 'There's my brother, moaning about money again.' There was strife over Alfred's spontaneous notions to buy other magazines with shaky financial prospects. Harold's rating of some of his brother's own creations as 'rags' occasionally soured the collaboration. He wanted to 'knife' any title that was not an instant money-maker. His attitude to buying the London *Evening News* was that it was only worth their while if they could pick up the paper for a song.

In 1895 Harold was overwrought by panic that an economic collapse might engulf the country, pleading with his brother to sell out and secure what they had already made. But ten years later he was the principal architect of the Anglo-Newfoundland Development Company, which guaranteed supplies of the wood pulp needed for the newsprint swallowed in vast quantities by Alfred's publications. It was a notable contribution to the stability of the Northcliffe empire, and to Harold's own bank account and future financial manoeuvrings.

The alliance survived the bickerings over money and their disparity in temperament. It came near to breaking point only in Northcliffe's last year when he broke the rule that family discord should never reach the ears even of their closest associates. Harold had telegraphed him in France reporting the anxiety throughout the newspaper trade at wage demands from the printing unions. Alfred wrote to his secretary, H. G. Price, marking the envelope *Secret*: 'Any person in my office who accentuates my brother's tendency to panic will earn my most permanent hostility ... it is with much difficulty that, in view of my mother's advanced age, I have succeeded in averting family friction.' He said that if the printers tried to dictate *how* he should run his business, he would fight them. 'But I am not likely to join combinations of rich men for grinding down poor men.'[1]

---

[1] *Northcliffe* by Reginald Pound and Geoffrey Harmsworth, Cassell, London, 1959.

On Northcliffe's death in 1922 Harold, Lord Rothermere, became the most powerful newspaper proprietor in the country. He had acquired sole control of the *Daily Mirror* in 1914 and founded the *Sunday Pictorial* in 1915. Now the *Mail*, the daily newspaper with the largest sale, was his, a prospect Alfred had bewailed, prophesying that Harold would ruin it. *The Times* happily escaped from a new Harmsworth embrace, but some provincial newspapers fell into his lap. At fifty-four, an angry, embittered, rich man, with no philosophy of life beyond self-indulgence and self-preservation, he appointed himself a political sage, signposting the path for future generations. The expert in profit and loss became a prophet challenging elected governments and commending false gods to the worship of the public.

Rothermere told Bernard Falk: 'My brother used to argue that he alone was responsible for what the *Daily Mail* said and I in my turn took the same line.' Advertising revenue and circulation figures were the departments that mattered to him. He had no aptitude for journalism and no time for editors with individuality or a whiff of independence. The civil servant who came of age among rats on Tower Hill was now a man of authority: the wartime director of the Army Clothing Department (1916–17); the first Minister for Air (1917–18), fusing the Royal Flying Corps and the Royal Naval Air Force into the Royal Air Force; Director of Propaganda to Neutral Countries (1918). He had been given a viscountcy for his trouble, an honour he had long coveted but pretended to receive with haughty indifference. 'On the principle of refusing nothing,' he wrote to Alfred, the first viscount in the family, 'I shall accept it, although this kind of decoration has little value in these times.' His ownership of the newspapers he was about to debase ruled out any wearisome opposition from within. His personal wealth far outstripped Northcliffe's; he was therefore able to buy the best branded goods in the Harmsworth shop window as well as inherit the tradition of subservience to The Chief created by his brother. He was a political buffoon and bully, and he had other faults.

A wartime episode had demonstrated his judgement of men, especially demagogues. On 25 July 1915 he wrote in the *Sunday Pictorial*:

'Although we are not short of leaders, we do not sufficiently employ them. Take the case of Mr Horatio Bottomley, whose tonicsome utterances in this journal give inspiration and comfort to the most lugubrious souls. Mr Bottomley exercises an enormous influence with his pen and voice. Are recruits wanted? He gets them. Is there a strike to settle? He can pour oil on troubled waters. Is there a cause to plead?

He pleads it successfully . . . Yet his great talents are most exercised "unofficially". He is a force in the State. His services should be utilised more and more by the Government.'

Fortunately, the Government ignored his advice. In 1922 Mr Bottomley was sentenced to seven years' penal servitude for financial swindles in which he cheated thousands of ex-servicemen through his Victory Bonds. Yet, when the rogue was set free, Rothermere was able to stomach the idea that his *Sunday Dispatch* should publish Bottomley's prison memoirs for a fee of £12,000. 'I have paid, but . . .' was the headline.

Rothermere's first post-war campaign was innocent enough, though tedious for his readers and conducted with ranting repetition. 'SQUANDERMANIA' was the keynote. The government could not spend a pound without a rap over the knuckles from the sombre brother who had balanced Northcliffe's ledgers. Battleships? Outdated. The Singapore naval base? A white elephant. Even air power, his cherished cause, must undergo close scrutiny. On defence matters he talked a great deal of sense in the role of The Great Pruner and Moderniser, well briefed by experts in the Services. He could also be merely silly, denouncing labour exchanges as pensioners' clubs; not a single Harmsworth, after all, was on the dole. He attacked a national health scheme. A medical service for all? Unemployment pay? Over Rothermere's dead body.

The Anti-Waste League (President: Lord Rothermere) had some success at the polls when he sponsored his own parliamentary candidates. The public were badgered to buy *Solvency or Downfall*, a reproduction of his exhortations. A South African Bantu, seeing an advertisement for the pamphlet in *Overseas Mirror*, sent off his money expecting to receive a reliably salacious novel; it was clear from his letter that he was more interested in downfall than solvency.

Like another Press baron, Beaverbrook, the Messiah from New Brunswick, Rothermere's script-writers ransacked the Bible for the language in which the prophets of old couched their forebodings. The titles of his manifestos in the newspapers were 'Has the Day of Reckoning Come?' and 'The Seven Lean Years'. The day of reckoning had not come for Harold Harmsworth, nor the seven lean years, but the manner in which he conducted his public life at this time dismayed his associates. He moved from his hotel suite into a modest flat. The message was frugality. His co-directors endured austerity meals, water instead of wine as the host discoursed upon the coming bankruptcy of Britain. One night he spotted Alexander Campbell, his *Daily Mirror* editor, in a seat at the

Russian Ballet, summoned him over in the interval and harangued him on the country's impending collapse. 'The House of Commons,' wrote Rothermere, 'must listen to the irresistible cry of the people. How shall it help us that our arms were carried to victory, if the fevered Squandermania which followed success in the field drags us down to national bankruptcy?'

No vacuum was caused, so far as the man of decision and action was aware, by the death of Northcliffe, the fall of Lloyd George's Coalition Government, and the sudden retirement and death of his successor at No. 10, Bonar Law, all in a period of two years, 1922 and 1923. One of Bonar Law's early callers during his brief Tory administration was Rothermere, said to be demanding an earldom for himself and a Cabinet post for his surviving son, Esmond, then a Conservative MP, as the *quid pro quo* for his support of the new government. Esmond, the second Viscount and a positive improvement on the first, was not present at the market place but is on record as a disbeliever of the story. J. C. C. Davidson, later Lord Davidson, was within earshot as Parliamentary Private Secretary to Bonar Law. He said that he heard what had occurred from the Prime Minister 'within seconds' of Rothermere's departure, and it is related in *Memoirs of a Conservative*, the book about Davidson by Robert Rhodes James.[1] The account cannot be dismissed as incredible; the Harmsworths had conducted similar foraging expeditions in the past and there were to be others in the future. The door they were shown is still at No. 10 Downing Street. As for the readers of the *Daily Mail*, Rothermere inflicted upon them a series of attacks on Bonar Law's policies which suddenly dried up when Lord Beaverbrook intervened on behalf of his Canadian friend; Law was born in the province where Beaverbrook was reared, New Brunswick.

The only consistency traceable in Rothermere's political attitudes is that as his wealth increased so did his fear of Socialism, driving him further to the Right with only one momentary lapse or threat in 1929 which no one took seriously. The peaks and troughs of his thinking along the way run off the graph. The curves occasionally end up as circles. From 1914 the *Daily Mirror* was Liberal, then in 1922 fervidly anti-Socialist. In that election all factions except one, Ramsay MacDonald, were accorded a special *Mirror* issue; social reform was anarchy, a message Rothermere was then able to trumpet also in the *Daily Mail*. Bonar Law's Tory government did not last long, nor, because of cancer, did Bonar Law. Rothermere's advice in the election of December 1923,

[1] Weidenfeld & Nicolson, London, 1969.

that the older parties should unite against Socialism, was rejected and the Liberals incurred his wrath for 'committing suicide'. The country threw Stanley Baldwin's Protectionist policy overboard and the result of the polling was a negative confusion; no majority for any party and the certain defeat of the Government on the reassembly of Parliament in the New Year. When George V sent for Ramsay MacDonald on 24 January 1924 to form a government the spectre of the social revolution Rothermere feared became a reality.

Long before his delirium Northcliffe was pursued by the daemons of his hallucinations; the Germans were after him, and he fitted a secret catch in a door that would ensure his physical deliverance. Rothermere's daemons were more tangible; the spendthrifts, the malingerers and the social reformers were after his money and power. All that made his life bearable was in jeopardy, and there was no escape door. He viewed the future with gloom, and what he feared with some reason was Communism in Europe and Socialism in Britain. The new power and insolence of the working classes was disturbing the money markets. His answer to the wild talk about social welfare was stringent national economy and lower taxation, a free hand for the business entrepreneurs, the creators of wealth. Pruning. Retrenchment. Discipline. His retort to friends or relatives who tried, but only once, to counsel him was 'Teach your grandmother to suck eggs.' The King took a less alarmist view. He wrote in his diary: 'Today 23 years ago dear Grandmama died. I wonder what she would have thought of a Labour Government!' A few weeks later, having met some of the new Ministers, he wrote to his mother: 'They have different ideas to ours as they are all Socialists, but they ought to be given a chance and ought to be treated fairly.'[1]

Britain's first attack of Socialism was a mild affair, hardly meriting any thoughts of a 'sell out' or of emigration by so prominent a patriot as Rothermere, though it was probably at this jittery stage of his life that he started gambling on Wall Street to build up a reserve fortune in the New World, just in case. MacDonald was Prime Minister of a minority government, by courtesy of an uneasy alliance with the Liberals in the Commons. Labour was in office but not in power, in willing double-harness with the civil servants in their Ministries, trying to demonstrate that Labour (treated fairly) could govern; they were suitably dressed for State occasions by Moss Bros. Eleven members of a Cabinet of twenty were of working-class origin. It frightened Harold Rothermere; it was also an affront to the natural ruling class, the amiable aristocrats with the

[1]*King George V, His life and Reign* by Harold Nicolson, Constable, London, 1952.

goodwill and time to spare to run the country on weekdays, the scions of the wealthy groomed for leadership in the best public schools, and the intellectuals honed in the ancient universities to direct the nation's business. In inclement political weather the old wound to their dignity still troubles them.

At the end of September the first Labour government was defeated by 364 to 191 votes, snuffed by a vote of censure on its action in dropping the prosecution of a British Communist charged under the Incitement to Mutiny Act of 1797. A violent controversy over a commercial treaty with Russia, to be followed by a settlement of Russian debts and a guaranteed loan to Russia by England, had also raised suspicions that the milk-and-water Labour administration was over-sympathetic to the Communists. It was the old and new story: was a British Labour government outwardly conducted by moderate men really under the domination of its left wing, and was the left wing dominated by camouflaged Communists or fellow-travellers? Rothermere had no doubt of the answer to that question and was determined that the Socialists should not only get out but stay out. He played a role which Northcliffe would have envied in the famous 'Zinoviev Letter' election which followed in October 1924, nine months after the emerging power of Labour first flickered in Westminster and Whitehall.

The letter, dated 15 September, was on notepaper headed 'Executive Committee, Third Communist International. Presidium. Moscow', addressed to the 'Dear Comrades' of the Central Committee of the British Communist Party, and signed 'With Communist Greetings, President of the Presidium of the IKKI, Zinoviev'. It was marked 'VERY SECRET', not surprisingly in view of the contents. The theme of the letter was 'stirring up the masses of the British proletariat', conveying instructions on seditious activities and outlining the requisite conditions for the complete success of an armed insurrection in Britain. 'From your last report,' said the letter, 'it is evident that agitation-propaganda work in the Army is weak, in the Navy a very little better . . . It would be desirable to have cells in all the units of the troops, and also among factories working on munitions and at military store depots.' Zinoviev was concerned that the Military Section of the British Communist Party further suffered from a lack of specialists, 'the future directors of the British Red Army'.

Copies of the letter were in possession of the Foreign Office, the Conservative Central Office, and the *Daily Mail*. The Prime Minister, MacDonald, and the Foreign Secretary, Henderson, but not their Cabinet colleagues, had known about it for a fortnight before it became public property. The PM had drafted, but not finalised until the document could be authenticated, a protest to the Soviet Embassy in London. Then, on a Saturday morning four days before polling day, when the exhausted MacDonald had reached Aberavon on his electioneering tour, the *Daily Mail* bombshell burst:

MOSCOW ORDERS TO
OUR REDS

GREAT PLOT DISCLOSED

'PARALYSE THE ARMY
AND NAVY'

AND MR MACDONALD
WOULD LEND RUSSIA
OUR MONEY

The remainder of the headlines made it clear, and truthfully so, that the Foreign Office had issued the document only after the *Mail* had spread the news.

Rothermere's newspaper wasn't selfish about its scoop. Some things, even in Rothermere's world, were above the sordid considerations of commercial competition; notably documents, authentic or otherwise, which would sabotage the Socialists. The *Mail*, taking its readers into its confidence, said:

'A copy of the document came into the possession of the *Daily Mail*, and we felt it our duty to make it public. We circulated printed copies to other London morning newspapers yesterday afternoon. Later on the Foreign Office decided to issue it, together with a protest, dated yesterday, which the British Government has sent to M. Rakovski, the Bolshevik Chargé d'Affaires in London.'

The mandarins in the Foreign Office appear to have panicked, releasing the Zinoviev Letter before it had been authenticated and without the Prime Minister's authorisation, and publishing the protest to the Soviet Embassy before it had been finalised or approved. Or was there some more sinister motive for their rash action on the eve of the election, an intrigue against Labour by permanent officials?

The rest of the Tory Press were grateful for the nugget from its rival. The *Daily Mirror* ('Net Sale Much the Largest of any Daily Picture Newspaper'), at that time yapping at the *Mail*'s heels, announced

'RUSSIAN CALL FOR BRITISH REVOLT' and asked the pertinent question: 'Is it correct that Mr MacDonald and Mr Henderson have been in possession of the Zinoviev letter for some weeks? If so, will they kindly explain why publication was delayed until today.' The *Daily Express*, which had been sniffing out Bolshevik plots to seize power in Britain since 1919, when they were short of rations even in the Kremlin, printed its Page One headline in dramatic red on polling day:

DO NOT VOTE 'RED' TODAY!

The *Manchester Guardian* doubted the authenticity of the letter and wondered why the Tory Central Office had been in possession of it before it was officially released by the Foreign Office. Alone, two days before the election, the Labour *Daily Herald* called it a clumsy and demonstrable forgery, probably emanating from White Russians in touch with the British Secret Service. Unfortunately, the *Daily Herald* itself had been exposed three years earlier for accepting Russian subsidies. It was the role of the *Daily Mail*, not unduly irked over questions of authenticity, to extract the maximum propaganda value from the windfall. On the front page, illustrated with a pen-and-ink drawing of Zinoviev resembling Rasputin's grandfather, and tossing in the anti-Semitic titbit that his real name was Apfelbaum, the paper published this groaningly over-loaded comment as the second paragraph of its news story:

> 'The letter is addressed by the Bolsheviks in Moscow to the Soviet Government's servants in Great Britain, the Communist Party, who in turn are the masters of Mr Ramsay MacDonald's Government, which has signed a treaty with Moscow whereby the Soviet is to be guaranteed a "loan" of millions of British money.'

How the British Communist Party, which at that time had 3,500 card-carrying members, was to accomplish its assignment has never been explained. Nor has the Red Letter ever been established as genuine. The case for forgery rests upon the incorrect description of individuals, faulty phraseology, and the fact that the original of a document with so many convenient copies has never been produced. It was certainly the intention of the Third Communist International that their British comrades at that time should conduct such a conspiracy: it was also the ambition of the British comrades to do so. The only fact that is beyond question is the fate of the unhappy Apfelbaum, alias Grigori Evseevich Zinoviev. He was one of the first Bolsheviks, prominent in Lenin's time. He was also the chief defendant at the first of Stalin's show trials in 1936, the year of the Great Purge. He was shot.

Like most election scares, the Zinoviev affair was not a decisive factor in the election. In spite of it Labour increased its total vote by a million, but two million more people went to the polling booths than in 1923 and the majority of them wanted the Socialists out. Half way through the ten months between the elections Baldwin cunningly renounced Protection; it would have to wait for indisputable evidence that 'public opinion is disposed to reconsider its judgement'. The Liberals, already confused, disheartened, split and in decline, were now deprived even of their Free Trade banner. With their help this time, Baldwin and the Tories were restored to power for more than four years under his second leadership as Prime Minister. Rothermere looked elsewhere for inspiration.

The coming in 1922 of the first of the European post-war dictatorships quickened his pulse. Britain must, of course, expand her air power, but Benito Mussolini—the one and only journalist to create an authoritarian state—was heralded by the *Daily Mail* as being of the calibre of leader desperately needed, a man of authority able to enforce his iron will to reverse the drift into anarchy and economic chaos. Europe needed a proliferation of Mussolinis to stem the menace of the Communists and check the debilitating influence of the political pinkies and social softies. In March 1926, the year of the General Strike in Britain, an article in both the *Daily Mail* and the *Sunday Pictorial* indicated the direction of Rothermere's fears and thoughts. It was entitled 'Do We Need a Mussolini?', but cautiously concluded that despite the genius of *Il Duce* there were some 'practical' objections to a dictatorship in Britain. He had a plan he considered more subtle at that stage, the appointment of Three Strong Men to run the nation's finances *free from any interference from Parliament*. That was startling enough, but it was the first sortie. In June 1927 he was contemplating One Strong Man in Britain, sending this letter to David Lloyd George, out of power for five years but not out of politics:

'May I suggest that in your public utterances you should make a move from your present standpoint and travel the road—the road almost invariably pursued by all great democrats—towards a very modified political dictatorship. Even a small advance along this road will secure you the support of the inner core of the Conservative Party. Artistically done your movement will be very difficult to detect and almost before you know where you are you will be back to the days of December 1918 when you were regarded as the saviour of the country. It is too early to start a Lloyd George boom but I believe that in six months' time it will be possible for myself to inaugurate such a boom personally over my own signature.'[1]

Rothermere had moved from three strong men to one, from a dictatorship to which there would be 'practical' objections in Britain to a 'very modified dictatorship' which, with sufficient artistry, would be difficult to detect, all under the auspices of a Rothermere 'boom'. By such subterfuge nations lose their freedom, and have, and still do. In a decade when the same panacea is sought by reasonable people who have lost their dignity and sense of direction ('What we need is another Churchill'), and by frustrated patriots with military medals who dream of Secret Armies, it is instructive to continue this political post-mortem on Rothermere.

He was not alone in his contempt for the standard of British governments between the two world wars; half the nation, for different reasons, were also dissatisfied or angry. Stanley Baldwin was the symbol of statesmanship for fourteen years of that period, thrice Prime Minister, still nostalgically revered by elderly High Tories for his firm handling of the General Strike in 1926 and his diplomacy in the Abdication Crisis of King Edward VIII a decade later. His lethargy in handling the economic drift and social injustices of his time was legendary. His inactivity in the face of growing German power and aggression was nearly fatal to his country. He concealed the need for rearmament, and then in November 1936 confessed his cynical motive; the need had become apparent in 1933, but he felt he could not have won an election and retained personal power on such a programme. The secret of his appeal was his imperturbability, the pipe-smoking 'Honest Stanley' image, a solace to the apathetic and the well-to-do. Rothermere had every right to be impatient and a duty as a right-wing activist to use his newspapers to administer the kiss of life to the moribund Tory Party, stimulating thoughts that might lead to a new and virile leadership, but his actions were fickle and unethical. Lloyd George described working with Northcliffe like going for a walk with a grasshopper. Baldwin's experience of Rothermere was even less companionable, a *pas de deux* with a scorpion. In a signed article, lovingly displayed in his newspapers, Rothermere commended Baldwin to his readers as 'one of the greatest Prime Ministers who ever held office'. Four years later the same readers were incited to adjust any foolish notions they might hold about Baldwin's ability. 'Mr Baldwin,' wrote Rothermere, 'is a completely incompetent person who got into high office by an accident of post-war politics.' The run-up to the 1929 election, which ended

[1] The letter is among the Lloyd George Papers in the Beaverbrook Library.

Baldwin's second term of office as Premier, demonstrated the sillier and uglier rather than the dangerous side of the publisher's political inanity.

His first approach was through the chairman of the Conservative Party, who informed Baldwin on 13 September 1928 that Rothermere had decided to support the Labour Party at the coming election, but would rally to the Conservatives instead if Baldwin were to slip into a speech a sentence of sympathy for Hungary.[1] He could, if he wished, reverse the policies of his newspapers because of a current whim or pique, a matter of some importance since the *Daily Mail* that year was selling two million copies a day, passing through the hands of five million people. The gambler with his personal fortune of twenty-six million pounds figured that Labour would probably win the election, but Baldwin was too shrewd to believe that Harold would welcome the burglars into his own home. Rothermere also demanded of Baldwin to be told in advance the names of the next Tory Cabinet. Lloyd George told Northcliffe, who made a similar demand in 1918, that he 'would not dream of such a thing'. Baldwin's reply to Rothermere was reserved for a public occasion. The clumsy Harold did not share with the readers of the *Mail* his confidences on these occasions; they knew when, but not why, the weathercock revolved.

At this stage in 1929, the second exercise of restricted power by Labour after the narrow defeat of Baldwin, Rothermere resolved to rejuvenate the Tory Party with dynamic policies and a new leader: two examples of the policies were 'No more surrender in India' and 'No diplomatic relations with Moscow'. The new idea was active participation in politics in harness with Beaverbrook and his *Daily Express*. An article in Rothermere's *Pictorial* by G. Ward Price, a notably articulate journalist who was his mouthpiece and frequently his 'ghost' writer, advocated that Baldwin be deposed as Conservative Party leader and Beaverbrook appointed in his place. Rothermere's *Daily Mail* quickly endorsed this 'interesting suggestion', which encouraged Ward Price to return to the subject in the *Pictorial* on 5 January 1930. Only one year after Rothermere had taunted the Tory leader that he might support Labour, one of his principal newspapers was blasting Baldwin, of all people, for having made 'costly but futile bids for popularity by adding to the country's burden of pensions and doles', and giving the vote to 'millions of flappers who promptly helped to put the Socialists in office'.

Price again nominated Beaverbrook for the Tory leadership, and at a public dinner held shortly after, when the Press barons were both in

---

[1]*Memoirs of a Conservative* by Robert Rhodes James.

attendance, Rothermere magnanimously endorsed his own newspapers' promotion of Beaverbrook. Beaverbrook in his speech acclaimed Rothermere's influence and judgement as 'the great master of popular opinion' and as 'the greatest trustee of public opinion that we have seen in the history of journalism'.

In February 1930 the *Daily Mail* launched the United Empire Party to contest half the Parliamentary seats in the country at the next election; nobody in Rothermere's entourage had the wit or nerve to remind him that during the Squandermania campaign he had scornfully asked, 'Can we now afford to subscribe £5,000 a year to an institution called the Empire Parliamentary Party?'

Beaverbrook was Baldwin's most dangerous, persistent and consistent adversary, assailing him at public meetings as well as in his newspapers, a more wily and politically lethal opponent than the great master of popular opinion. In the first of two memorable ripostes to the Press barons the Tory leader, on both occasions Leader of the Opposition, paid particular attention to the Harmsworth end of the axis. He named three Press proprietors, Hearst in America and Rothermere and Beaverbrook in Britain.

'There is nothing more curious in modern evolution than the effect of an enormous fortune rapidly made and the control of newspapers of your own ... We are told that unless we make peace with these *noblemen*, candidates are to be run all over the country. The Lloyd George candidates at the last election smelt; these will stink.'

He was speaking at Caxton Hall on 24 June 1930 to Conservative MPs and candidates, many of whom, as readers of the *Mail* and *Express*, had guiltily shared the doubts over the efficacy of his leadership. On the morning of the meeting, the *Mail* had confidently said that Baldwin's performance would be his 'swan song', furthermore that the hour had come, and it had produced The Man (Beaverbrook). The dramatic moment at the meeting came when Baldwin during his speech fumbled in his pockets for a document, skilfully heightening the air of expectancy, nervously fiddling with his spectacles, affecting uncertainty, and then saying: 'Here is a letter from Lord Rothermere.' As he read it out in measured tones, pausing as the cock crowed thrice with his terms for loyalty, the emotions of the audience escalated from excitement to astonishment and rage in somewhat less than half a minute. The letter said:

'I cannot make it too abundantly clear that under no circumstances whatsoever, will I support Mr Baldwin *unless* I know exactly what his

e last days of the pre-Hitler regime the
Jewish government officials in Germany
Israelites of international attachments we
to key positions in the German adminis
erman ministers only had direct relation
h case the official responsible for conveying
licy to the public was a Jew. It is from such
eed Germany.'

ed and used as propaganda by the Nazis

nce Rothermere wailed 'the Jews are every-
oubted whether at the outset he grasped the
ess in condoning Hitler's Jewish policy. The
n Nazi Germany was not merely a recurrence in
on a more ghastly scale of the oppression of the
Russia, Poland and Roumania: it had a novel

usands who earlier fled to Western Europe, the
itain were refugees from religious, not racial
ostatised and embraced Christianity, as some did,
ociety and their suffering would have ceased or
no guarantee. Only the Jews themselves who
ould resolve the problem of how far and how soon
with their new environment, surrender to modern
odernise their precepts of Judaic orthodoxy, and
of Western culture as well as enjoy its opportunities
Only the Gentiles who had been conditioned to
heir inferiors and as the scapegoat for any ills that
d hasten the pace of their social acceptability.
persecution was minimally inspired by personal
minority with a different faith ('The Jews killed
of life, but overwhelmingly in most European and
nti-Semitism was ordained by the State and sanctified
classic example was Tsarist Russia, an Orthodox
where Christians enjoyed full rights and Jews were
ss subjects, periodically reminded of their status by
ged by the sovereign. 'As long as I am Tsar,' said
ast of them all, 'the Zhidy [Yids] of Russia shall not have

alism of the first two decades of this century expressed

---

policy is going to be, *unless* I have complete guarantees that such policy will be carried out if his Party achieves office, and *unless* I am acquainted with the names of at least eight, or ten, of his most prominent colleagues in the next Ministry.'

Northcliffe had never put his demands in writing. Beaverbrook delivered his threats in public. Rothermere had dictated the baleful 'unless' conditions of a blackmailer, signed them, and delivered them. A professional extortioner would have known better; from a public man the letter was horrendously indiscreet, transforming Baldwin's swan song into a political spectacular. The Lord had delivered his enemy into his hands. 'A more preposterous and insolent demand was never made on the leader of any political party,' he told his cheering audience. 'I repudiate it with contempt, and I will fight that attempt at domination to the end.' The approval in Caxton Hall from his own party was echoed in the Commons that same night when both sides of the House rose and cheered.

The story of the alliance of the Press barons, its abrupt demise, and of Baldwin's second and shattering denunciation on 18 March 1931 is part of the Beaverbrook story in Chapter V, but the place of dishonour he reserved for Rothermere is relevant here. Said the Tory Leader:

> 'I have used an expression about an "insolent plutocracy". These words appeared in the *Daily Mail* of yesterday week: "These expressions come ill from Mr Baldwin, since his father left him an immense fortune which, so far as may be learned from his own speeches, has almost disappeared. It is difficult to see how the leader of a party who has lost his own fortune can hope to restore that of anyone else, or of his country."
>
> 'I have only one observation to make about that. It is signed, "Editor, *Daily Mail*". I have no idea of the name of that gentleman. I would only observe that he is well qualified for the post which he holds. The first part of that statement is a lie, and the second part of that statement by its implication is untrue. The paragraph itself could only have been written by a cad. I have consulted a very high legal authority, and I am advised that an action for libel would lie. I shall not move in the matter, and for this reason: I should get an apology and heavy damages. The first is of no value, and the second I would not touch with a barge-pole.'

The rise of Hitler and the National Socialists in Germany further whetted Rothermere's appetite for authoritarian government in Britain, and this time his advocacy was more strident. A 3,000-word despatch on a news page of the *Daily Mail* of 24 September 1930, signed by him, was headlined:

GERMANY AND INEVITABILITY

A NATION RE-BORN

YOUTH ASSERTING ITS POWER

It was addressed from 'Munich, Tuesday, the birthplace and power house of Nazism'. He informed his readers that the generation of Germans then coming into political power was a type which few foreigners knew at all. Its members had little experience of the war. Reparation debts, lost territories, and enforced disarmament were the only political topics they heard discussed around them. They found themselves heirs to a great nation strong in natural resources, population, diligence, and technical skill, but plunged in profound depression by overwhelming defeat in war. They had set themselves to build a new nation. And then came the clarion call:

'With the same vigour as they have developed their bodies by physical culture, with the same energy as they worked long hours at factory, office or farm, these young Germans have organised themselves to take an active part in their country's affairs. They have discovered, as, I am glad to know, the young men and women of England are discovering, that it is no good trusting to the old politicians. Accordingly they have formed, as I should like to see our British youth form, a Parliamentary party of their own.

'We can do nothing to check this movement, and I believe it would be a blunder for the British people to take up an attitude of hostility towards it ... Moderate opinion in Britain and France should therefore give full appreciation to the services which the National Socialist Party has rendered to Western Europe.'

In one paragraph of the same despatch Rothermere disclosed from Munich his thoughts on Britain:

'Under Herr Hitler's control the youth of Germany is effectively organised against the corruption of Communism. It was with some such purpose that I founded the United Empire Party in England, for it is clear that no strong anti-Socialist policy can be expected from a Conservative Party whose leaders are themselves tainted with semi-Socialist doctrines.'

the revulsion by Christians against 1,500 years of official Jewish subjugation. In theory, and certainly legalistically, the post-war year of 1919 brought enfranchisement and liberty to Jews throughout the world, a recognition of their equal political rights by all Christian countries. The ghetto gates were opened and the mass brutalities ended. In no country had assimilation progressed more encouragingly than in Germany. Less than one per cent of the population was Jewish, twenty-seven per cent of their marriages were with non-Jews, and the most distinguished Jews in Europe were contributing notably to the national culture and well-being in the arts, learning, banking and the manufacturing trades. Residual anti-Semitism lingered on, but only as an expression of individual ill-will, snobbery or envy. It lingered less in Germany than in England, with its petty unwritten but elbow-nudging rules about who could join the golf clubs or enter the famous public schools.

Hitler's crime against humanity, which Rothermere grossly mis-represented to the British people, was that he reversed at one stroke the process of integration and assigned the Jew again to the role of scapegoat, denouncing him, together with the liberals and social democrats, as traitors, wholly responsible for the downfall of Germany. What was novel and evil about the Nazi creed was that the Jews were pronounced guilty of original *racial* sin, denied redemption by apostasy or physical escape as refugees unless they had money and influence. They were trapped. By a series of laws they lost their citizenship completely, were forbidden to marry with Germans, were banned from state schools, public parks, libraries and museums. They could engage in hardly any professions or businesses, could own no land and associate with no non-Jew. Their property was confiscated and they were driven back to the ghettos.

Rothermere, by dwarfing the problem to local tussles about how many Jews had this or that job in government departments, was acquiescing in an historical rejection of the modern Christian basis of Western civilisation, and in the negation by State authority of the rights of human personality because of racial origin: the Jews were 'non-Aryan'. In 1938 a book for children was published in Germany entitled *The Poisonous Mushroom*, describing the Jews as the poisonous mushrooms of humanity. On 10 November of that year *Kristallnacht*, the night of the broken glass, signalled the first act of the final solution. Nazi gangs swinging truncheons jumped from lorries to smash up Jewish shops in Berlin. 7,500 places of business in Germany were demolished. 150 synagogues were burned down. Between 30,000 and 40,000 Jews were arrested and many were killed by sadistic guards. In 1978, recalling that infamous night, Chancellor Helmut Schmidt of West Germany spoke of the horror in a solemn address delivered in a Cologne synagogue, one of those razed by the Nazis. 'Forty years ago today,' he said, '30,000 Jewish fellow-citizens were arrested, mostly to be dragged off to concentration camps. Ninety-one Jewish people were murdered and very many were tortured. Most of the Germans alive today are innocent. But we have to bear the political legacy of the guilty and draw the consequences from it. It was a staging post on the route to Hell. Young Germans should know that it all began with the search for scapegoats.' The final act was Auschwitz, Majdanék, Treblinka, Buchenwald and Bergen-Belsen, the genocide of six million.

During the unfolding of the Nazi creed in all its aspects, once youth was triumphant in Germany and a nation was re-born, there was nobody in Britain—in spite of some formidable rivalry—who more consistently misread the portents and misled the public than Viscount Rothermere from the moment Hitler became Führer.

The *Daily Telegraph*, the *Manchester Guardian* and *The Times* condemned the persecution during Hitler's first year of power. The contrast between the editorial attitudes of the *Guardian* and Rothermere's London *Evening News* is illuminating. On 4 October 1933 the *Guardian* said:

'We have repeatedly heard in our own columns of "the other side": of the undue preponderance of Jews in the professions, of the many foreign Jews who flocked in after the [First World] war, of the Jews involved in this or that "scandal". Were it all true, which it is not, how would it justify the relentless grinding down of the Jewish race, which lives in Germany, so far as it lives, as all private and public reports show, in misery and terror?'

The previous day the *Evening News* was counselling Britain on what its attitude should be to an anti-Nazi protest meeting at the Albert Hall, to be addressed by Professor Albert Einstein, the German-born American physicist, supported by Sir William Beveridge, Sir Austen Chamberlain, and the Bishop of Exeter:

'The lecture is a piece of alien agitation on British soil; its promoters ask nothing better than that it shall make bad blood between this country and Germany . . . Intelligent and patriotic people will stay carefully away . . . not because they necessarily approve of everything done under the Hitler regime but because "fair play" as they see it means allowing the Germans to run their own country in their own way exactly as we demand the right to run our country in our own way. It will be time for British agitation when British interests are assailed.'

1934 was the vintage year of Rothermere's folly. Suffering from what would now be called an attack of selective amnesia, he forgot that the *Daily Mail* under Northcliffe in 1919 had pressured Lloyd George to drive the defeated Germans into the ground as an act of vengeance. Now, under Rothermere, the same newspaper was telling its readers a different tale, urging Britain to envy and emulate her rebirth as a nation. On 21 March he advocated that Tanganyika, the Cameroons and Togoland should be restored to their former colonisers. 'Though this proposal may not be popular,' he wrote in the *Mail*, 'I am convinced that it is wise. We cannot expect a nation of "he-men" like the Germans to sit forever with folded arms under the provocations and stupidities of the Treaty of Versailles . . . To deny this mighty nation, conspicuous for its organising ability and scientific achievements, a share in the world of developing backward regions of the world is preposterous.' Publicists and politicians more intelligent than Rothermere were saying the same thing, and had indeed said the same thing (unlike the *Mail*) when the Treaty was signed. The most prophetic cartoon of all time was drawn by Will Dyson in the *Daily Herald* of 1919: Clemenceau, the Tiger, leaving Versailles with David Lloyd George, President Woodrow Wilson and Orlando of Italy, turns aside and says ominously: 'Curious. I seem to hear a child weeping.' Above the head of the child, partially hidden by a pillar of the Palace, is a halo with the words '1940 Class'.

Had Rothermere confined his advocacy on the Nazi issue to a revision of the Treaty terms, his other manifold absurdities might have been forgotten; but Harold, unlike *The Times*, was not bothered about ethics. *The Times* stated its position in august terms: 'Europe in fact is placed in the dilemma of having to refuse to force what reason suggests should at least in part be conceded, or else of yielding to extremism what earlier was refused to moderation.' Such niceties did not trouble Rothermere.

When, on 30 January, Hitler was appointed Chancellor, annihilating all opposition within six weeks by the operation of government boycotts and purges of anti-Nazi elements, Rothermere wholeheartedly welcomed the news; nor did he question the events of 30 June, the blood-bath which eliminated Roehm, the storm troopers and General Schleicher under the vague indictment, untried, of treason and homosexuality. Hitler originated or sanctioned the massacre, but Rothermere was not surprised when the strong men took action. In 1934 he also proclaimed, principally in the *Daily Mail* and dutifully reflected in the *Mirror* and *Pictorial*, that 'Nearly all the news regarding the Nazi regime published in our most responsible journals is pure moonshine,' 'We and the Germans are blood kindred,' 'Herr Hitler neither drinks, smokes nor eats meat.' After a visit to Hitler he returned to assure the British public that his hero was 'simple and unaffected and obviously sincere . . . There is no man living whose promise given in regard to something of real moment I would sooner take.'

The Führer, already identifiable as a psychopath, an oppressor and a mass murderer, was projected by Rothermere to the readers of his newspapers, a mighty slice of the British public, as an abstemious vegetarian whose word was his bond. By the same precept the massacre of the Armenians would have been condoned on the grounds that Abdul the Damned was a keen anti-vivisectionist, and Rasputin forgiven his trespasses because he viewed the clubbing of baby seals with disfavour. Yet nobody in that vast newspaper enterprise protested to the point of resignation. No director, or editor, or cosseted relative, or journalist, or printer, or commissionaire declared that enough was enough and silently stole away or noisily denounced the deceiving of the British people. The proprietor's word, like Hitler's, was absolute. Ironically, the only complaint was from Adolf Hitler himself. In December 1935 he wrote to Harold Rothermere pleading for restraint:

'You ask me . . . whether I do not think that the moment has now come to put forward the German colonial wishes. May I ask you, dear Lord Rothermere, not to raise this point now because looking forward to closer collaboration with Great Britain I do not want to give the impression [that] I wanted to avail myself of the present situation of your Government and its many difficulties, and of the British Empire, to exercise a certain pressure.'

At the height of his political imbecility Harold Harmsworth had a considerable propaganda machine to deploy. The editorial policy of the *Daily Mail* was under his total command from 1922 until his formal retirement in 1937, when he was succeeded by his son, the Hon. Esmond Harmsworth. Its significance was that it was the only popular British daily newspaper with a predominantly upper-class and middle-class clientele. In March of 1931 he placed the *Daily Mirror* and *Sunday Pictorial* businesses under the control of John Cowley, an accounting clerk who was among the flotsam washed ashore when the Harmsworths bought the London *Evening News*. Cowley continued to represent the controlling shareholder until Rothermere, believing the *Mirror* was going broke and would cease publication, disposed in 1935 of the Daily Mail Trust shares and of his own. Between 1931 and 1935 Cowley and his co-directors, though the *Mirror* and *Pictorial* had been stipulated in a letter from Rothermere to be 'entirely' under their control, were still too scared of him and unsure of themselves to question the use of the papers for his anti-democratic crusades in the first half of the Thirties. They did not even have the courage or wit to publish opposite or other views. They also licked the jackboot, and the appeal of both the *Mirror* and the *Pictorial* to a wider social readership than the *Daily Mail* vastly increased Rothermere's sphere of influence.

Now that the trains in Italy were running on time and Mussolini was dreaming up the new Italian Empire, and Hitler was purifying the Aryan 'race', Harold Rothermere was awaiting with impatience the portent of Youth Triumphant in Britain. In the early 1930s he observed a comet so dazzling in the political sky that it seemed to promise hope, and possibly deliverance, for the most unhappy of the world's rich men. Sir Oswald Mosley, whose philosophy was that the real division in politics was not between parties but between the modern mind and the pre-war mind, had embarked upon the fifth of his brief political lives. Ex-Tory MP, ex-Independent MP, ex-Labour MP (a member of the 1929 MacDonald Government), he was sickened in 1931 by Labour's rejection of his cure for unemployment and started his own new but short-lived Socialist party. It was annihilated at the polls in the 1931 election. Mussolini and Hitler had begun as disillusioned Socialists, and Rothermere spotted his man. His offer of support to Mosley in 1931 was not rejected; acceptance was prudently postponed. Rothermere was kept at bay, but the publisher who urged Lloyd George to 'travel the road almost invariably pursued by all great democrats' and the politician with one more road to travel were reaching what Mosley described as their overt companionship and political association. It was the association of a political buffoon and a political romancer.

Mosley was in the Rothermere orbit for many years, originally meeting him at discussions organised by the younger and brighter Tory MPs in the early post-war years. Beaverbrook and Lloyd George were among the elder statesmen who attended these functions, and to a lesser degree Churchill. The *Daily Mail* was not as respectful to Mosley the Socialist in the later 1920s as in the 1930s, especially when he successfully fought Smethwick for Labour in 1926. Sir Oswald, sixth baronet, was generally regarded at that time as a socialite, wealthy and arrogant, a shallow dressy demagogue who had never soiled his hands. His first wife was the daughter of Marquess Curzon of Kedleston, Lady Cynthia, a beautiful and popular Mayfair ornament whose presence at the hustings in the December rain in Staffordshire did not enhance Mosley's pose as the champion of the proletariat. His accent and bounce contrasted curiously with the earthiness of his opponents, a former railwayman (Conservative) and the son of a miner (Liberal). The *Daily Mail*, which hailed Mosley as the Saviour of Britain eight years later, giggled its way through the Smethwick election, setting the tone for the rest of the Tory Press at the opening meeting. Sir Oswald was described as immaculately dressed. Cynthia, known as 'Cimmie' to her upper-crust admirers, which didn't help, happened to be wearing a dress bought for a song in India, embellished with tiny circular mirrors appliquéd on to the sleeves; the observant *Mail* reporter said she was elegantly gowned, discarding her magnificent fur coat to reveal a 'charming dress glittering with diamonds'.

Other Press vignettes, not all in Rothermere's newspapers, portrayed Cimmie's Hyde Park sentiments delivered in a Park Lane accent, and Sir Oswald, more familiar to the public with his elegant Savile Row suits and Ronald Colman moustache, performing his part as a West End Keir Hardie in an old overcoat and a battered hat and calling Lady Cynthia 'the missus'. Cimmie had no better luck the next year when, a Socialist to the core, during that social season anyway, she was adopted as Labour candidate for Stoke-on-Trent. The Conservative MP she was chosen to dismount was a colonel who had once been a navvy.

Mosley was a Wykehamist and a Sandhurst officer with personality, intellect and courage; he did not allow his powerful oratory, often from the roof of a van, to be silenced by bricks or bottles from hecklers. When he founded the British Union of Fascists in 1932 he was represented to the readers of the *Daily Mail* and other Rothermere journals as a man of sterling character whom they would not be likely to confuse with the 'phoney' they had read about in the same newspapers eight years back. 1934 was the year when he judged he wanted Press support. The telegram promising it came from Monte Carlo, where Rothermere was relieving his anxieties about the future with the best of everything money could buy—the choicest on four legs to eat and swill down with Château Mouton-Rothschild, and on two legs for diversion. He welcomed the Fascist movement as the only alternative to Socialism; so at first did a number of respectable Conservatives. There was nothing alarming about Mosley's economic policies—expansionism, planning and a managed currency. Nor was the Corporate State he advocated utterly alien to the consensus view. His demand for stronger armed forces to protect Britain especially appealed to Rothermere. But what attracted Mosley's twenty thousand adherents and indicated their level of intelligence was the Italian-style black shirt they were entitled to wear as members. The BUF also attracted anti-Semites, ignoramuses and thugs, who enjoyed the violence provoked by the Fascist marches.

On 15 January 1934 Rothermere signed a long article in the *Daily Mail* entitled: 'HURRAH FOR THE BLACKSHIRTS!' He told his readers: 'We must keep up with the spirit of the age. That spirit is one of national discipline and organisation . . . Britain's survival as a great power will depend on the existence of a Great Party of the Right with the same directness of purpose and energy of method as Hitler and Mussolini have displayed.' A *Daily Mail* editorial said later that 'Sir Oswald Mosley at his meetings has only expressed with one or two exceptions views that are identical with those of the robuster minds in the Conservative Party.' On 22 January it was the turn of the *Daily Mirror* to join the marching Fascists, publishing another article by Rothermere:

> 'Timid alarmists all this week have been whimpering that the rapid growth in numbers of the British Blackshirts is preparing the way for a system of rulership by means of steel whips and concentration camps.
>
> 'Very few of these panic-mongers have any personal knowledge of the countries that are already under Blackshirt government. The notion that a permanent reign of terror exists there has been evolved entirely from their own morbid imaginations, fed by sensational propaganda from opponents of the party now in power.
>
> 'As a purely British organisation, the Blackshirts will respect those principles of tolerance which are traditional in British politics. They have no prejudice either of class or race. Their recruits are drawn from all social grades and every political party.'

The piece was headlined 'GIVE THE BLACKSHIRTS A HELPING HAND', and closed with a list of the addresses of Blackshirt premises where embryo Fascists could enrol. A later article announced that young men might join the BUF by writing to the Headquarters, King's Road, Chelsea, London, SW.

The alliance with the British Fascists was not a permanent aberration. Rothermere fled long before Sir Oswald was able to train the new recruits drummed up by the Harmsworth newspapers, or evolve the Great Party of the Right. He had no time, in the five months of Rothermere's observance of the comet, to satisfy the 'panic-mongers' that the BUF respected the traditional British principles of tolerance. The fanfare which greeted the Saviour was followed by a boisterous campaign which petered out sooner than Mosley expected. Rothermere's excitement over the BUF waned for the same sort of material reasons which had inspired it. The talk of youth and idealism was rousing patriotic stuff, innocuous enough, but his blanket endorsement of Fascism in Italy, Nazism in

Germany, and Blackshirts in Britain was incautious, and—in the minds of those less politically naive—dangerous. Advertisers in the *Mail* and other sections of Rothermere's newspaper orchestra became uneasy, and some of the powerful advertisers were powerful Jews. Rothermere gave money to the British Fascist movement, which was potentially and eventually anti-Jewish, and the Jews provided a large slice of his income. The notorious Blackshirt rally at Olympia in June 1934, boosted in advance in the *Daily Mail* as stirring, provoked ugly clashes between the bullyboys in Mosley's bodyguard and the Communists, frightening scenes that were not impeccably in the tradition of British tolerance. Rothermere pulled out a safe two years before the Public Order Act of 1936 prohibited political uniforms and empowered the police to ban political processions and demonstrations. The Great Party of the Right was strangled in its cradle by Jewish advertisers and the Conservative Government which passed the Act.

How did the alliance appear to Mosley? Sir Oswald, still living in 1979 in restless retirement at Orsay, near Paris, eager at eighty-three to answer the call, has devoted some of his time to writing his engaging memoirs.[1] He strives to treat his Chief Propagandist and financial benefactor with respect and gratitude, though he discloses in passing that Harold's largesse did not equal Lord Nuffield's £50,000 cheque to the movement. Mosley begins by listing the familiar virtues which were duly recorded in Rothermere's own newspapers when he died. He was a *genuine* patriot, presumably in the sense that in England all newspaper proprietors are genuinely patriotic, all surgeons eminent, and all Roman Catholics devout. He was concerned with 'the way things were going'. He was 'a great business executive, dynamic in all his dealings, and he passionately wanted to get something done for England'. Viscount Rothermere emerges none the less as a political fool, more politely described by Sir Oswald as 'a financial genius but a political innocent, unwilling to accept advice on subjects of which he knew little or nothing'.

Sir Oswald would have played it differently had Rothermere given him any indication of what he was going to do. He writes that he would have 'naturally suggested a more discreet discussion of this phenomenon, a rather hostile enquiry in the first instance, asking what the Blackshirt movement was all about, followed by some reports of my speeches which would offer a gradual explanation and would appear to convert the *Daily Mail* at the same time as the public in a reasonable and convincing process

[1] *My Life* by Sir Oswald Mosley, Nelson, Sunbury-on-Thames, 1968.

. . . Politics are a subtle business . . .' But subtlety, unlike patriotism and financial wizardry, were not Harold's forte. The sudden telegram from Monte Carlo, and then, says Mosley, 'The headlines came pelting like a thunder-storm.' There was no consultation; just 'Hurrah for the Blackshirts!'

The subsequent history of the BUF suggests that the public did not swallow the message, unlike those on Rothermere's payroll. G. Ward Price was then much in the company of Mosley. The ideas men in the newspaper promotion department drummed up obvious Northcliffian stunts. Their daftest gimmick was a beauty knock-out for women Blackshirts. 'Rothermere was staggered not to receive a single entry,' says Sir Oswald. 'I was embarrassed to explain that these were serious young women dedicated to the cause of their country rather than aspirants to the Gaiety Theatre chorus.' There were, in fact, few beauties except the Leader's wife among them. Rothermere's own idea of how to raise large funds for the BUF, a commercial project, also fell apart, and Sir Oswald gives in *My Life* the authentic version of this curious enterprise:

'He came to me one day with an extraordinary proposition. He prefaced the proposal with the statement that he had made two large fortunes in newspapers and in the Newfoundland pulp business, and with my help would make a third, which would be the largest of the three.'

The wheeze was cigarettes. Any competent manufacturer could pack and roll them. The problem was merely distribution because the monopolists in the trade operated tied shops. Why shouldn't the vigorous young men in the Blackshirts' hundreds of branches become the distributors for the new Rothermere King Size gasper, profits to be split fifty-fifty between his lordship and the BUF? The genuine patriot who passionately wanted to get something done for England while he was netting his third and largest fortune splashed £70,000 on the machinery and lured a production expert from the tobacco combines into the project. Mosley records the death of the cigarette bubble and departure of Rothermere as the chief of his supporters:

'I warmly welcomed his proposal . . . Then came a sudden message that he could not proceed, and had decided to sell the machinery for what it would fetch. I went to see him in a hotel he frequented, and found him in a relatively modest apartment, an imposing figure of monumental form lying flat on his back on a narrow brass bedstead; it seemed an incongruous setting for one of the richest men in the world.

'Lord Rothermere explained that he was in trouble with certain advertisers, who had not liked his support of the Blackshirts, and in company with many other people had now heard of the tobacco business and liked it less. This was war, and I reacted strongly. The card to play with Rothermere was always his brother Northcliffe . . . I said: "Do you know what Northcliffe would have done? He would have said, 'One more word from you, and the *Daily Mail* placards tomorrow will carry the words: JEWS THREATEN BRITISH PRESS; you will have no further trouble.'" The long struggle fluctuated, but I lost. He felt that I was asking him to risk too much, not only for himself, but for others who depended on him. He was a patriot and an outstanding personality, but without the exceptional character to take a strong line towards the end of a successful life . . .'

The last reference to Rothermere in *My Life* was Mosley's observation that the experience made him more than ever reluctant to be dependent for political finance on the caprices of the rich. The overt companionship fell apart. They disengaged with the civil exchange of letters which customarily marks the departure of a Minister from a government. Rothermere instead celebrated Christmas that year, 1934, with the Nazi leaders in Berlin. He was photographed smiling with Hermann Wilhelm Goering, the founder of the brown-shirt storm troops, organiser and commander-in-chief of the Luftwaffe. A portrait of the Führer dominated his desk and a globe of the world in relief on an ornate stand was at his side.

The shot-gun marriage with Fascism in Britain, and the quick divorce on the grounds of commercial incompatibility, were further indications of Rothermere's political instability. He was now an obsessional Russophobe, and the demands he made on his readers became more conflicting. Dr Franklin Reid Gannon, the American who wrote *The British Press and Germany, 1936–1939*,[1] concluded after a study of the files of his newspapers and other available evidence, that 'Lord Rothermere was very near to being unbalanced on the issue of Communism, and constantly importuned Ward Price to write articles' on the theme. The USSR was the ogre and Nazi Germany the saviour of mankind. Four conspicuous pieces in the *Daily Mail* in 1936 establish the wild range of its proprietor's hopes, fears and fantasies:

January: To acclaim Hitler's third anniversary as Chancellor on the thirtieth of the month, columns of storm troopers goosestepped past his

[1] Clarendon Press, Oxford, 1971.

window at night-time bearing torches in a demonstration staged by Joseph Goebbels. Only one British newspaper participated in the adulation. The *Daily Mail* said:

'This is a memorable date in the history of Europe . . . Germany by [Hitler's] magnetic influence and the strenuous exertions of her people, has been placed once more in the forefront of the nations. Communism, which in 1933 was such a menace to the States of Central Europe, is dead and is not likely to return to life so long as his vigorous hand is in control. The enemies who so persistently predicted his early fall have had to confess their complete want of foresight. At the end of three years of power he is stronger than ever and more popular with his countrymen.'

July: In its solitary reference between the years of 1933 and 1939 to the potential peril the Nazis might hold for Britain the newspaper warned in an editorial: 'It is madness for Great Britain to remain unarmed when Germany and Italy are armed to the teeth and able at any moment to attack our vital interests.'

August: When Herr von Ribbentrop, Hitler's friend, was appointed the representative of the Reich at the Court of St James's, the *Mail* hailed him as 'A Welcome Ambassador' whose 'moderation and tact have been greatly appreciated in Britain'. (One example of his moderation and tact was that on several official and social occasions he greeted King Edward VIII with the Nazi salute.)

September: Ward Price stated in an article that Bolshevism was a greater threat to the British Empire than National Socialism. If Hitler did not exist, he said, 'All Western Europe might soon be clamouring for such a champion.'

Rothermere was not alone in holding this view, and he did hold it openly. What was alarming about the man was that his reaction to events was the product of predilection, prejudice, fear and self-interest, bereft of any measured assessment of the trends; further, that he had an audience of ten million readers. The one service he rendered his country was to press without much success for British rearmament; even in the year 1936–37 the national expenditure on arms was less than half of Germany's. The rest of his policies made nonsense even of his call for rearmament. There was no conceivable threat at that time of an invasion of Britain or of her Empire by the USSR. He had financed the design of a superior bomber aircraft and presented it to the nation naming it Britain First, the slogan of the British Union of Fascists. But until a matter of months before war in 1939 precious few of Britain's bombers in service could reach even Berlin, and Moscow was three times that distance. The danger from the USSR was the seepage, with the active encouragement of the Kremlin, of Communism as a revolutionary doctrine to other countries including Britain: the answer to ideological warfare was not bombers but social reform and justice which Rothermere's newspapers consistently opposed. Rearm against whom? There was every reason to rearm against Nazi Germany, but Rothermere presented Hitler to the British people as a sincere statesman with a justified grievance against the Versailles strait-jacket, and the Nazi storm troopers as the emblem of Youth Triumphant. There was no incentive for his compatriots to dig deeply into their pockets to protect themselves against an international terrorist he told them was a friend of Britain. He did not ponder where Hitler would turn when he had subjugated Europe and Russia. The immediate threat to Britain and her Empire, and to democracy and Western culture, was not Bolshevism but the German ersatz brand of National 'Socialism'. Yet such was Rothermere's fear of a Communist invasion that he contemplated setting up a private estate in central Hungary as a retreat.

A contemporary view should be mentioned. In the *News Chronicle* in August 1937, A. J. Cummings wrote:

> 'There is nothing in modern politics—not even in German politics—to match the crude confusion of the Rothermere mentality as revealed in the Rothermere Press. It blesses and encourages every swashbuckler who threatens the peace of Europe—not to mention direct British interests—and then clamours for more and more armaments with which to defend Britain, presumably against his lordship's pet bully.'

The *Daily Mail* was the only popular British newspaper which actually supported and condoned Nazi Germany. Rothermere sent his special correspondent Ward Price as his emissary to hob-nob at the courts of the dictators. In exclusive interviews given prominence Hitler and the other Nazi leaders were provided with a platform to disguise their policies in Europe. Price, to his credit, abhorred in private the brutalities of the totalitarian regimes; to his discredit he presented in public their alibis. His defence was he reported accurately what they said, 'leaving British newspaper readers to form their own opinions of their worth'. It has never been denied that Price was the author of the Nazi eulogies which appeared under Rothermere's name and which were calculated to bend the readers' opinions in favour of Hitler and Mussolini.

The *Daily Mirror*, then entirely free of Rothermere's influence, was fiercely anti-Nazi; Cassandra's column and the editorials by Richard Jennings were among Winston Churchill's favourite morning reading.

There was no such radical change in the policy of the *Daily Mail* in 1937 when its proprietor retired, at least from the active conduct of the newspaper. A student would have observed less emphasis on Hitler's sincerity and purity, an even more strident demand for rearmament, but no admission that the newspaper had been fooling the public since the Führer came to power. The message was still that Europe was none of Britain's business and that strength and isolation were the prudent stance. The *Anschluss*, the incorporation of Austria in the German Reich in March 1938, was headlined in *The Times* as 'The Rape of Austria'. The *Daily Mail* recorded the event as a demonstration of 'the speed and effectiveness of power politics'. It published not one word about the confrontation between the Austrian Chancellor Kurt von Schuschnigg and a raving Adolf Hitler at his mountain retreat at Berchtesgaden, or of the uncompromising Nazi demands on its neighbour. It said the settlement was founded upon facts, a natural settlement achieved by peaceful negotiation. The *Anschluss* itself was merely an occasion for another exhortation about Britain's own defences: 'Arm, arm, arm! That has been the lesson of the past few years. That is the lesson which is underlined and emphasised by Austria today.' A situation which should have inspired the blindest isolationist to think again about collective security was used by the Rothermere Press to preach the opposite gospel: 'Today the resolve of the British people will be to have nothing to do with the situation in Central Europe. Not one British soldier, not one penny of British money, must be involved in this quarrel which is no concern of ours. Britain must concentrate on building up her strength, ready to exert it to the last man and the last penny if her direct interests are threatened.'

Czechoslovakia was next on Hitler's list. On 23 May 1938 the *Mail* declared that any kind of pledge that France would fight would only inflame Prague which might then be tempted to take irrevocable action at other people's expense. The paper rejoiced in any move which absolved Britain from moral responsibility or intervention—the mediation mission to Prague by Lord Runciman in July, Neville Chamberlain's visits to Berchtesgaden, Godesberg and Munich in September, culminating in the Munich Agreement of 30 September which incorporated Sudetenland in the German Reich. It was all none of Britain's business: all that Britain needed was more arms.

By the reckoning of most of the British appeasers in the Press, Parliament and the stately homes, 1938 exhausted Hitler's 'justifiable territorial demands'. The *Daily Mail*, however, clung tenaciously to Rothermere's delusions even when the Nazi troops marched into Prague on 15 March 1939 and incorporated Memel into the German Reich on 22

March. It told its readers that when the rearmament it had advocated was completed it would matter little what happened on the Continent. It conceded that by exceeding his own racial claims Hitler had indeed created speculation as to what he might do next. The voice of the *Mail* became inaudible as the gathering storm broke, though Viscount Rothermere was still sending fawning cables to Hitler, addressing him as 'Leader', long after war was inevitable.

The story ended in 1940 when, as a gesture, Beaverbrook's Ministry of Aircraft Production cooked up a meaningless mission to Canada for Rothermere though he was sick and seventy-two, morose and disillusioned. Doctors halted the journey and ordered him to the sunshine of Bermuda where he died on 26 November; dropsy was diagnosed and the post-mortem indicated cirrhosis. The same year Sir Oswald Mosley and his second wife, Diana Mitford, daughter of Baron Redesdale, were interned with 763 of his followers under the Defence Regulations. The German blitz on London began with nightly bombings from 7 September to 2 November. Before he lost consciousness Rothermere said: 'There is nothing more I can do to help my country now.'

There is not a single book on his life, authorised or irreverent. Northcliffe and Beaverbrook left mountains of letters and memoranda, taking care to ensure their preservation, anticipating their niche in the history of their time. Rothermere destroyed the evidence as he went along, leaving no fingerprints or footprints except in the files of his newspapers and in letters kept by the recipients. On the last journey in the liner from New York to Bermuda he looked again at the secret papers he carried with him and threw them out of the porthole.

IV

HENRY ROBINSON LUCE

'I am a Protestant, a Republican and a free-enterpriser, which means I am biased in favour of God, Eisenhower and the stockholders of Time Inc.'

'I want good editors with independent minds. I like to see independent thinking. If it's going the wrong way I'll straighten them out fast enough.'

Henry Robinson Luce, with his second wife,
Clare Boothe Luce, in 1964.

Luce, the 'grizzled tycoon',
who reached thirty million minds through his magazines.

'Harry, now that you've got America, how do you like it?'

Tom Matthews was riling his former boss, Henry Robinson Luce, co-founder and then proprietor of the *Time-Fortune-Life* publishing emporium, at their last-but-one meeting in New York in 1953. Matthews, a frustrated poet of talent and originality, had been enmeshed for a nerve-tingling, teeth-chattering, brain-washing quarter of a century in the Time Machine and was showing signs of metal fatigue due to the repetition of stress cycles of maximum intensity. He began as a cog, Religion Editor, and was soon jacked up to foreman of the cultural departments, responsible for 'a Religion writer who hated religion, a Cinema writer who despised the movies, a Music man who said he hated music, an Art man who knew nothing about pictures.'[1] He was jacked up again as chief stoker in Dante's Inferno, the National Affairs Department, finally changing his dungarees for the strait-jacket worn by the chief engineer running the whole clattering contrivance; well, almost running it. It was Managing Editor (later Editor) T. S. Matthews, but always Editor-in-Chief H. R. Luce.

Matthews wasn't, however, suffering from mental fatigue. He gave an account of that dinner with the portentous, uninterruptible Luce in a letter to an old *Time*hand:

> 'Alas, I took no notes; alas, I had had several drinks . . . Well, I'll tell you what I do remember . . . We reminisced. Somewhere in the course of the—I almost said conversation, but you will understand—the discourse, I decided that I might as well get a few things said. These, as I remember them, are the few things. "Harry," I said, "now that you've got America, how do you like it?" Of course you want to know what his reply was; so do I. There must have been a reply, or at least an answering spate of words, but what it was I cannot tell you. Anyhow, I regard that as one of the few blows landed during the entire bout. As a dead-game sport, I can now admit that he jarred me once; he said (or words to this effect), "By what right do you put me on the moral defensive?"

[1]His own words in *Name and Address*, An Autobiography by T. S. Matthews, Anthony Blond, London, 1961, the source of other quotations from Matthews in this chapter.

'I remember bringing one haymaker right up from the floor: I told him that he was kidding himself about the power of the Press; the Press had no power of accomplishment, though it did have a negative power—to debase taste, harm individuals, etc. That should have laid him out, but it never fazed him. What an iron jaw! The only other punishing punch of mine I can remember I clumsily blocked myself. I reminded him of a series of meetings I had once engineered between him and a little gang of subversives which ended with Harry answering the question "Under what circumstances would you make *Time* a political instrument?" His answer was: "If I thought the Republic was in danger." Which at the time we thought unexceptionable. But on this last-supper occasion I pointed out (I *hope* I did, at least; I can't be sure) that as a Republican he had come to the point of believing that the Republic was in danger whenever the Republicans weren't running it.

'Well, that's about it, or all I can recall of it . . . Anyhow, we shook hands on the sidewalk, and—parted friends. Eh? What did you say?'

A chance meeting five years later in New York led to the final dinner. 'I felt again some of my old fondness for this grizzled tycoon whose hard-shell opinions hadn't become any softer. Though we raised our voices it was not from temper but because we had both become rather hard of hearing.'

Luce I met but once at a cocktail reception staged by his London bureau. He was ill at ease in the atmosphere of phoney conviviality where he could hear scarcely a word above the noisome champagne bubbles, the crackle of cheese straws, the sucking of olives stuffed with pimentos. He said he looked forward to a long talk with me which never took place; Lord Beaverbrook had permanently poisoned him against the *Daily Mirror*—besides, it supported Labour in Britain.

The successive heads of the *Time* bureau in London, most of whom I have known, have been journalists of high calibre and personal integrity. They were forever being embarrassed by the published versions of what they had reported, commented upon, or foretold in their despatches. They never knew how their copy would emerge after its journey on the conveyor belt at headquarters. Condensation by rotary cutters with multiple teeth—for reducing length of cable, however short—was fearsome enough, but not the only hazard. Truth, emphasis and balance rarely survived the processes of trimming, swaging, ultrasonic grinding, shearing, broaching, punching and buffing by desk-bound Yale graduates who usually hadn't visited Europe even on vacation but were skilled at operating a battery of communication machine tools. The stated objective of the magazine was 'to keep men well-informed': the truth did not consistently emerge but the end product was never dim-witted or dull.

In the competitive world of publishing the philosophy of Harry Luce was unique and not insincere. The co-founder of the brittle news-magazine believed that no nation in history, except ancient Israel, was so obviously designed as America for some special phase of God's eternal purpose. He said the founding of America was a Providential occurrence. He was dedicated to America's high destiny, yet dissatisfied with America from earliest manhood; America was not being as great and good as he knew she could be and believed was intended to be. He talked of God and the Scriptures in his public speaking and writing, inspired by what he called 'the American proposition', the flowing together of eighteenth-century French libertarianism and revealed religion. He believed the American proposition to be essentially spiritual and moral, that 'the American capacity for successful co-operation is directly related to our country's constitutional dependency on God'. Co-operation embraced the running of a booming business and making a fortune.

The restless prober presided over his publications from an elegant but austere suite on the thirty-fourth storey of Rockefeller Center, in a cluster of Manhattan skyscrapers. The titles he chose reflected his aspirations, but he attended church on Sundays at home and abroad and prayed on his knees at bedtime. He was a militant Presbyterian obsessed with God and success, also with success and God. He was a capitalist with thirty-three million dollars invested in the company and an annual dividend income from that source alone of one and a quarter million dollars. To the executives of Time Inc. he said, disarmingly: 'I was brought up to think that if anything was wrong in America it was that too many people were too rich and rich people were apt to be more sinful than other people.'

Luce's father, Henry Winters Luce, was a tall, red-haired individualist, the son of a wholesale grocer in Pennsylvania. In his last year at Yale he shelved his legal ambitions and changed course. God willing, he wrote, he proposed to go to the foreign field and witness for Him as best he might in the uttermost parts of the earth. He chose China. His unquestioning faith coincided with the period when the proselytising fervour of the American Protestants, blessed by successive Presidents and financially nudged by big business in search of new markets, had reached its crescendo of impudence. Christianity to them was transcendent. Confucianism ('Do not do to others what you do not wish them to do to you') was a heresy. Buddha was an impostor, Nirvana a hallucination, and his one hundred and fifty million adherents in four countries were dupes to be shown the light of American super-religion and super-culture. The rough-hewn New World, still groping to establish moral standards of its own, exported missionaries and their pious spouses in their thousands to civilise the oldest surviving civilisation, uninhibited by the fact that the Chinese were the first in AD 105 to manufacture the paper on which their Bibles were printed. The Americans did not enjoy a monopoly in their Holy Crusade. The British were also active in the market for souls.

Only the missionaries were surprised that their crusade against sacred beliefs dating from the sixth century before Christ provoked oriental doubt and discourtesy. The Confucians were confused because, for one thing, half a dozen Western religions worshipping the same god appeared to be in rancorous rivalry. In 1895, two years before the Reverend Dr Henry Winters Luce arrived on the Shantung peninsula with his bride, a YWCA worker, eleven missionaries were murdered in China; in 1900 the Boxers, a secret society pledged to cleanse China of all foreign devils, rose in rebellion, massacring the representatives of God and Mammon as if they were one and the same. Nearly two hundred missionaries and fifty of their children were killed. Thirty thousand of their Chinese converts were slaughtered by burning or torture. The German Minister was beaten to death in the street and fanatical Boxers in their thousands surrounded the legations in Peking, laying siege. The Luce family fled with difficulty and danger to Korea until the rebellion was put down by European troops using modern refinements of the gunpowder invented by the Chinese themselves in the tenth century. Then the family returned to the mud-brick walls of the Christian compound in Tengchow to continue their life of service among the heathen.

Henry ('Harry') Robinson Luce was conceived in America and born in Tengchow in 1898, the first of four children. The guiding principle of the family was Calvinism, relating everything to a dependence on God and the observance of public righteousness. He was reserved as a boy, a stutterer, but bright, precocious and studious. His father's next station was at Weihsien, where Harry began his journalistic career with a hand-written newspaper for the children in the compound. He often said later that he loved China, but was immunised against illusions about her. He remembered the decay of Chinese civilisation that the rich tourists and intellectuals didn't see or comprehend. On walks as a child he had seen the stone towers where the poor Chinese abandoned the babies for whom neither Confucius nor God had provided enough rice; family planning was post-natal.

At his first school in America, Hotchkiss, where he was nicknamed 'Chink', he met Briton Hadden, his partner in the foundation of *Time*. Harry became editor-in-chief of the school's *Literary Monthly* and then assistant to Hadden, the managing editor of its weekly newspaper, the *Record*. It was a partnership of collaborating rivals rather than an alliance of natural friends; the same happened at Yale where Briton Hadden was chairman of the board of the Yale *Daily News* and Harry the editor. The jobs were by election, prestigious and salaried, and by the end of their time the Yale newsmen were covering world events and stimulating controversy in their university newspaper; the First World War ended too soon for them to serve and demonstrate their patriotic fervour. They also planned to start one day an enlightening periodical of their own to remedy the parochialism of their compatriots. They graduated superlatively with the class of '20 at Yale, Luce voted 'most brilliant' and Hadden 'most likely to succeed', both members of the university's most secret senior society, Skull and Bones, all sworn to help each other through life's tribulations.

Hadden elbowed his way into the office of Herbert Bayard Swope ('One does not swope until swopen to'), editor of the New York *World* and demanded to know when he could start as a reporter. 'Mr Swope,' he said, when shown the door, 'you are interfering with my destiny': he got the job. Luce had saved $4,000 from his pay on the Yale *News*, invested the loot at Oxford studying history, then toured Europe. His first professional job was on the Chicago *Daily News* in 1921 as Ben Hecht's legman on his famous column *One Thousand and One Nights in Chicago*. A tip-off from a Yale classmate to Luce and Hadden that reporters' jobs at $40 a week were going for the asking on the Baltimore *News*, reinforced by a message from Hadden to Luce—'If we're ever going to start that paper, this looks like our chance'—brought them together again, as reporters but conspiring to go into business on their own account.

Time, the Weekly News-Magazine was born on borrowed money on 3 March 1923, a tremendous achievement for two twenty-four-year-old tyros determined to become tycoons. Yale money came from Skull and Bones admirers, and Yale staff. It was most brilliant and most likely to succeed; it was also brash. The prospectus told Americans they were for the most part badly informed because no publication had adapted itself to the time which busy men were able to spend on simply keeping informed. *Time* was interested in 'HOW MUCH IT GETS OFF ITS PAGES

INTO THE MINDS OF ITS READERS'. It would deal *briefly* with 'EVERY HAPPENING OF IMPORTANCE', presenting these happenings as 'NEWS' (fact) rather than as 'comment'. Yet *Time*, giving both sides, would clearly indicate which side it believed to have the stronger position. Among its prejudices would be a respect for the old, particularly in manners, an interest in the new, particularly in ideas. To keep men well informed—that, first and last, was the only axe the magazine had to grind. Said the prospectus.

The toss of a coin selected the editor, Hadden winning. The idea was to swop every year, but business pressures kept Luce out of the chair for three years. 'Had I won the toss,' he was fond of saying, 'the magazine would have evolved differently.' Differently, but not so successfully so soon.

Luce was unlovable, flinty, aloof, scholastic and socially rude, insensitive to the feelings of others and capable of mental cruelty to his employees. His foresight and timing were of a high order, but what made him a formidable journalist and publisher was his insatiable curiosity, appeased only by travel, questioning and reading. He disliked small talk and made big talk dull, resenting interruptions to his monologues. In later years he scorned a deaf aid because 'If ten people are talking around me I can understand seven of them and the other three probably don't matter.' As a young man he was prudish about women. Briton Hadden was flamboyant, aggressively gifted, gregarious, a free-ranging bachelor. The partnership was therefore mutually agonising.

The conception of *Time* was among the most original and successful in the history of publishing. It had its own style or stylistic gimmicks, almost its own language invented by Briton Hadden. The news was aimed at readers straight between the eyes, delivered in short bursts as if from a verbal machine-gun; more intelligible and titillating than cablese but equally time-saving, angled on personalities rather than issues or principles. There was no verbiage, no 'on the other hand'. Words like *and*, *the* and *a* were chopped to convey brevity and pace. 'He said' was taboo: people quoted *said* nothing at all, they snapped or gruffed, sneered or croaked, or gushed, or burbled. Explaining *Timesque* while biogging balding founder Harry Luce, baldomed scribe and erstwhile *Time* neophyte John Kobler guffawed:

'Two basic ingredients of early *Time* style, the double epithet and the inverted sentence, Hadden adapted from the *Iliad* and the *Odyssey*. But whereas the Homeric epithets are poetic ("rosy-fingered Aurora, Zeus the cloud-gatherer, fleetfooted Achilles"), *Time*'s were abrasive ("snaggle-toothed, hog-fat, purse-potent, moose-tall, weed-whiskered, kinky-bearded ... beady-eyed"). The Homeric line sings ("Then to the city terrible and strong,/ With high and haughty steps he tower'd along"), *Time*'s versions were merely acrobatic ("Ghostly was His Eminence's mission").

'Under Editor Hadden's prodding, and later Editor Luce's, the repertory of attention-getters grew to include:

'The tantalising picture caption. "Perfumer François Coty and his divorced wife. For her smell work, $5,200,000." *Time* once carried a story about the artificial insemination of cows solely in order to be able to caption the picture of a prize seed bull "Cuckolded by a capsule".

'Compound words, "Cinemactor" (Lon Chaney was the first, and Gloria Swanson the first "cinemactress"), "cinemaddict", and so on *ad nauseam* ... euphemisms that skirted libel like "great and good friend" for mistress; the repetition of phrases until they became *Time* trademarks like "As it must to all men, death came last week to ..." and "in time's nick".[1]

Hadden's New Language arrested the attention of the masses and curdled the purists until *Time* itself tired of the capricious captions and up-ended sentences and tried with some difficulty to learn English again. Cassandra of the London *Daily Mirror* called *Time*style 'as vile a piece of mangling as ever stripped the heart out of prose'. It was also encouraged to reform by Wolcott Gibbs's parody in his *New Yorker* profile of Henry Luce: 'Backward ran sentences until reeled the mind ... Where it all will end, knows God.'

Hadden's ambition was to be a dollar millionaire by the age of thirty. He was, and died at thirty-one in 1929 of a streptococcal infection. He thus tactfully averted the consequences of an incipient clash between the personalities of the co-founders; they were growing further apart.

1928 was the turning point for *Time* with over a hundred thousand readers. Then profits soared. By 1964 the corporation owned forty-five per cent of the seventy-million-dollar Rockefeller Center. The circulation was nearly three million, the weekly picture magazine *Life* sold seven million copies, *Sports Illustrated* a million, and *Fortune*, the stylish, handsomely produced monthly business magazine, four hundred thousand. There were international editions of *Time* and *Life* and a clutch of other acquired publications. Luce reached the minds of thirteen million paying readers. Assuming conservatively that his attractive

[1] *Luce* by John Kobler, Doubleday, New York, 1968.

products were *read* or *seen* by twice or thrice that number, including the patients in doctors' and dentists' waiting rooms, hospitals and lunatic asylums, he reached thirty million minds, principally in America but to a significant extent throughout the world. He profoundly influenced American taste, aesthetically, morally and domestically, extending the horizon of his readers on modern medicine and science and on the culture of earlier civilisations. The 'uplift' picture-series in *Life* were of permanent value, dedicated to raising public taste. 'I might even say,' said Robert M. Hutchins, a former Chancellor of the University of Chicago, 'that Mr Luce and his magazines have more effect on the American character than the whole education system put together.' In a television interview Mr Luce himself was cautious. He thought the question of whether he had too much power for one man was a very abstract question. How could power be measured? It couldn't be weighed. He conceded he had 'influence perhaps and upper responsibility', but he associated power more clearly and semantically with public office. It could not be said of Luce that he exercised power or influence without responsibility or through ignorance. His judgement, on one issue in particular, could exhibit spectacular bias, but the quest for the minutiae of knowledge was his driving force.

Time began as a literary mugger, stealing news, rewriting it, interpreting it, adding a dose of imagination and packaging it in one of the twenty-two editorial departments. The source was the daily newspapers, notably the *New York Times*: fortunately for Hadden and Luce the US Supreme Court had decided while they were still at Yale that news a day old was public property: i.e., non-copyright. There was no fear of a charge of plagiarism over the letters Hadden faked in the early days, supposedly from readers. As it developed, the magazine planted its own correspondents in the power centres of the world and Luce took no mean view of his status running in parallel with, though not a member of, the Washington Establishment. When history did not evolve in South Vietnam as ordained by *Time* and Washington, Luce said to an Assistant Secretary of State, 'I see we're both in trouble.' He said in 1940 to his first correspondent in Berlin, 'Remember, when you get there, you're second only to the American Ambassador.' In an inter-office instruction in 1963 he wrote, 'I hope you will be able to follow-through on a purposeful study of our South American policy and personalities. By "our" I mean both Uncle Sam and Time Inc.'

He was on 'Dear Harry' terms with the American Presidents, and with the industrial and banking tsars of his time. He bought and published, with the persuasive influence of the fattest chequebook in the business, the memoirs of Churchill (who asked Luce to sail back to England on the *Queen Mary* with him), the Duke of Windsor, President Truman, General Douglas MacArthur: they were all his contributors. Statesmen the world over cleared their desks for an off-the-record chat. He described Frederika of Greece as his favourite Queen. He celebrated *Time*'s fortieth anniversary at the Waldorf ballroom in New York with fourteen hundred guests plus three hundred whose portraits had appeared on *Time*'s cover. When Walter Guzzardi, his Man in Rome, conducted him to the chamber in the Vatican where Pius XII was ten minutes late for the appointment, Luce said, 'Goddamn it, Walter, where the hell's the Pope?'

An appearance on *Time*'s cover indicated to a vast audience that the subject, if an American, had acquired national significance; the appearance of a foreigner established that he had attained world significance. *Time*'s Man of the Year was an accolade that had no equivalent in Press approbation throughout the world. President John Kennedy was aware as a Democrat of the value of praise or even of a square deal from Republican Harry Luce and his 'goddam magazine'. He brazenly courted favour from *Time*, *Life* and *Fortune*, obsessed especially by the influence of the weekly magazine and granting its Washington reporter special access to the White House and personal contact; he virtually moved in with the family, seeing some of the President's major speeches in advance. Luce liked Kennedy and was a close friend of his father. He told Father Joe that President Jack would be 'forgiven liberal transgressions on domestic issues but that if he were soft on Communism he would have to destroy him, that was all there was to it'. Luce specialised in savaging the reputations of Democrats.

His egocentricity was chronic and the quickest way to rattle him was to accuse him of deceiving the public. He dismissed objectivity as a 'myth', and he gave the game away in answers to two separate interviewers:

> *Luce on truth*: 'Do you imply that there are always two sides to a question? Are there not more likely to be three sides or thirty sides? If I should answer that a man ought to speak and print the truth as he sees it, would you consider that to be a pretty good starting point?'
>
> *Luce on prejudice*: 'I am a Protestant, a Republican and a free-enterpriser, which means I am biased in favour of God, Eisenhower and the stockholders of Time Inc.—and if anybody who objects doesn't know this by now, why the hell are they still spending thirty-five cents for the magazine?'

The product packaged, boosted and sold as a news-magazine was in fact a biased views-magazine, printing not the truth as one man saw it but the fantasies he hoped would materialise, assessing men's characters by their political party labels. He was a standard-bearer of the Right, exorcising all who were left of centre as unpatriotic or evil and therefore to be undermined by character-assassination in his magazines.

The influence of a successful publisher and news manipulator crosses frontiers and can be significant in the issue of war or peace, cold war or détente. Luce's gifts and activities as a mind-bender—or, as Theodore White called him, a 'skull-basher'—focused upon the attitude of the United States towards China and the USSR, America's phobia over indigenous Communism, and internal political affairs, where he was fiercely anti-Democratic Party. He had axes to grind other than the original objective of keeping men well informed, and—unchallenged—he would have ground them mercilessly. The brake on Luce at his worst was provided, paradoxically, by Luce at his best. The professional excellence he insisted upon in his publications could never have been reached by sycophants, time-servers or hacks, however well rewarded. The men immediately around him were his intellectual equals. Their only disadvantage in the arena was that Luce happened to own it and laid down the rules of combat. Alistair Cooke, Britain's best guide to American civilisation past and present, was nudging the truth about how Lucepress began and developed when he wrote in the *Guardian* of Luce's death: 'The staff was no longer a nest of skylarking college rebels but a palace guard of the American establishment, conservative, tough-minded, scholarly, unfooled.' He probably exaggerated the rebellious-ness of the pioneers, at that time the favoured sons of Yale; he certainly exaggerated the conservatism of their successors, the product of a later and more liberal university vintage. It was they who eventually loosened the strait-jacket policy of Republicanism-right-or-wrong and dared to nobble some of Luce's hobby-horses.

Luce's method was to seek to conquer all by argument rather than to issue orders. He saw the mission of Time Incorporated as achieving 'a consensus of opinion and conviction . . . and sometimes try to evoke it in the nation'. When he was not pontificating, which was often, he was encouraging debate. He said he wanted good editors with independent minds. He enjoyed contention when it didn't bore him: the only proviso was that he was the referee and the vote of the Editor-in-Chief rated higher than the others. 'We cannot evade the demand [*his demand*] for a general coherence and a clear sense of responsibility [*his responsibility*].' Like most people, Luce put his point less elegantly in a television interview: 'I want good editors with independent minds. I like to see independent thinking,' he told an interviewer. 'If it's going the wrong way I'll straighten them out fast enough.' Tom Matthews eventually rejected the inequality of reaching a consensus view with Harry Luce and departed from Rockefeller Center. I guess he would not fault the verdict of another *Time* executive: 'Things did appear in the magazines that Luce had not seen and might not have liked. The kind of men Luce needed to run his enterprises would not have stayed, myself included, had they always fought only to lose.'[1]

On one issue Luce was intractable until the last scene of the last act. The worst disservice he rendered the American nation was his obduracy over China. I examine the deceit in detail because there is no example that illustrates more clearly how one man manipulating the media had to learn that he could fool all of the people some of the time, and some of the people all the time, but could not, however desperately he tried, fool all of the people all of the time. The story of the Influential American and the Chinese Warlord deserves to go on record as the classic reminder to newspaper and magazine readers that, in spite of the limitations of the camera, the printed word can lie.

Harry Luce rated himself the infallible sinologist. He thwarted or suppressed his writers and editors when they surfaced with a contrary prognosis of events in China, and pilloried government ministers and advisers who didn't see things his way. On Far Eastern affairs he was impervious to fact or logic. He mounted a prodigious propaganda campaign which sold a false bill of goods to the public—the notion that Chiang Kai-shek was a lasting unifying force beloved by his people instead of a comma in Chinese history, a ruler under whom corruption flourished and land reform was delayed. Of two thousand years of Chinese development Luce got the half century which ended in 1950 wrong. He pursued his objective years after it was manifestly unattainable and obnoxious. He would not accept that God apparently favoured his adversaries.

Luce could hardly be chivvied for not comprehending the cataclysms between his birth in Tengchow and his departure at fourteen to be educated in the West—one rebellion, two local wars, two revolutions, and a fallen dynasty later. Nine-tenths of China's population knew less of what was going on than young Harry. He often said he felt sentimental about China, and certainly he could not resist the lure to return. His

[1]*How True* by Thomas Griffith, Atlantic-Little, Brown, Boston and New York, 1974.

conviction grew that a dedicated American of his stature could arrest the course of social conflict in the world's most populated country: maybe he saw himself as a twentieth-century Marco Polo, not seeking knowledge and buying up Eastern treasure like the Venetian, but dispensing American wisdom and largesse free.

He was thirty-four on his first revisit in 1932, and a great deal had happened when his back was turned. Civil war traditionally followed the end of a dynasty. The revolution which disposed of the last Chinese Emperor in 1911 produced a republic only in name. There was a central government which couldn't govern because the provincial warlords held the military and political power. China was disunited but the revival of the nationalist spirit was there to stay, with two revolutionary parties contesting for the leadership. The Kuomintang (Nationalist Party), founded by the legendary Sun Yat-sen, and the Communist Party, created only in 1921 and including Mao Tse-tung obscurely on its list of members, were able to maintain a fitful alliance so long as Dr Sun lived. The course of the game of Power Mah-jong was really resolved when Sun and his ally Chiang Kai-shek, a professional soldier trained in Tokyo, turned to Soviet Russia for arms, advice and money. Moscow welcomed the prospect on its border of a friendly regime already in alliance with the Chinese Communists. Chiang soon found himself with a Soviet-trained Chinese army and a Soviet-inspired military academy at Whampoa, near Canton. He spent four months in the USSR studying the Red Army and other Soviet institutions. He absorbed the Leninist gospel on imperialism as the highest state of capitalism, and saw in Lenin's ideas the key to China's mass poverty and weakness as a nation. He was grateful for the guns and ammunition; unlike the Chinese Communists, he rejected the notion of sovietisation. The devolution of power to workers' councils of discussion, decision and action had no appeal to a military autocrat, however sincere he may have been at that time for social reform.

Because of his military power Chiang was able to outmanoeuvre a Communist coup for the leadership of the Kuomintang and seize it himself when Sun Yat-sen died in 1925; a private army, 50,000 strong and loyal, is a more persuasive argument than a political exhortation. He sustained Russian aid and held the factions together until 1927. Then, with his army, he threw out the Communists from the Kuomintang in a bloody coup of his own, scattered the remnants, including Mao Tse-tung, and resolved to exterminate them. He subdued the rival warlords, occupied the ancient capital of Peking in 1928, and established a new central government in Nanking.

There were some changes in China, and Chiang's Nationalist Party was responsible. The long-term programme was the late Dr Sun's—military unification leading to political tutelage directed by the Kuomintang, leading to unfettered democracy at the final stage. Chiang had some political as well as military achievements to his credit. China was developing the appurtenances of modern civilisation—communications and banks, currency reform, legal institutions. He also moved modestly towards technical innovation in agriculture, essential to a nation whose peasantry represented eighty per cent of its population. There were public health measures against contagious disease and an attempt to establish a system of education with some relevance to the twentieth century. On the international level he succeeded in renegotiating some of the concessions coerced by foreigners before the 1911 revolution. But Nanking was still a parody of republican government; its power was not absolute and some provinces still exercised autonomy.

In 1931 there were two ominous events. The Chinese Communists proclaimed 'a soviet republic' in the territory they still held. To 'protect her interests' Japan invaded and occupied Manchuria, and later north-east China and what is now known as Korea, enthroning a puppet emperor, P'u Yi, the last of the Manchu emperors who had been pensioned off in Peking at the age of six.

That was the scene when Luce returned in 1932. There was no meeting with Chiang Kai-shek, but he was impressed by what he heard and witnessed. He did not sense that the 1911 revolution was still fermenting. Authoritarianism in government never repelled him, and the General-issimo's recent conversion to Christianity was a factor in the mind of the missionary's son. God may not have chosen Chiang as his shield against the godless Communists; Luce did so on His behalf. *Time* no longer treated the general as just another Chinese warlord; the affinity between the two men, with no personal contact, began at this time.

'In 1932,' said Luce, 'the biggest example of progress that I have ever seen was the difference between the China I had left as a child and what I saw twenty years later.' In his typewritten notes to the publishing office in New York he made his first reference to Chiang: 'Wide and far among the Chinese is the belief that Chiang is reincarnation of a great sea beast which used to live in the waters and sun himself in the sands near Ningpo, Chiang's birthplace. Dictionary gives iguana as translation of Chinese word for this beast . . .' *Time* henceforth nicknamed Chiang 'Iguana'—Chiang ('Iguana') Kai-shek.

The nine years before Luce's next visit in 1941 presented an exacting test of the Iguana's prowess as soldier and statesman. He rejected the obvious duty and opportunity of unifying the Chinese nation against the Japanese threat to the mainland and embarked upon a ferocious five-year civil war while the enemy were at the gates. Between 1930 and 1933 he launched five campaigns against the Chinese Communists. His strategy, unique in military history, was to deploy his army against his compatriots and deal with the common enemy later. In 1934 the Kuomintang army overran the new Communist positions in south-east China and Mao Tse-tung led what remained of his defeated forces across the country. The celebrated Long March was in fact the Long Retreat. They tramped through the southern and western provinces, arriving one year later in north Shensi, numerically depleted but strengthened in their resolve. Mao was now their undisputed leader and Chou En-lai was Party Secretary.

Chiang thus established himself as a commander of no historical account and as a statesman of provocative ineptitude long before the Second World War began. The revolutionary vision of Sun Yat-sen was a memory; the 'unfettered democracy' was mentioned no more; the promised social reforms were forgotten. Mao was amassing his Red Army in the north, recruiting Nationalist deserters as well as the peasants, and the Japanese, entrenched and unmolested in the vast territories they seized and extended in north-east and north China, were building up their resources and preparing their next move. Chiang's final folly in his campaign against the Communists, a plan to launch yet another, and as he hoped final, assault upon them in 1936, was squashed by a revolt of his own generals and the northern warlords who had accepted him as their nominal commander-in-chief. They arrested the Iguana and compelled him—'or else'—to agree to their demand for a united front that included Mao's Communist army against the foreign invader. Disastrously late, because of Chiang's vain attempt to impose his own authoritarian regime on China before engaging the Japanese, an uneasy pact was reached between the Nationalists and the Communists in the early summer of 1937. The Communists recognised the Nationalist Government's authority. The Nationalists recognised the territory held by the Communists to be largely self-governing. Mao placed his reconstituted armies at the Nationalist Government's disposal with some reservations. This was the move that Harry Luce, the missionary's son, never under-stood. The suspension of civil hostilities held good in name, but not always in practice, until 1945. It was not a submission by Mao to Chiang: Mao knew that, in a China overrun by the Japanese, Communism would be strangled in its cradle. The Japanese, not Chiang, achieved Chinese unity.

In July 1937 the Japanese launched a full-scale invasion of the Chinese mainland when the Second World War was still two years away for the British and four for the Americans and Russians. The *blitzkrieg* tore China apart. When Nanking fell Chiang moved his government to Hankow, and when Hankow fell it withdrew to Chungking in the extreme west. It was a military-manual base for a defeated army. The province of Szechuan was a rich agricultural area protected by some of the world's highest mountains, physically secure except from aerial bombardment but also severed from all sources of supply except by air. As a national hero, if he had ever achieved that stature outside the pages of *Time* and *Life*, Chiang was discredited. He was hated by millions of Chinese because of one simple act as an orthodox soldier. To retard the advance of the invaders, he blew up the dykes of the Yellow River, forcing the water to alter its course and find a new mouth to the Yellow Sea; the devastation was calamitous, but was only one example of his 'scorched earth' policy. The surrender of a huge area of central and southern China to the Japanese had not made him popular. Neither of Chiang's armies, Nationalist or Communist, was in a position to risk major battles. Chiang's design was simply to hold together some sort of Nationalist Army as a recognisable entity until—a fair hope—American interest might be aroused.

Mao's strategy was shrewder. As a master of guerrilla tactics, which he had already practised on the Nationalists before the civil armistice, he was able to operate with success on two fronts. The Japanese advance and the Nationalist retreat were a golden opportunity for the Communists. They were active behind the Japanese lines in the rural areas, sabotaging communications, blowing up bridges, derailing trains, causing havoc in limited but lightning raids. More significantly for the future of China they were setting up self-defence pockets in the villages, living with the peasants and earning their trust, establishing local soviets. How Mao Tse-tung expanded the influence of the Communists in the agricultural communities while the army commander who had failed them was beleagured in Chungking became the theme for the bizarre 'modern revolutionary opera' I saw in Peking in 1973, entitled *The Red Lantern*. The last three scenes are: 'Advancing Wave upon Wave', 'Ambushing and Annihilating the Enemy', and 'Forward in Victory'. The script of the final scene reads: 'As the curtain rises, red flags flutter against a clear blue sky. The guerrilla leader walks down the hill slope. Knife-grinder enters with Tieh-mei. All the guerrillas enter. Solemnly, Tieh-mei hands the code to the guerrilla leader. Brandishing their rifles and swords, all rejoice in their victory. Tieh-mei holds aloft the red lantern while crimson light radiates. The curtain slowly falls.'

Harry Luce had been more successful on China's behalf in the United States than Chiang had been in China. He had appointed himself the Iguana's Ambassador Extraordinary, the architect of his fame in the wealthiest nation and throughout the world. The Luce magazines had given saturation coverage to the struggle or disastrous withdrawal under Chiang's leadership, with more, much more, to come. He had galvanised American voluntary aid to China, fusing eight jostling charities into a central fund, United China Relief, raising millions of dollars, including a quarter of a million from *Time*'s brainwashed subscribers.

Hitler's war in Europe was less than two years old when Luce's plane touched down on the runway at Chungking on 8 May 1941. Britain, unconquered but threatened, was standing alone: so was China, unconquered but severely mauled. *Life* had published pictures to show there was a Chungking blitz as well as London's. The plane had flown from Hong Kong over Japanese-occupied territory and in the city Luce experienced a Japanese air raid that killed forty Chinese. His status as a traveller was as official representative of United China Relief and he was accompanied by Clare Boothe Luce, his second wife, accredited as photographer-correspondent of the magazines. They were formally received by the Generalissimo—now called the Gimo in Lucepress—and Madame Chiang Kai-shek.

'You got the feeling,' wrote Luce, 'that there was no person in the room except the man who had just entered it so quietly. We stood up. A slim wraithlike figure in khaki moved through the shadow and there were a few distinct grunts of encouragement. "How . . . How . . ." ("Good . . . Good . . .") The Madame then introduced us . . . He went and stood before his armchair next to where I had been carefully placed . . . motioning us to be seated.'

There was every reason for Chiang to grunt 'How . . . How.' What the admiring Luce had achieved for the Nationalist Government he would continue to achieve for a few more distinct grunts of encouragement. Luce saw Chiang as the leader who would Christianise China and bring it closer to America, crush the Japs when granted sufficient military equipment and liquidate the Communists in Asia into the bargain. They were allies in a triple cause. Fearing God. Hailing America. Hating the Communists. The truth was that Chiang was militarily impotent. The Sino-Japanese war was in its second phase, a stalemate that lasted from 1939 to 1944. Japan had already relegated the conflict to a care-and-maintenance basis with other business in mind elsewhere.

'An hour later we left,' Luce wrote, 'knowing that we had made the acquaintance of two people, a man and a woman, who, out of all the millions now living, will be remembered for centuries and centuries.' The rival empresses were accomplished ladies, elegant, radiant, ambitious, theatrically regal; Mei-ling at forty-nine a mature oriental beauty and Clare at forty-two a maturing occidental beauty.

Chiang had divorced his first wife and married into the fabulous family presided over by the westernised, cultured and wealthy Charlie Soong. Soong was educated by a pious benefactor in America as a Methodist missionary, but he deserted the pulpit for the market place when he returned to his native land, reaping millions of yuan as a shrewd merchant. He sired three fortunate daughters and a son. The eldest daughter, Ei-ling, married Dr Kung Hsiang-hsi (Yale), who occupied many posts in Chiang's government, including the highest, and was now Minister of Finance. He fanned the interests of Standard Oil in China and raked himself a fortune. The second of Charlie's girls was the widow of Dr Sun Yat-sen. The youngest, Mei-ling, became Chiang Kai-shek's bride in 1930 at the peak of his grandeur two years after he occupied Peking. She also had been educated in America, at Wellesley, a leading woman's college where Luce's two sisters had graduated. As a symbol of serenity and later on as a fund-raiser in America, she was rated as worth ten divisions to the Gimo. Her brother, T. V. Soong, a wealthy banker trained at Harvard, was Chiang's present Premier (another of the Chinese Nationalist gods, like Chiang, who ascended the Valhalla of *Time*'s cover portraits with a sanctimonious account of his exertions on the people's behalf). Sun Fo, a son of Dr Sun Yat-sen's first marriage, also served in high office in the administration. It was when Chiang married Mei-ling Soong—and the Soongs married Chiang's government—that he was baptised a Christian, forswearing concubinage. There is surely a Chinese character for nepotism.

There was nothing newsworthy in the progress of Clare Boothe, the cool blue-eyed blonde from Connecticut (father, a vaudeville fiddler; mother, ex-chorus girl) until she caught the eye of the man who added Brokaw to her name. He had three qualities and one drawback. He was prominent in the New York Social Register, rich and a bachelor; he was also an alcoholic. She had been divorced for five years when she met Harry Luce, filling in her time as an editor of *Vanity Fair* and as an aspiring playwright, acclaimed as 'drenchingly beautiful' by Cecil Beaton and more discerningly assessed by an appreciative Frenchman as 'a beautiful façade, well constructed but without central heating'. Clare was sharp-tongued and witty. She rated Harry Luce as a dull man at their first encounter and as enormously rude at the second: he had pulled out his watch and said: 'Good night. Time to go to bed,' not 'Good evening.

Time to go to bed.' The mutual attraction was talk about journalism and politics rather than sexual magnetism. Harry fell short of the average woman's notion of the whirlwind lover, but Clare was no average woman. She had been planning a picture magazine for years; he was already the owner of *Time* and *Fortune*, about to give birth to *Life* itself. A generous settlement eased the parting from his first wife, the lighthearted (and unpunctual) Lila Hotz, and in December 1935 *Time* was able to announce the wedding at the ages of thirty-seven and thirty-two in the same issue that reviewed with 'mild censure and faint praise' her first disastrous play. It was called *Abide With Me*, and the honeymoon lasted longer than the show. By the time of their visit to China in 1941 Clare had earned a million dollars with her second play *The Women*, a lethal study in bitchiness, and had been twice elected to Congress. She was too smart by half to attempt to change Harry's rugged, sunless personality, but assumed control of the exterior decorations. The publisher, renowned for his baggy trousers and greasy slouch hat, suddenly appeared in the list of America's ten best-dressed men. Luce, in *Timese*, was spruced.

When the four ambitious people gathered in Chungking, Madame Chiang was interpreter as well as hostess. At a suitable moment she offered a charming tribute to Clare's beauty. There was an exchange of gifts; *from* the Luces a bound portfolio of photographs of the Chiangs and their leading ministers (Luce recorded that Chiang grinned from ear to ear) and a bountiful supply of Madame's favourite cigarettes; *to* the Luces a jade Tang horse for Harry and embroidered Chinese silk pyjamas for Clare.

Luce fatuously described Chiang as the greatest ruler Asia had seen for 250 years, the equal of K'ang-hsi, the second and greatest Manchu Emperor renowned in Chinese history for his conquests, diplomacy and intellectual influence. He was much impressed by what he saw of the Nationalist army on his visit with Clare to one of the confrontation areas; they glimpsed the Japanese heavy artillery on the cliffs of the Yellow River. He was pixilated by his hero but not utterly sycophantic. He had the candour, or vanity, to offer criticism and advice to the ruler. From his Chungking correspondent and from foreign diplomats he had heard evidence of the tyranny, inefficiency and corruption of the regime, and conveyed to Chiang in his farewell letter a little, only a little, of what he had heard:

'Your speech to the Kuomintang headquarters some weeks ago calling for reform was much admired in America, but does not seem to have been taken very seriously here. If a drastic reform in the attitude of some sections of the Kuomintang is possible, it would seem to be desirable at once. I am told that the best young men and women dislike both the Communists and Kuomintang parties and feel politically homeless.'

That was true of the Kuomintang. The high living of Chiang's élite and the misappropriation of such American official aid as was reaching Chungking by air over the mountains were common knowledge.

Luce reported to an American audience in San Francisco on his return to the States. The Chinese, he said, had qualities that were invincible. 'Free China' was bitterly and desperately at war. Japan was not 'bogged down': it had been stopped cold in its tracks by the soldiers of China. In Washington he lobbied personally among President Franklin Roosevelt's ministers for more military aid, determined to see China triumphantly emerge from the war 'a stronger, more excellent nation, linked to the US in an honourable partnership' led by Chiang.

In Chungking he had met for the first time Theodore H. White, waiting in attendance in his khaki shorts and sun helmet with the reception party on the tarmac. White had majored in Chinese history at Harvard, served for a while as a writer for the Chinese Ministry of Information and was now at twenty-six chief reporter for Time Inc. in the Far East. Luce took him back to New York to help in the campaign he was planning for the magazines.

The invasion of Russia by Hitler's panzer divisions on 22 June 1941 brought Marshal Timoshenko to *Time*'s cover, with the loaded comment inside: 'The time gained was no gain unless urgent use was made of it. No good use would be made of it if the US, pleased to see Nazism fighting Communism, relaxed its defence efforts.' The 30 June cover of *Life* was an eye-catching portrayal of the beautiful Madame Chiang, the same issue publishing ten thousand words of Harry's own prose illustrated by Clare's own photographs reporting their visit. The theme was both heroic and tragic, a story of bravery and sacrifice in spite of martial need; neither America nor Japan had entered the world war, but the Americans were heavily tutored in China's role in the 'defence' of the United States. The General Chen Cheng dominated an issue of *Time* as the Defender of Chungking; it made a change from Chiang himself. The piece, written by Theodore White, called for aid to China, artillery and scouting planes. White also wrote four articles for *Fortune*, educating top businessmen on the importance to America of China and the importance to China of Chiang Kai-shek. *Life* rounded off the campaign in March 1942 with

White's profile of Chiang, hailed as the leader of 'the restless masses of Asia', a statesman and military figure who might in the future exercise 'greater influence than any other single being of our age'. At this stage White shared Luce's high estimation of Chiang.

There was no need for Luce to exercise pressure in Washington in a political sense, because the official policy of the Roosevelt administration already acknowledged Chiang as the leader of resistance to Japan and the symbol of future Chinese unity: the pressure was for more military aid.

1941 was the pivotal year of the Second World War. One month after Luce's departure from Chungking the Nazi-Soviet non-aggression pact of 1939, barely two years old, was shattered by Germany's invasion of Russia and the Russians entered the war on the side of the Allies. Six months after Luce's departure Japanese planes launched their attack on the US naval base at Pearl Harbor, Hawaii, and America entered the war. The second of these events was of immeasurable importance to Chiang Kai-shek. China became part of the Allied front and her government was seated on the Allied Pacific war council.

Japan's initial successes were spectacular. Hong Kong, the Philippines, the Netherlands East Indies and Malaya all fell and Burma was invaded. From Malaya the Japanese successfully stormed the 'impregnable' British naval base of Singapore in February 1942. The British guns were facing the wrong way, out to sea. China was no longer alone in her plight, but the question of supplies was the cause of strenuous wrangling among the Allies. Churchill was dubious about China's importance as a major partner. The high command was divided on the rival merits of air power and land armies in the war against Japan, an issue that sharply affected what could be spared for Chiang's Nationalist army. Supplies, in any case, were desperately scarce.

There now occurred in 1943 one of those wartime happenings hard to credit in retrospect. Madame Chiang emerged from the squalor and desperation of Chungking upon the world war scene, visiting the United States in person. She travelled from China in an American aircraft sent for her and her queenly entourage, and was formally met at the airport by Harry Hopkins, the President's special representative. When she appeared before both the House of Representatives and the Senate, *Time* genuflected, portraying the scene in deferential prose to which its readers were unaccustomed:

'She knew that what she said might not have great effect on strategies already determined. But it could have—and in her first appearance it certainly did have—more effect than anything which has yet happened in giving one great people the kind of understanding of another great people that is the first need of a shrinking, hopeful world.'

The Roosevelts received the Wellesley graduate as their guest at the White House and the President devoted hours to her supplications. *Time*'s gratitude for his gesture was an attack on his complacency about China's plight and meanness to Chiang's Nationalist Government. Madame appeared yet again on the cover.

Life was also wheeled into position for Luce's new propaganda explosion. Madame Chiang—'this beautiful woman, clad in black and ornamented with flawless jade'—was the subject of a full-page feature and a full-page editorial urging action on her case for more aid for her husband. The magazine described her 'first night' at Congress with a degree of hyperbole that would have shocked Harry Luce had the subject been anything but China and the heroine anyone other than the most gifted of the sisters Soong:

> 'She had all the art of the greatest of divas . . . Senators, without exception, said they had never heard anything like [her speech]. Many said they never expected to hear anything like it again. It was almost as though a modern Sappho had charmed them with emerald phrases and her own pearly beauty . . . Congressmen were wholly captivated by her personality, amazed by her presence, dizzied by her oratorical ability . . . The most famous woman in the world . . . If the Generalissimo could take the Japs as Madame took Congress, the war in the Pacific would be over in the bat of an eyelash . . .'

The objective of the mission was to touch America's heart and loosen her purse strings for more military aid and donations from the public at a stage of the war when supplies for China's ground forces were low on the list of Allied priorities. China was portrayed as the heroic nation united behind Chiang, eager and able under his divine leadership to transform the Far Eastern scene to the immediate advantage of the Allies. It was the gospel according to Luce, but Madame Chiang Kai-shek was also Mei-ling Soong; her American pilgrimage was the most astonishing and extravagant of all the wartime jamborees, unparalleled in pomp and circumstance by any of the summit meetings of the Western war leaders. Stories appeared in the newspapers which must have raised doubts in the minds of the most generous of the United China Relief contributors. The gracious and eloquent lady beseeching alms for the destitute Chinese paraded a wardrobe that made even the richest American women goggle.

W. A. Swanberg described the sumptuousness of her progress:

'The richness and variety of her dress were dazzling. When she went to New York for treatment of a skin trouble, she took over the entire twelfth floor of the Harkness Pavilion for herself and entourage, ensuring privacy. She brought her own silk sheets, which were changed daily. When she was a White House guest, she annoyed Mrs Roosevelt by her queenly habit of clapping her hands when she wished a household employee, as she did in China. She startled the President, when he asked what would be done in China if miners struck as they were doing in the United States, by drawing a hand across her throat.'[1]

The ballyhoo was intensive, with New York as the high spot of the tour. At the Waldorf Madame occupied a suite in keeping with her insistence on the best hotel in every city. The United China Relief fund always picked up the tab, obliged to squander dollars collected for starving Chinese. The American Stratoliner flew her back to the Gimo with one small courtesy unfulfilled: she forgot to thank Paul Hoffman for the seven million dollars United China Relief was raising in that year alone under his chairmanship.

Her next appearance on the international stage was at the Cairo Conference at the end of the year, where Chiang and she sat with Churchill and Roosevelt, less dazzled by her fashion parade than the pressmen. It was the Generalissimo's one and only attendance at high table during or after the war. Churchill had misgivings, but Roosevelt insisted.

Madame Chiang's stately tour of the United States began in February. Concurrently, more fissures had appeared in the Chiang Proposition. On 22 March a dispatch from Theodore White appeared in *Time* disclosing the appalling muddle of the Chiang regime. Describing the famine in the province of Honan, White told of 'dogs eating human bodies by the roads, peasants seeking dead human flesh under the cover of darkness, endless deserted villages, beggars swarming at every city gate, babies abandoned to cry and die on every highway'. He estimated that of Honan's thirty-four millions there had been three million refugees and that in addition five million would die before the new harvest could be gathered. White attributed the tragedy to the insistence of Chiang's army on extracting a grain tax from farmers 'in the face of known crop failures and compounded by the government's tremendous miscalculation in not

[1]*Luce and His Empire* by W. A. Swanberg, Scribner's, New York, 1972.

sending grain into the province in time'. The Honan tragedy could not be blamed on the Japanese blockade, on inflation, or attributed to an Act of God. *Time*'s exposure and White's personal intervention with Chiang brought immediate action. The speed of the aid from existing resources at the Generalissimo's command in China was incontrovertible proof of the earlier inefficiency and indifference of his government.

Time did publish White's harrowing dispatch about the unnecessary famine, but the views of Harry Luce on this exposure of the truth appeared only in a private letter to White:

> 'In Chungking you are, of course, daily confronted with all the things that are not being done as well as they should be. But just think, Teddy—the great fact is that Chungking is still there! That's the fact you have to be concerned about explaining . . . You have always had immense faith in China and in the Generalissimo . . . Perhaps you felt that you had communicated too much faith—or a too easy faith. I simply write to say you need have no such fears. It is still the faith—and not the defects of the faith—which it is most of all important to communicate.'

The policy line was that avoidable suffering should not be over-stressed.

A second witness now emerged who should have caused Luce more discomfiture. Pearl Buck, a Nobel and Pulitzer prize-winner for her writing, the daughter of American missionaries, was known and loved by the American people for her first book on China, *The Good Earth*. She was concerned that the resplendent pilgrimage of Madame Chiang might blind her compatriots to the realities of wartime China, and requested Luce to publish an article. Her plea for greater aid to China appealed to Luce. What disturbed him was her insistence on an understanding of what was happening in China itself. She disclosed the oppressive bureaucracy, the suppression of free speech and the increasing official corruption under the Nationalist Government.

Luce set down his agonising thinking on paper. He was aware of the faults or evils in Chinese administration and would welcome anything that could be done. 'Now, let the general approval of China be open to widely conflicting views, involving the basic integrity of the leaders in China—and I hate to think of the hash that can be made out of the situation from both left and right.' Could they, being the leaders, have done substantially better—or substantially worse? Yet Luce did not on that occasion want to be 'found guilty of having misled the American people'. Pearl Buck's article appeared in *Life*.

Theodore White filed further critical dispatches on the Chiang regime and was recalled early in 1944 from Chungking to rest and write, in America, about the current China scene for *Life*. He was free from Chinese but not American censorship. His request to the Pentagon for the publication of his *Life* article was accompanied by this note: 'I know that I reflect the views of the staff of the American Army in Asia. I have been chided many times personally by Lt General Stilwell for the lush and unrealistic tone of all American public writing on China and its war effort.' Stilwell was Chiang's American Chief of Staff, under Chiang's command.

Theodore White wrote for *Life*, and *Life* published on 1 May an appraisal of the Generalissimo's conduct of affairs. By inference Chiang was blamed for the political deadlock in Chungking and Madame Chiang for falsely representing China to the American people. The Nationalist Government was controlled by a corrupt political clique that combined some of the worst features of Tammany Hall and the Spanish Inquisition. Two brothers practically controlled the thought of Chiang's China through a combination of patronage, secret police, espionage and administrative authority. Then came the most damning indictment of Chiang Kai-shek. In White's computation ten divisions of Chiang's best troops who might have been fighting the Japanese invaders were in the province of Shensi sealing off the Chinese Communist armies, depriving Mao's troops even of medical supplies. The American Government was attacked by White for broken promises over supplies to the Chinese armies and the article concluded with a demand for greater American aid. White wrote to Luce:

'When I came back to New York, I was told that you would never let anyone publish anything like the things I wanted to say. I was scared as Hell, Harry, at what I thought would be an inevitable clash between my convictions and your policy.'

There was a third witness to the reality of events in China—General Stilwell himself. He called Chiang 'the Peanut' and regarded him as the main obstacle to the unification of China and her co-operation in a real effort against Japan. Any man less obdurate than Luce would have conceded he had mistaken and miscast his man. As an intellectual he was usually susceptible to argument if not to persuasion; over China his judgement was awry and his balance thrown. He was prepared merely to adjust but not to reverse his policy.

In Washington there was a more realistic appraisal. Far from Chiang being still accepted as the leader of resistance to Japan and the symbol of

postwar Chinese unity, there were misgivings on both counts. As for
unity, which simply meant an accommodation with Mao's Communists
to defeat the common foe, Chiang's principal military exercise was to
confine the Communists around Yenan, the seat of their rival
government. There was little doubt where Chiang would wish to deploy
future aid from the Allies. The economic position in China was grievous
because of Japan's stranglehold, chaotic because of Nationalist mis-
management and corruption.

An inhibiting factor in Luce's campaign to save China for God was his
lack of rapport with President Roosevelt. Three powerful magazines were
a formidable weapon in bending the minds of the public. The White
House was less malleable, and *The World of Time Inc.* records that by
1943 'the President detested both Luce and his wife and the feeling was
reciprocated. The Luce magazines were among the President's severest
critics, and now Mrs Luce sat among his political opponents in
Congress.'

There began in 1944 a series of high-powered government missions to
China and personal intercessions with Chiang, reflecting the anxieties
and disillusionment of the White House. Chiang was pressed to reach an
armistice with the Communists in the interests of winning the war against
the Japs and to accept General Stilwell in command over Chiang of all
China's forces, Nationalist and Communist. Roosevelt sent his Vice-
President to Chungking as one of his emissaries, but with no
success—Nationalist China wanted the military aid but it was not a
banana republic. The greatest ruler since Emperor K'ang-hsi would not
suffer loss of face, and if the Communist armies were to receive a fair
share of supplies how would they be used? Stilwell was recalled at
Chiang's insistence, virtually dismissed. To Theodore White and the
unhappy American residents in Chungking his military execution was a
betrayal of American and Chinese interests. White told Luce that Chiang
could no longer tolerate a group of men whose standards of honesty,
efficiency and responsibility were so strikingly at variance with his own
apparatus; the Gimo had outlived his historical usefulness, was not only
ignorant but unaware of his ignorance. White reported a turning against
Chiang such as he had never believed possible. He urged no more
meddling by Lucepress in Chinese internal affairs, disassociation from
the Kuomintang, and a keen alertness for the development of any group
in China who would give the people decency in administration.

Time's cover story of 13 November 1944 on the Stilwell dismissal
disregarded White's interpretation. It quoted a dispatch to the *New York*

Times from Brooks Atkinson which also described the dismissal as 'the political triumph of a moribund, anti-democratic regime more concerned with political supremacy than in driving the Japanese out of China'. *Time* sneered at Chinese Communists 'and their sympathisers' who never reported the censorship, iron discipline, concentration camps and secret police in Mao's Yenan: 'If Chiang Kai-shek were compelled to collaborate with Yenan on Yenan's terms, or if he were forced to lift his military blockade of the China Communist area, a Communist China might soon replace Chungking. And unlike Chungking, a Communist China (with its 450,000,000 people) would turn to Russia (with its 200,000,000 people) rather than to the US (with its 130,000,000) as an international collaborator.' Chiang's refusal to reach a rapprochement with the Communists was totally supported. White's facts from the spot, the view of the Joint Chiefs of Staff on Chiang's failure, and President Roosevelt's own reappraisal were sunk without trace as far as the readers of *Time* were concerned by pro-Chiang propaganda. The tug-of-truth between White and Luce in a series of brutal cables and letters is recorded in Robert T. Elson's *The World of Time Inc., 1941–60*, and I quote some relevant exchanges in the following pages.

White: We have indulged in an all-out attack on the Yenan Communists and have whitewashed Chungking. I can't believe it.
Luce: Keep your shirt on until you have full text . . . Your views have always been respected here but I do not think it becomes you to get angry if for once your editor does not instantly follow your instructions.

White talked of resignation to preserve his integrity, but was appeased by the publication in *Life* on 18 December 1944 of an article under his own name describing his visit with other correspondents to the Communist-occupied areas. The by-line indicated personal freedom of opinion: it did not indicate, and certainly not on this occasion, Lucean approval. White's attitude to the Communists was sympathetic. He sought to make Americans realise that there were reservoirs of strength, courage and honesty in the Chinese people that could still be mobilised. He urged United States co-operation with the Communists against the Japanese. The Party was willing to go to any lengths to be friends with the USA, and if their friendship were reciprocated, wrote White, it could be a lasting thing.

White: It is still my intention to resign if *Time* wilfully fails to tell the story.

Luce: You seem to assume that I am a supporter of Kuomintang. Nothing could be further from the truth. We have consistently distinguished between the good and the bad in Kuomintang and you will recall that in April 1941 I told Generalissimo his Kuomintang was thoroughly unpopular and for ample reason ... I deeply regret the pain and embarrassment you have endured in past few weeks and we hope that 1945 will be the best year ever for you and for *Time* in our Asiatic assignment.

Time was, in fact, wilfully failing to tell the story; it was still avowing Chiang's current policies and smearing those who differed as Communist sympathisers.

1945 brought peace for every country in the world except China with its own civil war. In Europe and the Far East the war was going away with a roar not a whimper. Churchill, Stalin and Roosevelt met in Yalta in February to plan the closing stages of the war in Europe—and, as a by-product, the future of Far Eastern affairs affecting China. Roosevelt died, the Russian and American armies linked up in Europe, Mussolini was executed by Italian partisans, Hitler committed suicide, Berlin was taken and all the German forces unconditionally surrendered. Events were no less dramatic in the Far East. The first atomic bomb exploded at Hiroshima on 6 August, killing 78,000 people, and the second at Nagasaki on 9 August, killing 74,000 and injuring 76,000; the same month Japan surrendered unconditionally to the Allies.

There was no peace or unconditional surrender in the offices of Time Inc. or in the bureau in Chungking concerning immediate affairs in the Far East. White had warned *Time* that Japan still had the power to convulse all Asia and urged that the surrender of Japanese garrisons in China must be in accord with a plan that would satisfy the Communists as well as the Kuomintang, Mao as well as Chiang. The planning of a major cover story in exultation of Chiang triggered White's next confrontation with Harry Luce and Luce's with the truth.

Luce (to his editors): White's gloomy cable is that of an ardent sympathiser with the Chinese Communists.
White: China this week [is] entering the gravest crisis ... It is true, indeed, that Chiang Kai-shek is the key personality ... But if Time Inc. adopts the policy of unquestioningly, unconditionally supporting his hand we will be doing a monstrous disservice to millions of American readers and to the Chinese whose personal concern this is ...

Luce (to White): We desired nothing except non-partisan reporting. We realised this might be an unreasonable request in view of your avowed partisanship . . . Such a policy obviously doesn't include efforts to over-throw the duly recognised President of China.

White: In past years every major treatment of China problem displayed divergence our views and [that cable] was attempt [to] alert you to that fact and underscore it.

White's draft profile of Chiang for *Time*'s cover piece drew a parallel between Chiang and Stalin—an analogy that hardly supported Luce's view that White was an ardent Communist sympathiser. The charges White levelled were unequivocal. Chiang permitted his government to impose upon the people one of the most merciless and brutal of totalitarian systems. The misery and bitterness engendered were capitalised by the Communist Party to create a system and army of its own. By the policy of no compromise Chiang had forced the Communists into what might become total, abject subservience to the Soviet Union. Unless the Communists could be convinced that Chiang's promises and concessions offered an adequate guarantee for laying down their arms there could be no peace.

The monstrous disservice to millions of American readers and to the Chinese was duly rendered by Henry Luce. *Time*'s cover story reported that Chiang's government was firmly and popularly supported and could establish an effective administration. It was a lie as well as a disservice. Outraged by the doctoring of his stories in the head office in New York, White stuck a notice on his door in Chungking: 'Any similarity between this correspondent's dispatches and what appears in *Time* is purely coincidental.'

Time's portrait of China, with Luce directing the brush work, was a curtain-raiser for his visit in October 1945. He was flying to Chungking at the personal request of Chiang Kai-shek: Theodore White, at the personal request of Luce and to the relief of the governing clique, was flying in the opposite direction, never to return as *Time*'s correspondent.

Luce placed on record what happened after dinner with the Generalissimo and the Madame:

'Had wonderful conversation with the Generalissimo, mainly of a philosophical nature. For the first time, I learned what the concept of "freedom" meant in Chinese thought. The Generalissimo, discussing the Chinese character for freedom, said it connoted (1) movement and (2) naturalness. The character suggested a fish in the water—moving

freely and naturally . . . After the Generalissimo retired the Madame
and I talked for an hour or so. Her main point: the Government now
has a terrible responsibility not to disappoint the hopes of the people.'

Few Americans other than Luce were ever taken in by Chiang's talk of
freedom or by the Madame's concern for the people. Others were
shocked by the contrast between the poverty of the millions and the
luxury of the living standards of the dictator and his henchwoman, of the
Soongs, and the rest of the chosen who constituted the inner circle. There
was evidence all around him of rapacity, misappropriation and
decadence; Chungking was a black market flogging American aid stolen
or diverted by corrupt officials.

Mao Tse-tung and Chou En-lai were prominent in Chungking at the
time of Luce's visit. Chiang had fought the Communists for eighteen
years, since 1927, and twice driven them away in disarray and defeat: they
were still there, more of them with more arms. They were ready to
negotiate unity under the mediation of the American Ambassador Patrick
Hurley but in no mood to be trampled underfoot by the Nationalist
Government.

The military reality was that the armies of Chiang and Mao were
manoeuvring for the final trial of strength. The Nationalists were
spreading their areas of control and re-aligning their supplies.
Communist guerrillas were sabotaging the rail links. Mao now had half a
million men under arms, not the quarter-million at the start of the war; he
had set up soviets in the large areas he already controlled, and his political
commissars had been talking with the peasants about nationalism and
land reform rather than about Communism. Chiang's forces had been
maimed by the Japanese. United States troops were still supporting
Chiang in occupying garrisons surrendered by the enemy, with US
Marines having to hold some of them until Chiang's troops arrived. The
only stabilising influence in Chiana was the presence of the American
military.

The political reality was that each of the contesting parties wanted full
power and was chary of compromise. The Communists would accept a
coalition government with the Kuomintang on equal footing but not a
part in a multi-party administration in which they could be out-voted;
the Communists were also insisting on legalised redistribution of the
land.

Another reality was the Russo-Chinese agreement of 1945, reached a
few months before Luce's visit. *Time* said the treaty had 'for the present
kicked the props out from under the Chinese Communists', a hope which

proved to be nonsensical. Luce himself thought the treaty could be one of the most fruitful ever made; he still had not grasped what was happening and was likely to happen. The Friendship and Alliance sworn in the thirty-year treaty with Chiang's regime was not honoured by the Soviet Union for one year. The Russians seized the bulk of Japanese technical industrial machinery in Manchuria to deny it to Chiang, and handed over to Mao the surrendered military equipment; they also delayed the reoccupation of Manchuria by Chiang's troops.

The Generalissimo took care to ensure that Luce enjoyed top treatment throughout his visit. At a dinner in honour of Mao, attended by three hundred guests, he alone was not Chinese. At this dinner the publisher had his first personal contact with the Communist leaders. 'Mao was surprised to see me there and gazed at me with an intense but not unfriendly curiosity,' said the diary. 'His remarks: polite grunts.' Luce also had 'a nice talk, completely frank' with Chou En-lai. 'He said we hadn't been very nice to them recently. I said that was too bad because we had a world wide battle on our hands with world-wide left-wing propaganda—and it was as nasty as skunk. At my request, he said he would put me in touch with the Communists . . . in Shantung.'

Luce's last formal service before leaving for home was to write, deferentially, to Madame Chiang. He advised her that the Nationalist Government, while being generous to the 'true Communists' in all that concerned peaceful political activity, would have a 'popular mandate' to proceed vigorously, though soberly, against lawless military activity of every sort. Luce told a cluster of Chinese reporters in Peking that it would be reasonable to be optimistic about the future of China, though there was nothing he had heard or seen to justify such a view.

What deeply disturbed him was the attitude of the American GIS serving in the theatre. He was concerned that they would go back to America with their own impressions of the Gimo and his government. He recorded with dismay in his diary the banter of the sergeants in an army truck that rescued him when his jeep broke down outside Chengtu. The talk was unflattering to Chiang's China. One sergeant shouted to a battalion of soldiers carrying guns: 'The war's over; so now you're going to fight.' Another gave the truck-load of GIS a lecture on the relative merits of two government-inspected whorehouses in Chengtu.

Luce was right to be concerned. The portrayal of China foisted on the American public by Lucepress on the occasions, which were many, when they had suppressed or trimmed the cables of Theodore White, would be blown sky high by the American soldiers on the spot; especially the fable that the Nationalist Government had firm popular support. The GIS called Chiang 'Chancre Jack'. Yet Luce's answer to the demand in America to bring the boys home on the grounds that they had no rightful role in an imminent civil war was a further flight from reality. An editorial in *Life* pleaded for American intervention and aid to Chiang to be sustained, even to the extent of employing US troops to protect China's railroads from Mao's guerrilla raids.

Luce was already being warned by his senior associates that Time Inc. was damaging its reputation by its continuing commitment to Chiang, but on this issue he would still not be deflected.

The redeployment or disposal of Theodore White was among the domestic office problems awaiting Harry Luce's return to New York. Harry liked and respected Teddy's honesty, but he was not to be returned to China for *Time*; no question of that. His request to go to Moscow as correspondent was rejected and Luce wrote confidentially to his top editors: 'What he offers to us is a highly specialised service. I am not buying it at this time.' White had been forbidden to tell the truth about Chiang in *Time*: what he wrote elsewhere in a book was denounced as bias, smeared by inference as Communist propaganda.

Events in China vindicated White's judgement. Chiang's triumphal return to Peking, Shanghai and Nanking, where he again sited his government, was embarrassingly delayed by military preoccupations which no longer involved the Japanese. There were signs in Washington, too, of growing irritation over the intransigence of Chiang and the incompetence of his regime.

Harry S. Truman as Vice President moved into the White House on Roosevelt's death, and won the Presidency in 1948 in his own right against the virulent campaigning and predictions not only of *Time* and *Life* but of the whole American Press. In 1945 he brought General Marshall, the wartime US Chief of Staff, the man he called the greatest living American, out of retirement to be his envoy in China with orders to seek to reconcile the irreconcilable. Luce eagerly seconded two of his Washington bureau to the mission, both at Marshall's request; one to spearhead Marshall's endeavours, the other as Chiang's political adviser to tutor the Gimo into adopting more liberal measures that would not offend American opinion.

Luce himself was now so involved and committed that he could not bear to be away from the China scene for more than a year. When he arrived at Nanking in October 1946 the Communist forces and the Nationalists were actively fighting in some areas in spite of Marshall's 'cease fire' plea. Mao's terms for a cease fire were the withdrawal from key front-line positions of all Nationalist troops. The Communists were deeply suspicious of Chiang and partially suspicious of American mediation; 'mediating' on whose side? They criticised Marshall as 'a two-faced reactionary villain', though Marshall at the time was warning Chiang that he was over-extended and could not sustain a long war that would cause economic collapse.

Luce's reception could not have been excelled for the President of the United States himself. The 'mediators' were still in congress and he met them all—the Gimo and Madame, Chou En-lai as Mao's principal negotiator, General Marshall, and the new US Ambassador, J. Leighton Stuart, an old friend and also the son of a missionary. Premier T. V. Soong put on a banquet for Luce. He was Honoured Guest of the Chiangs and also at a dinner hosted by K. C. Wu, Mayor of Shanghai (and friend of Chiang). The Minister of Information, to whom Luce could teach nothing of the art of gilding a Chinese lily, spoke eloquently of his virtues at another dinner.

There were divisions among the Americans as well as the Chinese. Marshall still favoured mediation, and had told Truman he would stay two months more to try to achieve conciliation. Stuart advocated American support of Chiang including American troops. 'We had the ironic situation of the man of God favouring military action and the soldier unwilling to use his sword,' said Luce. There was no doubt where Luce stood.

At an Embassy dinner on 31 October Luce and his *Time-Life* writers were talking of certain victory for the Nationalist Government, stating emphatically that the Communists were all but beaten. But on that journey, for the first time, Luce's faith in the eventual outcome was shaken. Twenty years later he admitted: 'I must record the utter confidence as well as the good humour with which Chou En-lai spoke to me. While he didn't say so in so many words, I had the chilling feeling that he expected soon to be in control of all China. At the end of my stay, I figured he was right . . .' He also said: 'History says that the Communists took over mainland China in 1949. I have trouble remembering that date, because as far as I am concerned the Communists had won in 1946, when the Marshall mission ended.' What Luce confessed twenty years later was precisely what he concealed from his readers at the time.

General Marshall attributed the failure of his one-year mission to the 'reactionaries' in the Kuomintang Party and to 'irreconcilable Communists'. He pleaded with the Chinese liberals to unite to produce some good government under Chiang's leadership, but Luce was infuriated to hear from his Washington bureau what Marshall really thought. On his return from China Marshall took office as President Truman's Secretary of State, and in an early off-the-record briefing to the American Press spoke disparagingly of the Chiang regime. He condemned the corruption in Nanking. He said the us could not afford to be dragged through the mud by all-out, unreserved support of such a government.

Luce would still not face reality. Lucepress had been guilty so far of deceiving readers by the suppression of truth. The later admission that he knew Chiang had lost to the Communists in 1946 puts his future propaganda on Chiang's behalf in an even more reprehensible category, extracting public money under false pretences for a lost and seedy cause.

Luce always worked closely with the China Lobby in Washington, which now redoubled its campaign to squeeze more us dollars for Chiang. Lucepress was the publishing arm of the lobby and Harry Luce was its inspiration leader. Its thrust was anti-Communism. Its activities were varied and brash, influencing appointments in the administration through a clique in Congress that included the notorious Senator Joe McCarthy, the Grand Inquisitor of anti-Communism. It enjoyed the support of patriotic organisations like the American Legion and vested commercial interests like the us Chamber of Commerce. Another of its more picturesque adherents was the Committee of One Million Against the Admission of Communist China to the United Nations. 'Less famous workers for Chiang crowded around the Chinese Embassy in Washington. Eight hundred thousand dollars allotted to the Embassy by Taiwan for public relations, augumented by another million arranged for by Madame Chiang, enabled the hiring of expensive publicity men. Both T. V. Soong and H. H. Kung now lived in New York and were influential in the cause . . .'[1]

It was soon apparent that Truman's appointment of Marshall as Secretary of State was an obstacle to the publisher's role as Chiang's principal wire-puller in America. He continued to deceive the public and the hotheads in Congress about the state of affairs in China, but not the administration in a practical way. Marshall knew that a no-policy attitude to the most populated nation in the world could not be the final stance, but there were more pressing matters, such as the rehabilitation of war-shattered Europe. It was the year the United States assumed the leadership of the world, and *Time* had no alternative but to hail General Marshall as Man of the Year, with curmudgeonly noises-off from Harry Luce. Even at the moment of partial triumph, when in April 1948 the

[1] *Luce and His Empire* by W. A. Swanberg.

Foreign Assistance Act gained Congressional approval, Luce's bitterness remained. Marshall's European recovery plan was authorised and China was given nearly $350 million in economic aid and $125 million in special grants for military aid. Among the useful gifts at this time were 230 American planes. Marshall, though right, had been defeated on the Far East issue principally by Luce's ceaseless propaganda through his magazines and the China Lobby, but the Chiang regime had deteriorated too far, the aid came too late, and even Luce knew it. This was the twilight of his god.

The American economic mission despatched to China found nothing but chaos wrought by Chiang's bureaucracy. In some areas they couldn't even spend the money. The conquest of Mukden by the Communists ended the grip of the Nationalist Government on Manchuria. Luce had to publish in *Life* in late October a report from his own correspondent: 'Until I came to Nanking I had not realised how completely the Chinese of the cities have lost confidence in Chiang Kai-shek . . . China is very nearly lost.'

The confused state of Henry Luce's mind as history was nudging Chiang Kai-shek into the wings is disclosed in an office memorandum and in a letter reproduced in *The World of Time Inc*. His instruction to his Foreign Editor as the Communists enveloped more of the mainland lacked his usual lucidity. It bore the same forlorn desperation as the last note of a suicide. He had always opposed collaborating with the Communists; now he was prepared at the moment of Communist victory to countenance even coalition:

> 'If [coalition] is what the Chinese want—or have to take—with their desire for "peace at any price"—then that's up to them . . . We are sorry it turned out this way. We think it might have turned out differently . . . if, as it might, the Chiang Government had done a real job of reform in connection with all-out American aid . . . A strong note of regard for the Chinese people can be struck . . . May be they will find, as they hope, that Communism will be de-fanged in its encounter with the fluidly stubborn character of China. We wish them well. We wait and see.'

The cause of his remorse was that he had not bent minds far enough. When the editorial appeared in *Life* it conceded that Nationalist China was dying—America's fault not Chiang's. The editors were certain that if their interest and belief in China had been shared by most Americans or by the US Government the Communists and their masters in Moscow would at that moment be losing Asia, not winning it. Like a madman crying in the wilderness, Luce sent his last exhortation to Chiang in December 1948 in a letter written, he said, at the request of a number of friends of China:

'*First*, declare that the Yangtze will be defended under your personal leadership. *Second*, give to the ablest man in China, not counting yourself, the task of forming an entirely new government whose primary requisite shall be a capacity to govern. *Third*, let the Government be representative of all non-Communist elements in China. *Fourth*, let there be a mighty demonstration of loyalty to this government by governors of provinces, mayors of cities, leading intellectuals and other representative men. *Fifth*, let this government establish itself on the mainland of China in Canton or some other place, at a safe distance from the Yangtze front line so that there could be assurance that it would have at least six months in which to administer government while the loyal soldiers of China . . . defend the Yangtze.'

What happened in the first six months of 1949 mocked the delusions of Harry Luce. In January Peking was occupied by the Communists. In August they crossed the Yangtze and took Nanking, the Nationalist capital. Shanghai also fell and in August Mao announced the establishment of the Communist People's Democratic Republic. They then captured Canton and Chungking, where the government had taken refuge. In December the Nationalists fled to the island of Formosa— Chiang Kai-shek, Mei-ling, half a million of his shattered army, an immense concourse of government officials, and as many well-to-do civilian refugees as could knife or bribe their way onto the transports. On 8 December he declared the city of Taipei on that island the new Nationalist capital.

The Gimo and his government never saw the mainland of China again, but Luce ensured that he remained a thorn in the side of the American administration. Far from being the end of the story, Chiang became a embarrassment on the international scene. Luce provoked or supported every move by Washington which favoured the Nationalist 'ghost' government, withheld recognition from the new regime and blocked the People's Republic of China from its place on the UN Security Council. Luce created and sustained the fantasy that Chiang's hideout in Formosa (Taiwan) with its fourteen million inhabitants was China, and that the tarnished clique around him constituted China's official government; Mao, governing five hundred million on the mainland, was a pretender to be dislodged as soon as America gave Chiang sufficient military muscle.

The leading lights of the China Lobby had a formal toast, demonstrated on one occasion at a dinner at the Chinese Embassy in Washington by Senators McCarthy, Knowland and Bridges; they sprang to their feet and chanted in unison 'Back to the mainland'. It was all over, but Harry Luce was still unprepared to retire from the pulpit. 'As I am in a position to testify,' he wrote retrospectively, 'the great mass of the Chinese people were not yearning for land reform or anything else.'

The first nation to recognise the new Communist republic and reach a treaty with her was predictably the USSR, providing credit, industrial and technical aid. The United States, nominated by Mao's government as the arch imperial enemy, understandably hesitated, and a new event of a startling nature postponed recognition *sine die*. A crisis in Korea led to Luce's gravest act of irresponsibility in Far Eastern affairs.

Korea, annexed by Japan in 1910, had remained under her control until 1945 when the Japanese surrendered to the Soviet troops north of the Thirty-eighth Parallel and to the US forces south of it. The line had no ethnic, political, or even geographical significance; the 'Thirty-eighth' was an arbitrary division by mutually suspicious allies of temporary areas of responsibility. The promise of the Cairo conference in 1943, endorsed in 1945, that Korea would be free and independent had not been fulfilled by the time of Mao's victory in China in 1949; worse, a stalemate had been reached internally and externally. The Soviet Union and Communist China recognised and aided a northern Communist government set up at Pyongyang and the US and United Nations recognised Syngman Rhee's elected government at Seoul. Both regimes claimed to be Korea's legitimate government and the nationalist rivalry between them erupted in a civil war in 1950 with explosive international overtones. In June of that year, inspired by the Communist take-over of China, the North Koreans (Russian-trained) crossed the Thirty-eighth Parallel and fought their way south in a fully-fledged offensive against the South Koreans (US-trained and equipped).

Truman immediately took 'police action'. He ordered support for South Korea by the US Air Force and Navy and within a week landed forces from his occupation army in Japan. His third measure angered Chiang Kai-shek: Truman sent the US Seventh Fleet into the Formosa Strait to keep the Chinese Communist and Nationalist governments apart while America's attention was distracted. Chiang petulantly complained he was fettered in any actions he might take against the mainland Communists. He made sure that Luce knew, through a *Time-Life* correspondent, that he had unlimited confidence in General Douglas

MacArthur and would be happy to place the fate of Formosa and of Nationalist China in his hands. He could see another chance of retaining the albatross around America's neck and knew that his Ambassador Extraordinary would convey the message. Six months later additional credit and support arrived from the US to enable Chiang to re-train and modernise his army.

The United Nations Security Council passed in the absence of the USSR delegates a resolution requesting all members of the UN to aid the South Koreans, and General MacArthur was placed in command of the UN forces (US and South Korean ground forces, British and Australian fleet units). On 1 October 1950 Mao warned that should 'the imperialists wantonly invade the territory of North Korea' China would not stand idly by. MacArthur's forces did invade north of the Thirty-eighth Parallel and the Chinese army—farcically called 'volunteers' by Peking—did intervene in force.

In November in New York a frightened John Foster Dulles, then assistant to Secretary of State Dean Acheson, told a shocked Harry Luce that the American Army ('the only army we have') had been surrounded, and also a Marine division. He put the question: 'Should we ask for terms?' Luce recorded in his diary: 'I could not believe my ears and that is what I said.'

Where did Luce stand in the great divide between President Truman and General MacArthur? Truman and the United Nations allies jettisoned any notion of 'liberating' the whole of Korea and limited their objective to a restoration of the original position: the immediate risk was all-out war with China and possibly, if not probably, war with Russia as well. MacArthur was a fearless and militant commander, and his rule as 'Emperor' of defeated Japan had emboldened his confidence and pride. He assessed the situation as 'an entirely new war', advocated carrying the fight to Red China and wanted to use Nationalist forces from Formosa in his battle order. Moreover he voiced in public his outrage at the restrictions placed on him. All of this while the UN armies were retreating southwards in chaos, with more retreats to follow before the allies could reverse the disaster and push northwards again.

'The Editors of *Life*' was the pseudonym which endowed one man's prejudices and delusions with an aura of wisdom and perception. On this occasion they, or he, lost their sanity. MacArthur's call for the widening of the war was ratified by Luce's publications; the general was deified. On 11 December 1950 the Editors of *Life* declared: 'World War III moves ever closer . . . The Chinese Communist armies assaulting our forces . . . are as truly the armies of the Soviet Union as they would be if they wore the Soviet uniform.' On 8 January 1951, the same magazine said: '*Life* sees no choice but to acknowledge the existence of war with Red China and to set about its defeat, in full awareness that this course will probably involve war with the Soviet Union as well.'

The adulation of MacArthur was accompanied by an attack on the US Secretary of State, Dean Acheson: 'It is terrifying, it is wrong, that this proud priest of "coexistence" with Soviet Communism . . . should still be in a position to shape the President's most vital conceptions and statements of American foreign policy.' *Life* even expressed the view that there were strong reasons for believing that America had a good chance of winning the struggle without atomic war—a frank avowal that atomic bombs should be used if the good chance of winning receded. Luce no doubt had it in mind that some months before the Korean war began President Truman had announced his decision to go ahead with developing the H-bomb.

Truman was already concerned about MacArthur's insubordination as a general challenging his government's policies, chafing at civilian control of the military. The last straw came when the military position was nearing stabilisation by the UN forces in Korea under General Matthew Ridgway, and MacArthur sent a letter to the minority leader in the House of Representatives, promptly read out on the floor of the House, deploring the concept of a limited war, declaring bombastically 'there is no substitute for victory'. Truman sacked MacArthur. Luce continued to extol MacArthur and his policy: 'He was ousted for no petty reason but because he chose to challenge the whole drift of events and the dominant attitudes of the Government of the United States.' The words this time were written by Harry Luce himself, and Luce was among the few MacArthur asked to visit him when he returned, deposed, to New York. He wanted to make the general *Time*'s Man of the Year for 1951, but Tom Matthews won the argument.

The Korean war consisted of one year of fighting and little talking, and two years of talking with sporadic fighting. The truce was signed in July 1953 after Eisenhower succeeded as President. The human toll was over a million killed, two and a half million homeless, and damage to property totalling one thousand million dollars. What would have happened if MacArthur's grand strategy, endorsed by Luce, had prevailed is a horrifying hypothesis to contemplate. 'Carrying the fight to Red China' would have been instantly condemned by the United Nations, depriving the United States of her allies and moral supporters, including Britain. It meant the bombing to ashes of Peking, Shanghai, Nanking and all the major Chinese cities, ports and railroad links. That would have produced chaos and vast human suffering, but not victory. Huge populations of peasantry cannot be annihilated or even cowed by bombs, as America learned to its humiliation and high cost later in Vietnam. The Chinese, inured more than any other nation to centuries of deprivation, even famine, would have survived as a people long after America was disillusioned, bankrupt and exhausted.

On the fundamental issues in the Far East in his lifetime, Luce was wrong; politically, sociologically, militarily. He had an abundance of historical knowledge but no sense of history. His vanity would not allow him to disengage and admit his folly, even to press the 'blab off' switch. Like a psychopathic killer he returned to the scene of the crime.

Harry Luce visited the Chiangs three times in Taiwan. In 1952 the Gimo was next call after the Japanese Prime Minister during a flying world tour to shake off the labours of the Eisenhower election. 'Give us the tools,' said Chiang, 'and we will finish the job of reconquering Red China.' The publisher was photographed inspecting the Nationalist army under training for the return to the mainland. In 1960 he called again at the end of another world tour and inspected the Nationalist air force. The Chiangs were living in conditions of modest opulence on American largesse, and on each occasion honoured their benefactor in the style to which he was accustomed in their presence. His seventh and final reincarnation in China, at any rate in his mortal lifespan, took place in Taiwan in 1964, three years before his death. Chiang Kai-shek was now seventy-eight and the Madame seventy-two, ghosts but still breathing, with memories but little to say. The two people Luce once said would be remembered for centuries had already been forgotten by the world. All the courtesies, and such splendour as could be conjured up, were accorded to the man who had tried to make them legendary heroes but who had achieved nothing for China. Any idea that the position could be reversed with Chiang again ruling in Peking or Nanking was fatuous. The publisher again solemnly reviewed the Nationalist armed forces who would never fight. The Gimo appointed a bemedalled major general and a rear admiral as escorts on Luce's journey around the island; they had little else to do. Presented with the Golden Key to Taipei, he told the local Press: 'You are not attacking the mainland tomorrow, but the prevailing attitude of the American people is pro-Republic of China and anti-Chinese Communists.'

Matthews niggled Luce on the China issue, but with no more success than he expected. He wrote in his autobiography:

'Luce was one of several Americans I knew who had been born in China and whose faces seemed to bear the inscrutable stamp of their birthplace. That may have been my imagination, but in other ways he showed undoubted traces of his early upbringing.

'His feeling for China I never altogether understood. I believe he loved the country and the people, and I have heard him really eloquent on the subject. And yet, long before China's defection—or kidnapping, from his point of view—into Communism, he must have misunderstood China just as badly as his hero Chiang Kai-shek did. Luce was stubborn and headstrong, but facts and logic could usually persuade him; on this issue alone he went beyond the bounds of reason. At the climax he pitted his faith in the China he had known against the present facts reported by his principal correspondent on the scene; it was a heavy responsibility for a journalist to take, but he took it. When the facts went against him and he was proved wrong before the world, he had to have a villain, someone who could be held responsible for "losing" China to the enemy, and his villain was to hand; the Democratic administration in general, Roosevelt and Acheson in particular.

'Luce's fidelity to Chiang Kai-shek does credit to his loyalty, whatever it says about his intelligence or his partisanship as a journalist.'

How Dean Acheson in particular had to pay the price as the villain when Luce was proved wrong about China severely fractures the sincerity of the publisher's role as a Christian intellectual. The vendetta was as merciless as any other vendetta inflicted by a Press proprietor, typical of many conducted by *Time* and typical of the ferocity of Luce's political bias. The denigration of Acheson by Lucepress would rate a chapter in any manual on character assassination.

His crime in Luce's eyes was that as Democratic Secretary of State in charge of foreign policy he had sold Chiang short and therefore encouraged the Communists in China and driven China into the Russian Communist orbit. The able, patriotic Secretary, his diplomatic colleagues and advisers, were personally held responsible for a turn of history that was predictable and comprehensible to most thinking people except Luce and the bigots of the China Lobby—including, curiously, Richard Nixon, who as President years later was destined to make America's first friendly gesture towards Mao's China. Sinologists like Professor Owen Lattimore, who had devoted their time and talents to advising Washington on Far Eastern affairs and interpreted events with perception, were branded as if they were guilty of treason to Uncle Sam.

The Truman–Acheson policy of encircling Communism with military might, and then, having 'contained' it, co-existing with it, was presented to Luce's readers in terms of the abuse of its advocates. Those who rejected the MacArthur–Luce World War III concept of carrying the fight to Red China, probably involving Soviet Russia itself, were represented as going soft on Communism, as treacherous fellow travellers who in high office or even government service were an active or potential menace to national security.

In a communication to his editors Harry Luce called Acheson 'an irresponsible (if not worse) internationalist'. In the magazines he was pilloried and his resignation demanded. *Time* specialised in physical characteristics calculated to arouse suspicion: 'The familiar bony face, the hawk nose, the moustache, the Homburg; his blue, slightly protuberant eyes.' His virtues were coldly enumerated to suggest that here in Acheson was the antithesis of the All-American Man: 'tall, elegant, unruffled, punctilious and polite'. The news magazine loaded its profile of the Secretary of State with half-truths, lies and elbow-nudging hints, death from a thousand innuendoes. It was worded in the traditional *Time* past tense which, to the uninitiated, had the flavour of a reported fact: 'What people thought of Dean Gooderham Acheson ranged from the proposition that he was a fellow traveller, or an abysmally uncomprehending man, or an appeaser, or a warmonger who was taking the US into a world war, to the warm if not so audible defence that he was a great Secretary of State . . . Charges that the State Department had housed [Communist] party-liners and homosexuals had obviously stuck.' The State Department under Acheson had abandoned Chiang to his enemies, aided Mao, and continued hopefully to stroke the fur of the Red leader.

What the readers of *Time*, six million of them, learned by insinuation was rammed more brutally down the throats of the eighteen million readers of the more popular *Life* in case they might miss the point: 'It was Acheson who was Truman's chief adviser on basic policy, and Acheson was also Truman's chief alibi-ist . . . Acheson would not only have let Formosa go to the Communists, he might have recognised the Communist Government of China, if he could have got away with it—and he still might.'

This brand of vicious political journalism had few equals in the world, and Acheson was but one of the slain. Most of the leading Democrats— Franklin Roosevelt, Harry S. Truman, Adlai Stevenson—expected and received the same kind of treatment in varying degrees from the man whose high ideal was to achieve in his publications 'a consensus of opinion and conviction and sometimes try to evoke it in the nation.'

Luce was not always aloof. Occasionally he would ignore the chain of command and send for young journalists whose work had appealed to him; they were honoured but relieved when the brief interview was over. He would preside at office luncheons to which his editors were called to meet visiting personalities like Jean Monnet and Golda Meir or Lord Beaverbrook. Aspiring home-front politicians, including John F. Kennedy, were often on the menu. The editors rarely got a word in and sometimes not even the guests.

Two buzzes on the phone meant Luce was on the line, but his principal mode of communication with his staff was the morning memo, or notes scribbled on a yellow legal pad, conveying an idea he wanted to be followed up or some criticism. His top executives would not claim over the years to have mollified the proprietor's granite prejudices and wilder vanities, but he could not always rely on the best of them to perform as obedient pencils in his hairy, hurrying hand. A few could be as rude as Luce, as independent as he was autocratic. If anybody is ever moved to compile an *International Anthology of Offensive Office Memoranda* this example of vituperation by Matthews merits consideration:

'There are several possible answers to your memo of yesterday on Harry Bridges: (1) tear it up and throw it in the wastebasket (as Alex did); (2) remonstrate with you (as John Billings did); (3) say nothing; (4) tell you to go to hell—as I have been very strongly tempted to do.

'I honestly think I have listed all the possible answers. No decent human being would answer your memo by accepting it (I mean of course its tone and manner—*not* your views on Bridges). You have written it as if to dogs, not to human beings. And you thus make a great mistake.

'If you're really degenerating into a barking boss, you'll soon have behind you only the anxious, stupid, dishonest subservience that kind of boss can command. But you will no longer command either my respect or my services.'

Matthews admits he kept forgetting or wouldn't admit that *Time* was not only Luce's invention but his property. He believed *Time* was a public trust that should not be subject to the whims or dictates of one man. Others used 'effective ways of circumventing some of Harry's bad-tempered fiats, his ill-conceived or impossible notions', but on the occasions when Matthews did reluctantly force the issue he always wondered why it had to be him. It had to be him over the Lucepress treatment of Adlai Stevenson, the Democratic Governor of Illinois, and for several cogent reasons.

The 1952 Presidential election was a microcosm of Lucean and *Time* ethics in all previous elections, with the additional flavour that on this occasion somebody stood up for the innocent man being publicly lynched and was prepared to be counted. It was the breaking year for Harry Luce and Tom Matthews as Dwight Eisenhower and Adlai Stevenson moved towards their nomination as Republican and Democratic candidates for the White House. Nobody in the ring at *Time* was a tongue-tied innocent, certainly not Matthews. He wasn't by nature a man of passionate political conviction, but he did believe the product should be a news-magazine as advertised and not a crudely biased views-magazine as sold over the counter. As managing editor for nine years he had been an effective hatchet-man, as dexterous a launderer of the facts as the rest of the hierarchy during elections and the anti-Communist crusade. He was a brilliant writer and independent thinker; a third factor sustained his morale and elevated him above the wage-slaves who had to take 'No' as an answer from Luce—his personal fortune from the family Ivory Soap business. As well as a share of the lucre he seemed to have inherited the special selling quality of Ivory as 'the soap that floats'. His hyper-sensitivity over the treatment of Adlai Stevenson, the best potential President America never had, was due to his high regard for the man and to a friendship that went back to their years as classmates at Princeton.

Luce merely had to choose between 'Fighting Bob' Taft and General 'Ike' as Republican candidate and it was no disadvantage to Eisenhower, at that time on active duty in Paris as Supreme Commander, Allied Powers in Europe, when Robert T. Elson was able to report to head office after a private talk with him in Paris : 'He would like to see a start made on a Pacific security pact but recognises the formidable spiritual and moral factors . . . in rallying oriental resistance to Communism . . . He is friendly to Chiang and would put no obstacle in way of Chinese undertaking to liberate themselves from Mao's tyranny.' There were other factors in his choice of Ike, but China was still important to Luce, and Eisenhower would be easier meat for him and the China Lobby than Roosevelt, Truman or Marshall had been. Luce liked Ike and Ike liked Chiang, another professional soldier.

Harry Luce was travelling a great deal that year. He crossed the Atlantic to England with Churchill in the *Queen Mary* in January. Winston was again Prime Minister and Anthony Eden his Foreign Secretary after they had both been out of office for six years: Luce was anticipating a tougher British line against the USSR. There were other journeys, a tour of eight countries in the Far East and a more leisurely three-week holiday in Spain with Clare, but Harry found time for two talks in Paris with Dwight Eisenhower. During one of his absences from the Rockefeller Center Tom Matthews published a cover story on Adlai Stevenson in *Time*, the most complimentary piece the Governor of Illinois was ever to read about himself in any publication owned by Luce.

Stevenson had not been nominated nor was it certain he would be. The moment seemed opportune to Luce, none the less, to ease Matthews out of the managing editorship, the post that gave effective control of the magazine under Luce as Editor-in-Chief, and to promote him to the 'editorship' with no specific powers at all. Not quite right; he was put in charge of the cover stories, a move which soon caused a problem. When Stevenson was nominated as Democratic candidate the second cover story in one year had to appear about him. Matthews found himself battling for the exclusion of a distressing incident in Stevenson's childhood: he and his cousin were playing with a gun which discharged, killing the cousin. It was that sort of piece.

From then on, says Matthews, 'there was no holding *Time*. The distortions, suppressions, and slanting of its political "news" seemed to me to pass the bounds of politics and to commit an offence against the ethics of journalism.' The files of *Time* before and during the Eisenhower-Stevenson election of 1952 substantiate the charge, but with Matthews effectively manacled Luce had no reason to fear that his editorial executives were not accepting his dictum that objectivity was a myth.

All human virtue was attributed in successive weekly issues to Eisenhower by the crisp word-spinners of the National Affairs department. Ike was portrayed as innately kind and modest; he had great humility and clarity, force, sincerity, spontaneity and charm. Months before he won the election the general was hailed as a statesman. He was a vigorous campaigner, a great American soldier disclosing political greatness, a man of unique experience. Every cry of 'Attaboy' and 'Go to it' from the crowd was recorded. The crowd liked Ike and *Time* liked Ike's exorcism of defeatism and his vow to cleanse the Washington set-up of subversives from top to bottom. Two of the Lucepress writers were seconded as his speechwriters and *Life* photographers acquired the skill of capturing only those moments when the candidate was smilingly confident.

Eisenhower's senatorial running mate as Republican Vice Presidential candidate, a thirty-nine-year-old lawyer born of Quaker parents in

California, was also accorded a *Time* cover story. His virtues were listed with a thoroughness which might well have unnerved the Pope. Well, said Lucepress, he seemed to have everything including good looks and effectiveness as a barrier of Communism. An essential quality in the All-American Male, especially during the hustings, is aggressive modesty or modest aggressiveness, so he was described as having 'a manner both aggressive and modest'. Attractive family background. Deep sincerity and religious faith. Taught at Sunday school. Patriotism? Full marks. Good war record; was under bombardment. *Time* was able to assure its readers that back home in California (where he began and ended his career) 'the folks were confident'. They were not so confident, nor was Eisenhower, when the Vice Presidential candidate was accused by the *New York Post* of illegally benefiting from an $18,000 private fund raised by his wealthy supporters, but he got away with it, just, with a television spectacular in which he denounced 'the Communist smear' and took the precaution of appearing on the screen with his wife and dog. His name was Richard Milhous Nixon. On that occasion, not for the only time, the Quakers' pious son was facing political extermination. Luce's magazines stood at his side with heart-rending loyalty; the headline in *Life* was: 'NIXON FIGHTS, WINS, AND WEEPS.' Nixon had 'established himself as a new force in the party with a prestige seldom enjoyed by a Vice Presidential candidate'. Even Eisenhower was applauded on the grounds that his 'command decision' in not jettisoning Nixon dispelled any lingering doubt of Ike's executive ability. The iniquities of Luce's magazines on such occasions as these made the indigenous African political press read like *Crockford's Guide to the Clergy*.

The Lucean dispensation did not extend to Harry S. Truman, the retiring Democratic President, when he campaigned for Stevenson in that 1952 election. There were allegations in the news-magazine of Trumanism and Truman tactics; he was denounced for making weird charges, pouring reckless abuse upon Eisenhower, attempting to swing Jewish and Catholic votes (shame!) and doing his demagogic best as a rabble-rouser.

The subtlest skills of Harry Luce's demolition squad were predictably reserved for the Democratic candidate himself. Stevenson was a lawyer of international standing who had established a commendable record in the affairs of the United Nations before he became Governor of Illinois in 1948. For a while he had served in his family newspaper business and occasionally considered working for Lucepress itself. The battery of cameras used by the *Life* photographers covering the Stevenson campaign all seemed to develop the same technical fault; they could only succeed in snapping Adlai with his mouth open, or in some ungainly pose. He could not be parodied as a mountebank or a fool, or undermined as an active or potential 'Red' (well, we'll see), so the *Time* men got it about right from Luce's point of view in the second cover story when they stirred up doubt with the cover headline: '*Does he make sense to the American people*?' The implication was that not making sense to the American people was an impeachable offence, and the long piece inside did not come to the conclusion that he *did* make sense. He was the most articulate American in public life at that time, but when Luce's piranhas had had their weekly fill little remained of the man's personality or integrity. He was 'thrown on the defensive'; he 'set out to explain'; he was a man who felt there were two sides to most questions; he 'tried desperately'. He laughed nervously and swallowed manfully. He would have to face the facts of life. He was unfitted for the job. He was, unlike Ike the world warrior, a Washington operator. As a candidate appearing before the great American public he did not rouse his audience, and anyway his crowds were far smaller than Ike's. It was pointed out, ridiculously, that ten months ago Stevenson was not even a name in the national consciousness, whereas Eisenhower had been dealing with the European heads of state. A new version was given of his fight against corruption in Illinois, previously applauded by *Time*. The second cover story said: 'He has never so much as slapped the wrist of the Cook County Democratic organisation, the most corrupt and powerful of existing big-city machines.' For the record, the youthful tragedy with the gun was omitted.

John Sparkman, his Vice Presidential running mate, was laughed out of court as 'a connoisseur of coughdrops'. All that remained to be done was to smear Adlai Stevenson with indelible red ink. It was implied that he moved in a circle of 'subversives'. He didn't 'make sense' to the American people to such an extent that he had suggested the possibility of parleys with the USSR. He was close to the 'Acheson faction' who 'watched the victories of Mao with feelings ranging from complacence to connivance'. The innuendo was treason, and in case the dumbest reader of *Life* still didn't get the point he was reminded that 'on the periphery of this faction one finds the trail of Alger Hiss', a minor government official accused of spying.

One of the prides of the proprietor of *Time*, *Life* and *Fortune* was that he had served as Editor-in-Chief during three crisis Presidencies. In the election of Dwight Eisenhower he played a role far beyond the rights and duties of legitimate publishing to help to achieve the first Republican victory after the party had lost five successive Presidential elections over twenty years. To Luce it was of paramount importance that a Republican should be put in the White House, 'almost any Republican', and he conducted the campaign with a bias that exceeded all his previous efforts.

I have mentioned Theodore White and Tom Matthews as the brave dissenters in the Luce camp. There were some who survived, notably Thomas Griffith, National Affairs Editor, 1949–51, then for five years Foreign Affairs Editor. Luce once actually conceded in the privacy of an editorial dinner that *Time*'s coverage of an election had been biased in favour of the Republicans; his guests were surprised when he explained away the ruse as 'a little cheating, as in bridge'. Griffith felt in February 1956 that there was a great deal of cheating in the treatment of American affairs and wrote to Luce to tell him so:

> 'I for one am no longer satisfied to do the best I can in my own area and wear blinkers about the rest. The plain fact is that National Affairs is not only bad in itself, it is hurting the rest of the magazine. It is dishonest, and its dishonesty is spreading a cynicism through the rest of the magazine. This cynicism, in this form, is a new thing in the halls of *Time* in my twelve years here . . . National Affairs forfeits trust in the area most people can catch us out in . . . *Time* used to "cheat" a little in the campaign's final month, and did so guiltily; now it's a four-year proposition.'[1]

Griffith was dealing with the period of Eisenhower's term of office when the Democratic national chairman sneered at it as the house organ of the regime. 'We are getting into worse and worse habits,' said Griffith, 'and like dope users, increasing the dosage.' He advanced two arguments even Luce could not brush aside: (1) *Time* did not have the power to win elections, only to hurt itself; (2) the 'many good things' about the Eisenhower Administration would be better celebrated if the reader could trust *Time* not to omit the bad. Griffith was surprised when summoned the next morning to be told by Luce that he agreed things had gone too far. The editors of National Affairs were changed and so was the policy. Griffith recognised the change was real; though there were later lapses he deplored, he acknowledged that *Time*'s entire coverage was 'never again so blatantly distorted' in favour of the Republicans. Had the hard-shell opinions of the grizzled tycoon really become softer?

In the 1960 election, Nixon versus Kennedy, Time Inc. declared its Republican allegiance as an organisation reasonably enough on *Life*'s

---

[1]*How True* by Thomas Griffith.

editorial page, but Griffith, temporarily editing *Time*, was able to hold the balance in political *reporting* in the magazine with such dexterity that even Arthur Schlesinger Jr, the Harvard historian working in John F. Kennedy's Democratic camp, was able to say, 'This is the best *Time* political coverage since 1936, the best and the fairest.'

'Surprising enough, the way to put out a "fair" *Time* in election year had to be invented,' wrote Griffith. He acknowledged the support of an emerging influence of maximum importance in the organisation, Hedley Donovan, then of *Fortune*. It was Donovan who inherited Harry Luce's mantle when the co-founder yielded the title of Editor-in-Chief at the age of sixty-six in April 1964. The new chief stated his policy in the presence of Luce at a dinner for the staff to mark the event:

'The vote of Time Inc. should never be considered to be in the pocket of any particular political leader or party. The vote of Time Inc. is an independent vote. Not an independent vote in the sense of some snooty or finicky disdain for political parties. And certainly not independent in the sense of any wishy-washy confusion as to what we believe. But independent in the sense that we are in no way beholden to any party.'

Griffith, then holding the highfalutin title of Senior Staff Editor of all Time Inc. publications, which meant he was deputy to both Luce and Donovan, had shown the boss in advance just that one paragraph from his successor's speech: so Harry didn't spring to his feet or walk out. The grizzled tycoon led the applause. Donovan's soothing praise the same evening for Luce's 'talent for sharing authority without diluting it' was a calculated touch of the forelock so far as the past was concerned. Now, at last, Luce was devolving authority, calling himself Editorial Chairman, exerting an influence on the publications during his remaining few years but investing in the new Editor-in-Chief the final policy vote.

Lyndon Baines Johnson was already President, promoted in November the previous year by Lee Harvey Oswald, who peered through his telescopic lens in Dallas, Texas, and assassinated John F. Kennedy. In October 1964, five months after the spring cleaning in Rockefeller Center, Johnson won the election against the Republican Barry Goldwater with an unprecedented majority of fifteen million votes. For the first time in its history of forty-one years Time Inc. supported the Democratic candidate for the Presidency. During the election Luce was journeying in the Far East, visiting the Generalissimo and Madame Chiang Kai-shek for the last time.

In 1967, the year of his death at sixty-nine, Luce was asked whether General MacArthur was right or wrong about Korea and beyond. 'Was MacArthur right? Of course he was. It was both ridiculous and immoral to allow the murderous Chinese bombers to have "sanctuary" beyond the Yalu. Sanctuary? How blasphemous can you get!'

He died suddenly of a coronary occlusion in the early hours of 28 February after spending some of the evening watching a favourite television programme, 'Perry Mason'. He was in St Joseph's Hospital near his retreat at Phoenix, Arizona. The nurse who hastened to his aid when he yelled out and collapsed in the bathroom said that his last cry was 'Oh, Jesus.' At the memorial service in the Presbyterian Church in New York where Harry had worshipped for forty-three years the Reverend Read brought his eulogy to an end with the John Bunyan hymn:

> 'He'll fear not what men say;
> He'll labour night and day
> To be a pilgrim.'

In 1972, five years later to the day of Luce's death, Richard Milhous Nixon, Republican President and former stalwart of the Chiang Kai-shek American lobby, boarded his plane at Peking to return to Washington after a week of amicable talks initiated by the United States with the leaders of Communist China. The readers of *Time*, *Life* and *Fortune* magazines saw on their television screens the pictures of a grinning Nixon shaking hands with a beaming Chairman Mao Tse-tung, signalling the close of twenty-seven years of hostility. On 1 January 1979, diplomatic relations were established. The United States acknowledged that 'Nationalist' Taiwan was an integral part of China and that the Communist regime was China's only legal government: the American defence treaty with Taiwan was severed. The Coca-Cola Corporation hoisted the red flag of the People's Republic of China among the national emblems of its other customers, but *Time* did not repeat its jest about Coca-cola-nisation.

V

BEAVERBROOK

William Maxwell Aitken

'I run the paper purely for the purpose of propaganda, and with no other motive.'

'It is my purpose to break up the Conservative Party if it does not adopt the Empire Free Trade policy.'

'The *Daily Express* stands for more life—more hope—more money—more work—more happiness.'

'There will be no war.'

'Why don't you start a vendetta against somebody? *That's* the way to get people reading your column.'

'Do justly, love mercy, and walk humbly.'

Lord Beaverbrook at his country mansion,
Cherkley, with his two favourite instruments,
the telephone and the dictaphone.

'I am the victim of the Furies,' wrote William Maxwell Aitken, Baron Beaverbrook, to a friend. 'On the rockbound coast of New Brunswick the waves break incessantly. Every now and then comes a particularly dangerous wave smashing viciously against the rock. It is called the Rage. That's me.'

The character of the abrasive Canadian who acquired the *Daily Express* and London *Evening Standard* and founded the *Sunday Express* has been described by a variety of people in extravagant degrees of loathing or affection. One of his friends said, 'Everything that anyone said about Max is true—the best things and the worst things.' His mood and conduct reflected the part he was performing. He was an actor-manager; he wrote his own heroic scripts and played half-a-dozen major roles simultaneously, including 'I am the cat that walks alone.'

A. J. P. Taylor's massive biography, or history, of Beaverbrook is now the standard work of reference on the subject,[1] though there is scarcely a political memoir of the last half-century that omits his name. Taylor is critical as well as admiring in his interpretation of all the letters and documents but totally at a loss to explain why many people regarded Beaverbrook as indescribably wicked, an evil man: 'To enjoy mischief and even to appear irresponsible is surely a long way from being wicked.' He loved Max Aitken when he was alive, and when he learned to know him better from his records he loved him even more. He constantly reminds the reader of Max's role as a foul-weather friend; sustaining Churchill and Haldane when the Tories forced their exclusion from the Asquith Coalition in the First World War; befriending the first Earl of Birkenhead, Samuel Hoare, Edward VIII in the Abdication Crisis, Leslie Hore-Belisha when he was sacked as War Minister, Churchill when he was in the wilderness though their policies were opposed. In his newspaper activities Beaverbrook was also a foul-weather friend to journalists—I was among them—if not to the victims of his newspaper policies. Alan Taylor's homily on the Rage's attitude to power is less convincing: 'Beaverbrook was not interested in power except in the sense

Beaverbrook by *A. J. P. Taylor* FBA, Hamish Hamilton, London, 1972.

of being able to ensure that his orders were carried out.' Genghis Khan and Abdul the Damned would have conceded, with a chuckle, that they took the same view.

Max Aitken's lovability was not universally acclaimed. Andrew Bonar Law, whom he manoeuvred into No. 10 Downing Street, called him a curious fellow. He played a decisive part in making David Lloyd George Prime Minister, but Ll.G. said no man in any party trusted Max. When he appointed the Canadian as Minister of Information in 1918 the severest critic was Lord Salisbury. He described Aitken to backbenchers as a very wicked man, and when challenged by Edmund Goulding to justify the gibe merely added, 'Oh, ask anyone in Canada.' For fifty-five years, with few estrangements, Winston Churchill enjoyed his boisterous companionship and acknowledged his energy, confidence and ability to get things done in a crisis, but Churchill was sorely taxed by Beaverbrook's tantrums as Minister of Aircraft Production in 1940, his bullying and bickering and threats of resignation when his orders were opposed by Ministers with equal claims on resources. Clementine Churchill considered that Birkenhead, Beaverbrook and Brendan Bracken over the years brought out the 'worst' in Winston and she deplored their influence.

Cabinet Ministers of other parties, who had to endure Beaverbrook in coalition during the Second World War, some in silence, expressed their views in due course. To Clement Attlee he was 'The man in public life most widely distrusted by men of all parties; he had a long record of political intrigue and political instability, with an insatiable appetite for power.' Ernest Bevin settled for 'The most dangerous man in British public life.' Stafford Cripps, the most austere of the wartime Socialists, said in 1942 that 'the way Beaverbrook turned his bright young men into drunkards was done out of sheer sadism. He certainly had an intentionally demoralising effect on his young men and young women.'

Lord Reith, who exhibited the Christian virtues ostentatiously in public and confided his darker thoughts to his diary, reserved a special place of hatred in his heart for the Rage: 'What a dreadful man he is; one of the worst I ever met. Evil he seems . . . How I dislike that man. I think I would oppose anything he wanted . . . disgusting . . . an impossible fellow.' On 16 September 1941, when Beaverbrook was turning frying pans into Spitfires, Reith wrote in his diary: 'Today [as Minister of Works] I was asked to approve £1,300 for a special train for Beaverbrook and Co going to the North of Scotland en route for Moscow. I hope Beaverbrook gets killed en route. It would be a splendid release and escape for this country.' He also wrote, 'to no one is the vulgar designation shit more appropriately applied'.[1] Reith was frustrated and envious, a proud and vain man who saw himself as Prime Minister and also dictator of Great Britain; he despised those around him, including Churchill, and his judgement on individuals cannot be seriously taken into account. Harold Macmillan had no illusions about the more 'distasteful aspects' of Beaverbrook's character, yet learned as his Under-Secretary at the Ministry of Supply 'to appreciate the extraordinary gifts of this strange and wayward genius'. It was not to his discredit, at any rate, that Hermann Goering, head of the Luftwaffe, called him *ein gefaehrlicher bursche*, a dangerous fellow. A woman's view came from Rebecca West, who knew him well through her friendship with H. G. Wells: 'Max was a honey, but he didn't add up.'

In Fleet Street Beaverbrook was regarded less horrifically than in Westminster. His whimsicality and eccentricity were accepted by journalists with favour. The omnipotence and omnipresence of the driving force behind his publishing empire were apparent before one even crossed the threshold. He was demanding, exacting, tyrannous, vindictive and malicious; yet all or most of the excesses of the master journalist were forgiven by the men and women who worked for him because of the success of his publishing enterprise and his impish sense of fun. The victims of his malevolence usually resided outside the encampment.

I met none of the bright young men he had 'turned into drunkards' or 'demoralised', but many he had driven to distraction prematurely or who exhausted themselves in his service. Three of the editors of his newspapers died at fifty-six or thereabouts. I did meet the young men he encouraged or forcibly fed with his own notions, and my personal experience of his capacity for encouragement of the young is no doubt typical of many.

Halfway through the war he said would never happen I was ordered as a seconded infantry officer to London by air in 1943 for three days (to receive my next orders) after the advance of the Desert Rats from El Alamein to Tunisia. 'Why not tell the country what you've been telling me about the campaign?' said Grigg, the Secretary of State for War: 'I'll ring the MOI.' On the morning after my performance for the captive blacked-out audience of the BBC, Beaverbrook phoned me: 'D'ya know who this is? The Prime Minister and I listened to your Eighth Army broadcast last night and Winston thought it was great stirring stuff. Goodbye to you.'

[1] *The Reith Diaries* edited by Charles Stuart, Collins, London, 1975.

He approached me at the end of the war to join the *Express* organisation, and then, when I was unemployed for two hours just before Christmas in 1949, immediately invited me to what he called 'the sunny side of the Street'. The Fleet Street edifice, veneered in black glass, where the *Express* newspapers are still produced, faces south.

The speed with which he acted was one of the attractive aspects of the man. I had telephoned Arthur Christiansen, the Editor of the *Daily Express*, to inform him that the tone of the correspondence between Harry Guy Bartholomew and myself in the rival newspaper group indicated my imminent departure. Christiansen phoned Beaverbrook at his winter retreat in Montego Bay, Jamaica. Within two hours I had joined the *Express* organisation and within six hours a cable reached me from the Beaver: 'It is with enthusiasm that I welcome you to our house where you will be happy and contented. I have sought your companionship for long. Beaverbrook.' His intention was that I would eventually follow John Gordon as editor of the *Sunday Express*. He twice appointed me editor but omitted to tell John Gordon; another interesting facet of his character.

When I arrived on my first visit as an employee at his top-floor apartment in Arlington House near the Ritz Hotel, overlooking Green Park, he said, 'Hugh, bring your chair over here. Not there—here !' The accent was a pleasant, soft and persuasive Canadian twang; I learned on other occasions that it would easily become harsh and domineering when raised in anger. We sat opposite each other and the invitation to 'Come closer' was repeated until our knees touched. The siting of the chairs was a matter of meticulous stage-management. The lighting seemed to play upon his face alone. He was not apparently expecting me, with uplifted right hand, to swear by Almighty God to speak the truth, the whole truth, and nothing but the truth (according to the policies of Lord Beaverbrook); he was silently exhorting me to see the truth in his face. He narrowed the lids of his eyes and peered into mine; having no alternative I peered steadfastly back. The prophet was casting his spell on a newcomer half his age. He was administering a mute oath of allegiance. Or was Mephistopheles promising to show Dr Faustus all knowledge and all experience in return for his immortal soul? Or was it a ritualistic absolution from my sins of the past when, in some unthinking moment, I had doubted his dictum of Empire Free Trade?

Halfway through the two-minute ordeal I prided myself that lesser men might have cracked, sobbed fitfully, and confessed that under the influence of government hospitality they had indeed commended the British Council for sending Welsh harpists and long-haired poets to policy is going to be, *unless* I have complete guarantees that such policy will be carried out if his Party achieves office, and *unless* I am acquainted with the names of at least eight, or ten, of his most prominent colleagues in the next Ministry.'

Northcliffe had never put his demands in writing. Beaverbrook delivered his threats in public. Rothermere had dictated the baleful 'unless' conditions of a blackmailer, signed them, and delivered them. A professional extortioner would have known better; from a public man the letter was horrendously indiscreet, transforming Baldwin's swan song into a political spectacular. The Lord had delivered his enemy into his hands. 'A more preposterous and insolent demand was never made on the leader of any political party,' he told his cheering audience. 'I repudiate it with contempt, and I will fight that attempt at domination to the end.' The approval in Caxton Hall from his own party was echoed in the Commons that same night when both sides of the House rose and cheered.

The story of the alliance of the Press barons, its abrupt demise, and of Baldwin's second and shattering denunciation on 18 March 1931 is part of the Beaverbrook story in Chapter V, but the place of dishonour he reserved for Rothermere is relevant here. Said the Tory Leader:

'I have used an expression about an "insolent plutocracy". These words appeared in the *Daily Mail* of yesterday week: "These expressions come ill from Mr Baldwin, since his father left him an immense fortune which, so far as may be learned from his own speeches, has almost disappeared. It is difficult to see how the leader of a party who has lost his own fortune can hope to restore that of anyone else, or of his country."

'I have only one observation to make about that. It is signed, "Editor, *Daily Mail*". I have no idea of the name of that gentleman. I would only observe that he is well qualified for the post which he holds. The first part of that statement is a lie, and the second part of that statement by its implication is untrue. The paragraph itself could only have been written by a cad. I have consulted a very high legal authority, and I am advised that an action for libel would lie. I shall not move in the matter, and for this reason: I should get an apology and heavy damages. The first is of no value, and the second I would not touch with a barge-pole.'

The rise of Hitler and the National Socialists in Germany further whetted Rothermere's appetite for authoritarian government in Britain, and this time his advocacy was more strident. A 3,000-word despatch on a news page of the *Daily Mail* of 24 September 1930, signed by him, was headlined:

GERMANY AND INEVITABILITY

A NATION RE-BORN

YOUTH ASSERTING ITS POWER

It was addressed from 'Munich, Tuesday, the birthplace and power house of Nazism'. He informed his readers that the generation of Germans then coming into political power was a type which few foreigners knew at all. Its members had little experience of the war. Reparation debts, lost territories, and enforced disarmament were the only political topics they heard discussed around them. They found themselves heirs to a great nation strong in natural resources, population, diligence, and technical skill, but plunged in profound depression by overwhelming defeat in war. They had set themselves to build a new nation. And then came the clarion call:

'With the same vigour as they have developed their bodies by physical culture, with the same energy as they worked long hours at factory, office or farm, these young Germans have organised themselves to take an active part in their country's affairs. They have discovered, as, I am glad to know, the young men and women of England are discovering, that it is no good trusting to the old politicians. Accordingly they have formed, as I should like to see our British youth form, a Parliamentary party of their own.

'We can do nothing to check this movement, and I believe it would be a blunder for the British people to take up an attitude of hostility towards it ... Moderate opinion in Britain and France should therefore give full appreciation to the services which the National Socialist Party has rendered to Western Europe.'

In one paragraph of the same despatch Rothermere disclosed from Munich his thoughts on Britain:

'Under Herr Hitler's control the youth of Germany is effectively organised against the corruption of Communism. It was with some such purpose that I founded the United Empire Party in England, for it is clear that no strong anti-Socialist policy can be expected from a Conservative Party whose leaders are themselves tainted with semi-Socialist doctrines.'

Istanbul, or thought in their ignorance that the United Nations was a noble concept, or kissed the faded hem of the Fabian Society, or shaken Earl Mountbatten of Burma by the hand. Had I at last acquired the artifice of silence, or was I mesmerised? No word was spoken, and I was therefore able to concentrate upon the remarkable head a foot or less away from me. It was round, with a mouth so broad that it seemed to reach his ear on each side; like a melon chopped but not severed by a machete. The brow and the lines dividing his cheeks from his nose and upper lip were deeply furrowed. The skin was leathery, permanently tanned in the sunshine of Montego Bay and Cap d'Ail, where he took his asthma and friends for the winter. The eyes were piercing and his features immobile for the first minute of the seance. I noticed that the collar of his shirt was slightly frayed and his tie loosely knotted. The second minute was occupied with a display of his range of moods, all facially expressed. Doubt. Suspicion. Anger. Ruthlessness. It is all magnificently captured in Graham Sutherland's portrait. The final expression, the most startling of all, transformed the Three Wise Monkeys— 'Hear No Evil, See No Evil, Speak No Evil'—into One Wise Monkey reversing their policies. Then the mouth broke apart in a pleasing puckish grin and the eyes opened wide and he laughed.

'Hugh,' he said, 'have you seen my electric rum-cocktail mixer? Jamaican rum and West Indian limes. The limes are absolutely paramount.' I had passed the loyalty test and within a few months was appointed to the inner circle of the Policy Committee, the sanctum where the chosen few were vouchsafed untramelled freedom to agree with what the master said.

William Maxwell Aitken had three careers in his lifespan. The first, as financier in Canada, made him a millionaire by the age of thirty. In the second, as a politician in Britain, he exerted influence behind the scenes rather than achieving personal success in Parliament. In the third he became a multi-millionaire newspaper proprietor. His appointment as a Cabinet Minister in the 1914 war sprang from his friendship with Bonar Law and David Lloyd George, and from his propaganda performance for the Canadian forces in Europe. His three ministerial appointments in the 1939 war were the result of his friendship with Churchill, his drive and ability as an organiser, and his fame as a Press baron. His political career from 1910 until 1918, however, was a self-contained phase of his life with no relation to his subsequent high jinks as a newspaper owner.

He was a son of the manse, born in 1879 at Maple, Ontario, where his Presbyterian father had emigrated from Scotland. At twelve he was selling newspapers in Newcastle, New Brunswick, to grab a little personal capital. At seventeen, working in a law office, he began a lifelong association with Richard Bedford Bennett that had two influences on his future. Bennett, who became Conservative Prime Minister of Canada, interested him in politics: he also advised his restless young friend to forget the law and sell bonds. In Edmonton Aitken first tried his luck as a small businessman, collecting and distributing cargoes of meat. At twenty in the Maritime Provinces he was an insurance company inspector, staying up late, gambling and drinking away the earnings. At twenty-one he made his great decision in life, and from that moment onwards never faltered in his resolve. He dedicated his gifts to Mammon, the pursuit of wealth—and of power through wealth—and of more power through more wealth. He prided himself that he had 'an intuitive perception of the real and not the face value of any article'. He embraced the creed that men as well as things had their price.

The chain mail of the financier fitted him as if it had been riveted by a bespoke armourer. Human need was a golden opportunity for exploitation and personal gain. The men who crossed his path or stood in his way would be pushed aside or crushed. The Holy Grail was profit, with no sleepless nights over the ruthlessness required to attain it. He sanctified his plans with the kind of prose usually reserved for nobler causes: 'The battles of the market-place are real duels, on which the realities of life and death and fortune or poverty and even of fame depend. Here men fight with a precipice behind them.' He had psychological and physical assets in his quest for Canadian dollars. He was a salesman with a flair for persuasive patter; a cunning negotiator, wooing the confidence of both sides and concealing his own hand; his energy was inexhaustible. The objective to be a dollar millionaire did not appear fanciful to him or to those who knew him.

His coming of age marked his entry into big-business circles, first as secretary and then associate of John L. Stairs, senior partner of the leading finance house in Halifax, Nova Scotia, president of steel and banking companies, friend of other rich men. During his travels selling bonds Max spotted a bank for Stairs' bank to take over, netting the salesman his first ten-thousand-dollar profit. Stairs and his well-to-do friends launched a holding and investment company with Aitken as managing director, floating companies to supply electric light, power and transport, buying up land around the expanding city to sell at a handsome rake-off. Aitken repeated the exercise in the West Indies, his first solo assignment. His cut in the estate when Stairs died was $50,000, but the taunts that the end of Stairs was the end of 'little Max' were stillborn.

In 1906, when he was twenty-six, he found Halifax too shallow and smooth a pond for a barracuda to swim in. The city columns of the Montreal newspapers were already calling him a sort of financial infant prodigy. Montreal was the money-makers' Mecca. The great Canadian boom was beckoning.

There was a business of a different nature to attend to first. The young adventurer had been advised that to make his mark in that city he must establish himself as a respectable man with wife and family, and Aitken's attitude to marriage was as materialistic as his attitude to a money deal. He had 'no compelling desire for marriage'. It was 'to some extent a matter of convenience with me', and the lady was ungallantly depicted in something he wrote later but did not publish as having a more lively interest in him than he had in her. But as a shrewd investor he took good care to make the best marriage possible and acquire the most attractive female property in town. Miss Gladys Drury at nineteen was not only charming and cultivated; she was also the daughter of the first Canadian to command Halifax garrison as a general. Her family, rated among the country's most distinguished, was not flattered that Gladys accepted a young financial pirate as her suitor. During the honeymoon, briefly in New York and then in the West Indies, the bridegroom was able to conduct a certain amount of business as well as lavishing affection and gifts on his bride. In Cuba he bought the Puerto Principe Electric Light Company for $300,000, 417 acres of land, the old Mule Tram franchise, and the electric railway franchise.

The honeymoon over, it was back to business. The same year Mr and Mrs Aitken occupied an apartment in Montreal, but Gladys was soon to learn that most of her time during the next four years would be spent alone in that apartment, or alone with her servants and everything she wanted, except her husband, in the country house he established across the bay at Halifax. The Drury family were now on Max's list of beneficiaries, so there were no complaints of his neglect from them. He celebrated his first wedding anniversary by buying himself a seat on the Montreal Stock Exchange, becoming an investment banker and devoting half of the $700,000 he had so far garnered in buying control of the staid, long-established Montreal Trust Company. He sold it two years later at a profit of $200,000. What he had also achieved was entry into, if not acceptance by, the fringe of the élite of the banking fraternity. He re-acquired the Royal Securities Corporation he had managed in Halifax and returned to the more flamboyant sport of company-promoting with his own money backed by other speculators.

By 1910, at thirty, he was a millionaire in sterling. How? The answer is—mergers. It was this financial spree that led Salisbury in 1918 to say, 'Ask anybody in Canada' when challenged to justify his allegation that the man from the Dominion who had become a British Cabinet Minister was very wicked. How 'wicked'? How did he achieve the wealth in Montreal that led to his power through wealth in London?

What happened in the United States a decade earlier, until halted by public anger and legislation, now hit Canada. The financial highwaymen, who knew little and cared less about the industries they manipulated from the stock market, made glittering fortunes. They called it rationalisation. It was, quite simply, the creation of *near* monopolies, the capitalist version of Socialist nationalisation, engineered for private gain with government acquiescence and pickings for helpful politicians in the know. The public interest didn't figure in the prospectuses, though the interest of the public was patently involved in the hundreds of mergers that affected human needs, from iron and steel to beer and boots, silk and soap, bread and milk. The highwaymen bought on borrowed money and sold quickly. Max Aitken didn't create the conditions: he was in the right place at the right time and exploited his luck more daringly and on a bigger scale than his rivals. Working with different syndicates he set up combines with a capital greater than $100,000,000 over a period of twelve months, and the financial stage where he operated had one resounding advantage. The combines were created in tariff-protected industries, eliminating most of the competition at home and all from overseas and therefore offering rich rewards for the few who moved quickly and boldly. The guile of the game was always to leave a handful of companies, the weakest, outside the combines, so that a semblance of indigenous competition remained: in those circumstances the politicians could be relied upon, or persuaded by political conviction or financial participation in the harvest, to maintain the tariffs.

Max Aitken set out on a safari into the merger jungle for killings throughout Canada. The result was a slaughter that would have earned the grudging respect of John D. Rockefeller in America. He displayed the organising zest and ability that gains the accolade of genius in the financial world, though not elsewhere. He set up mergers in cast-iron, railroad freight-cars, grain-elevators, paper milling and in other juicy sectors. Nobody except Aitken himself knew how many fingers he had in how many pies during the hectic year of 1909. He was operating as a slick businessman with no more strength or 'pull' than he could exert by his wits, energy, cunning and commercial vision. The opprobrium and enmity he incurred were caused by his last and biggest two deals in Canada, the formation by him of the Canada Cement Company and the birth of the Steel Company of Canada in which he played a different role. The most distinguished character in the cement scramble was Fleming, but the principal role was Aitken's. Sir Sandford Fleming, born at Kirkcaldy, Scotland, and then eighty-two, was Canada's authority on railway surveying and engineering, still the legendary figure of the Canadian Pacific Railway, a national personality in politics and a sharp financier though long retired. The CPR, Canada's greatest enterprise, had a cluster of directors on the board of the Bank of Montreal. What was good for the Bank was good for CPR, and what was good for CPR was good for Canada. When Fleming's son and two associates approached Aitken it began to look as if what was good for CPR was good for Aitken. The invitation was for the young company promoter to look into the affairs of three cement companies in which they held investments with a view to merger. Merger? The terms and conditions for his services were agreed. The notion of a cement combine was alluring enough, but to be *invited* to organise a new company of which Fleming would agree to be Honorary President, with CPR and the Bank of Montreal hovering benignly in the wings, was irresistible.

The Canadian economy was busting its seams. Cement was in demand for new houses, administrative buildings and factories, and (the mergerer's blue heaven) there was a tariff against importing cement. The companies who were producing the stuff in Canada weren't producing enough. Fleming himself happened to be the head of a cement concern that was virtually bankrupt, and William Maxwell Aitken was also no sucker. An enterprising holding company registered as the Bond and Share Company bought eleven cement companies for $16,592,250. It sold them to the new combine for shares and mortgages valued at $28,993,400. The chairman of the Bond and Share Company was Mr Aitken: the organiser of the combine was Mr Aitken. The retrospective view of O. D. Skelton, a Canadian economic historian, is worth quoting:

'This epidemic of mergers was accompanied by serious evils both in promotion and in operation. The investor to his cost found that, while a few of the new companies were prudently financed, the majority were over-capitalised . . . There was little question that there was a huge gap representing the extortionate profits of promoters and vendors. The cement combine was perhaps the most flagrant instance.'

Canada woke up to the monopoly racket just as slowly as America ten years before. There were doubts and murmurs, and after the cement deal Aitken was formally warned by a Minister of the Liberal Government that he would incur strictures if he embarked upon further mergers. Max went to earth, but not for long. One of his favourite stories as Lord Beaverbrook was of how he increased his fortune in a steel deal; the details varied in his versions though the grin was consistent.

Aitken wasn't creating the merger this time; he jockeyed himself into the position in which a merger could not successfully take place except on his terms, an even more lucrative exercise. The tip-off that the United States Steel Corporation was casting covetous eyes at the Montreal Rolling Mills, the finest steel-finishing company in Canada, dismayed Max the Patriot and enraged Max the Financier. He smartly bought the Mills at the asking price, $4,200,000, not unduly perturbed that he didn't have the money at the time. Nobody was more peeved than the other Canadian steelmasters, two of them linked with CPR, who were busily but secretly hatching their own merger, the Steel Company of Canada. They hadn't reckoned on 'the big-headed, big-mouthed, bumptious youngster from the backwoods', as Tom Driberg described him, sitting menacingly at their table. The in-fighting was so rough that the ring was moved, to avoid distractions, from Montreal to a hotel suite in New York.

Round One: They had no objection to Aitken's demand for one-third of the equity (mere speculation) but returned to their corner when he wanted $5,000,000 for the Mills. The pirate was trying to extort almost a million-dollar profit on a property he had just bought and had visited for only two days. *Round Two*: The CPR steelmasters and their friends were more attentive when Aitken casually mentioned that in the event of no deal he would talk with the companies excluded from the projected Steel Company of Canada and also, of course, with the United States Steel Corporation. His second offer was $4,000,000 on account for the Mills, $200,000 less than the purchase price, with an assessment of the Mills by independent valuers; anything above that $4,000,000 to go to him, any less to be repaid by him to the combine. The agreement was signed on the spot, with the steelmasters preening themselves on winning the fight. *Round Three*: The independent valuation was $6,000,000.

Between his purchase of the Montreal Rolling Mills and the sale, Aitken had dashed over to London for a week, selling bonds and borrowing $5,000,000 from Parr's Bank on his personal securities. That was just in case he had to produce the money. The $4,200,000 for the purchase of the Montreal Rolling Mills was never handed over; the combine paid the bill. Aitken pocketed two million profit and with some personal interest watched its shares grow sixty times in value over the decades. He always had an intuitive perception of the real and not the face value of any article.

The Steel Company of Canada went into business on 17 July 1910. On the evening of the same day Mr and Mrs Maxwell Aitken left Montreal by automobile for New York, never to return to Canada as residents. He had an appointment at Saratoga Springs, New York State, to talk business with the head of Price Brothers, the pulp and paper manufacturers, then boarded a Cunarder for England. A Daimler awaited the Aitkens at Fishguard to drive them to London, with leisurely stopovers on the way.

Just as Halifax was too smooth a pond for a barracuda, the whole of Canada did not offer sufficient sustenance for a man-eating shark. There is, however, no justification for the remark attributed to Lord Northcliffe: 'Max only just got away in time from the arm of the law.' There was no legal action against him or threat of action. The speculators he had outwitted were glad to see him go, but any suggestion that he dared not return is disproved by the fact that he did temporarily return on several visits until the outbreak of war in 1914, involving himself in further business deals. The biographers of Aitken, with the exception of A. J. P. Taylor, confuse the chronology of his business buccaneering in Canada to a degree that suggests a rapid withdrawal was prudent after the cement deal. The truth is that the financial conspirators in that legal but sharp encounter did not fall out until 1911; at a time of gross inconvenience to a rising politician in Britain. The Canadian newspaper attacks on Aitken had not begun when he and Gladys Drury, the loyal, loving, patient and neglected wife, occupied their suite on the Cunarder. Aitken might have been expecting the tumbrils to roll; the only certainty is that his own version of why he cut and ran from Canada existed only in the mind of Max the Romanticiser. It wasn't because he decided to abandon finance for politics; he could have achieved that ambition in Canada. Nor did he emigrate to become the champion of Empire in the Mother Country; that notion came later.

The opportunist had matured at an early age and was searching for new and wider opportunities. He wasn't 'on the run', but he was running. At thirty, when most men's political convictions are fossilised, the only major political idea in Max Aitken's head beyond affairs in Canada, where he had promoted the career of Richard Bedford Bennett, was that Free Enterprise had served him well and any *ism* that challenged his own interest was an abomination to be destroyed. Few people outside 'the City' knew much about him when he arrived in England in July 1910, or would have heard of him for some considerable time had he arrived without his bank balance. What was remarkable was the rapidity of his rise in a country where skulduggery was conducted beneath the veneer of gentlemanly codes unfamiliar to the Rage.

THE PREROGATIVE OF THE HARLOT

Aitken blasted his way into English political circles and upper-crust society with cheque-book and charm. The Empire was the link with Rudyard Kipling, an early friend in Britain who gave him a letter of introduction to his cousin, Stanley Baldwin, believing Aitken would find him 'a delightful fellow'. Knowing Bonar Law meant knowing Birkenhead and Lloyd George and Churchill, and the City had no bars against a millionaire. His initial relationship with Bonar Law was financial, but Law eased Aitken's entry into politics as a candidate at Ashton-under-Lyne.

Aitken's personality and egotism were in the same range as those of General MacArthur, with sentimental moments. He had a hobby that endeared new friends, including Kipling, to him. Without their knowledge he invested on their behalf money they couldn't spare, unassumingly handing over the profit: if the speculation soured they didn't hear of it. Or did he invest any money on their behalf? Was the welcome dividend a concealed gift? Was he Santa Claus, and why? F. E. Smith, later Lord Birkenhead, was one of his beneficiaries, and Bonar Law was not the poorer because of his association with magnanimous Max. Yet not all who benefited were useful to him; he could be generous without any apparent motive.

He bought the controlling share of Rolls-Royce and was soon impressing Lord Northcliffe, a motoring pioneer. He renewed his acquaintance with Andrew Bonar Law, to whom he had carried a letter of introduction on his first London visit in 1908 and sold five thousand dollars' worth of Nova Scotia bonds. Law, the son of another Presbyterian manse in New Brunswick, was a Member of Parliament of ten years' standing, a pillar of the Unionist Party, and an ironmaster. The friendship that developed between them had a tremendous impact on both their lives. Finance was the link and the politics followed. Law produced £100,000 as his stake in a syndicate set up by Aitken to trade in Price Brothers newsprint shares; the cement and steel millionaire had not wasted his time in Saratoga Springs. The temperaments of the two men were dissimilar and there was a twenty-year gap in their ages, but Aitken was as attracted by the older man's political influence as Law was attracted by Aitken's financial acumen. Within four months of Max's arrival as a resident Bonar ordered the Unionist Central Office to sniff out a suitable Parliamentary seat for his friend, 'a keen Imperialist'.

In December 1910 Aitken, W. Max, (Unionist) became MP for Ashton-under-Lyne with a majority of 196 over the Liberal candidate. He was valiant for Tariff Reform. In 1911, the year Bonar Law became Leader of the Unionist Party, ousting Balfour, the Chief Whip Sir

Alexander Acland-Hood had two peerages, two Privy Councillorships, two baronetcies and six knighthoods in his pocket for the Coronation List. Aitken, in England for less than a year and a backbench MP for only a few months, was offered his knighthood for services to come; the Unionists were short of funds. Lord Derby, the 'King of Lancashire' and the Unionist leader in that county, was displeased, believing the honour should go to an MP selected by him. Aitken was already making enemies.

At the moment he was being honoured so precipitously in Britain a whirlwind of cement dust was engulfing his name and reputation in Canada. The buccaneers had fallen out. Fleming, angered by Aitken's reluctance to buy his own cement company, now considered that twelve million dollars was too much to pay for what he ironically called 'promotional' expenses. He resigned as Honorary President of the Canada Cement Company and applied to Sir Wilfrid Laurier, a Liberal and the first French Canadian Prime Minister of Canada, for a government inquiry into the deal. Aitken had not in fact netted the lion's share of the twelve-million-dollar difference between the buying and selling prices of his string of cement companies; his associates in the slick transaction had their cut. Some of the newspapers in Canada were not concerned with such niceties; they turned upon him with fury, asking how near he had gone to the brink of illegality in his deals, calling into question the morality of the vast transformation of Canadian commercial practice for personal gain.

It was Aitken's Coronation honour that inspired the attack on him and his business methods in the *Toronto Globe* of 4 July 1911:

'The Knighting of Sir Max Aitken was probably not inspired by anyone in Canada. We should be greatly surprised to learn that the Government of Sir Wilfrid Laurier had anything to do with it.'

When concern was voiced in the Canadian Parliament, Laurier damped down the dust by suggesting that those aggrieved should go to the courts for their remedy. The dust did not settle so conveniently in Britain. The facts were paraded by A. G. Gardiner, the editor of the Liberal *Daily News*, and Aitken, ignoring Law's advice, replied in public in Manchester. The text of his rhetorical performance was simply— 'Gentlemen, these statements are false. (*Cheers.*) And more than that . . .' He denied he was responsible for an advance in the price of cement in Canada. He said his profit amounted to not one-twentieth, not one-thirtieth, and not one-fortieth of the amount stated. He also mentioned that the *Daily News* was the chief journal of fiction published in all England.

The figures he quoted on cement prices before-and-after were disputed in Canada; like any bonds salesman he stretched the years to prove his point. Fleming had been dead for six years when Aitken, then Lord Beaverbrook, referred to Canadian cement (no names mentioned) in his jaunty book *Success*, published in 1921:

> 'All the immense engines for the formation of public opinion which were at the disposal of the opposing forces were directed against me in the form of vulgar abuse. And that attack was very cleverly directed . . .
> 'I am prepared now to confess that I was bitterly hurt and injured by the injustice of these attacks. But I regret nothing. Why? Because these early violent criticisms taught me to treat ferocious attacks in later life with complete indifference.'

Aitken's indifference to criticism was a pose known to everyone near him. 'In future,' he said at Manchester in September 1911, 'curs may bark at my heels. I have not time to pick up stones to throw at them. The barking and howling does not bother me.' It did bother the barkers and the howlers: throughout his life he pursued them in unbridled vengeance with missiles ranging from flints to monumental mason's headstones.

There is evidence that he was anxious not to over-publicise some aspects of his past. After a short acquaintance with Churchill he sought to ingratiate himself by offering to organise a journey to Canada for the prominent British MP as his guest, honourably saying there was an objection to himself that Churchill must know about. He said in a letter that he had created all the big trusts in Canada; none of them bad, but the cause of frequent and sometimes very offensive attacks by the Western farmers. He didn't care, though Churchill might not like an intimate connection. The letter ended with a curious request: 'Please don't tell anybody I admitted I organised any trusts.'

The reasons a visit by Churchill did not take place are not known. What is known is that Beaverbrook's attempt to suppress his Canadian financial operations was futile. Saying that he liked Aitken personally, and describing him as a man of very high commercial ability as well as being thoroughly patriotic and public spirited, Churchill told the Liberal Chief Whip that Aitken would like to be appointed one of the British Commissioners on the Imperial Commission probing the Empire's trade resources. Aitken, if appointed, was willing to vacate his Parliamentary seat. He was not called upon to do so. The reply to Churchill came from the Prime Minister, Asquith himself, on 26 December 1911:

'Aitken is quite impossible. I take it that his Canadian record is of the shadiest, and when (at the instance of the Tories) he was made a Coronation knight, Albert Grey wrote to us that throughout the Dominion there was a howl of indignation and disgust.'[1]

Albert Grey was Earl Grey, Governor-General of Canada. As the representative of the Crown in the Dominion it is not likely he withheld from the Palace the report he sent to the Premier. That year Grey was succeeded by Prince Arthur, the first Duke of Connaught. Did Connaught neglect to attach interesting cuttings from the *Toronto Globe* and other newspapers to one of his private letters to his nephew, the King? And the Palace can scarcely have missed the profile of the immigrant written by Mr Gardiner in the *Daily News*.

Lord Beaverbrook, the expanding Press baron of the post-war years, was not as sensitive or secretive as the aspiring Sir Max about such matters. His earlier attempts to present the cement deal as a Sunday picnic—trivialising his personal profit, denying that cement prices rose, complaining he was bitterly hurt by the attacks—all vanished in a mighty guffaw. He told a bolder story just after the 1926 General Strike when advocating the merging of all British coal mines into a combine. His opponents exhumed the cement controversy, but this time he was not fighting an election in Ashton-under-Lyne. 'I was not concerned with the consumer one way or the other,' he said. 'My interests were two-fold : the first to make money, and the second was to sell the public a sound security . . . I succeeded in both these objects. I made a large sum of money and the value of the shares far exceeds today the price at which I put them on the market.'

Take that. And that. And that. But it was a different story.

I select Buckingham Palace as the vantage point for monitoring the progress of the Rage until the end of the First World War. King George V acceded in 1910, when Aitken arrived in London, and was crowned in 1911, when Aitken took his seat in the Commons. The young Canadian provoked a degree of irascibility in His Britannic Majesty and disapproval in Lord Stamfordham, the King's Private Secretary. For a man who 'at heart had a plain radical contempt for the glitter of rank and title' he collected honours with breathtaking speed and consistency, always hesitating, consulting his associates, but accepting.

[1] *Winston Churchill* by Randolph Churchill, Vol II, Heinemann (C. and T. Publications, Ltd), London, 1967.

Sir Max's refusal of a baronetcy in 1915, when Bonar Law joined Asquith's Coalition Government, bore the hallmark of self-effacement. He wrote that he was obliged to Law for the proposal, but must definitely decline because he felt certain the honour would be criticised on the grounds of their personal friendship; he did not want even a small thing like that to weaken Law's position at that time. The facts buckle the halo. Canada's wartime Prime Minister, Sir Robert Borden, rejected Law's suggestion that Aitken's name should appear on the colonial list for their highest order of chivalry; he had claimants of his own. So Law had to do what he wished to avoid, to recommend Aitken for a baronetcy on the personal list he shared as Unionist Leader in the Coalition Government with the Liberal Prime Minister Asquith. It was when Asquith said 'No' that Aitken wrote his letter of refusal, *at Bonar Law's request*. It is probable that news of this abortive transaction reached the ears of Stamfordham. It is also probable that from his own sources, including Bonar Law, the future Baron Beaverbrook was aware of the grumbling opposition of George V to the next three flights in his apotheosis. They occurred at yearly intervals, like the call of the cuckoo, beginning in 1916. The Royal displeasure mounted, establishing a Guinness record in gracelessness and disfavour.

They were awards to Aitken the wealthy and wily politician. He had not yet made his mark as a powerful and wily newspaper proprietor, yet Bonar Law had had reason to be grateful for his financial advice and political stimulus since 1910, and David Lloyd George was soon to come within his ambience. He was due for another gong, and this time Borden was willing—at Law's request—to commend Sir Max for his work as official Canadian Eye Witness in the European war, publicising his compatriots, and as Canadian military representative at the War Office; Lieutenant-Colonel Sir Max Aitken was now to be seen, when appropriate, in khaki.

On this occasion, the Duke of Connaught forwarded the recommendation from Canada with a private letter in which he stated, accurately or inaccurately, that Borden 'regretted an honour being conferred on a man with a Canadian reputation such as the particular individual possessed', and the King was unimpressed by the citation. Another snag was that the highest honour available on the colonial list was a KCMG and Sir Max had been assured a baronetcy, a recurring honour for his son, and his son's son. Law therefore had to place his name again on the list he shared with Asquith, and A. J. P. Taylor discovered that the King then 'objected that Aitken should appear on the Canadian list or not at all'. Objection ignored; baronet he became, and one year later his name was again before the reluctant monarch. This time the situation was Gilbertian, and finally ironical.

Lieutenant-Colonel Sir Max Aitken, Bt, MP, in his favourite role as a political puppeteer with Bonar Law at the end of the strings, had done more than any of the other conspirators to edge Asquith out of his wartime Premiership and Lloyd George in. The new Coalition was an urgent requirement to galvanise the country's war effort. Northcliffe was 'noises off', but Aitken was 'on stage', or more precisely in the prompter's box. He had reason to believe from the lips of the new man expected at No. 10 that he would become President of the Board of Trade, the department organising troop movements to France and in the forefront of the war effort. Incautiously, he told his constituency chairman in Ashton-under-Lyne of his impending elevation to the Cabinet and advised him to plan ahead for a by-election. Then he learned by chance from a Whitehall mandarin that Lloyd George's wheeler-dealing with the leading Tories he needed in his Coalition meant the Board of Trade going to Albert Stanley, later Lord Ashfield. Lloyd George offered Aitken a minor job which was refused, and then a peerage as balm to ease the wound to his dignity and the blow to his ambition. 'Why Aitken?' demanded Lord Derby. 'There are many Lancashire MP's with stronger claims to peerages than him.' But Aitken had to go to the Lords because the party needed his safe Lancashire seat for the man who had snatched his promised Cabinet job, Albert Stanley. The final drollery came from King George V. Asked for his consent to the peerage he demurred. The thruster was in the unenviable plight of being deprived of ministerial office, losing his Parliamentary seat, and being locked out of the Lords though he had already chosen his title; he had paddled and fished in Beaver Brook as a boy.

Harold Nicolson described the solemnity accorded the matter at Buckingham Palace, omitting the name of the angry Lord-in-waiting:

'The King when asked for his consent replied that he did not "see his way" to approve of this honour, since he did not consider that the "public services" of the individual in question "called for such special recognition". Mr Lloyd George replied that any refusal would "place him in a position of great embarrassment" and begged Lord Stamfordham to discuss the matter with Mr Bonar Law. The latter divulged that, not only had the individual himself been informed of his intended elevation, but that the Conservative Association in his constituency had been told . . .'[1]

[1]*King George V, His Life and Reign* by Harold Nicolson, Constable, London, 1952.

Stamfordham informed the Prime Minister in a letter that he could not conceal from him His Majesty's surprise and hurt that this honour should have been offered without first obtaining his consent. It is a piquant reflection on the peculiarities and vanities of the British Establishment, at that moment in instant danger of extinction, that the new Prime Minister was obliged to exercise his mind over protocol as well as national survival. Lloyd George did not reply to the King's rebuke and refused to put his views in writing. He did, however, make a promise in private audience that he would not fail to communicate His Majesty's views verbally to the members of the Cabinet. Thus ended the wrangle between the monarch and the premier on whether a boy who sold papers at the age of twelve should be allowed to join the humblest of the five ranks of the peerage, wear a stoat's winter coat as a collar to his scarlet mantle, enjoy exemption from jury service and the right of personal access to a sovereign who would not wish to meet him, and lose (with lunatics) his right to vote in a general election. In Canada Sir Max's elevation was treated as a joke.

The embarrassment at Buckingham Palace continued. Peer he became in December 1916, and one year later the name of the eager beaver was again before the King. The Aitken/Sir Max/Sir Max Aitken, Bt/Lord Beaverbrook File in Stamfordham's office was well-thumbed. Beaverbrook certainly knew about, and wrote about, the third Royal rebuff in February 1918, when Lloyd George appointed him Minister of Information in the last year of the war. He would not accept the role without a ministerial rank to guarantee authority, and Lloyd George agreed he should become Chancellor of the Duchy of Lancaster. King George disagreed. Beaverbrook told his version of the rumpus in one of his historical books:[1]

'A powerful complaint came from Buckingham Palace. This concerned my position as Chancellor of the Duchy. It was reported that the King was disturbed by the idea of a Presbyterian administering the ecclesiastic preferments of the Crown. I did not believe it. But of a certainty he was animated by no great personal liking for me.

'I was told that he was really hostile and that his dislike flowed in part from the old story when Balfour lost the leadership of the Tory Party [to Bonar Law] that behind the scenes was the "little Canadian adventurer". Then again when Asquith tumbled down there was the charge of "intrigue" which the fallen Liberal Ministers had spread.'

[1]*Men and Power, 1917-1918* by Lord Beaverbrook, Hutchinson, London, 1956.

The supposed objection on Presbyterian grounds, cited by nobody other than Beaverbrook, was flattering fiction; neither Jews nor Catholics, or for that matter the Highland 'Wee Frees', were refused the Duchy on the grounds of faith. It was the 'little Canadian adventurer' legend that was worrying Buckingham Palace. They had their own information about the odium surrounding the earlier honours. Stamfordham defined the King's hostility in a letter to the Chief Whip of Bonar Law's party when Beaverbrook's dual appointment was disclosed. 'His Majesty,' wrote the Private Secretary, 'expressed much surprise that, considering past circumstances, he should now be asked to agree to Lord Beaverbrook presiding over the Duchy, which, as it were, is the personal property of the Sovereign and entailing closer relations between the King and its Chancellor than with many of his Ministers . . .'

The Duchy was appropriated to the Crown in 1461 as part of the Royal inheritance; its Chancellor's duty is to administer the estates for the sovereign's wellbeing, handing over the revenues annually. The phrase *considering past circumstances* could only mean, offensively, past circumstances in relation to the proposed Chancellor. Stamfordham concluded: 'I must again assure you that the Prime Minister in saying that he was thinking of employing Lord Beaverbrook in the Propaganda Department, never referred in merely any way to the Duchy of Lancaster . . .'

Beaverbrook was happy to record that Lloyd George sent 'a firm answer back', expressing his certainty that as a first-rate businessman Lord Beaverbrook would administer the Duchy well. Beaverbrook's Royal itch lasted longer than the Palace's Beaverbrook itch. The little Canadian adventurer didn't forget.

The approaching armistice in November 1918 released him from Westminster to launch his third and most explosive career as a newspaper proprietor in Fleet Street. Previous experience was sparse. *The Canadian Century*, a puny highbrow weekly he founded himself, was of no account. In London he bought the pink-hued *Globe*, an ailing London evening newspaper, for next to nothing, squandered £50,000 on it and then gave some industrialist £5,000 to take it out of his sight. The significant sortie was his involvement with the *Express*, edited by Ralph D. Blumenfeld, and also in financial difficulties. In January 1911, Beaverbrook approached Blumenfeld to canvas the support of the *Express* for Bonar Law and also to report his own activities so that the paragraphs might be reproduced in newspapers in Ashton-under-Lyne and Canada. A result of their association was a Beaverbrook loan of £25,000 to the paper. In November 1916, at Blumenfeld's suggestion, he bought the controlling shares of the *Express*, inheriting its debts and committing himself to further expenditure on newsprint. As always, he sought advice and hesitated before he moved. Lord Rothermere, warning him of the financial risks and personal effort involved, told him to go ahead, thus creating the greatest competition Northcliffe's *Daily Mail* ever faced. Northcliffe himself was less encouraging, seeking to frighten him off:

N: 'How much are you worth?'
B: 'Over five million dollars.'
N: 'You will lose it all in Fleet Street.'

By 1954 the circulation of the *Daily Express* rose from probably less than 250,000 to over four million. In the same time the newspaper bought for £17,500 achieved a market value of over £7,000,000. The new proprietor's object was solely to use the Press for political propaganda to influence the political leaders: the quest was for power. In December 1918 Beaverbrook founded the *Sunday Express*. 'I may claim,' he wrote, 'to have become a full-blooded journalist just before the General Election of 1918.' And he began as he intended to go on, using his newspapers as the new base for his political intrigues, wooing other Press proprietors to dinner with Lloyd George at No. 10 Downing Street to marshal support for the Coalition Government at the polls.

Beaverbrook was nearly forty when he set his hand to establishing his newspapers as permanent institutions that would assure his influence and preferably make a profit. The heady wine of newspaper power was pleasing to his palate. His newspapers became the absorbing passion of his life. To the *Express*, Daily and Sunday, he devoted his energy, cunning, leadership and ideas, and he knew that the only way through was to achieve an excellence that would dwarf the records set by Northcliffe. He was happy to plough the first profits of the *Daily Express* back into the newspaper, but his blooding on the more sombre aspects of proprietorship came swiftly with the newspaper he created. Blumenfeld's estimated risk of £20,000 to launch the new *Sunday Express* escalated to £150,000 in the first year and £300,000 in the second while the initial circulation of 300,000 fell to 155,000. Two million pounds of his Canadian resources were drained before the paper moved into the black.

The *Daily Express* developed as a human interest paper in pursuit of the *Daily Mail*, visibly weakening under the control of the first Lord Rothermere after Northcliffe's death in 1922. The *Sunday Express*, when it got its second wind after four years, offered well-advertised, circulation-raising big-name series, lapsing rarely to the level of Mrs

Thompson's love letters to the murderer Bywaters and rising occasionally to H. G. Wells's record of his journey to Communist Russia. Financial scandals were a speciality, fascinating the chief shareholder more than the readers. The policy of both papers was to avoid raw sex and the sordid and to peddle romanticism and escape, ever yearning for the good and gay life of High Society beyond the reach of its readers but now within the grasp of the proprietor.

The *Sunday Express* was long in the doldrums with a mortality rate among its early editors equalled only by Rothermere's *Daily Mail*. The biggest flop in the chair was James Douglas, the same Douglas who later made his name on the same paper as the apostle of spontaneous moral indignation. He upbraided Lord Dawson of Penn, a Royal physician and Lloyd George's as well, for defending birth control, which moved Ll.G. to write to Dawson: 'When Beaverbrook holds up hands steeped in the blood of the slaughtered commandments to express horror at your speech it beats the record for disgusting hypocrisy.' Beaverbrook was happy to foist sanctimonious nonsense on his middle-class readers while conducting his private life as a parody of the unctuous Douglas dictum.

In 1922 he announced that the *Express* stood for 'More life—more hope—more money—more work—more happiness—the creed which is going to redeem Great Britain from the harsh aftermath of war, and set her feet once again on the path to prosperity.' Who was against more life, hope, money, and happiness, then or now? He chose the cosy course of being furiously anti-Labour in any election and naggingly anti-Conservative when the Conservatives were in government.

Ralph Blumenfeld was respected in his own profession and outside, but too absorbed in politics and too much of a gentleman to evolve the sort of newspapers that could reflect Beaverbrook's personality and attract the vast audience he was seeking. Beaverbrook said that he carried the *Daily Express* to greatness with the aid of a bell-hop and a piano-tuner—E. J. Robertson and Beverley Baxter, both Canadians. He met the first when Robertson was financing his own education at college as a hotel worker during vacation, an established Canadian custom. Baxter, when he met Beaverbrook for the second time on a ship returning from England to Canada, was a piano salesman with ambitions to become a concert pianist and/or professional singer. Robertson became the shrewdest management man of his time in the newspaper industry in Britain, and Baxter did his sophisticated best when the Beaver turned him into a journalist and editor successively of the daily and Sunday papers.

The editorial excellence of the products was not conspicuous until John Gordon from Dundee became editor of the *Sunday Express* in 1928 and Arthur Christiansen from Lancashire of the *Daily Express* in 1933. Baxter, in his time, dropped into the office to peruse the proofs of the last edition in white tie and tails after an evening at Covent Garden, a West End theatre, or a late dinner with his cultured friends. Christiansen worked in the office at night in his shirt sleeves. Beaverbrook needed those two professionals who knew how to organise the flow of news, how to present the goods in the supermarket, and sustain an atmosphere of perpetual suspense. They buttressed the Beaver as a newspaper tycoon until he became a full-blooded journalist himself, and he paid them well to do so.

As an impresario Beaverbrook assembled around him a galaxy of writers and cartoonists without equal in the newspaper world: Hannen Swaffer, David Low, licensed to caricature the boss and his policies in his cartoons, Valentine Castlerosse, the gossip-writing Irish viscount nurtured by the baron and described by Lady Astor as 'Beaverbrook's Buttons'. There were H. V. Morton (*In the Footsteps of Christ*: Next Week—*The Mount of Olives*), J. B. ('Beachcomber') Morton, James Agate, Sefton Delmer, Osbert Lancaster, Giles, Nathaniel Gubbins, Strube and his 'Little Man' and dozens of book, film and theatre reviewers.

Frank Owen was Beaverbrook's 'ghost' on economic policy, and the brilliant, subtle George Malcolm Thomson, still now writing his own books at the age of eighty, wrote the boss's articles and editorials on foreign affairs. Beaverbrook persuaded Arnold Bennett, Bertrand Russell and the acid pessimist Dean Inge to become his contributors as well as H. G. Wells. Inge wrote regularly in the *Evening Standard* on the imminent collapse of Christian civilisation and Bennett reviewed books in an elegant weekly article; to be mentioned even disdainfully by the master was the foundation of many a novelist's career. Rayner Goddard also wrote for the *Evening Standard* on crime and punishment while sitting as Lord Chief Justice. When my brother, Percy Cudlipp, was editing the Beaver's *Evening Standard* in the inter-war years the anonymous contributors to its Londoner's Diary included Robert Bruce Lockhart, Harold Nicolson, Malcolm Muggeridge and Randolph Churchill.

The Beaver's success as a journalist was that he had the same insatiable curiosity as Northcliffe and Luce. His newspapers knew what was going on, but apart from the news of the day, large areas of which were presented without bias, the readers could never be sure *they* knew what was going on. Political news and opinion were subject to the chief shareholder's fiat. The personal beliefs of the writing journalists who laboured near the sun were shrivelled by its heat. They wrote with the courage of his convictions, Beaverbrook's, and wrote in his style, influenced by American newspapers and magazines and, curiously, the Old Testament. They consoled their consciences with an easy cynicism and a fat cheque. But, hell, it was fun for them.

The Beaverbrook familiar to the British public and the publishing world emerged as soon as his newspapers were successful. He knew a millionaire need never be lonely; he also found that newspapers opened more doors than cement or steel. Politicians, industrialists, film magnates, famous writers, actors and actresses, and the darlings of Society were at his beck and call and he was the generous host. People of real talent or true independence in public life were impervious to Beaverbrook's Law, but only the foolish or the brave went out of their way to insult the *Daily Express*, the *Sunday Express*, or the *Evening Standard* and make an enemy of him. Who wouldn't be a Press baron in London rather than a company promoter in Montreal or a bonds salesman anywhere in the world?

The Hyde Park Hotel was his abode until it lost its convenience as a permanent address. The Vineyard, a small Tudor house in Fulham, seemed more appropriate, with a film projector in the dining-room and a tennis court, a compact London HQ where he could meet his political and financial contacts in privacy. Lloyd George, Bonar Law, Churchill and Birkenhead were frequent visitors; he did not lack less serious company. Entertaining on a more lavish scale was for the weekends at Cherkley Court, a monstrosity of a house he bought near Leatherhead and tarted up with a tennis court, swimming pool and cinema. The latest films were borrowed by his reviewers from the movie companies in London and his favourites like *Destry Rides Again* (the Western with the sultry, leggy Marlene Dietrich as the saloon songstress and sexpot) were shown again and again. Prurience was a change from Presbyterianism.

With Gladys and his sons and daughter parked away at Cherkley, he enjoyed the Roaring Twenties as a playboy with a purpose. The powerful, the promising, the storytellers, the witty and the beautiful were welcome at his table : he did not suffer the foolish or the plain. He became a figure in the social scene, flitting between Deauville and Monte Carlo with his guests. He became a racehorse owner, acquired a yacht, and multiplied his millions by an entry into the film industry. These were the roisterous years in the Beaverbrook saga, and his sexual track-record was not the least of his accomplishments; he did not expend all his energy on money-making. Alan Wood, an Australian who became a *Daily Express* war correspondent in 1943 and stayed in the group as a policy writer, made a shrewd observation on these affairs:

'It seemed that Beaverbrook would take special delight in tumbling the pride of society women. One of his editors was a little disconcerted on one occasion, on being summoned to get some instructions, to find Lady ------- sitting on his lap, caressing his face with her hand the whole time Beaverbrook talked. Another editor complained that what annoyed him most, on being woken early in the morning by Beaverbrook shouting criticism down the phone about something in the paper, was to hear feminine laughter in the intervals of Beaverbrook's sallies, and to realise that the performance was simply designed to amuse some girl with him.'

Mr Wood took the solemn view that a public man's private life should be treated as his own affair, but before hurrying on to other aspects of Beaverbrook's career he did record for posterity this romantic interlude:

'The talk of the town was to touch on several of Beaverbrook's affairs, beginning with a muscial comedy actress who had taken part in a film made about the time of his period as Minister of Information. She described him as her best lover since Little Tich, her first; she liked to describe his habit of giving a great shout of laughter every time and it was gossip about this affair which largely accounted for Beaverbrook's later unpopularity in provincial Ashton-under-Lyne, where Lady Beaverbrook was idolised.'[1]

The forgiving Gladys sent signals of distress when he overtly made Mrs Jean Norton, a noted beauty, his regular mistress and attendant at social engagements; and one event, in those playboy years, caused distress to Beaverbrook himself. In December of 1927 his wife died from heart failure at forty-two. Sir Thomas Horder broke the news and it is said that the Rage cried like a child. The letters that passed between them in the final years give evidence of her enduring love for him and of his sense of guilt. He railed against the doctors for forbidding him, to avoid excitement, to visit her as she was dying. He erected an illuminated cross at Cherkley 'to remind me that I'm a Christian', he told Hannen Swaffer. Birkenhead wrote of Gladys Drury:

'She had a beauty, a poise, and a judgement which would have recommended her to any society in Europe at the most critical moment

[1] *The True History of Lord Beaverbrook* by Alan Wood, Heinemann, London, 1965.

of that society . . . She was essentially womanly, and being womanly she was incredibly understanding. She made allowances easily and generously.'

Lady Beaverbrook died at Stornoway House, a residence of some elegance near St James's Palace, overlooking Green Park. Her 'My Lord dear Lord' and 'My Beloved One', as she endearingly addressed him in her domestic notes, had acquired the property in 1924 when she had complained of her isolation at Cherkley Court between the weekend parties. Beaverbrook now abandoned the Vineyard in Fulham and transformed Stornoway into his London home and office, installing half a score of secretaries.

William Maxwell Aitken's character was enigmatic or complex only to those who took him at his own valuation or were well-rewarded to pretend so to do. The aura of Old Testament Prophet was sustained throughout his life in Britain by his biblical allusions and quotations. They became tedious, but who dared say so?

'I hoped to see the British Empire united in one economic unit. Again and again the prospect seemed almost realised, but on every occasion the golden gates closed on it.'

'I have touched the ivory on the golden gates with my finger tips, but I have never got within.'

'The Temple of Success is based on the three pillars of Health, Industry and Judgement . . .'

'How long, O Lord, how long must we listen to those who give us false counsel and persuade us to walk in ways that bring us to low estate and bitter humiliation? How long must we submit to this leader, Mr Baldwin?'

Only the credulous believed there was any deep religious conviction. He had learned the Bible like a parrot in his father's Presbyterian church and studied the good book for oratorical rather than spiritual inspiration throughout his life: it was an ingredient of the personality he decided to project. He wrote *The Divine Propagandist*, setting out his own thoughts on the meaning of Christ to mankind, but the moral force of His life and His teaching had no discernible impact on the private or public life of the author of that slim volume. As soon as his Presbyterian mumbo-jumbo is taken at its real and not its face value, the man behind the tanned, furrowed mask becomes comprehensible. Aitken was the political equivalent of Edward G. Robinson in the film *Little Caesar*. To an uncanny degree he physically resembled the stocky, growling Hollywood actor; they had the same jaunty walk, and in their moments of rage their nasal accents were similar. Ronald Neame, casting his film *The Magic Box*, tried to get Robinson to play the Beaverbrook part. Little Caesar was a small-time hoodlum and Lord Beaverbrook was a company promoter, politician, and newspaper tycoon, but they shared a determination to get to the top by any means at hand.

Max's political perception was acute, and mischievous. His support was invaluable, and mercurial. His mental gifts were adulterated by his addiction to intrigue. He liked to be the 'honest broker' with a foot in both camps, negotiating a peace that suited himself. Hugh Kingsmill called him 'Robin Badfellow' and few praised him without qualification. The menace of the man, with his roaring personality and his talent for communication, was the unreality of his 'causes'. The public would have been hoodwinked had they bought his newspapers for political guidance instead of for entertainment. Imperial economic unity, or Empire Free Trade, was an impracticable pipedream. Splendid Isolation from Europe was a panacea that scared the feathers off even the most senile of ostriches. The rest of his policies were transient attitudes, dictated by expedience or headline heroics, that sprang from his basic misconceptions. Percy Cudlipp, when editing the *Evening Standard*, observed to me in a moment of disillusion: 'No cause is really lost until we support it.'

Beaverbrook's vendetta against Stanley Baldwin was an example of the use of his newspapers to stalk and seek to destroy a public man who would not bend to his will. The vehemence of his denial that there was ever a vendetta was the sort of ruse that led people to call him enigmatic or complex. It was a lie, with the evidence in his newspapers and public speeches.

Friendship with the straitlaced English country gentleman, a leading Westminster figure for fourteen years and Prime Minister three times, was unlikely to blossom from Kipling's cheery introduction. They were both rich, Beaverbrook vastly more so, and Baldwin hadn't played Monopoly on the Montreal Stock Exchange. The member for Bewdley, Worcs. (Harrow and Trinity College, Cambridge) inherited his constituency from his father, Alfred. The only son also inherited Alfred's iron and steel engineering company, Baldwins, Ltd, and some collieries, but not until Stanley had run the business himself for twenty years. The gaiety and roguery of Max was a passport to the affections of other brilliant roguish men. The homespun Stanley Baldwin shunned such frivolity; his name was never in the guest books at the Vineyard or Cherkley Court. His private life was blameless.

Aitken put Baldwin's foot on the first rung of the political ladder when he produced a short-list of three MPs for the post of Parliamentary Private Secretary to Chancellor Bonar Law in 1916. They chuckled Stanley into the job because he was listed as 'rich, reticent, and neutral in character'; just the man. In 1918, when he was on the second rung as Joint Financial Secretary to the Treasury, it was his duty to defend the Minister of Information, then under fire for enrolling big-business buddies as heads of departments. He said Beaverbrook was a man of very strong personality, adding unfelicitously that the magnetism which came with that personality 'either attracts or repels'. He referred to the English dislike of self-advertisement and deftly mentioned that he could speak with perfect freedom because there was no intimacy between them. What the junior minister said to a hostile House of Commons fell short of idolatry. He did his duty as Government spokesman, no more and no less, in one sentence: 'Lord Beaverbrook has taken on a most difficult, delicate, and thankless task . . . Give him a fair chance, and judge him by results.'

It was not friendship at first sight, nor hatred. But the feud that lasted twelve years until the Abdication Crisis of 1936 ended with the hostility between them deeply etched. 'Reconciliation?' said Beaverbrook. 'Reconciliation? I never want to be reconciled to him. Baldwin could do so many diabolical things and get away with them. He used to make me so frantic.' Baldwin's scepticism towards Beaverbrook developed into contempt and then loathing. The countryman who enjoyed Mary Webb's rustic novels and puffed at a pipe had a natural antipathy to the political swashbucklers who fascinated London society and bartered their talents in coalitions. He had a crusade of his own; to purge the body politic of what to him was the corrupting influence of the wayward geniuses.

Beaverbrook's friend, ally and political jemmy was Bonar Law until his death. Law headed the first post-war Tory Government and with Beaverbrook's approval Baldwin became Chancellor of the Exchequer. Without Beaverbrook's influence or opposition he succeeded to the Premiership in 1923, outmanoeuvring Lord Curzon when Law was forced to stand down some months before he died of throat cancer. Sir Thomas Horder, his own physician, told Beaverbrook of the nature of his friend's ill health and said the end would be soon; he swayed and stumbled, deeply distressed.

'Something was severed in my political associations,' wrote

Beaverbrook in *Politicians and the Press*; 'I had never cared much for the purely political life, but Bonar's charm, his urbanity, his wisdom, his firm and reasonable attitude towards all problems, held me like a silken chain.' He over-dramatised that friendship of convenience. The dying Bonar said to Max, who was at his side throughout the final months, 'You are a curious fellow.' It was the end of Beaverbrook's influence behind the scenes because Lloyd George had fallen from power and Churchill was changing his party allegiance. Until Churchill came to supreme power in 1940 Beaverbrook's only weapon was his newspapers. The go-between moved into the shadows, but not the go-getter. His papers were prospering, setting up their own printing plants in Manchester and Glasgow as well as London. The ownership of newspapers, he said, was only for the very strong, the very healthy, the very vigorous; he could have added, in his case, the very cunning and very vindictive.

Baldwin told his biographer G. M. Young that what was 'between' him and Beaverbrook was Bonar Law; they 'both fought for his soul'. Certainly their last act in unison was as pallbearers when the man called the Unknown Prime Minister was buried in Westminster Abbey after shrill demands by the *Express*, supported by the *Mail* ('Get Rothermere on the phone') that Law should be accorded that honour. The first rift was caused by Baldwin's inept handling as Chancellor of Britain's war debts to America. His neglect to consult or inform Beaverbrook before or after that or any other decision was sufficient cause for ill will. His resolve to fight another election within a year of Bonar Law's carefully orchestrated victory of 1922, ignoring warnings by Beaverbrook and others, was an act of defiance.

The importance of Beaverbrook at that time to most of the leading politicians except Baldwin is indicated by the guest list at a Cherkley party just before polling day. Lloyd George and Churchill were there, and Austen Chamberlain and Birkenhead—the old coalitionists and, incongruously, Arnold Bennett. Beaverbrook's ploy that weekend was to inspire an amalgam of Conservative and Liberal Free Traders under Lloyd George's leadership, a new centre party that he forlornly hoped would eventually espouse Imperial Preference by a stretching of the rules. Unfortunately Arnold Bennett blew the gaffe to a reporter that the meeting had taken place; didn't mean to, but did. How absurd, said Beaverbrook when the news was published, to represent that social occasion as a sinister intrigue.

In the 1923 election Baldwin lost Bonar Law's overall Tory majority. The Labour Party, as the second largest in the House, formed a government for the first time in its history. Churchill, fighting for the last time as a Liberal, lost his seat. There was no doubt who would pay the price for the shambles. Vendetta? Beaverbrook disavowed such nonsense; he said he had always been ready to agree with Baldwin when he was right. The launching date of the anti-Baldwin campaign can be pinpointed as 17 February 1924, when the reds from under the beds first sat on the right-hand side of the Speaker in the Commons and Beaverbrook sneered in the *Sunday Express* not at them but at the leader of the Tory Party:

'Mr Baldwin is in the descending scale of values . . . Now that he is stripped of power and *patronage* he must rely on his own capabilities as a parliamentarian in opposition. Here his qualifications have so far proved of second rank—suited to a minor post, adequate for an Under-Secretary but far below the level of a Prime Minister or a Leader of the Opposition.'

The next irritation for the Tory Leader occurred in March 1924 when Churchill, unhorsed as a Liberal in Dundee, decided to select another mount. The local Tory association in the Abbey Division of Westminster, right on Parliament's doorstep, were either off their political heads or following Baldwin's guidance, or both, when they rejected him as official Tory candidate. He fought the by-election as an Independent Constitutionalist advocating Conservative social reform and, to secure the support of Beaverbrook and his newspapers, Imperial Preference. The *Express* and the *Mail* campaigned for him with enthusiasm and he scored only forty-three votes fewer than the official Tory candidate. It was the first time these newspapers, hitherto loyal to the Conservative Party in elections, had strayed. What was their real intention? Beaverbrook, for one, was soon seeing Churchill as the man to oust Baldwin from the Tory leadership. The former Tory MP and former Liberal MP, now seeking to return to the Tory fold as an agile floor-crosser, was also a politician with panache and twenty-two years of Parliamentary experience, much of it as a Minister.

The 'rich, reticent neutral' struck back with a ferocity that astonished his admirers and critics and caused a political sensation, choosing—even more astonishingly—a newspaper as his vehicle. Behind the façade he had the capacity and will for revenge. On 18 May 1924 the *People*, then an independent conservative newspaper controlled by another Canadian financier, Colonel Grant Morden, appeared with the headline:

BALDWIN TURNS AND RENDS
HIS CRITICS

After the opening stanzas dealing with the Party's social programme, the interview with Our Political Correspondent was bitingly personal:

'I was determined that never again should the sinister and cynical combination of the chief three of the Coalition—Mr Lloyd George, Mr Churchill, and Lord Birkenhead—come together again. But today you can see the signs of the times.

'If his [Birkenhead's] health does not give way he will be a liability to the Party. But can a leader in opposition shut the door to an ex-Minister? [The health hint about Birkenhead referred to his inordinate thirst.]

'I am attacked by the Trust Press, by Lord Beaverbrook and Lord Rothermere. For myself I do not mind. I care not what they say or think. They are both men that I would not have in my house. I do not respect them. Who are they?

'Besides, all this intrigue—this Churchill plotting—is bad for the Party, for all the young men who are looking to Toryism for the salvation of the country. What do these intriguers want? Simply to go back to the old dirty kind of politics. Not while I'm leader of the Party.'

The frankness of the interview was unprecedented. Baldwin, of course, repudiated it, and a formidable legal adviser was soon at his elbow, Sir Douglas Hogg, the first Viscount Hailsham. Baldwin issued a denial to the Press Association to circulate to all newspapers. He wrote a personal letter to everybody mentioned including the time-honoured phrase: 'I hope you will know me well enough . . .' He was deeply distressed, grossly misrepresented, etc. Nobody who knew about newspapers considered for a moment that such an interview with all its implications could conceivably have been faked. It had been arranged by officials of the Conservative Central Office. Beaverbrook, who knew about newspapers, was the one man to whom Baldwin addressed his personal disclaimer who did not reply.

The story of why Ramsay MacDonald's first Labour Government crumbled and how the Tories were swept back to power with a majority of 211 over all other parties combined in the 'Zinoviev Letter' election of 1924 was related in Chapter III. Baldwin was in Downing Street for the second time. Churchill, who had fought and won a Tory seat but not this time as an advocate of Imperial Preference, was appointed his Chancellor of the Exchequer; the simple countryman knew that the wayward geniuses had their price. The omens were favourable to Beaverbrook, but not for long. In his favourite role as Iago he calculated that Baldwin had foolishly opened the door to his successor as leader of the Conservatives, but Churchill's first budget—returning to the Gold Standard—ruptured the friendship. It was the first prolonged quarrel between Churchill and Beaverbrook, who now again had no friend at court.

His next manoeuvres were erratic and transparently mischievous. They can scarcely have bent the minds of his readers, though each of his capers was inflicted upon them. David Low depicted Beaverbrook and Rothermere in his cartoons as the Wicked Uncles and Baldwin as the innocent Babe in the Wood. In May 1925 Beaverbrook wrote an article in the *Sunday Express* with the headline: 'The Government Arraigned'. 'I never thought,' he said, 'that Baldwin himself would be so good or his Government so bad.' It was the kiss-and-clout technique. At the same time the *Daily Express* was prophesying that independent Conservatives would again emerge, supported 'quite likely' by the *Express*. Baldwin concentrated on the clout, awaiting the next opportunity.

Could a political party possibly survive when the most popular papers that nominally supported it were engaged in ridiculing the leader? The *Spectator* asked and answered the question in October 1925: 'The persecution of Mr Baldwin has passed beyond reason and decency . . . [but] the Press is less powerful than it seems to be . . . Mr Baldwin passes serenely on his way without paying any attention . . .' *Truth* reminded Beaverbrook that 'responsibility goes with power'. The editor of the *Weekly Westminster*, a Liberal, was more pungent in a remark about his book *Politicians and the Press*: 'This trivial little book . . . displays the working, at the heart of our national life, of a dangerous, irresponsible, and corrupting power.'

In 1928, surviving a car crash, Beaverbrook asked Baldwin to divide £25,000 on his behalf between any medical institutions the Prime Minister would care to select. The cat was playing with the mouse, beguiling it with a pussy-pat before he made his next pounce. He did not know that Mrs Baldwin was encouraging Stanley in his more aggressive postures with cries of 'Tiger Baldwin . . . Tiger Baldwin'. He did not grasp then, or until too late, that he underestimated his man. Lloyd George, excluded for the rest of his time from public life by Baldwin, had dismissed him as of little or no account; Lord Curzon was bitterly shaken when the mediocrity he regarded as of the 'utmost insignificance' was summoned to Buckingham Palace to succeed Bonar Law as Prime Minister. The slow-moving, non-pretentious, you-can-trust-me Englishness of the man appealed to the British public. The politicians who tried to topple him never realised that when roused the iron from his father's foundry could enter his soul. This was no cat-and-mouse frolic: the steel speculator was challenging the ironmaster.

There was applause in his own three newspapers, nowhere else, when the Beaver re-entered the political arena in 1929 with an apology for his absence. The greatest world financial depression of all time was developing after the collapse of the New York stock exchange. The British unemployed drew attention to their plight with a hunger march from Glasgow to Trafalgar Square. The disclosures of Clarence Hatry's fourteen-million-pound frauds, chicken feed by current standards, led people to question the integrity of big business and the City. India was granted Dominion status. The word *apartheid* was heard for the first time in South Africa. Italy elected an all-Fascist parliament and France laid the foundations of the Maginot Line. In Britain Stanley Baldwin's Government reached the end of its term of office and the second Labour Government, still with a slender majority and MacDonald as its leader, came to power. In the literary world that year R. C. Sherriff's *Journey's End* seemed to express the mood and the events more than J. B. Priestley's *The Good Companions*.

At the close of Baldwin's second Government (October 1924—May 1929) *The Times* had said that 'In the Parliaments of the last fifty years only two or three will be found to rival in quality and quantity the output of the past four years.' The British public threw the Conservatives out. The achievement of the five-power Locarno Pact, recognising European frontiers and outlawing the use of force, had less impact in the industrial areas than the unwavering continuance of 1,200,000 unemployed. The Government had introduced the 'flapper vote' and the young were more significant than in any previous election. Yet Baldwin's appeal to the electorate was 'Safety First', proclaimed on hoardings throughout the land with posters illustrated with the immobile face of Honest Stanley, with pipe. He once claimed that his worst enemy could never say he did not understand the people of England: his best friend could never say he was capable of inspiring them.

The Labour Party were no more inspired in that election. The reply to the 'Safety First' slogan was the political cliché 'It's Time for a Change'. The only spark of imagination came from Lloyd George and the Liberal Party, now united under his leadership. The cry was '*We Can Cure Unemployment. We Mobilised for War—Let us Mobilise for Prosperity.*' The total vote for the Conservatives was higher than for Labour, but Labour won 288 seats against the Tories' 260 and the Liberals' 59. The high Liberal vote had undermined the Tories. King George V for the second time summoned Mr MacDonald to Buckingham Palace.

The Tories were inconsolable, and the Wicked Uncles displayed some ingenuity in their recriminations before they again fell upon Mr Baldwin in person. The *Daily Mail*'s lament was that 'Conservatism as it was led before the General Election was not Conservatism. It was the semi-Socialist policy that went down in the great defeat.' The paper opposed the provision of any vacant seats in future for 'semi-Socialists such as Captain Harold Macmillan', who had lost Stockton-on-Tees. Beaverbrook deplored that neither Baldwin's Tories nor MacDonald's Socialists hardly mentioned the Empire in the election. On 30 June 1919, one month to the day after the election, he was asking, 'Who is for the Empire?' In the *Sunday Express* he wrote: 'I stand in the dock with all those I indict. The fiscal union of the Empire will only be achieved by a crusade carried on by those animated by the crusading spirit.' On 7 July he said that the Crusade should be independent of all parties.

Summer is a close season for newspaper campaigning, and Beaverbrook was committed to a vacation trip to Russia with Arnold Bennett, Lady Louis Mountbatten, Mrs Jean Norton, and a few other friends; he was the first former British Cabinet Minister to visit the first Communist country. His return at the beginning of winter was the signal for activity. The readers of the *Express* were not, of course, told about the wheeler-dealing behind the scenes in November 1929. Beaverbrook's only link and leak in the Cabinet, Sir Samuel Hoare, compèred the first meeting between Beaverbrook and Neville Chamberlain, an avowed opponent of Empire Free Trade; he had three objections to the policy—obsolescence, impracticability, mischievousness. His offer was that the Conservatives would not declare themselves *against* food taxes.

On 11 November, Armistice Day, Baldwin, pressed by Neville Chamberlain, proposed a meeting at his home at Upper Brook Street; the man who said he would never have Beaverbrook in his house was making that one concession. On most occasions they were evenly matched but at this confrontation the guile was Baldwin's and the innocence Beaverbrook's. The Tory Leader put his cards, or one of them, on the table; he urged his unwelcome guest to present the Empire Free Trade case in the House of Lords so that it could be discussed in a Parliamentary fashion with dignity, and Beaverbrook agreed. The trap was that oratory had no place in the Lords, and Beaverbrook was no debater; Baldwin, if he intended to yield at all, would not be yielding to a Press baron vulgarly hollering in a newspaper. The meeting itself was courteous on both sides.

Beaverbrook initiated a debate on 19 November and their lordships heard him with curiosity. He was not a familiar figure in the Upper House though the subject was: the warring of the old members over Free Trade and Tariff Reform had begun when Max Aitken, aged twenty-one, was dedicating his life to Mammon in Halifax, Nova Scotia. The discord in the

Press reports about their lordships' response is of interest. The *Daily Telegraph* observed 'opposition from all sides'; the *Liverpool Post and Mercury* thought 'the audience was cold'; the *Daily Express* said that Lord Beaverbrook was 'warmly cheered from all sides of the House'. The loudest cheer ever heard in that assembly is a muttered 'hear hear' or a clearing of the throat.

There was another example a few days later of over-reaction, or proprietorial reporting, by the *Express*. Baldwin, addressing a Tory rally in London, expressed the customary sentimental thoughts about Britain's Imperial role in the world. Then, lazily proffering an olive branch, he told his supporters: 'We owe a word of gratitude to one not always a supporter of our party, Lord Beaverbrook, for bringing before the country once more that idea . . . of a united Empire. I pay tribute to his courage—rare in one of his profession—in offering a subject he believes in to criticism in its proper place—the Houses of Parliament.' His reference to Beaverbrook was as likely to provoke a jeer as a cheer. He did not espouse the cause of Empire Free Trade, but the readers of the *Daily Express* were presented the next morning with these headlines:

MR BALDWIN'S GREAT EMPIRE SPEECH
NEW CONSERVATIVE POLICY
STRONG TRIBUTE TO LORD BEAVERBROOK
MR BALDWIN'S PLEDGE
VISION OF A UNITED COMMONWEALTH

Baldwin was too suspicious of newspapers to be misled by that sort of hyperbole, especially in big type in that paper. Even if he mused, fleetingly, that the Crusader might be hanging up his sword and shield and joining the big battalion, the next three months dispelled that notion. Beaverbrook realised that the private meetings had merely achieved a private offer that the Tories would not utterly reject food taxes. The Lords debate achieved nothing. He resolved forthwith to use the weapons he knew best, Press power and public propaganda. On 10 December the national and provincial newspapers carried large advertisements for the Empire Crusade Register. A second advertisement appealed for members, and a fighting fund was launched with Beaverbrook's £25,000 (of which he handed over only £10,000), Rothermere's £5,000, and a target of £100,000.

The Empire Crusade was conducted with all the gusto, ill will and propaganda muscle at his command. The First Crusade in history, sponsored by Pope Urban II and led by Peter the Hermit and Walter the Penniless, a knight, traversed Europe to Constantinople. The Empire Crusade of 1930, led by Max the Millionaire, a baron, traversed the United Kingdom, and in the re-play the Saracens were represented reluctantly by the Old Harrovian Baldwin. The baron established himself as a formidable orator in the evangelical mould, and the meetings, ballyhooed in advance in his newspapers and enthusiastically reported, attracted the crowds: there was no rival television until 1936. Businessmen and Parliamentary candidates seeking prominence appeared with him on platforms, certain of a mention in the *Express*. Occasionally a New Zealander or an Australian materialised, no Indians or blacks. The readers were assured by its editor that they were the makers of history in supporting the movement and were urged to sign membership forms free of charge. The Crusaders reached a modest numerical strength of 200,000 and Max pronounced the result of a fortnight's brainwashing of his readers as 'immediate and overwhelming'. Significantly, no leading politician, none nationally known, jumped to his side on the platform; some made sympathetic noises.

What Beaverbrook was doing had never been done before. He was using his newspapers as the launching pad for a new political pressure group, contesting by-elections with its own candidates and in other cases supporting candidates who acknowledged the cause. The Crusade had a registered membership, a national organisation, and money; it published its own manifestos. The Fourth Estate was sabotaging the Third Estate and the effect upon the ethics of his newspapers, reflecting upon the integrity of the Press as a whole, was deplorable. A. J. P. Taylor, who loved the man, does not disguise his revulsion at Beaverbrook's professional conduct at this time:[1]

> 'He now forgot his doctrine that the first duty of a newspaper was to tell the news of the day. Instead it became the duty of his newspapers to tell only the news of the Empire Crusade. Each day he sent instructions to report the speech of some politician who inclined towards Empire Free Trade . . . Beaverbrook's own speeches were set beforehand and were accompanied by a flamboyant account of the meeting and of its success. Speeches of opponents were not reported. When Sir William Bull expostulated against this policy of suppression, Beaverbrook replied on 19 December 1929: "It is impossible to open the columns of the *Daily Express* to those who are against us. And for this reason—our space is limited and we need every inch of it for the

[1]*Beaverbrook* by A. J. P. Taylor.

purpose of putting forward the views of our supporters. In every campaign in which I have been engaged I have been advised 'Open your columns to the opposition.' My reply has been 'Go to the opposition newspapers.'"''

Beverley Baxter, still editor of the *Daily Express* but not for much longer, protested many times about injuring the paper. When Beaverbrook was planning to develop the Crusade into a new political party, Baxter tried again on 14 February: 'Tactically this may be necessary, but we are a Conservative paper, with a million Conservative readers.' Beaverbrook called him an infernal fellow, and told L. S. Amery, whose important (i.e. supporting) speech had been missed by the *Express*, that the truth was that an editor of a newspaper was only useful so long as he worked honestly and earnestly in furtherance of the political programme.

What was the political programme, how valid, how attainable? The problem was British survival in a changing world. Beaverbrook's answer was Free Trade between all the countries of the Empire with tariffs against all foreign goods. Potentially it was an exciting concept to the simple and hopeful in a country with over two million unemployed, but Beaverbrook hadn't thought it through; worse, he did his thinking on the hoof, shifting his ground as obstacles emerged. Why, he asked, did America become so suddenly wealthy? Because it fulfilled its domestic needs by mass production for a vast protected federal market. Britain should therefore develop its Colonies and persuade its Dominions to increase their demands for her exports of coal, machinery and textiles, in return taxing or excluding all food imports except those from Empire countries; Empire and home-grown food would meet Britain's needs. It would put up the price of food to the British consumer (the 'stomach tax') but the other benefits—self-sufficiency and guaranteed markets for Britain's exports—would more than compensate. To hell with the foreigners: 'Who is for the Empire?'

The facts belied the theory. The farmers of Australia and Canada were keen enough on an exclusive market for their agricultural produce in thickly-populated Britain, but the Empire industrialists were now embarking on their own Industrial Revolution; as for the goods they couldn't yet manufacture themselves, they wanted the best and cheapest and had no reason to care whether the imports were British, German or American. For Britain, which survived by exporting, protection was perilous, inviting punitive measures from 'foreign' countries. Even more alarming was Beaverbrook's idea that taxes on non-Empire food should be slapped on the English unconditionally so that the Dominions would be shamed or 'inspired', rather than 'bribed' into Empire Free Trade. His off-the-cuff replies at Empire rallies were sparkling stuff; good fun for the orator and the audience, but he had no serious replies to serious arguments. Within a few months he was confessing that all they could reasonably expect from the Dominions was a gesture of Imperial Preference for Britain's goods.

His wishful thinking was not wrecked by Baldwin's obduracy; Empire Free Trade was rejected by all political parties in Britain and by every major country in the Empire. It wasn't practical economics or politics. Empire Free Trade was chicanery. Apart from Canada, Beaverbrook did not visit a single Dominion or Colony except Jamaica in his eighty-five years; he merited no more attention than a bearded nut in Trafalgar Square carrying a placard proclaiming that 'Judgement is Nigh', but he owned newspapers.

Throughout the Empire campaign he operated as an Unholy Trinity—a newspaper proprietor suppressing the opposition case, a public orator making ever wilder threats, and a political intriguer always available at short notice for a deal. Rothermere's mouthpiece, G. Ward Price, had already advocated in 1929 the dethronement of Baldwin as Tory Leader in favour of Beaverbrook, dismissing his peerage as a temporary obstacle that could be overcome by the abolition of the hereditary principle, 'making it possible for all peers to sit in the House of Commons'. On 5 January 1930 with his *Daily Mail* nodding in approval, Rothermere's *Sunday Pictorial*, via Mr Price, prolonged the absurdity. 'The conviction is fast spreading among Conservatives,' he wrote, 'that their next leader must be found outside the established hierarchy . . . the name of Lord Beaverbrook becomes steadily more prominent . . . *There is no man living in this country today with more likelihood of succeeding to the Premiership of Great Britain than Lord Beaverbrook.*' Rothermere solemnly endorsed the prophecy in a public speech at a dinner in the presence of Beaverbrook himself, and far from deprecating the notion the tenant proposed for No. 10 Downing Street effusively praised his host's influence and judgement. Beaverbrook told an American friend of his very great fear that his 'present complications' might land him at No. 10, but apart from this lapse he was too shrewd, at that time, to take the idea seriously: no one else did. The obvious successor to Baldwin was Neville Chamberlain.

The provincial audiences enjoyed the barnstorming. The politicians were less easily aroused. Beaverbrook had to admit: 'Mr Snowden has poured out his scorn. Mr Lloyd George has been moved to put on all his war paint and cut some of his most comical capers. Mr Baldwin looks another way, while some of his lieutenants fulminate and threaten . . .'

He saw Baldwin on 5 and 12 February, pressing the cause and seeking a compromise. Would Baldwin object if the Crusade put up Empire Free Trade Conservative candidates? *Yes; disastrous.* Would he object if the Crusade tried to get Empire Free Trade candidates before the selection committees? *Yes; he wouldn't countenance such a course.*

On 18 February Beaverbrook announced that the Empire Crusade had begat the United Empire *Party* and Rothermere cabled his enthusiastic approval of the 'prairie fire'. The Party was a joint enterprise of the Wicked Uncles, sponsored by the *Mail* and *Express*, proposing to contest half the Parliamentary seats at the next general election, a move that could tear the Tory Party asunder and make a mockery of Baldwin's leadership. Beaverbrook declared: 'We shall oppose every Parliamentary candidate, no matter of which party, who does not adopt and further the policy of Empire Free Trade.' The threat became more sinister when he harangued the little Baldwins and their wives in Gloucester: 'It is essential to save the country even at the expense of wrecking every political party.' Any Communist soap-box performer making such threats would assume there was a Special Branch man in the audience and a local bobby taking notes.

Concurrently, the enemies were involved in more private talks. Baldwin could not 'look another way' any longer. His object was to split the Beaverbrook–Rothermere axis and he dealt through an intermediary with Beaverbrook alone. To a gathering of Conservatives in the Hotel Cecil on 4 March the Leader of the Conservative Party in opposition declared that if the Tories won the next election they would hold a referendum (Beaverbrook's suggestion) on food taxes. Beaverbrook phoned Rothermere as the speech was coming over the tapes. Churchill arrived unannounced at Beaverbrook's London suite, declaring his satisfaction that they could now work together again. Beaverbrook phoned Baldwin thanking him for his 'wholehearted and generous advocating of our policy'. He was so certain the conversion was wholehearted, though only a referendum was offered, that on 8 March 1930 he announced the parting of the ways with Rothermere and the end so far as he was concerned of the United Empire Party; it was now unnecessary to put up Empire Free Trade candidates and the subscribers would get their money back. One cause of the split was that Rothermere had insisted on harnessing hobby horses of his own to the basic idea of Empire Free Trade, nonsenses such as 'No more surrenders in India' and 'No diplomatic relations with Russia'. Baldwin had dis-united the United Empire Party. Rothermere announced that the Party 'will by no means cease', and the Wicked Uncles now went their separate wicked ways, campaigning unilaterally.

They were still underestimating the Babe. Baldwin was as wily in small print as Beaverbrook in headlines. This was his commitment on 4 March: that after the next election an Imperial Conference should meet in an atmosphere of perfect freedom, and '. . . if there should emerge any form of agreement, arrangement, treaty . . . that does give us great benefits and that demands in return a tax on some articles of food from a foreign country—that whole issue could be put clearly before our people' in a referendum. It was an if-but-maybe deal; he wasn't buying a second-hand car from Beaverbrook, he was selling one to him. Beaverbrook even agreed that the deal should not be presented to his readers as a triumph for the United Empire Party or for Press power. Baldwin addressed him as 'My dear Max' and thanked him for 'playing the game'.

The euphoria was short-lived. Had the Crusader surrendered everything for nothing? Was Baldwin assuming the referendum would destroy food taxes and therefore Empire Free Trade? Was he cheating, as Rothermere alleged? The answer soon came when the Conservative Central Office issued a pamphlet giving assurances to the public *against* the imposition of food taxes; further, it changed the emphasis of Baldwin's canny statement of 4 March by implying that the initiative should come from the Dominions. Beaverbrook reacted with a towering rage, refusing to appear at a Crystal Palace meeting where he was billed to speak on the same platform as Baldwin unless the pamphlet was withdrawn. The meeting was cancelled. Then the Conservative Leader, with an eye on the next election, publicly declared where he stood on food taxes: against. 'We have to rule that right out. It would be madness at the present time.'

If the readers of *Express* newspapers were not by this time schizophrenics it was not the proprietor's fault. The visionary Free Trade plan for Dominion co-operation became a device to impose upon the Colonies. The gimmick *for* the referendum was jettisoned because the Conservative Leader used it 'as a shield instead of a sword'. The Fleet Street gibe was that the titles of the papers were to be changed to the *Daily* and *Sunday Suppress*, and a world-weary Civil Service wit at the Ministry of Works penned a quatrain:

> When round for public works we look
> Two pressing jobs at once appear:
> To damn for ever Beaver Brook
> And drain the mud from Rother Mere.

By-elections, under the influence of Beaverbrook rampant, became boisterous affairs commanding the attention of all newspapers. He dramatised his sincerity by selling his house at Newmarket and disposing of his racehorses 'on account of his duties in connection with the Crusade', giving up one string of losers for another. On 24 June 1930 Baldwin struck a note of asperity at an assembly of Conservative MPs, candidates and party supporters at Caxton Hall, London. He began with his usual sporting metaphors: 'I have been very busy working for the party, making speeches all over the country. While I have been away a good many have been at work "queering the pitch". I can use that expression to you as I can use the expression "playing the game". I cannot use it to that section of the Press, because the words would convey no meaning to them . . .'

This was the speech in which he likened Lord Rothermere and Lord Beaverbrook to America's Mr Hearst. 'The control of newspapers of your own,' he said, 'seems to destroy the balance—the power of being able to suppress everything that a man says that you do not like, the power of attacking all the time without there being any possibility of being hit back; it goes to the head like wine, and you find in these cases attempts have been made outside the province of journalism to dictate, to domineer, to blackmail . . .' Rothermere suffered the most savage public lashing on this occasion for his 'preposterous and insolent demand' to know in advance of the election Baldwin's policy and the names of his proposed Cabinet Ministers as the price of *Daily Mail* support. (See page 159, Chapter III.)

The Crusader was displeased, but not for long dispirited, by the *Mail*'s clumsy announcement on the morning of Baldwin's speech that 'the hour has come, and it has produced the Man'—the Rt. Hon. Lord Beaverbrook.

There was no doubt about the Crusader's ardour. The by-election at North Norfolk, where Lady Noel-Buxton (Labour) was fighting Mr Cook (Conservative candidate and Empire Free Trader), was a rum example. Her ladyship, well known and well liked locally, won with a reduced majority her husband's former seat, and the peaceful citizens of the cathedral city of Norwich and its surrounding villages were entertained by a Barnum and Bailey political circus the like of which they had never seen before.

Beaverbrook arrived in a three-car motorcade to set up his headquarters at the Blakeney Hotel, accompanied by secretaries and, of all people, the rotund Lord Castlerosse. Valentine's principal role was to be rude to Lady Noel-Buxton—'The best thing about Lady Buxton is her tongue; there is a fine shrewish touch about it.' Lord Rothermere also popped up to see Beaverbrook during the affray, adding to the drama and the speculation. Beaverbrook was practising his oratory at public meetings, to become a formidable and polished performer in later years. There is a revealing photograph taken in Norwich of him with right arm aloft, fist clenched, jacket flapping, legs astride, bawling into a microphone. Three sides of the table were draped with Union Jacks, and one of the diversions was a black box that emitted an eerie buzz once a minute; after every buzz Beaverbrook shouted, 'The country has just spent another £1,000 on imported food.' The *Manchester Guardian*, later to call him the Pedlar of Dreams, then settled for 'a transatlantic revivalist with a true touch of the seer'. The seer told a heckler that he could see truth in his eyes and urged him to 'Come along and help me.'

The success of the campaign was in disuniting the Conservative Party. Neville Chamberlain made peace moves in July, proposing concessions by both Baldwin and Beaverbrook, but they were abortive and hostilities reopened. The campaign's principal failure was in the attempt to unite the Empire. The Dominions did not want Free Trade and were soon to demonstrate their rejection of the Beaverbrook policy at the Imperial Conference in London, September–October 1930. The estrangement between the Crusader and his old friend R. B. Bennett, Canada's representative as Conservative Premier, was due to financial differences that excluded any mutual manoeuvring behind the scenes in spite of Beaverbrook's efforts. Bennett turned down Empire Free Trade flat: 'In our opinion it is neither desirable nor possible, for it would defeat the very purpose we are striving to achieve.' He was prepared to talk about Imperial Preference. Prime Minister MacDonald wasn't. Baldwin was, but rejected any tariff on foreign wheat. The other Dominion Prime Ministers ignored the issue.

It was Baldwin who took the punishment. Beaverbrook declared: 'It is the same old jig. Let us concern ourselves no more with Mr Baldwin: I do not mean to do so.' At a public meeting during the South Paddington by-election the same month he stepped up the attack: 'Mr Baldwin is the champion of all backsliders. We believe we have brought him to grace; we lift up our voices in a hymn of rejoicing; and we have hardly got through the first line of it before we see him crawling down the aisle again.'

Beaverbrook spoke eleven times at the rough-and-tumble by-election, making his shrillest threat: 'It is my purpose to break up the Conservative Party if the Conservative Party does not adopt the policy.' Yet the most savage attack of the contest came from the first Lord Hailsham, twice in his career Lord Chancellor, who spoke only once. He explained later that he hadn't meant physical shooting, but what he said was this: 'Lord Beaverbrook is compared to an elephant trumpeting in the jungle. I am inclined to compare him to a mad dog running along the streets and yapping and barking, and I would remind his Lordship that the best way to treat a mad dog, if you can't muzzle him, is to shoot him.'

Beaverbrook held no monopoly as a critic of the Leader. Neville Chamberlain, Chairman of the Party, secretly wanted him to go but was not disloyal. A group of young, bright MPs openly advocated a change, and the dissatisfaction erupted when seventeen 'braves' called for a Party meeting of peers, members and supporters to hear their case for Baldwin's resignation. He did not attempt to divert or delay the challenge. The meeting on 30 October was faced with a resolution drafted by Chamberlain expressing confidence in Baldwin, who had nobly insisted on a secret ballot: 116 voted against, an uncomfortably sizeable minority, but 462 voted for. Unfortunately for the Leader, on the day of the mutiny the Empire Crusade candidate running against the official Conservative candidate in South Paddington won by 941 votes.

Baldwin might have been dancing the same old jig; Beaverbrook never hesitated to change his jig. Protection for British agriculture became the dominant theme instead of Imperial Preference. The slogan of Empire Free Trade remained, but the cause now had little to do with the Empire and even less to do with Free Trade. His tactics for 1931 were to concentrate solely upon by-elections instead of rampaging across the country at excitable moments. East Islington in February was an example of the havoc he was causing. With two Tory candidates in the field and Tory loyalties divided, Labour held the seat. As soon as he knew that the Tory Crusader had notched up eleven hundred more votes than Mr Baldwin's official candidate Beaverbrook had the audacity to blame Baldwin for splitting the vote since he represented the Tory minority. There was gloom at the Party Central Office and restiveness among the backbenchers. The frustration of Opposition was no substitute for power and the fruits of office.

There is no record in British affairs more comforting to politicians, especially beleaguered party leaders, than the survival of Stanley Baldwin from 1929 to 1931. Loyalty towards an election-losing leader is a rationed commodity in the Tory Party, and the fragility of Labour in power kept the question of the leadership in the forefront. He was pestered by the emotional appeal of a phoney cause and undermined by the two popular pro-Tory papers. He had secured his vote of confidence in 1930 with Chamberlain's help. Now, in 1931, the issue of India's future was exacerbating more political strife, with Churchill opposing official policy and resigning from the Shadow Cabinet. The Tory Right opposed the leadership over India and the Tory Left were impatient at the lack of a reformist policy. Throughout Baldwin's career his strength had two bases—the diversity of his political opponents within the party, pulling in different directions, and his acceptance by the public regardless of party as a plodder they felt they could trust, honest if uninspiring.

A new revolt stirred against him six days after Beaverbrook and his Press propaganda machine had been in action in East Islington.

Chamberlain was already 'getting letters and communications from all over the country';[1] then on 26 February 1931 he received a disturbing memorandum from the chief agent of the Party, Sir Robert Topping, requesting that the Leader reconsider his position and indicating the need for new leadership. Chamberlain consulted his principal colleagues and, with their agreement, reluctantly showed the letter to Baldwin on 1 March. The laconic entries in Neville Chamberlain's diary should be embroidered and framed above the beds of all men and women who aspire to Downing Street, next to 'The Lord is My Shepherd':

'Everyone I think except Willie Bridgeman was of the opinion that S.B. would have to resign.'
'1 March 1931: 4.30, S.B. has decided to go at once.'[2]

'At once', in Baldwinian terms, did not mean today or tomorrow; he was never a man in a hurry. He listened to Willie, agreeing to wait a while and see. He was still there on 18 March when the situation reversed dramatically in his favour. Within six months he was Lord President of the Council in a National Government, where he remained securely for four years until he became Prime Minister in 1935. He voluntarily retired in May 1937, succeeded at last by Neville Chamberlain.

Ironically, it was Beaverbrook who saved Baldwin by his intervention in a by-election at St George's Westminster, a Tory stronghold. Labour and the Liberals saved their money and did not even put up candidates, but the Empire Crusaders entered the ring. There was some difficulty, owing to Baldwin's precarious position, in pressuring an official Tory candidate even for so safe a seat. Several refused: who wanted to be labelled a Baldwinite just then, when he was going, going, and nearly gone? The issue was really the leadership, not India or food taxes, regardless of the nonsense in the *Mail* and *Express*. Beaverbrook knew it. So did Stanley Baldwin.

---

[1]*Life of Neville Chamberlain* by Keith Feiling, Macmillan, London, 1946.
[2]Ibid.

He detested the vulgarity of electioneering but suspended his susceptibilities on this occasion. Why not take a pot shot at the mad dog he couldn't muzzle, and at the other mad dog, Rothermere, whose newspaper was libellously suggesting to its readers that it was 'difficult to see how the leader of a party who has lost his own fortune can hope to restore that of anyone else, or of his country'. Baldwin chose 18 March, the eve of poll at St George's, seventeen days after he had decided to go at once, to speak at a rally in the Queen's Hall in favour of Alfred Duff Cooper, who had loyally stepped into the breach as official Tory candidate.

Baldwin's theme was persecution by newspaper, and he spoke of his ordeal:

'I have said little. It is not worth it. I am going to say something today. The newspapers attacking me are not newspapers in the ordinary sense. They are engines of propaganda for the constantly changing policies, desires, personal wishes, personal likes and dislikes of the two men.

'What are their methods? Their methods are direct falsehood, misrepresentation, half-truths, the alteration of the speaker's meaning by publishing a sentence apart from the context, such as you see in these leaflets handed out outside the doors of this hall; suppression and editorial criticism of speeches which are not reported in the paper. These are methods hated alike by the public and by the whole of the rest of the Press . . .

'What the proprietorship of these papers is aiming at is power, and power without responsibility—the prerogative of the harlot throughout the ages.'

The sentence that expressed Baldwin's savage scorn was written by his cousin Rudyard Kipling, Max Aitken's first friend in England, the man who told him he would find Stanley a delightful fellow. They had parted company in 1918 over the Irish question, Beaverbrook on that occasion being in the right. It was no consolation to the Old Testament Prophet weaned in Maple, Ontario, that the voice was Jacob's but the hands were the hands of Esau.

'For once in his life,' wrote Harold Macmillan, who was present on this notable St Crispin's Eve, 'Baldwin was angry.' The exorcism of the harlots still lives in political and newspaper history, and its potency produced instant results. The next day Duff Cooper won St George's with a majority of 5,700 votes. Baldwin's agony as the tormented Leader was over and Neville Chamberlain had to sustain his strained loyalty for another six years before he could succeed him. Of permanent significance, the baleful influence of proprietorial journalism was diminished. The personal prestige of Beaverbrook and Rothermere as Press barons, which rarely extended beyond mutual genuflection, plummeted: so did their power, though not their pride or arrogance.

Nothing is final in politics, even victory or defeat in war, and certainly not in lesser matters. Beaverbrook and Baldwin were never to meet again; the brief 'My dear Max' interlude in 1930 never recurred. Yet within a week the backslider and the harlot were engaged in an arm's-length assignation, with Neville Chamberlain again the political pimp. Within ten days the Conservative Central Office formally announced an amicable settlement. Within a month Beaverbrook was smoothly deprecating and deploring the appearance of dissension in Conservative circles. Baldwin said nothing; Kipling was busily engaged on correcting the proofs of *Limits and Renewals*, published the next year.

Beaverbrook glorified the formal exchange of letters between himself and Chamberlain as the 'Stornoway Pact' of 31 March 1931, implying the triumph of Empire Free Trade. Neither the Empire, nor Empire Free Trade, nor Imperial Preference was mentioned in the concordat. Baldwin merely authorised Chamberlain to say that the present Conservative policy for the development of British agricultural production was to employ all, or any, of the methods Beaverbrook had enumerated— quotas, or the prohibition of foreign foodstuffs, or duties on foreign foodstuffs. He also agreed to ask the electors for a mandate for such a purpose. Beaverbrook claimed that the Conservatives were now committed to the complete campaign for food taxes, the price he said he had always demanded for a cease fire: the claim was bogus. Once again, his the headlines, Baldwin's the small print. The Stornoway Pact at least pulled down the curtain on Empire Free Trade, or lowered it for an interval to enable the readers of the *Express* to relieve themselves.

The Crusade was formally buried by the economic avalanche that overwhelmed Britain a few months later in August 1931, tearing apart MacDonald's Labour Government (and the Labour Party) and replacing it with a National Government with MacDonald as Prime Minister and Baldwin as Lord President.

Beaverbrook was now dancing yet another jig: 'I ask you to give your confidence to Mr Ramsay MacDonald and his colleagues . . . Ask no question. Seek no pledges. Trust in Mr MacDonald's leadership. Rely on Mr Neville Chamberlain.' But not, by interference, trust or rely upon Mr Baldwin. A year later he was again at his throat: 'He really is at heart a Socialist. He really is. He is our enemy.'

Beaverbrook never shed his pose as the Old Testament Prophet, but a new dimension was added to the act: the eccentric rich man. He had a spell as vegetarian, then as teetotaller. He became an exhibitionist, dictating letters clad only in a panama hat to a male secretary, continuing talks with his minions while sitting in the toilet or soaking in the bath, conducting conferences as a barber cut his hair. He was a compulsive host, but would never dine or wine at the homes of friends or in restaurants; he had to be in charge of the conversation. Like the other newspaper multi-millionaires he enjoyed ill-health, consulting famous physicians and thumbing through *Diseases of the Heart* as a book at bedtime; he had one serious experience, but the rest of his maladies were psychosomatic. He frequently announced his retirement from his newspapers—'I'm like a shipbuilder who has built a ship but will not be her captain. As the vessel glides down the slipway he says "Farewell".' He was forty-eight and his eldest son, Max II, was seventeen when the first full-dress rehearsal of the Farewell Performance was staged in 1927. When he was nearing seventy, reviving again the rumour of his imminent departure, Young Max, then Vice-Chairman of the enterprise, told a reporter that it had been an annual event for twenty years. Beaverbrook thought it was fun, keeping them guessing and talking. New opportunities to display his capacity for mischief and his zest for organisation still lay ahead for the man who didn't retire at forty-eight.

His final clash with Baldwin arose in the Abdication Crisis of 1936. The upheaval caused by King Edward VIII's determination to marry the vivacious American lady with two husbands still living is within the memory of senior citizens, and the intimate details of the wooing are now familiar to television viewers.

Beaverbrook had never been invited to Buckingham Palace. Beyond a cursory acquaintance, including one visit by the Prince of Wales to Stornoway House with a mutual friend, he had never been near the Royal circle and had little knowledge of the sovereign. But several succulent aspects of the situation that winter beckoned the conspirator. King George had resented handing him the key of the Duchy of Lancaster; now his unconventional son and successor, at loggerheads with the Establishment, sought Beaverbrook's advice and aid. Above all there was the compelling incentive that the Premier, lampooned as Bumbling Baldwin in the *Express*, was now also the King's enemy. Edward's happiness, the threat to the standing of monarchy, and the developing constitutional predicament were of less concern to Beaverbrook than the opportunity to challenge his adversary yet again in an unexpected and august arena.

He was involved at several stages of the crisis. The King, summoning him to Buckingham Palace on 16 October, besought him to use his good offices to protect Mrs Simpson from prominence in the British Press over her petition for divorce. Beaverbrook, at that time assured by the King's own lawyer that there was no intention between them of marriage, called a secret and hurried Fleet Street conference where, with Lord Rothermere's son Esmond at his side, he repeated that assurance. The meeting achieved what the Duke of Windsor later described as 'the miracle I desired—a "gentleman's agreement" among editors to report the case without sensation'. Over lunch at Fort Belvedere on 26 November, having sped back from America at the King's request, Beaverbrook learned not only that Edward was determined to marry Wallis but that he had already suggested to Prime Minister Baldwin a morganatic marriage, making Mrs Simpson his wife though not Queen. Unsuccessfully, Beaverbrook urged patience and delay and a withdrawal of the offer: the case for delay, urged also by Churchill, impressed the King but not Wallis. The scenario was complete and the outcome inevitable when the King insisted on marriage, Mrs Simpson preferred morganatic marriage, and Mr Baldwin insisted that the King could not marry Mrs Simpson and remain on the throne. Baldwin moved with speed and the Cabinet decided to seek the views of the Dominion Governments on the suggestion of a morganatic marriage, with the wording of the cables in Baldwin's hands. The third meeting, the next day, between the King and Beaverbrook was described in the Royal autobiography.

'Max Beaverbrook . . . hurried to Buckingham Palace in a state of agitation unusual for him. "Sir," he explained, "you have put your head on the execution-block. All that Baldwin has to do now is to swing the axe." He looked searchingly at me. "Have you seen the cables to the Dominions?"'[1]

He hadn't, but it dawned on him they were 'hardly likely to be compassionate pleas' on behalf of his proposal. The advice had come too late and had no effect on the crisis.

The word used by the Duke of Windsor in describing Beaverbrook's next move was 'conspiracy'. Determined that Bumbling Baldwin must not emerge the victor, his plan was that Mrs Simpson should renounce the marriage and thus postpone 'the great decision', depriving Baldwin of his triumph and allaying public excitement; later on, if the King's ardour

[1] *A King's Story* by the Duke of Windsor, Putnam, New York, 1947.

had not cooled, as it had with other married women, the marriage stakes could be reopened. The question of abdication would at least be postponed, and given time anything might happen. At Beaverbrook's instigation Mrs Simpson retreated to the South of France where his intermediary persuaded her to announce her readiness to withdraw forthwith from a situation rendered both unhappy and untenable. Then Edward sent his message to Wallis, 'Wherever you go, I will follow you'; her ring was more important to him than his crown.

As soon as the silence ended Beaverbrook chose propaganda ahead of truth in his newspapers. With the sole object of embarrassing the Prime Minister he encouraged his editors to clamour for a morganatic marriage long after he knew the King's proposal had been rejected by Baldwin, the Cabinet and the Dominion Governments. When Mrs Simpson, pressured by him through Lord Brownlow, announced from Cannes her offer to withdraw, he was already aware of the King's attitude to such a course. Yet the *Daily Express* proclaimed, 'END OF THE CRISIS'— again misleading the public on a matter, it might be claimed, of national importance. Keeping faith with his readers was a low priority. His admission that he ran his newspapers purely for propaganda was demonstrated on this occasion to the degree of absurdity.

The Abdication established that Beaverbrook was a clumsy courtier who understood human frailty more than loyalty. Enlisted by the King, he was so intent on de-bagging Baldwin that he worked in the last resort behind the King's back, forfeiting his trust. But he was not crestfallen. 'I wouldn't have missed it for worlds,' he said; 'it was fun.' One of his jokes at the time was that it was a pity Mrs Simpson couldn't marry Lord Rothermere and become the Queen of Hungary.

Stanley Baldwin ('When I was a little boy in Worcestershire reading history books I never thought I should have to interfere between a King and his mistress') was politically on his hands and knees by 1936; dispirited, languid, confused, taking a rest. He had publicly confessed that in the general election the previous year he concealed the need for rearmament, apparent since 1933, because he felt he could not have won and retained personal power on such a programme. Honest Stanley Baldwin, the Man You Can Trust, the high priest of Safety First, had cynically put national safety last. The Hoare-Laval Pact, appeasing Mussolini over his aggression in Abyssinia, had also stunned public opinion and split the Tory Party. His handling of the Royal crisis restored his name to general esteem and the approval of the House of Commons was demonstrated in all parties by its hostile reception to Winston Churchill's plea for patience and delay. He was the luckiest Prime

Minister of all time. A few days before the Abdication, Edward VIII excommunicated himself from the constitutionalists by telling the unemployed miners of South Wales that 'Something must be done' about their misery. Must? The *Daily Mail* exploited the phrase to harass the Government, and the King did not endear himself to the Ministers deciding his fate.

Beaverbrook's major disservice to his country and to Western civilisation was the deployment of his newspapers for five decades in the 'cause' of Splendid Isolation. It was the basis for his jeering onslaughts against the League of Nations and the United Nations, and against the individual advocates, like the pre-Suez Anthony Eden, of any semblance of international co-operation. His gospel was a national menace during the rise of the European dictatorships, unique in its reckless disregard of current evidence, history, and even of common sense. When the only shield against Germany's diplomatic and then military aggression was collective security, his newspapers preached salvation in going-it-alone. He advocated rearmament, but sought to sell his readers and the country the myth that Britain was safe so long as it kept its nose out of Europe's business.

The final manifestation of the Splendid Isolation policy was the opposition of the *Express* newspapers, year after year, to Britain joining the European Economic Community. The project was the quintessence of everything he stood against—Continental ties, embroiling Britain with 'the brawling Europeans'. The pro-Marketeers were well aware of the power of his propaganda when Harold Macmillan's Government first opened the abortive negotiations in 1961, and so was Macmillan himself. He received reports that Tory MPs with marginal seats were falling into 'the spider's web'. He had always maintained a personal relationship with the Beaver but at no time doubted the man's penchant for mischief and verbal mayhem. After a dinner at the Australia Club in 1962, where he spoke with Robert Menzies about the Common Market, Macmillan sighed to his diary: 'Naturally, the *Express* has completely mis-represented both my speech and Bob's. Sentences are taken out of their context and printed in heavy type. The qualifying sentences are suppressed. Jokes are turned into serious points and *vice versa*.'[1] Edward Heath later suffered from the same subjective sub-editing. Other tenets of the Beaverbrook Code of Campaign Conduct were invoked; every morning, noon and sabbath there was a fusillade of facts in his

[1]*At the End of the Day* by Harold Macmillan, Macmillan, London, 1973.

publications selected with bias. How far he misjudged the numerical strength of the Little Englanders was demonstrated in 1975, three years after Britain joined the EEC. The result of the public referendum was that 67.2 per cent were in favour of Britain staying in the European Community.

Beaverbrook was against British intervention abroad on any pretext whatsoever. His policies sustained Britain's inter-war governments in their myopia and lethargy and were a lethal factor in the country's military nakedness in 1938. There is considerable evidence that his activities did not corrupt *public* opinion. The gulf between Beaverbrook and the public over Italy's threatened aggression against Abyssinia was demonstrated by the results announced on 28 June 1935 of the Peace Ballot, an unofficial plebiscite organised by the League of Nations Union. In excess of ten million votes supported economic sanctions with only 600,000 against: nearly seven million were in favour of military sanctions—war against the aggressor—with 2,351,000 voting 'no'. In September, when the League was agonising over the issue of sanctions against Italy, Beaverbrook wrote in the *Daily Express*: 'We cannot, we will not, we must not police the world alone.' And a few days later: 'War cannot stamp out war. War breeds war. Do not be led into courses by hatred of dictators ... Let the people who are misgoverned rid themselves of their autocrats.'

The folly of Splendid Isolation culminated in Beaverbrook's personal assurance to his readers that 'There will be no war.' In the year of Munich, 1938, his newspapers were peddling the twin policies of appeasement and optimism while paying lip-service to rearmament. The poster at the front of the sandwich-board Messiah said 'Rearm'; the poster at the rear said 'Relax'.

When he met the American journalist Quentin Reynolds in Miami early in the year he was already rehearsing 'the policy'. He told Reynolds, who knew better, that talk of a major war was absurd. We wouldn't have one for a long time. Germany wasn't ready, France was a pacifist country, Russia couldn't afford a war, and Italy couldn't stand up a month against any first-rate army or navy. No, there wouldn't be a war. On 12 February an *Express* article entitled 'DON'T TALK WAR' made the curious assertion that 'The present worries of Europe only make war more unlikely.' On 10 March an editorial said: 'Welcome Herr von Ribbentrop, Hitler's Foreign Minister. You have the right to believe that he comes here as an Ambassador of peace, sincerely seeking it.' The readers were anaesthetised with the promise that 'Mr Chamberlain means peace for the British people,' as if that were the end of the matter.

They were told that 'Germany is not as strong as Britain. The Germans are not likely to make war against us. They have no money ... They have no petroleum ... they have no rubber.' In the *Sunday Express* of 20 March 1938 Lord Beaverbrook said: 'Peace is with us. Let us enjoy it with a good cheer. For we shall have happy days for a long time to come.' The Biblical phraseology was no doubt seductive to some readers of that newspaper, and there was more to come for the weekday students as they dead-headed the daffodils in their gardens at the close of spring. The voice of authority became more strident on 23 May in the *Daily Express*:

'Britain will not be involved in war. There will be no major war in Europe this year or next year.

'The Germans will not seize Czechoslovakia.

'So go about your own business with confidence in the future, and fear not.

'Provide us with the airplanes, anti-aircraft guns, and ammunition.

'Develop our own Imperial resources and give our races prosperity and happiness at home.'

On 15 August Beaverbrook was quoted by Hearst's International News Service: 'Germany cannot and will not march into Czechoslovakia to fight ... When war does come, British interests will not be involved and Britain will not be in it.' He was telling the British public that there would be no major war in Europe and the Americans that when war did come Britain would not be involved; he was telling everybody that the Germans would not seize Czechoslovakia. He repeated in the *Daily Express* of 1 September: 'There will be no European war.' His assertion was (1), if the Czechs refused concessions, France and Russia would not support them; (2) if they did make concessions Hitler would shrink from war with France and Russia. Further, that even if the Führer himself wanted war his generals would not allow it.

When Neville Chamberlain flew to Germany to meet Hitler at Berchtesgaden Beaverbrook ordered the *Daily Express* to be joyful at the news and provided champagne for his guests at Stornoway House to acclaim the mission. When Chamberlain, on his next mission, flew to Munich to confer on 29 September with Hitler, Daladier, the French Premier, and Mussolini, there was more champagne at Stornoway House. No representative of the Czechoslovakian Government was present at the meeting in Munich, but the Nazi right to enter that country was endorsed. Chamberlain surrendered and the Munich Agreement incorporated Sudetenland in the German Reich. On 30 September the *Daily Express* published across seven columns on its front page the slogan: 'THE DAILY EXPRESS DECLARES THAT BRITAIN WILL NOT BE INVOLVED IN A EUROPEAN WAR THIS YEAR OR NEXT YEAR EITHER.' The paper was not alone in its euphoria over Munich: its folly was that it persisted in its lullaby for the first eight months of the following year. The British newspaper with the largest daily sale, 2,500,000, could not have performed a more useful service to the Nazis if it had been owned by Joseph Goebbels.

In the year of the war, 1939, as Hitler's grand strategy became abundantly clearer, Beaverbrook's thinking became more hysterical, or certifiable. His newspapers had the task of bending their readers' minds in opposite directions. 'There will be no war' was sounded incessantly, and the call for rearmament became shriller. He wrote in the *Express* of 18 January 1939: 'Neither Germany nor Italy will invade France or seize French territory. Such an enterprise would be madness . . . Britain has nothing to fear at home or abroad.'

He opposed the pledge to Poland. He was still a Splendid Isolationist. He believed the Polish Pact would make war inevitable. Yet the *Daily Express* continued to declare 'There will be no war.' The slogan last appeared twenty-eight days before Germany invaded Poland and thirty days before Britain and France declared war on Germany, and less than two months before Poland was partitioned between Germany and Russia.

In July Beaverbrook set off on a scheduled holiday in Canada, returning to England a few days before the war officially began. The only positive step he took at this time was to advocate Winston Churchill's return to government as a Minister, a step which had long been urged, and first urged, by the *Sunday Pictorial* and *Daily Mirror*. He said, when he arrived in Quebec on 11 August: 'I would not be out here if I did believe that war was imminent.' If war should come, he added, the British people were psychologically prepared for it. On 14 August the *Express* leading article declared: 'The storm has not yet broken. And the *Daily Express* believes that Hitler will keep the peace this year.' The chairman of Express Newspapers, E. J. Robertson, himself decided to drop the slogan and urged the guru to return to London.

In assessing what Beaverbrook really thought, as opposed to his deception of the British public, the interview he gave his personal friend, Roy Howard of the American Scripps-Howard group of newspapers, is significant. The date was April 1939. 'So far,' said Beaverbrook, 'the menace to Britain depends upon the threat to bomb London. Now London is in a position to meet and delay that menace.' He talked knowledgeably about the relative strengths of Britain and Germany in fighter and bomber planes and had plainly reflected upon London's vulnerability to air raids. 'I believe,' he said, 'that war in Europe depends ultimately upon the attitude of the British people. They will not put up indefinitely with threats and menaces. The war spirit may finally possess the people. If this spirit does arise, it may force the Government to take drastic measures. I hope very much that the day is far removed, but the English people won't stand indefinitely the injustices, persecution and abuses now being perpetrated in Europe.' He wrote to Quentin Reynolds on 26 April 1939 saying that we were all living on a great keg of gunpowder, with some burning fuses about, with nobody knowing when the blow-up would come.

None of the comparative realism of that interview and that letter was ever reflected in his newspapers in Britain. Beaverbrook, not for the first or last time, held his readers in contempt. At editorial conferences where the braver of his executives and leader writers expressed their misgivings he always replied: 'If we're right, everyone will praise our foresight. If we're wrong—nobody will remember.'[1] Dead men told no tales, but those who did survive remembered.

'There will be no war' was the most dishonest and indefensible of the *Express* campaigns, the subject of angry criticism long after the war was over. Editor Arthur Christiansen wrote in 1961: 'It seemed to me to suit the spirit of the time and the spirit of the people. It gave hope and reassurance that the worst need not befall. Was that so very wrong?' Yes. When Beaverbrook himself was calling for rearmament the soothing slogan, repeated *ad nauseam*, engendered national sloth and the climate of false security. The claim that it reflected the spirit of the people was bogus; the fear and detestation of Hitler and the Nazis were surging among the British people long before the first signs of resistance and serious preparation in Chamberlain's Government. 'There will be no war' suited the spirit of the advertisers who knew their customers would be less likely to buy new motor cars, furniture, carpets and cooking stoves if in a few months' time they might be dented by bomb blast, covered in rubble, or blackened by incendiaries.

In the spring of 1939 a visitor to Stornoway House observed men digging a hole in the garden, preparing a private air raid shelter for the occupant which for some reason was never completed. In the autumn of 1940 Stornoway House was shattered and burnt out by a German bomb.

---

[1] *Beaverbrook, A Study in Power and Frustration* by Tom Driberg, Weidenfeld & Nicolson, London, 1956.

Beaverbrook's contribution to the war effort as Minister of Aircraft Production and in other Cabinet appointments, sustaining Churchill, does not concern us in this study. Here was the verdict of the man who appointed him:

'All his remarkable qualities fitted the need. His personal buoyancy and vigour were a tonic. I was glad to be able sometimes to lean on him. He did not fail. This was his hour. His personal force and genius, combined with so much persuasion and contrivance, swept aside many obstacles.'

He created internecine Whitehall warfare; bullied and bawled; feuded with the formidable Ernest Bevin, Minister of Labour, who distrusted him, over the deployment of skills; pirated warehouses Lord Woolton had requisitioned for the storage of food. Critics niggled that the instant production of planes was the fruit of plans he inherited rather than initiated. When Churchill referred to Beaverbrook's 'magic' a Cabinet Minister said the principal stock-in-trade of a magician was illusion. But he produced results and exuded confidence in the darkest hours of the struggle for survival. The propagandist aspect was vital.

As a newspaper proprietor before he took office, he behaved with a sabotaging wildness difficult to reconcile with rational thought or judgement. His newspapers mounted a puerile campaign against the official blackout, an elementary precaution in a target as vulnerable to air bombardment as Britain. Food rationing was opposed as a dreadful iniquity and a *Daily Express* editorial on 19 November 1939 urged the public to revolt against it. If any citizen should have been tapped on the shoulder for seditious talk in the first year of the war he was Beaverbrook. One of his complaints against the blackout was that two members of the *Express* staff had, collectively, broken a leg and an arm. Food rationing, inevitable in a mini country encircled by sea and submarines and threatened with shortages, was denounced as a panic measure that smacked strangely and smelled strongly of a combination of Socialism and Fascism: the word-spinners were always available to Beaverbrook to translate his notions into printable editorials for a fee and pension. Rationing was introduced so that all the people might be fed, but they were told by the *Express* that 'The cry for rationing and registering springs from a mad passion to regiment the public.'

His newspapers opposed an expansion of the British Army: 'The Government plan a mighty army. Millions of men in khaki. What for? To please the French . . . Let the public show their determination to resist the proposal.' The future Minister of Aircraft Production wailed against the purchase of planes from America: 'American planes are not good enough for fighting. We should buy no more from that country. Even if there should be an expansion on a huge scale we are going to get very bad work as a result.'

After twenty-one months of what he called 'high adventure' in office, successively as Minister of Aircraft Production, Minister of State, Minister of Supply, then briefly of War Production, he was again the maverick, pressing in his newspapers support of Stalin's insistence on an immediate Second Front, an invasion of Germany in the West to relieve the pressure on the Eastern Front. To ensure world-wide publicity for the enterprise he announced his campaign at a gathering organised by the American Newspaper Publishers' Association in New York: 'Strike out to help Russia! Strike out violently—strike even recklessly!' He was telling the joyous diners in New York: 'How admirably Britain is now equipped in weapons of war for directing such an attack on Germany, I well know.' When he resigned as Minister in February 1942, his letter to Churchill ended with the words: 'In leaving, then, I send this letter of gratitude and devotion to the leader of the nation, the saviour of our people, and the symbol of resistance in the free world.' Now, for public consumption everywhere, he said: 'Of our own great leader, Mr Churchill, I read in all the newspapers and I am told here and there, wherever I go, that he will fall before the summer is out. You must help me to kill that bad rumour. Such a disaster we cannot contemplate in Great Britain.'

Mr Christiansen, working in his shirt sleeves in London, did not miss the story. His newspaper recorded the speech with the headline: 'THE BEAVER'S CALL SWEEPS AMERICA.' Nor was the *Express* tardy in setting up mass public rallies in Britain to demand the Second Front Now, repeating the technique of the Empire jamborees. One of the orators was Michael Foot, then editing the *Evening Standard*, and the Prophet himself materialised on the platform.

Mr Churchill was entitled to reflect that his friend was showing his gratitude and devotion in an eccentric manner. By denying the 'bad rumour' that Churchill would fall he added credence; worse, the announcement by a man of Beaverbrook's prominence, so recently a leading Minister, that Britain was admirably equipped at that time for such an attack on Germany raised the expectations of the public falsely and raised Stalin's suspicion of duplicity by the Allied powers. Why the delay in relieving Nazi pressure on the Eastern Front?

Operation Overlord of 1944 could not have been launched in 1942 and Beaverbrook knew it. In a BBC broadcast six months before he resigned as

Minister in February 1942, he told the British people that 30,000 more tanks were essential before the Western Front onslaught could be unleashed. The chilling obscenity of the Second Front Now hysteria was de-bunked by Driberg:

'At a great Anglo-Soviet demonstration at Birmingham, Beaverbrook said: "The Army is, in my opinion, equipped ready for the job and wanting to do it." Unfortunately, this stage of his campaign coincided with severe military reverses in North Africa. Beaverbrook's Birmingham rhetoric did not sound so convincing to a public stunned by the news that, contrary to all expectations, Tobruk had fallen and 25,000 British troops had surrendered—especially when Alan Moorehead, the distinguished war correspondent of the *Express* staff itself, reported that the Army, in Libya at any rate, was *not* "equipped for the job", that it was inferior to the Germans in tanks, in guns, and in aircraft (lacking dive-bombers in particular). These revelations of inadequate equipment shook the Government and the prestige of Churchill himself: but Beaverbrook also felt their repercussions, for there were many to recall, as *The Economist* did, that he had been, "at one time or another, responsible for the ordering and manufacture of all these items of equipment".'[1]

Rommel rolled the British Army back to Egypt; hardly an auspicious omen. The bloody failure of the raid on Dieppe in the summer of the same year silenced the belligerent Second Front civilians, and Beaverbrook's return to the Cabinet in September 1943 silenced him and his newspapers.

The Moral Rearmament Movement founded by Dr Frank Buchman, the American evangelist, embraced absolute honesty, purity, love, and unselfishness to achieve the moral regeneration of mankind. It also specialised in soul-cleansing confessions, and one of the souls it fumigated was Peter Howard's. Indeed, he became a pillar of the movement.

Peter Howard was an engaging personality, at one time the most dexterous of all the political mischief-makers whose work appeared under the pseudonym 'Cross-bencher' in the *Sunday Express*. He was the third of the troika of Beaverbrook fledgelings, the others being Michael Foot and Frank Owen, who together wrote—under another pseudonym 'Cato'—the best-seller *Guilty Men*, exposing all the Municheers and

[1] *Beaverbrook* by Tom Driberg.

Neville Chamberlainites except Beaverbrook. Then Howard, his soul cleansed and in a mood of spiritual revolt, wrote *Innocent Men*, easing his conscience with a confession: 'Did I conduct feuds and vendettas? Certainly I did. If I heard that anyone had criticised my employer or my newspaper, I would wait for weeks, maybe months, until the moment arrived to hang my victim's hide on the fence and take vengeance on him.'

There were many victims of his employer's vengeance. The Socialist Harold Laski had a good deal to answer for. He had written to Baldwin that his victory over Beaverbrook was a victory 'for the forces of sheer decency in public life'. In the 1945 post-war election the *Express* decided that 'Laski' sounded more sinister than 'Attlee'. One of the scarifying headlines was:

SHALL THE LASKI '25' RULE GREAT BRITAIN?

The professor was then the chairman of the Labour Party Executive, which had twenty-five members. Ernest Bevin, as Minister of Labour in Beaverbrook's Aircraft Production days, had to pay for his intransigence. Geoffrey Dawson, editor of *The Times* and Baldwin's crutch in the Abdication Crisis, was frequently scorched. Earl Mountbatten of Burma was in a category of his own as a target of a Beaverbrook vendetta.

Once upon a time they had been friends, or not unfriendly; Lady Louis and Mrs Jean Norton ran the switchboard at the *Daily Express* during the 1926 General Strike; in 1929 they were among the party to Russia. In the early years of the war 'Dickie' had letters from Max applauding his naval exploits. The sourness erupted over Dieppe and Mountbatten's role as the last Viceroy of India, but Beaverbrook's claim that he criticised Mountbatten only on grounds of public policy was cynically silly.

A variety of reasons other than military led to the ill-fated raid on Dieppe on 19 August 1942. Churchill later described it as 'a costly but not unfruitful reconnaissance in force', as an indispensable preliminary to full-scale operations, probing German defences, testing the Allies' capacity to land a large force with tanks on a heavily defended coastline. The political factor fell far short of sound wartime strategy; a well-publicised diversionary raid on the Continent, it was argued, would appease the important doubter in the Kremlin and the naggers on the home front. The psychological factor was the inactivity then frustrating the Canadian troops in England, forbidden by their government to take part in the Middle East campaign and therefore confined to ceaseless training. Dieppe was to be the opportunity for those men who were raring to go.

Mountbatten was Chief of Combined Operations and Montgomery was General Officer Commanding in Chief, Southern Command, head of the land forces earmarked for Dieppe during the planning stage. The portents which attended the previous spectacular and fruitless British aggressions in Norway and Greece were again present. Montgomery's demands for massive air cover and heavy naval bombardment before the landing were not met: the Mediterranean was Churchill's priority theatre of war for equipment and no heavy ships were allotted by the Navy. Mountbatten decided the June rehearsal was unsatisfactory and insisted on more preparation. July's weather inflicted two more postponements. Montgomery, concerned about security after those delays, wanted to call the raid off for all time and announced a cancellation to his officers. Luckily for his own reputation he was ordered to Egypt early in August to take command of the beleagured Eighth Army.

Seven thousand troops took part in the raid, mostly Canadians. The fighting lasted only nine hours, but the statistics tell the sad tale of one of the bloodiest encounters of the war: 4,963 of the Canadian 2nd Division landed on French soil, 3,369 became casualties, and more than 900 lost their lives. The raid was swiftly repulsed by the German occupiers of France.

The darker aspects of Beaverbrook's nature—the egocentricity, the pitiless extravagances, the visitation of vengeance upon a scapegoat—that led more compassionate men to regard him as capable of evil were all manifested in his reaction to this folly of war. He believed Dieppe was the deliberate slaughter of his Canadian compatriots in a 'futile and foolish attack' launched to discredit his cause of the Second Front Now. He held Mountbatten personally responsible. There was a confrontation between them soon after the event when they were guests at the London apartment of Averell Harriman, Special Representative of the US President. The American was distressed at the scene and told Churchill about it. Beaverbrook later admitted that at a private gathering he had allowed his bitterness to outrun his discretion and that his verbal assault on Mountbatten was ill-tempered. The Chief of Combined Operations was in no way involved in the political expediency of the exercise. Dieppe was approved by the Prime Minister and the Chiefs of Staff. Mountbatten and his planners had in fact advocated landings to the west and east of the French port with the object of encircling the most heavily defended sector: it was the Army who insisted on a frontal attack. Churchill's defence, that the reconnaissance in force was an indispensable preliminary to full-scale operations (if so, why wasn't it repeated more successfully elsewhere during the next two years?), was rhetorical moonshine for the consumption of a restive House of Commons. He would not as a military historian have written that a preliminary gallop over the mile-long course at Balaclava would have reduced the suicidal risks or casualties undertaken by Cardigan's Light Brigade.

The relationship was fitfully restored when Mountbatten, appointed Supreme Commander in South-East Asia, consulted the publisher on public relations in that theatre of war. They corresponded occasionally, and Beaverbrook in 1945 complimented him on his 'splendid services'.

The second eruption concerned Mountbatten's historic role in India, when Beaverbrook's rage had even less justification: Mountbatten, again, was carrying out orders. In March 1942, the Churchill wartime Government promised India full independence after the war. Viscount Mountbatten of Burma (the country he had reconquered from the Japanese) was the obvious choice as last of the Viceroys. He was appointed by Attlee's post-war Labour Government in March 1947, and by August the same year succeeded in liberating British India, transferring power to Indian hands and partitioning the sub-continent into the two new Dominions of India and Pakistan. The mission was fulfilled with diplomacy and dispatch, so much so that the provisional government of India requested his appointment as the first Governor-General, representing King George VI; he fulfilled the role as Earl Mountbatten and then returned to the Navy. It was a remarkable achievement darkened by one thunderous cloud. The partition, and the division of the Punjab and Bengal, aroused fanatical religious rivalry. For two months there were communal riots, mass migrations, massacres, then an uneasy acceptance of the new era. The combined patience and diplomacy of God, Allah, and Krishna ('Whatever god a man worships, it is I who answer the prayer') had failed before and have still failed to reconcile Muslim and Hindu: the sailor also failed.

Beaverbrook's newspapers maligned him as the man who 'threw India away'; by his hasty action and 'failure to define boundaries' he was held responsible for 'terrible disasters'. Beaverbrook moaned: 'There are many forces working for the Empire's disintegration. We have Lord Mountbatten acting as a Santa Claus in India.' The reproach became part of the mandatory diet of editorials in the Beaverbrook papers for many years. The vendettas, once mounted, were permanent; even when there was nothing to forgive, nothing was forgotten. The cure for infection by the viruses of Beaverbrook's hatred or envy was not discovered in his lifetime. Surgically, he specialised in reopening old wounds.

The publication in 1948 of *The Canadian Army, 1939–1945, an Official Historical Summary* was the sort of opportunity he would never miss. His

London *Evening Standard* was entrusted to review the volume, devoting a half-page to the article and concentrating to the exclusion of all other activities of the Canadian Army on what happened at Dieppe in 1942. A strategic blunder. An utter failure. An ill-conceived and badly-planned adventure. If the Dieppe disaster proved anything it proved that the Allies were not yet ready to launch an all-out attack on German-occupied Europe, but the *Evening Standard* reviewer reached the remarkable conclusion that 'It would have been better to have launched the full-scale attack and secured a permanent toe-hold in France. The plan was there, ready . . .' Colonel C. P. Stacey, who wrote the history, could only have been surprised at this appraisal.

When Mountbatten's appointment as First Sea Lord, the same supreme naval post from which his father was obliged to resign during the First World War, was announced in 1954, the *Observer* made this comment: 'It is pleasant to see the complete ineffectiveness of the campaign waged against Mountbatten by the Beaverbrook newspapers for the last ten or twelve years, a vendetta that has borne all the appearances of personal spite.' A. J. Cummings, a political opponent of Beaverbrook but under the influence of his 'magic', headlined his column in the Liberal *News Chronicle*: 'STOP SNIPING AT LORD LOUIS', but his hope that Beaverbrook would change his mind about this 'brilliant man' was not fulfilled. Vendetta? No; differences over public policy. 'He is subject,' wrote Beaverbrook in June 1955, 'to the same measure of attack as any other public man who may transgress the high principles which the *Express* sets in all matters concerning the British Empire.'

In May 1958, Old Max wrote to Young Max (his son, Sir Max Aitken, DSO, DFC, who succeeded him on his death as head of Beaverbrook Newspapers): 'Print these statements, simple statements. Don't Trust Mountbatten in Any Public Capacity. Together with a further quotation from Mountbatten's speech in Canada where he said he took full responsibility for Dieppe. Four thousand set forth and three thousand did not return.'[1]

In common decency, as Chief of Combined Operations, Mountbatten did not wish in public and least of all in Canada to protect himself by arguing that his plan of operation was not executed and that the raid was starved of naval and air support. Beaverbrook placed the worst possible interpretation upon his shouldering the full responsibility. In personal savagery he rivalled Northcliffe's pursuit of Haldane. One of his periodic

---

[1] *Beaverbrook* by A. J. P. Taylor, FBA.

quarrels with Churchill was solely due to some justified praise Winston had bestowed on Mountbatten.

We began with the proposition that 'Everything anyone said about Max is true—the best things and the worst things.' There is abundant evidence for the worst and less for the best. Harold Macmillan, who had contact with him at stages of his own career, in and out of office and occasionally serving under or near him in a ministry, is an impressive witness because he neither praises nor condemns wholeheartedly:

'I felt instinctively that he was a man whom it was wise to treat with a certain aloofness, for there were aspects of his character which I found distasteful. He had a streak of vindictiveness and even cruelty. But he was equally capable of extraordinary kindness, and often his kind actions were towards those from whom he could gain no personal advantage and who could never repay him in any form. His charm could be, if he chose to exert it, almost irresistible. All men, I suppose, have in their moral make-up good and evil. Yet most of us are, to be frank, of a somewhat indeterminate nature. Beaverbrook sometimes seemed almost a Jekyll and Hyde . . . If there were aspects of his character which repelled, there were others that were intensely attractive. While I served him and until the end of his life I received from him nothing but kindness . . . Perhaps I was fortunate, but this was my experience.'[1]

Others were less fortunate. Ernest Bevin could cut him down to size, but Churchill did not try. The streak of vindictiveness and even cruelty was exhibited privately in his treatment of his Cabinet colleagues : Attlee, no coward, once said to him in Churchill's presence, 'What have I done to you that you should treat me like this?' The same streak was frequently exhibited in public in the vendettas conducted in his newspapers. Nobody burst into spontaneous tears on Beaverbrook's behalf when he declared with feigned self-pity at an election meeting : 'Everybody knows the trouble I've seen. If ever a man has been maligned, misinterpreted, misreported, and attacked, I am that man.' There would have been universal accord if he had somewhat adjusted the heartcry confessionally to, 'Everybody knows the trouble I've been. If ever a man has maligned, misinterpreted, misreported, and attacked, I am that man.'

There was a code of honour controlling the blood feuds in Corsica and Sicily in the eighteenth century. The motive was to avenge a murdered

[1] *The Blast of War* by Harold Macmillan, Macmillan, London, 1967.

relative or friend, or a woman's honour, as a duty or privilege. The vendetta was brought into disrepute by the Mafia in the nineteenth century, defying established justice with the dagger, and by the British and American Press lords in the twentieth, abusing their power for personal ends in feuds where they were in no danger of losing a drop of their own blood unless they tortured beyond endurance a man like Mrs Baldwin's 'Tiger'. Beaverbrook was the most vicious, unleashing his passion to extraordinary lengths. When he visited the *Express* newsroom to await the result of the St George's by-election he saw a picture of Stanley Baldwin stuck on the wall. 'Take that picture down,' he shouted, 'I will not have it here!' The staff were embarrassed by his rage.

Beaverbrook and the skilled operators he recruited and inspired enhanced the technical achievements of modern journalism in news gathering and notably in presentation, displaying a panache never seen before. He and the first Lord Rothermere also emasculated the integrity and public standing of the popular Press by the policies they conducted for their 'causes' and against their 'enemies'. In his vendettas the Beaver favoured refined and protracted torture, the fierce light at midnight and darkness at noon, rather than the clumsy stab in the back inflicted by the unsubtle Rothermere. One repellent diversion of Mr Hyde was his persecution of the second and last Sir John Ellerman, a shy, sick recluse whose interest in life was the scientific study of rodents but who also happened to be Britain's richest man. His wealth, his business activities, his hobby, his houses, his journeys were the subject of persistent scrutiny in Beaverbrook's newspapers. He was rarely newsworthy and hated publicity, yet he could not put his head outside a door without being pursued by reporters and photographers on the Beaver's payroll. Ellerman, in an agonising talk with me ('All those millions, and this persecution by the Press, are driving me crazy. I can't stand it any more'), said the cause of the vendetta was a quarrel Beaverbrook had with his father. Beaverbrook told me he had never known Ellerman's father, never had business conversation with him or any relation with him whatsoever; he merely had the pleasure of his acquaintance, nothing more; he was 'a short stout little Jew, he didn't attract anybody or please those he came in contact with'.

Were Dieppe and India the cause of the implacable hostility to Mountbatten, or instruments to gratify a private grudge? A. J. P. Taylor concluded that 'It is difficult not to feel that more lay behind . . . none of Beaverbrook's friends could discover what it was. Something about Mountbatten touched Beaverbrook on a raw nerve.' Driberg wrote, 'It is possible that Beaverbrook's feud springs from a deeper, earlier, and more personal source.' There was, in fact, no mystery: I accept the simple explanation that follows, given to me by Lord Mountbatten himself. In the early day Beaverbrook was eager to befriend Mountbatten, and did, in the same way that he was ready to patronise the rising stars in politics, regardless of party. Mountbatten was prepared to be encouraged but not patronised. He would be nobody's protégé. He listened to advice but exercised the right to reject it. He understood more than most the value of newspaper publicity but preferred an arm's-length relationship with Press proprietors. He was at nobody's beck and call and Beaverbrook resented it. Hence the spleen in his newspapers until 1963 when Macmillan achieved a reconciliation between them.

There was nothing enigmatic about Beaverbrook's attitude to the Royal Family. It was the subject of a brief altercation in Canada a few years before his death. Sir John Elliot, Blumenfeld's son, tells the story in his postscript to Alan Wood's *The True History of Lord Beaverbrook*:

'He asked me what I thought of the paper now. I offered one criticism. I asked him why he, who had so sure a journalistic instinct, published now and then what seemed to many people to be attacks on the monarchy, whom the British people loved and respected. I told him I believed it did the paper—and him—much harm.

'He stopped in his tracks, and for a moment said nothing. Then explosively: "The *Express* never attacks the Queen! She is a fine young person, and she plays her part well. It is the principle of royalty that is out of date. 'Holy Cows' may still be necessary for India; they are an anachronism in Britain."'

There is evidence, from Driberg, that though any sentimental or mystical concept of kingship was alien to him, he accepted monarchy as a convenient and expedient arrangement. The petty side of Beaverbrook's character again supplies the answer: he never forgot the grumbling opposition of George V to his own ascent in the social scale during the First War. His emergence as the King's Man in the Abdication Crisis did not confuse Edward VIII about his true motives. He thought Beaverbrook was interested, no doubt, in supporting a King who had 'tramped the outer marches of the Empire', but he observed in his memoirs that 'An additional impulse was furnished by his long-standing enmity for Mr Baldwin.'

The *Express* newspapers were as enterprising as their rivals in expanding sales by the lavish coverage of glamorous or poignant Royal events. In the intervals between they were noted for their waspish comment, inspired by the chief shareholder. Whacking Mountbatten was some recompense for having been whacked himself by the late King George V; occasionally it was implied that as the uncle of Prince Philip the Earl Mountbatten was a sinister influence behind the Throne. Beaverbrook's newspapers were tediously vigilant in exposing any whiff of inefficiency or discourtesy on the part of the Palace, though the errors were occasionally those of officials. It was the fashion of the time (less so now) to attribute sin to the advisers as if the Royals were their puppets on a string. They were taken to task by Beaverbrook's newspapers for selecting the wrong date for the Coronation of the present Queen, to suit the convenience of Her Majesty and her consort rather than that of the readers of the *Daily Express*. The criticism of Prince Philip moved him to refer to the *Express* as 'that bloody awful newspaper'. Any columnist writing for Beaverbrook's newspapers, including John Gordon, knew that he could come in from the cold by a spontaneous fit of anger about a new lick of paint on the Royal yacht *Britannia*. Why wasn't the allowance paid to Prince Philip made public? What is the Queen Really Worth?—relating to her private fortune—was a recurrent theme: the best years of the lives of many a city editor and economic expert were wasted on that inconclusive probe. 'No,' Beaverbrook would say, 'it must be more than that,' and resurrect the subject a few months later as if it had never been mentioned before. The nagging of the Royals was unjust to them and distasteful to his readers: what did that matter? There was no reason known to Beaverbrook why Royal blood should not be spilled in a vendetta; the fact that they could not reply was their concern, not his.

Beaverbrook had the same freedom of speech in his newspapers as any stump orator on a soapbox at Hyde Park Corner; no more, no less. It was his own affair when he squandered his gunpowder on foolhardy campaigns. It was everybody's affair when he used his influence, whether unwittingly or from some Machiavellian or merely mischievous motive, to weaken national resolve and resistance.

The Empire Free Trade bubble created havoc in the Conservative Party; otherwise it caused no more harm than the activities of the Flat Earth Society or the spotters of unidentified flying objects. The potential danger of his policy for Splendid Isolation was limited by the common sense of the British public rather than by any lack of energy or skill on his part as a propagandist. 'There will be no war' was at its best an irresponsible gamble and at its worst a cruel deception. Beaverbrook was telling his American friends in private that nobody knew *when* the blow-up would come; concurrently, his newspapers were assuring their readers that a blow-up would not come because Germany wasn't ready for war and could not come because even if Hitler himself wanted war his generals would not allow it. The slogan appeared in the *Daily Express* until a few weeks before the outbreak. The European dictators could not have hoped or prayed for a more efficient Fifth Column in Britain than that created by the principal Press barons, aided and abetted by the appeasement policy of *The Times*: Beaverbrook considered it 'the duty of newspapers to advocate a policy of optimism in the broadest sense'—not, therefore, their duty to tell the truth.

When war did come there was no hint of contrition from the leading deceiver, no attempt to make amends. The man who said there would be no war was soon embarking upon campaigns that, had they prevailed, would have ensured there would be no victory. Perversity is a mild explanation of his opposition to expanding the British Army when war was declared and to buying American planes : as soon as he was Minister he ordered American planes on a vast scale. He beat the drum in favour of the pettiest discontents, and his incitement to the public to revolt against wartime food rationing bordered on sedition. Opinion surveys conducted by Mass Observation showed that a large majority in all classes was decidedly in favour of rationing, more so after the *Daily Express* campaign than before it.

It would be pleasant, but it is difficult, to absolve the Beaver from any charge of cant. The man who told Churchill in a letter that he had created all the big Trusts in Canada, asking him not to tell anyone else, became in Britain the vociferous champion of the 'small man' in business, insisting on free competition, pillorying the 'Co-op' and the chain stores for pushing the High Street shopkeepers out of business. '*Instinctively,*' he declared in his newspapers, 'I am on the side of the little man and against the great big fellow. I am on the side of the little minnow against the great big trout. I am on the side of the little pig against the big bad wolf. I am on the side of the little trader and against the co-operative society.'

Beaverbrook approached death with some reluctance and delay but with his accustomed histrionic majesty: 'The days of our years are three score and ten. I have passed the allotted span. Every hour further is a bonus to me from the Almighty.' Some bonus; it lasted another fifteen years. There may have been some reluctance on the part of the Almighty to speed his parting from the earth.

At this stage of his life there was some ribaldry among the friends of the Old Testament Prophet about his future. H. G. Wells had earlier expressed the view that if Max got to Heaven he wouldn't last long: 'He will be chucked out for trying to pull off a merger between Heaven and Hell ... after having secured a controlling interest in key subsidiary companies, of course.' Randolph Churchill said, 'It would be damned ungrateful of him if he *didn't* believe in Hell, seeing that they've been getting the place ready for him specially all these years.' Beaverbrook acted the final scenes with superb artistry and no noticeable humility. He read the Bible even more diligently as he contemplated the Life to Come, quoting this as a favourite passage: *'God shall bring every work into judgement, with every secret thing, whether it be good, or whether it be evil.'* He knew that Elijah was carried up to Heaven in a whirlwind (II Kings 2:11), and would not have been surprised if some such exit as that was in store for him. He did not, to the end, lose his puckish sense of fun; nor did he conceal his uncertainty as to his destination. I was present at the Positively Last Farewell Performance of William Maxwell Aitken, Baron Beaverbrook. A banquet was staged at the Dorchester Hotel on 25 May 1964 to celebrate his eighty-fifth birthday. Lord Thomson of Fleet, another ebullient Canadian and the proprietor of *The Times*, was the host. There were six hundred of us, of all ages and most professions, happy or proud for one reason or another to be at the last gathering of the tribe, regarding the guest of honour either with awe or, with qualifications, affection. I was able to reflect, like Harold Macmillan, that I had received nothing from him but kindness, knowing others were less fortunate. Nobody present, I reckon, has forgotten the nerve-tingling atmosphere of the occasion, as spellbinding as the last act of a Verdi opera without the need for scenery or music or lighting effects. The compelling personality of the man, now physically frail and dying, was undiminished. Everybody knew, including Beaverbrook, that it *was* the last performance—but not, far from it, *The Death-bed Repentance*. He arrived at the hotel in a chair, walking to his place on the arm of his son, bracing himself for a display of oratory equalled in my experience only by Lloyd George, Winston Churchill and Michael Foot. We heard his definition of the good journalist:

'First, he must be true to himself. The man who is not true to himself is no journalist. He must show courage, independence and initiative. He must also, I believe, be a man of optimism. He has no business to be a pedlar of gloom and despondency. He must be a respecter of persons, but able to deal with the highest and the lowest on the same basis, which is regard for the public interest and a determination to get at the facts.'

The timing of his sallies and asides was professional, the voice strong, the grin whimsical, the gestures dramatic. His theme was 'The Apprentice'—an apprentice to finance in Canada, to politics in England

and to journalism in Fleet Street. He had thought, at last, he would be Master, fancy free; instead he became 'the slave of the black Art', never to know freedom again. The peroration was perfection:

'This is my final word. It is time for me to become an apprentice once more. I have not settled in which direction. But somewhere, sometime soon.'

There was a brief silence while the audience shuffled to its feet, uproarious applause, and then an emotional rendering of 'For he's a jolly good fellow'.

Beaverbrook returned to Cherkley that night and died after two weeks on 9 June. His son, Max Aitken II, told me that his father, just before he became unconscious, handed over to him a box of papers he described as secret. Young Max, accompanied by George Millar, the Beaver's secretary in charge of his private office, took the papers to the hillside near Cherkley and set fire to them.

INDEX

Acheson, Dean, Secretary of State, 215, 216, 218, 219, 224
Agate, James, 252
Aitken, Sir Max, DSO, DFC, 276, 290, 297
Aitken, William Maxwell, see Beaverbrook, Lord
Alexander the Great, 131
American, the Boston, 57, 64
American, the Chicago, 57
American, the New York, formerly the New York *Journal*, 61, 65
Amery, Leo S., 266
Angell, Sir Norman, 125
Apperson, Phoebe Elisabeth, see Hearst, Mrs George
Archbold, John D., 71
Arthur, Sir George, 91
Asquith, Herbert Henry, 86, 88, 89, 95, 101, 102, 103, 105, 106, 113, 117, 118, 119, 244, 246, 247
Astor, Lady, 252
Atkinson, Brooks, 204
Attlee, Clement (Earl Attlee), 232, 287

Baldwin, Stanley, 10, 151, 155, 156, 242; 256-76 (the Beaverbrook vendetta); Premier, 257; 261, 262; Abdication crisis, 276-9
Balfour, Arthur, 118
Ballin, Herr Albert, 96-102
Bartholomew, Harry Guy, 234
Barthou, Louis, 136
Battenberg, Prince Louis Alexander of, 92
Baxter, Beverley, 251, 252, 266
Beaton, Cecil, 195
Beaverbrook, Lady (Gladys Drury), 237; in Montreal, 237; arrives in UK, 241; 1927, death of, 254
BEAVERBROOK, Lord (Sir William Maxwell Aitken, Bt.), 93, 120, 126, 127, 128, 149, 150, 157, 158, 159, 176, 180, 220
Chapter V: The 'Rage', 231; 'wickedness' charge, 231; foul-weather friend, 231; and power, 231-2; denounced by Attlee, Bevin, Cripps, Reith, 232-3; his three careers, 235; son of Canadian Manse, 235; selling bonds, 236; marries Gladys Drury, 237; turning ten thousand dollars into a million, 236-7; in the merger jungle, 258; Canadian Cabinet Minister's warning, 239; emigrates to UK, 241; his generosity to useful people, 242; the Bonar Law-Aitken axis, 242; Unionist MP, 242; honours in Britain, brickbats in Canada, 243; Asquith tells Churchill of Aitken's 'shadiest' Canadian record, 245; anger at the Palace, 245-9; enters Fleet Street, buys *Daily*

Express, founds *Sunday Express*, 249-50; political propaganda, 250; peddles romanticism and moral indignation, 251; Lloyd George on Beaverbrook's 'disgusting hypocrisy', 251; death of Gladys Drury, 255; vendetta against Baldwin, 256-76; death of Law, 257; Beaverbrook and Rothermere as 'The Wicked Uncles', 261; called a 'corrupting power', 261; under-estimates Baldwin, 261; Empire Free Trade policy examined, 266; Baldwin's denunciation, the prerogative of the harlot, 274; Abdication Crisis, 276-9; 'Splendid Isolation' and the EEC, 279-80; 'There will be no war', 280-3; Churchill extols his Cabinet service, 284; his Second Front campaign, 285-6; the personal vendettas, 287; Mountbatten, 287-91, 293; 'This is my final word,' 297
Begbie, Harold, 105
Bellew, Kyrle, 129
Bennett, Arnold, 252, 258, 263
Bennett, James Gordon, 69
Bennett, Richard Bedford, 236, 241, 271
Berriz, Colonel, 37, 38
Bethmann-Hollweg, Theobald von, 86, 87, 100
Beveridge, Sir William, 164
Bevin, Ernest, 232, 236, 291
Bierce, Ambrose, 13, 28, 58, 59, 60
Billings, John, 220
Birkenhead, Lord, 109, 231, 232, 242, 253, 254, 258, 260
Blackwood's Magazine, 93
Blanco, General Ramón, 42, 43, 51, 52
Blumenfeld, Ralph D., 94, 103, 249, 250, 251
Borden, Sir Robert, 246
Bottomley, Horatio, 93
Bracken, Brendan, 232
Bresci, G., 58
Brex, Twells, 94
Bridges, Harry, 220
Bridges, Senator Styles, 214
Brisbane, Arthur, 50, 58, 60, 66, 75
Bruce Lockhart, Robert, 252
Bryan, William Jennings, 57, 65, 71
Bryson, George Eugene, 36, 37, 40
Buccleuch, Duke of, 104
Buchman, Dr Frank, 286
Buck, Pearl, 201
Buckmaster, Lord, 102
Bull, Sir William, 265

Calhoun, Eleanor, 21
Campbell, Alexander, 149
Campbell-Bannerman, Sir Henry, 84, 85
Cánovas, Antonio, 29, 42

298

My Friend Leonard

My Friend Leonard

James Frey

W F HOWES LTD

This large print edition published in 2005 by
W F Howes Ltd
Units 6/7, Victoria Mills, Fowke Street
Rothley, Leicester LE7 7PJ

1 3 5 7 9 10 8 6 4 2

First published in the United Kingdom in 2005
by John Murray (Publishers)

A CIP catalogue record for this book is available
from the British Library

ISBN 1 84505 850 X

Typeset by Palimpsest Book Production Limited,
Polmont, Stirlingshire
Printed and bound in Great Britain
by Antony Rowe Ltd, Chippenham, Wilts.

my cup runneth over.

psalm 23:5

BEGINNING

On my first day in jail, a three hundred pound man named Porterhouse hit me in the back of the head with a metal tray. I was standing in line for lunch and I didn't see it coming. I went down. When I got up, I turned around and I started throwing punches. I landed two or three before I got hit again, this time in the face. I went down again. I wiped blood away from my nose and my mouth and I got up I started throwing punches again. Porterhouse put me in a headlock and started choking me. He leaned toward my ear and said I'm gonna let you go. If you keep fighting me I will fucking hurt you bad. Stay down and I will leave you alone. He let go of me, and I stayed down.

I have been here for eighty-seven days. I live in Men's Module B, which is for violent and felonious offenders. There are thirty-two cells in my module, thirty-two inmates. At any given time, there are between five and seven deputies watching us. All of us wear blue and yellow striped jumpsuits and black, rubber-soled slippers that do not have laces. When we move between rooms we walk

3

through barred doors and metal detectors. My cell is seven feet wide and ten feet long. The walls are cement and the floor is cement and the bed is cement, the bars iron, the toilet steel. The mattress on the bed is thin, the sheets covered with grit. There is a window in my cell, it is a small window that looks out onto a brick wall. The window is made of bulletproof glass and there are bars on both sides of it. It affords me the proper amount of State required sunlight. Sunlight does not help pass time, and the State is not required to provide me anything that helps pass time.

My life is routine. I wake up early in the morning. I brush my teeth. I sit on the floor of the cell I do not go to breakfast. I stare at a gray cement wall. I keep my legs crossed my back straight my eyes forward. I take deep breaths in and out, in and out, and I try not to move. I sit for as long as I can I sit until everything hurts I sit until everything stops hurting I sit until I lose myself in the gray wall I sit until my mind becomes as blank as the gray wall. I sit and I stare and I breathe. I sit and I stare. I breathe. I stand in the middle of the afternoon. I use the toilet and I drink a glass of water and I smoke a cigarette. I leave my cell and I walk to the outdoor recreation area. If the weather holds, there are prisoners in the area playing basketball, lifting weights, smoking cigarettes, talking. I do not mingle with them. I walk along the perimeter of the wall until I can feel my legs again. I walk until my eyes and my mind regain some sort of focus. Until they bring me back to where I am and to what I am, which is an alcoholic and a drug addict and a criminal. If the weather is bad, the area is empty. I go outside despite the weather. I walk along the perimeter until I can feel and remember. I am what I am. I need to feel and remember.

I spend my afternoons with Porterhouse. His real name is Antwan, but he calls himself Porterhouse because he says he's big and juicy like a fine-ass steak. Porterhouse threw his wife out the window of their seventh floor apartment when he found her in bed with another man. He took the man into a field and shot him five times. The first four shots went into the man's arms and legs. He waited thirty minutes to let the man feel the pain of the shots, pain he said was the equivalent to the pain he felt when saw the man fucking his wife. Shot number five went into the man's heart. From three o'clock to six o'clock, I read to Porterhouse. I sit on my bed and he sits on the floor. He leans against the wall and he closes his eyes so he can, as he says, do some imagining. I read slowly and clearly, taking an occasional break to drink a glass of water or smoke a cigarette. In the past twelve weeks we have worked our way through *Don Quixote*, *Leaves of Grass*, and *East of Eden*. We are currently reading *War and Peace*, which is Porterhouse's favorite. He smiled at the engagement of Andrei and Natasha. He cried when Anatole betrayed her. He cheered at the battle of Borodino, and though he admired the Russian tactics, he cursed while Moscow burned. When we're not reading, he carries *War and Peace* around with him. He sleeps with it at night, cradles it as if it were his child. He says that if he could, he would read it again and again.

I started reading to Porterhouse the day after he hit me with the tray, my second day here. I was walking to my cell and I had a copy of *Don Quixote* in my hand. As I passed his cell, Porterhouse said come here, I wanna talk to you. I stopped and asked him what he wanted, he said he wanted to know why I was here and why a County Sheriff would give him three cartons of cigarettes to beat my ass. I told him that I had hit a County Sheriff with a car going five miles an hour while I was drunk and high on crack and that I had fought several others when they tried to arrest me. He asked if I had hit the man on purpose. I told him I didn't remember doing it. He laughed. I asked him why he was here and he told me. I did not offer further comment. He asked what the book was and I told him and he asked why I had it and I told him that I liked books. I offered to let him have it when I was done with it and he laughed and said I can't read mother-fucker, fucking book ain't gonna do me no good. I offered to read to him. He said he'd think about it. A couple of hours later he showed up and sat on my floor. I started reading. He has been here every day since. At six o'clock, I walk with Porterhouse to dinner, the only meal of the day that I eat. It is usually foul, disgusting, almost inedible. The meat is mush, the bread stale, potatoes like water, vegetables hard as rock. I eat it anyway. Porterhouse eats seconds and thirds and fourths, which, by long-standing arrangements, he takes from the trays of other prisoners. He offers to get food for me, but I decline. When I am finished eating, I sit and I listen to Porterhouse talk about his upcoming trial. Like every other man in here, regardless of what they might say, Porterhouse is guilty of the crimes that he has been accused of committing. He wants to go to trial because until he is convicted, he will stay here, at county jail, instead of doing his time in state prison. Jail is a much easier place to live than prison. There is less violence, there are more privileges, most of the prisoners know they are getting out within the next year, and most sooner than that, and they want to be left alone. Once they're gone, they don't want to come back. In prison, there are gangs, rapes, drugs, murder. Most of the prisoners are in for long stretches and will most likely never be free. If they are ever free, they will be more dangerous than they were before they were imprisoned. They could give two fucks about rehabilitation, they need to survive. To survive they need to replace their humanity with savagery. Porterhouse knows this, but wants to remain human for as long as he can. A guilty verdict is coming his way, but until it does, he will stay here, and he will remain a human being.

After dinner I go to the payphone. I dial a number that was given to me by my friend

7

Leonard. The number allows me to make free long distance phone calls. I do not know where Leonard got the number, and I have never asked him. That has always been my policy with Leonard. Take what he offers, thank him for it, do not ask questions. Leonard is what I am, an alcoholic and a drug addict and a criminal, though he is not currently incarcerated. He is fifty-two years old and he lives in Las Vegas, where he oversees an unnamed organization's interests in a number of finance, entertainment and security companies. When we talk we do not discuss his business.

I always call Lilly first. Lilly with long black hair and pale skin and blue eyes like deep, clean water. Lilly whose father deserted her and whose mother sold Lilly's body for drugs when she was thirteen. Lilly who became a crackhead and a pillpopper and hitchhiked across the country on her back so that she could escape her Mother. Lilly who has been raped and beaten and used and discarded. Lilly who is alone in the world except for me and a Grandmother who has terminal cancer. Lilly who is living in a halfway house in Chicago while she tries to stay clean and waits for me to be released from this place. Lilly who loves me. Lilly who loves me. I dial the number. I know she's sitting in a phone booth in the halfway house waiting for my call. My heart starts beating faster as it does whenever I see her or speak to her. She picks up on the third ring. She says hello sweet boy, I say hello sweet girl. She says I miss you and I say we'll see each other soon. She asks me how I am and I tell her that I'm good. She's upset that I'm here and I don't want her to worry, I always tell her things are good. I ask her how she is and her answers vary from day to day, hour to hour, minute to minute. Sometimes she says she feels free, which is a feeling she has rarely felt but has always sought. She says she feels like she's getting better and healthier and can put her past behind her. Sometimes she says that she feels fine, that she is getting by and that is enough, that she's off drugs and has a roof over her head, she says she's fine. Sometimes she's depressed. She feels like her Grandmother is going to die and I am going to leave her and she is going to be alone in the world, which is something she says she cannot handle. She says there are always options, she'll weigh them when the time comes to weigh them. Sometimes she feels nothing. Absolutely nothing. She doesn't talk she just breathes into the phone. I tell her to hold on, that she'll feel again, feel better again, feel free again, I tell her to hold on, sweet girl, please hold on. She doesn't talk. She just breathes into the phone.

I met Lilly and Leonard five months ago. I was a patient at a drug and alcohol treatment center. I checked in after a ten year bout with alcoholism and a three year bout with crack addiction, which ended when I woke up on a plane after two weeks of blackness and discovered that I had knocked out my front four teeth, broken my nose and my eye socket, and torn a hole in my cheek that took

9

forty stitches to close. At the time, I was wanted in three states on drug, drunk-driving and assault charges. I didn't have a job or any money and I was nearly dead. I didn't want to go to the treatment center, but I didn't have any other options. At least not options I was ready to accept.

I met Lilly on my second day. I was standing in line waiting for detoxification drugs and she was standing in front of me. She turned around and she said hello to me and I said hello to her and she asked what happened to my face and I shrugged and told her I didn't know and she laughed. I saw her and spoke to her later that day and the next and the next and the next. The treatment center had a policy against male/female relationships. We ignored the policy. We talked to each other, slipped each other notes, met each other in the woods that were part of the center's grounds. We helped each other and understood each other. We fell in love with each other. We are young, she is twenty-four and I am twenty-three, and we fell in love. Neither of us had felt anything like what we felt for one another and we agreed that we would stay together and live together when we left the treatment center. We got caught with each other and we paid for the violation of the center's rules. Lilly left the center and I went after her. I found her selling her body for crack and I brought her back. I left a week later and came here. Lilly stayed for nine more weeks and has been at the halfway house in Chicago for a month. When I leave here, I am going to meet her.

I met Leonard three days after I met Lilly. I was sitting by myself in the cafeteria eating a bowl of oatmeal. He came to my table and accused me of calling him Gene Hackman. I didn't remember calling him Gene Hackman, which made him angry. He told me that if I called him Gene Hackman again, there was going to be a problem. I laughed at him. He did not take kindly to my laughing and he threatened me. I laughed again, called him an old man, and told him if he didn't get out of my face, I was going to beat his ass. He stared at me for a minute. I stared back. I stood up and told him to get the fuck out of my face or prepare to get his ass beat. He asked me my name and I told him. He told me his name and asked me if I was fucked-up. I said yes, Leonard, I'm fucked-up, I'm fucked-up real bad. He offered me his hand and said good, I'm fucked-up too, and I like fucked-up people, let's sit and eat and see if we can be friends. I took his hand and I shook it and we sat down and we ate together and we became friends.

Over the course of the following two months, which is how long I was at the treatment center, Leonard became my closest friend. When I walked out of the center shortly after finishing the process of physical detoxification, Leonard walked out after me. I told him to leave me alone, but he wouldn't do it. He followed me. I knocked him down, and he got up. I knocked him down again and he got back up again. He told me that he wasn't going to let me leave, and that if I tried, he would have me found and brought back. He told me it didn't matter how many times I left, he would have me brought back every single time. I looked into his eyes and I listened to his words. He is thirty years older than me but he is what I am, an alcoholic and a drug addict and a criminal. His eyes and words held truth, a truth that I knew and trusted more than institutional truth or medical truth or the truth of people who haven't seen the shit that I've seen. I went back to the center and I stayed at the center. I was leaving because I wanted liquor and I wanted crack and I wanted to die. I went back because of Leonard.

For whatever the reasons, and I do not know all of them, whenever I needed something or someone, Leonard was there. He watched over me and protected me. He helped me reconcile with my family. He gave me the best advice that I was given while I was at the center, which was to hold on. No matter how bad or difficult life becomes, if you hold on, hold on to whatever it is you need to hold on to, be it religion, friends, a support group, a set of steps or your own heart, if you hold on, just hold on, life will get better. He encouraged me to be with Lilly. He told me to forget about the fucking rules, that love doesn't come around that often, and when it does you've got to take it and try to keep it.

After Lilly left, she needed money to come back and stay at the center. Her Grandmother didn't have any more money. She had spent what she had to put Lilly there the first time, and Lilly didn't qualify for any of the financial aid programs. I didn't tell Leonard about Lilly's problems and I didn't ask him for help. He had done enough for me.

The morning he was leaving he asked to speak to me. I went to his room and he handed me a card. It had five names and five phone numbers on it. All of them were his, he said he used different names in different places.

He said call if you need anything, doesn't matter what it is or where you are, just call. I asked him why there were five numbers and five names on the card and he told me not to worry, just call if I need anything. After he gave me the card, he said he had something he wanted to talk to me about. I said fine, talk. He looked nervous, which I had never seen before. He took a deep breath. He said Kid, I have always wanted to be married and I have always wanted to have children. More specifically, I have always wanted to have a son. I have been thinking about this for a while now and I have decided that from now on, I would like you to be my son. I will watch out for you as I would if you were my real son, and I will offer you advice and help guide you through your life. When you are with me, and I plan on seeing you after we both leave here, you will be introduced

13

as my son and you will be treated as such. In return, I ask that you keep me involved in what you are doing and allow me to take part in your life. If there are ever issues with your real father, I will insist you defer to and respect him before me and over me. I laughed and asked him if he was joking. He said that he wasn't joking, not even close. I warned him that I tended to cause a lot of problems for the people in my life, and that if he could deal with that, I'd be happy to be his son. He laughed and he hugged me. When he released me he said he wanted me to go to jail and do my time and protect myself. He said not to worry about Lilly that she was going to be taken care of, that her financial issues had been resolved, that he hoped someday she would be better, that someday we would have a life together. I tried to object, but he interrupted me. He said what is done is done, now say thank you. I said thank you and I started to cry. I hoped that someday she would be better, that someday we would have a life together.

I talk to Leonard every two or three days. I call him if I can't get hold of Lilly, or I call him when I'm done talking to her. He always asks the same two questions: are you okay, do you need anything. My answers are always the same: yes I'm okay, no I don't need anything. He offers to come visit I tell him no. He asks when I'm getting out, I always give him the same date. He wants to have a party the day of my release, I tell him I want to see

Lilly, I want to be alone with her. When we hang-up he always says the same thing: look 'em in the eye and show no fear.

When I'm done with the phone, I go back to my cell. I do a hundred push-ups and two hundred sit-ups. When I am done with the push-ups and sit-ups, I walk to the shower. Most of the Prisoners shower in the morning, so I am usually alone. I turn on the heat from multiple faucets. I sit down on the floor. The water hits me from multiple directions it hits my chest, my back, the top of my head. It hits my arms, my legs. It burns and it hurts and I sit and I take the burn and I take the hurt. I don't do it because I like it, because I don't. I sit and I take the pain and I ignore the pain and I forget the pain because I want to learn some form of control. I believe that pain and suffering are different things. Pain is the feeling. Suffering is the effect that pain inflicts. If one can endure pain, one can live without suffering. If one can learn to withstand pain, one can withstand anything. If one can learn to control pain, one can learn to control oneself. I have lived a life without control. I have spent twenty-three years destroying myself and every-thing and everyone around me and I don't want to live that way anymore. I take the pain so that I will never suffer. I take the pain to experience control. I sit and I burn and I take it.

I finish my shower and I go back to my cell. I sit down on the floor and I pick up a book. It is a small book a Chinese book. It is a short book and a simple book called *Tao Te Ching*, written by a man named Lao-tzu. It is not known when it was written or under what conditions, nothing is known about the writer except his name. Roughly translated, the title means The Book of the Way. I open the book at random. I read whatever is in front of me. I read slowly and deliberately. There are eighty-one simple poems in the book. They are about life and The Way of life. They say things like in thinking keep to simple, in conflict be fair, don't compare or compete, simply be yourself. They say act without doing, work without effort, think of the large as small and the many as few. They say confront the difficult while it is easy, accomplish the great one step at a time. They say let things come and let things go and live without possession and live without expectation. These poems do not need, depend, create or define. They do not see beauty or ugliness or good or bad. They do not preach or implore, they do not tell me that I'm wrong or that I'm right. They say live and let live, do not judge, take life as it comes and deal with it, everything will be okay.

The lights go out at ten o'clock. I stand and I brush my teeth and I drink a glass of water. I lie down on the concrete bed and I stare at the ceiling. There is noise for about thirty minutes. Prisoners talk to each other, yell at each other, pray, curse themselves, curse their families, curse god. Prisoners cry. I stare at the ceiling. I wait for silence

16

and the deep night. I wait for long hours of darkness and solitude and the simple sound of my own breath. I wait until it is quiet enough so that I can hear myself breathe. It is a beautiful sound.

I do not sleep easily. Years of drug and alcohol abuse have sabotaged my body's ability to shut itself down. If I do sleep, I have dreams. I dream about drinking and smoking. I dream about strong, cheap wine and crack. The dreams are real, or as real as dreams can be. They are perverted visions of my former life. Alleys filled with bums drinking and fighting and vomiting and I am among them. Crackheads in broken houses on their knees pulling on pipes with sunken cheeks screaming for more and I am, among them. Tubes of glue and cans of gas and bags filled with paint I am surrounded stumbling and huffing and inhaling as much as I can as fast as I can. In some of the dreams I have guns and I'm playing with the guns and I am debating whether I am going to shoot myself. I always decide that I am. In some of the dreams I am being chased by people who want to kill me. I never know who they are, all I know is that they want to kill me and they always succeed. In some of the dreams I keep drinking and smoking until I am so drunk and so high so goddamn fucked-up that my body just stops. I know that it is stopping and I know that I am dying I don't care. I reach for the pipe and I reach for the bottle. My body is shutting down rather than suffer the continued consequences of my actions and I don't care. I never have good dreams or happy dreams or dreams in which life is good. I have no memories of good dreams or happy dreams or dreams in which life is good.

When I don't sleep, I lie on my bed and I close my eyes. I think about Lilly. I think about where she is and what she's doing. One of the requirements for her residency at the halfway house is that she have a job. She works the nightshift doing laundry at the hospital where her Grandmother is dying. She washes dirty sheets and dirty towels, used gowns and stained scrubs. On her breaks, she goes to her Grandmother's room. Her Grandmother has bone cancer, and it has spread throughout her entire body. She can't move without pain and she hasn't left her bed in two months. Her doctor has said that she will be lucky to live for another month. Lilly tells me she's on a morphine drip and she's incoherent and she doesn't know Lilly's name anymore and she doesn't remember anything about her life. Her mind has been consumed by her cancer as much as her body has been consumed by her cancer. It has overwhelmed her and there is nothing left. Just a shell of pain and morphine. Just a shell of what was once a life.

Lilly sits by her side and holds her hand and talks to her. It doesn't matter that she doesn't understand anything, Lilly sits and holds her hand and talks with her anyway. She tells her about the halfway house she hopes that it's working she can't wait to get out. She tells her about the job it isn't so bad she's certainly done worse. She tells her about me she misses me and she wishes I were there, she hopes I still love her. She tells her about the hope for a future with me and without drugs and with a sense of freedom and a sense of security. She tells her Grandmother about her fears. About the loneliness she's been alone forever she doesn't want to be alone anymore. About a return to her old life she would rather die than sleep with men for money. About me she's scared that we won't survive in the world away from institutions she's scared I'm going to leave her like everyone else in her life has always left her. About what life will be like when her Grandmother dies. She's scared because her Grandmother is the only person Lilly trusts and the only person that she is secure with and she can't imagine living without her. Sometimes Lilly can't talk anymore and she sits with her Grandmother and she holds her hand and she cries. She's scared and she can't imagine living without her. She cries.

I am leaving here in three days. I will have served my time, paid my debt to society. As I lie here in bed listening to the sound of my own breathing as I lie here fighting off dreams and drifting through the deepest night, I think about what I am going to do when the steel-door slams shut behind me. I am going to Chicago. I am going to Lilly. I love her and I want to be with her. I want to be with her now and tomorrow and every day for the rest of my life. I want to sit with her, talk to her, look

19

at her, listen to her voice, laugh with her, cry with her. I want to walk with her and hold her hand and put my arms around her and have her put her arms around me. I want to support her and have her support me. I want to stay away from drugs I can't go back and I want to help her stay away from drugs she can't go back. I want to forget about drinking and crime. I want to be a good, strong, sober man so that I can build a life. I want to build a life for me and build a life for her, a life for us together. I want to give her a home, a place where she feels secure and free. That is what she seeks, she seeks freedom. From her past, from her addictions, from herself. From her loneliness. I will do anything to give it to her.

I love Lilly. I love her blue eyes and her black hair and her pale skin. I love her damaged heart. I love what lives inside of her a spirit a soul a consciousness whatever it is I love it and I want to live with it for the rest of my life and I will do anything to make it happen.

I get out of here in three days.

Three more fucking days.

I lie in bed and I wait.

In the deep night.

Three.

CHICAGO

Lilly's Grandmother died two nights ago. Lilly found her when she went to visit during one of her breaks. She looked at Grandmother's chest it wasn't moving. She looked at her lips they were blue. She reached for her hand and it was cold. Lilly started screaming. When the doctors came and the nurses came she wouldn't let go of her Grandmother's hand. They tried to sedate her. She wouldn't take the drugs she just held her Grandmother's hand and cried. When the body was wheeled from the room, Lilly walked with it. Hand in hand all the way to the morgue. She sat outside the morgue for the next twelve hours. Crying.

I talked to her the next night. She was hysterical. She was sobbing and heaving, begging for me to come to her. I told her I would be there as soon as I could, I would be out in twelve hours. She said please James I need to see you, I need you right now, please, please, please, I need you right now. I said I'm in jail Lilly, I can't do anything here but talk to you. I'm being released in the morning and I'll be with you tomorrow night. She said I need you now James, I'm so scared and lonely, please.

She started crying harder harder harder. I tried to talk to her, but she couldn't talk to me. I told her I loved her and I was coming as soon as I could, that she'd be okay that we'd be okay that everything would be okay once we were together. She cried and I told her I loved her. She cried and I told her I loved her.

Her crying slowed and her breathing became normal. I asked her if she was all right and she said no. I asked her if she would be okay until I got there and she said hurry, please hurry. We said I love you, we both said it. We hung up the phone I wanted to say I love you one more time. I hope she'll be okay.

I have been sitting on the floor waiting for morning. I have been sitting on the floor waiting to be released from this place. I have stared at the wall and I have watched it turn from black to gray to white. When I hear noise the noise of other prisoners up and around, awake and starting their day, I stand and I walk to the sink and I brush my teeth and I wash my face. I finish and I take a deep breath, it has been a long night I'm worried about Lilly. I know there's nothing I can do until I am out of here. Nothing.

I sit back on the floor. I wait. A second a minute five minutes ten they are all a fucking eternity, it is taking too fucking long. I wait. Once the doors open I have an hour before the deputies come to get me and thirty minutes of release administration. I hope she's okay.

A buzzer. The day begins, the door opens. I stand and I pick up my books. I leave my cell and I walk to Porterhouse's cell, the door is open he sees me coming he stands to greet me. I ask him if he's ready to finish. He says yes. He sits on the floor and I sit on the edge of his bed. I read the last fifteen pages of *War and Peace*. When I am finished I close the book.

Porterhouse opens his eyes and nods his head and says that is one good motherfucking book. I smile and say yeah. I stand and I set the book on top of the other books, which are stacked next to Porterhouse's door. I start to walk out. He speaks.

James.

I stop, turn around.

Yeah?

Thank you.

No problem.

I stand outside of his cell and I look at my friend. He looks at me. He is going to spend the rest of his life in prison. He knows it and I know it. We will never see or speak to each other ever again. He knows it and I know it. He speaks.

Be good, motherfucker.

You too.

He smiles and he nods and I smile and I nod back. I turn around and I walk away. I walk to my cell and I sit down on the floor. I wait. I hate waiting, I hope they hurry, I sit and I wait. I do not wait long. Maybe fifteen minutes, which seems like fifteen hours. Two deputies show up and I greet them and I invite them in and they inspect my cell for general cleanliness and good order. They check to make sure that I haven't broken anything or altered anything or given anything away or stolen anything. They have a clipboard with a checklist. Sink, check. Toilet, check. Pillow, check. Towel, check. When they are finished checking, they shackle me and they walk me to Intake/Release. They stand with me while a clerk looks at his computer and makes sure that today is my release date, that this is not a mistake. The computer tells him that today is the correct day and the guards remove my shackles and I walk through a steel door. Another clerk meets and hands me a box with my belongings. I open the box. There is a pair of jeans a pair of wool socks a pair of scuffed black boots a white t-shirt a black hooded sweatshirt a wallet thirty-four dollars a pack of stale cigarettes a lighter a set of keys. I sign a piece of paper acknowledging that all of my possessions have been turned over to me. I step into a small room and I take off my jumpsuit, fuck that jumpsuit. I put on my clothes and I step out of the room and I sign another piece of paper and I'm done. A large steel-door opens and I step through it. I step through another, another. I step through another and I am outside and I am free. I take a deep breath. It is the middle of February the air is cold and clean. I take a deep breath, as deep as I can, I'm fucking free. I walk across a short expanse of concrete. I stop at a gate, which is part of a fifteen-foot razor-wire fence that surrounds the jail. I wait for the gate to open. It is moving too fucking slowly, I'm in a hurry. As soon as there is enough space, I step through the opening and start walking down the street. It is a barren street. No houses, no trees, no other buildings besides the jail. There are fields on both sides of the street with dead yellow scrub and drainage ditches. There is a lot of mud.

I walk as quickly as I can down the street, I walk jog run walk as fast my lungs allow. Before I came here and surrendered to the proper authorities, I went to North Carolina, where I lived before I went to the treatment center. I picked up my truck, my old blue battered truck and drove to a friend's house, a friend who was a professor of mine while I was in school. My friend makes moonshine in his basement and we used to drink the shine and smoke crack and get fucked-up together. He watched me get arrested on more than one occasion. He was happy when he heard I was coming back to serve time, happy that I was attempting to straighten out my life. Part of my sentence was a permanent revocation of my driving privileges in the state, permanent meaning for as long as I am still alive. If I get caught driving, it will be a violation of the conditions of my release and I will serve three to five years in state prison. He said I could leave my truck with him and he would drive me out of the state when I was ready to leave. I'm going to need someone to drive me out of here. I hope he's home. He better be fucking home.

Trees start appearing, an occasional house, a school, a gas station. My lungs hurt. I think about Lilly I hope she's okay. I look for a payphone the one at the gas station didn't have a receiver. I hurry to my friend's house I hope he's home I'll use his phone. I don't want to call my family or friends there will be time for them later. I want to call Lilly, I hope someone answers the phone I hope she's there. Tree lawn house fence barking dog rusty swing set car on blocks fast food heaven convenience store church. They are all a blur I'm moving as fast I can. I look for the correct street-sign I hope I'm going the right way. Continental Avenue. Brookside Lane. Cloverdale Street. Cherry Valley Road. I'll know it when I see it. He better be fucking home.

I come around a corner and I see my truck sitting in a driveway. I start running. Up the front walk front porch knock on the door look through the window nobody's home. I think about what to do. I don't want to wait. I don't want to wait. I don't want to fucking wait no no no no no I'm not going to fucking wait. If I'm careful I'll be fine. I'll drive cautiously, drive the speed limit, I'll be fine. Fuck it, I'll be fine.

I reach for the door. It's unlocked. This is a small town people still feel safe. I walk into the house, through a hall, into the kitchen. There is a phone on the wall. I pick it up and I dial. It starts ringing.

I wait for someone to answer there must be someone at that fucking halfway house who will answer the phone. Nothing. Ringing, ringing. Nothing. I want to talk to Lilly before I leave, I want to tell her I'm on my way. I want to hear her voice, make sure she's okay. I want to tell her I love her.

I hang up the phone try again. Nothing. Try again. Nothing. I look for a piece of paper and a pen I find them on the counter. I write a note it says Thank you for taking care of my truck, I'll be in touch soon. I leave the note in the middle of the kitchen table and I walk out of the house.

I walk to my truck. I take the key out of my pocket, open the door, sit down in the driver's seat. There's another pack of smokes on the passenger seat, I don't know if I left them or my friend left them, either way it's a beautiful thing, I can save what little money I have to spend on something other than smokes. I put the key in the ignition, turn it, the engine starts. I look at the dashboard clock it is eleven A.M. Chicago is five hours away. I told her I would be there by dark, I'll be early. The earlier the better. I hope she's okay. I want to hold her hand and tell her everything is going to be okay.

I back the truck out, start driving through the town. The highway isn't far, I know my way. I drive just above the speed limit. I know that if I drive too fast I draw attention, if I drive too slow I draw attention. I'm not nervous about driving.

29

I know the risk I am taking sitting behind the wheel. I am making a decision to take the risk because it is worth it to me. If I sit here and wait I will go fucking crazy with worry. I want to get to Chicago as fast as I can. If I get caught, I get caught. I will deal with it if it happens. I roll out onto the highway. It is not crowded. I pull into the right lane behind a large tractor/trailer. I turn on the radio. I find a station that has the news twenty-four hours a day. I haven't looked at a newspaper or watched television in three months. I have no idea what is going on in the world. I listen for a few minutes. Same bad news. I turn it off. I stare at the road. Time moves slowly when you want it to move quickly. Each minute is ten, each ten a thousand. I stay behind the tractor/trailer, drive three miles over the speed limit. I smoke my stale cigarettes one after another after another. I think about Lilly. I think about what it is going to be like when I see her again. I think about what it is going to be like when I stand in front of her door. Despite the circumstances, I know I'll have a big smile on my face. I'll knock and she'll say come in and I'll open the door and I'll step into her room. Hopefully someone will have been sitting with her, helping her, holding her hand, Lilly will pull away and come to me. She'll come into my arms. I'll close them and I'll hold her. She'll start to cry and I'll say I love you. I'll hold her for as long as she needs to be held. We'll deal with her Grandmother and her Grandmother's death. We'll get Lilly out of the halfway house and out of her job at the hospital. We'll find a place to live it doesn't have to be a palace, just has to be a place for us. We'll get jobs, make some money, be together, stay together, live together, deal together, just be together. We'll grow old together.

I cross the border of Indiana and Ohio. I smile. I'm safe now, I will not be back in Ohio for a long fucking time. I put my foot down, my old blue truck jumps, we go from sixty-three to eighty-three. I keep it at eighty-three because I know that if I get caught going eighty-five or higher, twenty-five miles or more over the speed limit, there's a chance that I will get arrested for reckless driving instead of speeding. Part of being arrested for reckless driving is that the trooper has the option of putting the offender in jail. If I go back to jail, even if it's for a couple hours, I'm fucked. I could give a shit if I get a speeding ticket. I'll tear it up and throw it out the fucking window as soon as the trooper who writes it is out of eyesight.

I drive eighty-three.

The miles start to add up. I see signs that have the mileage to Chicago on them. One hundred twelve miles. Eighty-eight miles. Sixty-three miles. Thirty-nine miles. I smoke my cigarettes and I smile I am almost there I smile. I turn the radio back on and I find a station that plays light hits, cheesy romantic ballads, lovey-dovey love songs. I sing along if I know the words. If I don't know the words, I make up my own. I'm getting closer sweet girl I'll be with you soon big kisses on your face my heart goes boom, forever and ever, oh yeah, oh yeah.

I cross the border into Illinois. The highway becomes bigger and more crowded. Smoke stacks and oil tanks dominate the land, the air smells like sulphur, gasoline. The sun is starting to drop, the sky is the menacing gray of deep winter. I should make it before it is completely dark. I should be there soon. I have the address of the halfway house and I have a general idea of where it is, somewhere on the north side of the city. Near down-town. It is a major street I should be able to find it without a problem. I start to get more excited. I smile. If I got in a wreck right now, I would do it with a smile. If someone shot me, I would take the bullet with a smile. If I got in a fight, I'd smile as I threw my punches. I am almost there, almost there. I love you, Lilly. Almost there.

I cross a large bridge I'm closer. I get off the highway I'm on a smaller road that runs along the edge of Lake Michigan. The lake is frozen. The ice is dirty and black. I can hear the wind screaming, I can feel it pushing my truck. My truck is a good truck a strong truck an old friend of a truck. My truck laughs at the wind, says fuck you wind, we've got somewhere to be, someone is waiting for us.

I take a ramp off the road into the center of the city. Towers of steel and glass on every side, crowded streets, horns. Pedestrians are heavily dressed, they lean slightly forward as they walk, they hurry to escape the bitter, bitter cold. I move inland, north and across the Chicago River. There are icicles hanging from the iron rails of the bridge, smoke and steam drifting through the girders. I look for Dearborn that is the name of the street.

Dearborn. She's on Dearborn.

I see it and I turn and I start scanning the buildings for an address. I start to get nervous, excited, scared. My hands start quivering trembling shaking. I can feel my heartbeat increase, it starts pounding, pounding. The last time I saw Lilly we were in a hallway at the treatment center. It was the day I was leaving. We stood in the hall and we held each other and we kissed each other and she cried and told me she was going to miss me. I told her to be patient that I would come to her as soon as I could. We said I love you, we held tight, we didn't want to let go. I walked away and Lilly stood and cried. I told her to be strong that I would come back to her.

I find the neighborhood, which was once the most glamorous in the city, fell into disrepair, and is now coming back. I see the building. It is a large stately home. Four floors, white columns, tall framed windows, a grand entrance. It is ragged, but still gorgeous, as if in a previous life it was an embassy or the home of a corporate titan. There is a small subtle sign in the front yard that has the name of the treatment center and in smaller letters reads Residential Extended Care.

I see an open parking space about half a block away. I drive down the street, pull into the spot. I see a florist at the end of the block. I fumble with the keys, my hands are shaking, I get out of the car. I walk to the florist and I open the door and I step inside. There is a woman behind the counter. She has gray hair and brown eyes, she is wearing a bright red turtleneck. She smiles, speaks.

Cold, isn't it?

Miserable.

You should wear warmer clothes.

I would, but I don't have any.

As I look around, I take a deep breath through my nose. I let it out, speak.

Smells nice in here.

Good. I'd be worried if it didn't.

I smile.

I need some flowers. I've got thirty-four dollars in my pocket. What can I get?

What would you like?

I don't know shit about flowers.

She laughs.

What's the occasion?

Reunion.

What type?

I smile again. I can't help it. Lilly is down the Street.

I just got out of my jail. My girlfriend is in that halfway house down the street. Her Grandmother

34

just died, and I want to give her something that will make her feel better.

The woman nods.

You want to cheer her up, and you probably want to show her that you love her.

I smile.

Yeah.

The woman steps from behind the counter, leads me toward a cooler. The cooler is filled with flowers sitting in white plastic buckets and arrangements sitting on shelves. She opens the cooler and she reaches into a bucket and she pulls out about twenty red roses, she pulls out every rose in the bucket. She closes the cooler. I speak.

I can't afford all of those.

She smiles.

I'm having a sale. How's thirty dollars sound?

I smile.

Thank you. Thank you very much.

Do you want them wrapped?

Is that what you do?

Yes, it is.

I smile again. I can't stop smiling.

I'd love to have them wrapped.

The woman steps back behind the counter. She reaches for some white paper, pulls it from a long roll, tears it along a sharp edge. She sets it on the counter in front of her and she sets the roses the beautiful red roses on top of it. I turn and I walk to the window. I look down the street toward the halfway house. It is almost dark, there are lights in the windows, on the front porch, along the front walk leading to the porch. Lilly is in there, in that house, I will have you in my arms soon. Beautiful Lilly, beautiful Lilly. I have missed you so much. I will have you in my arms soon. I have missed you so much.

I'm finished.

I turn around. The woman is holding the roses wrapped in paper, baby's breath surrounding them. I step toward her, reach into my pocket.

Thank you.

I set the thirty dollars on the counter, take the flowers. The woman smiles.

Have a good night.

Thank you. Thank you very much.

I turn around and I walk out of the shop. I'm smiling still smiling. I start walking down the street. It's cold, but I don't feel it. I start running, gradually faster, as fast as I can, I'm running and smiling. I turn up the walk, I'm on the front porch, I open the door, I step inside.

A simple foyer. Dark carpet, beige walls, a worn wooden desk, a cheery landscape on the wall behind. There is a woman sitting at the desk smoking a cigarette. She looks up at me. Her eyes are red and swollen.

She speaks.

Can I help you?

I step forward.

Is Lilly here?

She stares at me for a moment. Her upper lip quivers, she looks like she's about to break.

Who are you?

My name is James.

She looks at me, bites her lip. She takes a deep breath and stands.

Just a minute please.

She steps from behind the desk, walks to a door, opens it, leaves. I stand with my flowers and my smile and my pounding heart, my pounding heart.

The door opens and a man steps into the room. He's in his late thirties.

He has short dark messy hair, wears baggy jeans and a wool sweater. He has bags under his eyes, which are also red and swollen. He speaks.

James?

He reaches out a hand. I shake it.

I'm Tom. I'm the director of this facility.

What's up, Tom?

Would you mind coming back to my office?

Why?

I need to talk to you. I'd prefer to do it in private.

Where's Lilly?

Why don't you come back to my office.

I want to see Lilly, Tom.

Please, James.

I'm not going back to your office, Tom. Just tell me where the fuck Lilly is.

He looks at the floor, takes a deep breath. He looks up at me.

Before I tell you, I just want you to know that Lilly loved you very much.

She talked about you all the time and . . .

What the fuck is going on here?

He looks at me. He doesn't speak. His eyes are wet.

Tell me what the fuck is going on here.

He looks at me, bites his lip, takes a deep breath. My heart pounding.

Lilly.

His voice breaks.

Lilly.

His voice breaks again.

Lilly passed away this morning.

I stare at him. I am holding her roses.

What?

My heart pounding.

Lilly died this morning.

My heart pounding.

What happened?

Pounding.

She took her own life.

I stare at him. My heart, my heart, my heart. He stares at me, speaks.

I'm so sorry. I'm so, so sorry.

Her flowers slip from my hand.

What happened?

My heart.

We don't know. Her grandmother had just died. She was very shaken. We found her hanging from the shower faucet. She didn't leave a note.

I turn around.
I walk out of the House.
My heart.
My heart.
My heart.

No no no.
Suicide.
It is dark and it is cold.
No no no.
Suicide.
I start walking toward my truck.
No no no.
Suicide.
My legs start shaking. Yes, suicide. My chest starts shaking. Yes, suicide. My arms start shaking and my hands are shaking. Yes, suicide. My face is shaking. Yes, suicide. I take a step and my knees buckle. I try to take another, my legs won't support me. I fall, fall to the sidewalk. I try to get up, but I can't, yes suicide. I look around me. I'm on a street I don't know in a city I've been in twice. Yes, suicide. I came here for Lilly and she's dead, hanging in the shower, she's dead. Yes, suicide. She was supposed to wait for me. I told her I would be here she was supposed to wait. Yes, suicide. She hung herself in the shower, I can't believe this is happening. She's dead. She killed herself. I can't believe this is happening. She's dead.

I start crying. I sit on the sidewalk and I cry. It feels like there's a hole in my chest, it feels like everything has become a deep dark horrible fucking hole. There are tears, I shake. I lose my breath. There's a hole and I can't get out of it, I can't escape. I'm falling deeper, deeper, deeper. I cry, I can't breathe. I bury my face in my hands I feel tears dripping from my eyes and my nose, streaming across my cheeks, running down my neck. I was coming I got here as fast as I fucking could. She didn't wait for me. She went into the bathroom and she tied a knot a strong knot. I want out of this hole I want out I want to stop crying. She put her neck in a noose she knew I was coming to her she knew what she was doing to herself. She put her neck in the noose. Please please please let me out of this please. She strung herself up. She let herself down. She lost the ability to breathe. No, I can't believe this is happening, no. She put her neck in the noose and she hung herself and she couldn't breathe and she didn't stop, she didn't stop, she didn't stop. Why she didn't stop. Why didn't she fucking stop. I came here to help her I came here to give her everything. She hung herself. I can't stop crying I want to stop crying I can't stop. Hang, my beautiful Lilly, hang. I would have done anything for you. Hang my beautiful Lilly, hang. Let me out of this fucking nightmare please let me wake up, let me wake the fuck up. She stopped breathing. I'm not waking up. She stopped seeing thinking feeling she stopped breathing. I can't get out. She hung herself and she's dead. She hung herself and she's dead.

There is a church on the next block. I can see the steeple and I can hear the bells. The bells ring every hour. I can hear them above the wind.

The streets are empty. It's late and it's dark and it's cold as hell.

I am sitting on the sidewalk. I am crying. I have been here for hours. Just sitting and crying. The crying comes in waves. Tears, sobs, screaming. The crying hurts. Hurts my chest and my face, hurts the things inside that do not have names. Tears sobs screaming. Everything hurts. The same word over and over.

No.

No.

No.

Crying.

Sobbing.

Screaming.

I can't stop.

I can't stop.

The bells are ringing.

The wind is screaming.

Nine times I hear the bells.
And it starts to slow.
Gradually slow.
Slow, slow, slow.
I stop crying. I stand. My legs hurt and my chest
hurts. My face hurts, my eyes and lips hurt. I am
cold. I am shaking. It's dark and I am cold and
my entire body is shaking. I can see the building
down the street. The building where Lilly lived.
The building where she was supposed to be getting
better. The building where she was waiting for me,
the building where we were supposed to meet. I
can see the building. The building where she killed
herself. The building where she killed herself.

My lips quiver. A chill shoots down my spine. I
can see the building. I turn away and I start
walking down the street. I stop at my truck. I take
my keys out of my pocket. I open the door, climb
inside, shut the door. It is warmer inside, but not
much. I put the key in the ignition and I start the
engine and I turn on the heat and I wait and I
start to cry again. I start to cry. I want to stop,
but I can't stop. I want to take a deep breath and
tell myself that everything is okay, but I'm unable
to do so. I have no control over myself. I have no
control over my emotions. I have no control over
my body's need to express those emotions. All of
the time I spent sitting alone in my cell trying to
teach myself how to regulate my behavior is worth-
less, irrelevant. Lilly killed herself. Hung herself
in the shower. She's dead. She's fucking dead. It

doesn't matter that I don't want to cry. It doesn't matter that I want to stop. I can't do anything. I have no control. I cry and I wait for the heat. The heat comes and I sit in front of the vents and I stop shaking. The inside of the truck becomes warmer and warmer and I stop crying. My body needs a break, needs to rest, needs to try to let my mind and my heart accept what has happened. They don't want to accept it. They know one word. No. They keep telling me that I'm going to wake-up and find her waiting for me. No. They keep screaming she's not dead, she's not dead, she's not dead. No. She is the only person I have ever truly loved. She is the only person who made me want to live. She is the only person on Earth who could hurt me. She killed herself this morning. Walked into the bathroom and tied a knot and hung herself from the shower. It didn't matter what I felt, how much she meant to me, how much I loved her. It didn't fucking matter. She hung until she stopped breathing. She's dead. My mind and heart don't want to accept it. No. I reach for my pack of cigarettes. I take one out and I light it. I take a deep drag, hold it in, exhale. I stare out the window. I feel empty. I feel like my heart has been ripped out of my chest. I feel dis-connected, as if my body and mind are no longer part of the same vessel. I am exhausted. As I lift my arm to bring the cigarette back to my mouth, my arm is heavy, my hand is heavy, the cigarette is heavy. Everything I do takes great effort. I inhale

45

slowly. I feel the smoke traveling through my throat and into my lungs. I exhale slowly, feel the smoke coming back. I am so tired. What the fuck am I going to do. Somebody please help me.

I finish the cigarette, put it out. I look into the rearview mirror, see the house down the street. I want to be away. I put my truck into first gear. I want to be away from that House. I pull out of my parking space. I want to be away from that fucking house. I start driving down the street. I have no idea where I am and I have no idea where I am going. I just want to be away.

I drive. I smoke another cigarette. I turn on the radio and I turn off the radio. The neighborhoods all look the same. Row after row of brownstones. Tree-lined streets with sidewalks and overhead lights. I see churches and schools, fire stations and playgrounds. I see all sorts of small shops; shoe shops, clothing shops, candle shops, art and sculpture shops, real estate shops, book shops, garden shops. I see grocery stores and restaurants, convenience stores and gas stations. I see bars and liquor stores. On almost every block, I see either a bar or a liquor store. Beautiful bars filled with people drinking. Beautiful liquor stores devoted to alcohol. Beautiful establishments where I can make this nightmare go away. Beautiful bars and beautiful liquor stores. On almost every block.

I feel the urge. Drink. The instinct begins to assert itself. Destroy. My old friend the Fury starts to rise, it says kill what you feel, kill what you feel.

The Fury rises it says kill.

My hands start shaking. I can feel my heart beating. My teeth chatter. I take a deep drag of my cigarette, it doesn't help. I am an alcoholic and a drug addict. I have used substances to control and to kill my emotions and my insecurities and my rage for my entire life. I have spent the bulk of my existence using alcohol and drugs to destroy what I feel so that I wouldn't have to feel it. I have never felt like this before. Never even close. I know death, I have seen it and been close to it, but not this type of death. I know grief and sorrow and sadness, but I have never felt them so deeply. I know horror, but I have never cringed before it, I know self-destruction, but it has never made me shake. I don't know what I am going to do. There are beautiful bars and beautiful liquor stores on every block. I can make this all go away, the Fury says kill kill kill, it is time to destroy. I am an alcoholic and a drug addict. I can't deal with my feelings.

I pull over, park. I turn off the engine take out the key turn out the lights. I look up and down the block. There are two bars within eyesight, one liquor store. I have four dollars in my pocket and I have three reasonable options. Go to the most crowded of the bars and take half-finished drinks from tables when people stand and leave. Go to a less crowded bar and find a drunk. Drunks are stupid with their mouths and stupid with their wallets, and if I find one, I can probably get them to buy me a drink or several drinks. Fuck the bars, go to a liquor store. If they sell what I like to drink, which is cheap, strong, gutter wine, I could probably afford a bottle.

I need something now. I need to make this go away.

I open the door. Step outside. Close the door. It's cold, I look around me, I start shaking. The wind is screaming. I start walking. I walk toward a corner where there is a bar across the street from a liquor store. I can see people through the windows of the bar. They look young and happy. They are jumping up and down, dancing, moving to the beat of some cheery music. All I want is a drink, two drinks, as many drinks as it takes to make it all go away, to send me hurtling toward oblivion, to destroy. Fuck those happy people. Fuck that cheery music.

I walk toward the liquor store. It is on the opposite corner. It is a small store. It has a bright neon sign hanging above the door that reads Liquor, the windows are filled with bright posters of bikini-clad women holding beer cans. Behind the posters I can see rows and rows of bottles. Beautiful bottles filled with alcohol.

I open the door and I step inside. It is warm and bright with fluorescent light. There is a counter along the front wall, a man stands behind it.

There are cigarettes above the counter and candy bars below it. There is a television behind the man. It is broadcasting images of the store taken by cameras in each of the corners. I am the store's only customer. I can see myself on the television and I can see the man behind the counter on the television. He is staring at me. I ignore him. I start walking down one of the aisles.

The man watches me as I walk, I stare at a set of coolers along the back wall. The shit I drink is always in a cooler along the back wall, always hidden away so that respectable customers don't have to see it. It is of the lowest class of alcoholic beverages. Produced by liquor companies for poor drunks who need a strong, quick charge. Though it is called wine, it doesn't resemble real wine in any way. It is much cheaper, much more powerful. It comes in thick, squat bottles that are effective weapons when empty. It tastes like grape juice mixed with rubbing alcohol. Long term users of it often die from the effects that it has on one's internal organs. It burns holes in the stomach. It eats away the lining of the intestine. It causes cirrhosis of the liver. It is liquid death. Available in a pint or a quart. Sometimes a liter. Always in a cooler along the back wall.

I find four different types lining the bottom shelf of the corner cooler. I am familiar with all of them, have experienced the horrors of each. The worst of them, and the one I enjoy the most, is known as the rose. Its label calls it a fruit-flavored, ethanol-fortified dessert wine. I call it a quick ride to hell. It is available in one-liter bottles. At the height of my drinking, I could down three of the one-liter bottles before losing consciousness. At this point, having not had a drink in almost six months, one bottle will do everything that I need it to do. I need it to kill. I need it to kill.

I open the cooler pick up a bottle look at the price. Just under three dollars. With my remaining dollar I can get myself a bag of potato chips. This is not what I expected to be doing here. Getting drunk and eating chips on my first night of freedom, my first night in Chicago. Were it up to me, I would be with Lilly. Were it up to me I would be asleep in her arms. She's dead, in a cooler in some fucking morgue, and I'll never sleep in her arms again. The thought of it makes me sick, and it makes me want to join her. The rose will help me. It is time to start the killing. Time to fucking start.

I walk to the front of the store. The man behind the counter watches me the entire time. As I pass a rack of chips, I reach out and I grab a bag. I don't look at the flavor because the flavor doesn't matter. All I'm going to taste is the rose. I arrive at the counter and I set my wares down in front of the man and as he rings them up, I take the four dollars out of my back pocket. I set the money in front of him and he takes it and puts it in his register and he hands me a dime. I have ten cents to my name. Ten cents and a bottle of wine and a bag of chips and half a pack of cigarettes and a beat-up truck. The chips and the wine will be gone in twenty minutes. The cigarettes will be gone tomorrow. I'm starting to think I will follow them.

I walk out of the store. It's cold, the wind, the motherfucking wind. I walk to my truck, I open it, I get inside. It is still warm. I climb into the passenger's seat. I know that if I get caught drinking in the driver's seat I can be charged with Driving Under the Influence. It doesn't matter if the car is moving or not, I can still be charged under the laws of every state in America. In the passenger's seat they can charge me with open container in a motor vehicle, the equivalent of a parking ticket.

I settle into the seat. I light a cigarette. I open the chips put a few in my mouth chew. I set the bottle in my lap. I take it out of the brown paper bag that is holding it. I stare at it. My hands start shaking and my heart starts beating faster. Like Pavlov's dog I react when alcohol is in front of me. I smoke with one hand, hold the bottle with the other. I have a decision to make. Yes or no. The Fury is screaming drink, motherfucker, drink drink drink. The grief I feel says I will leave you if you feed me. My heart and my hands are shaking like dogs they want the taste. I know if I open the cap and put the bottle to my lips, pour and swallow, I will be taking a road from which there is no return. I know that once I have it in me again I will use it until I die from it. I was almost dead six months ago. Dead from the damage that hardcore drug and alcohol abuse cause to the

51

body, dead because I didn't want to live anymore. I chose life because of Lilly and Leonard and because once I tasted life again it tasted good, good enough to try to live it. Lilly is dead now. Dead by her own hand. The how and why don't matter. All that matters is the end result. Death. I can't believe I'm here. I can't believe I'm in this position. What the fuck am I going to do.

I stare.

I have no money.

I stare at the bottle.

I have no job, I have nowhere to live.

I stare at the bottle.

I am an alcoholic and a drug addict. I have been incarcerated for the last six months of my life in a treatment center and in a jail.

The bottle.

I am shaking. The Fury is screaming. The grief is overwhelming me please please please. I can make it all go away. I can kill it. Killing it will be the first step toward killing myself. Everything I have dreamed about and hoped for and wanted and expected is gone. It's dead and it's not coming back. There is no nightmare to wake from, this is my fucking life.

What am I going to do.

The bottle.

I start to cry.

What.

Cry.

There is sun streaming through the front window of my truck. It is bright, but it is not warm.

It is early morning and I am waiting. The bottle of rose is sitting on the seat next to me. It is still full.

I spent the night crying, staring at the bottle, smoking, cursing. I cursed God that motherfucker. I cursed myself I should have gotten here earlier. I cursed everyone I saw, I screamed at them and I cursed them. I cursed my truck it didn't do anything I cursed it anyway. I cursed the ground the sky the night. I cursed the bottle in my hand I cursed the parts of me that wanted it. I cursed them and I defied them and they cursed me and they tried to defy me. I cursed my shaking hand and my beating heart, I cursed myself, I should have known, I should have stopped her. I cursed the dime in my pocket. I cursed the potato chip bag. I cursed Lilly. I cursed Lilly how could she have done this to herself. I cursed and I cried. How could she have done this to herself.

It is early morning and I am waiting. The bottle

of rose is sitting on the seat next to me and it is still full. I am going to keep it. I am going to keep it so that if I decide to use it, it will be within reach. I made it through last night, but that does not mean I will make it through today or tomorrow.

I am waiting. I am waiting for the sun to move above me. I am waiting to hear the bells ring ten. I am waiting to call my friend Leonard. He told me that if I ever needed help he would give it to me I need help now. I have no money and no job and nowhere to live. I am waiting to call Leonard. I need help now.

I start the truck. I pull out of my parking space and start driving back toward the house. If I get hold of Leonard and he helps me, I will need to be near the house. The people there will know where Lilly is and who has taken her. I want to see her again before she is gone. I want to see her again.

I find my way back I see the house. I pull over and I park. I get out of the truck look around me. I see the flower store. I see the steeple that holds the bells. I see a park, the park is empty. I see a bank and a shoe store and a diner. I start walking toward the diner.

I open the door, step inside. It is warm and loud. It smells like bacon and eggs. There are people at every table eating, drinking coffee, talking. There is a short hall in the back of the diner I can see two bathrooms and a phone. I walk toward the phone, reach into my back pocket. I take out my wallet and I take a card from my wallet. The card has five names on it, five numbers. They all belong to Leonard.

I pick up the phone and I dial zero. I speak to an operator. I give her my name and the first number. I tell her I need to make a collect call. She puts it through, no one answers. We try the second number. No answer. We try the third, the call is denied. We try the fourth I hear Leonard answer.

Collect call from James?

Fuck yeah.

Thank you.

The operator hangs up.

My son.

What's up, Leonard?

You're out of jail and you're in Chicago. That's what's up.

Yeah, I'm here.

How is it?

Not good.

What happened?

I start to break.

I don't want to talk about it.

What's wrong?

I need your help, Leonard.

What happened?

I need help.

What do you need?

I need thirty thousand dollars.

What?

I need thirty thousand dollars, Leonard.

What the fuck is going on there?

You told me to call you if I ever needed help. I need fucking help. I need thirty grand.

Are you drinking?

No.

Getting high?

No.

What the fuck is wrong?

I start to break.

I need money.

He does not speak.

Please, Leonard.

He does not speak.

Please.

I hear him take a deep breath.

Where are you?

In a diner.

How do you want me to get it to you?

Thank you, Leonard.

You're my son. I'm going to take care of you.

Thank you, Leonard.

Now tell me how you want me to get you the money.

I give him the address of the house. He tells me that it will be there in an hour. I thank him, thank you, Leonard. He asks me if I want him to come to Chicago and I tell him no. He asks again if I'm drunk or high he wants to make sure and I tell him no. He says that though he does not need to know right now, at some point he'll want to know why I need so much money. I say fine. I thank him again and he says don't worry about it and I say thank you again and we hang up. Thank you, Leonard. Thank you. I walk out of the diner and I walk back toward my truck, toward the house. As I get closer, my heart starts beating faster. I think about what happened in the house, the images in my mind are clear. Hanging hanging hanging. I try to push the images away, but they remain, hanging hanging hanging. Every step is harder, every step is heavier. I start up the walk that leads to the door. every step. Hanging. I open the door step into the foyer. I want to leave, the images are clear. The same woman is sitting behind the desk. There are some red roses in a vase next to her. She looks up at me and I say hello and she says hello and she motions toward the roses and she tells me that she saved them for me. I thank her and I ask for Tom. She says he's out can I help you. There is a chair across from her I sit down. I want to leave, the images are clear. The bathroom where Lilly hung is in this house. I look at the woman and I speak.

I need some information.

I keep the flowers. They were for Lilly, not for the house. I keep them in water and I will use them. They were for Lilly.

I give all of her clothing to an organization that helps the poor. She did not have much, but maybe it will help someone.

I give her books to a library. She wanted to go to college and she had been studying for the entrance exams. She had seven books, all textbooks. What little money she had was in a box beneath her bed. I give it to a homeless woman who is sitting alone on a bench. The woman tells me it is enough to get her a place in a shelter for two months. I hope that time makes a difference.

She had a plastic Superwoman watch. I always thought it was funny that she wore it. I find it on a table next to her bed. When I find it, I cry. I hold it to my heart and I cry. I keep it in my pocket.

She had a hairbrush, a toothbrush. A tube of toothpaste and a bottle of shampoo and a bar of soap. I leave everything in the bathroom.

She had a simple silver necklace. It held a platinum cross. Her Grandmother gave it to her, it was her most cherished possession. I find it on a table next to her bed. When I find it I cry. I want to give it back to her. I want to give it back.

I don't have any photographs of Lilly. I don't have any photographs of the two of us together. The only documentation I have of our relationship is a large stack of letters, some written by me, some by her. This lack of documentation has made seeing her more difficult. Tom helps me. He speaks to an assistant medical examiner, he speaks to the medical examiner. He confirms that Lilly did not have any family aside from her Grandmother, who is in the morgue with her. He confirms that I was her boyfriend, and that I am the only person who is likely to claim her body. He helps talk the Medical Examiner into letting me see her. Just once, by myself. I am going to see her.

I walk down a hallway. A bright clean sterile hallway. At the end of the hallway is a large metal door. A man is standing in front of the door. He is wearing a white lab coat and latex gloves, an air filtration mask hangs at his neck. As I approach, he says hello and I say hello and he opens the door and he gestures me inside and I walk through the door and he follows me. The door closes behind us.

I am in a large open room. Along one wall there is a bank of stainless steel cabinets. Along another are three sinks and a large stainless steel counter-top. Along the back wall there are four rows of doors, each with a handle like the handles on large refrigerators. There is a stainless steel table in the middle of the room, a halogen lamp above it, a drain below it. There is a body on the table. A body that is covered by a white sheet.

I turn to the man.

Can I be alone?

Yes.

Thank you.

He motions toward a counter near the cabinets.

There are gloves and masks over there if you want to use them.

Thank you.

He turns and he leaves. I turn back to the body. I stare at it. I am scared.

My heart starts pounding, pounding to the point that it hurts. I am scared. I take a deep breath. Part of me wants to run. To get the fuck out of here, that is her body, her dead body beneath that sheet. Part of me knows that I need to do this. I have to see her. I have to see her. I have to see her.

I step forward, once twice, heart pounding. I step forward I am next to the table. I stand and I stare at the sheet she is beneath it. I place the palm of my hand in the center of the sheet. My heart is fucking pounding. I softly press so that I can feel beneath the sheet, my hand is somewhere on her stomach. I start moving it along the top of the sheet, along the contour of her body. She's beneath the sheet and I can feel her body. The

60

body I once held, the body I loved, the body that loved me. I run my hand up the curve of her neck, over her chin. I move it to the edge of the sheet, I put my other hand with my first. My heart is fucking pounding. My hands are shaking.

I start to slowly pull the sheet. I see her hair jet black so black it is almost blue. I slowly pull I see her skin, it was pale like porcelain in life, it is pale gray now. I slowly pull. I see her eyebrows black I see her lashes black. I see her eyes closed they were blue in life, beautiful clear deep-water blue in life, they are closed and I will leave them closed. I pull the sheet slowly her cheekbones strong and defined I pull past her nose I pull down and across her lips. Full and red they are still full. They are also quiet, calm, still, at rest. I pull the sheet down across her chin and off her face. I pull the sheet from her neck. She has a deep blue bruise around her throat. Whatever she used was thick, maybe a towel, I don't know, I don't want to think about it. I pull the sheet to her shoulders she is not wearing a shirt. I will not expose her naked flesh I will respect her in death as I respected her in life. I let go of the sheet and I set it just below her shoulders. I stare at her. She is quiet, calm, still, at rest. I love her now as I did before I love her now. In death and in life. My heart is pounding and my hand is shaking. I love her.

I stare.

I run my hands along the top of her head and through her hair.

I cry.
I feel the contours of her face.
I kiss my fingers and I press them to her lips.
I cry.
She is quiet.
Calm.
Still.
At rest.
I take her hand beneath the sheet. It is stiff and cold. I take her hand.
I am with her.
I hold her.
I love her.
She's at rest.
Cry.

They sleep in peace.
They sleep in peace.

G rieve.
I grieve alone.
Grieve.

I call my friend Kevin. Kevin is an old close friend, one of the closest friends that I have had in my life. We met at school and we lived together while we were there and he watched me as I fell apart and helped me as I started to pick up the pieces of my shattered life. He knew I was coming here, though he did not know exactly when I would arrive. He says welcome to Chicago and I say thanks and he asks me how I'm doing and I say fine and he asks me how it was he is aware of what I was doing in Ohio and I tell him it was fine. He knows about Lilly and he asks me how it's going with her and I tell him bad and he asks me what happened and I tell him I don't want to talk about it. He asks if I'm okay. I tell him I don't want to talk about it. I ask him when he'll be off work and he tells me seven and we agree to meet at his apartment.

Kevin lives on the north side of the city. His apartment is on the first floor of a four-story brownstone on a street lined with four-story brownstones. The neighborhood is full of people in their twenties working their first or second professional jobs, the streets are lined with suits and skirts and loafers. I find the building easily, park in front of it. I can see through the windows, I see a group of people smoking cigarettes and drinking. I get out of my car and I take a deep breath. I don't want to do this to see a group of people I'm nervous and scared I am used to being alone. I know I need to break the solitude to spend time among the living. I push the buzzer walk through the door into the hall he is waiting for me. He is smiling. He steps forward and he gives me a hug and he speaks.

It's good to see you, Buddy.

You too.

We separate.

Who's inside?

Some people who wanted to see you.

Who?

Come in and see.

You won't tell me?

Just come in.

I take a deep breath. I know I need to try and move forward with my life.

I step inside.

I see people I know, people I am friends with, people I am surprised to see. Adrienne and Ali. Two friends great friends, for several years we drank together and smoked together and laughed together and sometimes cried together. Erin and Courtney they were her friends, someone I was with in a different life. They were her friends and they became my friends. I don't know if they see her or speak to her and I don't care, it was a different life. David and Scott, older than me I used to drink and smoke and snort with them they are bankers now buttoned up and prim. Callie and Kim, they live with Kevin I used to sell them drugs, occasionally I used drugs with them. All of them know that I recently came out of a drug and alcohol treatment center, only Kevin knows about jail. They all seem happy to see me, they also seem scared to drink around me and smoke around me and be themselves around me. They ask me tentative questions. How are you is everything okay is it all right if I have this drink around you are you comfortable like this. I tell them I am fine. That the alcohol does not bother me, that they should be at ease. I keep a calm face and a relaxed demeanor. Inside I am not calm, this is all overwhelming. All the noise all the faces all the words. I have been alone for a long time. Alone and unsocial. This room is full of people I know and I like and who have come here to see me and it is overwhelming.

We go to a bar. All of us together we go to a bar. I shoot pool and smoke cigarettes and drink soda water. My friends shoot pool and smoke cigarettes and get drunk. As the night moves deeper I speak less and less. As the night moves deeper my friends lose the ability to speak. I do not judge them. I did what they are doing now every night for years. Got drunk and stumbled and slurred my words. I do not judge them, I am happy to see them.

We stay at the bar until it closes. We leave I say goodbye to everyone thank them for coming to see me walk back to the apartment with Kevin and Callie and Kim. They go to their rooms and they go to bed. I find some blankets in a closet and I go to the living room and I clear a space on the couch and I lie down.

I stare at the ceiling.

I start looking for an apartment. I look through the classified sections of the paper, I walk the streets and I look for rental signs, I go to local real estate offices and I look through the listings. I don't want much and I don't need much. Almost all of the money is gone. I want something simple and small and clean. Somewhere for me to sit and sleep and read. Somewhere for me to be alone. Simple and small and clean.

I find a place on my second day. It's on a small street only one block long. At one end of the street there are two giant steel giraffes on opposite corners, they're ridiculous and they make me laugh. At the other end there is a delicate little restaurant, its menu is written in Italian. Trees line both sides of the street, and though I know nothing about the neighborhood, it feels like somewhere that I could live for a while.

The apartment itself is in a large five-story building shaped like a U. It is a one-room apartment on the first floor. It has one brick wall, plain wood floors, an oven and refrigerator. There are three windows, all of them are barred, there are two doors, the doors

are in opposite corners. One of them leads into a
hall and the other to an alley where there are several
large dumpsters.

I meet the building superintendent. His name is
Mickey and he is about thirty. He is thin and effeminate and he has blond hair and blue eyes and he
wears pajamas. He says he is a painter who is
working as a super because he gets free rent, money
and lots of time to paint. As he reads my application, I see him occasionally glancing up at me. He
finishes and he tells me that he isn't usually allowed
to rent apartments to people without jobs. I tell
him that I intend to find one. He asks if I have any
references and I say no. He says he'll need to check
with his boss and I take all of the remaining cash
that I have and I place it in front of him.

That's a deposit and two months' rent and a bit
extra for you.

He looks down at the money, back at me.

How much extra?

Another month.

He looks me up and down.

You seem nice.

I chuckle.

And you seem like you won't be much trouble.

I laugh again.

He reaches out his hand.

Welcome to the building.

I shake his hand, smile.

Thank you.

We let go of each other's hands.

When do you want to move in?

Right now.

You're in a hurry?

I need somewhere to live.

He reaches into a file and takes out a lease. He asks me some questions, fills in the answers, I sign the lease. He hands me the keys.

Thank you.

You're welcome.

I stand.

I'll see you around.

He nods.

You certainly will.

I turn and I leave. I walk to my truck, which is parked on the curb outside the building. I get my clothes and my bottle and I walk back to the apartment. I open the door and I step inside. I set my clothes in a pile on the floor. I hold the bottle in my hand. I have taken it with me almost everywhere that I have gone in the last few days. I keep it with me as a test of my strength. I keep it with me in case I change my mind.

I feel like I want it now the rose. I feel like I want it all the time but more now more. I set it on the floor in the middle of the apartment. I open the door I am going to walk, walking calms me.

It is cold outside. The wind screams through the streets like a whip. It lashes at my face, penetrates my clothes, stings me shakes me hurts me. I start to walk. No agenda nowhere to go no idea how to get there. I just walk.

I pass the giraffes I say goodbye friends. I walk down a street called Broadway lined with pawn-shops, no dreams coming true here. I walk past Wrigley Field it's a baseball stadium dead in winter, old and silent and noble and dark. I walk under the elevated train tracks the ground shakes beneath them every five minutes the ground is shaking. I walk past people some I can't see they are hiding from the winter. I walk past store after store after store selling things I don't need. I walk past apartment buildings light and warm and offices light and warm and schools light and warm. I walk past a hospital. A police station. A firehouse. I just walk. For whatever the reason, it helps me forget. For whatever the reason, it brings me calm. As the day fades the temperature drops, the light disappears. I have been walking for hours, I make my way back to Kevin's apartment. I see him through the window drinking wine his roommates are smoking. I hit the buzzer go inside sit with them as they drink and smoke. I tell them about my apartment they want to celebrate.

We go back to the same bar we were in last night. We meet most of the same people. I sit with them as they drink and smoke. I have a glass of water. I want to drink, part of me wants to drink, one drink two drinks five drinks twenty. I want to drink because I know drinking will make it all go away. The pain I feel the sadness and sorrow and grief that are with me all day every second in every breath and beat of my heart in every thought in every step in everything I see and hear there is nothing but pain and sadness and sorrow and grief and I know drinking will make it go away. I also know it will kill me if I do it. Maybe not today or tomorrow but it will kill me. If I start I won't be able to stop. There is pain and sadness and sorrow and grief. I have a glass of water. I sit with my friends as they drink and smoke.

When it is time to leave I go back to Kevin's apartment with him. I borrow three blankets and a pillow. I walk back to my new apartment. It is bitter fucking cold and as I walk I wrap myself in the blankets and I clutch the pillow against my chest. I am tired. I don't know why I'm here or what the fuck I'm doing. I need a job and I need some money. I am lonely I miss Lilly so much, so much. It is the dead of night and it is bitter fucking cold and I don't know what the fuck I'm doing.

I find the giraffes I say hello. I find my building and I open the door and I find my apartment and I open the door. I step inside. I don't turn on the light and I don't take off my jacket or my boots. I lie down on the floor. The blankets are wrapped around me and I'm clutching the pillow.

I want to drink, but I know drinking will kill me.
I want Lilly, but I know she's not coming back.
I am tired and I want to sleep.
Sleep is not coming.
I lie on the floor.

Ineed a job and I need some money.

I find a paper and I look through the clas-sifieds. I write down addresses and walk around the city. It's cold and the wind is a whip but the walking calms me. I apply for several jobs. Two at bars working as a doorman. One at a clothing store working in the stock room. One at a coffee shop serving the coffee and working the register. Two at gas stations pumping the gas. I shake hands and I smile and I am told to wait. I give them Kevin's phone number. I wait.

At the end of the day I meet Kevin. He takes me out for pizza. I didn't eat today I'm flat fucking broke. After we eat, we meet our friends at the bar. They drink and smoke and I drink water and smoke. We shoot pool and talk and laugh, I am starting to be able to laugh again. I stay late sitting watching laughing smoking. I don't laugh much, but every now and then is fine.

The night ends and I walk back to Kevin's apart-ment with him, check the messages, nobody's called me. I walk home. It is home for at least the next two months I have nowhere else to go. I lie down on the floor and I wrap myself in the blankets and I clutch the pillow.

Sleep does not come easily.

Seconds become minutes become hours.

Hours.

I lie on the floor and I clutch the pillow.

I miss her.

I'm alone.

I miss her.

Dark becomes light.

I lie on the floor.

At last I sleep.

I sleep.

Sleep.

I hear my door open. I'm not sure if what I hear is a dream or not. I hear footsteps across my floor. I'm awake I know it's not a dream. I hear voices. Words being whispered someone's in my apartment. What the fuck is going on here. I hear words someone is in my apartment. I'm awake. This is not a dream. Someone is here.

I crack my eyes, look through the slits. My heart starts pounding. I see two pairs of leather shoes, expensive shoes. Who the fuck is here. I try to place the shoes, I can't. I try to place the voices, I can't hear them well enough to place them. I crack my eyes more, look up without moving my head. Why the fuck would someone be in my apartment. Cabinet doors start opening and closing. I look up more, more, more. I see the backs of two heads. I see a familiar bald spot. I open my eyes and I sit up and I speak.

Leonard.

Leonard turns around. He's wearing a black trenchcoat and black suit and he's holding a bag of coffee.

My son.

What are you doing here?

You remember Snapper?

How did you find me?

Had someone look. Wasn't hard.

How'd you get in here?

He motions to the man next to him.

Had him open the door. That wasn't hard either.

I look at the man, who has turned around as well. He's tall and thick and has short black hair and is also wearing a black trenchcoat and a black suit. I met him when he picked Leonard up from the treatment center. He's an intimidating man, a man who looks more like a bear than a person, a man I would avoid were he not with my friend.

How you doing, Snapper?

I'm okay, Kid.

I look back at Leonard.

What are you doing here?

Come here.

How'd you get in my apartment?

Just come here.

I stand.

What?

He motions me forward.

75

Come here.

I step toward Leonard, he steps toward me. He opens his arms and he puts them around me.

I'm sorry for your loss.

I start to speak, but I can't.

I'm so sorry.

I start to cry.

He hugs me.

I start to cry.

I cry.
In the shower.
As I brush my teeth.
As I get dressed.
Cry.

I've never experienced anything like this, nothing else comes close. Grief, sorrow, sadness, pain pain pain. A hole in my chest that cannot be filled. A wound that is leaking. A break that I can't repair, I'm broken and I can't repair myself and there's nothing I can do.

I cry as I get dressed.

I cry.

I take a deep breath, compose myself. I step out of the bathroom. Leonard and the Snapper are waiting for me. We leave the apartment and I lock the door and we walk to their car, which is sitting at the curb. It's new and large. A white, four-door Mercedes-Benz with black one-way windows. From what Leonard has told me, it is the only type of car that he will own, ride in or drive. He opens the front passenger's door and climbs inside. Snapper opens the driver's door and sits behind the wheel. I get in the backseat and Snapper starts the engine and we pull away from the curb. We drive out to the lake, head south down Lakeshore Drive toward the center of the city. I stare out the window, the lake is frozen, the trees without leaves, the wind strong enough that I feel it pushing the car.

Leonard turns around, speaks.

You hungry?

I look at him.

Yeah.

You look thin.

Jail food, and I haven't been eating much since I've been here.

I hate fucking jail food.

Snapper speaks.

Me too. That shit sucks.

Leonard speaks.

I always try to pay someone to bring me real food.

Snapper speaks.

Sometimes it works, sometimes it doesn't.

Leonard speaks.

I should have done that with you. Paid some motherfucker to bring you a Big Mac.

I laugh.

It's not funny. You're too thin. You look sick. We're going to fatten you up while we're here.

I smile.

Okay.

When we get where we're going, I'm going to

order you some bacon. A big plate of nothing but bacon.

Okay.

And then we'll get a big lunch.

Okay.

And then we'll get a big dinner. A huge fucking dinner. Steaks, spinach, cake, all kinds of tasty shit.

I laugh.

And you can bring your friends. However many you want. Everybody's welcome.

Laugh again.

It's good to see you laughing, my Son. It's good to see that. I'd be very scared if I couldn't make you laugh.

No reason to be scared, Leonard.

You just had a fucking bomb dropped on you. You seem okay, but that doesn't mean I'm not scared.

I'm fine, Leonard.

You keep saying that to yourself and eventually you will be fine, but don't try to lie to me about it now. I know you're not fine, and you shouldn't expect to be, and that's okay.

I look at him.

It's okay to be fucked-up, James.

And it all comes back. I look down, bite my lip, try to stop myself from crying.

It's okay.

I nod, try to hold back the tears. I turn away from Leonard, look out the window, he leaves me to myself. I try to hold back the tears, but I can't.

We drive south toward the city. The lake is frozen. I stare out the window, the tears run down my cheeks.

We reach a sweeping turn in the drive there is frozen beach on our left, we take a right into a mass of steel and stone and glass. We start to drive down Michigan Avenue, skyscrapers line both sides of the street. The sidewalks are crowded, people bundled and warm, nobody here is bothered by the cold. The Hancock lies ahead of us, grows larger as we approach, wide and strong a majestic tower of black steel, I try to follow it with my eyes it stretches beyond my line of sight. I look straight up. It rises higher.

We take a right off the avenue, Snapper pulls up in front of an elegant entrance with a red carpet and a black canopy. He stops the car, two uniformed bellmen open the side doors, a valet rushes to the driver's door. Leonard and I get out of the car. Snapper waves off the valet and pulls away. I ask Leonard where he's going and Leonard says that he's parking the car. I ask why he doesn't let valet do it, he says it is safer that way, nobody can access the car if the Snapper parks it. I sometimes forget who Leonard is and what he does for a living. Snapper parks the car.

We walk under the canopy, doors are held open for us. We enter a small oak lobby. We stand in front of an elevator and we wait for it, when it arrives we step inside. It is also oak, its carpet thick and deep, blood red. It is as nice an elevator as I have ever seen. Its control panel only has one button. Leonard pushes it and up we go very quickly my ears pop.

We stop. The doors silently slide open. We step into another lobby this one huge with soaring ceilings, expensive furniture, a subtle reception counter, three well-dressed concierges. We walk through the lobby toward a restaurant on the far side, it sits in front of a huge bank of windows with a view of the city and the lake.

We stop at the hostess stand. Leonard says hello, the hostess smiles and asks if he would like his usual table. He says of course, Madam, and there is no need for you to escort us. She laughs and we walk to a table for four near the windows. We sit down. A waitress comes she says hello to Leonard she seems to know him too. She offers him a menu and he says no thank you, I already know what we would like. She says okay and he orders a plate of bacon, a big plate of nothing but bacon. He orders a plate of sausage, a big plate of nothing but sausage. He orders blueberry pancakes, Belgian waffles, scrambled eggs, fried eggs. He orders a pot of coffee and a pitcher of water and three glasses of milk. He orders three omelettes, one with cheese, one with steak, one with spinach and tomatoes, and he orders corned-beef hash and hash browns and roasted potatoes and four types of toast. The waitress is laughing and so am I and Leonard looks at the ceiling and starts scratching his chin. He asks himself if he forgot anything and he thinks for a moment and he says ha, I did forget a couple of things. He orders a basket of scones and a basket of muffins. The waitress asks if that is all and he says yes, for now. She laughs again and she walks away.

The Snapper joins us. He sits next to Leonard, across from me. Leonard looks at him and the Snapper nods. Leonard turns to me, speaks.

Time to talk.

Something wrong?

I'm not sure, that's why we need to talk.

Okay.

Leonard looks in my eyes.

You drinking?

I shake my head.

No.

You doing drugs?

No.

After what's happened, I'll understand if you are.

I'm not.

And I'd rather have you be using, than have you lie to me.

I'm not lying to you, Leonard.

You sure?

Yeah.

Leonard looks at Snapper. Snapper reaches into one of the side-pockets of his trenchcoat and draws out my bottle of rose. He sets it in the middle of the table. Leonard looks back at me.

Care to explain?

I laugh.

It's not funny.

First you break into my place, and now you're stealing shit from it.

Yeah.

I shake my head.

That's fucked up, Leonard.

Why do you have it?

Because I've been thinking about it. I keep it on hand in case I decide I want it.

You don't want it.

We'll see.

Trust me, you don't want it.

We'll see.

No, we won't see. Drinking is not an option for you.

That's for me to decide, Leonard.

You want to die?

No.

That's what'll happen if you start again.

I know.

Do you think that's what she would want for you?

I haven't thought about it.

Maybe you should.

Maybe you should leave it alone.

She wouldn't want you drinking.

Shut the fuck up, Leonard.

She couldn't do it, but you know she'd want you to.

Shut the fuck up, Leonard.

Didn't she used to say that a second of freedom is worth more than a lifetime of bondage?

Yeah, she did. Now change the fucking subject.

She wasn't strong enough, James. She couldn't do it over the long term.

Shut the fuck up, Leonard.

But you can, and she would want you to, and you should remember that.

Fuck you, Leonard.

I reach out, take the bottle, set it on the floor next to my chair.

I appreciate the sentiment, and I'm not going to fucking talk about it anymore.

The food arrives. We eat in silence. The bacon is hot and crispy, the sausage thick and juicy, the pancakes with syrup sweet. I drink one two three cups of coffee. I look at my food or out the window, I do not look at Leonard or Snapper. The bottle is at my feet. The decision is mine.

I hear Leonard set down his fork and his knife, take a deep breath, let out a long sigh. He speaks.

James.

I look up.

Yeah?

You promise me two things and I won't bring that shit up again.

What?

Promise me you didn't spend the money I gave you on drugs or liquor.

I didn't.

And promise me if you do decide to drink, you'll call me and talk to me before you do it.

I can promise you that.

Leonard turns to Snapper.

You heard him, right?

Snapper nods.

Yes, I did.

Leonard turns to me.

You're going to have to deal with Snap if you break the promises.

I laugh.

Fine.

You laughed. That's good. I came here to have some fucking fun, and I want you laughing, and I want you having fun. It'll help.

I nod.

I know.

I want you to stay in the hotel with us tonight. I got you a room right next to our rooms.

You didn't need to do that.

I know I didn't need to, but I wanted to, and I already did. And feel free to take whatever you want from the mini-bar. The chips are tasty and the cola is cold.

I laugh again. Leonard keeps talking and we eat. We finish eating and we stand and Leonard leaves a hundred-dollar bill on the table and we walk to a bank of elevators in the lobby. We step inside Leonard hands me a key. The doors close and we move up quickly and silently. The doors open and we step out the hall is quiet and the walls are perfectly painted the lights dim the carpet thick. We walk to the end of the hall there are three rooms in a line. Leonard speaks.

You want to go down to the pool?

I speak.

I'm going to take a nap.

Take a nap? It's not even ten o'clock.

I'm tired.

Leonard looks at Snapper.

He's tired.

Snapper speaks.

So what, let him sleep.

Leonard looks at me.

How long you want to sleep for?

An hour or so.

We'll come get you in an hour. We'll go down to the pool, do some swimming, maybe some Jacuzzi.

Okay.

Leonard points to a door.

That's your room. I'm in the middle. Snap's over there.

I walk to my door, open it.

See you in a while.

I step inside, close the door, walk down a short hall. I pass a large bathroom and I walk into a large open room. There are three large windows across one wall I can see the skyline I can see the lake it is still frozen. There is a large oak cabinet against another wall. I walk to it and I open it. There is a large television sitting on a shelf in the upper half, a mini-bar is built into the lower half.

Sitting against the third wall is a giant bed. There are nightstands on both sides of the bed, there are phones on both of them. I walk to the bed and I pull the sheets down they are white and clean and soft, I kick off my boots and I sit down on the bed and I take off my socks. I climb under the covers, put my head on a pillow, close my eyes, clutch myself clutch myself.

The bed is soft and warm.

I think about Lilly.

Miss her.

Hate that I am here without her.

She would have loved this place.

This room.

This bed.

This comfort.

This warmth.

She never knew anything like this.

Never knew, never got the chance, never had a chance.

I wish she were here.

Would give whatever, everything.

For five minutes.

One smile.

One laugh.

One kiss.

Just one.

Alone.

I clutch myself.

Sleep.

Knock. I open my eyes. Another knock. I sit up,

get out of my bed, walk toward the door another knock. I open the door. Leonard and Snapper are standing in the hall. Both of them are wearing thick white bathrobes. Leonard is holding a small box. He speaks.

Time for the pool.

He hands me the box, steps past me. Snapper follows him.

Go put that on. We'll wait for you.

They walk into the room, I walk into the bathroom. I close the door, open the box. I take out a small bathing suit. It is a bikini bathing suit, small and thin with black and white stripes. I open the door, walk into the room.

Leonard and Snapper are looking out the window, have their backs to me.

Leonard.

They turn around. I hold up the suit.

What the fuck is this?

Leonard smiles.

Your bathing suit.

I'm not wearing this.

Why not?

You've got to be fucking kidding me.

What's wrong with it?

It's a fucking bikini bottom, Leonard.

He laughs.

Not it's not, it's a Speedo, it's a fine swimsuit.

What are you wearing?

He smiles, opens his robe. He's wearing the same suit.

What's Snapper wearing?

Snapper opens his robe. He's wearing the same suit. I laugh, shake my head.

No way, Leonard. I'm not wearing it.

Competitive swimmers wear them.

I'm not a competitive swimmer.

Europeans wear them.

I'm not European.

Motherfuckers with style wear them.

I'm not a motherfucker with style.

He looks at Snapper.

He doesn't want to wear it, Snap.

I heard him.

What do you think about that?

He ain't a swimmer and he ain't European and he ain't got no style. Why should he wear it?

Leonard turns to me.

Let's go. And bring your robe.

Where we going?

Snap and me are going to the pool. You're going to the gift shop to find another suit, then you're meeting us at the pool.

Okay.

Leonard and Snapper walk past me and out of the room. I grab my robe and follow them. We ride the elevator down and Leonard and Snap get out before me and I go further down and I go to the gift shop and I return the striped Speedo and I find a nice large, normal American bathing suit. I try it on it's two or three sizes too big. I have to tie it tightly tie it to keep it from falling down.

It's just my size, just the way I like it. I walk to the counter and a woman behind the counter asks for my room key and she charges the bathing suit to my room.

I go to the elevator, the pool. There are gray marble floors simple white walls. There are simple wooden lounge chairs along a wall and there is a Jacuzzi built into the floor at the far end. It is warm, and the crisp clean smell of chlorine is strong. Leonard is swimming laps in the pool and Snapper is sitting in the Jacuzzi. I walk toward the Jacuzzi. Snapper looks up, speaks.

Nice suit.

Thanks.

Fits nice.

I laugh, look toward Leonard.

What's he doing?

Swimming back and forth.

Why's he doing that?

He's been exercising like fucking crazy ever since he got out of the drug place.

Fuck that.

That's what I say. I go with him, but I don't do it.

Leonard stops at our end of the pool.

Nice suit.

Thanks.

You coming in?

No.

You're skinny, but you're in bad shape. You should exercise.

90

No thanks.

I'm going to do some more laps.

Go ahead.

Leonard turns and starts swimming, back and forth, back and forth. I get into the Jacuzzi it's hot. I close my eyes and lean back and let the heat soak in it feels good, relaxes me, calms me. When Leonard finishes his laps he gets into the Jacuzzi and me and him and Snapper sit and relax. It feels good.

When we've had enough we get out and we put on our robes white and thick and we go to the restaurant. People stare at us. Most of them are well dressed, some of the men are wearing suits and ties, we are the only ones in robes and bathing suits. We order a huge lunch cheeseburgers and fries and ice cream and we eat and when we're finished we go back to our rooms. Leonard and Snapper say they have some business they will meet me later. I take a nap. I dream about drinking and drugs. I get fucked-up in the dream, fucking blitzed in the dream, I can't walk or talk, can't function in any way. When I wake I feel awful, as if the dream was reality. I lie in bed. The last ten days have been a lifetime. I feel awful.

I get up take a shower watch TV wait. I eat some chips and drink a cola and the chips are tasty and the cola is cold. Leonard comes back tells me to call all of my friends we're going out for dinner he wants all of them to come. I ask him where we're going and he gives me the name of a famous steakhouse, says we're eating at eight o'clock. He says get on the fucking horn, my son, call your fucking friends, we're going to have some fun. I laugh and he leaves.

I pick up the phone, start making calls. I ask my friends to dinner they can all come. Kevin says our friend Danny is in town I say bring him along. I put on my boots walk to Leonard's room knock on the door. He answers he is wearing a black suit it looks expensive. I laugh, look at my clothes. Worn khakis, a black wool sweater, scuffed black combat boots. I look back at Leonard.

They going to let me in like this?

Hah!

I laugh.

What's that mean?

That means Hah!

Yeah, what's Hah mean?

Hah means of course they're going to let you in. You're with me.

You sure?

Yeah, I'm fucking sure.

He steps out of the room, closes the door, starts walking toward the elevator.

Where's Snap?

He stops, turns around.

Snap's not coming.

Why?

He's just not.

Understood.

I start walking toward the elevator, know that

there are things with Leonard that I should not question. He pushes the button and the elevator arrives and we go down walk through the lobby leave the hotel go outside. It's dark. It's cold. The wind. We start walking.

Five minutes later we're at the steakhouse. We walk through a set of large, unmarked oak doors. It's dark, the walls are wood, the carpet thick. It smells strongly of steak and cigars. I take a deep breath, we walk through a short hall to a reception stand. There is a man in a tuxedo behind the stand he steps around and greets Leonard calls him Sir and shakes his hand. Leonard introduces the man to me and we shake hands and the man says pleasure to meet you, Sir, which makes me laugh.

We are early, so the man leads us through the dining room to the bar. The dining room is large and open, candles on every table, white linens and silver, patrons in suit and tie, skirt and stocking. The bar is in a separate smaller room. It is large and oak runs the length of a wall. There are stools in front of it, there are small tables and low cushioned chairs spread through the rest of the room. Leonard shakes the man's hand and says thank you, the man bows and says my pleasure, Sir. We sit down at a table, the man leaves. Leonard reaches into the inside pocket of his suit-coat and removes two cigars. He offers one to me.

Cigar?

No thanks.

They're Cuban.

I don't like cigars.

I reach into my pocket, take out my cigarettes. Leonard stares at me.

How can you not like cigars?

Just don't.

Why?

Just don't.

Do you know how to smoke one properly?

No.

That's why you don't like them. You've never learned to enjoy them.

He hands me one of the cigars.

Time for you to go to cigar school, my son. Time for you to learn one of life's great pleasures.

I take the cigar, look at it. I don't want it, but know Leonard wants to teach me how to smoke it. He shows me how to cut it: find the tapered end, called the cap, cut leaving at least $1/_8$ inch of the cap remaining. He shows me how to light it: use a match, wait for the sulfur to burn away, do not touch fire to cigar, bring it close, use the heat. He shows me how to smoke it: do not inhale, draw in with your cheeks, hold it, enjoy the taste, exhale. I accidentally inhale a few times, and the smoke is strong and burning and it makes me cough. I don't like the taste, it is of smoke and dirt and sweat. Leonard tells me it is supposed to be a rich creamy taste with a medium body. I have no idea what he's talking about.

As my friends show up they are led to our table

in the bar. Leonard greets them all the same way. He stands and he says hello, hello my name is Leonard, it is wonderful to meet you. He shakes hands with Kevin and Danny and gives them cigars. He bows to the women and pulls out their chairs. Everyone is surprised by Leonard. I did not tell them much about him, just that he was my friend from rehab. I don't think they were expecting a cheery, friendly ridiculous man in his fifties who says things like drink it up, boy drink that cocktail the fuck up, or my oh my dear lady, your perfume is so delicious I feel like I'm going to faint.

When everyone has arrived Leonard stands and says it's time to eat like pigs my friends, time for a fucking feast. We stand as a group and walk into the dining room and sit at a table in the center of the restaurant.

There are immediately three waiters setting bottles of wine and water on the table, one of them sets a large crystal decanter filled with cola next to me. When they leave, Leonard stands again and raises his glass.

It is always a pleasure to meet strong young men and beautiful young women. I am honored by your presence at my table, honored that you have chosen to spend the evening with me. Let us all raise a toast to fine food, strong drink, delicious dessert and new friends.

Glasses are raised and the toast is made, hear hear, hear hear. As soon the glasses are back on the table, food starts arriving. There are jumbo

95

shrimp cocktails, small bowls with lumps of crab-meat, scallops wrapped in bacon, oysters, clams and mussels. There are salads, Cobb and Caesar and iceberg drenched in Roquefort. There are bowls of lobster bisque and French onion soup. There is food everywhere, hands reaching for food everywhere, smiles and laughs around the table, other patrons are staring at our table, we don't care.

The appetizers are taken away. We are given a moment or two of rest. I hear two of the girls talking to Leonard they ask him where he lives he says Las Vegas for part of the year, southern California for part of the year. They ask him what he does he says I'm a businessman. They ask him what type he says the type that doesn't like to talk about work away from the office. He asks them what they do, they both work at a clothing store. He says he loves clothing, has closets full of clothing, buys clothing everywhere he goes, loves loves loves clothes. They laugh. He stands and asks them what they think of his suit, he turns in a circle to give them a complete view. They tell him they think it's beautiful and he thanks them and he compliments them on their fine taste.

More food arrives. Family style platters of steak, lamb, chicken and lobster. Bowls of creamed spinach, sautéed mushrooms, asparagus. Plates of baked potatoes, mashed potatoes and hash browns. We eat, laugh, Leonard and I drink water and cola, my friends, now Leonard's friends, drink wine and cocktails. If a platter bowl or plate is ever empty, it is immediately replaced. When everyone is finished, dessert is delivered: ice cream and pie, chocolate cake and fruit. Leonard lights a cigar, the restaurant is now empty but for us. He motions for the concierge to bring more cigars, the man brings a small humidor to the table, it contains cigars of different sizes and shapes, cigars from different countries. Leonard walks around with the humidor and selects a cigar for each individual. When he is finished, he walks them through the same steps he taught me earlier. They listen to Leonard, follow his instructions, start tentatively. They are not tentative for long.

As we smoke, Leonard stands, motions for me to stand with him. We walk into the kitchen. He takes out a large roll of cash from his pocket and starts handing out tips to everyone, to the chef, to the sous chef, to the pastry chef, to the busboys, to the dishwashers. We leave the kitchen go to the bar. Each of the bartenders receives a handshake filled with money. We walk to the reception desk Leonard thanks the man slides him cash tells him that I am his son and that if I ever show up here he expects that I will be treated accordingly. The man thanks Leonard and says of course, Sir, of course.

We walk back to the table. The cigars are out, the glasses empty, the dishes are being cleared. Leonard helps the women put on their coats. He tells each of them it was an honor meeting you, he kisses each of their hands. We walk out of the restaurant and there are cars waiting for us. My friends all thank Leonard, tell him how amazing the meal was, tell him they hope to see him again soon. He is gracious to them, says it was my pleasure, you are wonderful young people it was my pleasure. He opens car doors, pays drivers, sends the cars away. The windows in the cars come down and everyone waves goodbye to him. When the cars are out of sight it is me and my friend Leonard. He speaks.

Thought we'd walk back. It'll help settle the food a bit.

Sounds good.

We start walking. It is colder, darker, the wind stronger.

You have nice friends, my son.

Yeah, I'm lucky.

Very polite, very interesting. The girls were all beautiful.

I'll tell them you said so.

You have fun?

It was the best night I've had in years, Thank you for doing it.

We'll do it again next time I'm in town.

We turn a corner. The hotel is in sight. I see Leonard's white Mercedes sitting in front of the hotel. Snap is in the driver's seat, the engine is running.

I speak.

Why's the car out there?

I need to go out for a while.
A little late, isn't it?
Sometimes I need it to be late.
I don't respond. We walk to the car. I nod at Snapper, he nods at me. I turn to Leonard.
Thanks again, Leonard.
No problem.
I'll see you tomorrow.
I'll come to your room when I wake up.
Cool.
You've got your key?
Yeah.
Goodnight, my son.
Thank you, Leonard.
Leonard turns, opens the car door, gets inside, closes the door. The car pulls away I watch it go.
Thank you, Leonard.
Thank you, Leonard.
Thank you.

For the next two days, we eat, sit around the pool, watch TV, sleep. I am rarely alone. When I am alone, and I'm not sleeping, I cry. I lie face-down on the bed and I cry. I stand in the shower and I cry. I stare out the window and I cry. It doesn't matter what I'm doing, or not doing, the littlest things set me off, everything sets me off. I cry when I'm alone. Whenever I'm alone. My bottle is always with me. An antidote to pain should I choose to use it. I keep it in plain view, on one of the nightstands next to the bed. I cradle it when I sleep. I have opened it twice, smelled, let it taunt me, let it enrage me. I do it because the test of it, the test of resisting it, makes me feel strong. Most of the time I feel like I want to die. The feeling of strength keeps me going.

On the morning of our fourth day in the hotel, Leonard shows up late for breakfast. When he arrives, he's wearing a suit.

My son.

What's up?

He sits.

Me and Snap are leaving in a little while.

100

Back to Nevada?

New York, then Nevada.

Why New York?

You remember the story I told you about my father? How he worked as a golf course maintenance man at a ritzy country club in Connecticut, just outside of New York, how he told me on his deathbed he wanted me to be successful enough to play that course someday, play it just like one of the members?

Yeah, I remember.

The older I get, the more anxious I am to do it. I got a line on somebody who might be able to help. I'm going to see him.

Good luck.

You gonna be okay without me?

Yeah.

You sure?

I'm a big boy, Leonard.

You need anything, you call me.

I will. Thank you.

You get close to picking up that bottle, you call me.

I will.

You know she'd want you clean.

I don't want to talk about it, Leonard.

She would.

I look away. He stands.

I gotta go.

Okay.

I stand.

Don't be mad at me, Kid. I'm just trying to help.

You are helping. It's just hard right now.

He nods. We hug each other, separate.

See you soon.

Thank you, Leonard. Thanks for everything.

He turns, leaves. I sit down, eat a huge breakfast, go back to the room, cry, take a nap, cry, leave.

I stop at Kevin's apartment. There are two messages for me. One from a bar, one from a gas station. I would rather work at the gas station. I call the gas station, the manager tells me to stop by so that I can meet him. I leave Kevin's, walk over, meet the manager. He's young, slightly older than I am. His hair is short, shoes shined, uniform clean and pressed. He asks me if I know anything about car repair and I tell him no. He asks me if I'm interested in a long-term position or short-term position, I tell him I need a job, have no idea how long or short a term. He nods, thanks me for coming, shakes my hand, I leave.

I call the bar. They give me an address, tell me to show up at four A.M. the next morning if I'm interested in the job.

I go home, sit on the floor, close my eyes, try to be still. It's harder than it was in jail. Harder because the same thoughts run through my head whenever I try to do it. I think about Lilly, about the last minutes of her life. I think about what was going through her head the moment she decided to die, as she tied the knots of her noose,

103

as she put the noose around her neck, as she hung and started to fade. I wonder if there were regrets, if there was peace. I wonder if she thought about me as she hung. I try to avoid the images, change the course of my thought, empty my mind of all thought. It doesn't work. I do not possess the necessary discipline. I sit, I think about Lilly and her death, I hurt. My body hurts, everything hurts.

After an hour I stand, shake, smoke a cigarette, leave. I go to Kevin's. We meet our friends at a bar, we shoot pool, they drink, I watch them. There is temptation every second of every minute of every five ten twenty thirty minutes every single second. Temptation to drink, to annihilate myself, to make the pain go away, to hurt myself more than I already hurt. It ebbs and flows, this temptation sometimes easy to resist sometimes difficult, sometimes so overwhelming that I know if I move I'm done. The only way to deal with it is to not move, to sit and wait, to hold on until it goes away.

My friends get drunk. I sit with them. They all have jobs so we leave the bar, they need a few hours' sleep before they go to work. I have three hours to burn. I keep walking up and down cold, empty, black streets, block after block, block after block. Occasionally I see another person, usually drunk, stumbling along the sidewalk. Occasionally I pass an open bar or convenience store. The only vehicles out are either cabs or cops, I can't afford a ride with either of them.

As I walk, I start to shake. My clothes are worn

and thin, I don't have a hat or gloves. The cold settles over me in layers, on my coat and pants, on my skin, beneath my skin, in my bones, in my jaw and teeth. I keep walking, hoping the longer I walk the warmer I'll become, but my theory is wrong. The cold hurts me and shakes me, makes me numb. The more numb, the better, the more numb the more comfortable. The numbness functions for me the same way the alcohol and drugs functioned for me. I am overwhelmed. Everything hurts. It hurts so much that I stop feeling. Everything is wiped away and the numb remains. I can deal with the numb. It is as it was before and it is the best I can do for myself. I walk and I walk and I walk.

I show up at the bar fifteen minutes early. Two doormen stand at the entrance. They're both in black, they both look cold, they're both scowling. They stop me as I start to walk in, one of them tells me they're closed. I tell them I'm here for the job. One of them laughs, the other says go around back, wait at the service door.

To get to the back, I have to walk around the block. There are two other men waiting, one white, one black, both young, neither looks happy. The black man paces, swears, hops up and down to try to stay warm. The white man stares at his feet, doesn't move, doesn't speak.

At four fifteen, the door opens. The doormen from the front lead us into a huge open room. Along one wall of the room, there are leveled risers with tables. The highest group of tables is surrounded by a red velvet rope. Along another wall, there is a stage. Above and at the edges of the stage are racks of lights and stacks of speakers, and at the back of the stage there is a DJ booth. Along a third wall is a long black bar. There are no stools in front of it. A group of bartenders and waitresses stand at one end of the bar talking drinking smoking laughing. A group of men with garbage bags are picking up trash.

We walk behind the bar, open a door at one end, walk into a bright hall.

There are five doors in the hall. One labeled Men one labeled Women one labeled Office two with nothing. One of doormen tells us to wait, knocks on the office door, the doormen leave.

We wait for a few minutes. We stand and stare at the floor, occasionally look at each other. The door opens. A middle-age man steps out. He's short and fat, has dark, thinning hair, bad skin. He's wearing a black and yellow sweatsuit, black leather loafers. He looks us up and down.

Here for the job?

White man nods, black man and I say yeah.

Any of you ever been janitors or done any clean-up work?

White man nods, black man and I say no.

I need people to clean my places. There's this one and two others. You pick up trash, mop the floors, wipe down tables, shit like that. Hours are from four to eight every morning. Pay is seven bucks an hour. If you do well, you might become a doorman or a barback. If you're no good, I'll fire you. If you're interested, get out there and start working. We'll process you when you're done.

I turn, walk back to the room, ask one of the men with garbage bags what to do, he tells me to do what he's doing. I get a bag, pick up trash, take it to a dumpster. I get a broom, sweep the floor, get a mop, mop the floor, get a bottle of cleaner, wipe down tables, chairs, countertops. The white man and the black man have also joined the crew, there are seven of us. It takes an hour to clean the club. When we're done, we walk down the street to another one. It's larger, flashier, there are cages hanging from the ceiling, four bars, two separate sections with tables, three separate levels. Process is the same: pick up trash, sweep, mop, wipe. Takes two hours. When we're done, we walk to a nearby bar. Bar is in the basement of a large residential building. Has pinball machine, pool table, two televisions which hang in corners, free popcorn, free food every night from seven to ten. Takes thirty minutes to clean. When we're done, most of the men leave. The white man, black man and I walk back to the office, fill out some paper-work, are assigned days. I get Thursday, Friday, Saturday, Sunday, Monday. From four to finish. Seven dollars an hour.

I leave, walk until I'm numb. I stop to talk to Lilly, tell her I miss her, tell her I love her. I leave, walk until I'm numb. Go home. Sleep.

My life becomes routine.

I work.

Sleep is still difficult I sleep for three or four hours a day. Usually sometime in the afternoon.

I walk in the cold, keep myself numb.

I cry less, cry less.

I go out with my friends every night. Go to bars, shoot pool, smoke cigarettes, watch them drink. Sometimes I talk, sometimes I laugh, both feel good. When I'm thirsty, I order a caffeinated cola drink, with ice and without a lemon. I start to feel more comfortable around people. The temptation is still there, always there, the urge to drink drug and destroy never leaves, but I'm getting used to it. It's like a rash, a nasty fucking rash, constant, annoying and painful. I'd like to scratch it till kingdom fucking come but if I do I die and I don't want to die.

When my friends go home I walk again, walk in the cold, keep myself numb, always numb.

I work.

Sometimes I read the Tao.

Sometimes I sit, stare at the wall, the wall is white.

Sometimes I feel too much, feel like I'm going to explode. All of me, all of what is inside of me, anger sadness confusion pain insecurity fear loneliness, heart soul consciousness, whatever words for some of what is inside me there are no words to describe, it swirls, it races, it taunts, it moves to the surface and pushes pushes, all of it pushes. I feel like I'm going to explode. I scream. At the top of my lungs. Long and hard, scream so that my lungs hurt, my throat hurts, my face hurts. I scream into pillows. I walk to the lake scream at the water. Stand in a park and scream into a tree. Doesn't matter where I am I just need to fucking scream. It makes me feel better.

My life is a simple routine.

Boss calls me into his office. I sit across from him. He speaks.

I need a doorman. Nobody else wants to do it. You interested?

Why won't anyone do it?

It's the late shift, nine to four. You gotta stand outside the whole time. The bar is on Chicago Ave., which is really fucking cold and windy, and you're gonna freeze your ass off. I'd need you Sunday, Monday and Tuesday nights. Those are the slow nights. The bartender and waitress are supposed to give you ten percent of their tips, but they don't make shit those nights, so you probably won't get shit. I'll give you a twenty-five cent raise, but it probably won't make up for it.

Sounds great.

I don't got time for fucking jokes.

I'm not joking. I'll do it.

He looks at me for a moment.

You start Sunday. Get there at eight, ask for Ted. He's the bartender, he'll tell you what to do.

I have a question.

What?

Is this a promotion?

What kind of question is that?

I've never gotten a promotion before. I'm wondering if I could consider this one.

Consider it whatever the fuck you want. Just show up at eight.

Thank you.

I stand, leave, start walking home. I smile for most of the walk, occasionally skip a few steps, occasionally snap my fingers. I have been fired from every job I've had in my life. There was usually yelling and screaming involved in my firings, always bad feelings on my employer's side, not one would give me a positive reference. Boss told me to consider my change of position whatever the fuck I want, I'm going to consider it a promotion, the first one of my life. I might not feel like it most of the time, I may be carrying around unbearable urges to drink and do drugs, I may be depressed and sometimes suicidal, I may be feeling a sense of sorrow and loss greater and more profound than any other I've felt in a life filled with sorrow and loss, but I'm getting better. I got a motherfucking promotion, goddamnit. It's time to celebrate.

I take a long, nonsensical route home. I weave through the wealthy neighborhoods of the North Side of Chicago. I walk past fancy stores, past clothing stores furniture stores I could give a fuck about clothes or furniture, past bookstores and art galleries I walk through them looking at beautiful things I can't afford, I look at the windows of real estate offices, they have listings hanging in silver frames greystone brownstone turn of the century rowhouse an excellent value. It's gonna go fast. I walk up and down the aisles of a gourmet grocery. I look at fruit and vegetables crisp and nearly ripe smells like a summer garden under fluorescent lights. I go to the cheese department cheddar Swiss mozzarella provolone Gruyère blue Brie feta cow milk goat milk semi-soft extra creamy crumbly mild stinky. I look at fish, pasta, tea that costs forty dollars an ounce, fish, eggs that cost two hundred, beef raised on beer at three hundred and twenty dollars a pound, they have twelve types of whipped cream forty types of coffee fifty different brands of chocolate, flowers that cost more than I make in a week. The colors the smells they make me delirious make me want to eat until I explode make me salivate drool my head spins my sight blurs.

I walk to the bakery section. I look at pastries and cakes, tarts and pies. My body craves sugar, always craves sugar. Years of alcoholism and the high level of sugar in alcohol created the craving, which I feed with candy and soda. I check my pocket, I have twenty-two dollars on me. I have twenty or so more dollars in my apartment. The cakes have the most sugar, sugar in the cake itself and sugar in the frosting. They come in two sizes large and small, they come in four types chocolate with chocolate frosting chocolate with white frosting white cake with chocolate frosting white cake with white frosting. I would like to buy one of each type in both the large and small sizes. I would have them put in nice white cake boxes and have the boxes closed with finely tied and looped string. It would be a struggle carrying so many boxes home, but I would persevere. At home I would open the boxes one at time and work my way through all eight cakes systematically, starting with the small ones and finishing with the large ones. I would forgo fork and knife and eat with my hands, licking my fingers and my lips along the way. Once I was done, I would most likely either vomit due to excess, which I have done many times in my life, or spend several hours in some sort of sugar-induced mania, maybe pacing in circles, maybe walking endlessly around my block, maybe babbling idiotically at random strangers on the street. Eventually I would shut down and sleep, happy and full, every cell of my body saturated with sugar, cake and frosting.

A woman in a white baker's outfit steps to the counter opposite me.

May I help you?

How much are the cakes?

Which ones?

I point to the cakes.

The birthday cakes.

The small ones are fourteen dollars, the large ones are twenty-one.

Large please. White cake with white frosting.

Do you want me to put an inscription on it?

Does it cost extra?

Nope.

Yeah, I would like an inscription.

What would you like it to say?

I think for a moment.

How about – Big Promotion, Jimbo!

She laughs.

Who's Jimbo?

Me.

What kind of promotion?

I work at a bar downtown. Got promoted from cleaning crew to doorman.

Congratulations.

In a couple years I'm going to be President of the United States.

She laughs, opens the cabinet, reaches for my cake.

I'll be right back, Mr President.

I will be anxiously awaiting your return.

She laughs again, turns around, puts the cake in a box and ties the box with a finely tied loop, hands it to me. I thank her and I go to the checkout line and I pay for my cake my beautiful cake.

I walk home. No more skipping and no more finger snapping, I don't want to hurt my cake. I do, however, smile, and I also greet people on the sidewalks with heartfelt and sincere hellos, how are yous, it's a beautiful days. As I walk into the building I see Mickey, the building super-intendent, walking out of it. His eyes are swollen and it looks like he's been crying.

Yo, Mickey. You want a piece of cake?

What?

I just bought a cake. You want a piece?

What kind is it?

White on white.

I need some cigarettes.

If you want cake, I'll be in my apartment.

Mickey skulks away. I go to my apartment. I open the door, go to my little kitchen, set the cake on the counter. I open it, my oh my it is a beautiful cake. I get two plastic plates and a knife. I cut two pieces away and set them on the plates. I take the rest of the cake and I sit on the floor next to my bed. I carefully pick it up and take a big bite out of it. I chew my bite slowly, savoring the light, moist, airy cake and the sweet, thick, creamy frosting. I take another bite, another another. It's a great cake. More than suitable for my promotion celebration.

About halfway through my eating of the cake, there is a knock at my door.

I stand, walk over, open it. Mickey is standing at the door, a pack of cigarettes in his hand. He speaks.

You have cake and frosting on your face.

I smile.

Is there any left?

I saved some for you.

He steps inside my apartment. I walk to the kitchen, get one of the plates with cake on it, get a plastic fork, give them to him. We sit on the floor, and as we eat, he tells me about his day.

He is miserable. His boyfriend broke up with him at breakfast, told him he needed someone with more ambition than Mickey, someone who wanted more out of life than a job as building superintendent. Mickey told him it was temporary, that he was working to make it as a painter, that he felt his dreams were going to come true. The boyfriend said I need more than your dreams, Mickey, and he walked out.

Mickey starts to cry. I eat my cake. I make sure to get some extra frosting on my face. When Mickey looks up, he sees me and he laughs. I speak.

If you don't eat yours . . .

He laughs, starts eating. As we eat, we talk, he asks me where I'm from I tell him Cleveland, he asks why I moved here I say I moved for a girl, he asks if we're still together I say yes we're still together. I ask him the same things he's from a small town in Indiana and moved here so he could be himself, could live as a gay man without being harassed, could try to make it as a painter. I ask him what he paints he says he'd rather show me than tell me. He finishes his cake and he stands and he leaves my apartment.

I keep eating, I'm almost done. Five minutes later Mickey comes back with a painting and sets it carefully on the floor in front of me.

It is a small painting, maybe six inches by six inches. The canvas is black at the edges. The rest of it is covered with tiny faces. Some are smiling, some are laughing, some are screaming, some are crying. The faces are painted in perfect miniature detail, they look like little photographs, and it's a beautiful painting, beautiful and horrifying, full joy and misery, laughter and sorrow. Mickey speaks.

What do you think?

It's great.

You want it?

Absolutely.

It's yours.

Thank you.

If you need a nail to hang it, I've got them.

Once I decide where to put it.

I'm gonna go. Thanks for the cake.

Thanks for the painting.

Sure.

And forget about the boyfriend, that shallow fucker.

He laughs.

Yeah.

He leaves. I finish my cake. When I'm done, I lick my lips and fingers and clean the excess from my chin and cheeks. I want to see Lilly. I usually walk to see her, but I'm tired, so I decide to take the train. I've never used the elevated train system of Chicago. I have been told it is simple and easy. I'm wary of it. Most of the time someone says something is simple and easy it turns out to be complicated and difficult.

I put on my warm clothes. Get my last twenty dollars from beneath my mattress, which is where I keep my money. I wrap the last piece of cake, carefully wrap it. I leave, walk to the nearest train station. I look at the map, colored lines weaving through and across each other. I find the station on the map, find Lilly's station on the map, buy a token, step to the platform, wait. The train comes, I make the transfer, arrive at Lilly's station. The trip is simple and easy. I now know how to use the elevated train. So much for my bullshit theory.

I walk, stop at a flower shop, spend eighteen dollars on red roses.

I give her the roses.

I give her the last piece of cake.

I tell her about my day. The best day I've had on my own in Chicago.

I got a promotion.

I went for a nice, long walk.

I spent my hard-earned money on something beautiful.

I ate that beautiful thing, and it was tasty.

I made a friend.

I was given a gift.

I learned something.

It was a great, great day.

I tell Lilly I love her, miss her. I spend my last dollar on a token home. Part of me expects Lilly to be waiting for me. I would give everything for her to be waiting for me. She's not. I'm alone. I lie down, can't sleep.

I wait for the darkness.

I start my new job. The bar is small, nondescript, in the lower level of a large building, beneath a clothing store. Eight steps lead from the street to the ten tables, two pinball machines, televisions in two corners continuously playing sports. There is a popcorn machine near the door, the popcorn is free. There are three employees working at any given time, a bartender, waitress, doorman. Bartender Ted and waitress Amy always work the same shift as me. They are boyfriend/girlfriend, and in between serving the dozen or so customers usually in the place, they stand at the corner of the bar smoking cigarettes, giggling, whispering and kissing. I stand outside. It's cold as hell and I'm always numb. I always have a roll of drink tickets in my pocket. I'm supposed to offer them to anyone and everyone who walks by the bar, they are redeemable for either a free shot of watermelon liqueur or a free kamikaze. No one in the first three days takes me up on the offer, so now I rarely bother. When I do bother I choose people who I'm sure will say no, such as children, the elderly, or the very very well-dressed, and I beg them to go inside, tell them my job is on the line, tell them I desperately need their help. Every single one of them says no. From midnight on, I only see a few people. I stand and shiver and smoke cigarettes. Sometimes I test myself to see how long I can go without moving, I can last about two hours. Sometimes I sing to myself, sing silly love songs with titles like Just Once, Secret Lovers, Lost in Love, Down on Bended Knee. I don't know how or why I know the words, I just do. Sometimes I flip a quarter over and over, keep track of how many times heads, how many times tails, for some reason there are usually more heads. Sometimes I talk to Lilly. Carry on long conversations with her. Talk about random things, the news, something I saw while I was walking, something I read. I talk to her about our plans the plans we made while I was in jail. Where we wanted to live, the jobs we wanted to get, maybe marriage, maybe kids, what the kids would be named, she wanted a little girl, I wanted a little boy. Sometimes I cry while I talk to her. Sometimes I get angry. Sometimes I feel stupid, but I keep talking anyway. Sometimes I just stop, I have her image in my mind, and I have to stop.

My shift ends at four. I punch out, leave. It's always dark, the streets empty. I walk south into steel and concrete canyons. I move up and down vacant blocks, stare up at fifty, eighty, hundred and ten story monoliths, watch streetlight shadows move across lower floors, kick deserted papers, cups and bags lying on curbs. I walk down the middle of wide boulevards, stand on the centers of iron bridges, sit alone in huge sprawling plazas, parks, long expanses of dead public grass. I am the only person awake, the city and its citizens are asleep, my footsteps my breath and the whistling screaming wind are all I hear. The city is reduced, ceases to be a city, becomes a museum. Objects aren't banks, law firms, hospitals, courthouses, shopping centers, apartment buildings, they are huge sprawling sculptures of marble limestone iron steel and glass, without purpose or use, just huge beautiful objects.

When I start to see other people, as the eyes of the city start to open, I leave, walk out to the lake, start heading north. It is always colder by the lake. The wind is always stronger. The cold shakes me and the wind stings my face. I walk until I find a bench and I sit the bench is always cold. I stare across the frozen expanse of ice and encased debris, sticks, logs, cans, there is a football opposite a beach, a lifejacket opposite a marina. I watch as thin girders of blue light start glowing, as the light turns yellow, pink, orange, as it spreads across the horizon. The sun appears, slowly rising, an edge, quarter, half circle. It becomes full and red, envelopes the sky, dominates it. It makes the monuments of this city, of any city every city, seem small and insignificant. It makes me feel small and insignificant. Makes me forget the past, dismiss the future. Makes my problems disappear, feel like nothing nothing nothing.

When I hear cars on the highway behind me I

121

stand walk home. As the normal day begins, my day ends.

I lie down in my apartment.

Sometimes I sleep.

Sometimes not.

I lie there.

Alone.

It is eight A.M. As I walk toward my building, I see a white Mercedes sitting at the curb. I enter the building, the door to my apartment is open. I step inside, see Leonard and Snapper standing in front of my refrigerator. The refrigerator door is open and there are brown paper bags on the floor.

Leonard.

They turn around.

My son, my son.

Leonard steps toward me.

How are you?

He hugs me.

I'm okay. What are you doing here?

Filling your fridge.

You came here to fill my fridge?

No, but when we arrived, we saw it was empty.

You gotta stop breaking in, Leonard.

Get a better lock and we'll stop breaking in. The lock you got is a fucking joke.

Snapper speaks.

I'm the one who actually does it, Kid, and it's real easy. You're lucky you ain't been robbed.

123

Leonard laughs.

Look at this place. Who would rob him? He's got nothing to steal.

I step toward the refrigerator.

What are you putting in there?

Snapper speaks.

We got shit from all five food groups.

Leonard speaks.

Fruits, vegetables, proteins, grains and dairys.

Snapper speaks.

We got them all.

I laugh.

It's dairy, not dairys.

I know, but it's funnier saying dairys. Say it.

Dairys.

I laugh.

Told ya. Dairys is funnier.

I laugh again.

Thank you. For all five food groups.

And that's not all.

Leonard opens the cabinets. They're filled with cans of soup, boxes of rice and boxes of pasta, jars of tomato sauce.

Snapper speaks.

I got something special for you in there.

He steps over, pulls down a box.

Rice-A-Roni. The motherfucking San Francisco treat.

I laugh.

Thanks.

Leonard speaks.

You're still too skinny, my son. If you're gonna be a doorman at a bar you're gonna need to gain some weight. We drove by last night and saw you standing out there and you do not look particularly menacing.

You drove by to see me?

We did.

Why?

That's why we're here.

To talk to me about my job?

Yup.

What about my job?

Let's go down to the hotel, get some breakfast. We'll talk down there.

I need some sleep.

Then get some sleep, come down for lunch.

What time?

One?

Okay.

Leonard turns to Snapper.

You finished?

Yeah.

Let's go. He needs some sleep.

Okay.

Leonard turns to me.

See you at one.

Snapper speaks.

See ya, Kid.

I speak.

Thanks for the food.

Leonard speaks.

Eat some of it. Right now. Get fat.

Snapper speaks.

Yeah, get fat.

I laugh.

Bye.

They walk out. I lie down, sleep, wake-up, take a shower. I am confident now I take the El train downtown, walk to the hotel from the train. I ride up the elevator, walk through the lobby, Leonard is waiting for me in the restaurant, I sit down with him.

Where's Snapper?

He's out working. You sleep well?

I never sleep well.

You will.

I guess.

You hungry?

Yeah.

Leonard motions for the waitress, orders steaks and French fries for each of us, turns back to me.

Now tell me, how the fuck you end up working at a bar?

I laugh.

Tell me how you know I work at a bar and I'll tell you how I ended up there.

I had someone looking out for you. They told me.

Who?

Doesn't matter.

You got some flunky following me around?

I'm just looking out for you.

I can look out for myself.

Why you working at a bar?

It was the only job I could get.

Come on, you're a smart kid. You can do better than that.

I applied for a few different jobs, nobody wanted to hire me. I don't exactly have a sparkling resume.

It's unacceptable.

It's fine, Leonard.

You're an alcoholic and you're a drug addict. You've only been clean a couple months. You can't work at a bar. It's crazy and stupid and dangerous.

I actually work in front of the bar. I stand there and pick my ass for hours on end. It might be stupid and it might be boring, but it's not crazy or dangerous.

Until you feel like you want a drink and you go inside.

I feel like I want a drink all the fucking time. And if I decide I want one, it won't be hard to get one, regardless of where I am.

It's unacceptable, my son.

You got a better idea?

I do.

What's that?

Come work for me.

I laugh.

Yeah, that's a great idea.

Why not?

Because I've got a record, because I'm trying to

stay out of trouble, because an arrest of any kind means I go away for three to five.

I got good lawyers, you won't go anywhere.

I laugh.

That makes me feel better.

It should. You'll have the power of an entire organization behind you.

I laugh again.

That's what I'm afraid of, Leonard.

I won't let you work at a bar.

It's not a matter of what you will or will not let me do.

I'll say it differently – I can offer you a much better opportunity than you have at the bar.

Gonna make me an offer I can't refuse?

Leonard laughs.

I can offer you a much better opportunity.

What would I do?

Pick things up and take them places.

I laugh again.

Pick things up and take them places?

Yes, indeed.

I wouldn't want to know what I might be picking up.

That would probably be best.

Our steaks come, we start eating. We do not talk about my new opportunity. We talk about basketball, we talk about the upcoming baseball season, we talk about the cold, he hates it. We talk about our steaks, they're good, we talk about our fries, they're hot and crispy. When we're finished, we order coffee and ice cream sundaes, he gets hot fudge, I get caramel. I finish my sundae, light a cigarette, speak.

Will I do anything legal?

Depends on your definition of legal.

How about according to your definition?

There are very few things illegal according to my definitions.

If I get caught, I'll be in big fucking trouble.

You won't get caught. And if you do, I'll take care of you.

I think, take a drag, take another.

My son.

I look up.

If you don't say yes, I'll buy the bar and fire you.

I laugh.

I'm nervous, Leonard. I'm trying to live a better life, trying to be a better person. I do not want to get locked up again.

I understand, and think that working for me will only help. You won't have any financial pressure, you won't have a boss screaming at you, you'll have as much time as you need to figure out your shit.

How long are you in town?

As long as it takes to get you to say yes.

What are you gonna do tonight?

I thought we'd take you to a firing range, make sure you're handy with a weapon.

You better be fucking kidding.

He laughs.

We're going out. Going to a basketball game, then having dinner. I'm gonna introduce you to some people that you should know.

Sounds cool.

What are you gonna do for the rest of the day?

I don't know. Go walk around.

You should give notice at the bar.

I'll think about it.

No thinking, my son. Just do.

What are you gonna do for the rest of the day?

Snapper's picking me up. We have to run some errands.

Errands?

He chuckles, nods.

Yes, errands.

What time should I meet you?

Seven.

Cool.

I stand.

Thanks for lunch.

Get fat.

I laugh.

See you at seven.

I leave. Down the elevator and outside. It's cold and gray, always cold and gray. I start walking. Think about where I want to go I have no idea. The temperature is below zero, I'm going to need to make stops every ten minutes or so, it's too cold too cold. I stop in a clothing store, they sell suits for thousands of dollars, a man in a security uniform follows me up and down the aisles. I stop in a coffee shop, I don't order anything just sit at a table in the corner and breathe. I walk into the lobby of a famous building built by a chewing gum company. The floor is marble, the walls are marble, the ceiling is marble. The walls and ceiling have been carved, covered with flowers, intricate patterns, saints, gods, little snarling gargoyles, big snarling gargoyles. I walk into a fast food restaurant, a comic book store, a jeweler I get followed by another guard. I keep walking, walk into an office building quickly walk out, walk into an art museum take off my coat. The museum is offering free admission, as it does one day a week, I start wandering through the galleries. I stand beneath angels and saints, beneath the son of god, beneath his mother, beneath beheaded martyrs, sobbing virgins, angry popes, beneath marching armies, generals astride their mounts, looted burning ravaged cities. I stare at dead game, fruits and vegetables in a market, Dutch fishing boats, Merrymakers in an inn, Rinaldo being enchanted by Armida. I stare at Cupid firing arrows, the Crystal Palace, at the Seine, at Bennecourt. I watch a woman at a piano she does not move just stares at the keys making music I can't hear. I meet Henri de Gas and his niece Lucie de Gas, I walk through Paris, rainy day, wait for the arrival of the Normandy train at the Gare Saint-Lazare. I confront the Portrait of Man. He stares at me. I stare back, waiting for answers. I get none.

I spend hours slowly moving from room to

room. I try to get as close to the paintings as possible. I close one eye and look at the individual strokes made by the painters. I close both eyes and try to smell the oil. I stand as far away as I can, walk forward the image coming gradually closer. I want to rub my hands along the surface, but don't want to set off an alarm or get arrested. Sometimes I talk to the paintings, to the figures in the paintings. I ask a farmer how's the weather, I ask a singer what's the song, I ask a baby what's your name, I ask a young woman why are you crying? I stand in front of Vincent's self-portrait. Vincent who knew pain and failure, who knew self-doubt and insanity, who cut off his ear, who shot himself. I know Vincent well. I have nothing to say to him.

I leave the museum at closing time. I walk back to the hotel, stopping along the way to get warm. When I arrive I wait in the lobby. Five minutes later, Leonard and the Snapper step out of an elevator, start walking toward me. I stand meet them halfway. Leonard speaks.

My son.

What's up?

Snapper speaks.

How ya doing, kid?

Good.

Leonard speaks.

Ready for some basketball?

Yeah.

Good.

We leave, go downstairs, pick up the car, drive to the stadium. The stadium is old and decrepit. It was built in the 1920s and is scheduled to be destroyed this summer, replaced by a newer version being built across the street. When we arrive we pull through rusted gates to an area of guarded parking, the parking lot where the players and team owners park. We get out of the car, walk into the stadium through a guarded door. We enter a series of tunnels beneath the main seating area of the stadium. We walk past locker rooms, training areas, administrative offices. We walk past men and women in uniforms rushing around I have no idea what they do. We walk out of a tunnel and onto the court. It's near game-time and the stadium is almost full. The game, as all Chicago basketball games are, is sold out. Leonard pulls three tickets from the inside pocket of his jacket, hands one to me, one to Snapper. He walks along the edge of the court, we follow him. He stops at three seats near the center, motions for us to sit.

Five minutes later the lights go out, loud music starts blaring through speakers hanging from the ceiling, the Chicago team is introduced and runs to their bench. The opposing team, which is from New York, enters without fanfare. Everyone stands while the national anthem is played, the game starts with the tipoff. Chicago's team is the reigning champion and their star player is considered the best basketball player in the world. New York can't keep up and they get obliterated. At half-time,

Chicago leads by eighteen, they win the game by thirty. Leonard acts like a little kid throughout, cheering, laughing, jumping up and down, eating popcorn, hot dogs and ice cream bars, drinking large cola after large cola after large cola. I skip the popcorn and hot dogs, I eat eight ice cream bars and drink seven large colas. Snapper doesn't eat anything, says he's watching his figure and waiting for dinner.

After the game we go to a restaurant. It's a simple Italian restaurant on the west side of the city, not far from the stadium. We walk in and Leonard and Snapper greet the owner, who leads us into a room behind the main dining room. The room has a long, simple table covered with a white tablecloth, there are ten chairs around it. We sit and the owner asks what we would like to drink, colas for Leonard and me, a glass of red wine for Snapper. Leonard looks at me, speaks.

You give notice today?

I shake my head.

Nope.

Why not?

Spent the day in a museum.

Snapper speaks.

What'd you see?

All kinds of stuff.

Leonard speaks.

Get more specific, my son.

Do you know anything about art?

Leonard looks at Snapper.

Do we know anything about art?

Quite a bit, actually.

Leonard turns to me.

We know quite a bit.

I laugh.

How?

How? We read. We go to museums and galleries. We pay attention.

I would have never thought . . .

Snapper speaks.

Tell him how we got into it.

Leonard speaks.

I have a house on the beach outside of LA. Every summer the town puts on this thing called the Pageant of the Masters.

Snapper speaks.

I love the Pageant of the Masters.

Leonard nods.

What they do is make stage sets that look actually like famous paintings.

So let's say they were doing The Last Supper by Leonardo da Vinci.

They'd get a bunch of men, dress them up so they look exactly like the Apostles in the painting. They'd get another fella and make him look like the Jesus in the painting. They'd put everyone at a table that looked like the table in the painting in a room that looked exactly like the room in the painting. Then they pose in painting poses and they sit there.

Snapper speaks.

It's beautiful.
Leonard speaks.
And tons of people come see the paintings, which have now been brought to life.
Snapper speaks.
They look so real it's crazy.
Leonard speaks.
We've been going every summer for years.
Snapper speaks.
And every summer it gets better and better.
Leonard speaks.
We're knowledgeable about everything from Pre-Renaissance work to the Post-Impressionists.
Snapper speaks.
They don't do modern art very well. Too hard to break a real person down into some form of cubism, pure abstraction or minimalism.
Leonard speaks.
They do Matisse and Modigliani. Don't forget about them.
Snapper speaks.
I shouldn't have forgotten Matisse, but Modigliani is boring.
Leonard speaks.
His work is not as dynamic as some.
Snapper speaks.
It's boring. Fucking boring.
Leonard turns to me.
What do you think, my son?
About Modigliani or this conversation?
Both.

I like Modigliani. I think those women are weird and gorgeous. I'm sort of shocked by the conversation.

Everybody thinks we're barbarians, but we've got soft, sensitive, sophisticated sides to us.

Snapper speaks.

I'm very soft, sensitive and sophisticated.

I laugh. The door opens, waiters start bringing in food, Platters of antipasti, mozzarella and tomato, fried calamari, fried zucchini, zuppa di clams, Caesar salad, crostini with chopped liver. There is more food than the three of us could eat, I ask Leonard if he's expecting anyone else. He tells me that there may be a few people stopping by to say hello.

We start eating. The smell of the food on the table and the smells drifting into the room from the nearby kitchen, garlic oregano olive oil peppers Parmesan pesto, roasting chicken beef and veal, sautéed spinach and scampi, strong espresso and chocolate, ignite my hunger I start eating. I eat slowly, one thing at a time, though the addict in me and the alcoholic in me say go go go more more more. As we eat, we talk, talk about the game we just saw, Leonard and Snapper debate the merits of this restaurant against Italian restaurants in Manhattan and the Bronx. As we finish the first course, the door opens and two men step into the room. Both are large, thick, menacing men, with short hair, simple dark suits. Leonard and Snapper rise, greet them, introduce them to me. Both slip me cards when we shake hands, which I slip into my pocket. I'm curious to know what the cards are, what they say, who these men are, but I know I should wait, look at them later, if they wanted me to look at them now, they would have handed them to me, not slipped them to me.

As more food arrives, large platters of food, spaghetti with meatballs, linguini with clam sauce, penne rigatoni pappardelle, chicken scarpariello, chicken contadino, chicken cacciatore, veal cutlets chops, veal saltimbocca, osso bucco, lobster oreganato, scampi fra diavolo, more people arrive. The table is filled, there are people standing around the table, in every corner of the room. I meet men some obviously Italian some not all wearing dark suits and wedding rings, I get slipped card after card. I meet women all beautiful some with the men, none wear wedding rings, I get slipped a couple of phone numbers. There are handshakes, kisses on cheeks, backslaps, laughter laughter laughter. There are cigars, cigarettes, red wine, white wine, beer, cocktails, colas for me I love an ice-cold cola. Leonard and Snapper are having a great time, laughing and happy, when I'm not talking to someone I'm watching them. Leonard commands the room everyone is aware of his presence when he talks to them, they listen, as he moves from person to person, group to group, the attention is always focused on him.

Hours pass quickly pass. It's late, the room is still crowded. I'm full, tired, wired on caffeine and nicotine. My clothes smell like deep, strong cigars. My shirt has stains on it grease and tomato sauce. My pocket is full of cards. I tell Leonard I'm going home I feel like I can sleep, he walks me outside. I speak.

You have a lot of friends, Leonard.

Most of those people were there to meet you.

Why?

You ask them what they do for a living?

No.

You look at those cards they gave you?

No.

Look at them when you get home.

Why?

Every card you got tonight is more or less a get out of jail free card. You come work for me and nothing is going to happen to you. Every person in there will guarantee it.

I laugh.

You're not gonna stop are you.

Not until you stop working at the bar.

I'll give notice tomorrow.

Leonard smiles.

Ha-ha! That's great news.

I laugh.

We don't use contracts, but I'm gonna give you a signing bonus.

I laugh again. He reaches into a pocket, pulls out a wad of rolled cash held together by a rubber band. He hands it to me.

I can't take this, Leonard.

Sure you can, and you're gonna.

No way. This is a ton of dough, I haven't done shit to earn it.

So what. Take it. It's your starting-up money.

No.

I hold the cash toward him. He shakes his head.

We've been through this before, my son.

What?

When someone wants to do something nice for you, don't argue, don't resist, don't say no, don't try to change their mind. Just smile and say thank you and think about how fortunate you are to have generous people in your life.

That's a lot of fucking money, Leonard.

Just smile and say thank you.

I put the cash in my pocket.

Thank you, Leonard.

It's good to have you, great to have you!

I laugh.

I need to go home.

Hold on.

He walks to a black town car sitting at the curb, knocks on the window.

The window rolls down, he speaks to the driver, shakes his hand, turns to me.

You have a ride.

I walk to the car.

Thanks for the game, dinner, the cash.

That's your signing bonus. You're gonna earn it.

I laugh.

Yeah.

Since I got you to quit, and take a real job, I'll be leaving in the morning.

Safe travels.

Thank you.

When do I start?

Not sure. Somebody will come see you.

And they'll also tell me what I'm supposed to do?

Yeah.

Cool.

See you soon, my son.

Thanks for everything, Leonard.

He nods. I get in the backseat of the car.

I go home.

My mother comes to visit me. My parents live in Tokyo and I don't see them very often. They are responsible for getting me into the treatment center. I haven't always liked them, and I have hurt them over and over and over through the course of my life, but they have always loved me. I am lucky to have them.

My mother sees my apartment, laughs. She asks me where I sleep, where I sit, I tell her the floor. She shakes her head and says not good, James, not good. She calls someone in Michigan, which is where they used to live, they still have a house it sits empty now. She asks the person about furniture in storage, how easy is it to access, she asks if they can send me a bed and a desk and a table. She hangs up, says I'll have a bed and a desk and a table in a few days.

We go downtown. We walk down Michigan Avenue. My mother and father are both from suburban Chicago, met here, were married here. They didn't have any money when they were married, they spent their honeymoon in a downtown hotel. As we walk, my mother points out restaurants they went to, parks where they sat, held hands, kissed, stores where they wandered, looking at things they couldn't afford, hoping someday, someday. It's nice to hear her memories, I like that she's sharing them with me. It feels like a door opening, a door to her, to my father, to their life. It's a door that I have never acknowledged before, a door that I'm happy to step through, a door I'm fortunate to have still be open.

We go to lunch. A fancy place, a place my mother knows and loves, she tries to eat there every time she's in town. We wait for a table, sit, napkins on lap, glasses of water. My Mom starts asking me questions. How are you doing, I'm okay. How are you feeling, depends, I go up and down, way up and way down, mostly I'm down. Is it hard staying sober, yeah it is, every second of every day is a struggle, I know I'll die if I do it, sometimes I feel like I want to die. Do you need help, no, I'll get through it, I gotta believe I'll get through it. She asks about Lilly, I just shake my head. She asks what happened, I just shake my head, say it didn't work out, I don't want to talk about it, can't talk about it. She says that's too bad, I had hoped that would work out for you. I cannot respond.

As we finish our meal, someone approaches our table. I vaguely recognize the person, but can't place him.

James?

Yeah?

David. From school.

I still can't place him, pretend.
Yeah, how you doing?
Good. What are you doing here?
This is my Mom. We're eating lunch.
He looks at my mom.
Nice to meet you.
Mom speaks.
You too.
He looks back at me.
I'm surprised to see you because I heard you
were in prison. For popping some cop.
My mom cringes.
Where'd you hear that?
I'm not sure.
As you can see, I'm not.
I guess. You living here now?
Yeah.
You wanna get together sometime?
Sure.
He reaches into his pocket, draws out his wallet.
You still partying?
I shake my head.
No.
He takes a card from his wallet, hands it to me.
If you ever get the urge, call me.
Will do.
See you later.
Yeah.
He walks away. I look at my mom. She speaks.
I hope you never call him.
I won't.

He seemed like an asshole.

I laugh. My mom has never spoken like that around me.

I have no idea who he is. I know I went to school with him, but other than that, nothing.

Good. He's an asshole.

I laugh again. We finish, leave, walk some more. My mom shares more of her memories, I listen, walk further through the door. We see the hotel where they spent their wedding night, a pizza place that my grandfather loved, a department store where my grandmother liked to buy presents. We see a jersey from the Chicago hockey team. My parents went to one of the team's games the night after they were married. They couldn't afford to do anything else, it was a big evening for them.

It starts to get dark, close to the time my mom will leave. Before she leaves, she wants to buy me some plates, forks, spoons, knives. Right now I use paper and plastic that I get from take-out restaurants. She thinks having normal possessions like plates, forks, spoons, knives will help normalize my existence, help me adjust more easily. We go to a store, look around, everything I like is black. My mom laughs, thinks it's strange that I like black plates and black utensils. I tell her that as much as she wants me to normalize, there are some parts of me that will always be a bit off. She laughs. We get all of the beautiful, semi-normal, black items.

We go back to my apartment. Put everything in the cabinets above my sink. My Mom has a car coming to pick her up, take her to the airport, she says she needs to go. I thank her for the day, a great day, probably the best day I have ever had with her. She smiles, starts to cry, she's happy, happy I'm alive, happy I'm becoming human, happy we can spend a day together without screaming. I give her a hug, walk her out, open the car door for her. The car pulls away.

I meet a man underneath the train tracks he calls himself a ragamuffin, the Ragamuffin King. He says he wanders the world looking for rags, beautiful rags, magnificent rags. I bow to him, the Ragamuffin King. I go to coffee with Mickey. I am the only straight man in the coffee shop. Mickey introduces me to his friends as his hetero buddy James. Mickey has a new boyfriend. An attorney who says he loves him, loves his paintings, wants him to do whatever he wants, just be happy. And he is, Mickey is happy.

I meet a man at a bar while I'm waiting for my friends. He says he's forty-five, he looks like he's twenty-five I ask him if he has a secret he says never get angry and be as immature as you can for as long as you can get away with it. A man sitting next to him laughs and says that's bullshit, the great secret is eat food and drink beer till you drop.

I see an old friend. He and I used to drink together, do drugs together, deal drugs together. He cleaned up for a girl, a girl he lives with now, a girl he loves, a girl he wants to marry. We laugh about old times, good times, bad times, he got out before they got really bad. We go to a punk show at an old abandoned bowling alley. The band plays on one of the neglected lanes, they're young and loud and they can't play their instruments and the songs are awful and they look like they're having a great time. We move into the pit, the fray, the moving circle of young angry men in black jackets and combat boots throwing elbows, high-stepping and slamming into each other. We get hit, we fall, get knocked around a bit. It's fun every now and then, getting knocked around a bit.

I meet a third man he's an old man he trips in the street he falls and I help him up, walk him to the curb. He shakes my hand says keep the faith, young man. I ask him what that means, he says keep running and don't let them catch you.

I sleep during the day. I still dream about drinking and drugs. Sometimes I wake to a hang-over, sometimes I wake to a trickle of blood from my nose, sometimes I wake scared and shaking.

I read, go to museums and visit Lilly in the afternoon. Sometimes I read to her, sometimes I talk to her, sometimes I just sit and remember the times, remember the times, remember the times.

I go out at night. Go to bars with my friends. I drink cola, smoke cigarettes, shoot pool, talk, sometimes don't talk, just sit and watch. I start to laugh more and more easily, start to feel more comfortable.

When the bars close, I walk, walk randomly through the empty city, walk among the buildings, through parks, along the lake. I sit on benches, the wind and cold hurt me, numb me, I stop feeling. There is peace in pain so overwhelming that it shuts down all feeling. It is the only peace I know.

I go back to my apartment.

Sleep.

Dream.

It's morning the phone rings. A man a voice I don't know tells me to meet him at a local diner.

I walk to the diner, sit in a booth, drink coffee, wait. A man walks into the diner he's in his late-twenties, clean-shaven, dark hair, well-dressed, but not flashy, a gold watch. He stops in front of my booth, speaks.

Your name James?

Yeah.

He sits down across from me.

You got a good memory?

Yeah.

You better.

Why?

This is how it's gonna work.

He reaches into his pocket, pulls out a small pager, pushes it across the table.

Keep the pager on you at all times. You'll get a page, call the number.

Always use a payphone, don't use the same one more than twice. When you call, you'll speak to someone who will give you instructions. Never write those instructions down, keep absolutely no record of them. If you fuck them up, it'll be your problem, so make sure you've got them before you hang up. When you do hang up, memorize the number on the pager, delete the number, follow the instructions. If you're driving, drive three miles over the speed limit, never faster, never slower. Always check the car to make sure all of the lights are working. If you get pulled over, don't say a fucking word. Ask for a lawyer and wait, tell the lawyer to get in touch with your friend Leonard. If the job goes well, and if you don't fuck up, when the job is done, call the original number to confirm. If you ever get a page that says 911, immediately stop whatever you're doing. Take whatever you're moving and put it in a safe place that is not your home. If it's a car, put it in a secure lot. If you get a page that says 411, stop whatever you're doing and wait for further instructions. Any questions?

No.

Do you want me to repeat what I just told you?

No.

Have a nice day.

The man stands and leaves. I order more coffee, some eggs, bacon and toast. I smoke a cigarette, read the paper, wait for the food. It arrives, I start eating, the pager goes off, two loud piercing beeps, two more, two more. I stand pick up the pager, walk to a payphone in the back of the diner. I drop in my coins, dial the number, there's a male voice after one ring.

Hello.

I got paged.

First timer.

Yeah.

You got a pen?

No, no pen.

Good. Good memory?

Yeah.

You better.

Voice gives me an address in a nearby suburb. Tells me to knock on the door, I will be handed a suitcase. Put the suitcase in the trunk of a white car sitting in the driveway, the keys are under the driver's side floormat. I am given a second address, which is in Milwaukee. Drive the car to the Milwaukee address, remove the suitcase from the trunk. Knock on the door, ask for a man named Paul, give him the suitcase, don't give it to anyone else, Paul is waiting for it. Drive the car back to the suburban Chicago address, leave it in the driveway, keys under the mat. Call to confirm.

I have the voice repeat both addresses. He asks me if I need them again, I tell him no, I got it. He says good, hangs up on me. I hang up, return to my booth, finish my breakfast, leave.

I take a commuter train north into the moneyed suburbs of Chicago. It's late morning, the train is almost empty. I'm nervous. My heart is racing, hands slightly shaking. I stare out the window, try to take deep breaths, try to stay calm. The few other passengers I see all look like FBI agents, middle-aged men in dark suits, and they all appear to be glancing at me, watching me. I tell myself that's bullshit, that I'm being paranoid, that nobody here gives a shit why I'm on this train, but I don't feel any better. Arrest scenarios roll through my mind I can see the cuffs, feel them on my skin, hear the cop reciting Miranda, smell the back of the car, feel a slight breeze as the door slams shut. I can imagine sitting with a lawyer, discussing my case, debating the merits of a plea agreement, trying to figure out ways to bring my sentence down. I can remember being processed, putting my few meager belongings into an envelope, changing into a jumpsuit, donning shackles, rambling down concrete and steel halls. My cell awaits me. I'm fucking nervous.

The train arrives at my stop, I get off, there are a couple of cabs waiting, I get inside one of them, give the cabbie the street name, he drives. We move through quiet neighborhoods full of large houses with wide lawns, manicured bushes, alarm system signs, foreign cars in the driveway.

I have him drop me on a corner. I start looking at the tastefully mounted numbers on porches and doors. I find my way to a large stone house with a white car in the driveway. I walk to the door, knock, wait, my heart is pounding. The door opens it's a middle-age man wearing silk pajamas. He does have a suitcase. He speaks.

Can I help you?

I'm here to pick something up.

What?

I wasn't told what.

You sure you got the right address?

My hands start shaking.

Yeah I'm sure.

I start to panic.

I don't think you do.

Panic.

This is the address I was given.

Panic.

By who?

I'm not at liberty to say.

This sounds awfully strange. You come to my door to pick something up, but you don't know what it is, and you won't tell me who sent you?

I'm just following directions.

Do you want me to call the police?

No sir.

They come quick in this town.

There's no need to call the police, sir. I must have made a mistake. I'll leave.

I turn, start walking away, can't run too obvious, I've got to get out of here now, how the fuck did I fuck this up, I've got to get out of here now now now.

Kid.

I stop turn around.

I'm just fucking with you. I heard you were new and thought I'd have some fun.

I smile, not because I think it's funny, if I could I'd hit this motherfucker, but because I'm relieved, and the smile is a nervous reaction. I walk back to the door. The man reaches behind and sets a battered brown suitcase in front of me.

You scared the shit out of me.

I couldn't tell.

You did.

You handled yourself well, stayed cool, no panic. If this ever happens for real, do exactly the same thing.

I hope it never happens.

Don't fuck up and it won't.

I pick up the suitcase.

Have a nice day.

You too.

I turn, walk toward the car. The suitcase is heavy, heavier than I expected, fifty pounds, maybe sixty. I hear the man shut the door behind me, I open the driver's door of the car, reach under the mat for the keys, find them. I put the suitcase in the trunk, get behind the wheel. As I pull out of the driveway I see the man is standing at one of his windows. He's smiling, waving at me.

I know the highway is to the west I start driving west. I take the map out of the glove compartment, look at it. Interstate 94 takes me straight up, if I keep going where I'm going I'll run into it. I set down the map, light a cigarette, settle in for the ride.

The ride is easy, boring. I smoke cigarettes, listen to the radio, occasionally sing along to a cheesy love song or a heavy metal power ballad or one of the many classic rock anthems. I try to find a station that plays punk, so I can yell and scream and shout obscenities, but I can't find one. Every fifteen minutes or so, I shout obscenities anyway.

I see Milwaukee in the distance. It's a small city, an old city, one that hasn't experienced any form of renewal. When I was a kid I used to watch a TV show about two women who worked in a beer factory in Milwaukee, aside from that I don't know shit about it.

I pull off the highway, look for a gas station. I pull in, ask for directions get them, start driving again, find the address, it is another beautiful neighborhood huge houses sitting along the coast of Lake Michigan. I pull into a long driveway. A row of hedges runs along one side of it, a yard the size of a football field runs along the other side. A massive stone house sits at the end, it looks like it belongs in England, Ireland or Scotland, not Milwaukee. I stop in front of it, get out of the car, get the suitcase, carry it to the front door. I knock and wait. I hear someone behind the door, the door cracks open, I hear a voice.

I'm Paul.

I cannot see a person.

Leave the case and get out of here.

I set the suitcase on the step. Paul tosses an envelope out, it lands at my feet. I pick it up, look inside it's filled with cash, I leave. The drive back to Chicago is simple, just smoke and listen to tunes and swear. I put the car back in the driveway, take the train back to the city. On the way back to my apartment, I stop at a payphone, call the original number on the pager, confirm delivery.

I'm shooting pool for money. Playing against a guy named Tony I've played him before I lose to him every single time. I'm in good shape this time, shooting at the eight ball, he's got three to go.

I'm in a bar called The Local Option. There's a front room, a back room. A bar runs along one wall of the front room, the pool table is in the back room. My friends are here. They're getting drunk.

As I wait for my shot, I hear my pager go off. I tell Tony I have to make a call, ask him if he'll wait for me, he laughs, takes the money off the rail, where it's supposed to sit until someone wins. I speak.

I'm getting that back next game.

He laughs.

We'll see.

I leave the bar. Walk down the street, look for a phone. I find one outside a dry cleaner, it's quiet I can hear. I look at the pager dial the number it's not a number I recognize. I wait, Leonard answers.

Ha-ha!

What's up Leonard?

What's up? What's up? My son successfully completed his first mission.

That's what the fuck is up.

I laugh.

How'd it go? Tell me how it went.

It was easy. I picked up the case, drove it to Milwaukee and dropped it off, went home.

That's it?

That's it.

I heard they were gonna have some fun with you. Shake you up a bit.

Yeah, that happened. The guy who gave me the case fucked with me, pretended I was in the wrong place.

Leonard laughs.

I bet you shit.

Sort of.

You meet Paul?

No.

Good. You're never supposed to actually meet anyone. That way if something happens, you can't testify against them.

I thought you said nothing would ever happen.

It won't, it won't. I'm just saying if. If, my son, never happens.

I hope so.

And forget you ever met that old fucker in his pajamas.

How'd you know he was in his pajamas?

He never leaves his house, and he always wears pajamas. That's how I know.

He's been forgotten.

Any idea what was in the case?

Nope. And I don't want to know.

Take a guess.

No.

Come on.

No.

What do you think it weighed?

I don't know.

Guess.

Fifty, sixty pounds.

Fifty.

Okay.

You know a million dollars in cash in twenty-dollar bills weighs twenty-one pounds?

I did not know that.

And a common suitcase weighs about six.

I didn't know that either.

You learn something new every day.

Thank you for that bit of knowledge, Leonard.

You get your money?

Paul threw me the envelope. I wasn't sure it was mine because there was so much.

Helluva lot better than seven fucking bucks an hour.

I laugh. The envelope had five thousand dollars in it.

Yeah, much better.

You did good, my son. You did good. I'm proud of you.

Thank you, Leonard.

You're doing okay otherwise?

Yeah. I was shooting pool in a bar when you paged.

Well go back, have fun. Say hello to your friends if you're with them.

They'll be happy to hear it.

I'll come visit again soon, my son.

I'll look forward to it.

Keep up the good work.

I laugh.

Thanks.

I hang up, head back to the bar, lose three more times to Tony. I wander for a few hours, spend a few hours with Lilly. I tell her about my new job. I know she wouldn't approve, she'd say you're moving too close to your old life, you gotta leave that shit behind. I tell her I know there are dangers, but I feel strong, each day I feel stronger, each day I don't drink or use I am stronger. I tell her it would be different if she was around. I tell her she made her decisions, and now I'm on my own, and I will make my decisions.

I take a car to St Louis. I don't know what's in the car, if there's anything in the car. Nobody tells me and I don't ask. I drive three miles over the speed limit. I leave the car in a shopping mall parking lot.

I move briefcases from the north side of Chicago to the south side of Chicago. I move briefcases from the south side to the north side. I ride the El train back and forth. I buy a set of nice clothing khakis black leather shoes a white oxford a blue sport coat, so that I look like a young ambitious commuter, so that people think I'm a law student or an apprentice currency trader or a young executive at a large multinational corporation, all of which, in a certain ridiculous way, I am.

I go back to Milwaukee.

Detroit.

Rockford, Illinois.

Sometimes I receive envelopes, sometimes I don't. When I do, the amounts vary, as high as five thousand, as low as five hundred, usually somewhere around three thousand. I don't have a bank account, so I keep the cash hidden around my apartment. I put the bulk of it under my mattress. I put more in a plastic Ziploc bag and place the bag in the tank of my toilet. I put more in a Captain Crunch cereal box, I bury the bills beneath the crunchy nuggets. I put the rest in an empty box of dishwasher detergent that sits beneath my sink. I never carry much cash with me because I don't want to draw attention to myself.

My friends ask me what I'm doing, ask me why I left my bar job. I tell them I left because it was too much to work in a bar too much temptation and torture. They ask how being in bars with them is any different I tell them when I was working I had to stand there I was bored out of my skull the boredom made me want to drink. When I'm in a bar with them I can occupy myself, talk, laugh, shoot pool, drink cola after cola after cola, that it is easier to be distracted. I tell them in a certain way it is easier when I'm with them because I see how they act when they're drunk and it reminds me of who I don't want to be and how I don't want to behave. They ask me how I'm making money I tell them I don't have much and what I do have is borrowed. They ask what I'm doing with my time, I tell them I'm trying to make it pass. And that at least is true. Sometimes all I want is for my time to pass.

M y phone rings. It is morning. I'm smoking cigarettes, staring at the fucking ceiling. I pick it up.

Hello?

My son, I'm coming to town. Good times are on their way.

What's up, Leonard?

I'm up, you're up, that's what the fuck is up.

When are you coming?

This afternoon.

You want me to meet you at the airport?

Remember that steakhouse we went to with your friends?

Yeah.

Meet me there. Six o'clock.

Okay.

And call some of your friends. See if we can meet them out after we eat.

Okay.

You want anything from Vegas?

Can you bring me a showgirl who'll make all my troubles go away?

I actually can.

I laugh.

That's okay.

You sure?

Yeah.

If you change your mind, I'll be here for another hour.

Okay.

See you at six.

Yeah.

I hang up, smoke, stare at the fucking ceiling. The ceiling doesn't have much to say to me this morning, can't tell me why I can't get off my bed, can't tell me why my sorrow is starting to feel like rage, can't tell me how I'm supposed to deal with it, can't tell me shit. I smoke, stare, wait, wait, wait, nothing.

Sometime in the afternoon I get up, take a shower, pull some cash from beneath my mattress, put on my nice clothes. I call my friends see what they're doing tonight they're going to a pool hall/bowling alley, I tell them I'll meet them around nine. I leave, start walking it's not as cold, spring is slowly asserting itself. It's harder to become numb, I have to walk longer, wear less, it still doesn't always work, my body has adjusted to the cold. It takes an hour to get to the restaurant. When I walk in the host greets me, says nice to see you again, sir. I ask if Leonard is here he says yes, let me show you to his table.

We walk into the restaurant it's early so it is almost empty. Leonard is sitting in the corner, facing out, he sees me stands.

My son! **My son!** MY SON!

I laugh.

Hello, Leonard.

Come sit, come sit.

The host guides me to the table, pulls out my chair. I sit down, I am also facing out. Host walks away. I speak.

So it's true.

What's true?

Men like you never sit with your back to the door.

He laughs.

No way.

No way what?

Back to the door. That's bullshit.

Doesn't look like bullshit to me.

I'm a people person, a motherfucking people person. I sit this way so I can see the people.

The people?

Yeah, the people. I love them. That's me.

I laugh again.

Where's Snapper?

I left him at home.

Why?

This isn't a business trip. I just came to see you.

Thanks.

Thought it would be good to spend time together just us.

That sounds cool.

How's life?

I laugh.

Which part of it?

Which part do you want to talk about?

I like my new job.

I knew you would. What are you doing with all the money?

Hiding it.

Under your mattress?

Yeah.

In a cereal box?

Yeah.

In the toilet tank?

Yeah.

You probably thought you were being real sneaky.

I did.

Not good, my son. Everybody knows those spots.

I also got some in a dishwasher detergent box. Keep it under the sink. You know that one?

No, never heard that one before.

If I get robbed, at least I'll have that.

You're not gonna get robbed. I'm gonna teach you how to deal with the cash.

Okay.

He reaches into his pocket, draws out a black leather wallet, passes it to me.

There's an Illinois driver's license in there. It's a valid license, and it will register on the State's computers. I got a picture of you that I took at the treatment center and doctored it a bit, it looks real. I also invented a name for you.

I take the license out of the wallet, look at it. It looks real.

James Testardo?

Yeah. Testardo means stubborn in Italian. I thought it would be funny if you could call yourself Jimmy Testardo.

I laugh.

Okay.

The address on the license is an empty house owned by a shell company I am very very loosely associated with, though there is no record of the association. Go to a bank, the bigger and more anonymous the bank the better, and get a safe deposit box. Whenever you go there, wear a hat or sunglasses or something that slightly alters your appearance. Put your money in the account, and put it in slowly and in manageable amounts, three, four, five thousand at a time. Never approach ten thousand, because at ten thousand the bank is required to notify the IRS of the deposit.

Once it's in there, take it out in cash as need be. Don't pay your bills with checks, always use money orders purchased with cash. If you start to accumulate too much, go buy something expensive, something in the three, four, five thousand range. Buy it with a credit card. If you don't have one, I can get one for you, in the Testardo name if you want it that way. Pay the credit card off in several installments using money orders purchased with cash. When you do buy something, I would advise buying small things, like watches or art or silver, jewelry, rare books, and don't go showing it off to people. Buy things you can sell for cash if you're ever in a jam, that can be moved quickly and easily. Use common sense and don't draw attention to yourself and you'll be fine.

I think I can handle that.

I know you can. You got any questions?

No.

You wanna order?

Sure.

Leonard motions for the waiter. We order lobsters and filets, creamed spinach and baked potatoes. We drink water, I drink cola, Leonard drinks diet cola. We talk about the upcoming baseball season, talk about our friends from the treatment center. One was a fugitive, he was caught and sentenced to life in prison, no parole. Another was beaten to death outside of a bar. A third is missing. A fourth committed suicide by shotgun. A few are still okay, still holding on, still struggling. I tell Leonard I spoke with our friend Miles, who is a Federal judge in New Orleans. He's still clean, feeling strong, taking care of himself. He's happy to be home, reunited with his wife and children, who he feared he might lose because of his alcoholism. Leonard smiles, asks me to tell Miles hello. He says he likes Miles, wishes he could stay in touch with him, but their respective positions prevent any sort of significant relationship.

Our food arrives, we eat. I ask Leonard about his ongoing quest to play golf on the Connecticut course where his father worked. He laughs, it's a bitter laugh, a laugh that masks anger and pain, he says no luck. I say sorry, he shrugs, says that's the way the world works, that people with privilege guard their privilege, that people take care of their own kind, that there are certain institutions that are exclusive whether it is right or not. He says it works the same way with his own organization, that only Italians can be full members, that there are no exceptions. I ask him what he's going to do he laughs again, the laugh different now anger mixed with menace, he says country club members do not take blood oaths, that there are certainly some that misbehave cheat on their wives sleep with whores run up gambling debts he is going to find one of them and have a conversation with that person and he will get in and play the course, just as his dying father made him promise he would.

We finish, our food is taken away. Leonard suggests we go to the bar for coffee and cigars. We stand as we walk away from the table he motions to the host we walk into the bar settle into two large plush comfortable chairs the host follows speaks to the bartender who walks into the bar's humidor. The bartender returns, hands the host a small box, the host walks toward us opens the box speaks.

Would you like a Cuban cigar?

Leonard smiles.

Matter of fact I would. Thank you.

Leonard reaches into the box chooses two cigars the host walks away.

Leonard takes a cutter from his jacket, carefully cuts the cigars, hands one to me, lights them.

You remember how to smoke?

Yeah.

I take a drag, swallow. The tobacco is sweet, strong, my mouth is immediately overwhelmed by it. I prefer cigarette tobacco. Leonard speaks.

These are good.

If you say so.

If you ever smoke a shitty one you'll be able to tell the difference.

I only smoke them with you.

Then you'll never smoke a shitty one.

Without having ordered it, coffee arrives. I take a sip, it's hot, strong, I feel it immediately, my heart starts racing.

Time for the serious talk, my son.

What's the serious talk?

I want to know how you're doing.

I'm doing fine.

What's that mean?

I don't know.

So you're not fine.

No, all things considered, I think I'm better than fine, much better than fine.

Explain.

I'm holding on, getting through the days, feeling stronger, feeling more comfortable with myself. I don't know how I'm doing it really, but I am, and each day is a step toward some form of normalcy and security, a step toward having a real life. If I was in hell before, I'm in purgatory now, and I feel like I can get to whatever's next. I still can't sleep right, I still have cravings all day every fucking day, I'm still nervous around and uncomfortable around people, and I still feel scared sometimes, but I'm okay with all of it. I've accepted that all this shit is just part of the price for my former life.

What are you scared of?

I don't know.

Yes you do.

When you've spent your whole life drinking and doing drugs, you learn how to do everything in a fucked-up way. I'm having to learn how to do everything over, and sometimes it's scary, and most of the time I feel scared.

If it makes you feel any better, I'm scared all the time too.

I laugh.

A big old tough guy like you? I don't believe it.

I used to think I was tough, but I've realized I wasn't. I was fragile, and I wore thick fucking armor, and I hurt people so they couldn't hurt me, and I thought that was what being tough was, but it isn't. What we're doing now is tough. Rebuilding, changing, having to deal with the damage, having to face the fear. If I make it through, then you can call me fucking tough.

You'll make it through.

We both will.

We'll see.

172

How you doing with your loss?

I miss her.

Did you think you wouldn't?

No, but I didn't think I would either, because I didn't think this was gonna happen. I was prepared for something else.

But it did.

Yeah, it did, and it fucking sucks and I miss her.

What do you miss?

I miss everything. I miss talking to her, hearing about her day. I miss her voice all gravelly and smoky, I miss hearing her laugh, I miss getting her letters, writing her letters. I miss her eyes, and the smell of her hair, and the way her breath tasted. I fucking miss everything. I miss knowing she was around, because it helped me to know that she was around, that someone like her existed. I guess most of all, I miss knowing I would see her again. I always thought I'd see her again.

You gotta respect what she did and that'll help you.

I don't know why the fuck you keep saying that.

It's true.

That's fucking crazy.

No it's not.

She killed herself, Leonard, threw in the fucking towel, and I feel sadness and confusion and a lot of hate, hate for myself for not being able to prevent it, and hate for her for actually doing it, but I don't feel respect.

You remember how she used to say that a second

of freedom is worth more than a lifetime of bondage.

Yeah.

She chose freedom, and you should respect her decision and admire her for being brave enough to follow through with it. It wasn't your kind of freedom, or my kind of freedom, but it was hers.

Suicide isn't freedom.

If all you feel is pain, and there's nothing but drugs to make it go away, and your choice is either living as addict or going out on your own terms, there's only one choice, and that's going out.

How about the third choice, which is dealing with the pain?

Not everybody can do it.

I look away, shake my head, clench my jaw. Leonard speaks.

You ever heard of the five stages of grief?

I look back.

No. What are they?

I don't know, I've just heard of them. Saw something about them on some ladies' show. I'm figuring you're going through them, and at some point you'll agree with me.

Fuck you, Leonard, and fuck your five stages of grief.

He laughs.

You want to get out of here?

Yeah.

He motions for the check. When it arrives, I reach for it. He speaks.

174

What are you doing?

I'm getting it tonight.

I reach into my pocket, get my cash.

No, you're not.

Yes, I am.

Unacceptable.

Not open to debate.

I pay for dinner. It's part of what I do.

Not tonight.

I have more money than you.

I look at the check, start counting the money.

You remember when you told me that when someone wants to do something nice for you, that you should smile and say thank you.

That only applies when I'm doing something nice for you.

Smile and say thank you, Leonard.

I put the cash in the check, close it. Leonard smiles.

Thank you, my son.

I stand.

Let's go.

Leonard stands, we leave. We take a cab north to meet my friends. We get out of the cab, walk into an old time bowling alley/pool hall. There are three rooms. One has a long oak bar lined with stools, the bar is probably a hundred years old. Another has the bowling alley, five lanes, all of them manual. Two men crouch at the end of the lanes and replace the pins when they fall and roll the balls back to the bowlers. The third room is large, open, has twelve-foot ceilings. There are ten pool tables in two lines of five that run the length of the room. Overhead lamps hang above each of the tables. Stools and bar tables line the edges of the room.

Leonard and I walk into the pool room, look for my friends. They're standing around a table in the corner, we walk over to them.

Though most of them have met him already, I introduce Leonard to everyone. He kisses each of the girls' hands, tells them they look beautiful. He shakes hands with the guys, says nice to meet you, nice to see you again. When the introductions are over, he motions to the waitress tells her bring more of everything, bring a pitcher of cola and two glasses, and keep it coming all night, just keep it coming.

We shoot pool, my friends drink, we smoke cigarettes, Leonard smokes a cigar, we laugh, laugh, laugh. We start shooting pool for money, five, ten bucks a game. Leonard is a disaster, loses three games. The rest of us are more or less equal, split the games, split the money. When Leonard's not playing, he's dancing with the girls, twirling them around, teaching them fancy steps, lathering them with compliments. The night moves on, my friends get more drunk. My friend Kevin suggests we raise the stakes, we agree raise them to twenty a game. Leonard starts playing again, destroys every single one of us, giggles to himself as he does it. I ask him what the fuck happened, he laughs, says he used to hustle pool and wanted to see if he could still do it. I laugh, say yeah, you can still do it, now stop, my friends aren't made of money.

Leonard stops playing, gives everyone their money back, tells them he used to hustle pool for cash, offers each of us a couple of tips. He starts dancing with the girls again. My friend Scott, who is bombed, walks over to me. He looks pissed. He speaks.

You better tell your buddy to stop dancing with my girlfriend.

He's harmless.

I don't like the way he's fucking dancing with her.

I can promise you he doesn't mean anything.

I don't care. Tell him to fucking stop.

Scott is a big man, six foot three well over two hundred pounds, and he has a bad temper. I know Leonard's not interested in his girlfriend, but I don't want any problems. I walk over to where Leonard and Scott's girlfriend, whose name is Jessica, are dancing. Scott follows me.

Leonard.

Leonard spins Jessica.

Leonard.

Pulls her in, gives her a dip.

Leonard.

He looks over at me.

Just a second.

Scott steps around me. I try to stop him, he pushes me off.

Stop dancing with my girlfriend, mother-fucker.

He pulls Jessica away. Jessica looks shocked, Leonard looks shocked.

No offense here, friend. No offense.

I'll kick your fucking ass if you touch her again.

You're misunderstanding this situation. I mean no disrespect.

Scott has no idea who Leonard is or what he does, has no idea the problem he's about to create for himself. I step toward him.

You gotta calm down, Scott.

He turns to me.

Fuck you.

Turns to Leonard.

And fuck you. I will kick your ass if you so much as look at her again.

People around have stopped playing, are watching.

You should watch yourself, kid. That temper is going to get you into trouble.

It's going to get you into trouble, old man.

Something in Leonard, who until now has been calm, changes. His face goes still, his eyes narrow, his body tenses. I have seen him like this before, once when I first met him in rehab, the other time when we got in a fight with two of the other patients there, one of whom was later killed.

You are making a big mistake, friend. You should turn now and leave.

178

Jessica starts pulling on Scott's arm and saying come on, come on, let's go. Scott stares at Leonard.

I'll fuck you up.

Leonard does not respond, just stares. Jessica pulls Scott away, they start walking toward the door, she's obviously upset, looks like she's going to cry.

I step toward Leonard.

Sorry about that.

Your friend shouldn't drink so much.

He can get a bit out of control.

Think I'm allowed to dance with the other girls?

I laugh.

Yeah, I think you are.

Good. Let's get back to the good times. That's why I came, for the motherfucking good times.

I laugh. Leonard walks over to Adrienne, asks her to dance.

She says yes.

I meet Leonard for breakfast, a late breakfast, we stayed out until four, Leonard dancing with the girls, me shooting pool with the guys, good times, good times.

Leonard asks me if I've spoken to Scott, I say no, I think it's best to leave it alone, he doesn't need to know about the potential consequences of his actions. Telling him would mean he would have to know what Leonard does for a living. Leonard agrees with me.

We leave the hotel. The sun is out. It's bright, warm, the streets are crowded with happy people, happy because winter is disappearing, happy because it's the first nice day in months. We walk down Michigan Avenue, occasionally stopping to look into the windows of expensive stores.

Leonard loves clothing, loves expensive clothing, loves tailored wool suits, handmade shoes, shirts made from Egyptian cotton, silk ties. He says that most people don't like wearing suits, and are uncomfortable in them, because they buy shitty, cheap, ill-fitting suits made from poor materials. He says a properly cut suit, made from quality materials, is the most comfortable thing one can wear. I tell him I prefer jeans and t-shirts, wool socks and combat boots, he laughs, says if you were my genetic son, you would think otherwise.

We end up at the art museum, the Art Institute of Chicago. We walk through the galleries of European paintings, we move through them in chronological order. We see six Giovanni di Paolo altarpiece panels depicting St John the Baptist, who looks like he's starving, wandering through a waste-land his golden halo shining. We see a bright silvery El Greco of the Virgin ascending on a crescent moon. We see eight gloomy Rembrandts, stern men in capes and feathered hats staring into a black distance, we see desperate Rinaldo being enchanted by the soreceress Armida in her billowing shawl as painted by Tiepolo. We see Turner, Manet, Corot, Monet, Renoir, Caillebotte. We see a dancing Degas, a strolling Seurat, a brooding van Gogh, once with his ear, once without. We see a Tahitian Gauguin and Leonard starts to cry, he just stands in front of it and he cries no words just heavy tears running down his cheeks. I stand with him, stare at the painting, which is of a young Tahitian woman, supposedly Gauguin's mistress, wearing a simple cotton dress, white flowers in her black hair, a fan in her hand. I don't speak, just let Leonard cry, he starts speaking.

Gauguin was a stockbroker in Paris, married, had five kids. One day he came home from work and told his wife he was leaving, that he was through supporting the family, that he had had enough. Just like that he fucking took off. He said he had always felt that he was a painter, so he moved into a rat-infested shithole and he started painting. His wife begged him to come back, his bosses told him he was insane, he didn't care, he was following his heart. He left Paris, moved to Rouen, went from Rouen to Arles, from Arles to Tahiti. He was searching for peace, contentment, trying to fill that fucking hole he felt inside, and he believed he could fill it. He died in Tahiti, blind and crazy from syphilis, but he did it. He filled his fucking hole, made beautiful work, made beautiful, beautiful work.

Leonard wipes his tears away.

It takes a brave man to walk away, to care so much that he doesn't care about anything else, to be willing to obey what he feels inside, to be willing to suffer the consequences of living for himself. Every time I stand before his work it makes me cry, and I cry because I'm proud of him, and happy for him, and because I admire him.

Leonard takes a deep breath, wipes away the last of his tears, turns and walks out of the room, out of the museum.

Leonard leaves, goes back to Las Vegas. My life goes back to normal, or what I consider normal, which is as normal as life has ever been for me.

I go to Kansas City.

Back to Detroit.

Indianapolis.

Milwaukee, three times to Milwaukee.

Northside. Southside.

Minneapolis.

Sometimes I drive, sometimes I ride the El, sometimes I take a bus. My friends start to wonder why I occasionally disappear I tell them that I need to be alone.

I spend my days walking endlessly walking. Spring arrives I don't have to wear a jacket the streets are crowded outdoor cafes full hot dog stands open on corners. I eat a lot of hot dogs. Extra mustard, hold the relish. When I'm not walking, I'm reading, for a few hours a day I sit and read. At home on benches on the grass in parks on the stairs of the museum I sit and read. I read the classics, or what are called the classics, try to catch up on what I missed in school.

I start to sleep more. I have fewer dreams. When the dreams come they aren't as bad, I don't wake up shaking, bleeding or vomiting, I don't wake up screaming, moaning or crying.

I gain weight. I look less like a drug addict and more like a poorly dressed young man.

I go to a punk club to see a band called The Vandals. I go with my friend Chris, who used to deal coke with me. We want to see them perform some of their hits, which include the classics *Anarchy Burger*, *A Gun for Christmas* and *Tastes Like Chicken*. They do not disappoint us. The guitars are loud and fast, the drums booming, the singer is on, his vocals moving effortlessly between yelling and very loud yelling. We march in the circle, high-stepping, throwing elbows, occasionally jumping into the middle and getting slammed.

At one of the breaks, Danny and Kevin show up with a group of girls.

Danny grew up outside of Chicago, in one of the wealthiest suburbs along the North Shore. He has known the girls, who are all well-dressed and have nice hairdos and wear diamonds and pearls in their ears, since childhood. They look horribly out of place and uncomfortable.

Chris and I walk over to them, say hello, their names are Molly, Rory, Mila and Brooke. I've met three of them before, though my memories of the meetings are faint. I ask them if they want a drink one of them asks me what kind of beer is available I tell her cheap beer. She laughs, says okay, one cheap beer please. I look at the other girls they agree, they'd each like one cheap beer.

I walk to the bar, Kevin comes with me. I speak.
What's up?
Nothing.
What are they doing here?
Danny wanted to bring them.
And they agreed?
I don't think they knew where they were going.
How long do you think they'll last?
They'll take one sip of the beer and leave.
I laugh. I order the beers, wait for them get them turn around. Three of the four girls are still there, talking with Danny and Chris, looking at the club's other patrons, young men with tattoos, shaved heads and Mohawks, like they're zoo animals. I walk back, hand out the cans, I ask if the fourth girl left. I hear a voice behind me.
My name isn't fourth girl, it's Brooke.
Okay.
I went to use the restroom.
I chuckle.
How was it?
It was disgusting, and it was also out of order.
There's a urinal in the men's room.
No thanks.
She takes the last can out of my hand, steps around me, moves toward Danny, starts talking to him. I turn back to the other three start talking to them. One of

them, her name is Molly, asks me how I've been and I laugh, tell her it's been a rough couple of years. She says she heard, was surprised when Danny told her they were meeting me tonight. I ask her how she's been, she says good, she's working for an interior design company and going to school for architecture. As I talk to her, I keep glancing at Brooke. Her hair is blond almost white, her eyes are ice-blue. She's tan, looks like she's been in the sun somewhere other than Chicago, she has pouty lips perfect teeth wears little makeup. I glance, I catch her glancing at me. I step away from Molly and toward Danny and Brooke steps away from Danny, goes to talk to Molly. I smile, know the little game that is being played here, a game that amuses me, that I haven't played for a long time. I step back and forth, she steps away every time I'm near her. She knows what I'm doing, doesn't acknowledge it, just steps away, steps away. The music starts again, Chris and I move back into the circle. We throw more elbows, get slammed, sing-along to all the hits. I know Brooke is watching me, I don't look toward her, know that not looking will frustrate her.

The music ends. Danny suggests we go to another bar, everyone but Chris and me are anxious to get out of this dump. We agree to leave pile into a couple of cabs I purposefully sit next to Brooke light a cigarette and ignore her.

We go to the Local Option. Our other friends are there, some other people we went to school with. Everyone is in the back room shooting pool I lay quarters down on the edge of the felt next

187

game is mine. I shoot pool and drink cola and smoke cigarettes for the rest of the night and Brooke and I both work very hard to ignore each other.

When the bar closes I leave start walking home. I walk alone my friends take cabs. For the first time in several hours I think about Lilly, I have never gone so long without thinking of her. I feel guilty, as if I've done something wrong, as if I have somehow betrayed her. I turn away from home and I walk to her and I tell her I'm sorry and I cry.

I hate myself for losing her.

I hate her for leaving me.

I don't have any answers.

Two nights later I see Brooke again she's with Danny I don't acknowledge her don't say a single word to her. I'm not playing a game, I am trying to be loyal, to be faithful, to honor Lilly's memory.

The next night I'm at the bar I see her again. She's with one of her friends, someone I don't know. She walks over to me, speaks.

Hi.

I nod.

You can't say hi to me?

I can.

I'm waiting.

Hi.

How are you?

Fine.

I turn, walk away, walk into the bathroom it's empty. I open a stall door close the toilet sit down on the lid. I hold up my hands, they're shaking. I light a cigarette, it doesn't calm me. My heart is hammering, I'm nauseous, dizzy. I put my head in my hands, close my eyes, take deep breaths. This shouldn't be happening, I'm not ready for this to happen and I don't want it to happen. I want to be with Lilly. I want to be alone. I'm safe alone and I can't be hurt alone. My heart is hammering. She could hurt me.

I stand walk out look through the bar she's gone. Part of me is relieved, part of me disappointed. I'm still rattled, my hands are in my pockets still shaking. I leave start walking. I want to talk to Lilly, need to talk to her, I'm scared to talk to her. I walk for an hour two three think. I buy flowers red roses at a 24-hour grocery store. I lay them down, sit beneath them.

I speak.

Hi.

I miss you.

I'm trying not to, but I do. I miss you.

I want to talk to you about something. I'm scared to do it, but it's going to come up sooner or later.

I met a girl.

I don't know her really, I've hardly spoken to her, and I don't know if anything will happen with her, but she's the first person to make me feel anything since you left me.

I'm sorry, I'm sorry.

I don't know what to do.

If you were here this wouldn't be happening.

I wish you were here.

I wish you hadn't left me.

I hate you for it.

But I'll forgive you, if you forgive me.

I love you, and will always love you, but I want to see her.

Forgive me.

As I dial my heart pounds hands tremble. First ring, second ring I think about hanging up. She answers.

Hello?

Hi.

Who's this?

You know who it is.

No, I don't.

Yes, you do.

It's eight in the morning.

So what.

Why are you calling so early?

Were you sleeping?

No, I wasn't. Is there something I can do for you?

You like baseball?

I don't really think about it much.

You ever been to a game?

No.

You want to go to one?

When?

Tomorrow.

What time?

One.
Cubs or White Sox?
Cubs.
Let me check my schedule.
I laugh.
Why are you laughing?
Why don't you give me your address.
There's a pause. My heart is still pounding, my fingers still trembling.
65 East Scott.
What's the apartment number?
There's a doorman. He'll call me when you get here.
I'll be there at noon.
I hang up. I smile. My heart pounds my hands tremble not because I'm nervous not anymore. I stand walk in a circle smile walk in a circle. I feel something other than sorrow and loss, confusion and uncertainty. I feel urges that I don't have to fight, that are not part of the horror of my former life, that are not going to kill me if I indulge them. I feel, something more, feel. I walk in a circle.

I take a shower smile in the shower. I spend the day walking around smiling, sitting in a park along the lake smiling, I eat a huge banana split in the afternoon I'm not full I eat another one smiling. I don't do anything, but when afternoon arrives, I want to sleep. Being lazy is very hard work and can be very tiring. I decide to try and take a nap. I can't remember the last time I took a nap. If I can actually do it, my body may be finally starting to recover, normalize.

I walk into my apartment lie down sleep. Sleep comes easily, deep sound dreamless afternoon nap sleep. When I wake it's dark I brush my teeth leave go to the bar to see if my friends are around they're in the back room shooting pool and drinking. I see Danny he walks over to me.

You call her?

Yeah.

You gonna see her?

I'm taking her to a Cubs game tomorrow.

He laughs.

No fucking way.

Yeah fucking way.

How was the conversation?

I called her and asked her if she wanted to go to the game. The entire thing lasted about two minutes. I was distant because I know girls like her get hit on all the time, and if you're not distant, they're not interested.

Do you know anything about her?

I know her name's Brooke. I know you grew up with her. I know she lives in a nice part of town, and she doesn't seem to have to work. I know some other things, but I'm not sure they're any of your business.

Like what?

I said I'm not sure they're any of your business.

He laughs again.

Come on.

I know that she's beautiful. I know that I get nervous around her. I know that she feels whatever it is that I feel.

Those are good things to know.

Yeah.

You want to know some more?

Like what?

She's from one of, if not the wealthiest family in Chicago.

I could give a shit about that.

She's also kind of tough, and won't tolerate any bullshit.

I don't intend to give her any bullshit.

She's also really picky.

No problem there, Danny. I'm the catch of the motherfucking century.

He laughs again.

If you ever meet her parents, I hope I'm there.

Why?

They're cool, but they're very conservative, old-money people. They'd probably freak out if you told them anything about your past.

I laugh, spend the next couple of hours smoking cigarettes, drinking cola, sitting in the corner watching the pool table, occasionally talking to one of my friends. I get tired, leave, think about going to see Lilly, walk home, decide to try and sleep, I need my motherfucking beauty sleep. It comes easily I close my eyes and I'm gone.

I wake up early. Shower with soap, put on clean clothes, get coffee, walk. I walk into the Gold

Coast, which is the wealthiest neighborhood in Chicago. It sits on the near north side, along the lake and just above Michigan Avenue and the shopping district. The streets are lined with ivy-covered brick, brown and greystone mansions built at the turn of the twentieth century by rich industrialists. European sedans sit at the curb, some of them have drivers in them. Women with children have nannies, men wear dark conservative suits and carry rolled newspapers. I walk up and down the blocks looking at the houses looking at the street names looking for East Scott. I find it, it runs parallel to the lake, a block off Lakeshore Drive. Compared to everything else in the neighborhood, Brooke's building is new, built in the sixties or seventies, twenty-five or thirty stories, simple white stone with large windows.

I walk into the lobby. A middle-aged man in a coat and tie sits behind a reception desk. He looks up, speaks.

Service entrance is around back.

I'm not here to perform any sort of service.

Can I help you with something?

I give him Brooke's name, he asks me my name, picks up a phone and dials. He speaks into the phone, hangs up, tells me she'll be down in a minute. I thank him, step outside, light a cigarette. I'm nervous, scared. I have never been on a date sober. Except for Lilly, I've never been with a woman sober. My time with her was spent in an institution where we were safe, where we

196

were shielded from the temptations and the self-created nightmares of the outside world, where we could pretend we were normal, where we could dream we had a future. It's different now, different because Lilly is gone, because I'm alone, because Brooke and I don't know each other, because I'm vulnerable, because I can be hurt. The nicotine doesn't make me less nervous or less scared. It doesn't make me invincible. It gives me something to do while I wait for Brooke to come downstairs.

I hear the door open behind me. I turn around. She's walking toward me she's wearing jeans, tennis shoes, a sweater, she's smiling she speaks.

Hi.

Hi.

I drop my cigarette, stomp it out. Nervous.

You ready to go?

Yes.

You want to walk or take the El.

Do we have time to walk?

Probably.

Let's walk.

We start walking, as we walk we talk, the small talk bullshit of first dates.

As we get closer to the stadium, the streets become more crowded. We don't have tickets, so I start looking for scalpers. I see three men on a corner pretending to be busy. I walk over ask them if they have tickets one of them asks me if I'm a cop I say no he gives me a price. I hand him some cash he gives me the tickets.

Brooke and I walk into the stadium. I offer to buy her souvenirs, a hat, shirt, perhaps you'd like a miniature bat, she laughs at me. We find our seats, they're in the upper deck along the third base line. We settle in I ask her if she knows the rules she smiles says I've never been to a game, but I'm not a fucking idiot.

They play the National Anthem, the game starts. A minute later, a beer vendor walks up our aisle.

You want a beer?

Didn't you just get out of rehab?

Not just, but not too long ago.

Won't it make you uncomfortable?

I'm not gonna have one, but if you want one, you should have it. Beer is part of the great American baseball tradition.

Okay, I'll have one.

I motion to the vendor, pay him, hand the beer to Brooke, she takes a sip.

How is it?

Good. Thank you.

Good.

Do you mind if I ask you a question?

Ask me whatever you want.

Why were you there?

Alcohol and cocaine.

Are you an alcoholic?

Yeah, I'm an alcoholic and I'm a coke fiend. I also have a record.

What kind of record?

Sold drugs, a couple DUI's, vandalism, a couple of assault charges, all kinds of stupid shit.

I'm sorry.

No reason to be sorry. Wasn't your fault, wasn't anybody's fault but my own.

How long were you there?

Rehab?

Were you somewhere else?

I went to jail when I was done.

How long were you in rehab?

Few months.

How long were you in jail?

Few months.

Which was worse?

Rehab was worse and it was also better. My body was fucked from too much liquor and too many drugs so I was sick for a long time and the sickness was a fucking nightmare. Once I started to feel better, I had to decide whether I wanted to live or die, and that was a hard decision because it meant coming to terms with a lot of pretty awful shit. After I made the decision I met a bunch of cool people and I started to get a bit more healthy and it was kind of amazing. Jail was boring and occasionally scary and a waste of fucking time.

How are you now?

At this moment I'm good, and I'm generally okay, but those are relative terms. Compared to normal people I'm a wreck, extremely troubled, extremely fucked-up.

She laughs.

At least you're honest about it.

If we become friends, you'd have found out sooner or later.

She smiles.

If?

I smile.

If.

As soon as the game starts the weather starts to turn. Heavy black clouds roll over our heads, we hear the quiet rumble of distant thunder. The temperature drops five degrees, ten degrees. The sun is gone, the wind back. I look at Brooke.

Think it'll pass?

The weather here is crazy. It could be sunny in fifteen minutes, or it could start snowing.

You want to risk it, or you want to take off?

The game just started. Let's risk it.

We stay, but don't pay much attention to the game. I ask her about her family, she has an older sister, a younger sister, she gets along with both of them, her parents are happily married. I ask her where she went to school she went to a small, private liberal arts college. I ask what she studied she says psychology, I ask her what she wants to do she says she doesn't know, she's trying to figure it out.

It starts to rain. Within fifteen minutes the rain turns to sleet. We're beneath the canopy of the upper deck, so we stay dry, but it's cold and I can see goose bumps on Brooke's arms. I ask her if she wants to leave she says let's stick it out, ten minutes later I ask her again, I don't want her to be uncomfortable, she says let's stick it out. I ask her again when the game is delayed and a tarp rolled across the field and she smiles and says, yes, I think we can leave now.

We walk out of the stadium, start walking back toward the city, we're both getting wet I try to hold the program over Brooke's head, it doesn't do much good. I lead her away from the stadium away from the bars away from the people she asks where we're going I say to a place I know.

We run a few blocks. We try to stay under trees or awnings so that we stay dry. We go to a small bar. I have been to the bar before, it's a dive with a pool table. I know it will be quiet. I know we'll be alone.

We walk in there are two people at the bar and the tables are all empty. I ask Brooke if she wants a drink she says sure I get her a beer, I get myself a cola. We walk to the back room which has the pool table and a few stools.

I look at Brooke, speak.
You wanna play?
Sure.
Do you know how?
Sort of.
Do you want me to teach you?
You can give me pointers.
I put the balls in the rack, hand Brooke a cue.
You wanna break?

Okay.

I take off the rack, hand her the cue ball, step back. She leans over, lines it up, cracks it, the cue ball blows the rest of the balls all over the table.

Doesn't look like you're gonna need many pointers.

She smiles.

We play for an hour. She slowly sips her beer, I drink five colas. We both smoke. She wins two games, I win three. We talk easily, no uncomfortable silences, no awkward pauses. She asks me how often I want to drink and use I tell her always. She asks me if being in a bar is hard I tell her I can get alcohol whenever I want, wherever I am, there are liquor stores on every block, being in a bar is no different than being anywhere else. She asks me if it's hard not drinking, I tell her it's miserable, that I spend a lot of my time crying, that sometimes I feel like I want to die. She asks me how I deal with it, I tell her I always know that at some point I will feel better and if I'm patient and hold on, that point will come. She asks me what I want to do with my life I tell her I have trouble getting through the day most of the time and I'm not really worried about it yet. She asks me how I make my money, I tell her I don't have much I scrape by doing bullshit jobs. I'm open with her, more open with her than just about anyone else, but there are some things she doesn't need to know, and there are some things I'm not going to tell her.

We leave around five. We get a cab I ride home with her. I spend the entire trip trying to decide if I'm going to kiss her. Though we talk to each other, I don't hear a word, don't have any idea what I'm saying. I just stare at her and think will she let me should I try will she let me should I try will she let me.

We get to her building, get out of the cab.

Can I walk you to your door?

Don't expect to be invited inside.

Who says I want to be invited inside?

She smiles.

Yeah, you can walk me to my door.

We enter the building, should I, get into the elevator, will she let me. She pushes the button for her floor, looks over at me.

Thanks for taking me to the game.

Thanks for going.

She smiles, we don't speak anymore, just awkwardly look at each other.

The elevator stops, doors open. We step out, start walking toward her door. My heart starts pounding my feet are heavy I'm nervous scared I want to kiss her don't want to get rejected I think she'll respond but you never know nervous scared. We stop at her door. She speaks.

This is it.

You have a nice looking door.

She looks at the door. It's a plain gray door with a number on it. She looks back.

I never noticed.

It's nice. I like it.
She laughs.
Thanks for a cool day.
Nervous.
My pleasure.
Scared.
See you soon?
Heart pounding.
Yeah.
She reaches out her hand, I take it, pull her toward me, kiss her. It is a simple kiss. Lips slightly open, a few seconds long. I pull away slowly, open my eyes. Brooke looks surprised. Sort of shocked. Sort of scared. I smile.
Bye.
I turn, walk to the elevator, push the button the door opens, I step inside, wait for the door to close. I don't turn around, look back or look up, I leave her with the kiss. The door closes, I immediately smile, take a deep breath, let it out. I push the button the elevator starts moving down. A rush runs through my body, something similar to the rush of speedy drugs, a rush of pleasure, security, joy, a rush of hope fulfilled, a rush of love or something that could be love.

I step out of the elevator still smiling leave the building still smiling. I start to walk down the street I think of Lilly my smile fades. Something inside hurts something between the happiness of moving forward and the sorrow of letting go. I go to a florist spend every cent I have on roses red roses.

I get down on my knees. Lay the flowers before me.

Hi.

I saw the girl I told you about.

It went well with her.

I haven't felt good about anything since you left, but today I did, I felt good, I finally felt good.

I want to see her again.

I need to see what happens.

I'm not going to come around so much anymore.

I miss you, and I wish you were here, and if you were this wouldn't be happening.

I start to cry.

You left me.

I cry.

You left me.

Cry.

I'm not going to come around so much.

Cry.

I see Brooke the next day.

Again the next day.

Again the next.

We go for walks, go to the movies, go for cheeseburgers at a cheap diner.

We go to a bar, shoot pool, smoke cigarettes.

After a week she lets me into her apartment. It's a two bedroom with views of Lake Michigan. Nice, but nothing extraordinary.

After ten days she lets me into her room. She has a soft white bed, she has clean beautiful sheets, she has more pillows than she needs. We lie on her bed and kiss, kiss, kiss long and deep we lie facing each other our legs entwined we kiss. We don't move beyond kissing I'm not secure enough to move beyond. I tell her I'm scared that she scares me that my emotions scare me that opening myself scares me. She asks about my past I tell her stories about dealing drugs about being arrested about being addicted about falling apart. I feel no pride in telling the stories, I feel no shame. It was my life, and now it isn't.

I meet her roommate Heather. Heather is nice

to me, but I can tell that she thinks I'm a hood-lum, and I can tell that she thinks Brooke could do better than me. I agree with Heather, Brooke could definitely do better than me.

I meet her friend Ned. Ned is openly hostile toward me. He tells Brooke that I'm going to hurt her, that I'm dangerous, unstable, insane. We have dinner with him in an attempt to calm him down, he doesn't speak to me except to occasionally correct my table manners. I ask Brooke if I can kick Ned's ass. She says no.

I stay with her for the first time I feel safe in her arms I sleep easily no dreams.

We rent movies.

Order pizza.

Hold hands as we walk.

Stay up late watch the sun rise.

Sleep through the afternoon.

See Danny, Kevin. They are both amused by what is happening between us. Kevin says it's just like the movies I say what movie he laughs, says Beauty and the Beast.

I don't work. I don't know why I'm not being called, don't know why I haven't had to go anywhere.

I make Heather laugh, once, twice, three or four times my sparkling wit starts to win her over. We both know Brooke could do better than me, but Heather starts to believe that maybe I'm not so bad.

We have another dinner with Ned. I know he likes sports I try to engage him. We talk about baseball, basketball, football. He loves the Chicago teams I know enough to carry on the conversation. At the end of the night, while I'm in the bathroom, he tells Brooke that maybe he was wrong about me. Later, when Brooke tells me, I say that I am happy he said it, because if he hadn't, despite your objections, I was going to kick his ass. She laughs at me.

I start to stay with her every night.

I go home in the mornings. I shower, pick up my mail, replenish my supply of cash. I am home one morning the phone rings I pick it up.

Hello.

Leonard speaks.

Harry motherfucking Houdini.

I smile.

What's up, Leonard?

Where you been, my son?

Been around.

Doing what?

Not much.

Hah! HAH!

I laugh.

What the fuck is that?

I say **HAH!** You've been running around with a little lady.

Maybe.

Maybe my ass. One of my reporters said you've been cavorting with a pretty young blonde.

One of your reporters?

I have people who report things to me. I call them my reporters.

And they watch me?

They check on you occasionally.

That's gotta stop, Leonard.

It's for your own good.

Stop having people watch me, Leonard.

Okay, okay, I'll stop.

Thank you.

Have you been enjoying yourself?

I laugh.

Yes.

Bet you don't miss working

Is this why I haven't gotten any calls?

I thought you deserved some time off to concentrate on more important matters.

Thank you.

You seem to have done well.

Yeah.

I'm impressed.

What do you know about her?

I know she's very attractive, I know she's very rich. I know she's from an old blue-blood family. I know you sound better than you have sounded in a long time.

You have someone watching her?

No, just did some checking.

No more of that.

I understand.

No more.

You're protective of her.

Yeah.

I'm happy for you.

Why?

If you're protective of her, it means you care for her. It's a good thing, a beautiful thing, if you're able to care for someone again.

You should come meet her.

Won't be anytime soon.

Why?

I'm doing some deals right now, significant deals, and I have to pay close attention to them. I'll come meet her when they're finished.

Okay.

Anything you need?

Nope.

You've got cash?

Enough for a year.

He laughs.

I doubt that.

I don't spend much.

You've got a girlfriend. You'll start spending.

I laugh.

She's not that way.

We'll see.

Anything you need?

No.

Stay in touch?

Of course.

Good luck with your deals.

Goodbye, my son.

I hang up, leave, walk back downtown. Brooke is waiting for me.

We are having dinner with Brooke's older sister Courtney and Courtney's husband. It's a test run for a potential meeting with her parents. We go to a fancy restaurant. I wear nice clothing, khakis and a blue shirt and a sport coat, the same clothing I wear when I am carrying something on the El and pretend to be a commuter. We sit down, we're early, I'm nervous. I feel like an impostor in my outfit, like an actor in costume, like I'm pretending to be something I'm not. Brooke and I talked about what I should admit and what I shouldn't admit, Brooke told me to be completely honest. She's right, I should be honest, but I want the sister to like me and I know she probably won't if she knows about my past. I know in many ways I shouldn't give a shit, I am what I am, but I do give a shit. I don't want to embarrass her.

We sit at our table, wait for her sister to arrive she's late. Brooke takes my hand, speaks.

You okay?

Nervous. You?

A little nervous.

No need for you to be nervous, I'm going to behave.

I know you are, and for whatever it's worth, Courtney's probably more nervous than either of us.

Why?

I've told her about you, she's nervous and excited to meet you.

What'd you tell her?

Just nice things. You have nothing to worry about.

Brooke motions toward the door. I turn, see a man and woman walking toward us. The man has dark curly hair, olive skin, is in his late twenties. The woman is a taller version of Brooke. Same blond hair, same blue eyes, same skin, same lips. Same air of reserve, same air of wealth. She's slightly taller than her husband, who walks a step behind her.

I stand say hello she smiles says hi, I'm Courtney, and this is my husband Jay, I shake each of their hands say I'm James we sit down.

The dinner is easy, comfortable. Courtney does most of the talking, she talks about her children, about her house on the North Shore, about how busy she is, about how much she loves her husband. Just before our food arrives, she asks if I mind if she orders wine I say no she asks how I'm doing with everything I know Brooke has told her about rehab I say well she orders a glass of chardonnay. She talks all the way through dinner, doesn't touch her food. I eat a steak it's great but I'm still hungry she doesn't touch her salmon if I could I'd reach over the table and take it and eat it.

We finish dinner her husband picks up the bill. We walk out together she gives me a hug gives Brooke a hug we say goodbye they leave. Brooke and I start walking back to her apartment. She speaks.

That went well.

You think?

Yeah, she liked you.

How do you know that?

If she didn't like you, she would have scowled at you and complained about everything and tortured Jay.

I laugh.

Poor fella.

Poor fella my ass, he knew what he was getting into when he married her.

I laugh again.

I'm glad it went well, glad you think she liked me.

She'll report back to my parents and tell them that you're completely acceptable.

Which is good.

Very good.

I motion toward my sport coat.

Now that I've done well, can I take this thing off?

No.

No? Why not?

I've never seen you dressed up before. I think you look handsome. Humor me and wear it until we get back to my place.

I smile, take her hand. A warmth and a chill roll through my body they settle softly they linger they scare me. I feel very close to Brooke, strong with her hand in mine, invincible to the rest of the world, but fragile to her, vulnerable to her, she could hurt me, she could hurt me, nothing else but she could hurt me.

We walk back to her place. We go to Brooke's room. Brooke shuts the door, lights a candle. I sit down on the bed she sits next to me. We stare at each other for a moment, silently stare at each other. We both start moving forward we close our eyes, reach, meet, hands breath lips bodies meet. There is something more this time, walls are down, armor discarded, defenses breached. There is something deeper faster more urgent in our hands in our breath in our lips in our bodies. We stand her hands run beneath my shirt my hands beneath her shirt around her back we briefly separate my shirt comes off we lie down. I can smell her hair, soap on her skin, perfume beneath her wrist. Her lips are soft against me, her hands firm. I take her shirt off. My chest against her chest I can feel her heart beating. I'm close to her in body and elsewhere I'm close to her.

I feel weak fragile vulnerable. She could hurt me. I'm close to her. I'm scared. She could hurt me. I can feel her heart beat, I can feel my heart beat, she could hurt me. I can't go through with this she could hurt me. I can't handle any more, any more she could hurt me.

I want to kiss her keep kissing her I haven't felt this good since Lilly since Lilly. I want to keep kissing her I start to panic I'm fucking terrified. I pull away.

Why are you stopping?

I can't.

What's wrong?

I just can't.

What'd I do?

Nothing.

Did I do something wrong?

I'm sorry.

For what?

I'm just freaking out.

Why?

I'm just freaking out. I'm sorry.

She stares at me. I look away. I'm embarrassed, ashamed, confused. My hands are shaking, my body is shaking. Her arms are around me she can feel me shaking I hate myself she could hurt me like Lilly hurt me I'm fucking terrified.

What's wrong?

I can't look at her.

What's wrong, James?

I shake my head, bite my lip. I don't want to cry in front of her I don't want to cry. She pulls me toward her, pulls my head into her shoulder holds me there.

I want to love her. I want to give myself to her. I want to take her in every way I want to be normal with someone to have a normal life with someone.

I don't want to be scared to love to give it and receive it. I'm tired of being fucking alone. I can't do it and I'm ashamed of myself. I speak softly speak.

It doesn't have anything to do with you.

Something before?

Yeah.

Do you want to talk about it?

No.

We can just lie here. You don't have to talk.

I'm sorry.

Just lie here.

We lie on her bed our legs entwined she holds my head against her shoulder. My heart slows, I stop shaking. Walls are up, armor on, defenses manned. She holds me I feel secure I'm safe again. She leans kisses my forehead.

You want a cigarette?

Yeah.

She pulls herself away from me. She stands walks to her dresser opens a drawer takes out a t-shirt. She puts it on and leaves the room. I sit up, lean against the headboard. I take a deep breath, stare at the sheets. I hate my weakness, hate my fear, hate myself. Brooke comes back into the room.

She's carrying a pack of cigarettes, an ashtray, a bottle of water. She sits in front of me, hands me a cigarette, I take it she lights it.

Thank you.

You want some water?

I take the bottle, take a sip.

Thank you.

You okay?

I shake my head.

No, not at all. I'm totally fucked-up.

Is there anything I can do?

I wish there was.

I'm sorry.

Don't be sorry. You've got nothing to be sorry about.

She leans forward, kisses my forehead. She moves so that she is sitting next to me. We smoke our cigarettes, take alternating sips from the bottle of water. I stare at the sheets, occasionally look over at her. She stares at the sheets, occasionally looks over at me. We finish our cigarettes, put them out. She takes the ashtray, sets it on the nightstand next to the bed.

She looks over at me, speaks.

You want to go to sleep?

Yeah.

We lie down next to each other. She leans forward again gently kisses my lips, puts her arms around me, lays her head on my chest. I watch her fall asleep. After about an hour, I get out of her bed. I walk into the living room, light a cigarette, stare out of her windows stare at the lake, smoke and stare at the lake it is quiet, black, still. I wish I could let her help me. I wish she could do something for me. I smoke and stare at the lake I'm scared, she could hurt me, she could hurt me.

I don't sleep well. I leave early the next morning. I kiss Brooke goodbye start walking try to walk off my fear it doesn't work. I walk all day walk until my legs hurt my feet hurt it doesn't work. I go back to my apartment read the Tao it doesn't work. I tell myself I have nothing to be scared of it doesn't work. I tell myself that she's not going to hurt me it doesn't matter. I tell myself I can deal with whatever comes I have been through worse endured worse it doesn't go away.

Brooke calls asks me how I'm doing I tell her okay. She asks if I want to meet her at a bar she's going out with Heather I say yes. Maybe I'll see her and feel differently, maybe, maybe.

I take a shower, change clothes, walk to the Local Option. I get there I see Brooke and Heather sitting at a table. I walk over to them as I walk I see Brooke looks upset. I arrive I speak.

Hi.

Hi.

Hi, Heather.

Hi, James.

I look at Brooke.

How you doing?
Brooke glances at Heather, looks back at me.
I'm fine.
I pull up a chair, sit across from her.
What's wrong?
Nothing.
Something's wrong.
It doesn't matter.
Yes it does.
She shakes her head.
Just tell me.
She glances at Heather again, looks back at me.
We were standing at the bar and some guy came up next to me and grabbed my ass. I asked him what he was doing and he said grabbing your sweet ass and he did it again.
Is he here?
It doesn't matter.
Is he here?
Heather points to three guys standing against the bar, speaks.
He's the one in the middle.
I stand up.
I'll be right back.
Brooke speaks.
What are you going to do?
Don't worry about it.
I start walking toward the three against the bar. A gate inside of me opens. I am flooded with rage, fear, aggression, an urge to protect and an urge to inflict, an overwhelming urge to destroy destroy

destroy. I know this feeling lived with it for years the Fury is back. I don't like it, it almost killed me before, it is back. My heart starts pounding. I clench my fists, clench my jaw. Every cell in my body tenses, prepares, tightens up, coils. My mind slows down my eyes focus on three men leaning against the bar. They are all about the same size as me, they are facing the bar, facing away from me. They wear pressed khakis, leather shoes, stiff-starched shirts, expensive watches. They have clean-shaven faces and short, conservative hair-cuts. They may wipe me out, I may wipe them out, maybe nothing happens. I'm trying to control myself, trying to prepare.

I stop a couple of feet behind them, speak.

Excuse me.

No response. I raise my voice.

Excuse me.

One of the others not the one in the middle turns around.

Yeah?

I want to talk to your friend.

He taps his friend on the shoulder, motions toward me. The one in the middle turns around.

Yeah?

My heart is pounding. I motion to Brooke and Heather, who are watching us.

Don't touch her again. Don't touch her friend.

His friends turn toward me.

What?

She doesn't want you touching her again. It was

inappropriate the first time, there shouldn't be a second time.

Who are you?

Doesn't matter.

Did she ask you to talk to me?

Doesn't matter.

I stare at him. He looks back at me. I'm nervous tense scared ready to go not sure what I'm going to do about his friends. He looks at each of them, looks back at me.

There are three of us and one of you.

I stare at him. Three of them, one of me. I don't know what I'm going to do.

I don't care how many of you there are. Don't touch her again.

We stare at each other. I see Derek reach beneath the bar for a short, thick, wooden club he walks toward us, speaks.

James?

I look up at him.

There a problem?

I look back at the one in the middle, he looks toward Derek, sees the club.

He speaks.

No problem.

He turns back to me.

Tell your friend I'm sorry.

Thank you.

I walk back to the table sit down with Brooke and Heather. Brooke speaks.

What happened?

He told me to tell you he's sorry.

What'd you say to him?

It doesn't matter. He's not going to touch you again.

She takes my hand.

Thank you.

Don't worry about it.

She can feel me shaking.

Are you okay?

I'll calm down in a few minutes.

She smiles.

Thank you for doing it.

I nod.

Sure.

I sit with them, drink a cola or two, smoke, wait to calm down. My hands stop shaking but the calm never comes. The Fury stays with me, taunts me, says drink motherfucker drink motherfucker, says destroy destroy, says I'm going to hurt you. I haven't felt like this felt the Fury like this since rehab I already feel fragile and vulnerable. I don't want to be in a bar right now. I want to make the Fury go away and alcohol destroys it. I want to drink. With each moment the need grows, grows, each moment is more of a struggle to resist. I need to leave. I want to drink. I need to leave. I wait for the three at the bar to leave first, I don't want Brooke alone with the one in the middle. They leave after an hour I watch them go I wait five minutes stand, look at Brooke, speak.

I gotta go.

What's wrong?

I just can't be here right now.

I'll come with you.

Stay here, have a good night. I need to be alone.

I lean over, kiss her goodbye, walk out of the bar. I start walking down the street. I want to calm down. I want this Fury to leave me. I want to feel safe, I want the urges to go away. This shouldn't be so difficult this shouldn't be bothering me. I know my problems are nothing. I know I have been through worse, seen worse, felt worse. I know my problems are minuscule and pathetic compared to other problems in the World. I know I should get the fuck over them and deal. Knowing, however, doesn't make a difference. If anything, knowing just makes me feel stupid, feel weak, feel worse.

I walk for hours, for the rest of the night. I walk and I look and I don't find anything no answers nothing. I'm the same person feel the same as when I walked out of the bar. I don't want to admit it but I know I can't go on I'm not ready to be with anyone but myself. She could hurt me. I am protective of her, feelings that strong are dangerous for me. I'm scared. I go to her apartment I say hello to the doorman he knows me now I go upstairs knock on her door. It's nine in the morning she should be up she answers the door in her pajamas. She smiles, speaks.

You don't look so good.

I'm not.

She invites me inside I walk into her apartment.

I walk into her living room sit down on her couch, she walks into the kitchen.

You want a cup of coffee?

Sure.

She pours two cups, puts some milk in her cup, walks in the living room.

She hands me one of the cups, sits down next to me. She kisses me on the cheek, pulls back.

You look sad.

I shrug.

What's wrong?

I look down, shake my head. I hate myself, hate my weakness, hate that I can't go on. She puts her hand on my hand.

What's wrong?

I look up, shake my head, bite my lip. She watches me for a moment, reaches for her cigarettes.

You want a smoke?

I nod. She hands me a cigarette, lights it, lights one for herself, looks at me.

You can't go on, can you?

No.

Why?

I just can't.

Did I do something?

I shake my head, bite my lip. I don't want to cry.

Then what's wrong?

I'm just fucked-up. Confused and scared and fucked-up.

A tear starts rolling down one of my cheeks.

It doesn't have anything to do with you.

Both cheeks.

And I wish it wasn't this way.

Tears down both cheeks she nods, leans forward, puts her arms around me, speaks.

I thought this might happen. I could see you hurting all the time and wanted to do something for you. I don't know what happened to you before, but I'm sorry, and I hope you can get over it, and if you need a friend, you know where I am.

I let her hold me and I cry. I'm sick of fucking crying there has been too much in the last year too much. I'm sick of crying. Brooke holds me and lets me and even though nothing is right and I hate myself for leaving her I feel okay because she's holding me.

I cry.

I'm so fucking sick of it.

I cry.

I find Leonard's card five names five numbers
I start at the top pick up my phone dial the
first number it rings rings rings a voice.
Yeah?
Mr Sinatra available?
No.
Voice hangs up the phone I dial the next number.
Ring ring a voice.
Hello?
Mr Kennedy available?
No.
Next number.
Mr Bob Hope please?
He's not here.
Next number.
Joe DiMaggio around?
Nope.
Final number.
May I speak to Leonard?
Who's this?
James.
He's not here. You want to leave a message?
Tell him I called.

Will do.

Thanks.

I hang up. Five minutes later my phone rings. I pick it up.

Hello?

My son, you called.

Yeah.

What's wrong?

Nothing. I want to go back to work.

Why?

I just do.

You left her, didn't you?

Why do you think that?

I can hear it.

Yeah, I left her.

I'm sorry.

Shit happens.

Don't try to be cool with me. You're upset. I can hear it in your voice.

You're right, I am upset. Nothing to do but move on, try to keep myself occupied. That's why I want to work.

I'll see what we got, maybe try to come visit later this week. Cheer your ass up.

That would be cool.

You need anything?

What I need I can't have.

That's the fucking truth. Keep away.

Call me if you're coming.

I will.

Thanks, Leonard.

Goodbye, my son.

I hang up.

What I need I can't have. I drink coffee smoke cigarettes read the Tao go for long walks wander the galleries of the art museum talk to Lilly don't sleep. Time moves slowly. What I need I can't have. I want to stay occupied. I wait for the phone to ring.

Knock on my door. It's around noon I'm lying in bed staring at the ceiling I get up knock again I stand in front of the door.
Who is it?
I hear Leonard's voice.
Mr Happy and his Cheer Squad.
I laugh, open the door. Leonard and the Snapper walk into my apartment.
I speak.
This is a surprise.
Leonard speaks.
We got some business in New York. We set up our travel schedule so we have an eight-hour lay-over.
I look at Snapper.
How you doing, Snap?
I'm the fucking Cheer Squad. Nothing better than that.
I laugh again. Leonard speaks.
Throw on some nice clothes and grab your credit card, we have an appointment.
Where?
Surprise.
What are we doing?

Bringing some beauty to your life.

What's that mean?

It means throw on some nice clothes and grab your credit card, we have an appointment.

I need to take a shower.

Fine. We'll wait.

I go into the bathroom, take a quick shower, go to my room, put on my nice clothes, Leonard and the Snapper and I leave. We walk to the curb get into a large white Benz start driving downtown. Leonard asks me if I'm hungry I say no, he says he's hungry we stop at a small restaurant he eats a green salad. He finishes the salad we get back into the car drive into the gallery district of Chicago park the car on the street get out of the car start walking down the street. Leonard speaks.

Do you know what happened to this neighborhood a couple years ago?

I have no idea.

The art market crashed and it, like every gallery district in the country, got fucking crushed. Do you know what that means for us?

I have no idea.

It means most of these galleries are on the verge of bankruptcy and they're desperate to sell their inventories and they're willing to make very, very, very good fucking deals. Do you know why we're here?

To buy art?

More specifically.

I don't know.

We're here to find you a Picasso.

You're kidding me.

Leonard looks at Snapper.

Am I kidding him?

Snapper looks at me.

He ain't fucking kidding you.

I look at Leonard.

I can't afford a Picasso.

You can't afford a painting. You can't afford a large drawing or an important drawing, but you can most likely afford something small.

Snapper speaks.

Picasso's work is surprisingly affordable.

Leonard speaks.

Snap has a couple of his own.

Snapper speaks.

I have a nice crayon drawing of a woman's head and a pencil drawing of a dove.

Leonard speaks.

And he got 'em cheap because dealers need to sell.

We stop in front of a building. Leonard speaks.

I did some research before we arrived. There's a place in here. High-end, but not super high-end. They have nice pieces in stock and they're in a deep, deep financial hole.

He opens the door and we step into the building. The gallery is on the second floor, we walk up a flight of stairs. Snapper opens a polished steel door we step into a large open room with white walls a gray wood floor and a lofted ceiling. Art hangs on the walls, some pieces are large abstract colorful some are small simple drawings, some are minimal monotone panels. In the back corner of the room there is a reception desk, behind it a door that leads into an office. Leonard looks at me, speaks.

Let's go back there.

We walk toward the office. As we approach it, an attractive woman in her late thirties steps out. She has short black hair, wears deep red lipstick, a black suit. She smiles.

May I help you?

Leonard speaks.

We're looking for Picasso drawings.

I have a few.

We'd like to see them.

Come with me.

We walk through the door into a small room. There is a large cabinet against one wall, the drawers are labeled with artists' names, a couple of small framed drawings sit on top of it. There are two chairs against another wall, a door against a third. The woman speaks.

Have a seat, I'll be right back.

Snapper offers us the chairs we sit. The woman walks through the door, quietly closes it behind her. I look at Leonard, speak.

This is fucking weird.

He laughs.

Why do you think it's weird?

The idea that I might be going home with a Picasso is just weird.

Get over it.

I laugh.

What do I do with it when I get home?

You put it on your fucking wall, what do you think you do?

What if someone steals it?

Leonard looks at Snapper.

Snapper?

Snapper looks at me.

You find 'em and you fucking shoot 'em.

I laugh. The woman opens the door. She steps into the room with one small drawing, probably eight by ten, and a slightly larger one, probably ten by twelve. She moves the drawings currently on the cabinet and replaces them with the new ones. We stand and look at them.

Leonard speaks.

If what you see doesn't move you, make you smile, make you happy, make you feel something, then fuck it, don't buy it.

I laugh. The woman laughs. I look back at the drawings. The woman speaks.

You feel anything?

I shake my head.

No.

I have more.

She picks up the drawings, leaves, comes back a few moments later with two more. I look at them feel nothing she leaves brings back two more nothing two more. I like one of them. It's two pieces of paper set on top of each other, a smiling male face is simply drawn in blue crayon across both of them. The word *papiers* is scrawled in gray pencil across the top of the lower piece of paper, the word *colles* is scrawled along the bottom of the top piece of paper. A large star, also in gray pencil, is haphazardly drawn over both pieces and the blue face, Picasso signed his name in large letters along the bottom. The work is about fourteen inches wide and twenty-eight inches tall, and it is housed in an old, ornate, black, carved-wood frame. I look at it and it makes me smile. I imagine Picasso sitting in a messy studio somewhere in France, I imagine him making it while he was bored, I imagine him sticking it in a drawer and forgetting about it. Maybe he gave it away, maybe he sold it when he needed some money, maybe someone found it after he died, I don't know how it ended up here, in this gallery in Chicago, but I look at it and it makes me smile and I know it's going home with me.

I ask the woman how much she tells me, Leonard says no way, that's above-market and he gives her a number. She responds they go back and forth back and forth until they arrive at an agreeable price. They look at me I smile and say okay.

I give the woman my credit card she says she prefers checks. I say I prefer credit cards she says okay she rings it up. I sign the slip. She asks me if I'd like it delivered, I say no I'll take it with me.

I pick it up, take it off the cabinet. Leonard and Snapper and I thank the woman and we walk out of the gallery. I carry the Picasso under my arm. I smile as I walk I have a Picasso under my arm I think it's completely ridiculous. Leonard looks at me, smiles, speaks.

You look good with that thing.

I laugh. He looks at Snapper, speaks.

He looks good with it, doesn't he?

Snapper speaks.

It really fits him.

Maybe he should come back tomorrow and buy another one.

Why not? You only live once.

That is certainly the truth. You only live once, buy Picassos whenever possible.

We laugh, walk down the street back to the Mercedes, get inside, pull away. We drive back to my apartment. Leonard says they have to get to the airport, they have a flight in a few hours. I say thank you for stopping it has been a great day. Leonard says no problem, we'll be back soon.

I get out of the car, they pull away. I walk into my apartment. I don't have a hammer or a nail so I lean my Picasso against the wall near my bed. I laugh every time I see it.

Spring becomes Summer.

I talk to Lilly. Sometimes I read to her, sometimes I just sit with her.

I go to St Louis.

Milwaukee.

North side, South side. Northside. Southside.

I go out every night. I go to bars with my friends. I smoke play pool watch my friends get drunk. I stay out late I still can't sleep when the bars close I walk through dark, silent, empty streets. I walk until it starts to become light. I sit by the lake and I watch the sun rise.

I sleep during the day, a few hours a day.

I read, look at art.

I go to Detroit.

Rockford.

Gary, Indiana.

I decide I want to write something. I have no idea what, I don't really care, I just want to try. I buy a computer. I sit down in front of it and stare at the screen. I open a word-processing document and with two fingers I type – What are you staring at dumbass? – over and over and over again. A woman stops me on the street and she says you won't always feel this way. I ask her what she means and she says I can smell your pain, I can smell it. I'm not sure if she's a genius or a lunatic. I turn and quickly walk away.

I see someone I used to know, someone I haven't seen for a few years. He sees me smiles walks over and says how's your fucking drinking problem, Frey? I say it's good, how's your drinking problem? He says he's broke and unemployed and it sucks, but it allows him to go out every night. I give him ten bucks, say have one on me, old friend, have one on me.

I go to Milwaukee again.

Rockford twice.

Minneapolis/St Paul.

I'm still too thin, I go on a special diet. I eat all of my meals at either The Weiner Circle, Taco/Burrito Palace #2, or The Olympic Gyro House. I only order items with red meat, I always order extra red meat, with most things I also order extra cheese.

A man offers to sell me a six pack of whoop-ass and a bottle of I know you can. I ask him how much? He says you ain't got enough, motherfucker, but I bet you can afford some of that lonely shit.

I visit Lilly. Sometimes I read to her, sometimes I speak to her, sometimes I just sit with her.

Summer becomes Fall.

I had my last drink one year ago, exactly one year ago. I took my last hit from a pipe one year and two days ago.

I am on the train going to the Northern suburbs. I have been to the house before. It is the house where I did my first pick-up, where the strange man in silk pajamas played a joke on me. I've been here three or four other times, each time someone different came to the door. I am supposed to get a briefcase and take it to the South side of the city.

It is late morning. The train is almost empty. I sit alone reading, occasionally glancing out the window, the sky is gray, the leaves have turned, they are starting to fall. It is starting to get cold.

I get off the train take a cab. I remember how to get there. I see the house large gray stone. I walk to the front door, knock, no one comes, I knock again, hear shuffling feet heavy breathing. I wait. The feet stop shuffling I still hear breathing. I knock again the door opens it's the pajama man again. He's wearing a pair of dirty white underwear briefs and a dirty white t-shirt, there are deep dark circles beneath his eyes. His nose is running and he's shaking and he looks like he hasn't slept in a long time. He is holding a nine millimeter pistol in one of his hands and he is pointing it at my face.

What do you want?

I am shocked terrified can't speak.

Who sent you here?

I don't want to die I immediately start shaking.

WHO SENT YOU HERE?

The black hole of the barrel is an inch from my face I can smell the metal.

I don't want to die I can't breathe move speak I don't want to die I'm frozen.

MOTHERFUCKER.

The man cocks the gun.

WHO THE FUCK SENT YOU HERE?

I don't want to die I piss myself. Urine runs down my leg, into my shoes, it keeps coming my bladder is done.

WHO?

He shakes the pistol fuck fuck fuck.

SENT YOU?

I don't want to die he shakes the pistol fuck me.

MOTHERFUCKER?

I've got to get away move move move if I don't get away I'm going to die.

I take a small step back. The man stares at me, the pistol is still aimed at my face. I take another small step I am so scared I don't want to die please please please. I take another step the man stares at me his finger is on the trigger please.

LEONARD SEND YOU?

Please another step please don't shoot me please.

LEONARD SEND YOU?

Another step don't shoot me please.

LEONARD SEND YOU?

I don't want to die. I don't want to die.

YOU TELL LEONARD.

Another step.

THAT I'LL SHOVE THIS GUN UP HIS ASS.

Another step.

AND BLOW HIS MOTHERFUCKING HEAD OFF.

Another step back. Another step, another step. The man watches me please don't shoot me please another step another step. Please please please let me get away. The man watches me, I'm almost gone. He lowers his gun, wipes his nose, shuts the door. I keep moving back until I reach the sidewalk. I turn and quickly walk away. My heart is exploding my legs are jelly. I'm shaking there is urine all over my legs and feet, my pants and my socks and my shoes. When I reach the end of the block I turn the corner I'm away holy fuck I'm away. I fall to my knees on a small patch of brown grass between the sidewalk and the street. I start vomiting.

I take the train home my pants are covered in piss. I buy a newspaper to keep over my lap so that the other passengers don't see my pants it's not a comfortable ride.

I call Leonard tell him what happened he is not happy. He tells me he's coming to Chicago to handle this personally he wants me to meet him at his usual hotel in the morning.

I spend the rest of the day chain-smoking cigarettes. I can still see the black hole of the barrel. I can still smell the metal. I can still hear the bullet entering the chamber. I can still feel the urine running down my leg.

Night comes I can't sleep. I can still see his eyes, hear his voice. He had his finger on the trigger and he could have killed me.

I go to the bank. Fill a bag with cash. I walk to the hotel it's a long walk. I want to burn away the fear I still feel it, it doesn't work I still feel it. I take the elevator up, go to the restaurant. Leonard and Snapper are sitting at a table waiting for me. They do not look happy. They stand as I approach them. Leonard speaks.

My son.
What's up, Leonard?
How you doing?
I'm good.
I look at Snapper.
What's up, Snapper?
You tell me.
Had a weird day yesterday.
So I fucking hear.
Leonard sits, we follow. Leonard speaks.
Have you eaten?
No.
Let's order, and then I want you to tell Snapper what happened.

We order, and unlike most of our meals together, the order is not excessive. After we order I recount yesterday's events. Midway through, our food comes and I continue to speak as we eat. Neither Leonard or Snapper interrupt. They just sit and quietly listen to me. When I finish, Snapper takes a deep breath, pushes his plate away, looks at Leonard and speaks.

You know what this means?
I do.
He's finally gone completely crazy.
I thought he was getting better.
Am I authorized?
Yes.
Snapper turns to me.
You're coming with me, kid.
I speak.

No way.

You owe him.

I don't care.

He stuck a fucking gun in your face.

I don't care, I'm not going.

I lean over and pick up the bag of cash, which has been sitting at my feet.

I set it in front of Leonard.

I also don't want to do this anymore. I brought you the money I owe you.

Leonard looks surprised.

You're gonna quit because some crazy fuck pulled a gun on you?

That's part of the reason.

What's the other part?

I feel good about staying clean. I feel like I can do it long term. Knowing that, I've got to figure out what I'm going to do with my life. No offense, but I don't want to be a deliveryman anymore, no matter how much I get paid. I don't want guns in my face. I want to try to have a normal life, or at least something that resembles one.

Holy shit. This is crazy. You should hear yourself.

I laugh.

What if I promoted you?

You know I can't really be part of what you do, and I don't want to be any more a part of it than I already am. I gotta do something on my own.

What?

244

I don't know, but I have enough money to take some time and figure it out.

Leonard motions to the bag of cash.

I don't want the money.

I owe it to you.

I want to know what you spent it on.

Just take it.

Why won't you tell me where you spent it?

I just don't want to.

Tell me what you spent it on, and you can keep it, and you can leave your job, and you can let Snapper deal with your friend in the suburbs. I agree with your intentions, and think it will be good for you to start dealing with the future, I just want to know where the money went.

I'd rather show you than tell you.

Fine. Show me.

You have a car downstairs?

Of course.

Let's go.

Leonard motions for the bill gets it signs it. We stand, I pick up my bag, we leave. Snapper gets the car he picks us up in front of the hotel. We start driving north and west it isn't far. I give Snapper directions we stop at the florist where I always stop, as soon as I walk through the door they know what I'm going to buy. I buy red roses beautiful red roses. Lilly loved them when she was alive, I hope she still loves them.

We pull through the gates. We are still in the city

but on its edges, we can see the towering skyline in the distance. Land spreads out before us, around us, there are thousands and thousands of stones. We drive slowly along a thin, winding road. It is quiet, still, empty. We turn off the main road onto a smaller road, drive for a moment, I motion for Snapper to pull over.

I step out of the car, Leonard and Snapper step out of the car. I lead them through the aisles. We do not speak. The only sounds are our steps and the chatter of small birds. Thirty yards in from the road I stop in front of two simple white stones. The stones are identical to each other. Words in simple print read—

Katherine Anne	**Lillian Grace**
Sanders	**Sanders**
1932–1994	**1970–1994**
You were Loved	**You were Loved**

There are dead roses in front of Lilly's stone. I pick them up and put the fresh roses in their place. I lean toward the point where the stone meets the grass, where I imagine she lies, her head resting on a pillow. I whisper hello, I love you, I brought some friends with me, you probably remember Leonard, he always asks about you, I hope you're well, I love you, I love you.

I step back, stand with Leonard and Snapper, who are staring at the stones, and I speak.

They didn't have any family except each other,

so I took care of them. I had them moved from the county morgue to a funeral home. I bought them dresses for burial, had them placed in silk lined coffins and I got these plots and the stones. They were Catholic, which I didn't know until after, so I had a Priest perform the services. Lilly had a shitty life, a shitty fucking life, and I thought I could change that, but I couldn't, so I wanted this, at least, to be nice for her.

I look at Leonard, tears are streaming down his face. He speaks.

They're beautiful.

Yeah.

I've never seen anything so beautiful.

I nod, start to tear up.

I'm gonna have roses sent here once a week forever.

You don't have to do that Leonard.

And these graves will always be tended.

You don't have to do that Leonard.

I know I don't have to, but I'm going to.

Thank you, Leonard.

He looks at Snapper, speaks.

Let's pay our respects, let them know we're thinking about them.

Snapper speaks.

I got a feeling they know.

I'm sure they do.

They step forward and they cross themselves, get down on one knee, start to pray. I don't believe in god, but I like to think that Lilly is in a better

place, so I get down on one knee and I close my
eyes and I pray.

I hope she knows.

That for her and only her, for her and only her.
I pray.

Fall becomes winter.

    I sit in front of my computer for hours I write what are you scared of dumbass, why are you scared?

A man at a bar tells me I look like a fly. I ask him why he thinks I look like a fly and he tells me that flies are born in shit and live in shit and he tells me that I look like shit and look like I've lived in, with and through shit, thus I look like a fly. I don't know what to say so I say thank you, my friend, thank you.

I meet a girl named Julianne she's Danny's friend she wants a roommate. We get along, she's from the South and her accent makes me laugh, I decide that I will be her roommate. We start looking for an apartment. We find a big apartment with two bedrooms, high ceilings, a living room dining room and kitchen, it should be expensive but isn't. We're trying to figure out why there is a loud rumble, and the building shakes and the windows shake and the floor shakes everything fucking shakes. Julianne wonders if we're having an earthquake, I laugh, walk to the back of the apartment, look out the window. The El tracks are ten feet away. I like the El tracks, like the shaking and the rumbling, like the apartment. I tell Julianne that I think we should move in, she agrees with me, we sign a lease. We move in and every fifteen minutes we rumble and shake, rumble and shake.

I meet another man at another bar he looks me in the eyes and he says I am mentally ill and unstable. I tell him I am mentally ill and unstable as well. He tells me that his doctors have advised him to never drink again, that it could kill him. I tell him my doctors have given me the same advice. He tells me that he goes to bars because he doesn't know what else to do with his life. I tell him I know the feeling and I buy him a cola, an ice cold glass of cola.

I sit in front of my computer.

Every fifteen minutes I rumble and shake.

Winter in Chicago is cold as hell.

Leonard's visits stop he hates the cold he avoids it. I talk to him once a week or so he calls me from strange places Venezuela and Costa Rica and Barbados, Guadeloupe and the Dominican Republic. I ask him what he's doing why he's traveling so much he says I'm TCB my son, T, C motherfucking B. I ask him what that means, he says it means taking care of business, taking care of motherfucking business.

Leonard calls tells me he's sending me a plane ticket he wants me to come to his beach house for the Super Bowl. I get the ticket, get on the plane, fly to LA, get off the plane. My friend Chris is picking me up. I went to college with him, lived with him for a year. He works at a golf course in Orange County. He wants to own his own golf course at some point, right now he works as an Assistant Greenskeeper. I ask him what that means, he says it means I mow fucking lawns all day.

I walk out of the terminal it's bright, warm, sunny. Chris is waiting for me at the curb I climb into his SUV he says what's up I say not much he asks where we going I say Orange County and I give him an address.

The drive takes just over an hour. We talk about friends laugh he asks me how I'm doing I say well, I ask him how he's doing he says fine all he does is work. I see a big sign for the Pageant of the Masters, it makes me laugh. We drive past an outdoor theater called the Irvine Bowl, which says it is the home of the Pageant of the Masters I

laugh again. We get to Laguna Beach. We get lost.
I call Leonard he gives us directions. We find his
house at the end of a dead-end street. It's a large,
white, contemporary house, all angles and glass,
built into the side of a cliff overlooking the ocean.
There are ten or so cars parked in the driveway
and along the curb. All of them are expensive
European cars: Porsches, Bentleys, Mercedeses,
Jaguars, BMWs.

We park, walk to the door, there's a man at the
door he asks for our names. I give him my name
and he lets us in. We walk through the door into
a large open living room. Everything is white,
the floors, the walls, the furniture, there are
white flowers in white vases, white lamps with
white shades, long white linen curtains on the
edges of the windows. There is a stairway leading
down at the back edge of the room, we hear noise
from below we walk to the stairway and descend.
We walk into another large open room. The front
wall of the room is made of glass, beyond the glass
there is a deck and beyond the deck open views
of the Pacific ocean. Along another wall there is a
pool table with black felt. Along a third there is
a bar a long white bar, a bartender in a white
tuxedo stands behind it serving drinks. Along
the back there is a huge television, the largest television I have ever seen, its image coming from a
projector hanging on the ceiling. There are three
large, soft couches in a U in front of the television.
There are about thirty people spread through the

253

room and on the deck, there are many more women than men. The men are diverse, black white and Asian, some in suits, some in shorts and t-shirts. The women are all white, all beautiful, most are blond. Most have surgically enhanced chests, and are all well-dressed, though some wear less than others. When we reach the bottom of the stairs Chris looks around and looks at me and smiles and says holy fuck, this is going to be fun.

I see Leonard on the deck he's smoking a cigar and talking to a man in his sixties with long white hair and a long white beard the man has a young blond girl with him. I walk toward Leonard he sees me raises his hand yells.

My son. My son has arrived.

The man and the blonde turn and look at me I laugh.

Hi, Leonard.

You just get here?

Yeah.

That your friend?

Yeah. Chris, Leonard. Leonard, Chris.

They shake hands. The man interrupts, tells Leonard they'll talk later. He walks away with the woman, who glances back at us. Leonard looks at Chris, speaks.

You live nearby, right?

Yeah.

You smoke weed?

Yeah.

You like fucking hot chicks?

Chris laughs.

Of course.

The guy who just walked away is the biggest pot dealer on the west coast and the woman is his wife, who's a porn star. She likes to fuck and he doesn't care who she fucks and I could tell by the look she gave you that she wants to fuck you, so if you want either weed or her, let me know.

Chris laughs again.

Seriously?

Leonard nods.

Yeah, but you better be ready.

Ready for what?

She stars in S&M porn films, and she might want to beat you up before she fucks you.

Really?

Yeah, and she can kick some ass. I've seen the results. It isn't pretty.

Chris turns around, looks at the woman, who is standing with her husband near the pool table. He turns back to us.

You got any beer? I think I need to have a beer and think about it.

Of course I've got beer, I've got whatever you want. Go tell the bartender and give me a minute with my son.

Cool.

Chris walks to the bar. Leonard turns to me.

Thanks for coming.

Thanks for having me.

This may be the last of these parties. I thought you'd want to see it and I thought you'd enjoy it.

Why the last?

Making some changes.

Care to elaborate?

Not yet.

Okay.

I look around.

Who are all these people?

Gambling fools, a number of whom will lose enormous sums of money to me tonight.

All of them gamble with you?

All of the men, and a couple of the women. The other women are either with one of the men or were hired by me to keep the men happy.

Which ones are hired?

You like one of them?

Just curious.

See the one talking to your friend?

I look at Chris, who is standing by the bar. He is talking to a tall blond woman, she's taller than him, who is wearing a short skirt and a tube top, neither of which covers much of her body.

Yeah, I see her.

She's a pro, and at some point in the next couple minutes she's going to lean into his ear and offer to go upstairs with him.

He's gonna shit.

If he's smart, he's gonna go upstairs. It'll be the ride of his fucking life.

I laugh.

You do this often?

As I said, this may be the last time, but I usually do it for the Super Bowl, the NCAA basketball championship and the Kentucky Derby, which are the biggest betting days of the year.

Why here and not Vegas?

Same reason I've never brought you to Vegas.

Which is?

I get followed around in Vegas. My every move is monitored by people whose sole aim in life is to figure out some way to lock me up. You're already a blip on their radar, but if you were to show up in Vegas, you would become a much larger blip, which doesn't need to happen. I have parties here because I can control what happens in this house and what people see and hear in this house. It's no coincidence that it's at the end of a one-way street, and that it's built into the side of a cliff. Both things make surveillance of it much more difficult. I also found these former spies from England who opened a spy shop that sells high-tech spy shit and they sweep it once a month for listening devices.

They ever find anything?

Yeah, but not in a while, which means the government has either given up on this place or is using shit my guys can't find. Won't matter soon anyway, because, as I said, these parties are ending.

And you're not gonna tell me why?

Not yet.

He takes a drag of his cigar, speaks.

Everything good with you?

Yeah.

Keeping busy?

Yeah.

Doing what?

I wrote a movie script.

Leonard smiles.

Hah! That's fucking great. Why didn't you tell me you were doing that?

I didn't want to be embarrassed if I couldn't finish it.

You want to be a writer?

I thought I'd try it.

Can I read this script?

No.

Why?

It's awful.

Come on.

No way.

It can't be that bad.

It's fucking awful. I showed it to a couple of people and everyone agrees, even though some of them won't say it directly.

Why'd you write a script? I thought you were gonna write a book.

Scripts are easier and take less time and I thought I might be able to make some money at it.

Most movies are awful, so it's probably perfect.

This is awful even on the movie scale of awful, and it wasn't supposed to be awful. While I was doing it, I thought it was brilliant. Nobody in their right mind would give me a penny for it.

There are plenty of people in Hollywood who aren't in their right minds. Some of them are here, right now, in this fucking house.

Trust me, even they would think it was awful.

You gonna write another one?

Yeah.

Good. You should write the dumbest, most commercial thing you can think of and I bet you'll sell it.

Maybe.

How's your money holding up?

I still have too much of it.

Go spend it. Buy something beautiful.

I saw a Matisse drawing recently.

I'll expect to see it on your wall next time I'm in town.

You should come soon. My friends miss you and they're hungry.

He laughs, motions toward the house.

Game's about to start, I gotta go in and take action.

Where's Snap?

Dallas is playing, and for some reason Snap, despite the fact that he is from New York, has always been a Dallas fan, so I got a pair of tickets for him and his brother and sent them.

You're a good man, Leonard.

He laughs.

No I'm not.

Yeah you are.

Let's go inside. I gotta get to work.

I follow him inside. Chris is still talking to the girl. Leonard walks toward the couches, a platinum selling R&B star is singing the National Anthem on the television. Leonard starts mingling with his guests, telling them jokes, laughing with them, shaking hands with them. I go to the bar, get a cola, find a seat, wait for the game to start. Almost immediately, Chris sits next to me, speaks.

Dude.

What's up?

That chick, I think she's into me.

I laugh.

What's so funny?

Are you into her?

Look at her. She's gorgeous. Of course I'm into her.

And why do you think she's into you?

She asked me if I wanted to go upstairs, have a private conversation.

What'd you say?

I said hell yes. She's grabbing her purse and we're going up.

I laugh again.

What's so funny?

I shake my head.

Come on, Dude. What's so funny?

She's a hooker, Chris.

No way.

Yes, way.

How do you know?

Leonard told me.

She's a fucking hooker?

Yeah.

I thought she was into me.

She probably was, though she gets paid to be into everyone here, literally and figuratively.

Goddamnit.

Get a drink. Let's watch the game.

He goes to the bar, gets a drink, comes back. As the game starts, most of the people in the house gather in the area around the television. Leonard is sitting in the middle of the couch taking bets. From where we are sitting we can hear the amounts fifty, seventy-five, one hundred thousand, we hear one man say two hundred and twenty-five, we hear another say four hundred. During the game, we hear more ridiculous bets. One man bets one hundred thousand dollars that Dallas will get a first down, he loses the bet. Another bets fifty that the other team's kicker will miss a field goal, he wins the bet. Leonard takes every bet offered, though he often adjusts the odds. There are bets on first downs, fourth downs, on extra points, passing yards, rushing yards, points above and below, there are bets on fucking everything. At half-time everyone goes upstairs, where a huge buffet has been laid out. There is prime rib, there are crab claws, there is Caesar salad, baked potatoes, creamed spinach. There are salmon steaks, there's pasta salad. There is a separate buffet with dessert

cakes and tarts and pies and cookies and choco-
lates and éclairs. We get plates of food, go back
downstairs, watch the halftime show. Chris meets
two other women one of them is a hooker, the
other is married to a record producer, I meet the
owner of a chain of car dealerships, an Israeli
weapons dealer, a man who exports used American
clothing to Japan, two professional gamblers, a man
who says he is Iranian royalty and had to flee the
Ayatollahs. Near the end of the show, Leonard sits
down next to me. I speak.

How's it going?

Bad right now.

Why?

Down 1.2 million.

Fuck.

I'll get it back.

That's a lot of dough.

Just wait. People start getting stupid in the
second half. You having fun?

Yeah, I am. This is ridiculous.

It is indeed.

You having fun?

It's work.

You should grab one of your girls, relieve some
stress before the game starts again.

They're not here for me. If you want one, though,
you can have my room.

No thanks.

Across the room, a man starts calling for Leonard.

I gotta run.

Cool.

He gets up, walks to the man. The game starts again. Chris shoots pool with two of the hookers, tries to decide if he wants to sleep with one of them or both of them or both of them at the same time. I try to convince him that he should have both of them at the same time, he decides against it, says it doesn't feel right to him. I tell him it would probably feel awfully fucking right while he was doing it and he laughs and says yeah, yeah, yeah.

As the game goes on Leonard's guests get more and more drunk, some of them start snorting coke off the coffee table, the bar, off compact disk covers, some of them start smoking weed. There are more bets, and the bets, fueled by liquor and drugs, are riskier and more ridiculous. Leonard starts winning more of them, makes his money back, starts racking up huge gains. By the time the game ends, which Dallas wins, Leonard is obviously happy, though it doesn't show because he keeps a straight face.

After the game the women turn on music, start dancing. The liquor is still flowing, the drugs are still out, some of the women start making out with the men, some of them start making out with each other, some of them stand on top of the bar, take off their shirts and dance. I have a red-eye and Chris has lawns to mow early in the morning, so we find Leonard he's on the deck smoking a cigar. I speak.

We're heading out.

You've had enough?

It was cool. I'm glad I came. Thank you for bringing me.

Of course. What are you going to do when you get home?

Write another dumb movie.

Make it really dumb.

I'll do my best.

And I'll come visit when I can or when I finish with my new business.

The secret business.

Leonard laughs.

You'll understand when I tell you.

Be careful.

I am being careful. That's why shit like this . . .

He motions toward the house.

Is ending.

I'm glad I got to see it.

He laughs.

If you stay a bit longer, you'll see a whole lot more.

I laugh. He puts his arm around me.

I'll walk you to the door.

Thanks.

We walk to the door. Leonard opens it we step outside. He speaks.

Safe travels.

You too.

He looks at Chris.

Good to meet you.

Thanks for having me.

You change your mind about those girls, let me know. It'll be on me.

Chris laughs.

Thanks.

Leonard looks back at me.

See you soon, my son.

Later, Leonard.

Chris and I walk to his truck get inside pull away. Leonard stands at the end of his drive, watches us go.

Later Leonard.

Winter becomes spring.

I write another movie script. I think it's great until I show it to my friends. They let me know that it is not great, not even close to great, that it should be thrown away.

I meet a girl named Tanya at the Local Option. She's small, blond, British.

She has bright blue eyes and she likes to laugh. Fifteen minutes after we meet she asks me if I want to take her home. I know I'll never love her, so I say yeah. We have a lovely evening together.

I buy the Matisse. It looks nice on my wall.

I celebrate April Fools' Day. The one day a year when we are reminded what we are for the other three hundred and sixty-four. Happy Fools' Day, motherfucker, happy April Fools' Day.

I see Brooke on the street. She's shopping, I'm walking. We talk for three or four minutes and it hurts me for three or four days.

I go out every night with my friends. We go to bars shoot pool, we go to clubs listen to music, we go to parties they drink, we go to dinner eat.

I still don't sleep well after a year and a half I

still can't fucking sleep. I read every night until four or five I read until my eyes fall until the rumbling and shaking lull me into black.

I bring Tanya home again and again I bring her home. She doesn't want anything from me or expect anything from me she's easy to be with and she likes to laugh and she makes me laugh. I bring her home again and again.

Spring becomes summer.

The phone rings I answer it. It's early in the morning I just fell asleep.

Hello?

My Son. MY SON. It's a beautiful, beautiful day!

It's not day yet, Leonard. It's still fucking morning. Early fucking morning.

Early to bed, early to rise, that is the man who wins the prize.

I laugh.

What the fuck happened to you?

Wonderful things.

Like what?

I'm coming to town. I'll tell you in person.

When are you coming?

Today. Meet me at the hotel for lunch.

Okay.

See you then, SEE YOU THEN!

I laugh.

Yeah, see you then.

I hang up the phone, go back to sleep. I wake up around noon, take a shower, walk down to the hotel. Leonard and Snap are sitting in the restaurant when I walk in they stand. Leonard speaks.

My son.

Leonard.

He hugs me, releases. I look at Snap.

Long time.

Been busy.

Good to see you.

You too, kid.

We sit. I speak.

What's the big news?

Leonard smiles, reaches into his pocket, pulls out a plastic card, sets it in front of me.

Phone cards.

I laugh.

Phone cards?

You got it. Phone cards.

So what.

So what? Think, my Son, think.

You want me to make a phone call?

No.

You want me to sell it?

No.

I have no idea. It's a phone card. I can buy one of those anywhere.

Leonard shakes his head.

Not one of these.

It's somehow different?

Leonard nods.

Where have I been traveling for the last several months?

All over the place.

All over the place where?

The Caribbean and Central America.

Why would I go there and what does that have to do with me and my business and phone cards?

No idea.

Think, my son, think.

Just tell me.

Leonard looks at Snapper.

He has no vision.

Snapper shrugs, speaks.

Some people don't.

It's obvious to me.

He ain't you.

Leonard looks back at me.

As you know, a large portion of my income is generated through the making and taking of bets. As you can imagine, the manner in which I take these bets, and the organization set up to handle and administrate them, is entirely illegal.

Right.

For a number of reasons, I don't want my businesses to be illegal anymore. The two primary reasons are that with the implementation of RICO laws, which are designed to put people like me away, my life has become increasingly more difficult. I'm tired of being followed, surveyed, I'm tired of fucking FBI agents harassing people who do business with me, I'm tired of having to monitor everyone I fucking know to make sure they're not ratting me out. I don't want to go to jail. I don't

270

want to die in jail. I have some things I want to do before I'm gone and I will not be able to do them if I'm in jail. If I legalize my business, I can't be sent to jail.

Perfectly understandable.

The other reason is the pledge I made to my dying Father, which was to play the golf course where he labored as a lawn-mower and play it just like one of the fucking members. As you know, I have had a very difficult time doing this. One of the reasons it has been so difficult is because I am a known criminal. If I stop being a criminal, and I can prove I have stopped being a criminal, it may open certain doors for me.

Also perfectly understandable.

In 1982, the Federal government ordered the break-up of AT&T, which held a monopoly on local and long distance telephone services. The break-up was ordered so that competition would be spurred and consumers would no longer be forced to pay rates that were much higher than they should have been. More recently, the Telecommunications Act was passed because the net result of the '82 break-up wasn't as positive as was hoped. The new act opens long distance lines to dozens of new phone companies, most of which will go out of business. A few won't, and a few will carve out specific little niches, and one of those niches is the phone card business.

Leonard picks up the card.

You buy a card, you have a specific amount of

money on the card, ten dollars, twenty dollars, fifty dollars, whatever, you make long distance calls through the card company's operators, you talk until the card runs out and then you buy another one. You with me?

I nod.

Yeah, I'm with you.

You understand where I'm going with this?

No I don't.

Leonard looks at Snapper, speaks.

He has no vision.

It ain't that, it's that you got a lot. That's why you're in charge.

He's my son, he should have it too.

Well he don't, and that's that.

Leonard looks back at me.

Do you happen to know what's legal in the Caribbean and certain parts of Central and South America that is illegal here?

I would imagine there are a few things.

You're right about that, but what that might be directly related to me?

Again, probably a few things, but I'm guessing from this conversation that you're referring to gambling.

Bingo! It's a fucking gambler's paradise down there. And what isn't legal becomes legal with a wad of hundreds slipped into the hands of the correct local official. I love it, I fucking love it.

I laugh.

So what does that have to do with phone cards?

Phone cards make it all legal, and let me make money off it regardless of the outcome of the bets.

How is that?

I recently relocated the bulk of the people who work for me in my gambling businesses to the Caribbean and certain parts of Central and South America, where what they do is entirely legal. I'm having everyone who places bets through my people buy phone cards from the phone card company that I now own, and I am charging very high rates for those calls. All of the money involved is moved through offshore banks, which are not beholden to the laws of this country, and the only person breaking the law in this equation is the individual placing the bet on American soil.

Really?

Let's say you were one of my clients. You go to a retail location that sells my phone cards. You buy a few of them. You call a number you've been given, that's been mailed to you from an offshore location. That number only receives calls through the operators who work for my phone company and who take calls using my phone cards. They put you through to someone sitting at a desk in a location where gambling is legal. That person takes your bet, and either takes a credit card number or provides you with wiring instructions for payment. You place your bet, you are given a confirmation number. The call costs you ten dollars per minute. You have broken the law by placing the bet, but no one on my end has broken the law because they are all working in places where their activities are legal.

You're sure about all this?

There are a few gray areas, but they're gray enough so that if someone wants to arrest me or tries to prosecute me, I'll tie them up in court for fucking decades.

Very impressive, Leonard.

I'm going to send the Federal Prosecutor in Las Vegas a note inviting him to come over to my house and kindly kiss my ass.

I laugh, Snapper laughs. Leonard looks around.

I hope those fuckers have someone watching or listening to us right now.

He lifts his middle finger, waves it around.

If so, this is for you, because you're not gonna get me, you fuckers.

I laugh again. When I stop, I speak.

Congratulations, Leonard.

Thank you.

I'm incredibly impressed.

Thank you.

We should celebrate.

Why do you think we're here?

Good. This time, though, I'm taking care of the check.

No, that's not how it works.

It is tonight.

No.

Leonard.

What?

I hold up a wad of cash.

This is the last of the money I made working for you. I've been keeping it so I could spend it on one of our dinners. You're going to shut the fuck up and let me take care of the check tonight.

He laughs.

Thank you, my son, thank you.

I cut up the fake driver's license throw it away Jimmy Testardo no longer exists.

I close the safe deposit box.

I get a job at a clothing store on Michigan Avenue. I work in the stockroom with a Filipino and two Mexicans. Most of my work is at night, after the store is closed. My co-workers and I are given a list by the manager with such tasks as replace flat front khakis, replenish and fold all fashion t-shirts, replace ribbon dispensers behind counter, sweep and mop entrance floor. It's a dumb job, and I don't get paid shit, but it feels good to work. I write another script. I send it to my friends I know they're tired of reading my awful scripts. I tell them this will be the last one.

I start sleeping, every second or third night I sleep easily, well. The shaking and rumbling of the train is a song that lulls me into six, eight, ten glorious hours of peace, silence and blackness.

I walk in the heat in the rain in the day night morning afternoon sunrise sunset I walk for hours. I walk along the lake and I jump into the water. I see a bench and I sit and have a smoke. I see an ice cream truck and I order the largest cone they sell. I take naps on the lawns of public parks, I listen to music played in bandstands, I read in the shade of trees in the shade of towering trees. I go to the zoo look at the animals, yo gorilla, what the fuck's up!

My friends tell me the script isn't bad might actually be good. It's a romantic comedy a love triangle between friends with a happy ending. I decide to try to sell it to Hollywood I don't know anyone in Hollywood, but so what I'll try anyway.

I wander the halls of the art museum the pictures are still beautiful and the galleries are air-conditioned I wander the halls.

I visit Lilly. Her flowers wilt in the heat so I bring more of them. I don't talk much, don't feel the need to talk anymore, just sit with her, it's good to know she's there, just sit.

I get fired from the job at the clothing store. The manager decided she wanted every article of clothing in the store, and there are thousands of them, taken off the shelves and re-folded. I ask her why she says because I said so. I try to organize a strike with the other stockroom guys and I succeed and we buy a box of doughnuts and sit on the floor in the middle of the store and refuse to work. She tells the other stockroom guys they can keep their jobs if they end the strike and she fires me and tells me if I don't leave the store immediately she's calling the police. I take the doughnuts with me.

My friend has a cousin that works for a famous director in Hollywood. I call her and I ask her to read my script, she says send it and I'll read it when I have some time. I call her once a week to remind her. She doesn't read it, so I keep calling her.

Leonard calls me tells me he's coming to town, he says he's touring with a rock band, they have a show in Chicago. I ask him what band he tells me I laugh ask him what the fuck is he doing touring with a rock band he tells me the singer is a friend and he felt like having a strange summer. I ask him if he wants me to meet him at his hotel, he says no he's staying somewhere else, he tells me where I start walking downtown.

The hotel is on Michigan Avenue, across the street from his regular hotel. Its lobby is also several stories up, above a high-end shopping center. I take an elevator to the lobby. The doors open to a vast room that takes up the entire floor of the building. Along one wall are the reception and concierge desks, along the other three are floor-to-ceiling windows. In the middle of the room there are tables and chairs, long, luxurious sofas, waiters and wait-resses carrying trays of appetizers and drinks. I look for Leonard, see him sitting on a sofa with several women and one man. I recognize the man as the singer of the band. I walk toward them, Leonard sees me coming, stands, yells.

MY SON, MY SON!

I wave, laugh. Everyone on the couch turns and looks at me.

MY SON HAS ARRIVED.

What's up, Leonard?

Living the rock 'n roll lifestyle, loving the rock 'n roll lifestyle.

I laugh again, sit down in a chair across from Leonard. He introduces me to the singer and the women. The singer, who also plays the drums, is in his early forties, has short graying hair, the slight accent of a Texas childhood, he wears jeans and t-shirt. None of the women are older than twenty, and on a scale of one to ten, they all rank somewhere around fifty. They each wear different versions of almost nothing, which is fine with me. Although Leonard seems perfectly comfortable with them, he doesn't really fit in. He is significantly older than all of them, and his clothes are more like those of an accountant. The singer and the girls are all drinking, Leonard has a pitcher of water. I order a cola and sit and listen to the singer tell stories about his life on the road as a rock star. He talks about trashing hotel rooms, orgies in the backs of buses, sets of twins, a set of triplets, about things in his contract that venues are required to provide, such as peanut butter cups stacked in perfect pyramids and cans of cola cooled to exactly thirty-six degrees. The girls hang on every word. Leonard seems to know the stories, adds certain details to them and says that's rock 'n roll, man, that's rock 'n roll at

280

the end of each of them. I just sit and laugh, though I'm not sure if I'm laughing with the singer or at the singer. At the end of a story about a particularly randy mother and daughter team, which draws big laughs and several oohs and ahhs, the singer says he needs to go upstairs and meditate before he leaves for the show. One of the girls asks him what kind of meditation he practices and he invites her to come upstairs with him so that he can show her. She obliges and they leave together.

The rest of the girls, now sitting with Leonard and me leave fairly quickly, each inventing a different excuse. When the last of them is gone, Leonard looks at me and he speaks.

What'd you think?

About him or them?

Them.

I love them all.

He laughs.

And him?

He was fine.

Leonard laughs again.

He's a dick.

I laugh.

He is, he's a dick.

Why do you hang out with him?

Because this is fun. I rock, I roll, I live it, I love it. And even though he's a dick, he's a fun dick.

I laugh.

You're doing good?

Yeah.

Anything new?

I got that girl in Hollywood to read my script.

Leonard smiles.

You just kept bugging her and finally she caved in?

I nod, smile.

Yeah.

What'd she say?

She said it's really good, that I could probably sell it, that I should move out there and try to keep doing it.

Leonard smiles, claps his hands.

That's fucking great.

There's more.

More, what kind of more?

After we finished talking about the script, we just kept talking. First night we talked for five hours. Next night five more. For the last three nights we've been up until dawn just talking.

What do you talk about?

I don't know. Everything and nothing. We just talk.

Talk for hours and hours and hours?

Yeah.

What's her name?

Liza.

That's a good name, a strong name. Are you in love?

I've never met her.

Are you in love?

I don't know.

My oh my, this is fucking wonderful. You're in love and you're moving to LA.

I'm not moving.

Why?

I'm just not.

Are you fucking crazy?

No.

You just got a new job, right?

Yeah.

What are you doing?

I work at a frame store. I'm the cashier.

That's a bullshit job.

Yeah it is.

You'd rather do that than be a writer?

No.

Then move to LA where you can make silly movie money doing what you want and spend time with the girl you stay up all night talking to.

I don't want to leave here.

Why?

I just don't.

You gotta let her go.

What?

You heard me. You gotta let her go.

This isn't about that.

You don't want to admit it, but it is.

No it's not.

You leave here and you leave her and you leave your memories and leave all those dreams you had behind and you finally let go.

Fuck you, Leonard.

She left you, you gotta leave her.

Fuck you, Leonard.

She did what she thought was right for her, you gotta do what's right for you. You respect her decision, and you know she'd respect your decision.

Fuck you, Leonard.

And if you don't leave, ten years from now you're gonna look back and regret it, and you're gonna hate yourself for being a coward and you're gonna hate Lilly for keeping you here and you'd know you fucked-up and blew it.

FUCKING DROP IT, LEONARD.

I'll drop it, but you should think about it, and we're going to talk more about it.

I look away. Leonard doesn't speak, just lets it sit there. I turn back, speak.

What time's the concert?

The opening band is at seven, but they're no good. They don't rock like a good band should rock, so fuck them. We should show up at around eight thirty.

You want us to meet you here?

Who you bringing?

My friend Erin.

Good, I like Erin. She dresses well, speaks well, has a nice smile and a nice laugh. I'll pick you up at seven thirty at your apartment.

I stand.

See you then.

Think about it, my son.

I walk home and I take a shower. I hang out with

284

Julianne she has a beer and I have a cola, I let her talk listen to her talk even though her accent has become familiar I still love to listen to it. Erin shows up a little early. She has a beer. We wait for Leonard who arrives at exactly seven thirty. We walk out of the apartment. There's a large black limo waiting at the curb, a uniformed driver standing near the open rear door. I look at Leonard, speak.

Black?

He speaks.

Yeah, black.

I thought you only drove white cars?

There's an exception to every rule and the exception to that rule extends to limousines, because white limousines are silly.

I laugh. We get into the limo and the driver closes the door behind us.

There's a fridge stocked with cola and champagne, a television, a stereo.

Leonard and I drink cola, Erin drinks champagne, and we listen to music by the band we're going to see as we drive out to the venue. When we get there we're waved into a reserved parking area and we're led to our seats, front and center, by a representative of the band. The show starts and the singer, who may be an asshole in his life, rocks the fucking house once he's on stage. I rock with him, Erin rocks with him, Leonard rocks with him.

We rock and fucking roll all night.

Live it, love it.

I think about leaving. I think about Lilly. I think about my life and what I want from it, I think about these things as I walk, as I work, as I eat, as I shower, as I read, while I'm on the phone, when I'm with my friends. My last thoughts before I sleep, my first thoughts as I wake, I think about leaving here.

I sit before her. I sit and I stare at the stone, at her name, at the dates of her life, at the words, You were Loved, at the words You were Loved. I sit before her and I remember the first time we met she smiled and said hello we were standing in line at the clinic medical unit and she turned around and she smiled and she said hello. I remember our first cigarette she said want a smoke, tough guy and she laughed at me. I remember the first time we were alone she came upon me in the woods I was broken and she held me and said you'll be okay, you'll be okay, and as long as she held me I was okay. I remember our first kiss, the way she tasted, her breath, the smell of her skin, the way my heart beat, beat, beat. I remember every minute of our time, every minute spent hiding from people who told us we shouldn't be together, every conversation, every kiss. I remember her eyes those beautiful blue eyes like deep water, I remember staring into those eyes and knowing. I remember how her hand felt small and fragile and stronger than I thought it could be. I remember her hair long and black a beautiful mess she used to hide it from the world with a baseball cap. I remember her smooth cold pale skin like marble the way my hands felt as they moved around it. I remember the scars on her wrists I thought were behind her. I remember crying with her and for her and because of her. I remember laughing with her and for her and because of her. I remember the peace I knew with her, the security I knew with her, the strength I knew with her, the hope I knew with her, the love I knew with her. I knew love with her, love like nothing before it. We had dreams, plans, we were going to spend our lives together. We carried each other through blackness and I thought through death and I was wrong. She did what she did. I don't hate her for it anymore. I'm going to do what I'm going to do. I start to cry. Some of the tears are sadness and sorrow, some are pain and rage, some are for loss, some for forgiveness and some of them, the best of them, are because I am fortunate to have known her at all. I lean toward the stone where she lies and I cry and I whisper I love you, Lilly, and I'll be back to see you, I love you, I'll miss you and I'll be back.

I stand and I walk away.

It's time to go.

LOS ANGELES

My second friend with the name Kevin lives in Los Angeles. He's an actor who lives in a Hollywood apartment and takes acting classes and goes to auditions and waits tables and struggles. We went to college together. He's twenty-six, but looks eighteen, he has dark wavy hair and blue eyes and big rosy cheeks. He likes to talk and he's funny most of the time and he's easy to be with most of the time and he wants to drive with me from Chicago to Los Angeles. It'll be good to have him.

He comes to Chicago and we pack up my truck and plan our route. We're going to cut straight across the Midwest, head south into New Mexico, cross Arizona, Nevada and California.

We leave early the next morning. As we pull out I stop at a random corner in a rundown neighborhood. I take my bottle of rose, the bottle I bought when I arrived, the bottle I've had during my entire time here, the bottle I've always kept as an option, and I leave it unopened on the corner. I hope somebody finds it, and I hope they enjoy it.

We drive straight west through hours and hours of farmland, hundreds of miles blend together in a sea of gently waving green and yellow, every red barn white farmhouse gray silo looks the same. We stop in Kansas City for the night, get up early, keep going. In Colorado we cut south, head into New Mexico. Kevin gets a message about an important audition, he needs to be back in LA sooner than planned. We decide to keep going straight to California, we'll stop for gas and food, we'll drive in shifts one sleeps while one drives. Kevin starts checking the fluids every time we stop for gas, he checks the oil, coolant, wiper. I tell him not to worry about it, that the car was just tuned-up and is in good shape. He tells me he's just being careful. We cross the mountains of New Mexico, drop into Arizona, it's two in the morning, I pull into a truckstop. I go inside for coffee and cigarettes Kevin starts checking everything again. Ten minutes later we pull out.

It is the middle of the night. We're in the middle of the desert. Kevin isn't talking anymore we're both tired he tells me he's going to sleep. I turn on the radio. I listen to someone talking about storm-troopers who fly around in black helicopters and kidnap and brainwash people who speak out against the government. It's part of a conspiracy controlled by the Freemasons and the Jews. I start to hear a strange ticking coming from the engine. I start to smell burning plastic. I laugh, think maybe the Freemasons and the Jews are after me. The ticking becomes louder, the smell stronger. There is a large BOOM, the engine immediately loses power, smoke starts pouring from beneath the hood, the smell is overwhelming. Kevin wakes up and says what's happened, what's going on, I tell him something seems to be wrong with the engine and I think it has to do with Freemasons and Jews, and I guide the car to the shoulder of the highway. We get out of the car Kevin is still confused.

What happened?

I don't know.

We've got to get away. I think the car is going to explode.

I think we're okay.

What's wrong with it?

I look at the truck. It is smoking less, it still smells awful.

I have no idea. Something bad happened.

How?

Did you put all the caps and shit back on?

Of course I did, I'm not stupid.

Just checking.

We stand and stare at the truck. The smoke is almost gone. We stand and stare for a couple of minutes. It is the middle of the night. We're in the middle of the desert. I look at Kevin.

Looks like we're fucked.

Try to start it.

It's not gonna start.

Just try.

I get in the truck, try to start it. Loud clicking

noises come from beneath the hood, it doesn't start. I get out.

Didn't start.

Maybe if we wait awhile.

We wait for ten minutes. Not a single car or truck passes us. I try to start the engine, same thing. Kevin speaks.

What do you want to do?

Sit here.

We sit there. A couple cars pass by, no one stops. Thirty minutes a state trooper pulls over. An officer gets out of the cruiser, for the first time in my life I'm thrilled to see a law enforcement officer walking toward me. He asks what we're doing we tell him the truck broke down. He asks where we're from and going and I tell him. He asks us if we know what's wrong with the truck I say no idea. He goes back to his cruiser, gets on the radio, speaks for a few minutes, comes back.

I called a mechanic I know who has a tow truck. He can come get you if you want, but it's not gonna be cheap. If you don't want to do that, you can wait till morning and the highway patrol will tow the car.

Can your guy get here faster?

It's the middle of the night and he's not close.

I don't want to wait till morning.

I'll call my guy. He can be here in an hour.

The trooper goes back to the cruiser gets on the radio, he comes back and tells us the mechanic is coming. He gets back in the cruiser and drives away.

We wait. I sit on the side of the road and smoke cigarettes. Kevin paces back and forth, he's worried we won't get back in time for his audition. An hour passes, two hours it is starting to get light when we see a tow truck approaching us. It pulls over behind us, a tall skinny man his arms covered with tattoos, a cigarette dangling from his lips, gets out of the truck starts ambling toward us he speaks.

Looks like you're having some trouble here.

Yeah.

What happened?

Funny noises and smoke.

Pop that hood the fuck up.

I reach in, pop the hood. He opens it, looks at the engine. Kevin and I stand behind him, watch him as he looks around the engine, he turns around.

You're fucked, man, fucking fucked.

What happened?

Your engine blew up.

How?

Was somebody messing around with it?

I motion toward Kevin. The man speaks.

He forgot to put the radiator cap back on and all your coolant evaporated and the thing, boom, blew the fuck up.

Kevin speaks.

Impossible.

Nah, that's what happened. I'm looking at it.

I put the cap on.

It ain't there, and as far as I know, they can't take themselves off.

Kevin gets angry, defensive.

You're not funny.

Ain't trying to be funny, just trying to tell you what happened, and what happened is there ain't no radiator cap on here and the motherfucking engine blew.

That's not what happened.

I look at the mechanic, speak.

How long will it take to fix it?

He thinks for a moment, speaks.

Probably a week, ten days. Ain't quick, this kind of job.

Kevin speaks.

A week?

At least, man. The engine is fucked, that shit is fucking fried.

Kevin turns to me.

I have to be back, I have to be back soon.

I look at the mechanic.

Any way to do it faster.

Nope.

Is there a truck rental place nearby?

In Flagstaff.

How far is that?

110 miles or so or something like that.

Can you tow us there?

I'll tow you to Japan if you fucking pay me, man. I'll tow you anywhere.

How much will it cost?

Well, it's four thirty in the morning and I fucking hate Flagstaff and my wife don't like me right now and I need some money to make her happy, so it's gonna be pricey.

How much?

Seven hundred fifty bucks.

No way.

Five hundred bucks.

Three fifty.

My wife's really fucking mad, man, I need five large.

Fine let's go.

The mechanic goes back to his truck, pulls it in front of my truck, starts hitching my truck to the towing mechanism on the back of his truck. Kevin is still angry, still doesn't believe this is happening, absolutely doesn't believe he had anything to do with it. I get in next to the mechanic, Kevin is next to me, we start driving toward Flagstaff.

We watch the sun rise over desolate flats. The mechanic talks and smokes he talks about his wife he says she hates him, about his two brothers he says they hate him, about his girlfriend he says she hates him. He talks about his truck he calls it Wayne it is his prized possession. He talks about shooting guns in the desert he's hoping to find someone who will sell him a bazooka so he can do some, he says, real true-to-life destruction-style shit. I listen to the mechanic and laugh for most of the trip. Kevin stares out the window, clenches his jaw and shakes his head.

We pull into Flagstaff. It is still early morning. Almost everything is closed we find a gas station with coffee and cigarettes and beef jerky. The mechanic drops us, with my truck, in the parking lot of a truck rental company. I write him a check, he says thank you and advises me to leave Flagstaff as soon as possible. I ask him why he says strange things happen around here. I ask him what he shakes his head and says man, just trust me, there is fucking ugly, scary, wack-ass shit in the air here. He gets in his truck and leaves us.

Kevin and I sit and wait. We have two hours until the office opens Kevin spends most of it cursing the mechanic and his faulty diagnosis. When the office opens I rent a large truck and a trailer and I push my poor broken-down truck onto the trailer. We start driving west. I haven't slept in twenty-four hours. The desert plays tricks with my mind with my eyes I see mirages, I see silver flashes, blue lights. I drink coffee, smoke cigarettes, turn the volume on the radio all the way up, hallucinate.

Once we enter Los Angeles County it takes four hours to go sixty miles.

When we pull into West Hollywood I can't think straight, see straight, walk straight. I leave the trucks my truck on the trailer and the big truck on the side of a street they take up half a block.

I call Leonard I told him I'd call as soon as I arrived. He wants to have lunch with me. He gives me the name of a restaurant, tells me he'll be there on Wednesday at one o'clock.

I get a ride to the restaurant. I arrive a few minutes early. I walk inside the Maitre d' is at a stand just inside the front door. I give him Leonard's name he tells me that Leonard has not arrived I should wait for him at the bar.

I walk to the bar, which is a few feet behind him. I sit down on a stool, look around me. It's crowded, noisy, I am the youngest person in the restaurant, and the worst-dressed. Most of the customers are middle-aged men in suits, the suits are all gray, black or navy blue they look like expensive suits. Most of the men are immaculately groomed perfect hair, smooth tans, manicured hands, those that aren't look deliberately ruffled, as if they spent the morning in front of the mirror making sure their hair was just the right kind of messy. The walls are covered with cartoon drawings of famous people almost all men who are regular customers, some are movie stars, some athletes, some famous directors and producers. I order a nice cold tasty cola and I wait for Leonard.

He arrives five minutes later he's wearing a suit, he's with the Snapper who is also wearing a suit. He sees me I stand we hug each other.

Welcome to California, my son.

Thanks, Leonard.

We separate, I shake hands with Snapper.

Welcome, kid.

Thanks, Snap.

The Maitre d' leads us to a table. We sit in a booth along a wall Leonard and Snap sit on one side, I sit on the other side. Leonard speaks.

Here you are, in the land of sunshine and dreams. You will either love it or hate it, and you will either flourish or fail.

I'm looking forward to finding out.

Love it, my son, and flourish. FLOURISH.

What are you doing in town?

I was seeing a nutritionist.

Why?

Because I want to live forever.

I laugh.

Seriously?

Yes, seriously. A proper diet may be the key to immortality. I would like to be immortal.

I laugh again.

That's crazy, Leonard.

Snapper speaks.

That's what I told him.

Leonard speaks.

To each his own.

You really think a special diet will make you immortal?

No, I don't, but I do think it'll keep me here awhile longer.

Probably.

Definitely. So, now I'm going to see this nutritionist once a week, on Wednesdays, for the foreseeable future.

I look at Snapper.

Do you go?

Snapper speaks.

Fuck no. I like cheeseburgers, pizza, fried chicken, ice cream, all the good stuff. I don't care if it kills me, I'm eating it.

I'm with you.

I'll dance on your graves, spin and yelp and sing happy gravedancing songs.

I laugh, Snapper speaks.

If I die, it won't be cause my fucking diet.

We all laugh. A waiter comes to our table says hello to Leonard says nice to see you again, sir he gives us menus we order. I get a ribeye and creamed spinach, Snapper gets a porterhouse, French fries, onion rings, tomatoes and onions and a blue cheese salad, Leonard orders a chopped salad. As we wait for the food Leonard asks about Liza I tell him it's too early to tell. He asks where I'm living I tell him I'm living at Liza's. He asks about my job prospects I tell him I may work shitty production jobs while I try to sell the script.

He tells me he has friends in Hollywood that will help if I want them to, I tell him I want to do this on my own. The waiter brings Snapper and me steak knives, refills our drinks. As he walks away another man walks toward us, Snapper sees him alerts Leonard to his presence.

The man is probably in his fifties, but looks older. He has dark wavy hair it looks like it's been dyed, he's extremely thin and extremely tan his skin looks like leather. He's wearing a suit and a sparkling watch and a pinkie ring. Snapper looks at Leonard speaks.

He still owe you?

Leonard speaks.

Yeah he does.

How do you want to handle it?

I don't want to deal with him. This is not the time or the place.

The man arrives at our table looks nervous slightly shaky he's starting to sweat he speaks.

Hello, Leonard.

Leonard looks at him, speaks.

It isn't a good time.

I need to speak to you.

It isn't a good time.

I'm sorry about my payments, I really am, I won't miss . . .

Snapper interrupts.

We're having lunch. We would like you to leave.

The man continues. Leonard looks away.

I'm sorry, Leonard. If you could just give me . . .

Snapper interrupts again.

We would like you to leave.

People at tables near us turn, start watching, Leonard shakes his head, the man continues.

Please, Leonard, please . . .

I see Snapper reach for his steak knife the man doesn't see it he's looking at Leonard who's looking away. BOOM. Snapper slams the knife into the table and pulls his hand away. The knife is sticking straight into the table it's wobbling a bit the man looks shocked. Snapper stands, towers over him, stares at him, speaks.

It isn't a good time.

Everyone near us is silent, staring, the man's eyes are wide and filled with fear, he turns and walks out of the restaurant. Snapper sits back down, takes the knife out of the table, wipes it with his napkin. Leonard speaks.

That guy's a fuckhead.

Snapper speaks.

Just say the word.

Fuck him. Let's enjoy our lunch.

Snapper chuckles.

Someday you'll let me.

Our food comes we eat Leonard eyes my steak I offer him some he says no. After we finish eating we order dessert Snapper gets cheesecake I get a hot fudge sundae Leonard gets a fruit plate. After dessert Leonard says I'll see you next Wednesday?

I say I'll see you next Wednesday.

I stay with Liza we talk for hours I get along better with her than any woman I've ever met we laugh and laugh we sit and talk for hours. As easy as it is to be with each other and as much as we like each other there's still something missing. We both feel it we both know it there's something missing between us and we both mourn it.

I take my battered truck to get fixed it's going to take ten days.

I drive around with Liza start to get a feel for the city. It's a strange city, unlike traditional cities. There is no central downtown. What is called downtown is a ghost town, empty but for a few high-rise office towers filled during the day. The only residents of downtown Los Angeles are the people who live in a self-governing ten block area filled with cardboard box houses and tents. The rest of the city is broken into small neighborhoods, though there is no feeling of neighborhood in them. The sidewalks are empty, people don't interact with each other. There is a feeling that people are living where they are and waiting to move somewhere better, that the dream is almost fulfilled, and when it is, they'll move to one of the wealthy areas of the city and finally make friends with those that live around them.

I find a house. It's a three-bedroom Spanish-style house on a busy street.

It stand out among the other houses on its block because the front yard is filled with garbage. I walk around the side of the house and the backyard is also filled with garbage. I look in the windows of the garage it's filled with garbage, I look in the windows of the house also filled with garbage. I ask one of the neighbors what's happening with this house she tells me no one has lived there for three years, occasionally a truck comes by and drops off more crap. I go downtown to the city tax office find out who owns the house call them. I ask them if they'd be interested in getting the house cleaned up and fixed-up, tell them I'll do it for free if they'll let me live there. The man tells me to meet him at the house later in the afternoon I meet him his name is Al he's a mechanic and inherited the house from his grandmother. He agrees to let me live there he also wants a small amount of rent fine with me.

I clean the entire house, the yard, the garage. I tear out carpets there are nice wood floors beneath them. I get a mattress, a desk and a table, somewhere to sleep somewhere to work somewhere to eat. I get a roommate.

His name is Jaylen. I know him from Chicago, where he was a wholesale weed dealer, never selling less than a pound at a time. He says he's through selling weed, that he wants to be a music video director.

I go out every night. Go out to bars with my friends, friends from the old days who have migrated here, all are working in some area of the entertainment industry. We go to the Three of Clubs, the Room, Smalls, DragonFly, the Snakepit, Jones, El Coyote. The bars are filled with beautiful young people it's as if the three best-looking people from every town in the country have come to Los Angeles. Everyone wants to be famous, everyone is well-connected. Everyone is just a step or two away they're waiting for that break it's almost there they can taste it fucking taste it.

I miss Chicago. I miss my friends, miss walking, miss seeing Lilly, miss living without ambition. Los Angeles is a lonely city. Everyone is focused on advancement success fame and money, it is hard to adjust to a culture based on always wanting more, on never being satisfied. I'm lonely, I miss my old life.

I see Leonard for lunch every Wednesday. He looks thinner and in better shape each time. Snapper and I both eat steaks and multiple side dishes and dessert, Leonard sticks with salad and fruit.

I decide I want a dog. I start paying attention to other people's dogs, to their temperaments, to their habits, to their needs, their cost. I meet a pitbull named Grace 2000. Grace 2000 is short and heavily muscled, white with brown patches, she has deep brown sparkling eyes. She's very excitable, runs in circles around my friend's house, loves to play catch.

Sometimes she bites the end of a spring attached to a thick branch of a tree and bounces from it. Sometimes she chases her tail. She never barks and she loves to give kisses. She's a fifty pound ball of energy and love.

I decide that I want a dog like Grace. I buy a paper, look in the classifieds, see ad after ad after ad, pitbull pitbull pitbull. One of the ads says Sons of Cholo. I didn't know what Cholo means or who Cholo is, but I like the sound of it, so I call the number and get an address. I start driving.

The address is in East Los Angeles, in a working-class Hispanic neighborhood. I park walk toward the house there are two men sitting on the front porch they're drinking beer and smoking cigarettes their arms are covered with tattoos. I stop in front of them, they stare at me, I say hello they nod.

I ask if they're selling the dogs, they say no habla inglés. I don't speak Spanish so I hold up the paper, say Sons of Cholo, they smile, nod, one of them stands up and motions for me to follow him.

We walk around the house. In the backyard there is a small fenced area.

Inside the fence is a small doghouse. The man whistles and a giant pit storms out of the doghouse and starts barking.

I've never seen a dog like him in my life. He's short and gigantic, has layers and layers of rippling muscle, his coat is the color of milk chocolate and he has bright green eyes. His head is huge and thick, as if carved from a block of stone, and it's covered with scars. He stands at the fence and snarles at me, his teeth are huge and a perfect white. I stare at him. He barks and snarls, looks like he wants to eat me, I am scared to death of him. The man taps me on the shoulder and points and smiles and says *Cholo, undefeated campeón.* He motions for me to follow him.

We walk to a garage. He lifts the door and puppies begin streaming out, adorable little chocolate puppies, small versions of Cholo, minus the scars, minus the snarling. They yip and tumble over each other, jump on my feet, bite at the bottom of my pants. The man points to the puppies and says Sons of Cholo.

I smile, sit down on the concrete. The puppies

run into my lap, start jumping on my chest, licking my face. A hierarchy has been established among them and the larger puppies start muscling the smaller puppies away. The smallest of them falls off my lap and immediately starts climbing back. He gets pushed off again, starts climbing again. All he wants is to get close enough to lick my face.

I stand up, the puppies start nipping at my feet again, I look at the man and point to the smallest puppy. The man nods and holds up three fingers. The price had been listed in the advertisement, I brought cash with me. I take it out of my pocket and hand it to him he picks up the puppy and hands him to me. We shake hands he says gracias I say gracias.

I walk toward my car. The puppy starts whining. The further we get from the garage, the louder the whining. When I open the driver's door, the puppy starts crying, looking toward the garage, where the other Sons of Cholo are still running around. I sit down in the driver's seat. I brought some puppy toys and puppy treats with me, I hold the little fellow in my lap and try to get him interested in them, he just looks toward the garage and cries. I give up trying to make him stop and I start the car and I drive away.

He sits in my lap on the ride back to my house. He cries and he shakes.

He pees on me, pees on the seat, pees on the floor. Son of Cholo is scared to death, and he pees all over me.

I call the puppy Cassius. He's a smart pup he knows his name after a few days. I potty train him in a week. He can sit, shake, stay, lie down in two weeks. He goes everywhere with me, rides shotgun in my truck, sleeps in my bed.

I go to parties with my friends. We go to apartments to the courtyards of apartment buildings to houses in the Hollywood Hills. When I meet new people the first question they usually ask me is what do you do? I tell them I am an unemployed aspiring writer and they realize I can't help them in any way and they can't use me in any way and they usually walk away from me.

I send out my script everywhere to everyone I meet who might be interested in it I call them follow up with them no luck no luck. Hearing people say no doesn't bother me, doesn't discourage me. I'm confident in what I can do and I believe that, to a certain extent, I'm playing a numbers game. If I get myself and my work in front of enough people, sooner or later someone will like it.

I go back to trying to write a book I spend most of my time staring at a blank computer screen.

Jaylen and I decide to fill the third bedroom in our house, figure it will be good to have someone to share expenses. Jaylen brings an old friend from Chicago to the house, his name is Tommy. Tommy is Korean, grew up in a small farm town forty miles west of Chicago, his father and mother are both doctors. Tommy dresses like a thug and talks like a thug with a thick inner-city accent. He wants to be either a rap-star, a deejay or a rap video director. I ask him if he ever feels like a phony with his clothes and his accent and he says motherfucker, I grew up in the fields, but my heart's from the motherfucking streets. I ask him if he's ever been in a fight, been arrested, held a gun or dealt drugs, he says he keeps it real with a peaceful vibe.

I see Leonard on Wednesdays he is always thinner, always looks healthier.

Leonard calls says it's a big, big day, round up some friends I'm taking you to dinner. I ask why it's a big day, he says I'll tell you when I see you. I ask when and where he says he'll pick me up at my house, round up some motherfucking friends. I call Liza, Mike, Jenny, Quinn, Mark, my friend Andy who is visiting from New York. Everyone meets at my house, Leonard arrives in his white Mercedes, Snapper is driving. There isn't enough room in his car so my friends drive their cars and I ride with Leonard. Leonard has a small briefcase at his feet. I look at it, speak.

That's not for me, is it?

Leonard speaks.

You're retired.

Good.

And I want to do this one myself.

Does that have to do with this being a big day?

Indeed it does.

I don't need to know anymore.

You can ask if you want.

I don't want to know.

You can ask.

That's okay.

Really, it's fine. Ask away.

No thanks.

Snapper turns around.

He wants you to fucking ask him, so ask him.

I look at Leonard, speak.

What does that briefcase have to do with the big day?

Leonard smiles.

My last truly illegal act.

I laugh.

Congratulations.

He nods.

It's a big fucking day.

Why are you bringing me and my friends with you?

For a celebration.

Are we at risk?

Of course not.

What's happening?

Russkies.

Russkies?

Yeah, the Russkies have come to town.

So what?

Leonard looks at Snapper.

You want to take this one?

Snapper nods.

Sure.

Leonard looks back at me.

He's taking this one.

I nod.

I got it.

Snapper speaks.

Russians are mean bastards, have always been mean bastards. They kicked Napoleon's ass, kicked Hitler's ass, kicked every ass they ever encountered. When people like us started coming over here, the Russkies were in Russia and had no interest. Then the Soviet Union kept 'em locked up for seventy years. Now those fuckers are free, and they see what we got, and there's fucking hordes of 'em coming over here, and like I said, they're mean fucking bastards. If I'm a six on the mean scale, they're twelves. They're greedy and aggressive, and now that we're legal, I think we'd just as soon step the fuck out of their way. We can't, however, just step away, because then we look weak and scared and then we get popped. So we work out a deal. We give them certain considerations that they want, they give us a bag of Russian sparklies that we sell. Everybody wins, everybody's happy, nothing bad happens. We're through with all the illegal rackets we had, and we can't get caught for nothing, except maybe tax cheating, which might happen, because this is gonna be the first year I ever filed a tax return, and the IRS notices that shit.

You have a good accountant?

He laughs.

I do, at least I think I do, and I better, or he's in trouble.

He chuckles again.

Tax return. I'm actually excited about it.

I laugh, turn to Leonard.

So what's in your briefcase?

Nothing. It's empty.

And you're trading it for one that looks like it, but isn't empty?

You learned well, my son. You were a natural.

I laugh. We turn on Sunset start heading east, away from the glamour of the Sunset Strip and into the reality of Hollywood. The apartment blocks are lined with decrepit buildings. Because it is night, there are hookers, women who are women and men who are women and some unknown, walking up and down the street, standing in small groups on corners, they wave and shake their asses and flash their tits and yell at us as we drive past them. Every other shop is a pawnshop, the windows are filled with guitars and amps and drumsets filled with the dead dreams of rock super-stardom. There is a Space Burger restaurant their burgers are out of this world, there is a diner filled with people sitting alone staring out the window. It's a common sight in Los Angeles, someone sitting alone staring out the window.

We pull off Sunset. We pull up to a valet in front of what looks like a Mosque. It's a large white building with a gold dome, it has spikes along the edges of the roof, iron doors with engraved Arabic words. We get out of the car. Snapper waves off the valet pulls down the street I look at Leonard, speak.

What the fuck is this?

Leonard smiles.

Belly dance!

Belly dance?

Yeah, belly dance!

My friends pull up get out of their cars. They seem to know the place I ask them if any of them have been here they say no. Leonard leads us inside. There is a large central room, it's a light room, an open room. There is a fountain in the center of the room, an ornate tile floor, mosaics cover the walls. There are smaller rooms off the central room, smaller rooms in every direction, they're dark rooms, thick dark oriental rugs cover the floors, they're lit by candles there are people sitting on cushions on the floor. Leonard greets the host who leads us to one of the smaller rooms. We sit on cushions around a low, circular table. A waiter brings us water and menus Leonard waves off the menus, orders for the table. Snapper joins us sets the briefcase near his feet.

Leonard introduces himself to my friends, introduces Snapper. He asks them where they're from, why they live in Los Angeles, how they know me. Snapper sits, doesn't speak, occasionally glances toward the entrance to our room, occasionally glances at his watch.

A first round of food is delivered. It comes on large round plates. The plates have sections for meats lamb and beef, thick flat bread, dark heavy sauces. None of us knows what it is or how to eat it Leonard tells us it's Persian we eat it with our hands just dip the bread and the meat into the sauces don't worry about the mess don't worry about manners. The food is rich, strong, spicy, my friends drink beer I drink water. As we finish the plates, I see Snapper nod to Leonard they both stand with the briefcase. Leonard excuses them they leave the room.

Our plates are taken away we wait.

Our drinks are refilled we wait.

Liza asks if I know where Leonard is I say I have no idea. Mark asks if we should order more food I say I'm pretty sure it's covered. More food arrives it never stops. We wait.

I think about going out to find them to make sure everything is okay, I laugh at myself know I'd last about five seconds against some mean fucking Russkie. I think about going to speak with the host I hear a bell, multiple bells, moving toward the entrance to our room. Above the bells I hear Leonard laughing, saying woohoo, woohoo, saying shake it shake it shake it. Everyone at the table turns toward the entrance. A belly dancer, in a traditional belly dancing outfit, her hips wiggling her stomach gesticulating cymbals on her fingers clashing clashing comes shaking into the room. She is followed by another dancer who is followed by Leonard hooting and laughing who is followed by a man with a guitar frantically strumming who is followed by two waiters with giant trays of food who are followed by a smiling Snapper carrying a

317

briefcase identical to the one he was carrying when he left the room. The belly dancers start moving around the table. The waiters set the trays on the table, start unloading heaping bowls of rice and platters with stacks of kebabs beef, lamb and chicken. Leonard follows the dancers, pretending to be one of them, making a complete fool of himself, knowing he's doing it, laughing. Snapper sits back down, smiles. My friends eat, drink, watch the show, laugh. Leonard sits and picks at a chicken kebab he says I'm watching my weight has the dancers start dancing again. Whenever I look at Snapper he nods and smiles, two or three times he mouths the words tax return, oh yeah, tax return, oh yeah. We stay at the restaurant for hours eating more drinking more listening to music watching the dancers laughing laughing laughing.

It's all legal now.

Snapper is going to file a tax return.

The phone rings I pick it up Leonard speaks.

MY SON MY SON MY SON.

I laugh.

Hi, Leonard.

How you doing?

I'm good. You?

I'm very upset with myself.

Why?

I forgot to give you the secret.

What secret?

The secret to kicking ass in dumbshit Hollywood.

You know it?

Of course I fucking know it.

I laugh again.

What is it?

Be bold.

Be bold.

But not bold, be fucking **BOLD**.

Okay.

Every time you meet someone, make a fucking impression. Make them think you're the hottest

319

shit in the world. Make them think they're gonna lose their job if they don't give you one. Look 'em in the eye, and never look away. Be confident and calm, be fucking bold.

That sounds more like the secret to kicking ass in life.

It is, but I was gonna wait and tell you that some other time.

Liza and her friend Mitch find a play they want to make into a short film. They ask if I want to direct it I say yes. Liza convinces the famous director she works for to fund half of it, her friend Mitch convinces the famous producer he works for to fund the other half of it. I'm not sure I'm a director, I have no real experience with actors and don't really know how a camera works, but I pretend to be one, and pretending seems to be all that matters in Hollywood. Pretend to be something, be convincing, and people will treat you differently, as if you actually are what you are pretending to be. It's a game, embarrassing and fake, but it is a means to an end here, so I play the game, and I quickly learn that I play it pretty well.

Tommy and Jaylen decide they're going to be deejay partners. They pool all of their money and they buy two turntables, a sound system and several crates of records. They stop working, spend all of their time smoking weed and spinning records.

Cassius grows and grows and grows. At four months he weighs thirty pounds at five he weighs forty at six he weighs fifty. The weight is all muscle.

His coordination lags behind his growth so he stumbles and trips and seems confused by his own size.

I start to sleep again. I get used to going to bed without the rumbling and shaking of the El train.

I go to meetings with development executives. I go to meetings with agents. Development executives are people who read scripts, hire writers to write or re-write scripts, agents are the people who arrange for the jobs and negotiate the deals. The meetings are general meetings, which means we say hello, nice to meet you, they tell me they've heard great things about me, I tell them the same thing, and we spend the next hour kissing each other's asses. I try to make an impression with everyone I meet follow Leonard's advice speak simply and directly and look everyone in the eye. Part of me hates going to the meetings they're fake and stupid and I feel insecure after each of them, part of me knows I need to and I have to if I want to work and make money. Part of me is happy that I'm doing something other than making deliveries, working a bullshit job or going for walks. It feels good to actually do something.

Tommy and Jaylen start throwing parties at our house. They set up the turntables in our living room and charge ten dollars to walk in the door. The parties start at midnight and end sometime near dawn. The parties keep me awake, I can't fucking sleep.

We finish the movie. Liza and Mitch want to have a screening and a party. The studio where they work has a theater they convince the man who runs it to let us use it.

I tell my parents, who I talk to once a week or so, they want to come to the screening. I tell Leonard he wants to come to the screening. Liza and Mitch send out invitations they say there's going to be a crowd of people at the screening, actors and directors and writers and agents and managers and producers. Most of them, Liza tells me, will be coming to see if they like my movie and want to work with me. I ask her how they know about me she tells me that she and Mitch have big mouths. I thank her, thank him. The days leading up to the screening drag I'm nervous. If it goes well I'll get work, if it goes poorly I'll be forgotten. I feel good about the movie but I also know that it's not going to change the world. If I fail, I fail. I've been through worse.

My parents arrive. They recently moved from Tokyo to Singapore, the trip to Los Angeles took twenty-six hours. I pick them up at the airport they're tired. I tell them I'll take them to their hotel they want to see where I live. I tell them I'll take them to their hotel. On our way we talk I ask them how the adjustment to Singapore has been, my Mom says it's a much easier place to live than Japan, everyone speaks English and they don't hate foreigners, my Dad says it's no different for him, an office is an office. They ask about Los Angeles I tell them it's fine I'm getting used to it, they ask about my friends here, they know them from before, I tell them they'll see my friends tonight. It's good to see my parents, it's easier than I expected it might be with them. Our relationship has been strained and difficult for most of my life, now it gets better and more healthy each time I see them. I know they love me they always have, I know they want the best for me they have always tried. It's good to have them here.

I drop them off at the hotel. I go home smoke cigarettes listen to Tommy and Jaylen practice, they sound worse than when they started, none of the beats match, the transitions from song to song are obvious and clunky.

Time is slow as it always is when I want it to be fast I have nothing to do but wait. I sit in my room can't think or talk on the phone because of the noise, if I make some money because of this movie I'm going to buy a bomb and blow those motherfucking turntables to bits.

I take a shower put on some nice clothing, the same clothing I used to wear when I was working for Leonard and was pretending to be a commuter. I laugh at the clothes they're dusty from lack of use I brush them off. I leave the house drive to the hotel pick up my parents. We drive to the studio, pull up to the gate, our names are on the proper list, the guard waves us through.

We park start heading toward the theater my Mom and Dad look around as we walk. Studios are large bland ugly places. The one we are on consists of a couple hundred acres of land dotted with what look like airplane hangars, a few simple office buildings built to look like houses, and a big, ugly, black tower. There is an amusement park attached to the studio where tourists pay for the privilege to be driven around the studio in long funny buses that look like giant golf carts. There are trucks and trailers parked outside of the hangars, casually dressed young people walk, ride bikes or drive golf carts, they all look like they're in a hurry. The tourists all stare at them, hope one of them is a star that they recognize from TV or the movies, my Mom asks where all the stars are, I tell her I don't know I've never seen one. My Dad asks what everyone is doing I say most of them are pretending to be busy so they don't get fired.

We get to the theater Liza and Mitch are standing outside. I introduce them to my parents, I take my parents inside and find them seats. People are starting to arrive I'm too nervous to sit down, I find Liza we walk around the back of the theater and smoke cigarettes. Five minutes before the screening is supposed to start we walk back to the front. There is a small crowd of people at the entrance, a few that I know, most I have never seen. Liza goes to talk to Mitch, I stand at the edge of the crowd wait for everyone to go inside, when they do I follow them. I stand at the door, wait for the lights to go out. I don't want anyone to see me I'm nervous, much more self-conscious than I expected to be. When the lights are out and just before the movie starts I slip in walk to the back row sit down.

I don't watch the movie, I watch people watching the movie. I watch their reactions, hope for laughs when laughs are supposed to come, hope to move them when I want to move them, hope I make them happy sad curious hopeful. The reactions are fine, not great not bad, though I doubt anything aside from being carried out on the shoulders of a cheering audience would have made me happy.

The movie ends the crowd claps. I stay in my seat in the back row while people file out of the theater. When they're gone and I am alone, I stand and I walk out. My parents, Liza, Leonard and a blond woman with Leonard are waiting for me. They all hug me congratulate me tell me it went great, tell me they're proud of me.

We walk to the party, which is at a nearby restaurant. As we walk, I meet the woman with Leonard, her name is Betty. She's tall, thin, probably in her forties but looks younger, she's wearing an expensive white silk suit and large diamond studs in her ears and a Cartier watch. I shake her hand it's soft, she smiles easily and often.

We arrive at the party. It's crowded Leonard finds a table for himself and Betty and my parents. I walk around thank people for coming.

Occasionally I stop by the table I hear bits and pieces of conversation. I hear Leonard talking to my parents he says I see him every week he's doing great. I hear him say I'm legit now, no more danger, no more illegality, I'm one hundred percent legit. I hear him say to my father I have a bunch of idiots working for me, complete and total idiots. I hear him say it'll be great, I'll pay you a fortune, a fortune, and you can live wherever you want, anywhere in the world. I watch my parents and Leonard and Betty from across the room. Leonard and my father look like they're engaged in a serious conversation, my mom and Betty are laughing and smiling. It's strange to see, my mom and dad and my criminal friend from rehab and his girlfriend sitting at a table together. Fucking strange.

At the end of the night I have a stack of business cards, people who said great work give me a call maybe we can do something together. My jaw hurts I'm not used to talking so much, I don't like talking so much. I'm glad this is over it seems to have been a success. I find Liza and Mitch and I thank them, thank them, thank them. I find my parents and Leonard tell them it's time to go we leave.

We walk to the cars we are all parked in the same place. I thank Leonard for coming he tells me he's proud of me. I tell Betty it was nice to meet her, that I hope we see each other again, she says the same thing to me.

They get in Leonard's car and drive away. My parents and I get in my car, I start driving them to their hotel. My father speaks.

Your friend Leonard is an interesting fellow.

Yeah, but you knew that already.

You know what he was talking to me about?

I'm scared to ask.

My mom starts laughing.

What's so funny, Mom?

She shakes her head, giggles.

What'd he say?

He wants me to come work for him.

I laugh, speak.

What's he want you to do?

Work for his *phone* company.

I laugh again.

You gonna do it?

I'm actually tempted.

No way.

My Mom speaks.

You should have heard his offer.

An offer you couldn't refuse?

My Dad laughs, speaks.

He said he stopped making those.

Yeah. So what was it?

A huge amount of money for six to twelve months of work.

Really?

My mom speaks.

It was a crazy amount of money.

Why only six to twelve months?

My Dad speaks.

He wouldn't say.

What would you do?

He wouldn't say that either.

Did he say anything?

That he needed someone he could trust who was outside of his organization and had extensive international business experience.

That's weird.

My mom speaks.

He's not exactly normal, James.

I chuckle.

Yeah.

I drop them off at their hotel. Leonard calls my Dad again the next day, says he would really love my Dad to reconsider his offer. My Dad says no thank you, Leonard, though I appreciate you thinking about me. I spend the next two days with my parents. We go to the beach, walk around Beverly Hills, eat at nice restaurants. I take them to my house when Jaylen and Tommy aren't there, they both think it sucks, when they say it I laugh. It's a good two days, it gets better with them every time we see each other. I take them to the airport my Mom cries tells me how proud of me she is, my Dad tells me to keep it up.

I call the people who gave me their business cards. Some of them take my calls some of them don't, some of them say they liked the movie, some of them dance around saying anything about the movie.

Tommy and Jaylen run low on funds can't afford weed anymore so they start growing it in our backyard.

Leonard cancels our Wednesday lunch once twice three straight times. He doesn't tell me why, just calls and says he can't make it.

I send my script to a dozen people two dozen people. I call them, follow up with them, a few of them like it, a few of them don't like it, nothing happens either way.

Cassius keeps growing it's shocking how fast he's growing. He still goes everywhere with me rides shotgun in the truck sleeps in my bed. Though he now looks like a large menacing pitbull he is a baby baby baby. He loves to give kisses, play tug-of-war, chase a ball, he'll do anything for a treat he's a huge musclebound baby.

I take a job working as a production assistant. It's

shitty work I drive around all day running errands for an asshole director who thinks he's saving the world with a shaving cream commercial.

Leonard cancels a fourth time, fifth time, sixth time. I wonder if something bad is happening or if he's just busy when I ask him he says he can't talk about it yet, he'll tell me when he can.

Tommy and Jaylen start selling the weed they're growing they figure it's easier than working. Our phone rings constantly there is a steady stream of people in and out of the house dull-eyed, slow-speaking, potato-chip-eating people.

A producer calls he read my script says he loves it. I've heard this before heard producers say they love it and I never hear from them again. I ask him if he's going to blow smoke up my ass or actually do something, he says he wants to buy it and make it. I ask him how much he gives me a number I say fucking sold, my friend, it is all yours.

Cassius and I move out.

My new house is in Laurel Canyon, which is a small neighborhood in the Hollywood Hills. There is one road into the canyon. The road is off Sunset, it is a two lane road that twists turns and is lined with huge overhanging trees and walls of rock. Houses built on stilts dot the rock, once you're into the canyon there are two roads that lead up further. The first road sits at a small intersection, there's a stoplight, a convenience store, a pizza place and a real estate office, the second road is several hundred yards up, there is a stoplight and the ruins of a stone mansion. The canyon is heavily wooded with pines oaks maples and cypress. It does not look like the rest of Los Angeles, it's cool dark and quiet, more like a forest than a city.

I live in a small house at the top of the first road. My house is pink stucco it has two bedrooms a bathroom a kitchen a living room. It has a small backyard that is dug out of the side of a hill, three cement walls hold the hill back and enclose the space. I don't have much furniture a mattress and a desk, I buy a futon and a television and a stereo. My neighbors are friendly say hello I recognize one of them as a drummer for a heavy metal band there's always noise coming from his house. I recognize another as a famous female porn performer there is always noise coming from her house. The couple next door are in their thirties, she's an actress, he's a composer. They're a brand of hippie found only in LA, they drive a Mercedes but say things like groovy, far out and dig it, man, dig it hard. Cassius and I are happy here we have a mellow life. I go back to trying to write a book no progress, he sleeps in the backyard chases flies tries to eat them. We take long walks through the hills. We watch TV on our futon. We get food from the store at the bottom of the hill, I like canned ravioli and fruit punch, Cassius likes beef-flavored kibble.

It's afternoon I am sitting at my desk drinking coffee smoking cigarettes trying to work, Cassius is on the futon watching a soap opera. We hear a car stop in front of the house. Cassius looks over at me I shrug tell him I don't know who it is we hear voices. Cassius looks at the door there's a knock. I stand walk to the door, Cassius stands walks to the door, I ask who is it, Cassius barks. Leonard speaks.

Open the door, my son.

I open the door. Leonard and Snapper stand in front of me.

Leonard speaks.

Your new house, it's a fucking palace.

I laugh.

Come on in.

They step inside. Cassius greets them both with a kiss on the hand he knows them they say hello to him. I speak.

You want something to drink?

What do you have?

I got coffee, and I got some beer and cola in the fridge.

Leonard speaks.

Cola please.

I look at Snapper. He speaks.

Why you got beer?

In case someone comes over and wants to drink it.

It don't bother you having it here?

I could give a shit. If I were gonna get drunk, I'd drink something a lot stronger than fucking beer.

He laughs.

I gotta drive. I'll have a cola too.

I get the colas from the fridge, hand them to Leonard and Snapper, speak.

What are you guys doing here?

Leonard speaks.

You never invited us up, so we decided to stop by.

Snapper speaks.

It hurt a little, Kid, the no invite thing.

I speak.

I figured you knew there's an open invitation, and I figured you'd stop by when you wanted to whether there was an invitation or not.

Leonard speaks.

You're right, we would.

Snapper speaks.

Invitations are still nice, though.

I speak.

From now on you're invited whenever you want.

Leonard speaks.

You got any plans tonight?

Nope.

Cassius have any?

I look at Cassius, who is back on the futon.

You got any plans tonight, Big Boy?

Cassius looks up, doesn't say anything. I look back at Leonard, speak.

I think he's free.

Leonard speaks.

Good, you're coming with us.

Where we going?

Las Vegas. I'm getting rid of my place there. I want to show you a night on the town before I leave.

You're moving?

Going to live at the beach house full time.

I look at Snapper.

You moving too?

I got a girlfriend in Vegas. I'm probably gonna split time between the two places.

You've got a girlfriend?

Don't sound so surprised. Lots of women like me.

Leonard speaks.

She's nice, works as an accountant for one of the casinos.

I speak.

Can I meet her?

Snapper speaks.

Maybe. I'll see what she's doing tonight.

Leonard speaks.

If we get there by tonight. Come on, let's go.

And you're sure Cassius can come?

Does he want to come?

I look at Cassius, speak.

You want to go to Vegas, Cassius?

He looks up at me again. I look back at Leonard.

He doesn't know those words. I've got to ask him another way.

I turn back to Cassius.

You want to go bye-bye in the car, Big Boy?

Cassius immediately jumps off the couch, runs over to me, starts panting, turning in circles. I look back at Leonard.

Do I need anything?

Everything will be taken care of.

Cool.

I put Cassius on a leash we walk out of my house get into Leonard's Mercedes start driving. The drive is simple. As soon as we're out of Los Angeles it's one long road that cuts through open, desolate desert. Leonard says he wants to set the mood so we listen to Frank Sinatra. Cassius sticks his face out the window, occasionally brings it back into the car and snorts and sneezes, immediately sticks it back out. The drive takes four and a half hours if you drive the speed limit, after three we start to see a dim glow hovering along the horizon. Leonard points it out, speaks. There it is, that mean and wondrous wench. The best place and worst place in America, a place where dreams come true, where people are destroyed, a place that doesn't care about the past and is a vision of the future, where capitalism is displayed in all of its glory and horror, where everything and anything can be bought, sold, traded or stolen, where some of the smartest and most ambitious people in the country come to make their fortunes, where some of the absolute worst and most despicable people in the country come to make their fortunes. It is corrupt, dirty and disgusting, and in five hundred years its massive buildings, thought of as garish and ridiculous, will be considered marvels. It is a giant carnival devoted to the glory of money and everything money can do, both good and evil, and there is plenty of both.

The dim grows and starts to form itself, becomes an outline of light. We pass bush league casinos on the side of the highway places for people who can't wait to get to the big casinos or need to make one last bet on their way out, we pass lonely gas stations, a ramshackle souvenir shop, one or two fast food restaurants. The light rises becomes brighter more defined, and very suddenly, we cross a line that separates an empty desert from a manic city.

We turn onto the strip. Both sides of the street are lined with massive, sprawling buildings covered in neon it's night and dark but looks like it's day. Leonard looks back at me.

Welcome to the Strip.

Wow.

When you see someplace you want to stay, let me know.

Aren't we staying at your house?

My house is a mess, all packed-up, boxes everywhere. I've been living in hotels.

Where?

All over the place. I move all the time, think it's nice to mix it up.

What do you recommend?

Whatever catches your eye.

I look out the window. Cassius climbs on my lap he looks out the window I ask him where he wants to stay he licks my face. We drive I see a huge black pyramid bigger than those in Egypt lights twinkling behind it. I see a ridiculous version of King Arthur's castle. I see New York City rebuilt a roller coaster winds its way through skyscrapers. I see what Leonard says is the biggest hotel in the world five thousand rooms every one offering the finest amenities. I see Monte Carlo, New Orleans, a hotel for pirates, a pink flamingo and a palace built in the image of Rome, though it doesn't look like the Rome I saw in Italy. I see the old-timey places, the new-timey places, big places giant places absurdly humongous places, rundown places sparkling places expensive places bottomed-out places. When we reach the end of the Strip we enter a dark area of grimy streets lined with convenience stores, hotels renting rooms by the hour, warehouses and hookers. I see another area of light a mile or so away I ask Leonard what it is, he says downtown Vegas. I ask him what it's like he says faded, lost and forgotten. I turn back look down the strip it is a perpetual wall of light. I look at Leonard, speak.

Which place is the most ridiculous?

Leonard speaks.

That's a tough question. What do you think, Snap?

Snapper speaks.

Excalibur has a magical medieval castle, a moat and a fire-breathing dragon. Circus Circus has exotic performing animals and the AdventureDome theme park. Mirage has the indoor jungle, Barbary Coast and Treasure Island are both full of pirates and buccaneers. They're all fucking ridiculous.

Leonard looks back at me.

They're all fucking ridiculous, my son. All of them.

Where do they have the best food?

Snapper speaks.

The Grand.

Leonard speaks.

I agree. Best food is at the Grand.

Let's go there.

Snapper nods pulls away we start driving back down the strip. I stare back out the window pay less attention to the buildings and more attention to the people, the hundreds of people thousands tens of thousands of people, on the sidewalks on footbridges that lead back and forth over the Strip in front of the casinos walking in and out. I stare at the people some looking around in awe some happily chatting some worried some quickly walking a few crying. I see Elvis, I see a couple just married he's in a tux she's in white, I see hookers lingering. I see a family hand-in-hand mother father four little children. I see a woman in a wheelchair an old man with a cane a blind man tapping a preacher pounding and screaming a hustler dealing cards people know they're going to lose but they play anyway. I see old young white black yellow red rich poor they're all looking for more more more, they're all the same and they all want more.

We pull up to the Grand the entrance lives up to its name. As soon as the car stops it is surrounded by valets. Leonard waves them off, Snapper pulls away, parks the car. Instead of walking toward the doors, Leonard turns and walks toward the sidewalk. I have Cassius on a leash we follow him.

He stops, speaks.

I want to tell you something before we go inside.

Okay.

You see all this.

He motions up and down the strip.

Yeah, I see it.

It's all a fucking charade. Built to lure you in,

tempt you, tease you, make you starry-eyed and dumb, make you think it's yours for the taking if you just throw down those next few bucks.

He turns to me.

You can do what you want, but the way I do it is I decide on a sum, the sum is an amount I won't miss. I play it until I'm either happy with my winnings, or I lose it all. I never go over, never spend more. The reason I do this is because this . . .

He motions up and down the strip again.

This was not built on losses, it was not built on losses. You understand?

The casino always wins.

He nods.

Yeah, the casino always wins. Goddamn sons of bitches. They should let me always win.

I laugh, he smiles. He turns back toward the entrance.

You ready.

Yeah, I'm ready.

We walk to the entrance, step into a huge revolving door it is silent between the swinging panes, for a second or two it's beautiful, light and silent. I step out of the door into the lobby, into flashing lights into noise from slot machines into music into laughing and cheering into the blast of air conditioning into plush carpeting into thirty foot ceilings into madness. Cassius looks around appears slightly confused, Leonard steps in behind us walks toward the reception desk we follow him.

341

He arrives at the desk asks for someone. The woman asks for his name he gives it to her she makes a call. Thirty seconds later a man in a suit steps out of an office behind the desk greets Leonard, shakes his hand, the man says it's great to see you again, how can I help you? Leonard tells him he'd like to stay for the night the man asks if anyone will be with him Leonard says we'll be three. Man asks if we have any bags Leonard says no we'll be purchasing whatever we need the man says excellent, let me know if I can help in any way. Leonard says please order a large porterhouse steak cooked well and a bowl of water and have them sent to our room immediately. The man looks at Cassius and laughs, says of course and steps to the desk, speaks with one of his coworkers. Snapper joins us, the man steps away from the desk, says follow me.

We go to an elevator. We ride to the top floor we need a key to open the elevator door. We step into a hall, a long hall with thick carpet, low lights, subtle neutral paint and two doors, one on each side of the hall just two doors. The man leads us to one of the doors opens it holds the door we go into the room.

It is not a room, not a suite, not an apartment. It is a mansion in the sky a beautiful series of rooms, bedrooms dining room living room multimedia room den kitchen bar sitting room. There are windows in every room offering views of the Strip of Vegas of the desert, the furniture looks like it belongs in a museum, the carpet is soft and thick, the drapes long and thick, the glasses at the bar crystal the refrigerators stocked. The man gives a brief tour gives us a card tells us to please call him if he can do anything for us he leaves. I let Cassius off his leash he starts running around smelling things. I look at Leonard.

This is incredible.

It's not bad.

What's something like this go for?

It doesn't.

It's free?

Yup.

You pay nothing?

Doubt anyone who's stayed here has paid for it.

Suite for high rollers?

High rollers, VIPs and people like me.

You're not a high roller or a VIP?

I'm something else, something that exists here but isn't often acknowledged to exist.

International superstar?

He laughs.

More like someone you don't want to piss off.

I laugh.

Are we expected to spend a bunch of money in the casino?

They're going to take care of us, and provide us with whatever we want, regardless of how much money we blow in the casino.

Whatever we want?

Leonard smiles.

Yeah, and you can get exotic in your requests if you would like.

How exotic?

As exotic as you can imagine.

I laugh again. Snapper walks into the room says he's hungry. Leonard asks if I'm hungry I say yes he asks if we want to eat in the room or in a restaurant. We decide to go to a restaurant. We wait for Cassius' steak. When it arrives I cut it into small pieces he eats it in about two seconds. I give him the bone he takes it runs around the room a couple of times jumps onto a couch starts chewing, he looks happy, like he'll be occupied for hours. We leave the room, take the elevator back downstairs, walk around, try to decide where we are going to eat, there are about twenty different restaurants. We go to a steakhouse. Snapper and I both have huge slabs of prime rib with spinach and hash browns, Leonard has a salad. After dinner we go to the casino Leonard wants to shoot craps. I have no idea how to do it Leonard tries to explain I say don't worry about it, just give me the dice and let me throw. He laughs hands me the dice I start to throw and my oh my do I fucking throw. Leonard handles the betting and we win again and again we start to accumulate a large stack of chips and a crowd around our table. With each throw the crowd either cheers or groans and we get many more cheers I keep throwing throwing we keep accumulating I have no idea how much we have at least ten times what we started with. We look at the pile and laugh. Leonard says you're my good luck charm, my son, let's quit while we're ahead.

We quit, cash out the chips, we have over ten thousand dollars in fifties and hundreds. Leonard asks me if I'm okay with money I say yeah, I'm doing well he says if you don't need it, let's give it away. We leave the casino walk out to the Strip.

We walk, look, we give a thousand dollars to an elderly couple, we give a thousand to a couple who just got married. We find some homeless men they're drunk we give them a few hundred dollars each. We see a family their car is broken-down we give them a couple thousand. We hand out money to whoever we see that looks like they're down, depressed, who looks like a few bucks will make them happier. Some of the people are thrilled thank us can't believe their luck, some of them don't want the money think we want something in exchange, some of them take it and quietly walk away. When we have a thousand or so left Leonard says we're keeping the rest for later we're going to need some throwaway money. I ask him why he says there's big fun coming, my son, big-ass motherfucking fun.

We walk back to the hotel, Snapper is having a drink with his girlfriend, Leonard wants to join them. I say let's give them some privacy, he says no, they're expecting us. We walk to a small quiet bar. Aside from the rooms it is probably the only quiet space in this entire complex. Snapper is sitting at a table for four with a small blond woman. They stand as we enter, Leonard speaks.

Look at Olivia, the most beautiful girl in the world.

The blond woman smiles it is a shy smile. Leonard gives her a hug they separate.

Olivia, this is my son James. James, this is Olivia, the most beautiful girl in the world.

She smiles again the same smile. She's short thin has dark brown eyes sandy blond hair. Her hands are soft, her nails immaculate, she wears a black skirt and a black blouse, she's beautiful in a simple natural way as if her beauty is something that she doesn't think about or let worry her. We shake hands, say hello, sit down. She looks at me speaks.

Dominic has told me a lot about you.

Dominic?

Snapper speaks.

She doesn't like my professional name.

I laugh.

I don't blame her.

She smiles.

Are you having fun in Vegas?

Yeah, I am.

You have good guides.

I laugh again.

Yeah, I do.

We sit talk laugh. Olivia is from Albuquerque, where her parents, Italian immigrants, opened a pizza parlor. She grew up working in the parlor, put herself through school, got her job in the casino when she graduated, has been there for six years. I ask her how she met Dominic she says she has a dog, a big, sweet, dumb as dirt Newfoundland who got off his leash one day and started wandering around her neighborhood. Dominic found him and brought him home. She says he seemed shy and nervous and sweet, and she thought he was handsome so she asked him out. They went to dinner and a movie that night. She took him to a romantic chickflick to see if he could deal with it and he laughed when he was supposed to laugh and clapped at the end. They had coffee afterwards, and when he took her home at the end of the night, Dominic didn't try to kiss her. She hoped he would ask her out again or ask for her number, but it didn't happen, and she went to sleep disappointed. The next day, when she got home from work, there was an envelope at her door. Inside the envelope, on a piece of handmade paper, someone had carefully transcribed a poem by Emily Dickinson called *It's all I have to bring to-day*, and beneath the poem there was a phone number. She called the number and Dominic answered and, she smiles and says, we've been together ever since. At the end of the story Leonard laughs, looks at Snapper, speaks.

You still remember the poem, Dominic?

Of course I do.

Recite it for James.

No way.

Come on.

Only for Olivia.

When did that become policy?

Olivia looks at Leonard, speaks.

When I said so.

Leonard laughs.

Since when are you the boss?

When he's with you, you're the boss. When he's with me, I'm the boss.

What about when he's with both of us?

Olivia smiles.

We both know the answer to that one, Leonard.

Everyone laughs, Olivia smiles and nods, holds her hands over her head like she's a champion. We finish our drinks. Olivia says she needs to go home, Snapper asks Leonard if we're okay without him for the night.

Leonard says yeah, we're fine, everyone stands Olivia hugs Leonard and me, she and Snapper leave. Leonard looks at me, speaks.

You tired?

What time is it?

Time doesn't matter here. You sleep when you're tired, not when a clock tells you you should sleep.

Is there anything else to do?

A friend of mine owns a strip club. I kept that dough so you could live in lapdance heaven for a couple hours.

You gonna join me?

I'm not much of a lapdance man.

I would have thought you liked them.

Nope.

Fuck it then.

You sure?

Lapdances are fun when your buddy's sitting next to you and everyone's laughing. There's something dark and sad about them when you're there alone hoping for something you're not gonna get.

Leonard laughs.

I could arrange that you get it.

That's dark and sad too.

He laughs again.

So what do you want to do?

Is there anything I've missed?

Is there anything you haven't seen that you want to see?

No.

We could go see a Sinatra imitator, or we could go to an all-night, all-you-can-eat buffet.

I'm good.

What do you want to do with the last thousand?

I don't care.

Let's put it on red or black and go to sleep.

Red.

Fine with me.

We go back to the casino bet red win bet red win we leave with four grand. We go back to the suite. Cassius is sleeping on the couch the bone is resting next to his sizable head. I wake him up we thank Leonard for a great night, a ridiculous night, we thank him. We go to our room the bed is huge the sheets are soft we go to sleep.

Cassius and I go home back to our little house in the hills. I spend my time in front of a computer, he spends his time in front of the TV. We go for walks three times a day, once in the morning, once in the afternoon, once at night. I eat most of my meals at home, I rarely go out with my friends. I read for three or four hours before I go to bed.

I have a good life, a simple life, for the first time in my life I'm happy and secure and stable. My Fury, which has shaped most of the twenty-five years of my life has faded without the fuel of drugs and alcohol, has faded as I have learned not to hate myself. Part of me is humbled by this life, this beautiful life. Another part of me feels incredibly fortunate. Part of me is waiting to fuck it up somehow, waiting to make some dumbass decision that destroys it, waiting for it to end. Part of me feels like it isn't complete without Lilly, this is what she and I dreamed of having together.

Sometimes I pretend she's here with me. I talk to an empty chair across the table, I wrap my arms around nothingness and tell her I love her. I tell her I'll be home in a little while when I leave, I tell her I'm tired and want to go to bed at the end of a long day. Even without her I have all I need, my little house, my big funny dog, my legally earned money, my time, my own time, my own precious time to do whatever I want to do. I have simple things, a simple life, all I need.

Leonard goes east for his annual attempt at a tee-time on the golf course where his father worked.

I see a drunk movie star drive his Porsche into a tree going ten miles an hour. He gets out of the car and starts kicking the door starts screaming nobody understands, nobody understands.

Cassius becomes friends with a squirrel who lives in a tree above our yard.

He sits and watches the squirrel jump from limb to limb, watches him collect acorns, watches him chatter and squeak, he spends hours watching the squirrel. I think Cassius is lonely.

I see a famous young actress, a shockingly beautiful young actress, gorging at a fast food restaurant, she disappears into the bathroom after eating six cheeseburgers.

I finish another script I like it.

I see a famous director throw an omelet at a waitress while screaming onions aren't mushrooms, onions aren't fucking mushrooms. The waitress walks away with egg in her hair, on her neck, on her shirt, tears in her eyes her hands are shaking. A minute or two later the manager of the restaurant walks over and apologizes to the director says the meal's on us please tell me what else I can get for you.

My friend Danny calls from Chicago tells me he hates his job, wants to do something new. I tell him to come to Los Angeles, it's the land of opportunity. He says what would I do, I say let's raise some money and we'll make a movie. He says that's crazy, I say it's crazier staying in a job you hate, he says you're right, I'm coming to Los Angeles.

Cassius and I are at the veterinarian's office. Cassius is having a regular semi-annual check-up. The vet asks me if I would ever consider having another dog, I look at Cassius, ask him he wags his tail says yes, Daddy, yes, Daddy, let's get another dog, please Daddy, yes. The vet says she has a young female pitbull that she found in a box behind a convenience store. I say bring her out, the vet leaves comes back two minutes later with a small, brindle pitbull her ears are sticking up her tail is wagging. Cassius licks her, they start jumping around barking and yelping. I ask the vet if she has a name the vet tells me she calls the little dog Bella. I say welcome to the family, Bella, I'm your new Dad, the big boy is your new brother.

A girl I know from school calls me asks me if I want to have dinner I say yeah, sure, I'll have dinner. Her name is Conner she's six foot two she likes a nice, strong cocktail and she likes to laugh. I ask her where we're going she tells me it's a bar that serves decent food in an outdoor courtyard. I ask her if anyone is coming with us she asks me if I remember her friend Allison. I ask if it's Allison skinny Allison and she laughs and says yes, that's her and I say yeah, I remember Allison. I ask her what time she says eight.

I work all day take a shower get dressed. I think about Skinny Allison on and off. She was tall, as tall as I am. She had long dark blond hair, olive skin. The first time I saw her she was eighteen, but looked fourteen, and in the two years we were at school together, she never aged. She was thin, long thin, delicate thin, fragile thin, thin like a runway model, thin the type that food wouldn't affect, thin that was somehow natural for her, as if her body would gain weight as she got older. I saw her occasionally she was usually with Conner

354

we never spoke. I never tried to speak to her because I knew she wanted nothing to do with me. She was from a nice, traditional Southern family, she did well in school. I imagined she would find a handsome, successful, stable man and live in a big house and have a beautiful family.

Cassius and Bella are sitting on the couch. I stop say goodbye to them they wag their tails and look up at me. If they could talk they'd say go on and leave, Daddy, we're going to have fun tonight without you, maybe we'll eat a pillow or chew our bones or try to catch squirrels or watch TV, go on, Daddy, leave. I give them hugs walk out to my truck drive down the hill to the bar.

I walk into the bar look around. I see Conner sitting at a table. I walk toward the table Allison is sitting next to Conner they stand as I approach them. I hesitate as I walk, blink a couple of times, try to keep my jaw from dropping, my knees from buckling, my eyes from popping out. Allison is not skinny Allison anymore. She's still thin but her body has filled out, there are curves beautiful curves. Her hair is longer, more blond. She's wearing light blue leather pants a white t-shirt. She's no longer a girl she's become a woman, a gorgeous, voluptuous woman. Men all over the bar are staring at her. I'm staring at her. I stop at the table speak.

Hi.

Conner speaks.

Hi. You remember Allison?

I look at Allison.

Hi.

She speaks.

Hi.

Long time.

Yeah.

How you been?

Great. You?

I laugh.

Been a long couple of years.

She nods.

So I've heard.

We sit, they're both drinking white wine, I order a nice cold cola. I talk to Allison ask her about her life. She's been living in Vail for the last two years, teaching skiing and working in an art gallery. She loves Vail, but wants to move, feels like two years in a ski town is long enough, that it's time to become an adult. I ask her where she wants to go, she says she isn't sure, maybe San Francisco maybe Santa Fe maybe Washington DC. I ask her what she wants to do, she says she needs to figure it out, maybe teach, maybe try to be a painter, maybe go back to school for landscape architecture. She asks me about my life I say it's good, never been better. She asks if it's true I got locked-up I tell her yes. She asks what I'm doing in Los Angeles I tell her, she asks if I like Los Angeles I say more and more every day. I ask her why it's not on her list of potential residences, she says she just can't imagine living here.

We order dinner they get salads I get a big fat fucking cheeseburger. We keep talking I ask about painting why she does it, she says she does it because when she is actually painting she forgets about the rest of the world, forgets about problems and insecurities, about failures and an uncertain future, about everything she just loses herself and paints. I ask who she paints like, she says she tries to paint like herself. I ask her who she likes, she says Matisse and van Gogh. I ask her why she says because Matisse paints beautifully and van Gogh paints painfully.

When the food comes, I can't eat. Allison intimidates me, makes me nervous, takes away my appetite. I take a few bites of the burger, try to look away from her, try to focus on Conner, try to seem cool and secure and distant even though I don't feel cool or secure, even though I don't want to be distant. What I want is to be next to her, to hold her, to be inside of her, to devour her, to disappear within her, to become part of her somehow, to become part of her. Part of what I feel is purely physical, a desire an urge a desperate clawing need, part of what I feel is something else, something that makes me smile, feel empty and full, makes my heart hurt. We finish dinner. I pay the bill they both thank me, we stand walk out. We wait for our cars at the valet, Conner asks me what I'm doing for the rest of the night, I tell her I'm going home getting in bed reading a book.

Allison asks me what I'm reading I tell her Paul

Bowles she asks me which book I tell her *The Sheltering Sky*. She smiles says she loves Paul Bowles, loves that book. I tell her I'll give her my report when I'm done she smiles says I'll look forward to it.

Our cars arrive. I ask them what they're doing tomorrow, Conner says she's not sure. I tell her to call me, that I might take my dogs for a walk in the Hills, that they can come if they want, she says cool. We get in our cars we leave.

I drive home and every second of the drive is spent thinking about Allison about how she looked in the first instant I saw her, about how she laughed she has a quiet shy laugh, about her smile she smiles like she's hiding something, about her leather pants her curves about painting I want to watch her paint about her reading I want to watch her read about the skinny girl that isn't skinny anymore, about what she would look like next to me with me beneath me on top of me about how she scares me she fucking terrifies me.

I get home the dogs are already asleep on top of my bed. I get into bed I stare at the ceiling I think about Allison, I close my eyes I think about Allison. I fall asleep thinking about Allison.

I wake up thinking about her. I try to work I can't work. I walk the dogs I want to go home I'm worried Conner might call I don't want to miss it. I brew some coffee my hand quivers as I drink it. I try to read, the words make no sense. I smoke cigarettes and stare at the wall and think about her. I hope Conner calls I want to see Allison again.

Conner calls we agree to go for a hike in the Hills. I ask the dogs if they want to go out, they jump up and down wag their tails run in circles. I ask them if they want to meet a girl Daddy likes they don't care. I ask them if they want to go bye-bye in the car they start barking.

We meet go for our hike. I let the dogs off their leashes they run away. It's hot I take off my shirt. Allison asks about my tattoos. I tell her they're like scars they remind me of things I've done, of how I want to live and how I don't want to live. Allison says I have a lot of scars. She smiles and she reaches out and runs her finger along the top of my left arm, along a faded black outline, she doesn't speak just runs her

359

finger along my arm, along my arm, along my arm.

We agree to meet for dinner. They're going to come to my house I'll drive us all to a nearby restaurant. They arrive we go to a local Italian place we eat, Conner and Allison drink wine I drink cola. We stay for three or four hours. I don't want to leave Allison I want to sit with her for the rest of the night, tomorrow, all of next week, for the next month, year. The bill comes I pay we go back to my house I have a few bottles of wine in the house for people who want to drink. Conner and Allison open one of them. We sit in the backyard it's a beautiful California night, warm still quiet clear. They drink, we smoke, talk about friends from school where they are what they're doing how they're doing, some are doing well some are disasters some have faded away. I ask Allison why we were never friends at school she laughs and says because you were psychotic and I was scared of you. I ask her if she's still scared of me, she says you're like your dogs, you appear kind and sweet and gentle, but I don't think I'd like to make you angry. I ask her if that means she's still scared of me she says she hasn't decided yet. I tell her to let me know if there's anything I can do to ease her fears, she smiles says okay.

It gets late two or three. Conner wants to go home. She's drunk I tell her she shouldn't drive they should stay here they can have my room I'll sleep on the couch. Conner wants to leave she walks out Allison follows her. I hear them arguing. I hear car doors open I hear them close. I hear Conner's car start, pull away. I hear a knock I walk to the door open it.

Allison is standing in front of me she speaks.
There's something you can do.
What do you mean?
To help ease my fear of you.
What's that?
She smiles.
Invite me in, I'll show you.

We have breakfast, lunch, dinner she stays the night again, we spend all of the next day together she stays the night again. She changes her flight so she can stay longer she picks up her bags from Conner we spend three more days together. We take the dogs for walks through the hills. We go to a gourmet grocery store Allison cooks a fancy dinner. We go to the movies sit in the back row hold hands share popcorn whisper to each other. We go see a band sit in the back row hold hands whisper to each other. We lie in bed for hours talking kissing exploring each other we lie in bed and stare at each other, her eyes are the same pale green as mine we lie in bed and we look into each other.

I convince her to stay for three more days. We drive up the coast. We get a room in a beachfront hotel we have plans to walk on the sand, swim in the ocean, sit in the sun, eat every meal outside. We never leave the room. We spend three days kissing touching exploring discovering we spend three days talking whispering laughing. We spend three days falling in love and I fall truly, deeply and absolutely in love with her. I fall in love with everything about her. I love her mind body smile, I love her walk long and graceful her voice soft and reserved. I love how she smokes, eats, I love her accent certain words have a faint Southern twang. I love the books she reads Paul Bowles and Jack Kerouac, the painters she admires Matisse, van Gogh and Michelangelo. I love that she went abroad alone lived in Florence and went to school. I love that she loves my dogs, that she's not scared of me anymore, that she makes fun of me and my past, says I'm nothing like what she expected, that I'm soft and sweet that I'm nothing like the monster she heard about. I love that I have never felt anything similar to what I feel when I'm inside of her, it's calm strength peace fulfillment fearlessness abandon satisfaction it's something I never knew with Lilly have never known with anyone. I love when I am near her I have to touch her, have to kiss her, have to have my arms around her, have her close to me next to me touching me. I love that when I am with her everything else disappears, I don't think care wonder or worry about anything but her.

We go back to Los Angeles. Allison says she needs to go home. I ask her to stay tell her I want her to stay please Allison stay with me. She has to go home. She doesn't know when she'll be back.

I drive her to the airport.

I walk her to the gate.

I kiss her goodbye.
I'm in love with her.
Please, Allison.
Stay.

The phone rings I pick it up.
Hello.
My son, MY SON, **MY SON!**
What's up, Leonard?
Where the fuck have you been?
Around.
Around my ass. I've left about ten messages.
I haven't checked 'em. Everything okay?
Yeah, but you missed lunch.
I didn't know you were back, didn't know we were having lunch.
Because you didn't check your fucking messages.
I laugh.
Sorry. How was it out East?
No good.
That sucks.
I've decided I'm going to have the entire course fucking torched. Burned to the fucking ground.
Really?
No. Fuck no. But I didn't get on and I'm pissed.
Sorry.
What have you been doing?
Met a girl.

Who?

Her name's Allison.

Nice name. How'd you meet her?

I went to school with her, knew who she was there. She was out here visiting a friend of hers and we all had dinner.

And?

And we had dinner the next night, then she stayed with me for five days, then we went to Santa Barbara for three days, then she went home.

My son, oh my son. This sounds serious.

Maybe.

Are you in love with her?

Madly.

Have you told her?

No.

Why didn't you tell her?

I don't know.

Why'd you let her go home?

I don't know.

Are you ready for something like this?

I feel like I am.

You're over Lilly enough to be with someone else?

I feel like I am.

I feel like I am isn't good enough. If you're going to tell this Allison that you love her, you need to be sure.

Who said I'm going to tell her that I love her?

Are you sure?

Why do you need to know?

I don't need to know, you need to know. Are you ready to love someone, and are you sure about her?

Yeah, I'm ready, and yeah, I'm sure.

I assume you have Allison's phone number.

Yeah.

We're going to hang up. You're going to call her. You're going to tell her that you love her, that you want her to move to Los Angeles, that you can't live without her. Then we're having dinner.

I laugh.

What if she doesn't love me, or she doesn't want to move here.

Then we will have a miserable dinner.

I laugh again.

We're hanging up now, my Son.

Okay.

And you're going to call her.

Okay.

And then you're going to call me back and we'll make dinner plans.

Sounds good.

I call Allison my hands are shaking I can see my heart beating I can hardly speak I call her she answers the phone. We talk for a few minutes. I wonder if she can tell I'm nervous scared I wonder if she can tell I'm shaking I hope not. I tell her that I love her. I tell her that I want her to move to Los Angeles. I tell her that I don't want to live without her. I tell her that I love her, I love her, I love her.

I fly to Virginia. I'm going to spend a week with Allison's family, help her pack, drive across the country with her. She picks me up at the airport I see her grab her hold her kiss her tell her I've missed her I'm so happy to see her I love her.

Her parents live in Virginia Beach. They live in a big, beautiful Southern house with white columns and a wide porch, on one side is a golf course on the other side is a quiet inlet of the Atlantic Ocean. They're conservative Southerners, people who believe in God, family, tradition. I like them, they seem to like me. I don't swear around them, never let them see my tattoos, avoid discussions about my past. I stay in a room on the side of the house opposite Allison's room. Every chance I get I drag her into closets into bathrooms into the attic, we sneak out of our rooms at night meet in the kitchen in the living room outside in the grass. I play golf with her father, go shopping with her and her mother, we go to their country club for dinner, Allison and I ride bikes take walks along the beach. It's a nice week, a mellow week, it feels like what our life could be like in a few years if we get married and live somewhere other than Los Angeles. It's an image I like it feels happy, comfortable. It feels right as right as any life I've ever imagined.

At the end of the week we pack the car, have a last breakfast with her parents, they cry and wave as we pull away. We've mapped out our trip in an atlas we're going a zig-zaggy route that takes us through the Southern United States. We're going to take our time at least a week, maybe two.

Our first stop is Richmond. We stay with Allison's brother, who is a lawyer for a large tobacco company. I met him in Paris several years ago we had drinks together a few times when I left Paris I ended up in rehab and jail when he left he went to law school. He's tall, blond, handsome, he wears pressed pants, starched shirts, lives in a pristine apartment, I imagine that he keeps an accurate checkbook and pays his taxes on time. He takes us out for dinner says he's tired of Richmond is tired of living in such a conservative environment is thinking of moving. I ask him where he wants to go he's says he's not sure maybe Los Angeles. I offer to throw his shit in Allison's trailer he can come with us. He declines.

From Richmond we go to Washington DC. We walk around Georgetown go to the National Gallery. Allison takes me to a bathing suit store she wants to buy me a leopard print Speedo, I ask her why she says because it's funny. I try one on walk around the store ask the other customers what they think of it. Most ignore me, two gay men tell me I look great, an elderly woman tells me to get away from her before she calls the police. I wear the Speedo as we drive out of town.

We decide to go to Memphis. Halfway there we stop at a cheap motel. We get a big room with a big bed it's the first time we've been truly alone since my arrival we take advantage of it. We arrive in Memphis tour Graceland eat barbeque listen to the blues on Beale Street. I feel bad for Elvis dying on the toilet in his big, silly, lonely house. I eat barbeque until I can hardly walk. I dig the blues and at times have known the blues but not right now, not right now.

We drive south through Tennessee and Mississippi. I walk into a backwater truckstop wearing the Speedo, truckers want to kick my ass, the clerk laughs and asks me if I am going to the beach. Further south to New Orleans we see my friend Miles Davis, not the trumpet player Miles Davis, my friend from rehab the Honorable Miles Davis, Federal Judge. Miles was my roommate at rehab. We spent a lot of sleepless nights talking, listening to music, he plays the clarinet he would play when he couldn't sleep. He helped me deal with my legal problems, talked to people for me, made calls for me and helped me avoid a stretch in prison. Aside from Leonard he's the only person I knew there who is still clean, the rest of our friends are either locked-up or dead. We stay in New Orleans for three days. I meet Miles' wife she's a

Doctor we have a huge cajun dinner with her and Miles. We go to a bar in the French Quarter where the waitresses look like beautiful women but are all men. We drink strong coffee eat beignets watch ragged magicians perform and drunk guitarists play and fortune tellers speculate and lie. We listen to jazz at night in dark smoky bars where the best musicians in the world play out their lives in obscurity. We walk through the gardens of former plantations the owners are still white the help is still black doesn't seem like much has changed. We eat Sno-Kones in the ghetto we wander through the zoo, what's up orangutan, I like that crazy hair. I'm sad to leave, sad to say goodbye to Miles. I could live in New Orleans, I don't mind the heat and noise and dirt, it's a beautiful decrepit debauched disintegrating paradise.

We drive north cross into Texas decide to try and make it across in one shot. Allison buys some books we turn off the radio she starts reading to me. Fourteen hours later we're through two books both Paul Bowles a gallon of coffee three packs of cigarettes and I can't see straight. Four more hours and we're in Santa Fe we see Allison's friends walk through the mountains spend a day at a spa get massages swim in a hot springs Allison gets treatments I have no idea what I just sit and read a book.

We go to Vegas. We're both tired we don't leave the room.

We drive from Vegas to Los Angeles. We pull up

to the house. Cassius and Bella have been staying with a friend he dropped them at the house earlier in the day. As I walk to the door I can hear them barking I don't know if they smell me or hear me but they know I'm home. I open the door they jump up and down run in circles, Cassius pees himself they give us kisses. I tell them Daddy's home now he isn't going away again. I tell them Daddy has Mommy with him she isn't going away again. Allison smiles I look at her put my arms around her, kiss her neck, speak.

I love you and I'm happy you're here and I don't want you going away again.

Allison's parents don't want her living with me until we're engaged we're not ready to get engaged she moves in with Conner. Their apartment is at the bottom of the hill about five minutes from my house.

Danny and I start trying to raise money for a movie. We call every wealthy person we know we tell them we have a great investment opportunity for them, some of them actually write us checks.

Allison starts working as an assistant for a producer at a studio. The producer is the son of the head of the studio, and has never actually produced anything, but has a big office and a large expense account.

I keep trying to write a book I spend most of my time smoking and drinking coffee and playing with the dogs and swearing.

Allison and I walk into a coffee shop. We see an ex-girlfriend of mine sitting at a table, the ex-girlfriend sees us. We all went to school together, the ex-girlfriend and Allison know each other. I have not seen the ex for three years, we split on terrible terms. The last time we saw each other I was bleeding, beaten, in handcuffs, on my way to jail. I look at her she looks the same, arctic blue eyes long thick blond hair. I say hello she says hello, Allison says hello she says hello to Allison. I have wondered what happened to her, where she was, what it would be like to see her. I feel nothing. I could give two shits about her. Allison and I order our coffees and we sit outside and smoke and laugh and look at each other and when the ex leaves none of us bother to say goodbye.

A yappy little beagle bites Cassius on the ass while I'm walking him and Bella down our street. The beagle snarls and barks jumps at Cassius, looks like he's going to bite him again. Cassius tries to ignore the beagle but the beagle keeps coming until Cassius lunges at him, puts his entire head in his mouth, shakes him a couple of times and tosses him a few feet away. The beagle shakes it off, appears to be fine, and runs away.

Allison and I are together every night. Most of the time we're at my house, once in a while we're at her apartment. She is the first person I have completely loved. I love her physically, emotionally, I love everything about her I love her more every day, more every day. Sometimes I wonder if this is it what my life would have been like if Lilly had lived. Sometimes I feel guilty because I'm happy. Sometimes I hate myself because when I'm with Allison, I stop thinking about Lilly, and I stop missing her.

Leonard wants to meet Allison. I invite him over for dinner, tell him we'll cook for him. He laughs, calls me a domesticated motherfucker, asks me what I know how to cook, I tell him absolutely nothing, Allison's in charge. He laughs again says he'd love to come I ask him if tomorrow is cool he says yeah.

Allison and I go to the fancy gourmet grocery store. She has a list she tells me what to get she checks to make sure I've picked up the right items she double checks as we wait in line.

She starts preparing the food in the afternoon. She makes a salad, mashed potatoes, an apple pie. While she's in the kitchen, I clean the house. I sweep the floors mop the floors, scrub every surface in the bathroom, wash the sheets wash the futon cover, pick up all the dogshit in the backyard and throw it in the woods. The smells coming from the kitchen make me hungry make me want to eat I take regular breaks to go into the kitchen and try to snack. Allison kicks me out I try again she kicks me out again. We take showers put on nice clothes survey the house to make sure everything is in order survey the kitchen to make sure everything is on schedule. Allison knows about Leonard knows what he does and who he is knows about my relationship with him knows how much he means to me. We both want tonight to go well she's nervous. I know Leonard will like her, I know she'll like him though she may be slightly intimidated by him. We hear a car pull up the dogs start barking car door opens knock knock knock. I open the door, Leonard is standing there with a huge bouquet of flowers, two bottles of wine one white one red. He speaks.

My son.

Come on in, Leonard.

Leonard steps into the house. Allison is in my bedroom. Leonard looks around, speaks loudly so that Allison can hear him.

I knew it, I knew it. This beautiful perfect woman was all a delusion, an invention, she doesn't exist.

I laugh.

I was always suspicious. This Allison sounded too good to be true. No one can be everything you said she is, gorgeous, smart, well-read, knowledgeable in the history of art, and willing to tolerate you. It's impossible, impossible.

Allison walks out of the bedroom. Leonard sees her.

Oh my.

Allison smiles.

Hi, Leonard. I'm Allison. I've heard a lot about you, it's nice to meet you.

Leonard drops to one knee.

My Lady, you're a vision. May I offer you flowers, and may I offer you wine, red if you please, white if you please.

Allison laughs, takes the flowers and wine.

Thank you.

May I stand?

She laughs again.

Of course.

Leonard stands, Allison walks into the kitchen puts the flowers in a vase. I follow her ask her what kind of wine she wants she says red I open the bottle ask Leonard if he wants a cola he says no, I stopped drinking cola, just water for me. I pour Allison a glass of wine, Leonard a glass of water, a glass of cola for me. Allison puts dinner in the oven, Leonard sits down on the couch. He looks at Allison, speaks.

Pretty Lady. Come sit with me.

Allison smiles, looks at me.

Can you handle yourself in here?

Yeah.

Allison sits with Leonard. I set the table, warm up the potatoes, put dressing on the salad. I hear bits of their conversation I hear them talking about Allison's hometown about women's clothing, which Leonard seems to know about for some reason. I hear then talking about art about wine I hear them laughing I hear them talking about me I try not to listen. I finish in the kitchen put the salads on the table tell them dinner is ready.

They walk over, Leonard pulls out Allison's

378

chair, we all sit down. Leonard raises a glass, speaks.

To my son, and to the beautiful, charming, intelligent young woman he has somehow convinced to spend time with him.

Allison and I laugh we all clink glasses we each take a sip. We eat the salad, eat dinner Allison makes beef tenderloin, eat dessert. Leonard asks Allison what I was like before rehab, she laughs and says she doesn't really know because she tried to avoid me as much as possible. Allison asks Leonard what rehab was like, he laughs and says it was great and awful at the same time. She asks how it was great, he says as ridiculous as it may sound, it was fun being institutionalized with a bunch of crazy drug addicts and alcoholics, we laughed a lot and told each other all kinds of crazy stories and became great friends. She asks why it was awful he says because nobody ends up there because they're healthy or sane or stable, nobody ends up there because they have a good life, and it's pretty miserable dealing with all the shit we've done to ourselves and other people and it's pretty miserable trying to figure out how not to do it again. She asks about our friends there Leonard tells her about Ed and Ted, Ed died in a fight and Ted is in prison for the rest of his life, about Matty the boxer shot dead outside a crackhouse, about Michael he blew his brains out with a shotgun, about John also now in prison for the rest of his life. Allison asks if Leonard knows Miles, Leonard says of course I do, he's a fine, fine man, I wish I could be friends with him. Allison asks why he can't, Leonard says our positions on opposite ends of the legal spectrum prevent any such friendship. Allison asks about his job, Leonard laughs, says if you're asking, you know, and that's all I'm going to tell you.

As I am clearing the table, Allison gets up goes to the bathroom. Leonard stands, starts helping me, speaks.

If she was my type I'd try to steal her from you.

That'd be a problem.

Thankfully she's not my type.

Do I have your approval?

Buy the ring tomorrow.

I guess that means yes.

That means yes yes yes yes yes, you're fucking crazy if you let her go.

I don't want to, but who knows.

What would stop you?

I don't know.

Lilly?

No.

Does she know about her?

Sort of.

What's that mean?

She knows of her, but she doesn't know details.

Why not?

I don't like talking about Lilly, and I don't with anyone but you, and I don't want Allison to feel like she has to live up to my memories of my dead girlfriend.

That might be a burden.
It would suck for her.
Yes, it would.
I love her and want her to feel comfortable.
I think you're being smart.
Thank you.
Allison returns, Leonard turns around.
Ah, pretty lady, we were just talking about you.
Allison smiles.
What were you saying?
James was telling me how much he loves you.
She smiles again.
I love him.
And I was telling him that if you were my type,
I would try to steal you from him.
Oh yeah?
Yeah.
You're charming, Leonard, but you wouldn't get
me.
I'm handsome too. Don't forget handsome.
Allison laughs.
Yeah, you're handsome too, Leonard, but I love
him.
Leonard looks at me.
You're lucky man, my son, lucky motherfucky.
I laugh.
A motherfucky?
Leonard nods.
Yeah.
What's a motherfucky?
That's you. You're a lucky motherfucky.

You ever use that one before?

Nope, just invented it, just for you, lucky motherfucky.

I laugh again, look at beautiful Allison, look at my friend Leonard, look at my doggies asleep on the floor, they're all in my house in Laurel Canyon in the hills above Los Angeles. I just had a great meal. I'm in love. I know I'm going to wake up tomorrow. I'm a lucky man. A lucky man.

Lucky motherfucky.

Allison, Kevin and I are walking the dogs up the hill toward my house. It's early Saturday morning, the sky is clear, the sun is shining. Allison has Bella I have Cassius Kevin is telling us about his job, he works for a former television star who now spends most of his life in the gym on the phone in front of the mirror. As we walk we hear a car coming up the hill behind us, we can hear it moving fast, we step toward the curb keep walking.

A small blue convertible roars past us, slams on its brakes about fifty feet in front of us. We walk toward it we see a man a light-skinned black man sitting behind the wheel he's staring at us. We keep walking when we're about ten feet away the man pulls thirty feet in front of us, stops, keeps staring. When we get closer he does it again. Closer he does it again.

Allison and Kevin are confused wonder why this is happening my instincts tell me that something unpleasant is about to happen. I pass Cassius' leash to Kevin walk toward the car the man is staring at me I speak.

Is there a problem?

The man pulls the brake on his car, opens the door, steps out. He's taller than me bigger than me he looks pissed. Allison and Kevin stop a few feet behind me. The man speaks.

Yeah, there's a problem.

What?

That your dog?

He motions toward Cassius.

Yeah.

Your dog bit my dog. Hurt 'im real bad.

What kind of dog do you have?

Got a little beagle named Elron.

I nod.

Yeah, my dog bit your dog after your dog bit him.

That's not what happened.

Yeah, it is.

No, it's not.

I was standing there. Your dog came running up, started snarling and barking, bit my dog, then came after him again, and my dog bit him back.

I got two hundred and fifty dollars in vet bills. What are you gonna do about it?

Show me the bills and we can try to work something out.

What's that mean?

It means I'll give you my address and phone number, and you can show me the bills and we'll work something out.

The man stares at me, I stare back. I'm not

scared of him, but have no interest in fighting him, or making anything out of this situation. We're neighbors. His dog, a twenty pound beagle, bit my dog, a ninety-five pound pitbull. My dog bit his dog back, and I don't doubt he hurt him, and the right thing to do is try to settle this amicably. The man turns around, opens his car door. He sits in the driver's seat, takes a pen and a pad of paper out of a backpack sitting on the passenger's seat, hands them to me. I write down my name, address, phone number, hand the pad back to him. He stares at me, speaks.

I'm glad you did that.

No problem.

He puts the pad and pen back into the backpack, takes out a pistol, looks up at me.

I said I'm glad you did that because I didn't want to go shooting anybody and I didn't want to go killing anybody.

What?

He shuts the door of his car.

You heard me.

I'm shocked. The gun is sitting on the seat, the man is staring at me, I speak.

Just show me the bill and we'll work something out.

He stares at me for another moment, starts the car, quickly pulls away. I turn around, look at Allison and Kevin. Allison is pale, looks terrified.

Kevin is staring up the street.

You okay?

Kevin shakes his head, speaks.

What was that?

The guy is obviously not right.

That's putting it mildly.

I look at Allison.

You okay?

She shakes her head, I step forward, take her hand it's shaking.

He was going to shoot us.

He wasn't going to shoot us.

I want to call the police.

We don't need to call the police.

I want to go home and call the police.

We'll go home. We're not calling the police.

We start walking up the hill. I know where the man lives I've seen his car in the driveway. We're going to have to walk past his house to get to my house, I'm hoping the car isn't there. It isn't we get to my house Allison has become increasingly more upset almost frantic. She speaks.

Call the police.

The police aren't going to do anything, Allison.

He threatened to kill us.

And if they go see him he'll deny it and nothing will happen.

Please, just call them.

It's a waste of time.

Kevin speaks.

I think you should call them.

I'll make a call, but it's not going to be to the police.

Allison speaks.

Who are you going to call?

Leonard.

What's he going to do?

I don't know. We'll see.

I pick up the phone, dial, wait, Leonard answers the phone.

Hello?

Leonard.

My son. Happy day to you.

Not really.

What's wrong?

Some motherfucker just threatened to shoot me, and maybe Allison, and maybe my friend Kevin.

What?

I tell Leonard what happened. Tell him about the car, the man, the gun, the threat. When I finish telling him, he laughs.

This is not funny, Leonard.

It's sort of funny.

Motherfucker had a gun. It wasn't funny.

Motherfucker might have had a gun, but he's nothing to worry about. He's not a tough guy.

He looked tough enough to me.

He might have looked tough, but he's no tough guy.

What's the difference?

A tough guy would have shot you, he wouldn't have threatened to shoot you. And he also violated one of the primary rules of a tough guy.

What's that?

Never show your gun, just empty it.

That's very comforting to know, Leonard.

It should be. The guy's probably not dangerous, just a bully.

How do you suggest I deal with him?

Your instincts were right. Pay the bill, settle the situation amicably, make it go away.

And what if that doesn't work?

Leonard laughs.

If there are any problems, call me.

Thank you, Leonard.

Tell Allison not worry.

I will.

I hang up the phone, turn to Allison and Kevin. Allison speaks.

What'd he say?

He told me to tell you not to worry.

What's he going to do?

Nothing.

What are you going to do?

When the guy brings me the bill, I'll work something out with him.

You should just pay it.

I probably will.

He scares me, James. I still think we should call the police.

Leonard is better than the police.

You promise?

We're going to be fine. I promise.

I don't hear from the man. No bill, no phone call, nothing. I stop by his house a couple of times when I see the car in the driveway. I knock on the door no one answers.

Leonard cancels three lunches in a row, switches our weekly lunch to every other week, starts arriving without Snapper.

Danny and I raise enough money to shoot our movie. We hire a crew, a cast, start pre-production, start shooting. Neither of us has any idea what we're doing, and because we don't have much money in Hollywood terms, almost no one on our crew has any idea what they're doing.

Allison hates her job wants to quit. I tell her she should quit, tell her she should take her time figure something else out, tell her she doesn't need to worry about money she can have mine. She says she doesn't want or need me to support her that she's fine on her own that she can pay her own bills. I tell her she can have whatever I have, take whatever she needs from me, that I don't care about money as much as her happiness, that I don't see it as support I see it as giving someone

I love a chance to make a change in their life. She's stubborn won't take anything from me she wants to do it on her own.

We keep shooting the movie the days are twenty hours long nothing goes right we fall behind schedule go over budget. Allison gets mad because we never see each other and when we do see each other I'm too tired to talk eat go out I'm too tired to do anything but sleep.

I see footage from the film realize that the film isn't very good realize that I'm no film director think that if I work harder I can somehow save my sinking ship I work harder harder harder every minute of every day is consumed with somehow saving what I've tried to create what Danny and I have spent other people's money to realize.

I spend less and less time with Allison she gets more and more angry.

I don't see Leonard at all.

Work harder and harder.

Sleep less and less.

We finish shooting the movie thank fucking god it's over.

llison's parents come to Los Angeles they want to see where she's living how she's doing. We pick them up at the airport show them Allison's apartment take them out for a fancy dinner. Next day we go to the beach show them Beverly Hills have them to my house I cook a chicken for them it's not very good. They're nice, polite people they play with Cassius and Bella, both of whom got baths prior to the parents' arrival, they pretend the food I make is edible.

Next day we drive to Newport Beach, an affluent community in Orange County. Close friends of Allison's parents live on an Island near there, we spend the day with them. We walk through the little town on the Island, sit on the sand, swim in the ocean, go for a boat ride. I do not take off my shirt in their presence, do not want them to see my tattoos. I do not swear try not to smoke.

Evening arrives we can either go back to Los Angeles or stay for dinner. Allison's parents want to stay we decide to go to a restaurant in Laguna, which is where Leonard lives. I want to call him, see him, I ask Allison, she doesn't think it would be appropriate, her parents want to spend time with her and me and their friends.

We drive south drive into Laguna we drive past the bluff where I can see Leonard's house we drive past a billboard for the Pageant of the Masters it's a photo of a living Seurat I laugh at the idea of Leonard and Snapper sitting in the crowd oohing and aahing. We drive past a restaurant I've heard them mention I can imagine them sitting on the front deck. I scan the sidewalks hoping to see them, the sidewalks are crowded no luck for me.

We pull up to the restaurant, valet my truck, wait for Allison's parents and their friends. They arrive, we walk into the restaurant. It has a tropical theme, looks like what I imagine a restaurant in Thailand would look like, wicker chairs with dark comfortable cushions, overhead fans, palm trees and large exotic flowers, candles everywhere. We're led to a table in a corner it's a large table with room for a couple more chairs. Almost immediately after we sit, I hear Leonard. I don't see him I hear him.

MY SON, MY SON.

I look around, don't see him.

I'M OVER HERE, GODDAMNIT. I'M OVER HERE, MY SON.

I laugh, continue to look around.

HERE HERE HERE HERE HERE.

I look toward the voice, see Leonard and Snapper walking toward our table. They're both wearing Hawaiian shirts, khaki shorts, docksiders. Snapper has a pair of black socks with his docksiders. They're both smiling, Leonard is waving.

My son, what are you doing here?

I stand up. Allison is smiling, shaking her head she's not angry just surprised, her parents and their friends look confused. I speak.

What's up, Leonard?

What's up? What's up? What's up is you're right in front of me, in my town. What a surprise.

I laugh, give him a hug, give Snapper a hug. Leonard looks at Allison, bows.

Beautiful lady, it's always a pleasure to see you.

Allison laughs.

You too, Leonard.

Leonard looks at Allison's parents and their friends, speaks.

And who do we have here?

Allison introduces everyone, Leonard bows to the women, shakes hands with the men, Snapper smiles and says hello. Leonard looks to the men, speaks.

Do you mind if we sit with you for a few moments?

Allison's dad says sure, Leonard motions to a busboy, shouts.

Garçon. Two more chairs. Immediately.

The busboy pulls over two chairs, Leonard and Snapper sit down. Allison's parents seem confused her mother looks at Leonard, speaks.

Your name is Leonard?

Yes, it is.

She looks at Snapper.

And your name is Snapper?

Yes, Ma'am.

What kind of name is that?

It's a nickname, Ma'am.

How did you get it?

I like to fish. I am an expert snapper fisherman. Thus the name.

She nods, and looks at Leonard.

And how do you know James?

We met several years ago. We were both on vacation at a luxury resort. We had lunch together one day, and we've been great friends ever since.

I try not to laugh, I look at Allison, she seems to be both amused and horrified. Her parents keep talking with Leonard we sit and listen to them.

Her mother asks.

Why do you call James your son?

If I had a son I would like him to be like James. Because I don't have a son, I have made James a son of sorts, and I like to call him my son.

Why don't you have children?

I've never been married, and didn't want to have a child out of wedlock.

Why didn't you get married?

I would have liked to, and I would have liked to have children, it just didn't work out for me, and I'm probably not suited for marriage.

Thankfully I met James and have experienced a form of fatherhood that has made me very happy.

Allison's father asks.

What do you do, Leonard?

I am a semi-retired business executive.

What type of business?

I'm the West Coast Director for a large Italian finance firm.

What type of finance?

We have interests in entertainment, tele-communications, we work with some unions, do some short-term, high-interest loans.

He looks at Snapper.

What do you do, Snapper?

I was a security guard, I became a collections officer, now I'm an executive assistant.

What do you assist with?

Whatever's necessary.

Her mother asks.

Do you see James often?

All the time, as much as possible.

Do you know his parents?

Wonderful people. Absolutely the best. I tried to get his father to work with me but he wouldn't do it. They're a class act, you'll love them.

Her father asks.

Are you able to discuss any of the deals you've done?

I could, of course, but our firm's policy is to be as discreet as possible. We do not like attention.

Allison's parents' friends seem confused and fascinated. Leonard tries to change the direction of the conversation, starts commenting on the women's hair, clothing, jewelry, starts flooding them with compliments.

He asks the friends if they've been to the restaurant before they say no, he smiles and says it's great you're going to love it. After a few minutes he looks at Snapper, nods, they both stand up. Leonard looks at me, speaks.

A wonderful surprise, my son.

I smile.

Yeah it was.

Lunch this week?

Yeah.

He turns to Allison.

You break my heart every time I see you.

She smiles.

Good to see you too, Leonard.

He turns to Allison's parents.

You are to be commended for having such a beautiful, intelligent, well-mannered daughter.

They both smile. Allison's mom speaks.

Thank you.

I hope to see you again, perhaps at a wedding.

They both laugh. Allison speaks.

Easy now, Leonard.

He laughs, steps back.

I hope you have a wonderful dinner.

Snapper speaks.

Nice to meet all of you.

They turn and walk away. I watch them walk away everyone at our table turns and watches them walk away, and when they're gone from view,

Allison's mom laughs and says I'm not sure how to top that, and we all laugh with her.

We start looking at the menus. Before a waiter arrives, the manager comes to our table with a bottle of wine. He speaks.

Your meal, with accompanying bottles of wine, has already been ordered for you.

He opens the bottle, pours some in a glass for Allison's dad, who sniffs it, tastes it, nods, says very good. The manager fills everyone's glass but mine.

When he's done he looks at me, speaks.

A cola will be here for you in a moment.

I laugh, say thank you. The friend of Allison's parents picks up the bottle of wine, looks at it, says wow, this is nice. As he hands the bottle to Allison's father, food starts arriving. There are plates of skewers beef chicken and shrimp, oysters with spicy salsa, seaweed salad, spinach salad with yellowtail, seviche. We share everything pass the plates amongst each other. As soon as we finish more food arrives bigger portions on bigger plates shrimp tempura, lobster tempura, black cod with miso sauce, whole fried snapper which makes me laugh, salmon teriyaki, beef tenderloin with pepper sauce. Whenever a bottle of wine is empty another appears immediately, whenever my glass of cola is empty, I get a refill. A waiter stands next to our table to take care of whatever we want, whatever we need. Allison's parents and their friends are overwhelmed by all the food the wine the service.

I've told Allison about meals like this with Leonard it's her first experience she thinks it's wonderful. When the entrees are gone and cleared we get dessert, chocolate cake, mango banana ginger and coconut ice cream, rice pudding and fresh fruit and strong coffee and subtle tea. After dessert Allison's father asks for a bill. The waiter leaves to get the manager. The manager comes to our table, speaks.

How was your meal?

Around the table he hears great, wonderful, amazing. He speaks again.

Is there anything else I can get for you?

Allison's father speaks.

The bill please.

That has been taken care of, sir.

I would like to take care of it, please.

I'm sorry, sir, but that's not possible.

I look at the manager, speak.

Thank you.

Certainly. Please let me know if you'd like anything else before you leave. The manager leaves, we stand up and leave. We say goodbye to the friends they get in their car and drive away, we get in my truck and drive away. Allison and her mother sit in the backseats, her father sits in the passenger seat. About halfway to Los Angeles, Allison and her mother are both asleep. Her father looks at me, speaks.

James.

Yeah.

I need to speak to you about something.
Okay.
And I need you to be honest with me.
Of course.
Your friend Leonard.
Yeah.
You didn't meet him at a luxury resort, did you?
No.
Did you meet him in jail or rehab?
I met him in rehab.
Why was he there?
Cocaine.
Does he still use it?
No, he's clean. Same as me.
And does West Coast Director of a large Italian finance firm mean what I think it means?
Probably.
Is that a good thing or a bad thing?
It is what it is.
And his executive assistant?
A wonderful man but also probably what you think he is.
The name Snapper doesn't have anything to do with fish, does it?
No, not a fishing reference.
Is my daughter in any danger?
Absolutely not.
Are you sure of that?
If anything, your daughter lives under a veil of protection. Leonard loves her, and would never allow anything to happen to her.

Are you involved in what he does?

No.

Does he really know your parents?

Yeah, they love him.

Allison's father looks out the window. It's dark, the highway is empty. He takes a deep breath, speaks.

It's a strange world we live in.

Yeah, it is.

He stares out the window. I drive. He turns back to me.

Will you please thank your friend Leonard for dinner, and tell him and his friend Snapper that we enjoyed meeting them.

I smile.

Yeah, I will.

We finish our movie it's not very good. We have a big premiere my parents come my brother comes Leonard comes there's a big crowd. At the after party people shake my hand pat me on the back give me their business cards tell me the movie was amazing, incredible, great. I smile say thank you but I know it wasn't very good. It hurts me to admit it, and it hurts me to accept it, my movie wasn't very good.

Allison hates her job more and more with every passing day and is more and more miserable with every passing day she comes home angry every night.

Leonard goes back to the East Coast to try to play the golf course. He says this time he's taking a briefcase full of cash with him. As I always do before his pilgrimage, I wish him luck, good luck Leonard good luck.

The script I sold goes into production, an actor from a popular television show about a group of friends in New York is the star. He hires his best friend to rewrite my script I read the new version and I hate it. I call a lawyer and I ask him if there's anything I can do about it, he reads my contract and says no and he tells me that when you take Hollywood's money you have to be prepared to eat Hollywood's shit. I don't like eating shit but I know I'm going to have to this time, so I go to my kitchen and I get a napkin.

I'm asleep. I hear the phone ring I'm asleep I hear the phone ring. Allison is sleeping next to me it's early Saturday morning we were out late last night. I hear her pick up the phone say hello. I open my eyes turn over. She has the phone to her ear I see her lose color I see fear register on her face I see her lips start to quiver she passes the phone to me her hand is shaking. I put my hand over it, speak.

What's wrong?

She shakes her head.

What's wrong?

She points to the phone.

Take it.

I put the phone to my ear, speak.

Hello.

You never paid my fucking bill.

I've heard the voice it's early I'm not awake yet. What?

You never paid my fucking bill.

I sit up. I know the voice it's my neighbor with the beagle, the blue car, the gun.

What are you talking about?

You never paid my fucking bill.

403

You never showed me the bill.

You knew how much the bill was, you know where I live, you should've fucking paid it.

I said if you showed it to me, we'd work something out. I'll still do that.

Too fucking late now.

What's that supposed to mean?

It means my cousin in the 68th Street Crips is on his way to your house right now to kill your fucking dogs and kick your ass.

What?

You heard me.

This is a huge fucking over-reaction.

Not the way I see it.

Just show me the bill and we'll work something out.

Too late for that.

He hangs up. I hang up. I look at Allison, who still looks terrified.

What'd he say to you?

He said put your boyfriend on the phone, bitch.

She takes a deep breath.

And I said what and he yelled put your fucking boyfriend on the phone you dumb fucking bitch.

You okay?

She shakes her head.

No.

Take a deep breath, calm down, everything is going to be fine.

What'd he say to you?

Doesn't matter.

I start dialing the phone.
Are you calling the police?
No.
Call the police.
No.
Phone starts ringing. Allison looks panicked.
Call the police, please.
Ringing. I take her hand.
No.
Ringing. She starts crying.
Please.
Leonard picks up.
Who dares to call me at this hour?
It's me. Did I wake you?
I've been riding my exercise bike for the last hour. What's going on?
I've got a problem, Leonard.
What's wrong?
I tell him about my conversation with my neighbor. When I'm finished he laughs. I speak.
This is not fucking funny, Leonard.
The guy's full of shit, my son. It's laughable how full of shit he is.
Sure didn't sound like he was full of shit.
He's definitely full of shit.
And how do you know that?
I've never heard of the 68th Street Crips. Now that doesn't mean they don't exist, but if they do, I can promise you that not one of them is going to risk serious fucking prison time to come up to nice, safe, leafy, lily-white, full of movie stars

Laurel Canyon to break into your house, shoot your dogs, beat your ass and somehow have to deal with your girlfriend. Gangbangers are crazy and dangerous, but they're not fucking stupid. Your obvious move here would be to call the police, who would roar up there and be sitting in your living room waiting for said supposed dog assassin to show up, at which point he would be arrested. A gang member would know that, and no gangster would be willing to risk it.

So what do I do?

Well, this guy is obviously fucked-up. And he may very well try to hurt you or the dogs, and if Allison is around, he may try to hurt her. That's not acceptable to me. I want you and Allison and the dogs to get in that shit-box truck of yours and drive down to the Four Seasons. I think Four Seasons are dog-friendly, and if they're not, they will be for you. By the time you get there, I will have called and gotten you a room. I'll try to get a big room if possible. Stay there until Monday. Do not leave. Eat your meals there, and if you need anything, clothes or books or whatever, have the concierge get it for you and charge it to the room. Have a nice time. Think of this as a little vacation. Take baths and swim in the pool and get massages and eat room service. Don't think about your asshole neighbor. When you get home on Monday, I will have taken care of your problem with him.

Thank you, Leonard.

I need you to do something for me.

Okay.

Get his address.

Okay.

And call me when you get to the hotel, so I know you're safe.

Okay.

I hang up the phone. Allison has been watching me listening to me she's still terrified I turn to her speak.

We're leaving.

Where we going?

Four Seasons.

The hotel?

Yeah.

Why are we going there?

We're going to spend the weekend there.

Why?

Leonard says it will be safe for us there.

And what do we do when we leave?

The problem will be taken care of.

What's that mean?

I didn't ask, and I'm not going to ask.

This is fucking crazy, James.

Do you want to stay here, see what happens?

No.

Then let's go.

We get up we move quickly we brush our teeth get dressed. Allison keeps some clothes at my house she packs them into a small bag with a toothbrush, some toothpaste. I get the dogs on their leashes we get in the truck drive down the hill. The blue car is in the driveway of the house Allison won't look at it I get the address. We drive to the Four Seasons, pull into the drive. The valet comes to my truck. He smiles at me like most valets smile at me and my truck, I'm not sure if they think the truck is cool or feel sorry for me for driving it. I don't really care either way.

We walk into the lobby. The dogs are excited, Cassius tries to take a piss in a potted plant. I pull him away we walk up to the reception desk. An attractive woman in her early thirties smiles at us and speaks.

Mr Frey.

Hi.

We have your room ready for you.

I laugh.

Thank you.

She hands me a small envelope with a keycard and mini-bar key.

If we can do anything to make your stay more pleasurable, please let us know.

Thank you.

We turn around walk to the elevators, take an elevator up, find our room, go inside. It's a small suite, with a bedroom and a sitting room with a couch and two chairs and a desk and a large bathroom with a marble tub and a shower and two sinks and soaps and lotions and big fat towels and thick robes. I let the dogs off their leashes they start running around smelling everything. I sit down on the couch, look at Allison, speak.

You okay?

She nods.

Yeah.

I look around the room.

Not bad.

She laughs.

Yeah, not bad.

I stand put my arms around her kiss her softly on the neck tell her I love her, she puts her arms around me tells me she loves me and we stand in the middle of the room silently holding each other.

We spend the rest of the weekend relaxing eating room service sitting by the pool watching pay-per-view movies taking baths lounging around in the robes. I get the dogs steaks cut them into little pieces, I take them for walks in the underground parking garage. They sleep in the bed with us we sleep well, easily, without worry.

Monday morning Allison and I have breakfast together, I drive her to work. I'm nervous as I go home start driving up the hill toward my house. I approach the man's house. I see a moving van parked on the curb. Men are moving furniture from the house to the truck. The blue convertible is filled with boxes. The man is standing in the door he is speaking into a cell phone. He looks nervous, scared. He sees my truck he immediately turns and walks into the house.

Two days later there is a For Sale sign in the front yard.

I don't see Leonard for two months. He calls me twice he doesn't sound well I ask him if he's okay he says yes, just busy, got some shit going on. I ask him if I can help in any way he says no.

The movie I shot doesn't sell we lose all of the investors' money.

Allison and I start fighting. We fight over everything. There's no good reason for the fighting, and neither of us wants to fight, but we can't seem to stop, and every day my heart breaks a little more, with each fight my heart breaks a little more.

I take a job writing a script for a children's movie. It's an idiotic job and I only do it for the money. I don't give a shit about it and after I turn in my first draft, I get fired.

Cassius and Bella get in a fight and tear each other up. I have to take them both to the vet they both get stitched, they both get infections, they both end up on antibiotics, they both end up with scars. I have no idea why they started fighting, and five minutes after I break it up, they're licking each other's wounds. Aside from Leonard and Allison, they're the best friends I've got, and when they hurt I hurt, and I can't imagine living without them, and the entire incident scares the shit out of me.

There's a huge storm with huge winds a huge tree in my backyard falls it falls through my fucking roof. I'm sleeping when it happens, it sounds like a fucking bomb exploded in my living room. I jump out of bed run into the living room there are tree branches and sticks and leaves everywhere I look up and I can see a black, black sky. I stand there and I look up and it rains on me and I stare up at a black, black sky.

Just before noon. I'm sitting in my living room. It took two weeks to fix the roof I stayed at Allison's we fought the entire time. I'm sitting in front of the television. I'm smoking a cigarette I'm drinking a cola the dogs are on either side of me. We're watching a talk show. Two sisters who are both married to their cousin, the same cousin, are fighting each other. They're throwing punches, screaming, scratching, pulling each other's hair. It's sick, but I enjoy watching it. The phone rings I pick it up. Leonard speaks.

My son.

What's up, Leonard?

I need to see you.

Okay.

I need to see you right now.

Where are you?

At a diner in Hollywood.

What are you doing there?

Doesn't matter, I just need to see you.

Okay.

Can you come now?

Sure.

He gives me the name of the diner I know where it is, I get in the truck drive down, park on the street, which is in a dangerous, rundown neighborhood. I walk into the diner see Leonard sitting in a corner facing the door. He stands as I walk toward him. He looks nervous, anxious.

He speaks.

Thanks for coming.

Of course.

He steps around the table, gives me a hug. We separate. I speak.

What's wrong?

Let's sit.

We sit down. He speaks.

Do you want anything?

No.

Everything okay with you?

Yeah.

Allison?

She's fine.

The dogs?

They're fine.

Work?

It's fine, Leonard, everything's fine.

Good.

What's wrong?

What makes you think something is wrong?

You've been away, I haven't heard from you. We're sitting in this shithole diner in a shithole neighborhood. You look nervous and you seem anxious and I can see your hand is shaking, which is something I've never seen before.

He nods.

You're good, my son, real good.

I laugh.

What's wrong, Leonard? Are you doing coke?

Fuck no. Never. You should know I'm done with that.

Then what's wrong?

I'm going away for a while.

Where you going?

I can't tell you.

Why?

I just can't.

Is this why I haven't seen you, and why when I've spoken to you, you've seemed fucking weird?

Yes.

Where you going?

I can't tell you.

Is someone trying to kill you?

No.

Are you going to jail?

No.

What the fuck, Leonard.

I'm sorry.

I don't understand this.

At some point you will.

When?

When I can, and I don't know when that will be, I'll get in touch with you.

And that's it?

Trust that I have to do what I'm doing, and that when I can, I will be in touch with you.

I look away, shake my head, bite my lip. I'm confused and angry and hurt I don't understand what's happening. I'm scared because Leonard is scared, nervous because he's nervous. I've never seen him scared or nervous before something bad is happening, something bad is happening. He speaks.

Do you trust me?

Of course I do.

I've got to go.

I don't want you to get killed, Leonard. And if you're locked up I want to come see you.

You said you trusted me.

I do.

Then trust that's not what's happening, and trust that I'll be in touch.

I look at him, nod. He stands.

Give me a hug, my son.

I stand, give him a hug. I don't want to cry I force myself not to cry. We separate, he steps away, speaks.

Don't be a dumbfuck.

I laugh.

No drinking, no drugs, no stupid bullshit.

I laugh again.

Okay.

Give Allison a kiss for me, and give those damn doggies some nice pats on the head.

I will.

Goodbye, my son.

He turns and walks out of the diner.

First month second month I pretend he's away on one of his trips, that he's busy, that our conversation at the diner didn't take place. That life is as it has been for the last three years, that he's going to call or start banging on my door or just appear in my living room. I pretend that life is as it has been.

I fail upward, only in Hollywood is failure rewarded. Often the bigger the failure, the bigger the reward. In my case, I wrote an awful movie made worse by a lame television star and his dumbass director best friend that was produced by a big studio and released in several thousand theaters all over America to resoundingly awful reviews and huge numbers of empty seats. I wrote, produced and directed a second movie that was so bad that it was deemed unreleasable by every distributor in America. I wrote a children's movie for a studio and the first draft was so awful that it immediately got me fired. Somehow, I keep getting work, and I keep getting work that pays me more and more money.

I re-write a thriller script. The script is terrible when I start, and is only slightly less terrible when I finish. I get fired again.

Danny meets an incredibly wealthy guy about the same age as us he's from an incredibly wealthy family. The guy wants to get into the movie business. Danny convinces him to fund a company for us. We open an office, hire a staff. I laugh every time I walk through the front door.

Three months nothing, four months nothing. I wonder where he is what he's doing, if he's running from someone, if he's in jail, if he's alive. I wonder if he's happy and laughing I doubt it, if he's pissed maybe, if he's scared yes, I think he's scared. I wonder if he's safe I don't know, I doubt it. Part of me clings to the notion that this is some sort of joke, that he's going to come through my door in a minute and yell my son, My Son, MY SON, that we'll laugh and laugh and laugh about how he fooled me. Part of me knows it's a defense mechanism, that I lost Lilly and though I've moved on, I've never recovered from it, and may never recover from it. I don't want to lose my friend Leonard. I don't want to lose him.

I decide to buy a house I want to live near the ocean. My mom comes to town to help me look for a house, Allison helps me look for a house. We find an old bungalow in Venice half a block from the beach. I take Cassius and Bella out to see the house they approve, Cassius asks if he can take surfing lessons, Bella wants a bikini. I buy the house move in. I hardly have any furniture so the house is almost entirely empty.

Allison and I keep fighting every fucking day there's a new fucking fight. She's mad at me because she wants to move into my house and I want her to move into my house but her parents won't approve of her moving in until we're engaged and I'm not ready to be engaged. All we do is fucking fight. I hate the fights. Hate myself for engaging in them. I try to stop, try to get her to stop, and for whatever reason, we can't stop.

Cassius and Bella have two more altercations. They hurt each other badly each time. I have their vet help me, I hire a trainer to help me, I hire an animal behavior specialist to help me. I love my dogs and I want them to be happy, I do everything I can to try to solve the problem. I talk to everyone I can who might be able to help me.

F ive six seven eight. Nine months. Nothing. Absolutely nothing. I check my mail nothing, voicemails nothing. I drive down to his house in Laguna someone else is living there. I call the customer service number on the back of one of his phonecards. I ask if he's available or if there is a contact number, they say they've never heard of him, I speak to a supervisor, they say they've never heard of him. I have no way of reaching Snapper. I know his first name is Dominic, I don't know his last name. I have no way of reaching Olivia, I know she works at a casino, I don't know which casino. I go to the steakhouse where we used to eat lunch, the Maitre d' greets me, says hello I haven't seen you in a while, I ask him if he's seen Leonard, he says no.

Allison and I break up. It isn't her fault and it isn't my fault. We still love each other but we can't get along and we're tired of fighting and we're tired of hurting each other and we need to be apart. I miss her. I miss everything about her. My life my heart my house my bed is empty without her, I'm empty without her. I cry myself to sleep at night. She's on the other side of town it might as well be the other side of the earth. I cry myself to sleep at night.

Ten months, eleven months, a year I haven't heard from him. I start to wonder if I ever will. I start to wonder if he's dead. If he is, I assume someone killed him. If someone killed him, I hope they did it quickly.

I want to get out of Los Angeles. I think it will be good for me to get out of town, get away from my memories of Allison and Leonard, away from my unhappiness, away from my emptiness. Danny and I decide to make a movie in Seattle. After my previous failures as a writer and a director, I decide that on this movie I'll function only as a producer. I move up there, bring the doggies with me, we live in a hotel.

Two days after we arrive it starts raining. It rains for sixty-three straight days. I hate it. The dogs hate it. We walk outside it's cold and gray we're immediately wet it fucking sucks. I made a mistake coming up here. I shouldn't have run away from my loss, I should have known it would run with me. If I could, I would go back. Go back to Los Angeles to Venice to my house to my life to whatever else I have and have to deal with, be it good, be it bad. I have to stay here for this movie there is too much of someone else's money involved to leave, I have to stay here for five or six months.

The movie is an absolute disaster. The actors are difficult, the crew hates each other, one of the

425

cameramen gets hit by a truck and breaks his arm, leg, jaw and cheekbone, one of our RV's gets stolen, we total a Seattle City Police cruiser, and, after a week, we're over-budget and behind-schedule.

Thirteen fourteen, fifteen sixteen. I assume he's gone, not coming back, dead, killed by someone for something in his past. I would have heard something by now. I would have heard something.

Cassius and Bella get in another fight. It's in the hotel room there's no rhyme or reason for it they just start fighting. Bella gets her throat torn I get my finger bitten. Bella ends up in the vet hospital my fingers swell they look like sausages I end up in the human hospital. When I get out I take Cassius to another vet who is also a behavioral specialist and a pitbull breeder. I just want my little boy, my mister big man, my best buddy to be better and to be happy.

The vet asks me about Cassius' history, his breeding, his life. He examines Cassius, takes him to his home for two days, brings him back, we meet in his office.

Cassius is three years old. He tells me that three is the age where male dogs reach full maturity. Cassius, the Son of Cholo, comes from a gene line of fighting dogs. Not all pitbulls are fighting dogs but Cassius is absolutely a fighting dog. He is genetically pre-programmed to be aggressive, to want to fight, to seek out fights. He will not change, and there is no way to change him, and the older he gets, the more aggressive he will become.

Cassius has grown to be almost one hundred pounds. He is all muscle, he is incredibly strong. The vet tells me I can try to micromanage his life, and keep him in the situations where he will not have outlets for his aggression, but that he will be unhappy and frustrated because he will not be allowed to do what his instincts are telling him he should do. I look at Cassius, who is sitting at my feet wagging his tail looking up at me.

I ask the vet what he thinks I should do, he tells me that he thinks I should put Cassius down, that it will be best for him, for me, for Bella. I don't want to accept the vet's opinion, but I know he's right. I look down at Cassius he's still sitting at my feet, I start to cry. He senses something is wrong he wants to make me feel better he jumps up starts licking my face. I put my arms around him and I cry and I tell him I love him, I love him so much, I tell him I'm sorry, I'm so sorry, I'm so sorry.

The vet tells me it will be painless, that I can be with him. We walk into an operating room Cassius jumps up on a steel table. The vet prepares the needle. I hold Cassius and I tell him over and over that I love him and that I'm sorry and that I'll miss him and he kisses me, kisses me, kisses me, he tries to make me feel better he has no idea. The vet inserts the needle, depresses the plunger. Cassius yelps like a little puppy, my big tough pitbull feels the sting, I hold him as his blood courses through his veins I hold him as he stumbles, as he falls, I hold him as he dies. I look into his eyes and I tell him I love him and I'll miss him and I'm so so so sorry. He dies in my arms and I hold him and I cry, I cry, I cry.

I am lonely and I am lost and I hate what I'm doing and I hate my life. I miss Lilly I still miss her. I miss Leonard I'm allowing myself to mourn him. I miss Allison I wish it could have worked with her I still love her. I miss Cassius and I hate myself for what happened with him. I am lonely and I am lost and I want to go home. I've spent my whole life moving, running, trying to escape, it doesn't fucking work. I want to go back to Los Angeles, I want to go home.

We finish shooting the movie. I have a week or two of work before I can leave, we have to shut everything down, return all of the equipment, clear the payroll, clear the bills. At the end of another long, shitty day I go back to the hotel to go to sleep. Bella and I walk in there's a stack of mail, most of it forwarded to me from Los Angeles. I start going through it bill, offer for a credit card, bill, another offer for another credit card. There's a postcard. It's a picture of the Golden Gate Bridge in San Francisco. I look at it, I don't know anyone in San Francisco who would be sending me this postcard, I look at it.

I have an idea maybe he's alive, maybe he's alive. I smile, you motherfucker Leonard, why did you wait so long, I smile.

I turn it over. It has my name on it, the address of the hotel where I'm staying, there is no note, just another address in the section where a note would be, an address in San Francisco.

I smile.

You motherfucker.

Why'd you wait so long.
I smile.

SAN FRANCISCO

I pack my shit there isn't much. I'm leaving Seattle as soon as I can.

Danny can handle the rest of the work without me.

I drive south through Washington, Oregon, Northern California. Bella rides shotgun, we stop for food, coffee, cigarettes, a walk every few hours, a bathroom break every few hours.

I cross the Bay Bridge into San Francisco. I'm staying with a friend from Paris, a woman named Colleen. Colleen has black hair, black eyes, always wears black clothes, looks like a movie star from the forties. She's seven years older than me, works at an Internet company during the day, makes paintings and collages at night. In Paris she made hats, shoes, clothes, worked at an advertising agency, and she was my only friend who wasn't a degenerate.

I find her house, which is in one of San Francisco's valleys. She gives me a hug, a big kiss, says James is in San Francisco, I'm so happy to see him. I laugh give her a hug, a big kiss. I drop my bags in her place, she wants to take me to lunch I tell her I need to go somewhere first, I give her the address. We get in my truck I bring Bella with us she'll be happy to see Leonard he'll be happy to see her. The address is on the other side of town, Colleen knows the general area. We drive up hills and down hills, up and down up a hill. We're on the street I look at the numbers on the houses. We're two blocks away, a block away. I see a white Mercedes sitting in a driveway I laugh. It's an old Mercedes, from sometime in the fifties or sixties, it's a small convertible in perfect condition. Colleen asks me why I'm laughing I just smile.

I pull over. I tell Colleen we may have to delay lunch, or at least switch the venue, I tell her I'll know in a minute. I get out of the car, Bella comes with me.

We walk toward the front door. The house is a small, two-story, white frame house with black shutters. The lawn is well-tended, there are flower beds on both sides of the front door. It is a nice, clean house, it's inconspicuous, there's no reason to give it a second look.

I step to the door, ring the bell. I'm excited to see my friend, my old friend Leonard. I wait for someone to answer, push the bell again. I wait, wait, no one comes to the door. I wonder if the bell is broken. I close my fist and I knock. I wait, nothing, knock again, nothing. I think about leaving a note, decide against it, I don't know the details of this situation. Bella and I walk back to the car. I'm not disappointed, I know he's here because of the Mercedes. I'll come back until someone answers the door. I'll keep coming back.

We go to lunch. I try again after lunch, there's no one home.

I try again before dinner, there's no one home.

I try again after dinner.

No one home.

I leave Colleen's house I tell her I'm going back to Los Angeles. If I don't find Leonard, I will go back, wait a few days, come back here.

I pull up to the house. It's a beautiful, clear, warm, sunny day. The convertible is sitting at the curb the top is down.

He's alive.

I look toward the front door it's open. I can see through a screen door into the house.

My friend Leonard is alive.

Windows are wide open.

Motherfucker disappeared for eighteen months, didn't say shit about where he was or what he was doing, I thought he was dead.

Curtains fluttering.

He's alive.

I hear the faint sounds of classical music. Bella's on a leash we walk to the door I press the bell. I wait. I see movement.

I smile, my friend Leonard is alive.

A man comes to the door. He's not Leonard. He looks like he's about thirty. He's tall, thin, has short blond hair parted to one side. He's wearing khakis, black leather sandals, a white oxford. He looks very clean. He stands at the door, speaks in a bitchy, effeminate way.

May I help you?

Leonard here?

How may I help you?

I have the postcard in my back pocket, I take it out, hold it up.

I got this postcard in the mail. It has this address on the back, I thought it might be from my friend Leonard.

May I see it?

Sure.

He opens the door enough for me to pass him the card. He looks at it, looks back at me, speaks.

Your name is?

James.

He motions to Bella.

And who is that?

Bella.

He looks at Bella, speaks.

Hi, Bella.

She wags her tail.

Isn't there another one? Cassius?

He died.

I'm sorry.

It sucked.

I'm sure it did. I know you loved him.

Who are you?

He opens the door.

My name's Freddie. I sent you that card. We've been waiting for you.

Is Leonard here.

Yes.

I step inside the house. There are pristine, pale wood floors. All of the furniture is white, there are thick, soft, white couches and chairs. There are impressionist prints on the walls, there are flowers everywhere. Freddie leads me through the foyer, the living room, I can see a deck. I can see Leonard, or what appears to be a faded version of Leonard, sitting on a chaise lounge on the deck, he's wrapped in a white cotton blanket.

As I walk toward him he turns to me. He smiles, lifts his hand, speaks, his voice is weak and scratchy.

My son. My son has arrived.

I walk onto the deck. Freddie stays behind, leaves us alone. I look at Leonard I'm shocked, speechless. He's lost thirty or forty pounds. There are open sores on his arms and neck. His hair looks dry and brittle, his skin is gray and sallow. He looks like he hasn't eaten in a month, like a skeleton, like a dead man. The only thing that remains unchanged are his eyes, which are clear and fixed, dark brown, alive.

My son, you found me.

I'm happy to see him but shocked. I smile.

You sent for me.

I lean down to hug him.

You don't have to touch me if you don't want to.

Fuck that, Leonard.

He laughs, I give him a hug, a strong hug. He feels small and fragile in my arms, feels like a child. He's skin and bones, smells like medicine, sickness, decay. He hugs me back, his arms are weak, incredibly weak.

It's good to see you, Leonard.

My son. It's good to see you too.

I pull away. Bella puts her front legs on the edge of the lounge, kisses Leonard's hand. He looks down at her, smiles.

Ooh, Bella, you little angel.

He leans down, she kisses his face.

Where's your brother? Where's the Big Boy?

He died.

Leonard looks up. He looks hurt.

What happened?

I shake my head. Leonard speaks.

Bad?

Yeah.

And how's Allison?

I laugh.

That was bad too.

She's okay, isn't she?

I assume so, though I haven't spoken to her in a while.

Big changes, my son.

I've been through worse, but it wasn't fun.

Big change never is.

Looks like you're experiencing some big changes too.

He laughs.

That's one way of putting it.

What's going on here, Leonard?

He laughs.

What's going on? Isn't that the fucking question.

You look fucking awful.

He laughs, coughs, speaks.

Pull up a chair.

I look around the deck there are a couple of other chairs I pull one of them over sit down.

You want the long version or the short version?

I'm not going anywhere.

He laughs, coughs, the cough gets worse. I look at him and I'm scared, I put my arms around him pat him on the back. He stops coughing, I pull away, he spits something unpleasant off the deck and into the yard. He laughs, speaks.

Pretty nice, huh?

What's wrong?

You ready?

Yeah, I'm ready.

He looks at me, takes a deep breath.

I'm gay, and I'm dying of AIDS.

I look at him. I don't know what to say. He speaks.

You okay?

I nod.

Yeah.

I'm gay, my son, and I'm dying of AIDS.

I heard you.

Surprised?

444

That would be one way to put it.

You can leave if you want.

Why would I leave?

I don't know what your position is on being gay, and I don't know what your position is on AIDS.

My position is that you're my friend, and if you're gay, you're gay, it doesn't make any difference to me, and if you've got AIDS, I'm sorry, and I'm going to do whatever I can to help you.

He smiles.

Thank you, my son.

You gonna give me the long version or the short version?

He smiles again, looks away, looks out across the deck. He closes his eyes, takes a deep breath as if he's gathering his strength, looks back.

I've always known. For as long as I've had memories, I've known. When I was a kid, I liked playing with girls more than boys and liked looking at boys more than girls. At the time I didn't know what that meant, though I did know that in a Roman Catholic Italian family, it wasn't considered right. As I grew up, got older, whatever it was I felt got stronger, and I had to work harder to ignore it. I went on dates. When I was old enough, I slept with women, I got engaged a couple of times, and just kept putting the weddings off. Although I love women, I love their company and their beauty, and could perform with them, I just couldn't follow through because it wasn't right for me. All the way through I overcompensated for what I felt,

445

which was a love for men, by being the meanest, craziest, most violent motherfucker anybody knew, that way nobody could question me or doubt me or even suspect me, because a person who did some of the things I did could never be a fairy, even though I was, and I am. What happened, because of the world I lived in, was that my violence made me more respected, and ultimately, more successful. That success locked me into my charade even more, because I was around more people, and they watched me more carefully.

I was in my early twenties the first time I slept with a man. He was a cab driver in New York. We were driving, talking, and he could tell somehow, and he propositioned me and I accepted, and it happened in the back of his cab, which we parked in an alley. I hated myself for it, fucking hated myself, and I hated him for being with me. I knew, though, that I would do it again, and I did, over and over and over, for the rest of my life, always with random men in random places, always with men who had no idea who I was or had any connection to me. I kept hating myself for a while, then I just accepted what I was, and I also accepted that I could never be open about it. If I was ever open, or if I got caught, I would get killed, because my business doesn't allow for weakness. Even though being gay isn't weak, that would have been the perception. Violent men, criminals, people like me, would have never allowed or tolerated or trusted or respected me, and at the first chance they got, they'd have put me in the fucking ground.

Somewhere along the way I picked up HIV. I have no idea from who or when. About six years ago I woke up one day and felt like something was wrong, so I took a test and it came back positive. When I got the result I left the doctor's office and I never went back. I know there are things I could have done with a doctor and drugs and combinations of drugs I could have taken to slow down the virus, and at this point they say there are things that can almost stop it, but if I had started going to a doctor, and had gone on a drug regimen, people would have found out. And again, if my associates had found out, they would have killed me.

I started thinking about what I have done, and I'll explain exactly what I've done soon, a few months after I met you and after you met Lilly. I remember very vividly you telling me about Lilly's desire to feel free from her addictions and the hell of her life, and her telling you that to her, a second of freedom was worth more than a lifetime of bondage. I thought about that every day, every fucking day, and then I started watching you and watching how you took responsibility for the mess you had made of your life, and how you rejected everything you were told would save you in favor of what you believed, which was that you had the power to make the decisions that would decide the course of your existence. What I learned from

the two of you was that freedom is worth sacrifice, and that I was in charge of my life and how
I lived it and that I could decide to do anything I
wanted to do. I wanted to escape, and be free,
free of my job, of my position, of my role. I
wanted out of the prison I built around myself.
I wanted to get the fuck out.

I started taking steps to do it when you were in
Chicago. I knew the virus would get me sooner
or later, so I was on a time schedule. My plan was
to try to legitimize some of my businesses, so that
I could make more money and hide it easier. I
also read that if I started living better by exercising, eating properly and living as cleanly as
possible, it might slow the virus down. That's what
all my diets were about, all my exercise plans, and
I don't know if they did anything or not. Once
the virus started mutating, I was going to disappear, which is what I did, so that, before I died,
I could live part of my life as a normal gay man,
albeit a normal gay man who was dying of AIDS.

That's what I've been doing since I last saw you.
First thing I did was get a fake passport and leave
the country. I knew once I was gone that people
would be looking for me, though not because I was
gay, they probably still don't know that, but because
I disappeared with a big pile of money. I knew if
they found me they would kill me. Being far
away, where no one knew me or would recognize
me, was important. I went to London, Paris, Rome,
Athens, Madrid, Moscow and St Petersburg. I

looked at beautiful art and saw the sights and went to gay bars at night and looked at beautiful men. I went to India and saw the Taj Mahal, went to China and saw the Wall, went to Japan and saw all sorts of weirdness. After seven months I came back to the States and settled here. I've been very careful since I've been here. I don't usually go out during the day. When I go out at night, I go to gay bars and restaurants with a predominantly gay clientele. I've been out on a few dates, I fell in love briefly, I've done some of the things I've always dreamed of being able to do.

Over the course of time I've also gotten sicker and sicker. As you can see, I'm not in good shape. I hesitated to contact you until recently because I didn't want you followed, and I'm sure at various points over the last year and a half you have been watched very carefully. Snapper, who is a wonderful man, but who is also a man with a nasty job that he does very well, would have known that you might be able to lead him to me, and that's probably what he's been doing since I left, trying to find me and kill me. I don't have much time left. If you leave when I'm finished talking, I'll understand, and I'll be grateful to you for coming at all. What I did was fucked-up, but it's what I did to complete my life, to be able to die happy. Now that I've seen you, I have only one thing left on my list of things to do before I die, which is play the golf course where my father worked and where I promised him I would play. To pull up, park my car in the lot, walk through the front door, and play that fucking course just like one of the members. I know that it isn't going to happen, and if that's all I haven't done, I'm fine with it.

Leonard stops speaking, slumps into his chair as if speaking has taken all of his strength. I look at him broken and dying, wasting away, sores all over his body, wrapped in his blanket, he looks at me I speak.

A lot of things make more sense now.

Like what?

No wife, no girlfriends. Your love of clothes and white cars. Why all of my girlfriends, romantic and platonic, wanted to be your best friend. The house in Laguna Beach, which is a gay town, that I thought you loved because of the view. Why you said Allison, who drops jaws everywhere she goes, wasn't your type. The Speedo bikini you used to wear when you went swimming.

He laughs.

The signs were there. It's fucking amazing nobody ever figured it out. And I still have that suit.

I understand it now.

He laughs again, it is a weak laugh.

Straight or gay I stick to my guns on it, it's for swimmers, Europeans, and motherfuckers with style.

I laugh.

I'm still not any of them.

Your loss. Someday you'll realize. Your loss.

Is Freddie your boyfriend?

No, though in a different situation I might want him to be. He's my care-giver, a nurse of sorts. He helps me deal with what's happening to me.

I look at him.

I'm sorry, Leonard.

For what?

I'm sorry you had to live like that for so long, sorry that you had to hide, and I'm sorry that you're dying.

I chose how to live as I've lived, and I'm choosing how to die as I'm going to die. You shouldn't be sorry. If anything I should be sorry, for keeping the secret from you and for disappearing on you.

No apology necessary.

Thank you.

Is there anything I can do?

Hang out with me. That's all I want. Some time with my son.

That's why I'm here.

Thank you, James, thank you.

Freddie orders lunch from an Italian restaurant. He sets up a table on the deck. We have mozzarella and tomato, pappardelle with boar ragu, veal chops, gelato. I eat like a pig, Leonard hardly eats at all. He feeds most of his lunch to Bella, pretends to eat the rest by pushing his food around the plate. I ask him about his travels, he smiles, calls for Freddie, asks him to get his books.

Freddie brings out a stack of books, sets them on a table. There are a few art books, a couple of photo albums, four or five weathered travel guides.

Freddie starts to walk away, Leonard speaks.

Don't you want to look at them with us?

Freddie turns around, smiles.

You've shown them to me about seventy-five times, Leonard. I think I can skip this viewing.

They both laugh, Freddie goes back into the house. Leonard stares at the books for a moment, smiles. He reaches for one of the travel guides.

Move your chair over here, my son.

I move my chair so that I'm sitting next to him.

We'll start with London.

London is a good place.

A great place. Much, much better than I expected. Everyone says the food is bad and that the English have terrible teeth, but I ate like a king and saw plenty of nice choppers.

I laugh.

And the accents. They're everywhere. Wonderful British accents.

Laugh.

He opens the book, opens one of the photo albums. There is a picture of him at a stadium surrounded by fans in red and white jerseys, with banners, hats, horns and beers.

I open to Wembley, where I saw the FA Cup final, which is sort of like the English version of the Super Bowl.

For soccer.

Yes, for soccer, though they call it football.

How was it?

Great. They're crazy about their football. They have to keep the fans of the teams separated by big fences or they'll attack each other. They make our fans look like poodles.

He keeps flipping through the books, opening a passage in a guide book to a corresponding photo, he starts showing me the highlights of his trip to London. He shows me his hotel, the Covent Garden, which he calls delightful. He reads me a passage about his favorite restaurant, which is the oldest fish and chips stand in the city. He talks about the London Dungeon Museum, there were fucking rats running in circles around the iron maiden, about the British National Museum, half of civilization under one big fucking roof, about the National Portrait Gallery and the Tate, my oh my they took my breath away. He talks about the weather it sucked but I didn't mind, about the friendly disposition of the city, it's like a cleaner, nicer version of New York.

He closes London we work our way through France. He says France is like a beautiful woman who knows she's beautiful, some people will love her beauty and arrogance, some people will hate it. Leonard loves it, says he spent two weeks wandering aimlessly around Paris drinking coffee and shopping and watching people and looking at the antique stands along the Seine, he spent two days in the Louvre and two in the D'Orsay, he spent another at the Musée Rodin. He ate every meal in a different restaurant, would just stop as he walked, pick places at random, he was never disappointed.

We move through the rest of Western Europe he says I loved it all, LOVED IT ALL. We move to Eastern Europe he says man, it's wonderful over there, we should have never been enemies with those people. We skip Italy he says he has another book for that part of his trip. I ask him if there's anything he didn't like about Europe he says the Greeks were mean and the weather in Russia sucked, other than that, I fucking loved it all. He opens the Asian guides, starts taking me through his Indian trip. He says India is a different world, one every American should be required to visit so that we understand how fortunate we are and how stupid we are. He says that despite the crushing poverty, the people are happy and hopeful and optimistic, and despite our own ludicrous wealth, we're depressed and unsatisfied and pessimistic. He talks about the cities you can't believe how many fucking people there are, the food it gave me the fucking shits, the art it's all religious, totally simple and pure, like early renaissance art, which may never have been exceeded. He says the Taj Mahal, the greatest and most magnificent monument to love the world has ever seen, is a fitting symbol for the country as a whole.

We open the book on China he tells me about Beijing it's huge and dirty and it smells and there are bikes everywhere, the wall it's so cool I can't even fucking believe it actually exists, the Forbidden City it makes every other palace in the world look like a steaming pile of dogshit. He tells me about Japan it's weird and noble and somehow simultaneously stuck in the past and in some version of the future, it's like everything is turned up to eleven.

We finish with the guide books and the photo albums, the last picture in the album is of a smiling Leonard sitting at a dinner table with a group of five hundred pound sumo wrestlers, there is enough food to feed fifty people. Leonard is still Leonard wherever he goes under whatever conditions, I laugh at the picture, he closes the albums.

He reaches for the art books, speaks.

Are you ready?

For what?

God, beauty, love. Perfection in multiple forms.

I motion to the books.

In those books?

He nods.

In these books.

That's a tall order, Leonard.

He smiles.

Order filled.

He opens the first book. The text is in Italian, there isn't much of it.

Leonard stops talking, starts slowly turning the pages, the pages are filled with color reproductions of paintings, frescoes, altars. I don't know or recognize many of the paintings, though I do recognize names: Botticelli, da Vinci, Caravaggio, Correggio, Ghirlandaio, Raphael, Tiepolo, Tintoretto, Titian. We spend a couple of minutes on each page. Sometimes Leonard will say where the piece exists, the Uffizi, Galleria Borghese, Santi Apostoli, the Pope's rooms at the Vatican, sometimes he'll point to a small detail, a drifting lock of hair, the reflection of a glass, a shading, a shadow, the look of a face.

We close the first book. Leonard carefully sets it apart from the guide books and photo albums. He opens the second book, which is on the work of Michelangelo. He moves more slowly through the pages, some of which appear to be stained in some way. We see the Pietà, David from twenty angles. We see the sketches for the Tomb of Julius II, the plans and corresponding photographs of the Laurentian Library. There is a page for each of the panels of the Sistine Chapel, the entire ceiling is spread across two pages. There are pages devoted to the details of the Last Judgment, the entire wall is spread across two pages. As we stare at the Last Judgment, tears start falling onto the pages. Leonard doesn't bother to wipe them away.

God, beauty, love. Perfection in multiple forms.

We stare at the pages and tears fall from Leonard's cheeks.

God, beauty, love.

Perfection in multiple forms.

I stay at Leonard's house. Bella and I stay in a guest room on the second floor. Freddie stays in another room on the second floor. Leonard has a bedroom set up in what used to be the dining room on the first floor. I carry Leonard to bed at night, carry him from his bed to the deck in the morning. We eat breakfast on the deck, he has sores in his mouth and all he wants is bread and water, he has trouble taking it down.

We play cards.

We watch baseball games, sports highlight shows. We rent movies Leonard has a list of movies he wants to see before he's gone *The Graduate, The Bridge on the River Kwai, E.T. – The Extra-Terrestrial, Annie Hall, Snow White and the Seven Dwarfs.*

We go out to a couple of gay bars. We go at night. We go to bars that are quieter, where they have seating Leonard can't stand up for very long. He drinks water, dances in his seat to the music, talks to other men, flirts with them, kicks me under the table when I tell him I think one of them likes him.

We take the convertible for drives through Marin

late at night. We drive with the top down Leonard stares at the hills the trees the vineyards the stars the moon the sky.

We make crank calls, pick up the phone dial random numbers start speaking absolute gibberish to whoever answers. They always hang up on us, we laugh and laugh and laugh and laugh.

I take him to San Francisco's art museum. It's early we're the first ones in line. He has trouble walking, I hold his hand as we wander through the galleries, he cries when we leave.

He asks me about my work I tell him I hate it. He laughs says you have discovered the ventriloquist that hides behind Hollywood's doll. I tell him no, I hate what I do because I went to Los Angeles to make some money so that I could try to write a book and somewhere along the way I got lost. He says quit, write a book, I tell him it's not that easy I have bills and responsibilities he laughs again and says it is that easy, quit your fucking job and write a fucking book. He asks about Allison I tell him that we still love each other but we're through, he asks if there's anyone else I say maybe, he asks who I tell him about one of my neighbors her name is Maya we're friends but nothing more. He says he likes the name Maya, it's a noble beautiful name.

We go to the beach at sunset. He sits wrapped in blankets shivering. I offer to take him home he says no, he wants to stay. We watch the waves crash, we listen to the wind scream, we watch the sun go down, we watch the sun go down.

Leonard asks me if there's anything I need to know before he dies, I think about it for a minute, turn to him, say what's the meaning of life, Leonard? He laughs, says that's an easy one, my son, it's whatever you want it to be.

We finish dinner we ordered Chinese.
Leonard hardly ate, he eats less and
less every day. Leonard seems distant,
distracted, I ask him if he's okay.

I was thinking about my friend Andrew.

Who's he?

He was my lover.

Your lover?

Yeah, my lover.

I laugh.

The person you fell in love with?

Yeah.

You should call him your boyfriend, not your
lover.

Why?

Lover is cheesy.

Leonard laughs.

You better watch out.

Why?

You're not allowed to call me cheesy.

I am if you use the word lover.

How many years have I been listening to you
wax poetic about your various girlfriends, oh I

461

love her and I can't live without her, oh she's so beautiful, oh her eyes, her eyes, her eyes.

I laugh.

A lot of years.

I'm going to call him my lover, Cheddar Boy, and you're not going to say shit about it.

I laugh again.

Okay, Leonard, call him whatever you want.

My lover.

Where is he?

Across town.

Really?

Yeah.

Why don't you see him?

I don't want to.

Why?

It hurts too much.

Why?

Because love hurts sometimes, and it hurts more if you know it's not going to work out.

How do you know it wasn't going to work out?

Look at me. It wasn't going to work out.

Who is he?

Just a guy. He's a lawyer. He's a little older than me.

A lawyer?

A lawyer. A corporate lawyer. He does work for technology companies.

And older?

I like older men. They make me feel young.

I laugh.

How'd you meet?

Freddie and I went out to dinner. He was sitting alone at a table. We asked him to join us.

Love at first sight?

Leonard smiles.

Yes.

First time?

No, but the first time I ever did anything about it.

What happened?

We ate dinner. He gave me his card. I called him the next day and asked him out. We ate dinner again that night. We talked about art, books, about each other's lives, about our childhoods, he grew up in an upper-middle-class family in San Diego and spent his childhood surfing and playing Little League. He came back here with me that night and stayed with me. We had dinner and he stayed with me every night for the next two weeks.

And then?

I sent him away. Told him not to call or ever come back here.

Why?

Leonard starts to tear up.

I'm already in too much pain. I didn't want to hurt that way anymore.

I'm sorry.

Leonard stares at the floor, starts to cry, starts to sob. I sit next to him, hug him, let him sob in my arms.

It's morning I get out of bed walk downstairs. In the week I have been here we've established a routine, I wake Leonard up, help him brush his teeth, wash his face, shave, help him out to the veranda, where I drink coffee and he drinks water. Leonard isn't in his room I walk out to the deck he's sitting on his chair. He's smoking a cigar, staring out across the backyard. He speaks.

My son.

What's going on, Leonard?

Sitting here, enjoying the morning, smoking a fine cigar.

Big day ahead?

You could say that.

You got plans?

You could say that.

Where's Freddie?

He'll be here in a little while. I told him I needed some time alone with you.

What's up?

He turns to me.

You still think about Lilly?

Of course. Every day.

What do you think about when you think about her?

I remember our time together. How she felt when I held her, how she kissed me, how she smiled, what her laugh sounded like. I remember holding her when she'd cry. I remember talking to her and writing her in jail. I think a lot about what our life might have been like, I invent scenarios that we would have experienced together. Sometimes I think about what it must have been like for her when she died. What she was thinking and feeling, why she did it.

Why do you think she did it?

She felt too much pain. She just couldn't deal with it.

And how do you feel about what she did?

A small part of me still hates her for it. A part of my heart is still broken. Most of me accepts that she did what she did because she thought it was right, and I respect her decision.

He nods, looks back across the yard. He takes a drag of his cigar, exhales, puts the cigar out in an ashtray.

That was a great cigar.

I smile.

Good.

My last one.

You want me to get you more?

I mean it's the last one I'll ever smoke.

Why?

He stares at me for a moment.

I'm going to ask you to respect the decision I'm making.

What are you talking about, Leonard?

I'm in too much pain, my son. I don't want to waste away anymore. I want to go out on my terms, with some dignity, before I turn into a wailing, delirious, drugged-up skeleton.

Don't do this.

We've had a good time here together, and this has probably been the best week of my life. It's only gonna get worse, and I'm not gonna let it.

No.

Are you going to respect what I'm going to do?

I shake my head.

No.

Please understand this, and respect it, and accept it, the same way you did with Lilly.

No fucking way, Leonard. You're not gonna kill yourself.

He stares at me, into my eyes, they are the only part of him that still has life, he stares at me, stares at me.

Please, my son. It's time for me to go.

What are you going to do?

I'm going to ask you to take Bella out for a walk. Stay away for a couple of hours. When you come back, I'll be gone.

I shake my head.

No way, Leonard.

I have a bottle of pills. They're pain pills that I received to deal with what's happening to me. I'm going to take the entire bottle. I'll go to sleep, and I won't hurt anymore.

Please, Leonard. No.

I'm not doing this to hurt you. You're the most important person in my life, the only person I've got in this world, the only person I love. You're my son, my motherfucking son, and I'm proud of you, and who you've become and how you conduct yourself, and I know you don't believe in this, but I'll continue to watch over you, and protect you, and I'll look forward to seeing you again.

He stares at me, into my eyes. He opens his arms.

Give me a hug, my son.

I step forward, let him hug me, start to cry. I don't want this to happen and I don't want to let it happen, I don't want to lose my friend, my best friend, the man who saved me, who helped me, guided me protected me watched over me took care of me I don't want him to die, I don't want him to die, I don't want him to die. He pushes me away I don't want to let go of him he pushes me away.

Be proud, be strong. Live honorably and with dignity. You can do anything you want to do. You're my motherfucking son. Always remember that.

Always remember that.

Tears stream down my face I'm having trouble breathing my hands are shaking I'm scared in shock I can't believe this is happening. He stares at me, into my eyes. I'm scared in shock I can't believe this is happening

I speak.

I don't want this to happen.

He chuckles.

I don't want this to happen either, but I'm in . . .

I interrupt him.

I DON'T WANT THIS TO HAPPEN.

I'm scared in shock I start to cry I start to sob.

NO. NO. NO. NO.

He stares at me. I look at him I sob I'm scared in shock I don't want this to happen please please please God if you exist save him, save him, save him and I will devote my life to you, please someone anyone stop this please just stop this I sob please please please.

Leonard leans over, puts his arms around me, he hugs me as I sob, hugs me as I sob. He waits until I stop sobbing he speaks.

If you're gonna cry, cry because of all the good times we had, and all the laughs, and all the fun shit we did, and cry because those memories make you happy.

I look up at him. He speaks.

We had good years, my son. Great years. The best of my life.

He stands he takes my hand, I stand and we look at each other for the last time, the last time. He speaks.

It's time now.

I start to cry again.

You gotta leave me. It's time.

I get Bella leave the house as I walk away my legs give. I fall I can't get up I can't move I sit on the grass and I sob uncontrollably sob uncontrollably sob uncontrollably sob. When I can I get up and I walk to my truck and I get inside and I close the windows and lock the doors and lie in the backseat and I hug my dog my little dog Bella and I sob uncontrollably sob.

Freddie knocks on the window I'm still in the backseat I don't know how much time has passed I'm exhausted, spent, I don't want to move can't begin to comprehend what's happened can't begin to comprehend what's in that house can't begin to comprehend that my friend Leonard is gone, my friend Leonard is gone.

I can't get out of the car. I feel safe in it, feel protected. I can't stop sobbing. Freddie calls an ambulance it comes they remove the body. I can't see it, can't look as they take him away. I sit in the backseat and I sob uncontrollably sob.

Freddie brings me food I can hardly eat. He takes Bella for walks. When it gets dark, I get out of the car go inside. As soon as I step through the door I start crying again I walk straight up to my room I lie in bed and I cry.

It's morning I'm awake I'm so tired I can hardly move. I go downstairs Freddie has coffee and cigarettes. We drink the coffee and smoke the cigarettes and cry together.

We start cleaning the house, boxing up Leonard's belongings there isn't much a few clothes, a few art books, a few pairs of slippers, we throw away medical supplies.

We eat lunch. I tell Freddie stories about Leonard we laugh between tears.

We clean.

We eat dinner we laugh between tears.

I cry myself to sleep.

I wake up. Coffee and cigarettes. Freddie gives me the number of a lawyer who set up Leonard's estate. Leonard asked Freddie to give me the number after he was gone. I call the lawyer make an appointment for the afternoon. I go see the lawyer, it's not Andrew the lawyer, it's a probate lawyer. He has an oak desk, oak walls, he wears a gray suit, has a gray-haired assistant who calls me Mr Frey. He tells me that Leonard has left two trusts. One of them, which is for me, has a significant sum of money in it. I tell him I don't want it, that I want to give it to the institution where we met. He tells me that it is a sum of money large enough so that I will never have to work again, never have to worry about money again. I tell him I don't want it, that I would like him to do whatever he needs to do so that the money goes to the institution where we met. He nods he tells me that the other trust is set up so that a pair of graves in Chicago will always be tended and will always have fresh roses. I ask him how long that will continue to go on. He looks at some papers, looks back at me says the instructions state there is a sum of money in place so that the graves will be tended for as long as the city of Chicago exists. I start to cry again. I sit in the lawyer's office and I cry.

I'm doing the last of the packing, cleaning, the doorbell rings. I walk to the door, open it. Snapper is standing in front of me. I'm terrified, absolutely fucking terrified. I think about slamming the door, but know it won't make a difference. If he is here to hurt me, the door won't stop him. He speaks.

Hey, Kid.

What's up, Snapper?

Not much. You?

You're a few days late.

He shakes his head.

No, I'm not.

Leonard's already dead.

I've known where he was for the last six months. I never would have hurt him. He was a great man, the greatest I've ever known. I'm here to pay my respects.

I step aside.

Come on in.

Snapper comes in, says hi to Bella, gives her a pat on the head. He asks if there's any alcohol in the house. There is a liquor cabinet, I look inside of it, tell him it's stocked. He asks for a scotch on ice and a glass of ice water. I get two glasses, get the ice, pour the scotch, pour the water. I give him the drink he tells me to keep the water. He asks to see the place where Leonard passed. I take him out to the deck. He reaches into his pocket, takes out two cigars, speaks.

Before he quit drinking, he drank scotch, after he quit drinking, he drank water. These are Cubans, they were his favorite. Let's smoke and drink in honor of our friend.

I smile, we toast, light the cigars. Snapper asks me about Leonard's last days I tell him, he says he wishes he could have been here with us. He asks where Leonard is now I tell him he's being cremated, that I'm picking up his ashes tomorrow. He looks at me, speaks.

I thought that's what he would do. That's good.

Why?

There's something you and I need to do.

What?

Can you get Bella back to Los Angeles, have someone take care of her down there?

Probably. Why?

He tells me why, tells me what we're going to do. We find Freddie. I introduce him to Snapper. I can see fear on his face I tell him everything's cool, that Snapper has come to pay his respects. I ask Freddie if he can take Bella to Los Angeles. He says he's not sure, Snapper takes a roll of hundred dollar bills from his pocket asks him if

476

five thousand dollars will make him sure. Freddie asks why, we tell him, he agrees to do it for free. The three of us go out for a steak dinner together. We order more food than we can eat, Snapper and Freddie drink a five hundred dollar bottle of wine, we leave a huge tip.

In honor of our friend.

END

I teach Freddie how to drive my truck. I give Bella a big kiss she licks my face they drive away.

Snapper and I pick up Leonard's ashes. They're in a box. We put the box in the backseat of the white convertible and we buy an atlas and we start driving east.

We drive across California into Nevada. We drive through Utah cross the mountains into Wyoming. We keep the top down, we drive fast, we take turns at the wheel, switch every few hours. Night comes Snapper sleeps I drink coffee and smoke cigarettes and drive, morning comes I sleep Snapper drinks coffee and smokes cigars and drives. We drive through Nebraska and Iowa and Illinois we drive through Chicago we've been driving for thirty-two straight hours. We switch back and forth one drives one sleeps we stop for food and coffee, cigarettes and gas. We keep driving the Mercedes is a strong car we drive eleven more hours through Indiana, Ohio, Pennsylvania, New Jersey. We drive into New York. We're both tired, spent, it's early morning we're almost there. We keep driving into

Connecticut. Snapper knows where we're going has driven past the entrance with Leonard too many times without going in this time will be different.

We approach a wooded drive there's a sign out front. We pull up to the drive Snapper's behind the wheel. He turns to me, speaks.

You ready?

I smile.

Yeah, I'm ready.

Ask Leonard if he's ready.

I turn around, look at the box, speak.

You ready, Leonard?

I stare at the box for a moment, look back at Snapper.

He's says he's been waiting for this day for a long fucking time.

Snapper smiles. We start moving down the drive, through the woods, we come out there's a parking lot to our left filled with Mercedeses and BMW's, Jaguars and Porsches, there's a Rolls sitting apart in a corner. To our right there's a clubhouse, a beautiful, sprawling white building with a columned entrance and a valet station. Spread out behind the clubhouse there's a golf course, we can see sparkling dew on the grass.

We pull up to the valet. A uniformed attendant steps forward. Snapper steps out of the car I step out of the car. I reach into the backseat and I pick up the box. The attendant looks at Snapper, speaks.

May I help you?

Snapper takes a bill from his pocket, hands it to the attendant.

Put it in the lot. Make sure it gets a good spot.

Are you playing golf?

We are.

Do you have clubs?

That's not for you to worry about. Just make sure the car gets put in a good spot.

The attendant nods, gets in the Mercedes, the last of Leonard's many white Mercedeses, and he drives it into the parking lot. We step toward the front door. There's another uniformed attendant at the door. He looks at us we've been driving for the last two days we don't look like we're here for golf. He speaks.

The service entrance is around back.

We step forward. I have the box in my arms. Snapper speaks.

Is this the front door?

Yes.

We're going to walk through it.

The attendant speaks.

Excuse me, Sir . . .

Snapper interrupts.

We're not here to cause trouble, we just need to go through that door. It can be difficult or easy, either way we're going through it. I would highly recommend you make it easy, because if you don't, I will make your life very fucking difficult. Once we're through, you're not going to notify or call anyone, and we'll be gone within thirty minutes.

Is that understood? The attendant looks scared. He nods, speaks.

Yes, Sir.

Snapper reaches into his pocket, hands him a bill.

Thank you.

The man takes the bill. Snapper looks at him.

You normally open the door for people?

Yes, Sir.

Then do it for us.

The man opens the door.

Thank you.

We walk through the door enter a foyer. There are beautiful polished dark wood floors, a mirror, an oak reception table with a huge bouquet, there is subtle flowered wallpaper. A hall stretches out in front of us we walk down it ahead of us there is a large room with couches, tables, chairs, a wall of windows looks out onto the golf course. We walk straight ahead through the room there are sets of French doors we open them walk outside.

It's a beautiful morning, sunny crisp clear. It will be hot later but it isn't now. There's a pro shop and cart station to our left, fifty yards away.

Without speaking we both start walking toward it. There's a putting green in front of it, there are three men on it lining up putts. Snapper looks at me, speaks.

Let's follow the rules while we're here.

We walk around the putting green, walk up to the cart station. A young man steps out from the station, asks if he can help us. Snapper steps onto a cart, gets behind the wheel. He looks at the young man, speaks.

We're taking this cart. You can pick it up in the parking lot in a little while. If you try to tell me I can't take it, I'll knock your fucking teeth out.

And if you call anyone and tell them we've taken it, I'll do much, much worse.

The young man nods, speaks.

Understood.

Snapper hands him a bill, speaks.

Thank you.

He turns to me, speaks.

You ready?

I nod, speak.

This one's for Leonard.

Snapper smiles, speaks.

This one's for Leonard.

He turns the key, steps on the pedal, we pull away. We drive straight through the course. We drive down the middle of the fairways. We ignore the golfers who are surprised by us, who yell at us, who ask what we're doing. As we pull away I open the box, and as we drive we take turns reaching into the box and spreading the ashes. We put ash on every tee on every fairway on every green. We spread our friend Leonard across the perfect, beautiful green grass of the golf course that he spent his life dreaming of playing, just like one of the members. With each handful of ash we say this is for you, Leonard, and both of us have tears running down our faces the entire time. We spread Leonard's ashes, our friend Leonard's ashes, our magnificent friend Leonard's ashes.

When we finish we pull the cart into the parking lot. We get out, we start walking down the drive that led us here. We leave Leonard's Mercedes in the parking lot, right where it belongs, right where it will stay until someone takes it away. We walk silently, for the first time in a long time we are both without some semblance of our friend. We have left him where he belongs, and where he will stay. When we reach the end of the drive, Snapper takes a phone out of his pocket, calls a taxi service. When he's finished with the call, we sit on the ground and wait. Neither of us speaks, we just sit and wait. Ten minutes later, two cabs arrive. We stand. Snapper looks at me, speaks.

I guess this is it, Kid.

I guess so.

He reaches into one of his pockets, takes out a card, hands it to me.

That's Olivia's business card. I wrote my number on the back.

I feel like an asshole. I didn't ask you about Olivia. How she's doing?

She's good. I'm trying to convince her to marry me.

Tell her I said hi, and that I said you're not as bad as you seem, and that I think she should marry you.

He laughs.

You call me if you ever need anything, or if I can ever help you in any way.

I smile.

I probably won't.

He smiles.

That's probably best.

Thank you, Snapper.

Thank you, kid.

We give each either a hug. We separate. Snapper speaks.

You going back to Los Angeles?

I'm gonna stop in Chicago for a few hours.

Visit your girl?

I gotta tell her Leonard's coming to see her.

He's probably with her already.

I hope so.

Snapper looks at me for a moment, nods, opens the door to one of the cabs, gets inside. It pulls away as I get into the other cab. The cabbie looks at me speaks.

Where you going?

Airport.

Which one?

LaGuardia.

Where you headed?

I'm going to see a friend, then I'm going home.

Thank you Maya, I love you Maya, thank you for our beautiful baby, I love you Maren. Thank you Mom and Dad, Bob and Laura. Thank you Sean McDonald. Thank you Kassie Evashevski. Thank you David Krintzman. Thank you Tobin Babst. Thank you Julie Grau, Cindy Spiegel, Roland Philipps. Thank you Nan Talese and Coates Bateman. Thank you Jenny Meyer. Thank you Mike Craven, Warren Wibbelsman, Elizabeth Sosnow, Jeffrey Dawson, Kevin Chase, Dan Glasser, Matt Rice, Josh Kilmer-Purcell and Brent Ridge, Susan Kirshenbaum, The Motley Crue of Hamilton, Nancy Booth, Eben Strousse, the Boys in the motherfucking GSL. Thank you Dave Massey, Megan Lynch, Larissa Dooley, Justin Maggio, Alex Morris, Feroz Taj, Dave Bernad, Nicole Young. Thank you Brooke. Thank you Lyssa. Thank you United Hudson Grocery and Mary's Marvelous. Thank you Bella and Preacher my little friends, my little friends. Thank you Miles, we're still going. Thank you Lilly, thank you Lilly. Thank you Leonard. Thank you, my friend. Thank you Leonard.